Business

and

Management

Business Organisation
and
Management

P. C. Tulsian
M.Com., F.C.A., A.M.I.M.A.
Head, Department of Commerce
Ramjas College
University of Delhi
Delhi

Vishal Pandey
A.C.A.

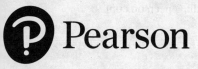 Pearson

ISBN 978-81-317-1634-2

First Impression, 2008

Nineteent Impression, 2019

Twentieth Impression, 2020

Published by Dorling Kindersley (India) Pvt. Ltd., licensees of Pearson Education in South Asia.

Head Office: 15th Floor, Tower-B, World Trade Tower, Plot No. 1, Block-C, Sector-16, Noida 201 301, Uttar Pradesh, India.

Registered Office: The HIVE, 3rd Floor, Metro zone, No 44, Pilliayar Koil Street, Jawaharlal Nehru Road, Anna Nagar, Chennai, Tamil Nadu 600040.
Phone; 044-66540100,
Website:in.pearson.com,Email:companysecretary.india@pearson.com

Printed in India by Rahul Print O Pack

PREFACE

This book adopts a fresh and novel approach to the study of Business Organisation and Management keeping in view the specific requirements of the students appearing in the B.Com examination of Indian Universities, and other professional examinations.

It follows a student-friendly approach enriched with pedagogical features for an easy comprehension of the subject.

The following unparalleled features impart distinct character to the book:

✓ The subject is presented in a self-explanatory manner so that even self-taught students may not feel any difficulty in understanding it.
✓ The matter is so presented that it serves as a tutor at home for all the students.
✓ Almost all the possible patterns of questions based on the standards of B.Com examinations of major universities are included in this book.
✓ Questions have been set at different levels of difficulty (i.e., easy, average and difficult levels) that are included for an easy and quick grasp of the subject.
✓ Questions have been put in a logical sequence.
✓ Includes revision questions for practice and revision.

We are quite confident that these features would make this book an invaluable asset for the learners. It is sincerely hoped that the students will find this book both instructive and enjoyable. We trust that this book will provide an easy way of understanding the activities involved in the industry and commerce which is the aim and objective of this book.

We wish to express our sincere thanks to several individuals and who have been a source of inspiration and support both personally and professionally, including Prof. P.K. Ghosh, Shri R.P. Tulsian, Shri N.D. Gupta, Prof. V.K. Bhatia, Shri Anil Jindal, Shri M.K. Sharda, Shri Rajiv Rustogi, Shri Sushil Jain, Shri Sunil Aggarwal and Shri Amarjeet Chopra.

We must concede that this book would never have been written without the support, encouragement and prodding of our family members. Many thanks to them.

Any criticism or suggestion for further improvement of the book will be gratefully acknowledged and highly appreciated.

AUTHORS

Contents

Part B   Management

16.   Nature and Significance of Management   **16.1**

17.   Principles of Management   **17.1**

18.   Planning   **18.1**

Part A   Business Organisation

1

Nature and Purpose of Business

MEANING OF HUMAN ACTIVITIES

Activities which human beings undertake are known as human activities. Some of these activities are undertaken to earn money but others are performed to derive personal satisfaction. All of us participate in various kinds of work from the time we get up from bed in the morning till the time we go to sleep at night. We get up from bed in the morning, brush our teeth, take bath and eat breakfast. Then children go to school or college to study, elders go to office or factory or shop or field to work and housewives work at home. In the evening all of us come back, take food, see entertainment programmes on TV and sleep at night. All the activities in which we, thus, participate from morning till night are called 'human activities'.

On examination of the human activities, one can find that some of these produce direct economic benefits e.g. working in office or factory or shop or field while others like brushing teeth, taking breakfast, going to school, playing, cooking food for the family, seeing entertainment programmes on TV, etc. do not produce any direct economic benefits.

Thus, human activities can be classified into two categories as under:

1. Economic Activities
2. Non-Economic Activities

MEANING OF ECONOMIC ACTIVITIES

Activities which are undertaken by people with the object of earning money are known as economic activities. These activities are concerned with production, exchange and distribution of goods and services.

Examples of Economic Activities

1. Production of goods by a manufacturer in a factory
2. Distribution of goods by a wholesaler
3. Selling of goods by a retailer
4. Transportation of goods by a transporter
5. Acceptance of deposits and lending of money by a banker
6. Insurance of risks by an Insurance company
7. Storage of goods by a warehouse keeper
8. Advertisement of goods by an Advertising Agency
9. Medical profession carried on by a Doctor
10. Legal profession carried on by a lawyer
11. Accounting profession carried on by a Chartered Accountant
12. Working as a nurse/doctor in a hospital
13. Working as Legal Officer in the Legal Department of a company
14. Working as an Accounts Officer in the Accounts Department of a company
15. Working as a teacher in a school

Economic activities can be divided into three categories—

1. Profession
2. Employment
3. Business

TYPES OF ECONOMIC ACTIVITIES OR OCCUPATIONS

Economic Activities are called occupations of people when the people are regularly engaged in particular economic activity or activities. The economic activities or the occupations of people can be classified into the following three categories:

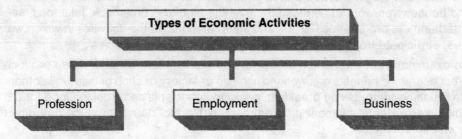

Types of Economic Activities

Profession   Employment   Business

Let us discuss these types of economic activities one by one.

Profession

Meaning of Profession — Profession refers to the activity which requires special knowledge and skill to be applied by an individual in his work to earn a living. It involves the rendering of personalised services of a specialised nature based on professional knowledge, education and training. The persons who are engaged in profession are called professionals.

Examples of Professionals and Profession

Professionals	Profession
1. Doctors	Medical Profession
2. Lawyers	Law Profession
3. Accountants	Accounting Profession
4. Engineers	Engineering Profession

Features of Profession — Profession is a specialised field which has the following features:

1. **Systematised body of knowledge —** Every profession has a systematised body of knowledge which can be learnt through instructions.

2. **Restricted entry —** Every profession has restricted entry on the basis of examination of education.

3. **Professional association —** Every profession has professional association of which membership is essential. Such association regulates the entry in the profession, grants certificate of practice, formulates and enforces code of conduct.

The various professional associations are given below:

Professions	Professional Association regulating the profession
1. Medical Profession	Medical Council of India
2. Law Profession	Bar Council of India
3. Accounting Profession	The Institute of Chartered Accountants of India (ICAI)
4. Engineering Profession	The Institution of Engineers (India)

4. **Dominance of service motive —** Every profession has dominance of service motive. True professionals serve their clients' interests through dedication and commitment.

5. **Code of conduct —** Professionals are regulated by formal code of conduct prescribed by the professional association of which they are members.

Employment

Employment refers to an activity in which an individual works regularly for another for an agreed remuneration under the rules of service. The persons who are engaged in the employment or service are known as employers. The persons who engage others to work regularly for them are known as employers. The remuneration paid by employer to employee is called salary or wages. The various examples of employment are given below:

1. Working as a nurse/doctor in a hospital
2. Working as a Legal Officer in the Legal Department of a company
3. Working as an Accounts Officer in the Accounts Department of a company
4. Working as Junior Engineer (JE) in Municipal Corporation of Delhi.

Business

Business activities refer to the activities which are connected with the production or purchase and sale of goods or services with the object of earning profit. The persons who are engaged in business are called businessmen or entrepreneurs. Similarly an organisation formed for the purpose of business activities is called a business enterprise or business organisation. The various examples of business activities are given below:

Types	Examples of Business Activities
1. Extractive Industries	Fishing, Mining
2. Genetic Industries	Dairy farming, Poultry farming
3. Manufacturing Industries	Manufacturing of Steel, cement, fertilizers, furniture, etc.
4. Construction Industries	Construction of buildings, bridges, dams, roads, canals etc.
5. Trade	Wholesale trade, Retail trade, Import trade, Export trade, Entrepot trade
6. Transportation	Land transportation, Air transportation, Water transportation
7. Banking	Acceptance of deposits and lending of money
8. Insurance	Insuring the risks attached to person or property
9. Warehousing	Preserving goods for the time gap between production/purchase and sale
10. Advertising	Providing information to consumers about the products through radio, newspapers, magazines, hoardings etc.

MEANING OF NON-ECONOMIC ACTIVITIES

Activities other than economic activities are known as non-economic activities. In other words, the activities which are undertaken for purposes other than the purpose of earning money, are called non-economic activities.

These non-economic activities are undertaken due to—

(a) personal satisfaction, (e.g. Meditation by a person)
(b) Physical requirements (e.g. engaging in sports activities for physical fitness)
(c) Social obligations (e.g. cooking food for family, working to help victims of flood and earthquake)
(d) Religious obligation (e.g. worshipping God)
(e) Love and affection (e.g. having dinner with family members)
(f) Patriotism (e.g. fighting for freedom of country)

DISTINCTION BETWEEN ECONOMIC ACTIVITIES AND NON-ECONOMIC ACTIVITIES

Economic Activities differ from Non-Economic Activities in the following respects:

Basis of Distinction	Economic Activities	Non-Economic Activities
1. **Basis**	Economic activities are based on **economic motives**.	Non-economic activities are based on **social or psychological motives**.
2. **Expectation of Money Income**	Money income is **expected** from these activities.	Money income is **not expected** from these activities.
3. **Purpose**	These activities are undertaken **for creation of wealth or assets**.	These activities are undertaken **for psychological satisfaction**.

CONCEPT OF BUSINESS

Literally speaking, the term 'business' means to be busy. Hence, business includes all occupations in which people are busy in earning income either by production or purchase and sale or exchange of goods and services to satisfy the needs of other people so as to earn income or profit.

Business relates to the creation of three utilities viz.

(a) form utility through processing
(b) time utility through storage
(c) place utility through transportation

CHARACTERISTICS OF BUSINESS

The essential characteristics of business are as follows:

1. **Deals in Goods or Services** — Business deals in goods and services. The goods may be consumer goods like bread, butter, milk, tea, water or capital goods like plant, machinery, equipment. The services may relate to transport, banking, insurance, warehousing, advertising and so on.

2. **Involves production or purchase and transfer or exchange or sale —** Business involves production or purchase and transfer, exchange or sale of goods and services. There must be a buyer and a seller. If goods are produced for self-consumption or presentation as gifts, such activities shall not be treated as business. There must be transfer or exchange or sale of goods or services between a buyer and a seller. The goods may be bartered or exchanged for money. Exchange of 5 kg wheat for 2 kg rice constitutes barter and sale of 5 kg wheat for Rs 50 constitutes exchange for money.

3. **Involves continuity and regularity —** Business consists of producing or purchasing and selling or exchanging goods and services on continuous and regular basis. Normally, an isolated transaction is not treated as business. For example, if Mr X sells his old Maruti 800 Car for Rs 50,000, it is not considered as business of Mr X unless it shows his tendency to indulge in trade of buying and selling cars.

4. **Based on profit motive —** Business activities are performed with the primary objective of earning profit. Profits are essential to enable the business to survive, to grow, to expand and to get recognition. For example, If goods are produced or purchased for distribution among poor families or victims of floods, earthquake or storms, it is considered as charitable activity and not business activity.

5. **Involves element of risk —** Business involves an element of risk. The possibility of incurring loss is termed as risk. Risk arises due to uncertainties of future. The element of risk exists due to a variety of factors which are outside the control of the business enterprise. Risks can be of two types:

   (a) **Insurable risks —** Risks whose probability can be calculated and can be insured e.g. risk of loss due to fire, flood, earthquake, theft.

   (b) **Non-Insurable risks —** Risks whose probability cannot be calculated and which cannot be insured against e.g. loss due to fall in demand, changing technology, changing fashions etc.

BUSINESS AS AN ECONOMIC ACTIVITY

Business is regarded as an economic activity for the following reasons:

1. **The objective of business activities is to sell the goods or services for profit.**

   If a farmer grows vegetables in his farm for self-consumption or consumption by family members, it is an economic activity but not a business activity. If he sells these vegetables in the market for a price, it will be considered as business activity.

   Income of business is the excess of revenue over the costs and is called profit.

   Thus, Profit of a Business = Revenue - Costs.

2. **Business Activities require use of scarce resources like capital, men, materials.**

   Business activities involve —

   (a) Introduction of ownership capital or borrowed capital

(b) Engagement of Employees

(c) Procurement and processing of Materials.

Payment for the use of these resources is to be made. For example, Interest for borrowed funds, salaries and wages of employees, purchase price of materials.

Thus, business always involves use of scarce resources.

3. **Business Activities satisfy various needs of businessmen and the general public.**

Business activities satisfy various needs of businessmen and their families by generating income in the form of profit. Business activities satisfy various needs of the general public by making available goods and services which they can buy to satisfy their needs.

Thus, business can be treated as an economic activity not only as a means of earning income by businessmen but also as a means of satisfying the wants of general public.

DISTINCTION BETWEEN BUSINESS, PROFESSION AND EMPLOYMENT

Business differs from the profession and employment in the following respects:

Basis of Distinction	Business	Profession	Employment
1. **Commencement of Establishment**	Business may be commenced with **entrepreneur's decision** and the necessary legal formalities (if any)	Profession may be commenced by anyone who is a member of concerned professional body and **holds certificate of practice**.	Employment commences **on joining duty** after getting letter of appointment and entering into service agreement.
2. **Qualifications**	Specific formal qualifications are **not required**.	**Professional qualification** and training are required.	Qualification and training are required **in some cases** and **not in all cases**.
3. **Nature of work involved**	It involves **production or purchase and sale** or exchange of goods and services.	It involves the **rendering of personalised services** of a specialised nature.	It involves **performing** the **work assigned** by employers under service contract.
4. **Capital/ Investment**	Capital is required **according to the nature and size** of business.	**Limited** capital is required for establishment of office to carry on profession.	**No capital** is required.

5. **Basic Motive**	The primary objective behind the business is **to earn profit**.	The primary objective behind profession is **to render service** besides earning income.	The primary objective is **to earn livelihood** by way of salaries or wages.
6. **Return/Reward**	Reward for carrying on business is called **profit**.	Reward for carrying on profession is called **professional fee**.	Reward for employment is called **wage or salary**.
7. **Element of Risk**	There **exists an** element of **risk of loss**.	There **exists an** element of **risk of not getting enough fee** to meet the expenditure on establishment.	**No risk exists** so long as the employer continues his operations.
8. **Transfer of Ownership/ Interest**	The owner of business **can transfer** ownership with necessary legal formalities, if any required.	A professional **can not transfer** his certificate of practice to any one else.	An employee **can not transfer** his job to anyone else.
9. **Code of conduct**	**No prescribed code** of conduct to be followed by businessmen.	A professional is **required** to follow the code of conduct prescribed by the professional body of which he is a member.	An employee is **required to follow** the rules prescribed by his employer.

INTERRELATION BETWEEN BUSINESS, PROFESSION AND EMPLOYMENT

Business, profession and employment are closely interrelated because business needs the assistance of professionals (e.g. Chartered Accountants for company Audit and Tax Audit, Cost Accountants for cost Audit, Lawyers for legal proceedings, Engineers for engineering works) and services of Purchase Managers, Sales Managers, Accounts Managers and assistants to carry on the business.

Similarly professionals require the services of assistants and require business houses to utilise their services.

Similarly, the persons seeking employment require business houses as well as professional firms to utilise their services.

Hence, it can be said that the activities of business, profession and employment are not competitive but complementary.

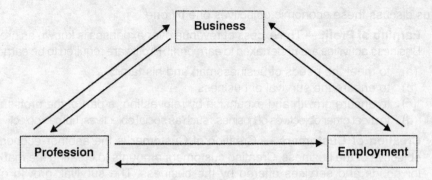

Figure: Interrelationship between Business, Profession and Employment

OBJECTIVES OF BUSINESS

According to **Henry Ford**, " business is not mere money chasing but it also should aim it serving the community."

According to **Urwick**, "Profit can no more be the objective of a business than eating is the objective of living."

Thus, 'service to community' is also regarded as another important objective of business in addition to 'Earning Profit.' No doubt profits are necessary for a businessman to stay in business, he ought to aim at something more for its survival and growth.

The objectives of business can be broadly classified into the following four categories:

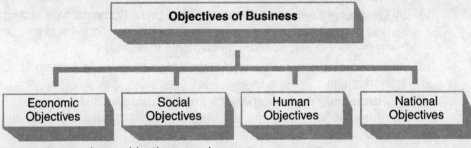

Let us discuss these objectives one by one.

ECONOMIC OBJECTIVES

Business, being an economic activity has primary objectives of economic nature. Some of the main economic objectives are discussed below:

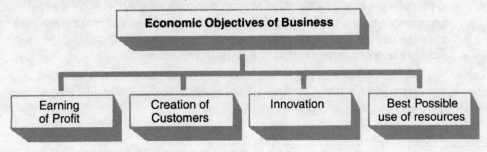

Let us discuss these economic objectives one by one.

1. **Earning of Profit** — The excess of revenue over expenses is known as profit. Business activities are undertaken to earn profit. Profits are required to be earned:

    (a) to meet the needs of businessman and his family
    (b) to ensure the survival of business
    (c) to ensure growth and expansion by reinvesting a part of the profits.
    (d) to meet other objectives of business such as social objectives, human objectives.

2. **Creation of Customers** — Creation of Customer is the another economic objective of the business. Creating customers amounts to creating the market for goods and services offered by the business. The survival, growth and expansion of business depends upon the number of customers who are ready to buy the goods and services offered by the business.

    If customers get goods and services of requisite quality, at reasonable price, at the right time and are fully satisfied, the business unit may be said to have created a market. Profitability depends upon the numbers of customers or the market share captured by the business unit. Thus, the business units must pursue the objective of creating customer.

3. **Innovation** — Innovation is the another economic objective which needs to be pursued by business. Innovation means changes which bring about improvement in products, process and/or distribution of goods. Innovation can be achieved in various ways such as —

    (a) *by introducing new products,* for example Pager, Mobile Phones, Digital Diary, Credit Cards.
    (b) *by introducing new process,* for example, Using Computer type-setting instead of hand composing, using power looms instead of hand looms, using tractors in place of hand implements in farms.
    (c) *by introducing new methods of distribution,* for example, e-commerce, Tele-shopping.
    (d) *by introducing new materials,* for example using transistors instead of Vacuum tubes, using micro chips instead of transistors in the manufacturing of computers, using Compressed Natural Gas (CNG) instead of diesel/petrol, using floppy diskette of 5.25" instead of punched cards, using floppy diskette of 3.5" instead of diskette of 5.25", using compact disc (CD) instead of diskettes of 3.5", using Re-writable compact disc (RCD) instead of simple CD's.

4. **Best Possible use of Scarce Resources** — The objective of every business is to make the best possible use of scarce resources such as men, machines and materials. The business should find ways and means of making the best possible use of resources at its disposal. The objective of making the best possible use of scarce resources can be achieved —

    (a) by making use of personnel employed in efficient manner,
    (b) by making full use of machines in efficient manner,
    (c) by reducing wastage of raw-materials

SOCIAL OBJECTIVES

Business being a socio-economic activity has some obligations towards the society also. Some major social objectives are:

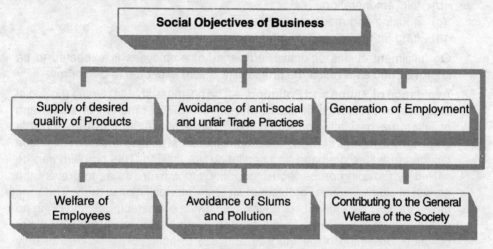

Let us discuss these social objectives one by one.

1. **Supply of Desired Quality of Products** — The important social objective of every business should be to produce and sell the goods of right quality of products at reasonable price. Quality may mean durability as in case of TV, Computer etc. or safety as in case of pressure cooker, washing machines, scientific instruments, or purity as in case of edible oils, medicines etc. Every business should satisfy the customers by providing them the goods of right quality at reasonable price. By achieving this social objective, the customer will be satisfied and satisfied customer will create new customers and hence the number of customers will increase and which in turn will increase the profitability of the business.

2. **Avoidance of Anti-social and Unfair Trade Practices** — The another social objective of business should be to avoid anti-social and unfair trade practices to earn profits. Anti social activities such as black-marketing, hoarding and unfair trade practices like over-charging, manufacture/sale of adulterated goods, giving misleading advertisements should not be undertaken by business for earning quick profits. All such activities earn a bad name and sometimes make the businessmen liable for penalty and even imprisonment under the law for the time being in force.

3. **Generation of Employment** — Generation of Employment is one of the social objectives of the business. This objective is achieved by employing people for different types of activities in the business. While fulfilling this objective, the business should give due consideration to poor or handicapped people so that the incomes of poor families can be increased and the handicapped people may be made useful to the society. The business units which pursue these objectives are in position to improve their public image.

4. **Welfare of Employees** — Welfare of employees should also be the social objectives of the business. This objective can be achieved by providing —

   (a) good working conditions for employees,
   (b) fair remuneration,
   (c) housing and medical facilities,
   (d) fund for future security after service,

   On fulfillment of this objective, efficiency of employees is expected to be improved and as a result the profitability is also expected to be improved.

5. **Avoidance of Slums and Pollution** — The business should pursue the social objective of avoidance of slums and pollution. The problem of slums and pollution are basically connected with industrialisation. It can be seen that some dirty dwellings come up around the industrial units where even minimum facilities of water, drainage and sanitation are lacking. This problem can be solved by providing proper housing facilities to workers so as to prevent the growth of slums. Another problem of air and water pollution is there. The toxic gases emitted the effluents of chemicals flowing out of factories and piling up of the industrial waste materials are the common causes of air and water pollution. Breathing of polluted air and use of polluted water are not only unhealthy but also cause incurable diseases.

   Every business should take the necessary steps so as to prevent air and water pollution in the interest of the society.

6. **Contributing to the General Welfare of the Society** — Business units should work for the general welfare and upliftment of the society. This objective can be achieved by making donations to schools, colleges, training centres, research centres, hospitals etc. The business units can also encourage intelligent students for higher education by providing them educational scholarships.

HUMAN OBJECTIVES

Since the efficiency and the success of the business enterprise depends on the motivation and ability of its employees, the business must also have some human objectives to safeguard the interests of its employees. Some of the major human objectives are as follows:

1. To provide fair remuneration to employees in terms of wages and salaries.
2. To provide better working conditions and environment to the employees.
3. To provide job satisfaction
4. To provide promotional/growth opportunities to the employees.
5. To provide for future security through Provident Fund and Pension
6. To improve the skills and develop abilities of the employees through training and development programmes.
7. To create opportunities for gainful employment of people
8. To help society and economically backward people and handicapped persons.

NATIONAL OBJECTIVES

Business being a part of nation has obligations towards nation also. Business should have national objectives which should be pursued to discharge its obligations to fulfill national goals. Some of the major national objectives are:

1. To promote social justice,
2. To produce according to national priorities,
3. To increase exports and add to foreign exchange reserves for essential imports,
4. To find out the better substitute for imports

ROLE OF PROFIT IN BUSINESS

No doubt, earning profit cannot be the only objective of business since the business has to pursue certain other economic social objectives. At the same time, the importance of profit can not be ignored since the other economic and social objectives cannot be pursued and achieved in the absence of profit. The importance of profit arises from the following:

1. **Provides the means of livelihood** — Profit is a source of income and provides the means of livelihood for the owner of the business. Profit is required to be earned to satisfy the needs of the businessman and his family members.

2. **Increases the Volume of Business** — Retention of profit is an internal source of funds. This internal source of funds is more dependable and cheaper source of financing than external sources of funds (e.g. from investors or lenders) since it does not involve explicit costs (e.g. floatation costs of raising funds through issue of shares and debentures, interest payable on debentures, dividend on shares etc.) A part of the retained profits can be used for increasing the volume of business through expansion (e.g. increasing the existing capacity of production of 1000 tons to 2000 tons) or diversification (e.g. start manufacturing stationery items alongwith existing line of publishing of books).

3. **Acts as an Index of Performance** — Profits act as an index of performance of those who manage the business. Profits indicate whether a business is being managed efficiently or not. In general, higher profits indicate the efficiency of management and lower profits indicate the inefficiency of management.

4. **Acts as Reward for Risk Bearing** — Profits act as reward for risk bearing. When a businessman starts his business by making investment, he not only anticipates profits but also assumes the risks of increasing losses as well due to uncertainties of business conditions. Profit is the reward for businessmen who bear the risks of business. Business is carried on in the anticipation of earning sufficient profits by overcoming the risks due to uncertainties of business conditions.

5. **Helps to Gain Reputation** — Profits help business to gain reputation (goodwill) in the market. After gaining reputation, the business is in position —

    (a) to raise funds more easily

     (b) to offer good remuneration to attract trained and experienced employees
     (c) to provide better working conditions
     (d) to provide more amenities to the employees

_____ EXERCISES _____

VERY SHORT ANSWER TYPE QUESTIONS

1. What is an economic activity?
2. Define 'Profession'.
3. Define 'Employment'.
4. Define 'Business'.
5. What is 'Non-economic Activity?

SHORT ANSWER TYPE QUESTIONS

1. Give five examples of economic activities.
2. List the types of economic activities.
3. Give two examples of profession.
4. Give two examples of employment.
5. Give five different examples of business.
6. Give five examples of non-economic activities.
7. Distinguish between economic activity and non-economic activity.
8. List the Characteristics of a business.
9. List the types of Business Activities.
10. State the Objectives of Business.
11. State the economic objectives of business.
12. State the social objectives of business.

LONG ANSWER TYPE QUESTIONS

1. Explain why business is regarded as an economic activity.
2. Define business. Distinguish it from profession and employment.
3. "The activities of business, profession and employment are not competitive but complementary." Explain.
4. Discuss the role of profit in business.

2 Structure of Business

CLASSIFICATION OF BUSINESS ACTIVITIES

Industry includes all those business activities which are connected with raising, producing or processing of goods. Industry creates form utility to goods by bringing materials into the form which is useful for intermediate consumption (i.e. further use as material in other industry) or final consumption by consumers.

Another explanation of the term 'Industry' — According to this explanation, the term 'Industry' is used to mean a group of factories producing similar or related goods and services. For example, all the factories which manufacture chemicals (such as Zinc Oxide, Zinc Chloride, Zinc Sulphate) are collectively called Chemicals Industry, similarly all the factories which manufacture automobiles (such, Two-wheelers, Three-wheelers, Cars, Tempos, Trucks, Buses) together constitute Automobile Industry.

It may be noted that the further discussion, will be with reference to first explanation and not the second explanation of the term 'Industry'.

Business activities range from making the materials available for production of goods to actual production of goods and then making the goods available for distribution.

These activities may be classified on the basis of size, ownership and function as follows:

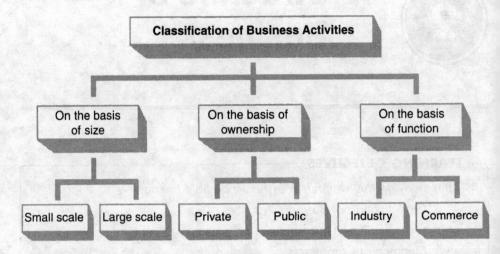

Let us these types of business activities as follows:

I. Classification of Business Activities on the Basis of Size

On the basis of size, business activities may be broadly grouped into two categories as follows:

(a) **Small Scale** — Small scale units require less capital, employ small number of workers and produce the goods on small scale. Some of the examples of business activities on small scale are given below:

    (i) Manufacturing textiles in handlooms or powerlooms

    (ii) Extraction of edible oil from oil seeds in 'Kolhu' or 'Ghani'.

    (iii) Manufacturing shoes by group of 2-3 cobblers

(b) **Large scale** — Large scale units require huge capital, employ large number of workers and produce the goods on large scale. Some of the examples of business activities on large scale are given below:

    (i) Manufacturing Textiles in a large Textile mill *(e.g. Raymonds, Grasim, Vimal, Reid &Taylor)*

    (ii) Extraction of edible oil from oil seeds in oil mills on large scale *(e.g. Suffola, Sunflower, Dalda Refined, Postman)*

    (iii) Manufacturing shoes on large scale *(e.g. Bata, Action, Liberty, Red tape, Woodland)*

II. Classification of Business Activities on the basis of Ownership

On the basis of ownership business activities may be broadly grouped into three categories as follows:

(a) **Private Enterprise** — An enterprise is said to be a private enterprise where it is owned, managed and controlled by persons others than government.

Private enterprise may be organised in several forms such as —

    (i)   Sole proprietorship *[e.g. Ram & Co Proprietor Mr. Ram]*

    (ii) Partnership *[e.g. Ram Chandra Krishna Chandra]*

    (iii) Joint Hindu family *[e.g. Ram Chandra & sons (HUF)]*

    (iv) Joint Stock Company *[e.g. Ram (private) Ltd; Ram Ltd.]*

    (v) Co-operative society *[e.g. Rajasthali Co-operative Store]*

(b) **Public Enterprise** — An enterprise is said to be a public enterprise where it is owned, managed and controlled by government or any of its agencies or both. Public enterprises may be organised in several forms such as —

    (i)   Departmental undertaking *[e.g. Railways, Post & Telegraphs, Public Works Department (PWD)]*

    (ii) Public Corporation [e.g. Industrial Finance corporation of India, Food corporation of India, Oil and Natural Gas Commission]

    (iii) Government Company *[e.g. State Trading Corporation (STC), Hindustan Machine Tools (HMT), Coal India Ltd.]*

(c) **Joint Enterprise** — An enterprise is said to be joint enterprise where it is owned, managed and controlled by government and private entrepreneurs.

III. Classification of Business Activities on the basis of Function.

On the basis of function, business activities may be broadly grouped into two categories as follows:

(a) **Industry** — Industry includes all those business activities which are connected with raising, producing or processing of **consumer goods** (e.g. bread, butter, *cheese, shoes,* TV) or **capital goods** (e.g. *machine tools, machinery, equipment)*

    The enterprises which undertake these industrial activities are known as **industrial enterprises**.

(b) **Commerce** — Commerce include all those activities which —

    (i)   establish a link between the producers and consumers of goods,

    (ii) maintain a smooth and uninterrupted flow of goods from producers to consumers.

    The enterprises which undertake these commercial activities are known as **commercial enterprises**.

CLASSIFICATION OF INDUSTRIES

Industries may be broadly classified into two categories as follows:

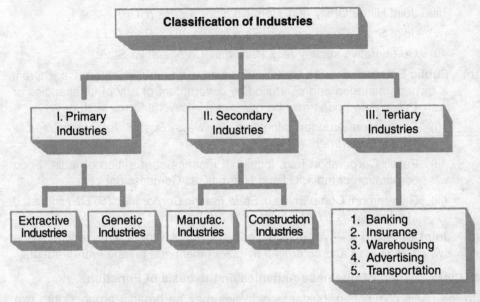

Let us discuss these types of industries one by one.

I. **Primary Industries** — Primary industries include those industries which are concerned with extraction, producing and processing of natural resources. For Example, the mining of iron ore or Gold is primary industry. Primary industries may of following two types:

 (a) **Extractive Industries** — Extractive industries include those industries which are concerned with the discovery and extraction of natural resources like minerals from mines, timber from forests, fish from rivers and seas. These industries are also called exhaustive industries because with every item there is depletion of resources and this wealth exhausts.

 The products of these industries are *either* directly consumed *(e.g. fish as food, coal as fuel)* or are used as raw-materials for further use in other industries *(e.g. iron ore is used in Steel Industry).* The activities involved in these industries may be carried out manually or mechanically. With rapidly changing technology, such activities have become highly mechanised.

 (b) **Genetic Industries** — Genetic industries include those industries which are concerned with reproducing and multiplying plants and animals with the objective of earning profit from their sale. The Activities involved in these industries are rearing, breeding of animals, birds and growing plants. Some of the examples of Genetic industries are as follows:

 (i) Nurseries which multiply and sell plants

 (ii) Poultry farming raising birds *(e.g. hens and ducks)* for meat and eggs

 (iii) Dairy farming raising milk from cattle *(e.g. cows)*

(iv) Animal Husbandry (*e.g. rearing of cattle for milk, grazing of sheep for wool and mutton etc.*)

(v) Farming to grow fruit trees of different kinds

(vi) Pisciculture i.e. growing fish in ponds, canals and rivers.

Difference between Extractive Industry and Genetic Industry — In the case of extractive industry, man can not add to the wealth which he withdraws from the earth, sea, and air, whereas in case of genetic industry, man not only adds to the growth but also reproduces the nature made goods.

II. **Secondary Industries** — Secondary Industries include those industries which are concerned with the transformation of the materials provided by primary industries. For example, the mining of gold is primary industry but manufacture of gold jewellery is secondary industry. Secondary industries may of following two types:

(a) **Manufacturing Industries** — Manufacturing Industries include those industries which are concerned with the conversion of raw-materials into finished goods. Generally the products of primary industries become raw materials for manufacturing industries. In other words, the manufacturing industries create form utility to the products of extractive industries.

Some of the **examples of manufacturing industries** are given below:

Products of Extractive Industries	Manufacturing Industries
1. Cotton/Jute	1. Textile Industry
2. Iron-ore	2. Steel Industry
3. Sugar-cane	3. Sugar Industry
4. Timbers from forests	4. Furniture Industry

Small Scale *vs.* Large Scale

Industrial Activities can be undertaken on a small scale or on a large scale. The various **examples of industrial activities** on small and large scale are given below:

Small Scale Industrial Activities	Large Scale Industrial Activities
1. Manufacturing Textiles in handlooms or powerlooms	1. Manufacturing Textiles in a large Textile Mill (e.g. Raymonds, VIMAL, Reid & Taylor)
2. Extraction of edible oil from oil seeds in 'Kolhu' or 'Ghani'	2. Extraction of edible oil from oil seeds in oil mills on large scale (e.g. Sun Flower, Sun Drop, Suffola, Postman)
3. Manufacturing Shoes by a group of 2-3 Cobblers.	3. Manufacturing shoes in shoe Factory on large scale (e.g. Bata, Liberty, Action, Woodland, Red Tape)

Types of Goods manufactured by Manufacturing Industries

Manufacturing industries manufacture basically three types of goods as follows:

(i) **Consumers Goods or Final Goods** — Goods which are directly consumed by consumers for example, bread, butter, cheese,

(ii) **Intermediate Goods** — Goods which are required to manufacture consumer goods or other intermediate goods for example, chemicals, steel, cement etc.

(iii) **Capital Goods** — Goods which are required to manufacture consumer and intermediate goods. For example, Machinery, Tools, Equipments.

(b) **Construction Industry** — Construction industries include those industries which are engaged in the construction activities. Some of the basic features of these industries are given below:

(i) the products of construction industries are immovabie. They are erected, built or fabricated at fixed rate.

(ii) These industries consume the products of manufacturing industries (e.g. bricks, cement, iron & steal) and extractive industries (e.g. wood, quarries)

(iii) These industries are labour intensive by nature. But with rapidly changing technology, the demand of heavy machines iike cranes, bulldozers etc. is increasing.

Some of the **examples of construction Industries** are given below:

```
1.  Construction of Office Buildings
2.  Construction of Residential Buildings
3.  Construction of Dams
4.  Construction of Roads
5.  Construction of Canals
6.  Construction of Railway lines
7.  Construction of Fly overs
8.  Construction of Bridges
```

III. Tertiary Industries — Tertiary industries includes all those activities which are concerned with providing services such as banking, insurance, warehousing, advertising, transportation etc.

MEANING OF COMMERCE

Commerce includes all those activities which —

(a) establish a link between the producers and consumers of goods, and

(b) maintain a smooth and uninterrupted flow of goods from producers to consumers.

To perform the aforesaid activities, the various hindrances of persons, place, time, risk, finance and information are to be removed.

The activities which remove such hindrances are as follows:

Activities Removing the Hindrances	Which Hindrances are removed	How Hindrances are removed
1. **Trade**	Hindrance of Person	Trade removes hindrance of person by making available goods to consumers from producers.
2. **Transportation**	Hindrance of Place	Transport removes hindrance of place by moving goods from the places of production to the place of distribution.
3. **Storage & Warehousing**	Hindrance of Time	Storage and warehousing removes the hindrance of time by facilitating the holding of goods after production till distribution.
4. **Insurance**	Hindrance of Risk	Insurance removes hindrance of risk by insuring the risks of loss or damage due to theft, fire, accidents etc.
5. **Banking**	Hindrance of Finance	Banking removes the hindrance of finance by providing funds to undertake various business activities.
6. **Advertising**	Hindrance of Knowledge & information	Advertising removes the hindrance of knowledge information by communicating information about goods to the prospective consumers.

Thus, commerce consists of activities which remove the hindrance of —

(a) Persons through trade

(b) Place through transportation

(c) Time through warehousing

(d) Risk through Insurance

(e) Finance through banking

(f) Information through Advertising

Small Scale *vs.* Large Scale

Commercial activities can be undertaken on a small scale or on a large scale. The various examples of such activities on small and large scale are given below:

Small Scale Commercial Activities	Large Scale Commercial Activities
Retail Traders buy and sell in small quantities.	Wholesale Traders buy goods in large quantities and sell in small quantities.
Transportation undertaken by a truck operator having one or two trucks.	Transportation undertaken by a transport company having a fleet of trucks.
Storage of goods on small scale in owned/hired godown.	Storage of goods on large scale in owned/hired warehouse.
—	Insurance companies insure the risks of loss or damage on large scale.
—	Banking companies provide on large scale.
Advertising undertaken by an advertiser on small scale.	Advertising undertaken by an advertising Agency on large scale.

FUNCTIONS OF COMMERCE

The functions of commerce are given below:

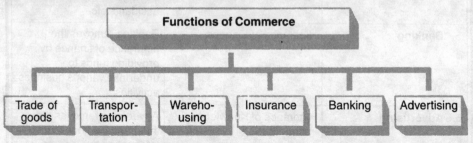

Let us discuss these functions one by one.

1. **Trade** — Trade removes the hindrance of person by establishing a link between the producers and consumers of goods. Traders buy goods from producers and sell goods to consumers. Thus, trade is an important function of commerce.

2. **Transportation** — Transportation removes the hindrance of place by moving goods from the places of production to the places of distribution. Thus, transport is also an important function of commerce.

3. **Warehousing** — Warehousing removes the hindrance of time by facilitating the holding of goods after production till distribution so that the goods may be made available for sale as and when necessary. Thus, warehousing is regarded as another important function of commerce.

4. **Insurance** — Insurance removes the hindrance of risk by insuring the risks of loss or damage due to theft, fire, accidents, floods, earthquake, storm etc. Entrepreneurs can protect themselves against these risks by taking relevant

insurance policy on payment of premium. Thus, insurance is also an important function of commerce.

5. **Banking** — Banking removes the hindrance of finance by providing funds to undertake various business activities. Entrepreneurs can increase the volume of business with the availability of funds. Hence, Banking is also an important function of commerce.

6. **Advertising** — Advertising removes the hindrance of knowledge by communicating information about goods to the prospective consumers. Thus, advertising is also an important function of commerce.

CLASSIFICATION OF COMMERCE ACTIVITIES

The whole range of commerce activities can be broadly classified as follows:

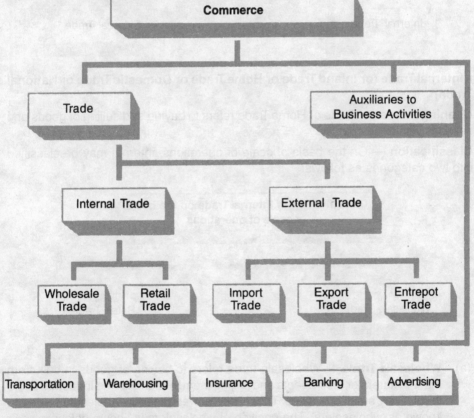

Let us discuss these commerce activities one by one.

TRADE

Meaning — Trade refers to the sale, transfer or exchange of goods and services for a certain price. Trade removes the hindrance of person by establishing a link between producers and consumers. The persons who are engaged in trade are called 'traders' or 'middlemen'. Goods acquire place utility through trade since the traders make the goods available to consumers in different markets. The position of traders has been shown below:

Classification — On geographical basis, the trade may be classified into two broad categories as follows:

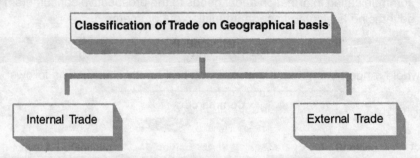

I. Internal Trade (or Inland Trade or Home Trade or Domestic Trade or National Trade)

Meaning — Internal Trade or Home Trade refers to buying and selling of goods and services within the country.

Classification — On the basis of scale of operations, internal may be classified into two categories as follows:

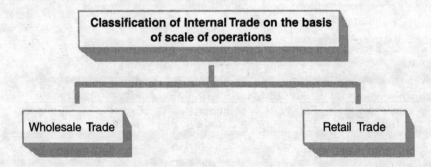

(a) **Wholesale Trade** — Wholesale trade refers to buying of goods in bulk from manufacturers or their agents and selling them to retailers and industrial users in relatively small quantities. Those who are engaged in wholesale trade are known as 'wholesalers'. The position of wholesalers is shown below:

Thus, the wholesalers act as middle men link between producers on one hand and retailers on the other.

(b) **Retail Trade** — Retail trade refers to buying of goods from wholesalers or manufacturers and selling them directly to the ultimate consumers. Those who are engaged in retail trade are called retailers. The position of retailers is shown below:

Producers → Wholesalers → Retailers → Consumers

Thus, Retailers act as middlemen between wholesalers on one hand and the ultimate consumers on the other.

II. External Trade (or Foreign Trade or International Trade)

Meaning of External Trade — External trade refers to buying and selling of goods and services between the nations of different countries or trade between agencies of the governments of different countries. It consist of export trade, import trade and entrepot trade.

Export Trade — It involves the selling of goods and services to other countries. For example, when M/s. P.P. Jewellers, an Indian firm, export gold plain jewellery to U.S.A., they are said to be involved in export trade.

Import Trade — It involves the purchasing of goods and services from other countries. For example, when M/s. Ratna Sagar, an Indian publisher, imports books from Frankfurt, they are said to be involved in import trade.

Entreport Trade — It involves importing the goods from one or more countries with the purpose of exporting them to some other country or countries. For example, when M/s Pustak Mahal, an Indian publisher imports some books from U.S.A. for the purpose of exporting them to Nepal, they are said to be involved in Entreport Trade. Singapore, Hongkong and Korea are important entrepot trade centres.

AUXILIARIES TO BUSINESS ACTIVITY

Meaning — The term 'auxiliaries to business activity' mean aid to business activity or supporting activities which removes various hindrances (e.g. hindrances of place, time, risk, finance and knowledge) which arise in connection with the production and distribution of goods. These auxiliaries support both industry and Trade.

Classification — The whole range of activities falling under auxiliaries to business activity may be classified into five categories as follows:

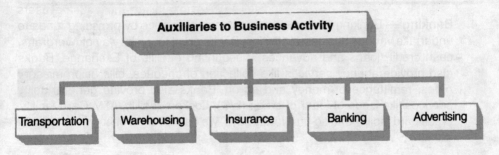

Auxiliaries to Business Activity

Transportation | Warehousing | Insurance | Banking | Advertising

Let us discuss these auxiliaries one by one.

1. **Transportation** — Transportation is an activity which is concerned with the movement of goods and passengers. Transport removes the hindrance of place and creates place utility by facilitating —

   (a) the movement of raw-materials from the areas of production to the manufacturing centres. For example, from Iron-ore mine to Iron & Steel manufacturing factory.

   (b) the movement of finished goods from the manufacturing centres to the selling centres for example, tea from Assam to rest of the country.

   (c) the movement of people who provide various services from their living places to their service centres where their services are required.

The various modes of transport are—

(i) Land transport-by Road, Rail, Pipeline

(ii) Water transport-Inland waterways, ocean transport

(iii) Air transport-Domestic Airlines, international Airlines

2. **Warehousing** — Warehousing refers to the function of preserving goods from the time they are produced to the time they are consumed. It removes the hindrance of time and creates time utility by providing facilities for storing goods after production /purchase for supply as and when required.

3. **Insurance** — Insurance removes the hindrance of risk by insuring the risks of loss or damage due to theft, fire, accident etc. Entrepreneurs can get themselves protected against these risks after taking relevant insurance policy on payment of premium to an insurance company. They can recover the actual loss subject to terms and conditions of insurance policy.

The various types of risk which can be insured may be grouped as follows:

Types of Insurance	Type of Risk
(a) Life Insurance	Risk of Death or old age
(b) Fire Insurance	Risk of loss or damage to property due to fire
(c) Marine Insurance	Risk of loss or damage to ship or cargo
(d) General Insurance	Risk of loss or damage due to theft burglary in a premises, risk of loss or damage due to accidents.

4. **Banking** — Banking removes the hindrance of finance by providing funds to undertake various business activities. Banks grant loans by way of overdrafts, cash credit, loans and advances, discounting of Bills of Exchange. Banks also provide agency services like collection of cheques, bills or promissory notes, remittance of money and so on. Banks also provide general utility services like issue of letter of credit (L/C), Lockers facility, ATM Card facility, credit card facility and so on. Now a days, we cannot think of business without banks.

5. **Advertising** — Advertising removes the hindrance of knowledge by communicating information about the products to the prospective consumers. It attracts and holds their attention, creates and sustains demands and wins their confidence. It helps in introducing new products in the market and in maintaining and increasing the sale of existing products. It educates consumers about the existence, features, uses and prices of existing and new products. Advertising can be done through various media of advertising such as —

   (a) Press Advertising-Newspapers and Periodicals

   (b) Radio Advertising

   (c) Television Advertising

   (d) Film Advertising

   (e) Outdoor Advertising

   (f) Direct Mail Advertising

http:/www.totalbizfulfillment.com/

———————————— EXERCISES ————————————

VERY SHORT ANSWER TYPE QUESTIONS

1. What is meant by Industry?
2. What is meant by Primary Industries?
3. What is meant by Extractive Industries?
4. What is meant by Genetic Industries?
5. What is meant by Secondary Industries?
6. What is meant by Manufacturing Industries?
7. What is meant by Construction Industries?
8. What is meant by Tertiary Industries?
9. What is meant by Commerce?
10. What is meant by Trade?
11. What is meant by Internal Trade?
12. What is meant by Wholesale Trade?
13. What is meant by Retail Trade?
14. What is meant by External Trade?
15. What is meant by Import Trade?
16. What is meant by Export Trade?
17. What is meant by Entreport Trade?
18. What is meant by Transportation?
19. What is meant by Warehousing?
20. What is meant by Insurance?
21. What is meant by Banking?
22. What is meant by Advertising?

SHORT ANSWER TYPE QUESTIONS

1. Give two examples of large scale business activities.
2. Give two examples of Public enterprises.
3. Give two examples each of industries and commerce.
4. Give two types of primary industries.
5. Give two examples of extractive industries.
6. Give two examples of Genetic industries.
7. Distinguish between extractive industry and genetic industry.
8. Distinguish between primary industries and secondary Industries.
9. Give two types of secondary industries.
10. Give two examples of manufacturing industries.
11. Give the types of goods which are manufactured by manufacturing industries.
12. Give two special features of construction industry.
13. Give two examples of construction industry.
14. Enumerate the functions of Commerce.
15. How does transport facilitate business activity?
16. How does warehousing facilitate business activity?
17. How does Insurance facilitate business activity?
18. How does Banking facilitate business activity?
19. How does advertising facilitate business activity?
20. Why do we insure goods?
21. How does advertising create demand?
22. Distinguish between a small scale industrial unit and a large scale industrial unit.
23. Is dairying a genetic or extractive industries? Give reasons in support of your answer.
24. Is furniture making extractive, manufacturing or construction industry? Give reasons in support of your answer.

LONG ANSWER TYPE QUESTIONS

1. Discuss various ways in which business activities may be classified. Give two examples each of such classification.
2. What is meant by auxiliaries to business? Discuss their significance for the growth of industries and trade.

Social Responsibility of Business & Business Ethics

3

MEANING OF SOCIAL RESPONSIBILITY OR SOCIAL OBLIGATION

Social responsibility means the obligation or responsibility of business to act in a manner which will serve the best interest of the society. It relates to the voluntary efforts of businessmen towards the betterment of the society.

FEATURES OF SOCIAL RESPONSIBILITY

The features of social responsibility are:

1. Welfare of Society;
2. Values of Society;
3. Aspiration of Society;
4. It goes beyond the limits of the country;
5. Social responsibility has significant influence on the social system;
6. Obligations and duties that business owes to society;
7. Business is no longer considered a tripartite venture i.e., owners, workers and consumers, but it has become a multiparty system; and
8. Business is part of society and community and therefore it has to serve society in many ways.

Difference between Social Responsibility and Legal Obligation

Social responsibility of business differs from legal obligation. Legal obligation may be fulfilled by complying with the provisions of relevant law but social responsibility is not covered by law.

CASE FOR/NEED FOR SOCIAL RESPONSIBILITY OF BUSINESS

Social responsibility is based on the assumption that what is good for society is also good for business. Increasing public awareness of their own rights has also contributed to the recognition of social responsibility by business enterprises.

The case for social responsibility of business is based on the following arguments:

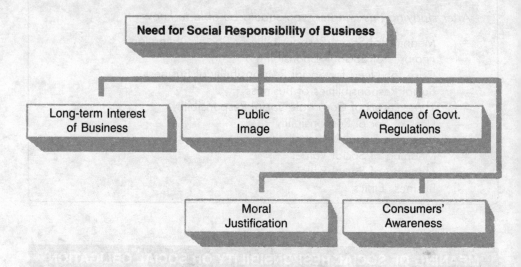

1. **Long-term Interest of Business** — Business being a part of the society must spend a portion of its profits to improve the social conditions. Improvement of social conditions creates an environment favorable for the long-run prosperity of the business. Business can bring the social improvements by taking necessary steps to control water, air & noise pollution, to develop educational facilities, to establish health centres etc.

2. **Public Image** — A business enterprise can build up its public image by undertaking activities to discharge social obligations. When a public image of business is built up, the business usually enjoys the support of the society which includes customers as well. As a result, the business is in position to increase its earnings.

3. **Avoidance of Government Regulations** — A business enterprise can avoid the need for government regulation if it voluntarily decides to discharge social obligation. For example, in case of manufacturing industries involving creation of air/water/noise pollution, the business enterprise should voluntarily take steps to prevent it. Where such voluntarily efforts are not made, the government may

order for the closure or shifting to some other place. Such closure or shifting may involve huge expenditure. For example, recently the Supreme court has issued such order for the closure of polluting units in Delhi City.

4. **Moral Justification** — On moral grounds also, the business enterprise should assume and discharge social obligations since it depends on society —

    (a) for physical resources
    (b) for human resources
    (c) for funds (capital as well as borrowings)
    (d) for disposal of goods and services
    (e) for common facilities like roads, water, power.

5. **Consumers' Awareness** — Due to increasing consumers' awareness of their own rights, business enterprise should assume and discharge social obligations. The various consumers' organisations educate the public about their rights as consumers. The various consumers' forums help the consumers to enforce their rights. It may be noted that the Consumer Protection Act, 1986 has also been passed. Now the business enterprise should supply the right quality of goods at reasonable price.

SOCIAL RESPONSIBILITIES OF BUSINESS

The social responsibilities of business is towards the following different groups of the society:

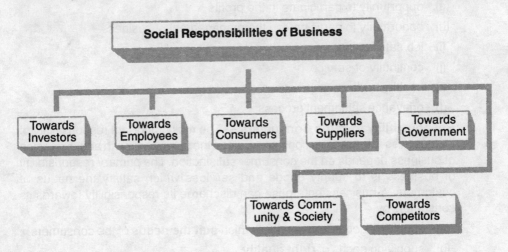

Let us discuss these responsibilities one by one.

1. **Responsibility towards Investors** — The primary responsibility of the business is towards the investors who contribute capital and bear the risks.

    Investors expect —

    (a) a fair and adequate rate of return on their capital
    (b) capital appreciation in the value of investment

(c) safety of capital contributed by them

(d) regular, accurate and upto date information about the working of the company.

(e) planned growth, solvency and optimum utilization of resources.

(f) respect their requests, suggestions etc.

(g) timely payment of their dues.

A business enterprise can discharge its responsibilities towards investors by taking the necessary steps for meeting the aforesaid expectations of the investors.

2. **Responsibility towards employees** — Another responsibility of the business is towards employees who contribute human capital. A business enterprise can discharge its responsibilities towards its employees by providing —

(a) fair remuneration to employees in terms of wages and salaries

(b) retirement benefits like gratuity, pension

(c) security of job

(d) opportunities for Self-Development and Promotion

(e) satisfactory working conditions,

(f) welfare amenities like housing accommodation, medical facilities, canteen facilities.

(g) opportunity to participate in the profits

(h) opportunity to participate in the management of business

(i) job satisfaction

(j) continuity of service

(k) healthy trade union practices

(l) grievance settlement process

3. **Responsibility towards Consumers** — The most important responsibility of the business is towards its consumers since the survival, growth and expansion of business depends on the consumer satisfaction. The primary responsibility of business is to supply goods and services which satisfy the needs of customers. A business enterprise can discharge its responsibility towards its consumers by—

(a) supplying goods and services which **suit the needs** of the consumers

(b) supplying goods of **right quality**

(c) supplying goods at **reasonable prices**

(d) ensuring **regular and adequate supply**

(e) attending to the grievances of consumers promptly and with courtesy.

4. **Responsibility towards Suppliers** — Every business enterprise has also responsibility towards its suppliers of materials and other items since the operating activities of the business depends on the materials and other items supplied by the suppliers. These suppliers expect fair price for the supplies,

reasonable terms of delivery and payments, regularity of payment according to credit terms. A business enterprise can discharge its obligations towards its suppliers by—

(a) giving them fair price for the supplies

(b) making regular payment as per terms of credit.

5. **Responsibility towards Government** — A business enterprise has certain responsibilities towards government in terms of compliance with the provisions of the law. A business enterprise can discharge its responsibility towards government by —

(a) Complying with the provisions of the applicable laws

(b) Paying all taxes (e.g. sales tax, Income tax, excise duties, custom duties), regularly and honestly

(c) Helping government in resolving national problems like development of backward and rural areas, reducing poverty, reducing unemployment etc.

(d) by using properly the national scarce resources

(e) by abating pollution

(f) by respecting community and citizens of the country.

6. **Responsibility towards the Community and Society** — A business enterprise has responsibility towards community and society as a whole. Business is expected to contribute to the safety and well being of the local community and public at large. A business enterprise can discharge its responsibility towards the community and society —

(a) by taking the necessary steps to control water, air and noise pollution

(b) by promoting and assisting educational, cultural and medical institutions so as to improve the standards of living of people

(c) by helping weaker sections of society by giving them preference while recruiting employees

(d) by providing for adequate safety precautions to avoid tragedies like leakage of poisonous gas from union carbide factory at Bhopal in Dec 1984

(e) by undertaking development programmes of backwards and rural areas

(f) by respecting human rights

(g) by donating funds for charitable purpose or any object of public utility.

7. **Responsibility Towards Competitors**

(a) Promote healthy competitive behaviour.

(b) Respect to both tangible and intellectual property rights.

(c) Foster ethical means and methods in business.

(d) Maintain healthy competition.

THREE LEVELS OF CORPORATE SOCIAL RESPONSIBILITY

Three levels of Corporate social responsibility are as follows:

Level-I : "Business has the responsibility to make a profit while dealing fairly and honestly."

Level-II : "Business has a responsibility to society with respect to its employees and products, and a responsibility to mirror the ideals and values of the society within its own microcosm."

Level-III : "It is a primary obligation of business to use its power to promote social ends perceived as moral."

USES OF SOCIAL RESPONSIBILITY

The uses of social responsibility of business towards society are as follows:

1. To give a clear picture of the whole business entity on the social responsibility aspect;
2. To make better understanding of social activities of entity on various segments such as employees, management, stock-holders, consumers, suppliers, investors, tax collecting authorities, law-makers, Government, public and community;
3. To protect environment;
4. Optimum use of national resources;
5. Welfare of employees;
6. To protect the assets of business;
7. To see welfare of community;
8. To respect the laws of the land;
9. Prosperity of Community;
10. Development of economy of a nation;
11. Improves the standard of living of people;
12. Fair price of goods to consumers;
13. Fair and healthy competition;
14. Social justice; protection of rights of workers; and
15. Quality Control.

ISSUES ON SOCIAL RESPONSIBILITY

The issues on social responsibility are as follows:

1. Environmental protection;
2. Equal Employment Opportunity;
3. Minimum wages;
4. Consumer productivity;
5. Affirmative Action;
6. Truth in Advertising; and
7. Occupational Safety and Health.

Conclusion — Business is created by society anticipating it would aid society. Society expects a lot of responsibilities and obligations. Although profit earning is essential for the survival of entity, it would spend certain amount of its earnings for the betterment of society and community. It is the obligation of business entity and decision-makers to take actions which protect and improve the welfare of the society as a whole along with their own interest. The scope of social responsibility reporting includes:

(i) Net income contribution;
(ii) Human resources contribution;
(iii) Public contribution;
(iv) Product or Service contribution.
(v) Environmental contribution.

The term contribution includes both benefits and costs associated with an organization's activities.

MEANING OF SOCIAL VALUES

Values on the basis of which members of a society judge each other's conduct or behaviour are known as social values. These social values determine what members of the society consider to be good or bad for the society. Social values in relation to business, include the following:

1. What are the characteristics of a good business?
2. What should be the objectives of a business?
3. How businessmen should carry on the business in the society's interest?

For example, if a business enterprise sells adultered goods or uses false weights or does not pay adequate remuneration to the employees, society considers it bad. On the other hand if a business enterprise sells quality goods at reasonable prices, society considers it good.

MEANING OF SOCIAL ETHICS

The moral principles derived from social values are called social ethics. These moral principles may also be called as the social codes of conduct or standard behaviour of members of the society.

BUSINESS ETHICS

The moral principles which should govern business activities in relation to society are called as business ethics. Business ethics suggest the ways and means of running a business which are morally justified. It prescribes principles which govern business practices and regulate the manner in which the business affairs should be conducted. Some of the examples of business ethics are given below:

1. Not to adopt dishonest means to earn profits.
2. Not to cause harm to others to earn profits
3. To sell genuine goods
4. To sell goods at reasonable prices
5. To pay taxes as an honest taxpayers

In *net shall*, the survival, growth and expansion of a business in the large run depend on the extent to which business ethics are being followed while conducting the affairs of the business.

Business Ethics refers to the business conduct or morals of standard. It is based on the cultural value system and the accepted ways of doing business in each society. Ethical norms are based on broadly accepted guidelines from religion, philosophy and legal system. Global managers are exposed to wide varieties of ethical problems. Therefore, understanding of ethical norms becomes essential for smooth operation of business.

Ethics is the study of decision making within a framework of a system of moral standards. The individual conduct that is considered 'right' and 'good' in the context of a governing moral code is called ethical behaviour. It is not only compatible with law but also confirms to a broader set of moral principles expected by all in the social group. Two basic questions arise in any examination of managerial ethics: (a) Can there be one fixed moral framework that can provide standards to guide managers every time they face ethical decisions? and (b) If a single set of standard is to guide managerial behaviour, which is the right set among the conflicting definitions of good and bad behaviour? As an example of ethical issue faced by companies, consider the case of pharmaceutical Burrough Welcome. It has come out with a drug AZT that slows the development of AIDS. The biggest issue is its pricing. At a cost of $3,000 for one year's dosage, many patients cannot afford it. The Burroughs contention is that it has kept the price as low as possible and that it has as much responsibility towards investors and employees as towards its customers. If it does not charge high enough price for the drug, it cannot pay adequate dividends to shareholders and cannot invest in research, impairing the health of the company and thus compromising the interests of its employees. A person whose value system gives more importance to relieving suffering might say that the price should be lowered. However, someone who believes that managers are obliged to repay shareholders as handsomely as possible might hold the view that a higher price is more appropriate. As this example shows, managers facing ethical issues are often feel pulled by conflicting interests.

_____ **EXERCISES** _____

VERY SHORT ANSWER TYPE QUESTIONS

1. What is meant by 'Social Responsibility'?
2. What is meant by 'Social Values'?
3. What is meant by 'Social Ethics"?
4. What is meant by "Business Ethics'?

SHORT ANSWER TYPE QUESTIONS

1. List the reasons for social responsibility of business?
2. List the different groups of the society towards business has social responsibilities.
3. List the social responsibilities of business towards Investors.
4. List the social responsibilities of business towards Employees.
5. List the social responsibilities of business towards Consumers.
6. List the social responsibilities of business towards Suppliers.
7. List the social responsibilities of business towards Government.
8. Explain briefly the concepts of social values and business ethics.

LONG ANSWER TYPE QUESTIONS

1. Give reasons to justify why business should assume social responsibilities.
2. Explain briefly the social responsibilities of business towards different groups of the society.

Factors to be considered for Starting Business

4

FACTORS TO BE CONSIDERED FOR STARTING A BUSINESS

The following factors should be considered for starting a business:

1. Identification of Business Opportunity
2. Market Assessment
3. Product/Service Design
4. Raw Material
5. Whether to make or buy the component comprising the final product
6. Technology and Selection of Equipment
7. Manpower
8. Utilities
9. Land and Building
10. Selection of Site
11. Working Capital Requirements
12. Requirement of Total Funds
13. Sources of Funds
14. What should be the form of organization
15. What is the Cost of Production?
16. What are Cost Break Even Point and Financial Break Even Point?
17. What is Profitability?
18. What are Funds from Operations?
19. What is Cash from Operations?
20. Implementation Schedule

Let us discuss these factors one by one.

1. Identification of Business Opportunity

The process by which an opportunity is identified is described as opportunity scanning or sensing and identification (OSI). An important tool in the identification of a business opportunity is the SWOT analysis. SWOT Analysis means analysis of our strengths and weaknesses in relation to opportunities in the market and competitive threats to the same.

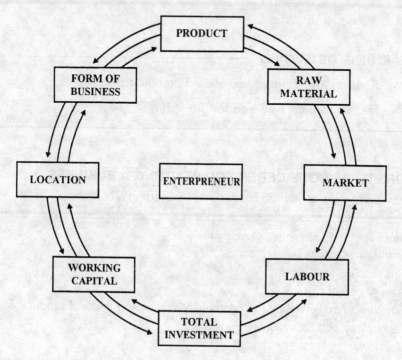

Figure 1 : Opportunity Identification an Interdependence Process

An entrepreneur would evaluate an opportunity somewhat as follows:

1. **What is the Status of Industry in the Economy?**
   (i) Present Production
   (ii) Present Demand
   (iii) Licensed & Installed Capacity
   (iv) Government Policies
   (v) Export Potential

2. How large is the gap between demand and supply in the market?

3. What is the nature of competition in the market for his product?

4. Is the product covered under any of the promotional policies of the government so that either entry into business or competition in the market are facilitated?

5. Are there any special product/service specific problems that he will face and can he avail of any part of promotional policies to soften the impact of these problems?

6. Based on all such product-market policy, policy-product-market type of analysis he will finally conclude that the opportunity is worth-investing-in.

    The same process is represented diagrammatically wherein the SWOT framework is shown and its visualization by an entrepreneur as not a static but maniputable framework.

Opportunity Identification through SWOT

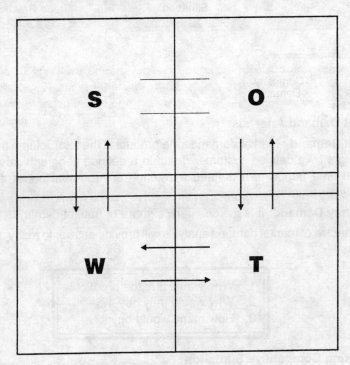

Figure 2 : SWOT Analysis

Notes:

i)   The four rectangles represent the subjectives and objective side of an opportunity respectively.

ii) Dotted lines which enlarges S and O can be due to

   a) Policies which help new, first generation self-employed entrepreneurs and hence add to their strengths.

   b) Policies of reservations of products etc. may enlarge the field of opportunities and contract that of thereats.

iii) The SWOT framework can be a manipulated framework.

2. Market Assessment

Three aspects needs to be covered in order to complete the exercises of market assessment:

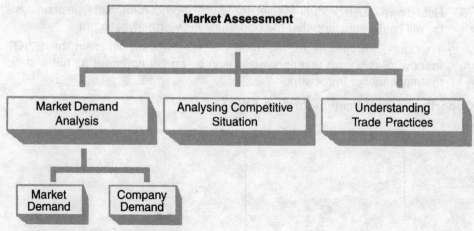

I. Market Demand Analysis

Market Demand : Market demand for a product is the total volume that would be bought by a defined customer group in a defined geographical area in a defined time period in a defined marketing environment under a defined marketing programme.

Company Demand: It is the company's share of market demand.

The exercise of market demand analysis will provide answer to many questions such as—

> 1. Who would buy the product?
> 2. Why would they buy it?
> 3. How many would buy it?

II. Analysing Competitive Situtaiton

In order to assess and understand the competitive situation, an entrepreneur should try to answer the following questions:

> 1. How many firms are in competition with him?
> 2. What are their market share?
> 3. What are the strengths and weaknesses of their products?
> 4. What kind of consumer image does each product enjoy?
> 5. What trade practices do the competitors employ?
> 6. Who are the major customers of each brand?

A study of this kind can be systematized by using a chart shown below. The exercise of preparing the chart may be quite tedious but the help it will provide in understanding the competitive situation would justify the work involved.

Competitive Products	Market Share	Product Price	Product Features	Product Image to Dealers	Discount Terms	Credit Major Customers
BRAND 'A' BRAND 'B' BRAND 'C'						

Figure 3: A framework for understanding the competition

This kind of rigorous analysis will bring to light where the entrepreneur can score over the competition, where the competition has an edge over him, and what are the areas of opportunities and threats. The analysis will help him tune his marketing efforts to the requirements to the customers and the trade. Correct understanding of the nature and extent of competition is essential as the whole process of marketing planning revolves around this understanding.

III. Understanding Trade Practices

In order to understand prevailing trade practices, an entrepreneur should try to answer the following questions:

1. Whether it has to reach the ultimate customers directly or through intermediaries (i.e. Marketing middlemen like Distribution, wholesaler, retailers, commission agents, brokers)

2. If middlemen are to employed what kind of middlemen are required?

3. How many middlemen are required ?

4. Places where middlemen are required?

5. How much selling load taken by each middlemen?

6. How much trade discounts are required to be offered?

7. How much cash discount are required to be offered?

8. What kind of gift scheme is to be offered for middlemen and ultimate customers?

9. How much credit period is to be allowed?

10. What are the prevailing sales tax and other legal implication in selling to the middlemen situated in different locations?

11. Whether some middlemen in some areas require for their own brand name to be put on the product.

12. What are the available modes of transportation to reach them.

3. Product/Service Design

The exercise of designing the product will answer to many questions such as-

1. What kind of **process** is required?
2. What kind of **quality** is required?
3. What **types of raw-materials** are required?
4. What **types of labour skills** are required?
5. What **kind of supervision** to manufacture the product required?

4. Raw Material

The excercise of raw-materials analysis will answer to many questions such as—

1. What types of raw materials are required for producing the proposed product?
2. What are the quality specifications of all such raw materials?
3. What are the chemicals, stores, consumables and packing materials required for producing the proposed product?
4. What is percentage of raw materials loss at each stage of production process?
5. What is quantity of raw materials, chemicals, stores, consumables and packing material required per unit of output?
6. What are the Sources of procurement? If the raw materials are to be procured from the international market, are there any restrictions on supply?

   Cost of raw materials for the first year, 2nd year and so on upto 10 years.
7. What is the Supply position? i.e. position regarding availability of the raw materials.

   Comment on availability of major raw materials-whether these materials are easily available or are occasionally or continuously in short supply.
8. If any tie-up arrangement required for procurement of raw materials?
9. Are there alternate raw materials other than what is proposed to be used? Have such alternative been examined? Provide details
10. What are prevailing prices of various raw materials, chemicals, stores, consumables and packing materials?
11. What other taxes, freight, duties, excise, octroi and such other charges are to be paid in addition to the price?
12. What is the length of credit period allowed by suppliers?

5. Whether to make or buy the component comprising the final product

Some of the factors influencing make or buy decision are:

1. What are the Idle facilities?
2. What are the Plant capabilities (Product quality, quantity and service, Personnel, equipment, future capabilities)?
3. What is the economic advantage?
4. What is supplier's reliability regarding Quality, quantity, service, schedule?
5. What are trade relations?
6. What are employment stabilization's?
7. What are trade union views?
8. What are alternative resource uses?
9. What are legal restrictions (Patents etc.)?

6. Technology and Selection of Equipment

Technology is the process of converting inputs (i.e. materials, labour) into outputs. The various factors for evaluating production process and equipment selection are as follows:

1. What are product/service requirements?
2. What is technological feasibility?
3. Financial considerations.
4. What are the Labour and skill requirements?
5. What capacity is to be installed?
6. Are new facilities compatible with existing facilities?
7. Are new facilities flexible?
8. What are raw material requirements?
9. What is the size and weight limits imposed by plant or building?
10. What kind of Maintainability required?
11. What are the spare parts inventory requirements?

7. Manpower

The excercise of manpower analysis will answer to many questions such as —

1. What are the requirement of skilled, semi-skilled personnel for production operations for the first year, second year and so on for upto first 10 years of project life?
2. Whar the requirements of administrative/managerial staff and marketing personnel?
3. What is the cost of manpower during first year, second year and so on for 10 years?
4. What is the position regarding availability of skilled manpower?
5. What is the scheme for training skilled manpower in case they are not readily available? Describe.

8. Utilities

The excercise of utilities analysis will answer to many questions such as—

1. What are the requirements of **power, water, fuel steam, compressed air** and other consumables: Quantity and value for the first year, 2nd year and so on upto 10 years?
2. What are the sources of said materials?
3. What is the position regarding availability of said materials?
4. What is the specific arrangements for electric power?
5. Effluents-type and quality of effluents, their treatment and disposal, investment in the effluent treatment and disposal. Government of India has since decided that any project proposal has to have a clearance of Environmental Authority set up by the government, i.e. Pollution Control Board in the states (PCB).

9. Land and Building

The excercise of Land & Building analysis will answer to many questions such as—

1. What is the area of land required?
2. How much constructed area is required?
3. What type of construction is required?
4. What are the building specifications?
5. What is the cost of land and construction of building?

10. Selection of Site

The location of a project is decided by comparing the relative cost advantages of setting up the project at various places. Normally, it is the nearness to the source of the raw materials or nearness to the basic infrastructure facilities or proximity to the markets for the finished products which determine the location of a project. **According to Weber's theory**, location of a project depends upon whether or not the raw-materials lose much weight in the production process.

Whether Raw-material lose much weight?	Where it may be economical to locate?
(a) **If raw-materials lose much weight in the production process.**	It may be economical to locate the project **near the source of raw-materials.** Thus, sugar factories are located near the sugarcane fields.
(b) **If raw-materials do not lose much weight in the production process.**	It may be economical to locate the project **near the market for the finished products.**

An ideal site is one where—

1. the unit cost of production and physical distribution is minimum
2. the profit is **maximum**
3. there is **opportunity for further growth and expansion**.
4. Political & underworld disturbances are absent or minimum.

The various factors for evaluating the location are as follows:

1. Availability of Materials
2. Availability of Labour
3. Easy Access to Markets
4. Competition.
5. Economics (Purchasing power of community, number of people employed in the area, per capita retail sales etc.)
6. Personal factors.
7. Geographic considerations.
8. Local laws and regulations

Selecting a facility location usually involves a sequence of decisions. The general procedure proposed by William J Stevenson for making location decisions consists of the following steps.

Step 1 → Determine the criteria that will be used to evaluate location alternatives, such as increased revenues or community service.

Step 2 → Identify factors that are important, such as location of markets or materials.

Step 3 → Develop location alternatives.

    i) Identify the general region for a location.

    ii) Identify a small number of community site alternatives.

A summary of the factors that affect location is provided in the following Table.

Factors	*Considerations*
Locations of raw materials or supplies	Proximity, modes and costs of transportation, quantity available.
Location of Markets	Proximity, distribution, costs, target market, Trade practices/restrictions.
Location of labour	Availability [general and for specific skills], age distribution of work force, attitudes toward work, union or nonuion, productivity, wage scales, unemployment compensationlaws.
Facilities	Schools, churches, shopping, housing, transportation, entertainment, etc.
Services	Medical, Fire and Police
Attitudes	Pro/cons
Taxes Environmental Regulations Utilities Development Support	State/local, direct and indirect State/local Cost and availability Bond issues, tax abatement, low-cost loans, grants.
Land	Cost, degree of development required, soil characteristics, room for expansion, drainage, parking.
Transportation	Type [access roads, rail spurs, air freight]
Environmental/legal	Zoning restrictions.

How to arrive at final decision?

Step 1 → Prepare a checklist for each of the following considerations.

    I. Basic Considerations (Development status of the town and its location with reference to enterprises needs)

    II. Physical Infrastructure considerations (Power, Water, etc.)

    III. Commercial infrastructure considerations (Telecommunication, banking etc.)

    IV. Social Infrastructure considerations (Housing, Health etc.)

    V. Financial Incentives considerations (Investment Subsidy, Income-tax concession etc.)

    VI. Site-specific considerations (Land, Price, Contours etc.)

Step 2 → Records the findings against each point in the checklist.

Step 3 → Make final decision on the basis of findings.

The checklists for each of the above considerations are given below:

I. Checklist for Basic Considerations

1. Location (City/Town/Village)
2. Population
3. Nearest large city (Name and Distance)
4. Connections to major cities (Rail, road, air-distance, Connection, Frequency)
5. Climate (Minimum/maximum temperature, humidity, minimum/maximum rainfall)
6. Distance from important geographical markets
7. Distance from major raw material sources and significance (or lack of it) of enterprise proximity to such sources.
8. Distance and connection to relevant ports (in case of export/import oriented enterprises)
9. Manpower: availability of required skills and prevailing wage rates
10. Overall industrial relations (strike/lockout/dispute in the area)
11. Law and order position in the area
12. Level of industrial development in the area and anticipated tempo.
13. Composition of industrial development in terms of types of industry and size/health of existing enterprises.
14. Proposed enterprise and govt. preference for type of industries at proposed location.
15. Whether ready built-up factory shed is available at the location and whether its size conforms to your need.

II. Checklist for Physical Infrastructure Considerations

1. **Land** — Availability and Price
2. Whether there exists an organized industrial estate.
3. **Water-supply** — Source (river, canal, tubewell), distance, quality (pH, Hardness), rate, common storage facility, operating authority (Public Works Department, industrial estate authorities corporation, municipality).
4. **Power Supply** — Nearest substation, feeder type (industrial/rural).
5. **Effluent** — Treatment and Disposal (if relevant): Disposal point (land, sea, river), arrangement for treatment (individual, common), drainage arrangement for conveying the effluent (open, underground), treatment and conveyance charge.
6. Approach road/internal roads
7. Street lighting
8. Responsibility for maintaining roads, drainage and street lighting (a single or multiple agencies).
9. Responsibility for maintaining roads, drainage and street lighting (a single or multiple agencies).

III. Checklist for Commercial Infrastructure Considerations

1. Telecommunication (availability of new telephone connections, manual or automatic exchange, STD facility, Telex facility, etc.)
2. Postal and telegram facility
3. Banking facility
4. Transport-operator facility
5. Weighbridge
6. Typing/photocopying
7. Courier
8. Waterhousing
9. Nearest offices of law-enforcing agencies (excise, sales tax, labor laws, factory inspection, pollution control etc.).
10. Nearest Offices of Industry-assisting agencies (State Finance Corporation, Industrial Estate Corporation, Raw material/Marketing Corporation, District Industry Centre which sanctions and disburses financial incentives).
11. Building/Electrical/Fabrication contractor facility.
12. Building material, spares parts and such other shops.
13. Motor-rewinding, painting, gas-supply and such other industrial services.
14. Technical educational facility (e.g. Industrial Training Institute, Polytechnic).
15. Professional resources position (Management/industrial consultants, financial/legal advisers, management/productivity associations).

IV. Checklist for Social Infrastructure Considerations

1. **Housing** — Availability, Quality, Price (ownership and rent), Public Housing (Actual and Planned housing by State Housing Board, Infrastructure Corporation or such other agencies).
2. **Education** — Primary, secondary and university education facility (quality, number of seats, ease of admission, medium of instruction).
3. **Health** — Dispensary, hospital, specialties.
4. **Recreational Facility** — Cinema, restaurant, library, parks etc.
5. Hotel Accommodation
6. Service Organisations: Rotary, Lion etc.

V. Checklist for Financial Incentive Considerations

1. Investment subsidy (from the Govt.)
2. Income-tax concession.
3. Sales tax exemption/interest-free sales-tax loan.
4. Promoter contribution (margin) and interest-rate policy followed by Finance institutions.
5. Electricity-duty exemption, local-tax exemption and such other incentives.

VI. Checklist for Site-specific Considerations

1. Whether the proposed site is a part of an organised industrial estate.
2. Direction of town-growth with reference to the site.
3. Non-agricultural status of the site.
4. Site-contours (levelled, hilly, pits, ravines, brick-kilns).
5. Site-shape (regular/irregular).
6. Immediate proximity of railway line, national highway, state highway.
7. Overhead telephones or powerlines or underground water/drainage/gas line passing through the site.
8. Access to national/state highway or other roads provided by the site.
9. Wind direction in relation to the site.
10. Soil-type.

11. Working Capital Requirements

The estimation of working capital requirements requires to answer the following questions.

1. What would be stock level of raw-materials?

   (Factors to be considered for this purpose include minimum & maximum consumption of raw-materials, delivery period)

2. What would be the stock level of work-in-progress?

   (Factors to be considered for this purpose include conversion process period)

3. What would be the stock level of finished goods?

   (Factors to be considered include demand pattern of finished goods)

4. What would be the level of debtors?

   (Factors to be considered include credit period allowed to customers)

5. What would be the level of pre-payments?

   (Factor to be considered include terms of advance payments)

6. What would be the level of cash-in-hand?

   (Factors to be considered include the frequency & quantum of cash payments to be made)

7. What would be the level of Bank Balance?

   (Factors to be considered include minimum balance as per commitment with the bank, the frequency & quantum of payments by cheque to be made)

8. What would be the level of creditors?

   (Factor to be considered include credit period allowed by suppliers)

9. What would be the level of outstanding wages, manufacturing expenses, office & Adm. Exp. and Selling & Distribution Expenses?

   (Factors to be considered include time lag in payment of expenses)

10. What is the total requirement of working capital?

11. How much is (a) permanent working capital, (b) Temporary working capital?

12. What are the sources of financing the requirements of working capital?

12. Requirement of Total Funds

What will be the Total Requirement of Funds for the project?

Give a break-up of the cost of land (including development cost), building, machinery's, miscellaneous fixed assets, technical know-how fees if any, preliminary/pre-operative expenses, margin money for working capital and contingencies and escalation.

13. Sources of Funds

1. What will be promoter's contribution?
2. Is any subsidy available from government/local authority?
3. What are the national and international sources of finance?
4. Is trading on equity beneficial? (i.e. whether Return on Investment exceeds the Rate of Interest on Borrowed Funds?)

14. What should be the Form of Organization

Your decision about choosing a specific form of ownership is guided by various factors such as:

1. Your personal capacity to take decisions, manage and control particular situations.
2. Your capacity to cover risk,
3. Your professional background which includes your educational background, technical expertise and experience or expertise in manufacture of proposed product, and
4. Your capacity to invest in your dream enterprise.

15. What is the Cost of Production?

A projected cost sheet should be prepared at different levels of capacity (say at 50%, 60%) over a period of 5 to 10 years. Foreign Exchange Cost (if any) should also be specified.

16. What are cost break event point & financial break even point?

Cost Break Even Point refers to that level (which may be expressed in terms of sales units, sales (rupees), Capacity %) at which the enterprise makes *neither* profit *nor* loss. In other words, BEP is the point at which contribution (i.e. sales *less* variable cost) is just equal to fixed cost. *Alternatively,* BEP is the point at which Total Sales Revenue is just equal to total cost (i.e. fixed cost + variable cost).

Financial Break Even Point refers to that level at which Earning Per Share is zero. In other words, FBEP is the point at which the enterprise is just able to meet its fixed financial commitments (i.e. interest & preference dividend).

17. What is Profitability?

A projected Income Statement should be prepared to ascertain profitability at different levels of capacity over a period of 5 to 10 years.

18. What is Fund from operations?

A projected Funds Flow Statement should be prepared to ascertain funds inflow & funds outflows and funds from operations (i.e. operating profit + depreciation) at different levels of capacity over a period of 5 to 10 years.

19. What is Cash from Operations?

A projected Cash Flow Statement should be prepared to ascertain cash inflows & cash outflows at different levels of capacity over a period of 5 to 10 years.

Cash inflow indicates how much money is coming into business from where and when. Cash outflow indicates how much money is going out of business, to where and when. If cash outflows exceed cash inflows, make arrangement to finance shortage. If cash inflows exceed cash outflows, make arrangement to utilize the surplus.

20. Implementation Schedule

Implementation schedule is an aid to ensure timely implementation of your business plan. Timely implementation is important because if there is a delay, it causes, among other things, a project cost overrun. A project meant to be implemented in 12 months at a cost of Rs 15 lakhs may entail an expenditure of Rs 20 lakhs, if there is a delay in implementation and this may jeopardise the financial viability of the project itself. Hence, the need to draw up a schedule and more importantly, to adhere to it.

It may be noted that project cost computation includes interest during construction period. The amount of such interest depends on your schedule for drawal of term-loan funds which in turn tied up with your implementation progress. Thus, implementation schedule is required to arrive at an estimate of interest during construction period.

Drawing an implementation Schedule consists of the following steps:

Step 1→ List the activities required to be taken prior to commencement of commercial production.

Step 2 → Ascertain the inter-dependence among these activities and hence the chain-effect of delay in carrying out one activity overall implementation schedule.

Step 3 → Identify the activities which can be carried out simultaneously.

Step 4 → Time required to complete each activity

Step 5 → Resources required to complete each activity

An interested entrepreneur can use Project Evaluation and Review Technique (PERT)/Critical path Method (CPM) to gain better insights into all implementations related operations and to ensure a closer monitoring of implementation progress.

EXERCISES

SHORT ANSWER TYPE QUESTIONS

1. List any five factors to be considered for starting a business.
2. List the factors to be considered accoding to Weber's theory of location.

3. What is an ideal site?
4. List the factors to be considered for evaluating the location.
5. How will you idenify business opportuniy?
6. How will you assess the market?
7. List the factors to be considered while designing the product.
8. List the factors to be considered regarding raw-materials?
9. List the factors to be considered while selecting technology and equipment/
10. List the factors to be considered regarding man-power.
11. List the factors to be considered regarding utilities.
12. List the factors to be considered regarding land & building.
13. List the factors to be considered regarding location of industries.
14. List the factors to be considered while estimating working capital requirements.

LONG ANSWER TYPE QUESTIONS

1. Discuss fully the factors to be considered while selecting the location of a plant.
2. Discuss fully the various entrepreneurial decisions which must be taken while promoting a new business enterprise.

Forms & Formation of Business Enterprises

5

MEANING OF PRIVATE SECTOR ENTERPRISE

A private sector enterprise or a private enterprise is one which is owned, managed and controlled by private entrepreneur(s). For example, business houses managed by Tata such as TELCO, TISCO, TATAPOWER, business houses managed by Birlas such an Century, MRPL, Birla Yamaha, Grasim Industries, business houses managed by Ambanies such as Reliance Industries, Reliance Petroleum, Reliance Capital.

CHARACTERISTICS OF PRIVATE SECTOR ENTERPRISES

The main characteristics of private sector enterprises are as follows:

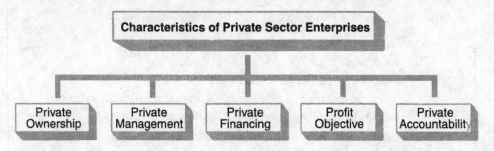

Let us discuss these characteristics one by one.

1. **Private Ownership** — Private Sector Enterprises are owned by private entrepreneur(s).
2. **Private Management** — The rights of its management vest in the owner but professionals can be employed for the efficient management of such enterprises.
3. **Private Financing** — Such enterprises are financed by the private entrepreneurs.
4. **Profit Objective** — Such enterprises are mainly guided by profit objective.
5. **Private Accountability** — Those who manage such enterprises are accountable to the owners for the performance of such enterprises.

FORMS OF PRIVATE SECTOR ENTERPRISES

Private sector enterprises may be classified into the following categories:

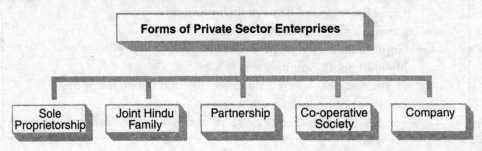

Let us discuss these forms of private sector enterprises one by one.

SOLE PROPRIETORSHIP – MEANING, FEATURES, MERITS & LIMITATIONS

MEANING OF SOLE PROPRIETORSHIP

A sole Proprietorship is a form of private sector enterprise that is owned, managed and controlled by an individual entrepreneur. This type of business organization is also called single ownership or single Proprietorship. Such individual entrepreneur is called as sole-Proprietor. The sole-proprietor arranges the finance, manages the business affairs, takes the profits or bears the losses.

FEATURES OF SOLE PROPRIETORSHIP

The main characteristics of sole-proprietorship are as follows:

1. **Individual Ownership** — Sole-Proprietorship form of organization is owned by an individual.

2. **Individual Management & Control** — Such organization is managed and controlled by the sole proprietor. Competent people can be employed for the efficient management of such enterprises.

3. **Individual Financing** — Such organization is financed mainly by the sole-Proprietor.

4. **Individual Accountability** — The persons (including sole-proprietor and employed managers) who manage the affairs of the business are accountable to the sole-proprietor. Sole-proprietor is the sole beneficiary of the profits. He has to bear the losses, if any.

5. **Unlimited Liability** — The liability of sole-proprietor is unlimited. In other words, if the business assets are not sufficient to meet the business liabilities, his private assets (after meeting private liabilities) are to be used to discharge the business liabilities.

6. **Minimum Govt. Regulation** — There are minimum government regulations to set up such form of organisation. For example, we can start a fruit stall or a cycle/scooter/photocopier shop without much legal formalities. However in some cases, a license may be required to be obtained for example, to start a restaurant, a licence from local authority is required. No specific regulation exists to form sole proprietorship.

MERITS OF SOLE PROPRIETORSHIP

The merits of sole proprietorship form of organization are as follows:

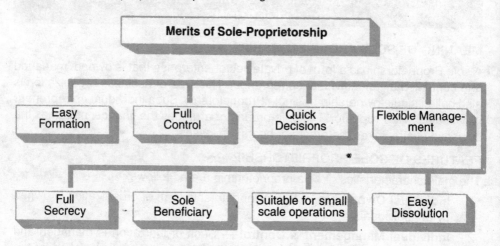

Let us discuss these merits of Sole-Proprietorship one by one.

1. **Easy formation** — It is very easy and simple to form sole-proprietorship. There is no specific regulation which governs the formation of sole-proprietorship.

2. **Full Control** — Proprietor exercises full control over the functioning and working of the business.

3. **Quick Decisions** — Proprietor takes quick decisions on various matters relating to business operations since he does not depend on others for decision making. This makes functioning of business simple and easy.

4. **Flexible Management** — The sole proprietor can easily bring about changes in the size and nature of activity according to the changing condition. This gives flexibility to business.

5. **Full Secrecy** — Full secrecy can be maintained since business secrets are known to the proprietor only.

6. **Sole Beneficiary of Profits** — All the profits of the business belong to the sole-proprietor. This motivates the proprietor to work hard and develop the business to get more & more profits since there is direct relation between effort and reward.

7. **Suitable for Small Scale Operations** — The sole proprietorship is very suitable for small scale operations. Such a business is also entitled to get certain concessions from government. *For example*, a small industrial unit may get loan at lower rates of interest, water & electricity at concessional rates.

8. **Easy Dissolution** — It is very easy and simple to dissolve sole-proprietorship. There is no specific regulation which governs the dissolution of sole-proprietorship.

LIMITATIONS OF SOLE PROPRIETORSHIP

The limitations of sole-proprietorship form of organization are as follows:

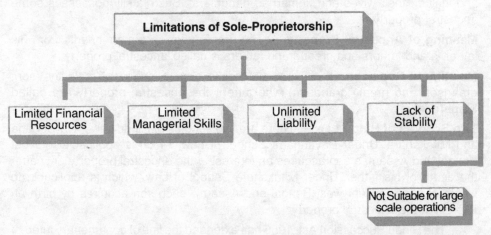

Let us discuss these limitations of Sole-Proprietorship one by one.

1. **Limited Financial Resources** — The sole proprietor has a limited capital and has limited capacity to raise funds because of limited personal assets. This limitation reduces the scope for expansion and growth of business.

2. **Limited Managerial Skills** — The sole proprietor has limited managerial skills and need not possess expertise in all areas like production, finance, marketing. This limitation reduces the scope for efficient management, expansion and growth of the business.

3. **Unlimited Liability** — The sole proprietor has an unlimited liability. He is personally liable for all business debts. In other words, if the business assets are not sufficient to meet the business liabilities, his private assets (after meeting private liabilities) are to be used to discharge the business liabilities.

4. **Lack of Continuity /Stability** — Such form of organization suffers from lack of continuity/stability since the continuity and stability of the business depends solely on one person. The illness of the proprietor may cause temporary closure of business and the death of the proprietor may cause the permanent closure.

5. **Not suitable for large scale operations** — Such form of organization is not suitable for large scale operations since the resources of the sole proprietor are limited. Since sole proprietorship usually operates on small scale only, the benefits of large scale operations are not available. This raises the cost of business operations.

JOINT HINDU FAMILY BUSINESS–MEANING AND FEATURES

MEANING OF JOINT HINDU FAMILY BUSINESS

Joint Hindu Family Business is a unique form of business organization prevailing only in India. It represents a business organization which is owned by the members of a Joint Hindu Family. It is also known as Hindu Undivided Family Business (HUF Business). It is governed by Hindu Law.

Meaning of HUF — According to the Hindu Law, "Hindu Undivided Family is a family which consists of all persons lineally descended from a common ancestor and include their wives and unmarried daughters". Such family possesses some ancestral property.

Meaning of Ancestral Property — The property which a man inherits from his father, grand fathers and great grand fathers is called 'ancestral property'.

Meaning of Coparceners — Three successive generations in the male line (son, grandson and great - grandson) who inherit the ancestral property are called 'Caparceners'.

Two Schools of Hindu Law — There are two schools of Hindu Law – Dayabhaga and Mitakshara. Under Dayabhaga School of Law, which is applicable to West Bengal and Assam, a son acquires an interest in the ancestral property only after the death of his father. Under Mitakshara School of Law, which is applicable to whole of India (except west Bengal and Assam), each son acquires by birth an interest in the ancestral property.

The Hindu Succession Act, 1956 has extended the line of coparcenary interest to female relatives of the deceased coparcener or male relatives claiming through such female relatives.

Meaning of Karta — The senior most Coparcener is called Karta who manages the joint family business.

FEATURES OF JOINT HINDU FAMILY

The main features of Joint Hindu Family are as follows:

1. **Creation** — It arises by status or operation of Hindu Law.
2. **Membership** — A male member becomes a member merely by his birth. The membership is restricted to three successive generations.
3. **Management** — The joint Hindu family business is managed by the senior most member of the family called Karta. The other members may assist him in the management of business.
4. **Liability** — The liability of the Karta is unlimited whereas the liability of other members is limited to the extent of their share in the property of the family business. Karta is personally liable if business assets are not sufficient to discharge business liabilities.
5. **Right to Accounts** — The member other than Karta do not have right to inspect and copy the account books, and ask for the account of past dealings.
6. **Dissolution of Business** — The Hindu Undivided Family continues to operate even after the death of a coparcener. Joint Hindu Family business comes to an end when the members so decide by mutual agreement.
7. **Implied Authority** — Only the Karta has implied authority to bind the Hindu Undivided family business by acts done in the ordinary course of the business of the firm.

PARTNERSHIP–MEANING AND FEATURES

MEANING OF PARTNERSHIP

Partnership grew essentially because of the limitations and failure of the sole-proprietorships due to limited financial resources and managerial skills.

Partnership is an association of persons who agree to combine their financial resources and managerial abilities to carry on a business and share the profits in an agreed ratio.

According to Section 4 of The Indian Partnership Act, 1932, *"Partnership is the relation between two or more persons who have agreed to share the profits of a business carried on by all or any of them acting for all."*

Meaning of 'Partners', 'Firm' and 'Firm's name'

The persons who have entered into partnership with one another are called individually 'partners' and collectively a 'firm' and the name under which their business is carried on is called the 'firm's name'.

Minimum Number and Maximum Number of Partners

The partnership Act specifies the minimum number (i.e. two) of persons to form partnership but is silent on the maximum number of partners. It is section 11 of the companies Act, which gives us the maximum limit. It states that any association having a membership of more than 10 in case of Banking Business or 20 in case of non-banking business must be registered as a corporate body failing which it would become an illegal association.

FEATURES OF PARTNERSHIP

The main features of partnership are as follows:

1. **Two or more Persons** — There must be at least two persons to form a partnership and all such persons must be competent to contract. According to Section 11 of the Indian Contract Act, 1872, every person except the following is competent to contract:

   (i) Minor

   (ii) Persons of unsound mind (e.g. lunatics, idiots), and

   (iii) Persons disqualified by any law to which they are subject (e.g., alien enemies, insolvents).

   However, the Partnership Act is silent about the maximum number of members that Partnership may have. It is Section 11 of the Companies Act which gives us the maximum limit. It states that any association having membership of more than 10 in case of Banking business or 20 in case of non-banking business must be registered as a Corporate body failing which it would become an illegal association.

2. **Agreement** — There must be an agreement to form a partnership. This agreement may be expressed (whether written or oral) or implied. This essential element is further clarified under Section 5. Section 5 provides that the relation of partnership arises from contract and not from status. That is why, a Hindu

undivided family carrying on a family business is not considered a partnership. The reason is that the coparceners of a Hindu undivided family acquire interest in the business because of their status (i.e., birth) in the family and not because of any agreement between them. Thus, partnership is voluntary and contractual in nature.

3. **Business** — There must exist a business. According to Section 2(b), the term 'Business' includes every trade, occupation and profession. For example, when two or more persons agrees to share the income of a joint property (e.g., rent from a building), it does not amount to a partnership because there does not exist any business. Similarly, an association created for charitable, religious or social purpose cannot be regarded as partnership because there does not exist any business. It may also be noted that an agreement to carry on business at a future time does not result in partnership unless that time arrives and the business is started.

4. **Sharing of Profits** — There must be sharing of profits. Unless otherwise agreed, sharing of profits implies sharing of losses as well. It may also be noted that sharing of profits is a prima facie evidence and not a conclusive evidence of partnership. That is why, everyone who share the profits of business need not necessarily be a partner. For example, a manager who receives a particular share in the profits of a business as part of his remuneration, is simply an employee and not a partner.

5. **Mutual Agency** — There must exist a mutual agency relationship among the partners. 'Mutual Agency' relationship means that each partner is both an agent and a principal. Each partner is an agent in the sense that he has the capacity to bind other partners by his acts done. Each partner is a principal in the sense that he is bound by the acts of other partners.

The mutual relationship of agency is emphasized in Section 18 of the Indian Partnership Act, which reads as under.

"Subject to the provision of this Act, a partner is the agent of the firm for the business of the firm."

Moreover, the use of the words' **carried on by all or by any of them acting for all**, in Section 4 of the Act clearly emphasizes agency relationship.

Such mutual agency relationship in case of a firm of X, Y and Z has been shown below:

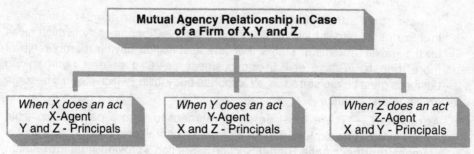

Fig. Mutual Agency Relationship in case of a Firm of X, Y and Z.

Because of the existence of mutual agency relationship amongst the partners, the law of partnership is also regarded as an extension of the general law of agency. It may be noted that the mutual agency relationship distinguishes a partnership from co-ownership and simple agreement for sharing profits.

6. **Unlimited Liability** — Partners have unlimited liability since the liability of the partner is joint and several. In other words, they are collectively and individually liable to the creditors of the firm. If the firm's assets are not sufficient to meet firm's debts, then firm's creditors can recover their debts from the private assets of one or all the partners.

7. **Joint Ownership and Control** — Firm is owned and controlled jointly by the partners since every partner has a right to take part in the management of the business.

8. **Non-transferability of Share** — A partner can not transfer his share in partnership to any other person without the consent of all other partners.

9. **Duration of Partnership** — The partnership may or may not have a particular duration depending upon the provision in the partnership agreement or mutual consent of all the partners.

PARTNERSHIP DEED

A partnership is formed by an agreement. This agreement may be expressed (i.e., oral or in writing) or implied. Though the law does not expressly require that the partnership agreement should be in writing, it is desirable to have it in writing in order to avoid any dispute with regard to the terms of the partnership. The document which contains the terms of a partnership as agreed among the partners is called 'partnership deed'. The deed is required to be duly sampled as per the Indian Stamp Act, 1889 and duly signed by all the partners. The partnership deed contains various provisions relating to various matters such as:

Examples of Contents of Partnership Deed

1. Name of the firm.
2. Names and addresses of all partners
3. Nature and place of business
4. Date of commencement of partnership
5. Duration of partnership
6. Amount of capital of each partner
7. Profit sharing ratio
8. Interest on capital
9. Interest on drawings
10. Interest on loan advanced by a partner to the firm
11. Salary or commission payable to any partner
12. Method of valuation of goodwill and other assets and liabilities in case of admission or retirement or death of a partner
13. Settlement of accounts in case of retirement/death of a partner or dissolution of firm.

Notes:

(i) The partnership deed must not contain any term which is in contravention with the provisions of the Indian Partnership Act.

(ii) The terms laid down in the partnership deed may be varied by to consent of all the partners.

REGISTRATION OF A PARTNERSHIP FIRM

Meaning of Registration

Registration means getting the partnership registered with the Registrar of Firm of the area in which the place of business of the firm is situated or proposed to be situated:

Procedure for Registration

The practical steps involved in the registration of a firm are given below in Exhibit 5.1

Exhibit 5.1 Practical Steps Involved in the Registration of a Firm

Step 1→ Obtain a Statement in the prescribed form from the office of the Registrar of Firms of the area in which any place of business of the firm in situated or proposed to be situated.

Step 2 → State the following information in the statement:

(a) the name of the firm;

(b) the principal place of the firm;

(c) the names of other place where the firms carries on business;

(d) the date when each partner joined the firm

(e) the names in full and permanent addresses of the partner.

(f) the duration of the firm.

Setp 3 → Get the statement duly verified and signed by all the partners or by their authorised agents.

Step 4 → File the Statement alongwith prescribed fees with the Registrar of the Firms of the area.

Step 5 → Obtain a Certificate from the Registrar.

When the Registrar is satisfied that the provisions of Section 58 have been duly complied with, he shall record an entry of the Statement in the register called 'Register of Firms' and file the statement. He shall then issue a certificate or registration.

It may be noted that if any change is made in the particulars filed with the Registrar, the same should be duly notified to the Registrar so that he can incorporate the same in the 'Registrar of Firms'.

Time of Registration

Since the registration of a firm is not compulsory, it can be effected at any stage, i.e., at the time of its formation or at anytime thereafter. Section 69(2) provides that no suit can be filed by or on behalf of an unregistered firm in a court. This means the firm must be got registered before any suit is filed in a court.

When does Registration becomes Effective

Registration becomes effectve from the date of filing of the duly signed and verified statement alogwith the prescribed form and not from the date of issue of certificate of registration since the act of the Registrar in recording an entry of the statement in the Register of Firms is only a clerical act.

Is the Registration of Firm Compulsory

Under the Indian Partnership Act 1932, the registration of a firm is not compulsory, But, indirectly, by creating certain liabilities (also termed as effect of non-registration from which an unregistered firm suffers, the law made the registration of firms desirable. The effects of non-registration of a firm are as follows:

(a) **No suit by a partner against the firm or the other partner**

A partner of an unregistered firm cannot file a suit against the firm or any partner of the firm to enforce any right arising from contract. For example, if a partner of an unregistered firm is not paid his, share of profits, he cannot claim it through the court.

Note: Section 69(1) prohibits the institution of civil suit and not the criminal suit.

(b) **No suit by the firm against third parties**

An unregistered firm cannot file a suit against a third party to enforce any right arising from contract For example, if an unregistered firm has sold some goods to a customer, it cannot file a suit against the customer for the recovery of the price of goods. On the other hand, if any unregistered firm has purchased some goods from a supplier, such supplier can file a suit against the firm for the recovery of the price of goods. Thus, it is only a suit by the unregistered firm or its partners against a third party, which is prohibited and not a suit by the third party against the unregistered firm or its partners. It may be noted that this disability can be removed by getting the firm registered before filing the suit. In case of **Puran Mul Vs. Central Bank of India**, it was held that a subsequent registration could not cure the defect that existed at the time of filing the suit.

(c) **No right to claim set off in excess of Rs. 100**

An unregistered firm or any partner thereof cannot claim a set off (if value exceeds Rs 100) in proceeding instituted against the firm by a third party to enforce a right arising from a contract. **For example**, if an unregistered firm owes Rs. 10,000 to X, a third party, X owes Rs. 1,000 to such firm, X files a suit against the firm for the recovery of Rs. 10,000. In this case, an unregistered firm cannot say that Rs. 1,000 should be adjusted against Rs. 10,000.

Rights not Affected by Non-registration

(a)   Rights of unregistered firm or partners thereof

   (i)   Right of firm or partner of a firm having no place of business in India.

   (ii)   Right to file a suit or claim of set-off if the value of suit does not exceed Rs 100.

   (iii)   Right of a partner to sue (a) for the dissolution of the firm, (b) for the accounts of a dissolved firm, or (c) for claiming share of the assets of a dissolved firm.

   (iv)   Right to enforce a right arising otherwise than out of a contract, e.g. infringement of a Patent right by a third party. The firm may file a suit to restrain the third party from misusing the Patent right.

(b)   Right of a third party to file a suit against the unregistered firm or partners thereof.

(c)   Power of an Official Assignee or Receiver or Court to realize the property of an insolvent partner.

Example: X and Y purchased a taxi and they were plying it in partnership. The firm was not registered. After 1 year, X sold the taxi without Y's consent and did not pay anything to Y. Y filed a suit against X to recover his share in the sale proceeds. X defended the suit on the ground that the firm was not registered. It was held that the suit was maintainable because it was for the realization of the assets of a dissolved firm.

DURATION OF PARTNERSHIP

On the basis of duration, the partnership can be *either* Partnership at will *or* Particular Partnership.

Partnership at Will

When there is no provision in partnership agreement for duration of the partnership, the partnership is called 'Partnership at Will'. A partnership at will may be dissolved by any partner by giving a notice in writing to all other partners of his intention to dissolve the firm.

Particular Partnership

When a partnership is formed for a specific venture or for a particular period, the partnership is called a 'Particular Partnership'. Such partnership comes to an end on the completion of the venture or on the expiry of the period. If such partnership is continued after the expiry of term or completion of the venture, it is deemed to be a partnership at will. A particular partnership may be dissolved before the expiry of the term or completion of the venture only by the mutual consent of all the partners.

TYPES OF PARTNERS

A person who deals or intends to deal with a firm, must know who the partners are and to what extent each partner is liable. To ascertain the extent of partner's liability, it becomes necessary to know the various types of partners which are given in Exhibit 5.2.

Exhibit 5.2	Types of Partners			
Actual or ostensible partner	**Sleeping or dormant Partner**	**Nominal Partner**	**Partner in profits only**	**Sub-partner**
He **takes an active part** in the conduct of the business.	He **does not take an active part** in the conduct of the business.	He **lends his name** to the firm without having any real interest in the firm. He *neither* contributes to the capital *nor* shares the profits or takes part in the conduct of the business of the firm.	He **shares the profits only** and not losses.	He is a **third person** with whom a partner agrees to share his profits derived from the firm.
He alongwith other partners is **liable to third parties** for all the acts of the firm.	He alongwith other partners is **liable to third parties** for the acts of the firm.	He alongwith other partners is **liable to third parties** for all acts of the firm as if he is an actual partner.	He alongwith other partners is **liable to third parties** for all acts of the firm.	He has no rights against the firm nor is he **liable** for the acts of the firm.
He **must give public notice** of his retirement.	He **need not give public notice** of his retirement.	He **must give public notice** of his retirement.	He **must give public notice** of his retirement.	There is **no question** of public notice at all since he is a third person and not a partner.
His insanity or permanent incapacity to perform his duties **may be a ground** for the dissolution of the firm.	His insanity or permanent incapacity to perform his duties is **no ground** for the dissolution of the firm.	His insanity or permanent incapacity to perform his duties is **no ground** for the dissolution of the firm.	His insanity or permanent incapacity to perform his duties **may be a ground** for the dissolution of the firm.	His insanity or permanent incapacity to perform his duties is **no ground** for the dissolution of the firm since he is a third person and not a partner.

Partner by Estoppel or Holding Out

A person is held liable as a partner by estoppel or holding out if the following two conditions are fulfilled:

(a) He must have represented himself to be a partner by word spoken or written or by his conduct (such type of representation may be called as active representation), or

He must have knowingly permitted himself to be represented as a partner (such type of representation may be called as tacit representation); and

(b) The other person acting on the faith of such representation must have given credit to the firm. It is immaterial whether the person so representing to be a partner, is aware or not that the representation has reached the other person.

Example I: *Ram*, a sole proprietor of Ram Shyam & Co. employed *Shyam* as manager. *Ram* introduced *Shyam* as his partner to *S*, a supplier of goods. *Shyam* remained silent. Treating *Shyam* a partner, S supplied the goods on credit. *Ram* failed to pay the price of goods. S filed a suit against both *Ram* and *Shyam* for the recovery of the price. Here, *Shyam* is liable as a partner by holding out because he has knowingly permitted himself to be represented as a partner and the *S* the supplier has acted on the faith of such representation.

Example II: *Pataudi*, a renowned sportsman assumed the honorary presidentship of a publishing business which brings out a sports magazine because other partners requested him to do. S, a supplier gave credit to this firm in the bonafied belief that Pataudi was a partner in a firm. Here, *Pataudi* is liable as a partner by holding out because he has knowingly permitted himself to be represented as a partner and the supplier has acted on the faith of such representation.

POSITION OF MINOR AS A PARTNER

Since a minor is not capable of entering into a contract, an agreement by or with a minor is void ab-initio *(Mohri Bibi v. Dharamodas Ghosh)*. Since partnership is formed by an agreement, a minor cannot enter into a partnership agreement. On the basis of the general rule that a minor cannot be a promisor, but can be a promisee or a beneficiary, Section 30 of the Indian Partnership Act 1932, provides as under:

"With the consent of all the partners for the time being, a minor may be admitted to the benefits of partnership."

An analysis of the above provision highlights the following three conditions:

(a) Before admission of a minor as a partner, there must be an existence of partnership;

(b) There must be mutual consent of all the partners;

(c) A minor can be admitted only to the benefits of partnership.

Note: There cannot be a partnership consisting of all the minors or of one major and all other minors. *[Shivaram v. Gaurishanker]*

MERITS OF PARTNERSHIP

The merits of partnership are as follows:

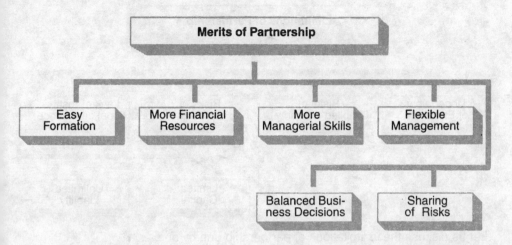

Let us discuss these merits of partnership one by one.

1. **Easy Formation** — It is very easy and simple to form partnership. The essential elements required to form partnership are at least two persons having capacity to contract, an agreement (Oral or written), lawful business, sharing of profit and mutual agency.

2. **More Financial Resources** — A partnership facilitates pooling of financial resources of all its partners. This increases the scope for expansion and growth of business.

3. **More Managerial Skills** — A partnership facilitates pooling of managerial skills of all its partners. This increases the scope for efficient management, expansion and growth of the business. For example, a partner having the experience of production, can look after production activities, a partner having the experience of marketing can look after marketing activities.

4. **Flexible Management** — The partners can easily bring about changes in the size and nature of activity according to the changing conditions. This gives flexibility to business.

5. **Balanced Business Decisions** — Since all partners participate in major decisions, there is lesser scope for reckless and hasty decisions. Decisions are taken after considering all the major aspects of the problem.

6. **Sharing of Risks** — The risks of partnership business are shared by partners on agreed basis. Hence, the share of loss in case of each partner will be less than that sustained in sole proprietorship. This motivates partners to undertake risks but profitable business activities.

LIMITATIONS OF PARTNERSHIP

The limitations of partnership are as follows:

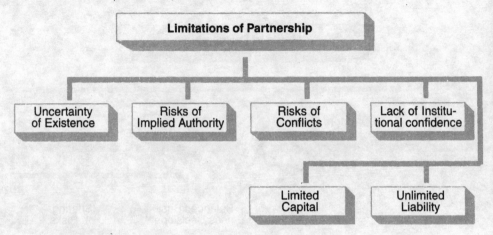

Let us discuss these limitations of partnership one by one.

1. **Uncertainty of Existence** — There exists uncertainty about the existence of a partnership firm since the death, or insolvency of a partner leads to the dissolution of firm unless otherwise agreed by the partners.

2. **Risks of Implied Authority** — Since each partner is an agent of the firm for the business of the firm, he can bind the firm and all other partners by his acts. A dishonest or incompetent partner may lend the firm into difficulties and other partners may have to pay for it.

3. **Risks of Disharmony or Conflicts** — There is scope for misunderstanding and conflicts among the partners. Such conflicts may cause delays in decision making and may lead even to dissolution of the firm. When some of the partners adopt rigid attitudes, it becomes impossible to arrive at a commonly agreed decision.

4. **Lack of Institutional Confidence** — Since the accounts are not published and publicised, the firm is not able to enjoy much confidence of banks and financial institutions. As a result, firm is not able to procure large financial resources.

5. **Limited Capital** — The capital raising capacity of partnership firm is limited since there is a limit of maximum partners (20 in non-banking firm and 10 in banking firm). Due to limited capital, the firm can not operate on large scale and hence the scope for expansion and growth is reduced.

6. **Unlimited Liability** — The most important limitation of a partnership firm is that the partners have unlimited liability. Because of this, not only their share in the profit & property of the firm, but also the private asset are subject to implied charge.

   Suitability — The partnership form of business organisation is suitable when the size of business is medium and when the partners can work in full cooperation with one another.

DISTINCTION BETWEEN SOLE PROPRIETORSHIP AND PARTNERSHIP

A sole proprietorship differs from a partnership in the following respects:

Basis of Distinction	*Sole-Proprietorship*	*Partnership*
1. **Formation**	It can be formed **at any time** when proprietor so decides.	It can be formed **by an agreement** between two or more competent persons.
2. **Specific Regulation**	There is **no** specific regulation which governs sole proprietorship.	It is governed by **The Indian Partnership Act, 1932**.
3. **Membership**	**Only one** member is required.	**Minimum** number of members required is **2** and **maximum** limit is **10** in banking business firm and **20** in other business firm.
4. **Extent of Financial Resources**	A sole proprietorship has **limited** financial resources.	A partnership has **more** financial resources due to pooling of financial resources of all its partners. This increases the scope for expansion and growth.
5. **Extent of Managerial Skills**	A sole proprietorship has **limited** managerial skills.	A partnership has **more** managerial skills due to pooling of managerial skills of all its partners. This increases the scope for efficient management.
6. **Existence of Business depends on**	The existence of the business depends upon the **life of the owner**.	The existence of business depends upon the **life, insolvency and retirement of partners**.
7. **Business Secrets**	Full secrecy is **maintained**.	Secrecy is **shared** by the partners.
8. **Sharing of Profits**	Profits fully belong to owner and are **not shared** with anyone.	Profits are **shared** by partners as per agreement.
9. **Sharing of Risk**	All risks are assumed by the owner and are **not shared** with anyone.	Risks are **shared** by partners as per agreement.

10. **Quickness in Decision Making**	**Quick** decisions are taken since he does not depend on others for decision making.	Decision making **may take time** since all partners in some matters and majority of partners in other matters have to participate in decision making.
11. **Scope for Reckless & Hasty Decisions**	There is **more scope** for reckless and hasty decisions since proprietor alone takes the decisions.	There is **less scope** for reckless and hasty decisions since all partners or majority of the partners take the decisions.

DISTINCTION BETWEEN PARTNERSHIP AND HINDU UNDIVIDED FAMILY

The partnership differs from Hindu undivided family in the following respects:

Basis of Distinction	*Partnership*	*Hindu Undivided Family*
1. **Agreement**	It arises from an **agreement**.	It arises **by status** or operation of law.
2. **Regulating law**	It is governed by the **Indian Partnership Act, 1932**.	It is governed by **Hindu Law**.
3. **Name of the persons involved**	The persons who from partnership are called '**partners**'.	The persons who are the members of the HUF are called '**Coparceners**'.
4. **Maximum limit**	The maximum limit of partners is **10** for a banking business firm and **20** for any other business firm.	There is **no** maximum limit of coparceners.
5. **Admission of new members**	A person can be admitted to the existing partnership **with the consent** of all other partners.	A male person becomes a member **merely by his birth**.
6. **Minor members**	A minor **can be admitted** to the **benefits** of partnership with the consent of all the partners.	A male minor bcomes a member merely **by his birth**.
7. **Female members**	A female **can become** a fullfledged partner.	A female **does not become** member merely by her birth.

8. Implied authority	Each partner **has** implied authority to bind the firm by acts done in the ordinary course of the business of the firm.	**Only the Karta has** implied authority.
9. Liability of members	The liability of all the partners is **unlimited**.	**Only Karta's liability is unlimited** and the liability of the other coparceners is limited only to their shares in the family property.
10. Right to demand accounts	**Each partner has a right** to inspect and copy the account books and ask for the account of profits and losses.	The coparceners have **no right** to ask for the account of past dealings.
11. Effect of death of a member	Unless otherwise agreed partnership is **dissolved** on the death of any partner.	The Hindu undivided family **continues** to operate even after the death of a coparcener.

CO-OPERATIVE ORGANISATION–MEANING, FEATURES, TYPES, MERITS & LIMITATIONS

MEANING OF CO-OPERATIVE ORGANISATION

Co-operative organisation is a voluntary association of person who come together to promote their common economic interests through the principle of self-help and mutual help. Mutual help means each for one and all for each.

According to Sec 4 of the Indian Co-operative Societies Act, 1912, Co-operative society is a society which has its objectives the promotion of economic interests of its members in accordance with cooperative principles.

A minimum of 10 persons are required to form a co-operative society. Co-operative organisations are required to be registered with the Registrars of co-operative societies of the concerned state in which the society's registered office is situated. There is no maximum limit for membership.

FEATURES OF CO-OPERATIVE ORGANISATION

The main characteristics of co-operative organisation are as follows:

1. **Voluntary Association** — A co-operative organisation is a voluntary association in the sense that person voluntarily come together to promote their common interests without any coercion or undue influence. Any person having a common interest can became a member. A member can leave the society as and when he decides after giving proper notice.

2. **Equal voting Rights** — Each member has one vote irrespective of the number of shares held by him.

3. **Democratic Management** — The management of co-operative organisation vests in a managing committee which is elected by the member in the annual general meeting. The general body lays down the broad framework of policy within which the managing committee has to function.

4. **Separate Legal Entity** — Like a company, a registered Co-operative organisation also enjoys a separate and independent legal entity which is distinct from that of its members. As such it can enter into any contract. It can sue and be sued in its own name. It has perpetual life. Its existence is not affected by the death, insolvency and lunacy of its members. Since law creates it, the law can only dissolve it.

5. **Service Motive** — The primary objective of any Co-operative society is to provide service to its members and not to earn profits.

6. **Distribution of Surplus** — Its profits are distributed in the form of dividend and bonus. After giving dividend on shares, and transferring a portion of profits to reserves, surplus profits are distributed by way of bonus. Such bonus is given in the proportion of the volume of business transacted by each member with the co-operative society. For example, in case of a consumer co-operative society, bonus is paid in the proportion of the purchases made by the members from the society. In case of a producer co-operative, bonus is paid in the proportion of the goods delivered for sale to the society.

7. **Capital** — The capital is procured from its members in the form of share capital.

TYPES OF CO-OPERATIVE ORGANISATIONS

According to the nature of activities performed, co-operative societies may be classified into different categories. The important types are given as follows:

Types of Co-operative Societies	Who form	Object of Formation	Main Activities
1. **Consumers' Co-operative**	**Consumers** who want to obtain household goods at reasonable price.	To eliminate middlemen and to ensure a steady supply of goods of high quality at reasonable prices.	1. Purchasing goods in bulk from wholesalers or producers. 2. Selling goods to members sometimes to non-members.
2. **Producers' Co-operative**	**Small producers** who want to obtain inputs for production and to sell their output.	To help the members in procuring inputs and in marketing the output.	1. Provides inputs like raw-materials, tools, equipment etc. 2. Sells their output to outsiders.
3. **Marketing Co-operative**	**Small producers** who want a steady	• To protect producers from	1. Pooling of output of its members.

		and favourable market.	exploitation by the middlemen in marketing their products. •To ensure a steady and favourable market for the output of its members.	2. Selling their output at best price. 3. Ensure honest trading practices in weighting, measuring & accounting.
4.	**Credit Co-operative**	Person **who** are in **need** of **credit**.	To provide loans to members at a reasonable rate of interest. To encourage the habit of thrift among their members.	1. Accepts deposits from members 2. Provide loans to members at reasonable rate of interest.
5.	**Farming Co-operative**	**Small farmers** who want to cultivate their land collectively.	To achieve economies of large scale farming and maximising agricultural output.	1. Consolidate the land holdings. 2. Provide modern tools and Equipments. 3. Provide good seeds, fertiliser and irrigation facilities.
6.	**Housing Co-operative**	Persons **who require** residential **houses**.	To provide residential houses to its members.	1. Purchase of Land. 2. Development of Land. 3. Construction of houses/flats. 4. Allotment of houses/flats to members.

MERITS OF CO-OPERATIVE ORGANISATIONS

The merits of co-operative organisations are as follows:

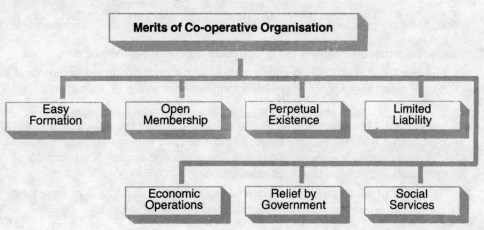

Let us discuss these merits of Co-operative Organisations one by one.

1. **Easy Formation** — It is easy and simple to form a co-operative society. Any 10 adult persons can form a co-operative society and get it registered with the Registrar of Co-operatives.

2. **Open Membership** — Any person having common interest can become its member. A member can leave the society at any time when he decides after returning his shares.

3. **Perpetual Existence/Stability** — It has perpetual existence. Its life is not affected by the death, insolvency or lunacy of any of its members. Since law creates it, the law only can dissolve it.

4. **Limited Liability** — The liability of its members is limited to the extent of capital contributed by them. They are not personally liable for the debts of the society.

5. **Economic Operations** — Due to voluntary services provided by the members and elimination of middleman, the operations of society become economical.

6. **Relief by Government** — The various reliefs are provided to such societies by the Government such as loan at lower rates of interest and taxability of income at lower rate, receipt of grants.

7. **Social Services** — Co-operatives encourage fellow feeling among members and impart moral and educative values which are essential for better living.

LIMITATIONS OF CO-OPERATIVE ORGANISATIONS

The limitations of Co-operative organisations are as follows:

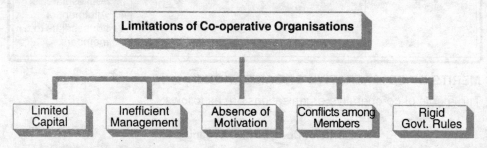

Let us discuss these limitations of Co-operative organisations one by one.

1. **Limited Capital** — Co-operatives have limited capital because the members do not invest much in its shares due to law rate of return on Capital invested by them.

2. **Inefficient Management** — The affairs of Co-operative society are not managed in efficient manner because the members who manage do not have business experience and qualified managers are not appointed on account of its limited capacity to pay adequate remuneration.

3. **Absence of Motivation** — Members are not motivated to put in their best efforts since there is no direct link between effort and reward.

4. **Conflicts among Members** — Over a period of time, conflicts arise among members and groupism takes place. The selfish motives takes place of service motive. When it becomes difficult to get full co-operation of the members, the co-operative becomes inactive in its operations.

5. **Rigid Govt. Rules and Regulations** — Excessive government regulation and control over co-operatives may adversely affect the flexibility of operations and the efficiency of management. For example, a co-operative society is required to get its accounts audited, to submit its accounts regularly to the Registrar.

COMPANY – MEANING, CHARACTERISTICS, MERITS, LIMITATIONS, TYPES

The company is one of the form of organisation. It has its distinctive characteristics and advantages which make it suitable for different purposes.

LITERARY MEANING

The term 'Company' implies an association of a number of persons formed for some common object or objects.

LEGAL MEANING

According to Sec. 3(1)(i) of The Companies Act, 1956. "Company means a company formed and registered under this Act or an existing company. An existing company means a company formed and registered under any of the previous Companies Acts."

The above definition is not exhaustive because it does not reveal the characteristics of the company.

Let us analyse some other definitions given in various judicial decisions to ascertain the characteristics of the company.

MEANING AS PER JUDICIAL PRONOUNCEMENTS

1. **According to Lord Justice Lindley** — "By a company is meant an association of many persons who contribute money or money's worth to a common stock and employ it in some trade or business, and who share the profit and loss (as the case may be) arising therefrom. The common stock so contributed is denoted in money and is the capital of the company. The persons who contribute it, or to whom it belongs, are called members. The proportion of capital to which each member is entitled is his share. Shares are always transferable although the right to transfer them is often more or less restricted."

2. **According to Chief Justice Marshall** — "A company is a person, artificial, invisible, intangible and existing only in the eyes of law. Being a mere creature of law, it possesses only those properties which the charter of its creation confers upon it, *either* expressly *or* as incidental to its very existence."

3. **According to Lord Haney** — "A company is an incorporated association which is an artificial person created by law, having a separate entity, with a perpetual succession and a common seal."

From the above definitions, it is clear that a company has a corporate and legal personality. It is an artificial person and exists only in the eyes of law. It has an independent legal entity, a common seal and perpetual succession.

CHARACTERISTICS OF A COMPANY

On analysing the aforesaid definitions the following characteristics of a company are revealed:

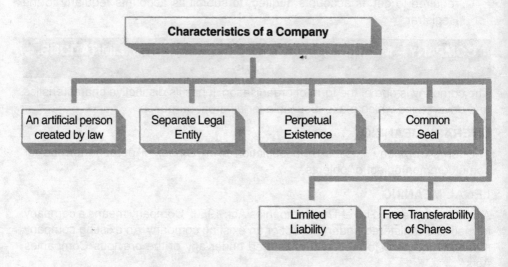

Let us discuss these characteristics of a company one by one.

1. **An artificial person created by law** — A company is called an artificial person because it does not take birth like a natural person but comes into existence through law. Being the creation of law, the company possesses only those properties which are conferred upon it by its charter (i.e. Memorandum of Association). Within the limits of powers conferred by its charter, it can do all acts as a natural person can do.

   Like a natural person —
   (a) The company can enter into contracts.
   (b) The company can enforce the contractual rights against others.
   (c) The company can sue in its own name.
   (d) The company can be sued in its own name.
   (e) The company can own and hold property in its own name.
   (f) The company has nationality. The registration of a company in a country determines the nationality of that company to that country.

   Unlike a natural person —
   (a) The company has no physical shape or form.
   (b) The company can not shake by hand.
   (c) The company can not marry.
   (d) The company can not smile or weep.

(e) The company can not take oath.

(f) The company can not be sent to jail.

(g) The company can not commit a crime like murder.

(h) The company has no citizenship because a citizen of a country is a personal right peculiar to human beings only.

2. **Separate Legal Entity** —The case of **Salomon v. Saloman & Co. Ltd. (1897) (AC) (22)** clearly established the concept of corporate personality as distinct and different from that of its members individually and collectively (known as the Doctrine of Corporate veil).

In case of **Saloman v. Salomon and Company Ltd.** Mr. Salomon was running a shoe business in England. He formed a company known as 'Saloman and Co. Ltd.' It consisted of Saloman himself, his wife, his four sons and a daughter. The shoes business of Mr. Saloman was sold to the company for £30,000. Mr. Saloman received from the company purchase price in the form of £20,000 fully paid shares of £1 each and £10,000 in debentures which carried a floating charge over the assets of the company. One share of £1 each was subscribed for in cash by each member of Saloman's family. Saloman was the managing director of the company. During the course of business, the company became liable for some unsecured loan. The company ran into financial difficulties after some time and went into liquidation within a year. On winding up, the assets realised £6,000. The company owed £10,000 to Mr. Saloman and £7,000 to unsecured creditors. Thus, after paying off the debenture holder. (Mr. Saloman), nothing was left for unsecured creditors. The creditors claimed priority over the debentures contending that Mr. Saloman and Saloman and Co. Ltd. were one and the same person, the company was only a facade to defraud the innocent creditors. Mr. Saloman should not therefore, be treated as a secured creditor. *The House of Lords* held that the company had been validly constituted and it had an independent existence distinct from its members. Therefore, Mr. Saloman was entitled to be paid his dues first as a secured creditor. It was observed that the business belonged to the company and not to Mr. Saloman. The company and Mr. Saloman enjoyed separate legal entities. The fact that the members were from one single family had no bearing upon the validity of the company.

The legal status of a company has been aptly described by the Supreme Court of India in ***Tata Engineering & Locomotive Co. Ltd. v. State of Bihar*** as follows:

"The corporation in law is equal to natural person and has a legal entity of its own. The entity of the corporation is entirely separate from that of its shareholder; it bears its own name and has a seal of its own; its assets are separate and distinct from those of its members; it can sue and be sued exclusively for its own purpose".

Effects — As a consequence of separate legal entity —

(a) The company may enter into contracts with its members and *vice-versa*. Thus, a member can be both a debtor and a creditor of the company at the same time.

(b) Its members can not be held liable for the acts of the company even if he holds virtually the entire share capital.

(c) Its members can not claim ownership rights in company's assets.

(d) Its members can not have any insurable interest in the company's properties.

(e) Its creditors' remedy for the recovery of their debts lie only against the company and not against its members or directors.

3. **Perpetual Existence** — The term *'perpetual existence'* means the continued existence. The death, insolvency or unsoundness of mind of its members or transfer of shares by its members does not in any way affect the existence of the company. Members may come and members may go but the company goes on forever. The company can be compared with a flowing river where water (members) keeps on changing continuously, still the identity of the river (company) remains the same.

   The company continues to exist even if all its human members die. According to Gower, 'even a hydrogen bomb can not destroy a company'. Since it is created law, it can be brought to an end by the process of law.

   Thus, a company still continue to exist for an indefinite period till it is wound up in accordance with the provisions of the Companies Act.

4. **Common Seal** — The term *'Common Seal'* means the official signature of the company. Since the company being an artificial person can not sign its name on a document, every company is required to have its common seal with its name engraved on the same. This seal acts as the official signature of the company. Any document bearing the common seal of the company and duly witnessed by at least two directors will be binding on the company.

5. **Limited Liability** — This specific characteristics of *'Limited Liability'* is possessed by limited companies and not by unlimited companies. In case of a **company limited by shares**, the liability of a member is limited upto the amount remaining unpaid (if any) on the shares held by a member. In case of a **company limited by guarantee**, the liability of a member is limited upto the amount guaranteed by a member.

6. **Free Transferability of Shares** — This specific characteristic of *'Free Transferability of Shares'* is possessed by public companies and not by private companies.

The shares of a public company are freely transferable. A shareholder can transfer his shares to any person without the consent of other members. Under the articles of association, even a public limited company can put certain restrictions on the transfer of shares but it can not altogether stop it. A shareholder of a public company possessing fully paid up shares is at liberty to transfer his shares to anyone he likes in accordance with the manner provided for in the articles of association of the company.

It may be noted that although restriction on the right to transfer may be placed in certain cases (e.g. in case of partly paid up shares) but absolute right of members to transfer shares can not be restricted and any provision in the Articles to that affect shall be void.

Sec 3(1) (iii) requires a private company to put restriction on transferability of its shares.

MERITS OF A COMPANY

The merits of a company are as follows:

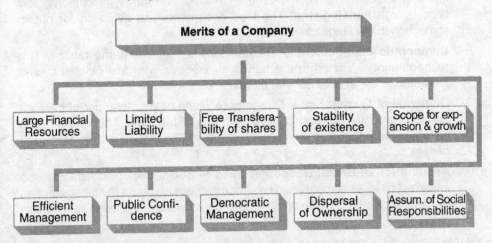

Let us discuss the merits of a company one by one.

1. **Large Financial Resources** — The company form of organisation has the main advantage of its ability to raise large financial resources. It can raise the share capital by issue of shares and can raise the debt by issue of debentures or raising loans. This facilitates the company to undertake business activities on large scale.

2. **Limited Liability** — The liability of the shareholders is limited to the face value of the shares held by them(in case of a company limited by shares) or the amount of guarantee given by them(in case of a company limited by guarantee). They are not personally liable if the company's assets are not sufficient to meet the company's liabilities. Persons who are not willing to take risk like this form of organisation. This facilitates the company to undertake business activities involving risks.

3. **Free Transferability of Shares** — The shares of the public company are freely transferable. Shareholders can sell their shares whenever they need cash or want to buy shares of another more profitable company. Thus, free transferability of shares provides liquidity to members' investment.

4. **Stability of Existence** — The company has perpetual existence. Its existence is not affected by the death, insolvency or lunacy of any of its members. Members may come, members may go but the company goes for ever. Since the law creates it, it can be wound up by law only.

5. **Scope for Expansion and Growth** — The availability of large amount of funds makes it possible for a company to undertake business activities on large scale. Undertaking business activities on large scale results in high profits due to economies of large scale operations. This in turn facilitates the expansion and growth of the company.

6. **Efficient Management** — The affairs of the company can be managed efficiently since the company is in position to employ experts professional managers due to availability large amount of funds.

7. **Public confidence** — A company enjoys confidence and trust of the public since it is required to submit various documents, returns, resolutions, and reports with the Registrar. The filed documents are available for public inspection in the Registrar's office.

8. **Democratic Management** — The company is managed democratically. The management is vested in the hands of directors who are elected by the members in the annual general meeting.

9. **Dispersal of Ownership** — Due to association of large number of persons as members, the ownership of company is widely held. This facilitates to distribute the benefits of the company's operations among a large section of people.

10. **Assumption of Social Responsibilities** — Social responsibilities are also assumed by large companies. These companies contribute to social activities by making donations, developing rural and backward areas, running hospitals etc.

LIMITATIONS OF A COMPANY

The limitations of a company are as follows:

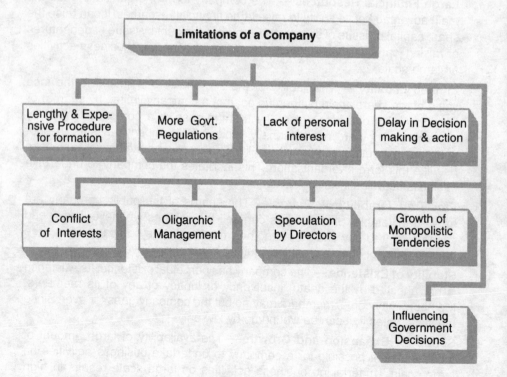

Let us discuss the limitations of a company one by one.

1. **Lengthy & Expensive Procedure for Formation** — Formation of a company is lengthy as well as expensive. It is lengthy in the sense that a lot of documents (e.g. Memorandum of Association, Articles of Association, Statutory declaration) are required to be prepared and filed. It is expensive in the sense that heavy fees for the preparation of required documents and for the registration is required to be paid.

2. **More Government Regulations** — A company is required to comply with various legal formalities at every stage of its working and to pay penalty for non-compliance of the legal requirements. It is required to spend considerable time and effort in complying with the various legal requirements.

3. **Lack of Personal Interest** — There is lack of personal interest in the management since day to day management is vested with the salaried executives who do not have any personal interest. This may lead to reduced motivation and result in inefficiency.

4. **Delay in Decision-Making and Action** — For a company, decision making process is time consuming since all important decisions are taken by either the Board of Directors or Shareholders in their meetings and it is difficult to arrange meeting all of a sudden. The delay in decision-making may result in loss of business opportunities.

5. **Conflict of Interests** — A company is bound to suffer when the interest of one group clash with the interest of other group or when individual interests clash with group interests for example, if sales manager does not sell what is being produced by production manager and production manager does not produce what is being demanded by sales manager, the company is bound to suffer unless such conflict is resolved.

6. **Oligarchic Management** — In actual practice, the management of a company is oligarchic and not democratic. Its management is controlled by a small group of persons who exploit the company to serve their personal interests.

7. **Speculation by Directors** — The company form of organisation gives scope for speculation in shares by directors. The directors can use the information about the working of the company to their personal advantage. For example, directors may buy shares when prices are to go up due to high profits.

8. **Growth of Monopolistic Tendencies** — Monopolistic tendencies may grow because of large size of a company. Then, it may eliminate competition, acquire major share of market and charge high prices.

9. **Influencing Government Decisions** — The large size companies generally become in position to influence government officials to make decisions in their favour because these companies are in position to offer lucrative incentives due to availability of large financial resources.

Suitability — The company form of organisation is suitable for those business activities which are to be carried on a large scale, require heavy investment with limited liability of members. For example, Iron & Steel Industry, Automobile Industries, Computer Industries.

DISTINCTION BETWEEN A PARTNERSHIP AND A COMPANY

A partnership differs from a company in the following respects:

Basis of Distinction	Partnership	Company
1. Separate Legal entity	A firm **does not enjoy** separate legal existence. Partners are collectively termed as a firm and individually as partners.	It **has** a separate legal existence. A company is separate from the members.
2. Nature of Liability	The liability of partners is **unlimited**.	Liability of its members is **limited** to the extent of face value of share held by them.
3. Prepetual Existence	It **does not** enjoy a long lease of life. Death, sickness, retirement of partners may affect its existence so as to dissolve it. Dissolution may take place on flimsy grounds.	It **enjoys** perpetual existence. Even an atom bomb cannot destroy a company unless it is wound up under the due process of law. Winding up may take years.
4. Minimum Number of members	Minimum number of partners is **2**.	A public company must have a minimum **7** members to start with.
5. Maximum Number of Member	Maximum number of partners may be **10** (in case of baking business) or **20** (in case of non-banking business).	There is **no limit** on the maximum number of members of a company.
6. Transfer of interest	A partner **cannot transfer** his share without the consent of other partners.	A member of a public company **may transfer** his shares as and when he likes. There is no restriction on transfer of shares.
7. Mutual Agency	There **exists** mutual agency. Each partner represents the other partners so as to bind and be bound to others.	There is **no agency** relationship among members of a company as they do not bind each other with their actions.
8. Distribution of profits	Profits are **distributable** among partners as per the partnership deed.	There is **no such compulsion** that profits must be distributed. Only when the dividends are declared that the members get a share of profits.

9. **Management**	The entire management lies **with all the partners.**	**Members cannot participate in management unless** appointed as directors. However, members may attend and vote at meetings while making the appointment of Directors, Auditors etc.
10. **Property**	Property of the firm is the **joint property** of all its partners.	Property of the company is **not the property of its members** as the company and members have separate legal existence.
11. **Remedy of Creditors**	The creditors of a firm can proceed **against the partners jointly & severally.**	The creditors of a company can proceed only against the company and **not against its members**.
12. **Restriction on Authority**	Restriction on a partner's authority contained in partnership contract **do not bind outsiders.**	Restriction on authority of directors contained in Articles **bind the outsiders** because they are deemed to have the knowledge of Articles.
13. **Compulsory Audit**	Audit of a firm is **not** compulsory under The Indian Partnership Act.	Audit of a company is **compulsory** under The Companies Act.
14. **Dissolution**	Firm can be dissolved at **any time by mutual agreement**.	A company, being the creature of law, can only be dissolved **by law**.

DISTINCTION BETWEEN COMPANY AND CO-OPERATIVE SOCIETY

A company differs from a Co-operative society in the follqwing respects:

Basis of Distinction	Company	Co-operative Society
1. **Formation**	Its formation is **difficult** as compared to the formation of a co-operative society due to many legal formalities.	Its formation is **easy** as compared to the formation of a company due to few legal formalities.
2. **Specific Regulation**	It is governed by The **Companies Act, 1956.**	It is governed by The **Co-operative Societies Act, 1912.**

3. **Minimum Number of Members**	Minimum number of members to form a private company is **2** and to form a public company is **7**.	Minimum numbers of member to form a co-operative society is **10**.
4. **Maximum Number of Members**	The maximum number of members in case of private company can be **50** and in case of a public company can be unlimited.	These is **no limit** on maximum number of members.
5. **Purpose of Formation**	The purpose of forming a company (other than licensed company) is to carry on a business and **to earn profit**.	The purpose of forming a co-operative society is **to render services** to its members.
6. **Voting Rights**	Its member has **as many votes as the number of shares** held by him.	Its member has **one vote** irrespective of the number of shares held by him.
7. **Payment of Dividend**	The rate of dividend is **first recommended** by the Board of Directors and **then declared** by the company every year.	A **fixed rate** of dividend is payable to its members as per the provision of the Co-operative Societies Act.
8. **Free Transferability**	Shares of a Public Company are **freely transferable**.	Shares of a Co-operative Society are **not so freely transferable**.
9. **Tax Liability**	Incomes of a company are subject to **Dividend tax**. **Minimum Alternate Tax** and **Corporate Tax**.	Specified Incomes of co-operative society are **exempted under section 80 P** of the Income Tax Act, 1961.

COMPANIES ON THE BASIS OF INCORPORATION

On the basis of incorporation, companies may be divided into the following three categories:

(a) **Chartered Company** — A company incorporated under a special charter granted by the King or Queen of England is called 'chartered company'. A chartered company is regulated by its charter and the Companies Act does not apply to it. The charter also prescribes the nature of business and the powers of the company. The familiar examples of chartered company are the East India Company and the Bank of England. This type of company cannot be formed in India now.

(b) **Statutory Company** — A statutory company is one which is created by a Special Act of Parliament or a State Legislature. Such companies are usually formed for achieving a purpose related with public utilities. The nature and powers of such companies are laid down in the Special Act under which they are created. However, the provisions of the Companies Act are also applicable to them in so far as they are consistent with the provisions of the Special Act. Such companies need not have a Memorandum of Association. A statutory company has also a separate legal entity and it is not required to use the word 'limited' after its name. The audit of such companies is conducted under the control and supervision of the Auditor General of India and the annual report of working is required to be placed before the Parliament or State legislature, as the case may be. Familiar examples of such companies are Reserve Bank of India, Unit Trust of India. The Life Insurance Corporation of India, State Trading Corporation, The Food Corporation of India, State Bank of India etc.

(c) **Registered or Incorporated Company** — A registered company is one which is registered in accordance with the provisions of the Companies Act of 1956 and also includes the existing companies. By existing company we mean a company formed and registered under any of the previous Acts. A registered company comes into existence only when it receives the certificate of incorporation. Registered companies are governed by the provisions of The Companies Act.

A registered Company may *either* be a private company *or* a public company.

I. **Private Company [See 3(1) (iii)]** — A Private Company means a company which has a minimum paid up capital of Rs 1,00,000 or such higher paid up capital as may be prescribed and which by its Articles —

   (a) restricts the right to transfer its shares, if any,

   (b) limits the number of its members to 50,

   (c) prohibits any invitation to the public to subscribe for any shares in or debentures of the company &

   (d) prohibits any invitation or acceptance of deposits from persons other than its members, directors or their relatives.

   Note: For the purposes of a limit of 50, present employees who are members & ex-employees who were members while in that employment & have continued to be members after the employment ceased, are excluded & the joint shareholders are counted as a single member.

Notes:

(i) Since the above mentioned **four** restrictions must be contained in the articles of a private limited company, it is necessary for a private company to frame its own articles.

(ii) A private company may be (a) a company limited by shares, or (b) a company limited by guarantee, or (c) an unlimited company.

(iii) In case a private company is a limited company, then it must add the words *'Private Limited'* at the end of its name.

(iv) If a private company does not comply with any of the restrictions contained in the articles, it ceases to enjoy the privileges granted to a private company.

(v) A private company must have at least 2 directors.

II. **Public Company [Sec. 3(1) (iv)]** — Public Company means a company which is not a private company. A public company may be said to be an association which —

(a) consists of at least 7 members,

(b) has a minimum paid up capital of Rs 5,00,000 or such higher paid up capital as may be prescribed,

(c) is a subsidiary of a company which is not a private company,

(d) does not restrict the right to transfer its shares,

(e) does not prohibit any invitation to subscribe for any shares in or debentures of the company.

(f) does not prohibit any invitation or acceptance of deposits.

Notes:

(i) There is no restriction on the maximum number of members. However, the maximum number of members depends upon the number of shares allotted.

(ii) A public company may be (a) a company limited by shares, or (b) a company limited by guarantee, or (c) an unlimited company.

(iii) In case a public company is a limited company, then it must add the words *'Limited'* at the end of its name.

(iv) A public company must have at least 3 directors.

Licensed Company or Association not for Profit [Sec. 25]

According to Section 25, the Central Government may by license grant that an association may be registered as a company with limited liability, without using the words 'limited' or 'private limited' as part of its name. The license will be granted only in the case of 'association not for profit'. In other words, the Central Government will grant the license only if it is satisfied that:

(a) the association about to be formed as a limited company aims at the promotion of commerce, art, science, religion, charity or any other useful object;

(b) it intends to apply its profits, if any, for promoting its objects; and

(c) it prohibits the payment of dividend to its members.

Such companies may be public or private companies and may or may not have share capital.

The Central Government may impose any terms and conditions that it deems fit for the grant of the license which shall be binding on the association.

COMPANIES ON THE BASIS OF LIABILITY

On the basis of liability, an incorporated company may either be (i) a company limited by shares, or (ii) a company limited by guarantee, or (iii) an unlimited company.

I. Company Limited by Shares [Sec. 12(2)(a)]

A company limited by shares is a company in which the liability of its members is limited by its Memorandum to the amount (if any) unpaid on the shares respectively held by them. The companies limited by shares may be *either* public companies *or* private companies. If a member has paid the full amount of shares, then his liability shall be nil. For example, suppose Mr. X buys 1000 shares of a company of the face value of Rs. 10 each. In this company his liability is fixed to the tune of Rs. 10,000 only. If he paid (when called by the company) Rs. 6,000 to the company. He is now liable to pay the only Rs. 4,000, this being the amount unpaid on his shares. When he has paid the entire amount of Rs. 10,000 (which means when his shares have been fully paid up) his liability shall be nil. The liability can be enforced against the members of the company during the existence of the company or during the winding up of the company.

Thus, the two main features of a company limited by shares are as follows:

(a)   The liability of its members is limited to the amount (if any) remaining unpaid on the shares held by them.

(b)   Such liability can be enforced *either* during the life time of the company *or* during the winding up of the company.

II. Company Limited by Guarantee [Sec. 12(2)(b)]

A company limited by guarantee is a company in which the liability of its members is limited by its Memorandum to such an amount as the members may respectively undertake to contribute to the assets of the company in the event of its being wound up. Such companies are generally formed for the promotion of commerce, art, science, religion, charity or any other useful object. The companies limited by guarantee may be *either* private companies *or* public companies.

Such a company may or may not have share capital. The main features of such company are as follows:

Types of Company Limited by Guarantee	Liability
(i) Company Limited by Guarantee not having share Capital	(a) The liability of its members is limited to the amount guaranteed by them. (b) Such liability can be enforced only after the commencement of winding up of the company and not during the life time of the company.
(ii) Company limited by Guarantee having share capital	(a) The liability or its members is limited to following two amounts: (i) The amount (if any) remaining unpaid on the shares held by them. (ii) The amount guaranteed by them. (b) The liability in respect of guaranteed amount can be enforced only at the time of winding up of the company and not during the life time of the company.

Note: The Articles of a company limited by guarantee must state the number of members with which the company is to be registered. [Sec. 27(2)]

III. Unlimited Company [Sec. 12(2)(c)]

An unlimited company is a company in which the liability of its members is not limited by its Memorandum. In other words, the liability of members is unlimited i.e., there is no limit on the liability of members. The members of such companies may be required to pay company's losses from their personal property. Because such companies have separate legal entity, its creditors cannot file a suit against the members directly. The creditors will have to apply to the court for the winding up of the company and then the liquidator will direct the members to contribute to the assets of the company to pay off its liabilities.

Such company may also be *either* public company *or* private company. Such company may or may not have a share capital.

Notes:

(i)   Such a company must have its Memorandum and Articles of Association.

(ii) The Articles of an unlimited company must state the number of members with which the company is to be registered. [Sec. 27(2)]

(iii) The Articles of an unlimited company having a share capital must also state the amount of share capital with which the company is to be registered. [Sec. 27(2)]

(iv) An unlimited company need not hold statutory meeting. [Sec. 165(1)]

(v)   An unlimited company having share capital may alter its share capital without any restriction. [Sec. 94(1)]

(vi) An unlimited company having share capital may reduce its share capital without any restriction. [Sec. 100(1)]

COMPANIES ON THE BASIS OF CONTROL

On the basis of control i.e., who effectively control the affairs of the company, the companies may be grouped as follows:

(i)   Government Company

(ii) Non-Government Company

(iii) Foreign Company

(iv) Domestic Company

(v)   Holding Company

(vi) Subsidiary Company

Let us discuss these companies one by one:

(i)   **Government company** — According to Section 617 of the Companies Act, a government company means "any company in which at least 51% of the paid-up share capital is held —

    (a) by the Central Government, or

    (b) by any State Government or Governments, or

(c) partly by the Central Government and partly by one or more State Governments, and includes a company which is a subsidiary of a government company as thus defined".

For example, Indian Telephone Industry, Hindustan Aeronautics Ltd. Even a subsidiary company of a government company is regarded as a Government Company. A government company registered under this Act is a non-statutory company and is not an agent of the government. Further, like any other company, it is governed by the provisions of the Companies Act. Section 620 of the Act, however, provides that the Central Government may by notification in the official Gazette direct that any of the provisions of this Act specified in the notification —

(a) shall not apply to any government company, or

(b) shall apply to any Government company, only with such exceptions, modifications and adaptations, as may be specified in the notification. A copy of such notification shall be laid before the Parliament.

Note: Sections 618, 619 and 619(A) of the Act cannot be exempted as these Sections specially deal with Government companies.

(ii) **Non-Government company** — A Company which may not be termed as a government company as defined in Section 617 is regarded as a non-government company.

(iii) **Foreign company** — A foreign company means a company which is incorporated in a country outside India under the law of that country. After the establishment of business in India, the following documents must be filed with the Registrar of companies within 30 days from the date of establishment:

(a) A certified copy of the charter or statutes under which the company is incorporated, or the memorandum and articles of the company translated into English,

(b) The full address of the registered office of the company,

(c) A list of directors and secretary of the company

(d) The name and address of any person resident of India who is authorised to accept, on behalf of the company, service of legal process and any notice served on the company, and

(e) The full address of the company's principal place of business in India.

(iv) **Domestic company** — A company which cannot be termed as foreign company under the provisions of the Companies Act should be regarded as a domestic company.

(v) **Holding and Subsidiary company** — According to Section 4 of The Companies Act, 1956, a company becomes the subsidiary of another if —

(a) that another company controls the composition of its Board of Directors; or

(b) that another company holds more than half of the nominal value of its equity capital or, in case of companies where preference shareholders have equal voting rights with the equity shareholders, controls more than half of the total voting power.

(c) that the first mentioned company is a subsidiary of any company which is a subsidiary of another company.

Example I — The equity share capital of S Ltd. is Rs 5,00,000 divided into 50,000 equity shares of Rs 10 each. H Ltd. acquires 25,000 equity shares on 1.4.20X1 and 5,000 equity shares on 1.7.20X1. S Ltd. becomes the subsidiary of H Ltd. by virtue of clause(b) on 1.7.20X1 and not on 1.4.20X1 because. H Ltd. holds more than 50% of the nominal value of the equity capital of S Ltd. on 1.7.20X1.

Example II — If US Ltd. is a subsidiary of S Ltd. which is subsidiary of H Ltd. then US Ltd, would also be the subsidiary of H Ltd. by virtue of clause(c) above. Here, H Ltd. is the ultimate holding company in relation to US Ltd. and US Ltd. is the ultimate subsidiary company in relation to H Ltd.

A company (let us call it Company S) is deemed to be a subsidiary of another company (let us call it Company H) only in the following cases:

(i)   When the company (Company H) controls the composition of Board of Directors of other Company (Company S).

(ii) When the Company H holds more than half of the total voting power of Company S.

(iii) When Company S is a subsidiary of a Company T, which in turn is the subsidiary of Company H.

MULTINATIONAL COMPANIES

MEANING OF MULTINATIONAL COMPANY

A multinational company is huge industrial organisation which —

(a)   operates in more than one country,

(b)   carries out production, marketing and research activities on international scale in those countries,

(c)   attempts to maximise profits world over.

ORGANISATION OF MULTINATIONAL COMPANIES

Subject to legal requirements, international agreements and commercial treaties, a MNC can organise its operations in different countries through either of the following five alternatives:

(i)   Branches (e.g. Head office in USA and Branch in India)

(ii) Subsidiary Companies [e.g. MNC (USA) acquires more than 50% voting power in an Indian Company]

(iii) Joint Venture Companies [(e.g. Maruti-Suzuki (Japan), TATA Mcgraw Hill)]

(iv) Franchise holders [(e.g. MNC (USA) given the franchise right to franchise holder of India)]

(v)   Turn-key Projects [(e.g. Handing over the project of construction of a Bridge in India to MNC (Japan)]

Examples of Multinational Companies:

1.	Coca Cola (USA)	2.	Pepsi Cola (USA)
3.	Sony (Japan)	4.	Sujuki (Japan)
5.	Brooke Bond (UK)	6.	Lipton (UK)
7.	LG	8.	National
9.	IBM	10.	Microsoft

Oligopolisation of Markets

As a result of their huge financial resources, latest technology and international reputation, MNCs are in position to sell number of products in number of countries. The emergence and spread of MNCs have brought about an internationalisation of production and investment. As a result, there has been growing oligopolisation of market and a rapid increase in the concentration of power across the markets at international level.

DISTINCTION BETWEEN PRIVATE COMPANY AND PUBLIC COMPANY

A private company differs from a public company in the following respects:

Basis of Distinction	Public Company	Private Company
1. **Use of the word 'Private'**	The name of the public company is **not required** to use the word 'Private'.	The name of the private company **must use** the word 'Private'.
2. **Minimum no. of members**	The minimum number of members required to form a public company is **seven**.	The minimum number of members required to form a private company is **two**.
3. **Maximum no. of members**	There is **no restriction** on the maximum number of members but limited to no. of shares.	The maximum limit of member is **50**.
4. **Minimum Paid up Capital**	It must have a minimum paid up capital of **Rs 5 lac** or higher paid-up capital as may be prescribed.	It must have a minimum paid up capital of **Rs 1 lac** or higher paid-up capital as may be prescribed.
5. **Restriction on Transfer of Shares**	The right to transfer the shares is **not restricted** by the Articles of Association.	The right to transfer the shares is **restricted** by the Articles of Association.
6. **Can it invite the public to subscribe shares or debentures?**	It **can invite** public to subscribe for its shares or debentures.	It **can not invite** public to subscribe for its shares or debentures.
7. **Can it invite or accept deposits?**	It **can invite or accept** deposits from any person.	It **can not invite or accept** deposits from persons other than its members, directors or their relatives.
8. **Compulsion of framing own Articles of Association**	It **can** either **frame** its own Articles of Association **or adopt Table 'A'** as its Articles of Association.	It **has to compulsorily frame** its own Articles of Association so as to include statutory restrictions.
9. **Is Delivery of**	Prospectus / Statement in lieu	**No** Prospectus / Statement

Prospectus/ Statement in lieu of Prospectus required? [Sec. 70]	of Prospectus is **required** to be delivered to the Registrar before allotting shares.	in lieu of Prospectus is **required** to be delivered to the Registrar.
10. **Is it required to Offer further shares to existing shareholders? [Sec. 81]**	It is **required to offer** further shares first to the existing share holders unless a special resolution is passed or approval of Central Govt. is obtained.	It **need not offer** further shares to the existing share holders.
11. **When can it Commence Business? [Sec. 149]**	It can commence its business only **after** obtaining the certificate of incorporation as well as the **certificate to commence business**.	It can commence its business immediately **after** obtaining the **certificate of incorporation**.
12. **Is it required to hold Statutory Meeting? [Sec. 165]**	It is **required to hold** statutory meeting and to send statutory report to share holders and file the same with Registrar.	It is **not required to hold** statutory meeting and to send statutory report to shareholders and file the same with Registrar.
13. **Place of holding AGM [Sec. 166]**	It is required to hold its AGM *at* its **registered office** or at some other place within the city, town or village in which the registered office of the company is situated.	It can hold its AGM **anywhere**.
14. **Quorum to constitute a valid meeting [Sec. 174]**	There must be **at least five** members personally present to constitute a valid general meeting of a public company.	There must be **at least two** members personally present to constitute a valid general meeting of a private company.
15. **Who can Demand for poll? [Sec. 179]**	In case of a public company, any **member** present in person or any proxy holding shares having **at least 1/10 of total voting power** or **at least Rs. 50,000 paid up capital** can demand for a poll.	In case of a private company **one member** present in person or by proxy (if not more than 7 such members are personally present) or **two members** (if more than 7 such members are personally present) can demand for a poll.
16. **Can it appoint Firm or Body Corporate to an office or Place of Profit? [Sec. 204]**	It **can not appoint** a firm or body corporate to an office or place of profit under the company.	It **can appoint** a firm a body corporate to an office or place of profit under the company.

17.	Minimum No. of Directors [Sec. 252(2)]	It must have at least **three** directors.	It must have at least **two** directors.
18.	Retirement of Directors by Rotation [Sec. 255(1)]	**Two-thirds** of the total no. of directors of a public company **must retire** by rotation.	Its directors **need not retire** by rotation. There can be permanent life directors.
19.	Is Statutory Notice required to stand for election as director? [Sec. 257(2)]	Statutory notice etc. is **required** for a person to stand for election as a director.	**No** statutory notice is **required** for a person to stand for election as a director.
20.	Is approval of Central Government required to effect increase in no. of Directors beyond 12? [Sec. 259]	Approval of Central Govt. is **required** for increase in number of directors beyond 12.	Approval of Central Govt. is **not required** for increase in no. of directors beyond 12.
21.	Can 2 or more directors be appointed by single resolution? [Sec. 263(1)]	Two or more directors **can not** be appointed by a single resolution.	Two or more directors **can be** appointed by a single regulation.
22.	Are directors required to file consent to act as director? [Sec. 264]	Its directors are **required to file** the consent to act as director within 30 days of his appointment with the Registrar.	Its directors **need not** file the consent to act as directors and as a result minor can also be appointed as director.
23.	Restrictions on appointment or advertisement of directors [Sec. 266]	Restrictions on appointment or advertisement of director contained in Sec. 266 **apply to** a public company.	Restrictions on appointment or advertisement of a director contained in Sec. 266 does **not apply** to a private company.
24.	Is approval of Central Govt. required to modify the provisions relating to appointment? [Sec 268]	Approval of Central Govt. is **required** to modify any provision relating to appoint-ment of managing, whole time or non-rotational directions.	**No** such approval of Central Govt. is **required** in case of private company.
25.	Can Articles require to hold qualification shares [Sec. 273]	The Articles of a public company **can require** the director to hold a qualification	The Articles of a private company **can not require** a director to hold qualification shares as this provision being contrary to Sec. 273 shall be void.
26.	Restrictions on powers of B.O.D.	There are certain **restrictions** on powers of	**Restriction** on Powers of Board of Directors **do not**

[Sec. 293]	Board of Directors of a public company.	**apply** to private company.
27. **Is there any prohibition against loan to directors?** [Sec. 295]	There is **prohibition** against loan to directors of a public company.	There is **no prohibition** against loan to directors of a private company.
28. **Can interested directors participate in Board Meeting?** [Sec. 300]	Interested directors **can not participate** in board meeting.	Interested directors **can participate** in board meeting.
29. **Is date of birth of directors required to be entered in Register? (Sec. 303)**	Date of birth of a director of a public company is **required** to be entered in the Register of Directors.	Date of Birth of a director of private company **need not** be entered in the register of directors.
30. **Restrictions on remuneration of directors [Sec. 309]**	There are **restrictions** on remuneration payable to directors.	There is **no restriction** on remuneration payable to directors.
31. **Is approval of Central Govt. required to change the remuneration of directors? [Sec. 310]**	Approval of Central Govt. is **required** to change the remuneration of directors.	**No** such **approval** of Central Govt. is required to change the remuneration of directors.
32. **Restrictions on appointment of M.D./WTD [Sec. 316]**	There are **restrictions** on appointment of Managing Director or whole time Director of a public company.	There is **no restriction** on appointment of Manager Director or whole time Director of a private company.
33. **Provisions relating to ascertainment of net profit & depreciation [Sec. 355]**	Provision relating to method of determination of net profits and ascertainment of depreciation **apply** to a public company.	Provision relating to method of determination of net profits and ascertainment of depreciation **do not apply** to a private company.
34. **Restriction on Inter Co. loans & Investments to other companies [Sec. 370]**	There are **restrictions** on making loans or investment by a public company to other companies.	There is **no restriction** as making loan or investment by a private company to other companies.
35. **Can Central Govt. excercise its power to prevent change in BOD? [Sec. 409]**	Central Govt. **can exercise** its power to prevent change in board of director which is likely to affect the company prejudicially.	Central Govt. **can not exercise** its power to prevent change in Board of directors which is likely to affect the company prejudicially.
36. **Can any person be Undisclosed Principal on company's behalf? [Sec. 416]**	**No person can** enter into contract on behalf of public company as undisclosed principal.	**A person can** enter into contract on behalf of private company as undisclosed company and need not give intimation to other directors.

PRIVILEGES OF AN INDEPENDENT PRIVATE COMPANY

The privileges available only to an independent private company (i.e. a private company which is not a subsidiary of a public company) are as follows:

1. **Minimum No. of Members [Sec. 12 (1)]** — A private company can be formed with **only two** members.

2. **Minimum Subscription [Sec. 69]** — A private company can allot shares **without** waiting for the **minimum subscription** to be received, since it is prohibited from offering its shares or debentures to the public.

3. **Delivery of Prospectus / Statement in lieu of Prospectus [Sec. 70]** — A private company **need not issue and deliver** prospectus / statement in lieu of prospectus to the Registrar, since it is prohibited from offering its shares/debentures to the public.

4. **Financial Assistance for Purchase of Own Shares [Sec. 77]** — A private company **can provide** financial assistance for the purchase of its own shares.

5. **Offer of Further Shares to Existing Shareholders [Sec. 81(3)]** — A private company **need not offer** further shares to the existing shareholders.

6. **Commencement of Business [Sec. 149 (7)]** — A private company can commence its business immediately **after** obtaining the **certificate of incorporation**.

7. **Holding of Statutory Meeting [Sec. 165(10)]** — A private company **need not hold** a statutory meeting or file a statutory report with the Registrar of companies.

8. **Place of Annual General Meeting [Sec. 166]** — A private company can hold its annual general meetings **anywhere**. It is not necessary for it to hold annual general meeting at the registered office or at some other place within the city, town or village in which the registered office of the company is situated.

9. **Provision of Sec. 170 to 186 to apply to General Meetings [Sec. 170]** — An independent private company **can exclude** the provisions of Sec. 170 to 186 by formulating its own provisions in its Articles to regulate its general meetings.

10. **Quorum [Sec. 174]** — Unless otherwise provided in the Articles of a private company, **only two** members personally present shall form the quorum of its general meeting.

11. **Demand for Poll [Sec. 179]** — In case of a private company **one member** present in person or by proxy (if not more than seven such members are personally present) or **two members** (if more than seven such members are personally present) can demand for a poll.

12. **No restriction on overall Managerial Remuneration Limit [Sec. 198]** — The **restrictions** regarding overall managerial remuneration **do not apply** to an independent private company.

13. **Appointment of Firm or Body Corporate To a Place of Profit [Sec. 204]** — The **restrictions** regarding the appointment of a firm or body corporate to a place of profit **do not apply** to an independent private company.

14. **Directors need not retire by Rotation [Sec. 255(1)]** — The directors of an independent company **need not retire by rotation**. In other words, it can have permanent life directors.

15. **No Statutory Notice to stand for Elections as Director [Sec. 257(2)]** — **No statutory notice** is required for a person to stand for election as a director of an independent private company.

16. **No approval of Central Govt. to effect Increase in Number of Directors [Sec. 259]** — In case of an independent company an approval of central government is not required for increase in number of directors beyond 12 or the number fixed by the Articles.

17. **Filling of casual vacancies among Directors [Sec. 262]** — The provisions relating to filling of casual vacancies among directors **do not apply** to an independent private company.

18. **Appointment of Directors by Single Resolution [Sec. 263(1)]** — In case of an independent private company, two or more directors **can be appointed** by a single resolution.

19. **Filing of Consent to Act as Director [Sec. 264]** — The directors of an independent company **need not file the consent** to act as directors.

20. **Restriction on Appointment or Advertisement of Directors [Sec. 266]** — Restriction on appointment or advertisement of a director contained in Sec. 266 **does not apply** to an independent private company.

21. **No approval of Central Govt. to modify the Provision Relating to Appointment [Sec. 268]** — **No** such **approval** of Central Govt. is required in case of an independent company.

22. **No approval of Central Govt. to Appoint M.D./WTD or Manager [Sec. 269(2)]** — **No** such **approval** of Central Govt. is required in case of an independent company.

23. **Qualification Shares [Sec. 273]** — The articles of an independent private company **can not require** a director to hold qualification shares as this provision being contrary to Sec. 273 would be void.

24. **Additional Grounds for Disqualification of Shares [Sec. 274 (3)]** — An independent private company **may** by its articles **provide** any grounds in addition to those specified in Sec. 274(1), for disqualification for appointment of directors.

25. **Restrictions on Powers of B.O.D. [Sec. 293]** — The **restrictions** on powers of B.O.D. **do not apply** to an independent private company.

26. **No prohibition Against loan to Directors etc. [Sec. 295]** — There is **no prohibition** against loan to directors etc. in case of an independent private company.

27. **No prohibition against Participation of Interested Directors [Sec. 300]** — An interested director of an independent private company **can participate** in Board meeting.

28. **No entry of Date of Birth of Director [Sec. 303]** — Date of Birth of a director of an independent company **need not be entered** in the Register of Directors.

29. **No restriction on Remuneration of Directors [Sec. 309]** — The **restriction** on remuneration of directors **does not apply** to an independent private company.

30. **No approval of Central Govt. to change the Remuneration of Directors [Sec. 310]** — **No** such **approval** of Central Govt. is required to change the remuneration of directors in case of an independent company.

31. **No Limit on Number of Companies of which one person may be Appointed Managing Director [Sec. 316]** — The **provision** of the Act limiting the number of companies of which one person may be appointed managing director **does not apply** to an independent private company.

32. **Provisions Relating to Ascertainment of Net Profits & Depreciations [Sec. 355]** — The provisions relating to ascertainment of net profits and depreciations **do not apply** to an independent private company.

33. **Restrictions on Inter-Company Loans & Inter Corporate Investments [Sec. 372A]** — The restrictions on Inter-Company Loans & Inter Corporate Investments **do not apply** to an independent private company.

34. **Power of Central Govt. to prevent change in B.O.D. [Sec. 409]** — In case of an independent private company, **Central Govt. cannot exercise** its power to prevent change in Board of directors which is likely to affect the company prejudicially.

35. **Undisclosed Principal on Company's Behalf [Sec. 416]** — **A person can** enter into contract on behalf of an independent private company as undisclosed principal and need not give notice to the other directors.

It may be noted that the moment a private company fails to comply with any of the statutory restrictions contained in its Articles or it becomes a subsidiary of a public company, it shall lose these special privileges.

FACTORS AFFECTING CHOICE OF FORM OF BUSINESS ENTERPRISE

The main purpose of discussing the features, merits and limitations of the various forms of private enterprises is to select a form of Business Enterprise that can effectively meet the business and entrepreneurial objectives.

Comparison of the various forms of organisation shows that none of these forms is ideal in all respects. Each form of organisation is good in some respects and not good in other respects. Looking for one best form of organisation for all kinds of business will be like looking for a shirt that fits everybody in the family. Thus, a particular form of organisation which is suitable in one situation may not be suitable in other situations.

The basic consideration which govern the selection of form of organisation is the attainment of the business and entrepreneurial objectives. Since those objectives vary from one business to another, no single form of organisation can be considered as the best suited for all kinds of business. However, the selection of a suitable form of organisation can be made after carefully considering the following factors:

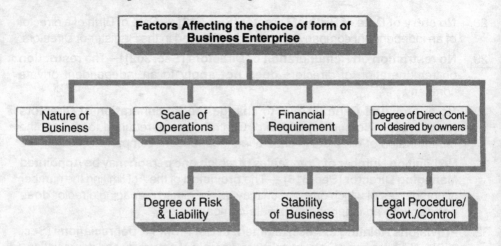

Let us discuss there factors one by one:

1. **Nature of Business** — The choice of suitable form of organisation is influenced by the nature of the proposed business since the organisational requirements are different for different types of business. If the nature of business require the personalised attention of the owner sole proprietorship may be quite suitable. If the nature of business does not require the personalised attention of the owner, partnership or company may be adopted. For example, for small business like hair dresser, dry cleaner, tailor, bakeries, electronic repair shop, sole proprietorship form of organisation is quite suitable.

2. **Scale of Operations** — The choice of suitable form of organisation is also influenced by the scale of operations.

Scale of Operations	Suitable Form of Organisation
(a) If scale of operations is Small	(a) Sole Proprietorship
(b) If scale of operations is Medium	(b) Partnership or Private Company
(c) If scale of operations is Large Scale	(c) Public Company

3. **Financial Requirements** — The choice of suitable form of organisation is also influenced by the financial requirements of the business.

Financial Requirements	Suitable Form of Organisation
(a) If Financial Requirements are Small	(a) Sole Proprietorship
(b) If Financial Requirements are Medium	(b) Partnership or Private Company
(c) If Financial Requirements are Large Scale	(c) Public Company

4. **Degree of Direct Control Desired by the Owners** — The degree of direct control desired by the owners also influences the choice of suitable form of organisation as under:

Degree of Direct Control Desired by the owner	Suitable Form of Organisation
(a) Sole Proprietorship over the business	(a) If it is desired to have a sole control
(b) If it is desired to have direct control over the business by some owners	(b) Partnership
(c) If there is no need for direct control	(c) Company

5. **Degree of Risk & Liability** — The degree of risk & liability desired to be assumed also influences the choice of suitable form of organisation as under:

Degree of Risk & Liability	Suitable Form of Organisation
(a) If risk is low and owner desire to bear the risk	(a) Sole Proprietorship or Partnership
(b) If risk is high and owners are not ready to bear the risk	(b) Company

6. **Stability of Business** — Stability of business also influences the choice of form of organisation as under:

Stability of Business	Suitable Form of Organisation
(a) If it is desired to have stability of business	(a) Company
(b) If it is not so desired to have stability of business	(b) Sole Proprietorship or Partnership

7. **Legal Procedure / Govt. Control** — Government control also influences the choice of form of organisation as under:

Degree of Govt. Control	Suitable Form of Organisation
(a) If much Govt. Control & regulations are not objected	(a) Company or Co-operative form
(b) If much Govt. Control & regulations are not desired	(b) Sole Proprietorship or Partnership

Inter-relation between the factors affecting the choice of form of organisation.

It may be noted that the above mentioned factors are inter-related and influence each other. For example:

1. **Financial Requirements of a business depend upon the nature of business and scale of operations.**

Nature of Business	Scale of Operations	Financial Requirements will be —
Trading	Small	Small
Trading	Large	Large
Industry	Small	Larger than in case of Trading
Industry	Large	Large

2. **Degree of Risk and Liability depends upon the amount of investment made in business**

Amount of Investment made in business	Degree of Risk and Liability will be —
(a) If the amount of investment made is Small	Low
(b) If the amount of investment made is Large	High

3. **Control and Sharing of Profit are related to the risk and liability.**

Degree of Risk & Liability	Degree of Control Desired	Whether Sharing of Profit Desired
Low	High	No
High	Low	Yes

_____ EXERCISES _____

VERY SHORT ANSWER TYPE QUESTIONS

1. Define Private Sector Enterprise.
2. What is meant by sole proprietorship?
3. Define Joint Hindu Family Business.
4. Define Partnership.
5. Define Partnership Deed.
6. What is meant by 'Partner by Estopple'?
7. Define Co-operative organisation.
8. Define Company.
9. Define a Statutory Company.
10. Define Private Company.
11. Define Public Company.
12. Define Licensed Company.
13. Define Government Company.
14. What is a Foreign Company?
15. What is a Holding Company?

16. What is a Subsidiary Company?
17. Define Multinational Company.
18. Name the company that may not have any share capital.
19. When shall a private company lose special privileges?

SHORT ANSWER TYPE QUESTIONS

1. Define private sector enterprise. Explain its characteristics.
2. Define sole-proprietorship. State its important features.
3. Give any three merits of sole-proprietorship.
4. Give any three limitations of sole-proprietorship.
5. Define Joint Hindu family business. Explain its important features.
6. Define Partnership. State its important features.
7. Outline the procedure for registration of partnership.
8. Enumerate three consequences of non-registration of a partnership firm.
9. Distinguish between Partnership at will and Particular Partnership.
10. Explain the terms: Sleeping partner, Nominal partner and Partner in profits only. Partner by holding out or estopple.
11. Distinguish between Sole proprietorship and Partnership.
12. Distinguish between Partnership and Hindu Undivided family.
13. Define co-operative organisation. Explain its main characteristics.
14. Enumerate the various types of co-operative societies.
15. Give any three merits of co-operative organisation.
16. Give any three limitations of co-operative organisation.
17. Define Company. Explain its main characteristics.
18. Give any three merits of a company.
19. Give any three limitations of a company.
20. Distinguish between a partnership and a company.
21. Distinguish between a company and a co-operative society.
22. Enumerate the types of company form of organisations.
23. Define 'companies limited by shares'.
24. Define 'companies limited by guarantee'.
25. Distinguish between a company limited by shares and a company limited by guarantee.
26. Define an 'unlimited company'.
27. List any five points of distinction between a private company and a public company.
28. List any five privileges available to an independent private company only.
29. List any five privileges available to any private company.
30. Name at least two government companies.

31. Name at least two statutory companies.
32. List the factors that help in choosing a suitable form of organisation.

LONG ANSWER TYPE QUESTIONS

1. What do you understand by sole-proprietorship? Outline its features. Explain its merits and limitations.
2. "One man Control is best in the world if that one man is big enough to manage everything". Explain the statement.
3. Define Partnership. Explain its main features, merits and limitations.
4. Describes the various kinds of partners in a partnership firm and discuss their rights and obligations.
5. Define Partnership Deed. Discuss its main contents.
6. Define co-operative organisation. Explain its characteristics, merits and limitations.
7. Explain the various types of co-operative societies.
8. What is a company? Explain its characteristics, merits and limitations.
9. A partnership firm has decided to expand its business which requires more capital and expertise. Should it take more partners or convert it into a private limited company? Give your advice with suitable arguments.
10. Distinguish between private company and public company.
11. Enumerate the privileges available to an independent private company.
12. Explain the factors determining the choice of the form of business organisation.

Public Enterprises

6

MEANING OF BUSINESS UNDERTAKING

A business undertaking is an organization through which business activities are carried out. In Layman's language, different terms are used for a business undertaking such as company, firm, concern, factory, mill, shop, plant etc.

TYPES OF BUSINESS UNDERTAKINGS

Business undertakings may be classified on the basis of size, nature of activities and ownership as given on next page:

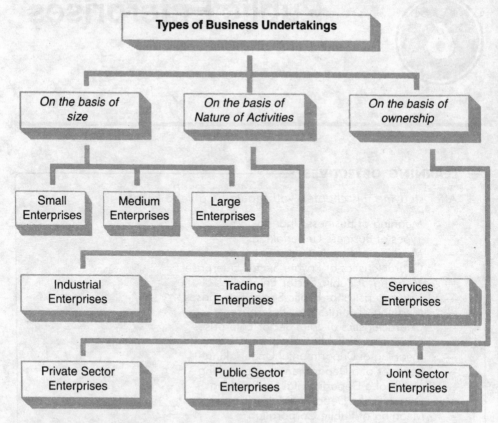

In this chapter, business undertakings on the basis of ownership are discussed.

PRIVATE SECTOR ENTERPRISES

MEANING OF PRIVATE SECTOR ENTERPRISE

A private sector enterprise or a private enterprise is one which is owned, managed and controlled by private entrepreneur(s). For example, business houses managed by Tata such as TELCO, TISCO, TATAPOWER, business houses managed by Birlas such an Century, MRPL, Birla Yamaha, Grasim Industries, business houses managed by Ambanies such as Reliance Industries, Reliance Petroleum, Reliance Capital.

CHARACTERISTICS OF PRIVATE SECTOR ENTERPRISES

The main characteristics of private sector enterprises are as follows:

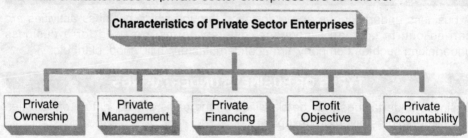

Let us discuss these characteristics one by one.

1. **Private Ownership** — Private Sector Enterprises are owned by private entrepreneur(s).

2. **Private Management** — The rights of its management vest in the owner but professionals can be employed for the efficient management of such enterprises.

3. **Private Financing** — Such enterprises are financed by the private entrepreneurs.

4. **Profit Objective** — Such enterprises are mainly guided by profit objective.

5. **Private Accountability** — Those who manage such enterprises are accountable to the owners for the performance of such enterprises.

PUBLIC SECTOR ENTERPRISES

MEANING OF PUBLIC SECTOR ENTERPRISES

A public sector enterprise or a public enterprise is one which is owned, managed and controlled by the Central Government or any State Government or any local authority.

They are also known as 'Public Undertakings' or 'Public Sector Undertakings'. The forms of organizing public enterprises are: Departmental undertakings (e.g. Railways, Post & Telegraph, PWD), Public Corporations (e.g. IFCI, LIC, Air India, Indian Airlines, Oil and Natural Gas Commission, Food Corporation of India)

Government Companies (e.g. State Trading Corporation (STC), Maruti Udyog Ltd., SAIL, HMT, Coal India Ltd.)

It may be noted that public enterprises and public companies are not the same entities. Public enterprises may or may not be in the form of companies. Public enterprises in the form of companies may be private companies or public companies depending upon the inclusion or exclusion of restrictive clauses in their Articles of Association.

CHARACTERISTICS OF PUBLIC SECTOR ENTERPRISES

The main characteristics of public sector enterprises are as follows:

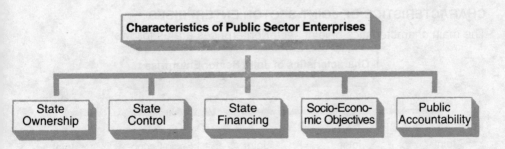

Let us discuss these characteristics one by one.

1. **State Ownership** — Public Sector enterprises are owned by the Central Govt. or State Govt. or jointly by both or Local Authority.

2. **State Control** — The rights of its management vest in the government. The majority of the directors and top officials are appointed by the government for the management of such enterprises.

3. **State Financing** — The whole or major source of financing such enterprises is the government. The funds are supplied from the government treasury or budget of the concerned Ministry Department or investment by government in the share capital of the enterprises.

4. **Socio-Economic Objectives** — Such enterprises are guided by both the profit and social objectives for the benefits of the community as a whole such as —

   (i) to set up basic and strategic industries (like steel and oil)

   (ii) to promote balanced regional development through the growth of economic activity in backward, rural and remote areas of the country

   (iii) to check the growth of monopoly and monopolistic tendencies in the private sector.

   (iv) To ensure adequate supply of essential goods at a fair price.

5. **Public Accountability** — Such enterprises are accountable to the public through the government. Their performance is subject to scrutiny of the Parliament or State Legislature and is evaluated by the committee on Public Undertakings or Public Accounts Committee or Estimates Committee. Their reports are presented for discussion in Parliament or State Assembly.

JOINT SECTOR ENTERPRISES

MEANING OF JOINT SECTOR ENTERPRISE

A joint sector enterprise is one which is owned, managed and controlled jointly by the private entrepreneurs and the government. For example, Cochin Refineries, Gujarat State Fertilizers Company. Such enterprises are organized to encourage private entrepreneurs to participate in industrial development jointly with the government.

CHARACTERISTICS OF JOINT SECTOR ENTERPRISES

The main characteristics of joint sector enterprises are as follows:

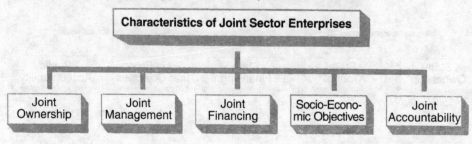

Let us discuss these characteristics one by one.

1. **Joint Ownership** — Joint sector enterprises are owned by private entrepreneurs and the government.

2. **Joint Management** — Such enterprises are mainly managed by private entrepreneurs.

3. **Joint Financing** — Such enterprises are financed jointly by private entrepreneurs and government. The proportion of capital to be contributed is decided by mutual consent.

4. **Socio-Economic Objectives** — Such enterprises are guided by both the profit and social objectives.

5. **Joint Accountability** — Such enterprises are accountable both to the private entrepreneurs and the government.

OBJECTIVES OF PUBLIC ENTERPRISES

The principal objectives of setting up public enterprises are as follows:

1. To achieve rapid economic development through industrial growth in accordance with the development plans.

2. To channelise resources in the best possible manner for economic growth.

3. To ensure balanced regional development of industry and trade.

4. To prevent the growth of monopoly and monopolistic tendencies in the private sector.

5. To prevent concentration of economic power.

6. To control the prices of essential consumer goods in the market to prevent public hardship.

7. To secure public welfare and to reduce inequalities in the distribution of income and wealth.

8. To mobilise public savings through financial institutions to meet the demands of public and private enterprises in accordance with planned priorities.

9. To provide satisfactory employment conditions to the personnel as model employers.

RATIONALE BEHIND PUBLIC SECTOR ENTERPRISES OR REASONS FOR GOVERNMENT PARTICIPATION IN BUSINESS

The reasons for government participation in business are given as follows:

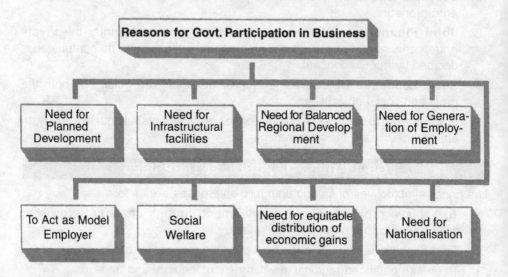

Let us discuss these resources one by one.

1. **Need for planned development** — Since the private enterprises are mainly guided by profitability and not by priorities of development as per Five Years Plans, it becomes necessary to establish public enterprises to give priorities to the growth of certain industries as per Five Years Plan.

2. **Need for Infrastructural facilities** — To bring about the rapid industrial development, it is necessary to develop those industries which facilitate the growth of other industries like transport, power generation, communication etc. Since these industries take a long time to complete, require heavy investment and yield low returns on investment, the private enterprises may not come forward and hence it becomes necessary to establish public enterprises to develop such infrastructure industries. The projects set up in this direction include Hindustan Machine Tools, Hindustan Shipyard, Hindustan Cables.

3. **Need for Balanced Regional Development** — Since private enterprises are likely to be concentrated in those regions where facilities are easily available, the backward regions would be deprived of the benefit of industrial development. Hence it became necessary to establish public enterprises to develop industries in backward regions to have balanced regional development in the country.

4. **Need for Generation of Employment** — The public enterprises helps in expanding employment opportunities by establishing industries in different parts of the country.

5. **To Act as Model Employer** — Public enterprises provide satisfactory facilities to the personnel as model employers in the form of housing, medical aid and other welfare amenities. They set an example for the private sector to follow in this manner.

6. **Social welfare** — Public Enterprises provide essential goods and services at reasonable prices and hence secure social welfare. For example, Fertilisers corporation of India and Food Corporation of India provide fertilisers and food grains at reasonable prices.

7. **Need for equitable distribution of economic gains** — The establishment of public enterprises prevents the growth of monopoly and monopolistic tendencies in the private sector and hence reduces the concentration of economic power.

8. **Need for Nationalisation** — To prevent the closure of sick units or to ensure proper utilization of funds, public enterprises were set up. For example, National Textile Corporation (NTC) was set up to take over the sick textile units. Banks and insurance companies were nationalised to ensure proper utilization of funds.

FORMS OF PUBLIC ENTERPRISES

There are three forms of organisations in Public Enterprises as follows:

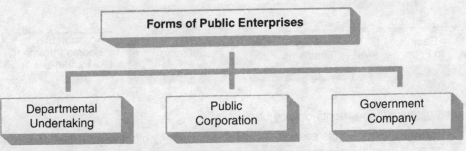

Let us discuss these forms of Public Enterprises one by one.

DEPARTMENTAL UNDERTAKING

MEANING OF DEPARTMENTAL UNDERTAKING

Departmental Undertaking is a public enterpirse which is organised, controlled and financed by the government in the same way as any other government department. **For example,** Railways, Post and Telegraphs, Public Works Department (PWD), Ordnance factories.

FEATURES OF A DEPARTMENTAL UNDERTAKING

The main features of a departmental undertaking are as follows:

1. **Formation** — Departmental Undertaking is created by the government and is attached to a particular ministry.

2. **No Separate legal Entity** — It is not a separate legal entity. It cannot sue and cannot be sued without government's consent.
3. **Management & Control** — It is managed and controlled by the concerned ministry of the government.
4. **Finance** — It is wholly financed by the government out of budgetary appropriations.
5. **No Borrowing Powers** — It has no powers to borrow.
6. **No Authority to use Revenue** — It has no authority to use its revenues. Its revenues are paid into the treasury.
7. **Accountability** — Concerned Minister is accountable to the legislature.
8. **Budgetary & Accounting Control** — It is subject to same budgetary, accounting and audit control as applicable to other government departments.

MERITS OF A DEPARTMENTAL UNDERTAKING

The merits of a departmental undertaking are as follows:

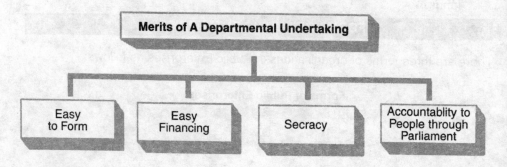

Let us discuss these merits one by one.

1. **Easy to form** — It is easy to form such undertaking since no registration or special legislation is required to bring it into existence.
2. **Easy financing** — It is wholly and directly financed through annual budget appropriations from the concerned ministry.
3. **Secrecy** — It is suitable where secrecy and control is very important such as atomic energy, defence industries.
4. **Accountability to people through Parliament** — The overall responsibility rests with the minister under whose ministry the undertaking functions. The concerned minister is answerable to the Parliament for the efficient operation of the undertaking. Any matter relating to such undertaking can be raised in the Parliament.

DEMERITS OF A DEPARTMENTAL UNDERTAKINGS

The demerits of a departmental undertakings are as follows:

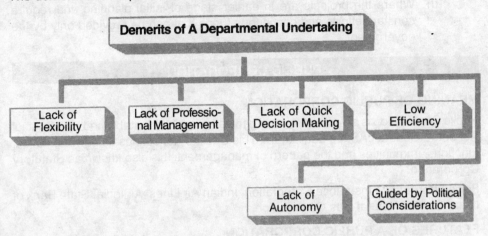

Let us discuss these demerits one by one.

1. **Lack of flexibility** — Departmental undertaking suffers from lack of flexibility since it is subject to rigid rules and regulations of government which do not allow any flexibility in the operations of the undertaking.

2. **Lack of Professional Management** — It also suffers from lack of professional management since the civil servants who manage it do not possess business experience and professional skill necessary for the management of a business.

3. **Lack of Quick Decision Making** — It also suffers from lack of quick decision making, since it runs on bureaucratic lines where number of files are handled by several persons. The transfer of file from one table to another takes time and as a result urgent decisions are kept pending.

4. **Low Efficiency** — It is not managed very efficiently due to lack of initiative on the part of the managers.

5. **Lack of Autonomy** — It also suffers from lack of autonomy since it works as a part and parcel of the government. Managers have no freedom to take important decisions. They have to refer for all important matters to the concerned minister.

6. **Guided by Political Considerations** — The operations of such undertakings are guided by political considerations and not business considerations. Sometimes Vote Bank becomes the considerations.

   Suitability — The departmental form of organisation is usually suitable —

   (a) Where the government desires to have full control over service sectors keeping in view public interest (e.g. Posts and telegraph, broadcasting etc)

   (b) Where maintenance of secrecy is regarded as a matter of strategic importance (e.g. atomic energy, defence industries).

(c) Where the basic purpose of an enterprise is to procure revenue for the government.

(d) Where the projects are in earlier stage of initial planning and require constant efforts and continuous funds that can be provided only by the government.

PUBLIC CORPORATION

MEANING OF PUBLIC CORPORATION

Public Corporation is an autonomous organisation which is established by a Special Act of the Central or State Legislature. This Special Act defines its powers, duties, functions, immunities and the pattern of management. It is also known as Statutory Corporation.

For example: Life Insurance Corporation, Indian Air Lines, Air India, State Bank of India, Oil and Natural Gas Commission.

FEATURES OF A PUBLIC CORPORATION

The features of a public corporation are as follows:

1. **Formation** — Public Corporation is created by a special Act of Central or State Legislature.

2. **Separate Legal Entity** — Like a Company, it has a separate legal entity. It can sue and be sued.

3. **Management and Control** — It is managed by the Board of Directors. Such Board is constituted according to the provisions of the Special Act which created public corporation.

4. **Finance** — It is wholly financed by the government.

5. **Borrowing powers** — It has powers to borrow funds from government as well as the public.

6. **Authority to use Revenue** — It has authority to use its revenue to meet its expenditure.

7. **Budgeting and Audit** — It has powers to prepare its own budget.

8. **Staffing and Terms of Service** — Its employees are not civil servants. They are governed by contract of service.

9. **Accountability** — It is accountable to the public through concerned legislature.

10. **Public Service Motive** — Its primary motive of formation is public service and not earning profit.

MERITS OF A PUBLIC CORPORATION

The merits of a public corporation are as follows:

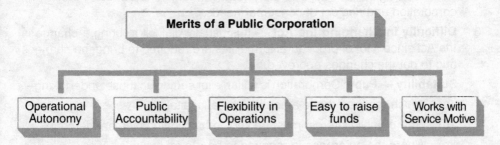

Let us discuss these merits one by one.

1. **Operational Autonomy** — Public Corporation works as an autonomous body within the provisions of the Special Act. It enjoys considerable degree of autonomy as there is no government interference in day to day affiars.

2. **Public Accountability** — The Management keeps public interest in mind while functioning since it is accountable to the public through the legislature.

3. **Flexibility in Operations** — It enjoys flexibility in operations since it is not subject to budget audit and accounting procedures of the government.

4. **Easy to Raise funds** — It can easily raise funds by issuing bonds since it is government owned statutory body.

5. **Works with Service Motive** — It avoids the defects of profiteering, exploitation etc. which are often associated with private enterprises. It works primarily with service motive and profit earning is only a secondary consideration. The profits generated by it are used for the good of the consumers and the community.

DEMERITS OF PUBLIC CORPORATION

The demerits of a Public Corporation are as follows:

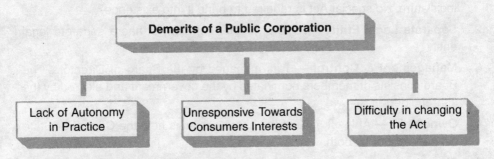

Let us discuss these demerits one by one.

1. **Lack of Autonomy in Practice** — The autonomy available in the eyes of law is not in practice enjoyed by public corporation. Most of the decisions are required to be taken in consultation with the concerned Ministry.

2. **Unresponsive Towards Consumer Interests** — Since public corporations do not have to face any competition, they ignore commercial principles in their working. This may ultimately lead to inefficiency and losses to the corporation and neglect of consumer needs.

3. **Difficulty in Changing the Act** — It is usually difficult to bring a change in the Act since a lot of procedural formalities are required to bring the changes and to get the changes approved.

   Suitability — Public Corporation is suitable for setting up those undertaking—

   (a) Which require a huge amount of initial capital,

   (b) Where public interest must be kept in functioning by management,

   (c) Where the enterprise is required to be run on business lines.

GOVERNMENT COMPANY

MEANING OF GOVERNMENT COMPANY

A government company is a company in which at least 51% of the paid up share capital is held by —

(a) the Central Government, or

(b) any State Government or State Governments, or

(c) Partly Central Government and partly by one or more State Governments.

Government company includes a company which is a subsidiary of such a company.

For Example — State Trading Corporation (STC), Hindustan Machine Tools (HMT), Maruti Udyog Ltd.

FEATURES OF A GOVERNMENT COMPANY

The features of a Government Company are as follows:

1. **Formation** — It is formed by complying with the provisions of The Companies Act, 1956. The government has the authority to exclude or modify certain provisions of The Companies Act by special notification duly approved by the legislature. No special Act is required to bring it into existence.

2. **Separate Legal Entity** — Like any other company, It has a separate legal entity.

3. **Management & Control** — It is managed by the Board of Directors. The Board consists of members nominated by the government and elected by the shareholders.

4. **Ownership** — At least 51% of the share capital is held the Central or State Government or by both.

5. **Finance** — It can raise funds from government or public.

6. **Staffing and terms of service** — Its employees are not civil servants. They are appointed by the company on its own terms & conditions.

7. **Operational Autonomy** — It runs an Commercial principles like, private

enterprise and enjoys higher degree of freedom from government interference. It can frame its own rules and regulation to govern its internal management.

8. **Annual Reports** — Its annual reports and accounts alongwith the audit reports are to be presented to the legislature as per The Companies Act.

9. **Appointment of Auditors** — Its auditors are appointed by the government on the advice of Comptroller and Auditor General of India (CAG).

10. **Borrowing Powers** — It has powers to borrow.

11. **Power to use Revenues** — It has powers to use revenue.

DISTINCTION BETWEEN GOVERNMENT COMPANY AND NON-GOVERNMENT COMPANY

The government company differs from a non-government company in the following respects:

Basis of Distinction	Government Company	Non-Government Company
1. Holder of Paid-up Share Capital	At least 51% of the paid-up share capital is held by the **Central Government or State Government or jointly** by the Central and State Government.	At least 51% of the paid-up capital is held by the **private persons**.
2. Who appoints of Auditor?	Its auditor is appointed by the **government** on the advice of the Comptroller and Auditor General of India (CAG).	Its auditor is appointed by the **General Body** of the members of the company.
3. Laying of Annual Reports	Its annual reports alongwith audit reports are laid **before the Legislature**.	Its audit reports are laid **before** its **General Body**.
4. Power of Central Govt. to exempt from Provisions of the Companies Act	The Central Government **has the power** to exempt it from any of the provisions of the Companies Act except the provision relating to Audit.	The Central Government **has no power** to exempt it from any of the provisions of the Companies Act.

MERITS OF A GOVERNMENT COMPANY

The merits of a government company are as follows:

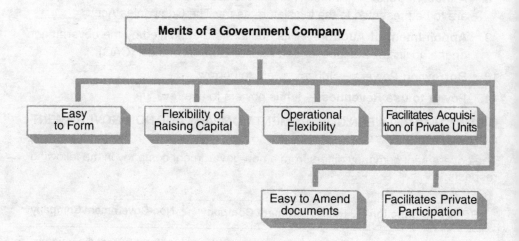

Let us discuss these merits one by one.

1. **Easy to form** — It is easy to form a government company after complying with the provisions of the Companies Act. No special Act is required to bring it into existence.

2. **Flexibility of Raising Capital** — It enjoys flexibility of raising of capital. It can raise funds from government and public.

3. **Operational Flexibility** — It enjoys flexibility in its operations. The evils of red-tapism and bureaucracy associated with the departmental form of organisation are avoided since the employees are not the civil servants. They take decisions and actions on prompt basis on any matter affecting its business. They manage it in efficient manner.

4. **Facilitates acquisition of private units** — It facilitates the acquisition of private units by acquiring at least 51% of paid-up capital of such units. For example, after acquiring equity of Burmah-Shell group, the government changed their name to Bharat Petroleum Corporation Ltd.

5. **Easy to amend documents** — It can amend its Memorandum and Articles by following the procedure laid down in The Companies Act, no approval of Parliament is required for such amendment.

6. **Facilitates Private Participation** — This form of organisation facilitates the private participation in the equity of public enterprises.

DEMERITS OF A GOVERNMENT COMPANY

The demerits of a government company are as follows:

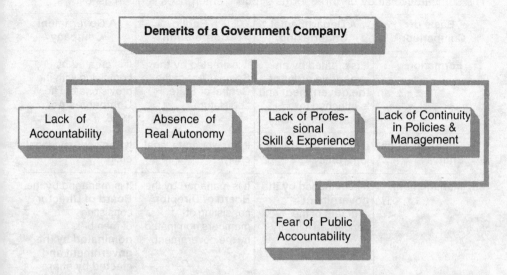

Let us discuss these demerits one by one.

1. **Lack of Accountability** — The government company evades constitutional responsibility because it is not subject to close scrutiny of the Parliament.

2. **Absence of Real Autonomy** — There is absence of real autonomy since the majority of directors are nominated by the government to represent the various ministries. The Board of directors is required to consult the concerned Government department on various policy matters.

3. **Lack of Professional Skill and Experience** — Majority of the directors nominated by the government do not possess professional skill and experience required for managing a commercial enterprise. As a result, It fails to achieve efficiency as required in private enterprise.

4. **Lack of Continuity in Policies and Management** — There is no continuity in policies and management since the management and chairman of these companies keep on changing and as a result the policies are also subject to change by these top officials.

5. **Fear of Public Accountability** — The top management may not take the initiative in entering into new areas of activities since they have the fear of public accountability.

    Suitability — The government company form of public enterprise is considered suitable —

    (a) When the private participation is required,

    (b) When the enterprise is to be run on business lines,

    (c) When the enterprise has to compete with other private enterprises.

COMPARISON OF THREE FORMS OF PUBLIC ENTERPRISES

The comparative study of three forms of public enterprises is given as follows:

Basis of Comparison	A Departmental Undertaking	A Public Corporation	A Government Company
1. **Formation**	It is created **by an executive order of the government** and is attached to a particular ministry.	It is created **by the Special Act** of the Central or State Legislature.	It is created **by** complying with the provisions of The **Companies Act,** 1956.
2. **Separate Legal Entity**	It has **no** separate legal entity.	It **has** separate legal entity.	It **has** separate legal entity.
3. **Management**	It is managed **by the government officials** of the concerned ministry.	It is managed **by the Board of Director** consisting of members nominated by the government.	It is managed **by the Board of Director** consisting of members **nominated by the government and elected by share holders.**
4. **Capital**	**100% capital** is provided **by the government** out of budgetary appropriations.	**Initial capital** is fully provided **by the government.**	**At least 51%** of the paid up share capital is provided **by the government.**
5. **Borrowing Powers**	It has **no** direct powers to borrow.	It **has** power to borrow funds from government and public.	It **has** power to borrow funds from government and public.
6. **Staffing**	Its employees are the **civil servants** (i.e. all government employees)	Its employees are **not civil servants** and are appointed **by the corporation.**	Its employees are **not civil servants** and are **appointed by the corporation.**
7. **Flexibility**	It **does not enjoy** flexibility in its internal working since it is subject to rigid rules and regulation of the Government.	It **enjoys** a great deal of flexibility in its internal working since it is not subject to budget, audit and accounting procedures of the Government.	It **enjoy flexibility** since it can frame its own rules and regulations.
8. **Degree of Autonomy**	It **does not enjoy** operational autonomy since it works as a part and parcel of the government.	It **enjoys** considerable degree of autonomy since there is no government interference in day to day affairs.	It **enjoys** substantial degree of autonomy.

CHANGING ROLE OF PUBLIC SECTOR

Despite the considerable role in the economic development of the country, the public sector has its ills and these are many. For instance over 100 of the 242 Central Public Sector Undertakings are loss making units with many of them terminally sick. In the present era of globalisation and liberations, it is required to bring reforms in public sector undertaking. The Government has realised the need of reforming the public sector undertakings.

Reforming, Public Sector Enterprise is neither a simple nor uniform process. Each enterprise is different from the other. The objectives are often different and for these reasons it is reqired to do different reform measure.

The measures for reforming the public sector undertakings are broadly divided into following.

1. Reforming Public Sector Enterprises by signing Memorandum of Understanding (MOU).

2. Green field Privatisation

3. Reforming Public Sector Enterprises by selling their assets either partially or wholly to the private sector or to the general public.

1. Reforming Public Sector Enterprises by signing Memorandum of Understanding (MOUs)

The system of MOUs was introduced in 1986 following the recommendations of the Arjun Sengupta Committee (1984). While there was no deying of the fact that the PSEs had performed a major role in areas like fertilizers, ship-building machine tools and heavy chemicals, but there was also much dissatisfaction with the fact that the generation of surpluses by PSEs was low and that in aggregate terms return on total investment made by them was poor.

Two of the major causes cited fo the poor financial performance of PSEs were

(i) the relationship between PSEs and the Government was dysfunctional.

(ii) the PSEs had to pursue a number of objectives that often conficted with each other.

It was against this background that the Government of India decided to adopt a system of Memorandum of Understanding (MOU) in 1986. The concept of MOU is very simple one. It is supposed to be a freely negotiated performance agreement between a public enterprises and Government acting as owner of the public enterprise enterprise in which both parties clearly specify their commitment and responsibilities.

The MOUs have progressively covered an increasing number of PSEs. From just 4 PSEs had signed an MOU in 1987-88, the number of PSEs expected to sign MOU in 1996-97 was 114. In 1995-96, 104 PSEs signed MOU with their concerned administrative ministries.

2. Greenfield Privatisation

Reforming PSEs as a process that aims at reducing involvement of the state or the public sector in the nation's economic activities by shifting the divide between public sector and private sector in favour of the later (Greenfield Privatisation) has made considerable progress since the introduction of the new economic policy (NEP) in 1991. The process of re-divide has been mainly through.

(i) **De-licensing :** For most of the PSEs, the market (customer) is also another public sector unit or goverment department. However, the new economic policies have dismanted the market structure on the supply as well as on the demand front. On the supply front, the delicensing of industries provides encouragement for direct foreign investment. This will result in an increase in productive capacity and shrinkage in market share for existing manufacturer. Apart from this, there will be erosion in the profit margin also.

(ii) **Reduction in Budget Allocation:** On the demand side, since most of the customers are government departments undertakings, the funding for fixed and working capial requirements were hitherto met from budget allocations. The reducion budget allocations will affect the asset acquisition and working capital programme of many PSUs. The PSUs output will therefore notice a contraction in the demand.

(iii) **External Air Grant:** Many infrastructure industries in the absence of the budget allocations, resort to external funding from multi-lateral and bi-lateral agencies. This, in turn, affects the market for domestic products.

(iv) **Anomaly in Duty Structure:** The recent reduction in customs duty, particularly in respect of the project imports, has eroded the market for the domestic capital goods industry as domestic manufacturers do not enjoy a similar reduction in excise duty nor are any specific benefits available to them.

(v) **Decision-making Systems:** The decision-making progress in PSUs has to be streamlined to respond quickly to market conditions. This calls for review of government policy, governing PSUs on procurement, investment, raising of resources and wage fixation. Similarly, PSU executives have to be provided with an even balance of authority and responsibility. At present, they have more responsibility than authority. This undermines quick decision-making.

3. **Reforming PSEs through disinvestment**

The Industrial Policy Statement of 24th July, 1991, envisaged disinvestment of part of Government holdings in the case of selected public enterprises in order to raise resources, encourages wider public participation and promote greater accountability.

Since the begining of the disinvestment in 1991-92 till 31st March, 1996 shares in 39 PSEs have been disinvested. The total amoung disinvested during the last 5 years from 1991-96 was Rs 9961 crore.

There is, however, a large gap between the amount planned to be raised and the amount actually raised. Except for the first year of disinvestment in 1991-92, in no other year could the government realise revenues greater than the targeted level of disinvestment.

In the Union Budget 1998-99, disinvestment in Public Sector Enterprises (PSEs) namely GIL, VSNL, CONCOR and IOC was announced. The CONCOR issue was introduced in the market in November, 1998 and raised Rs 221.65 crore. It was also announced that Government holding in Indian Airlines would be brought down to forty nine per cent over the coming three years. To underscore the Government's commitment in Public Sector Enterpries will be brought down to twenty six per cent. However, the Government will continue to retain majority holding in PSEs involving strategic considerations.

The Disinvestment Commission has so far submitted eight reports covering forty three PSUs. In its last report submitted in August 1998, the Commission has made specific recommendations for Air India Ltd. and Central Electronics Ltd, suggesting strategic sale for the former and deferment of disinvestment in the latter. Ten more PSUs have been referred to the Commission in November 1998. The Commission has undertaken diagnostic studies in respect of three undertakings for giving recommendations.

EXERCISES

VERY SHORT ANSWER TYPE QUESTIONS
1. Define Private Sector Enterprise.
2. Define Public Sector Enterprise.
3. Define Joint Sector Enterprise
4. Define Public Corporation.
5. Define Departmental Undertaking.
6. Define Government Company.

SHORT ANSWER TYPE QUESTIONS
1. Define Public enterprises. State its main features.
2. State the objectives of business enterprises in the public sector.
3. Give reasons to justify government participation in commercial activities.
4. Enumerate the types of public enterprises.
5. Define Departmental Undertaking. State its main features.
6. Name at least two departmental undertakings.
7. Give any three merits of a departmental undertaking.
8. Give any three demerits of a departmental undertaking.
9. When is departmental undertaking most suitable for organising a public enterprise?
10. Define Public Corporation. State its main features.
11. Name at least two public corporations.
12. Give any three merits of a public corporation.
13. Give any three demerits of a public corporation.
14. When is public corporation most suitable for organising a public enterprise?

15. Define Government Company. State its main features.
16. List any two points of distinction between a Government Company and Non-Government Company.
17. Name at least two government companies.
18. Give any three merits of government company.
19. Give any three demerits of a government company.
20. When is a government company most suitable for organising a public enterprise?

LONG ANSWER TYPE QUESTIONS

1. What are the objectives of business enterprises in the public sector? Give reasons to justify government participation in commercial and industrial activities.
2. Define departmental undertaking. Explain its main features, merits, demerits and suitability.
3. Define Public Corporation. Explain its main features, merits, demerits and suitability.
4. Define Government Company. Explain its main features, merits, demerits and suitability.
5. In what ways is the company form of organising a public undertaking superior to the departmental form?
6. Distinguish between Government Company and non-Government Company.
7. Attempt a comparative view of the three forms of organising public enterprises.

Formation of a Company

7

LEARNING OBJECTIVES

After studying this chapter, you should be able to know —

— Stages in the Formation of a Company
— Stages in the Commencement of Business of a Company
— Promotion – Meaning, Functions
— Preliminary Contracts or Pre-Incorporation Contracts
— Provisional Contracts
— How to Form a Company
— Certificate of Incorporation
— Effects of Registration
— Certificate of Commencement of Business
— Memorandum of Association – Meaning, Purpose, Form, Printing, Contents
— Contents of Memorandum
— Articles of Association – Meaning, Form, Printing, Contents
— Distinction between Memorandum and Articles of Association
— Prospectus – Meaning, Significance, Contents
— Matters to be Stated in the Prospectus
— Statement in Lieu of Prospectus

STAGES IN THE FORMATION OF A COMPANY

Basically, there are two stages in the formation of a company (whether private or public)

Stage 1   Promotion

Stage 2   Incorporation

The company is said to have been formed or floated from the date mentioned in the certificate of incorporation obtained under stage 2 since the certificate of incorporation is the birth certificate of a company.

STAGES IN THE COMMENCEMENT OF BUSINESS OF A COMPANY

The stages in the commencement of business of a private company and public company having no share capital are different from the stages in the commencement of business of a public company having a share capital since a private company and public company having no share capital can commence its business immediately after obtaining certificate of incorporation but a public company having share capital can not commence its business until it obtains the certificate of commencement of business.

There stages undoubtedly include the stages in the formation of a company. These stages are given below:

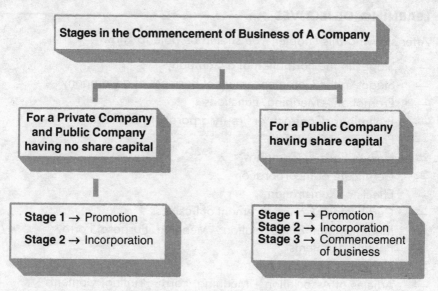

PROMOTION – MEANING, FUNCTIONS

Meaning of Promotion

Promotion is the first stage in the formation of a company. Promotion involves identification of a business opportunity or idea, analysis of its prospects and taking steps to implement it through the formation of a Company. *C.W. Gerstenberg* has defined promotion as the discovery of business opportunities and the subsequent organization of funds, property and managerial ability into a business concern for the purpose of making profits therefrom. Promotion stage comprises the following activities to be undertaken:

Activities Covered Under Promotion

1. Discovery of business idea or identification of business opportunity.
2. Detailed Investigation to find out the strong and weak points of the idea.
3. Organisation of resources.

4. Securing the cooperation of the required number of persons willing to associate themselves with the project.
5. Obtaining the consent of persons willing to act as first directors.
6. Appointing Legal Advisors.
7. Application for proposed name of the company.
8. Preparation of necessary documents like memorandum of association, articles of association.
9. Entering into preliminary contracts.
10. Filing of the necessary documents with the Registrars.

Meaning of Promoters

The Companies Act does not define the term promoters anywhere, it only refers to the liabilities of the promoters. A number of judicial decisions have defined the term 'promoter'.

1. **According to L. J. Bowen**, the term promoter is a term not of law but of business, usefully summing up in a single word, a number of business operations familiar to the commercial word by which a company is generally brought into existence.
2. **Lord Blackburn** states that "the term 'promoter' is a short and convenient way of designating those who set in motion the machinery by which the Act enables them to create an incorporated company."
3. **Justice C. Cockburn** described a promoter as "one who undertakes to form a company with reference to a given project and to set it going, and who takes the necessary steps to accomplish that purpose."

Thus, a promoter is one who identifies a business opportunity, idea, analyses its prospects and takes steps to implements it through the formation of a company.

A company may have more than one promoter. The promoter may be an individual, firm, an association of persons or a body corporate. For example, J.R.D. Tata was promoter of Tata Group, G.D. Birla was promoter of Birla Group, Dhirubhai Ambani is the promoter of Reliance Group.

Functions of Promoters

The various functions performed by the promoters include the following:

1. **To conceive business idea** — First of all the promoters conceive the idea of business.
2. **To make detailed investigation** — After conceiving the idea of business, they make detailed investigations to find out the weakness and strong points of the idea.
3. **To organize the Resources** — After satisfying about the profitability and feasibility of the idea, they organize the resources to convert the idea into a reality by forming a company. The steps to be taken in this regard include the following:

      (i)   Securing the co-operation of the required number of persons willing to associate themselves with the project (Note 7 persons are required to form public company and 2 persons are required to form a private company)

      (ii) Appointing Legal Advisors & other experts

      (iii) Entering into preliminary contracts

      (iv) Preparing detailed financial plan

4. **To obtain the consent of persons willing to act as first directors** — The first directors are generally appointed by the promoters. The promoters seek the consent of some individuals whom they deem appropriate so that they agree to be the first directors.

5. **To decide about the name of the company** — The promoters have to seek the permission of the Registrar of companies for selecting the name of the company. The promoters usually give three names in order of preference. The promoters should ensure that the name of the company should not be identical with or should not too closely resemble the name of another existing company.

6. **To get the necessary documents prepared** — The promoters on the advise of legal experts get the memorandum of association and articles of association prepared and printed.

7. **To arrange for filing of the necessary documents with the Registrar** — The promoters are required to pay the stamp duty, filing fee and other charges for registration of the company. The promoters are to see that the various legal formalities for incorporating the company are complied with.

PRELIMINARY CONTRACTS OR PRE-INCORPORATION CONTRACTS

Preliminary contracts are those contracts which are entered into by the promoters for and on behalf of the proposed company before its incorporation. These contracts are generally entered into by the promoters to acquire some property or some rights for the proposed company. **For example**, Contract with the vendor to sell his running business to the proposed company, contract for the Purchase of Property for the Proposed Company, contract for the grant of a lease for the proposed company.

PROVISIONAL CONTRACTS

In the case of a public company, contracts made after incorporation but before the grant of certificate to commence business are provisional and are not binding on the company until the company is entitled to commence business on the grant of the certificate. But on the issue of the certificate to commence business such contracts AUTOMATICALLY become binding, i.e., without any ratification.

HOW TO FORM A COMPANY

The various steps involved in the formation of a company are given below:

Step 1 →	**Consult —**
	(a) the latest edition of Directory of Companies together supplements updating it.
	(b) the Guidelines issued by the Department of Company affairs
	(c) The Emblems & Names (Prevention of Improper Uses) Act 1950
Step 2 →	**Select in order of preference at least four names which —**
	(a) are not identical with or too similar to the name of another registered company
	(b) are not attracting the provisions of the Emblem & Names (Prevention of Improper Uses) Act 1950,
	(c) are not in contravention of the Guidelines issued by the Department of Company affairs.
Step 3 →	**Apply to the concerned Registrar** of Companies to ascertain the availability of names in the prescribed Form No. 1A alongwith a fee of Rs. 500.
Step 4 →	**Get Ensured about the availability of name** within 14 days since the Registrar is required to inform the status of the application within 14 days.
	(a) **If available** — Complete all the formalities within a period of 3 months.
	(b) **If not Available** — Apply again (if satisfied with the reason for refusal given) or, Make an appeal against refusal
Step 5 →	**Get the Drafts of Memorandum of Association and Articles of Association prepared,** However a public company limited by shares need not prepare its own articles. It can adopt Table A as given in Schedule I of the Act.
Step 6 →	**Get the Drafts of Memorandum of Association & the Articles of Association vetted** by the Registrar.
Step 7 →	**Get the Memorandum Association & Articles of Association printed**
Step 8 →	**Get the Memorandum of Association & Articles of Association stamped.**
Step 9 →	**Get the Memorandum of Association & Articles of Association signed** by at least 2 subscribers in case of a private

company and 7 subscribers in case of a public company. Each subscriber shall also write in his own hand his address, description, occupation and numbers of shares subscribed for in presence of at least one witness who share attest the signature and shall write in his own hand his address, description and occupation (if any). These documents may be signed by an agent if he is authorized to do so by a power of attorney.

Step 10 → **Ensure that Memorandum and Articles of Association are dated on a date after the date of stamping.**

Step 11 → **Get Form No. 29** (in duplicate) duly filled up and signed to accord to consent of a person willing to act as director if he is so appointed by the Articles of Association of a public company having share capital [Sec 266]

Step 12 → **Get Form No. 18** (in duplicate) duly filled up and signed to give the notice of the situation of the registered office of the company if the subscribers have already chosen a registered office and they wish to give notice to the Registrar at the time of registration. *Alternatively* such notice may be given within 30 days of the incorporation of the company. [Sec 146]

Step 13 → **Get Form No. 32** (in duplicate) duly filled up and signed to provide particulars of directors, manager or secretary if they are appointed by Articles of Association and the subscribers wish to give notice to the Registrar at the time of registration. *Alternatively*, such form may be sent within 30 days of appointment of first directors.

Step 14 → **Get the Statutory Declaration** prepared in Form No. 1 Statutory declaration is a declaration to the effect that all the requirements of the Act and rules there under relating to the registration of the company have been complied with. Such declaration can be signed by any one of the following persons:

(a) an advocate of the Supreme Court or of a High Court; or

(b) an attorney or a pleader entitled to appear before a High Court; or

(c) a secretary, or a chartered accountant practicing in India and who has been engaged in the formation of the company; or

(d) by a person named in the articles as a director, manager or secretary of the company.

Step 15 → **File the following documents** with the Registrar of companies alongwith the forwarding application with necessary registration and filing fees:

(a) The **Memorandum of Association**, duly signed by the prescribed minimum number of subscribers, and duly stamped and signed by witness.

(b) The **Articles of Association** similarly signed, stamped and witnessed.

(c) A **copy of agreement**, if any, which the company purposes to enter into with any individual for appointment as its Managing Director or Whole-time Director or Manager.

(d) A **copy of Any other agreement**, if referred to in the Memorandum and Articles of Association in that case, it will form a part of the Memorandum and Articles of Association.

(e) **Power of Attorney** duly stamped and signed by the subscribers authorizing a representative to make amendments and/or alterations in the Memorandum and Articles of Association at the time of registration.

(f) A **Certified copy of letter of the Registrar of Companies, intimating the availability of the proposed name**.

(g) **Consent of director** to act in Form No. 29 (in duplicate) wherever necessary

(h) **Notice of the situation** of the registered office in Form no. 18 (in duplicate) wherever necessary

(i) **Particulars of Directors**, Managing Director, Manager and Secretary in Form no. 32 (in duplicate) wherever necessary

(j) **Statutory Declaration** in form no. 1

Step 16 → **Get the Certificate of Incorporation from the Registrar of Companies**

CERTIFICATE OF INCORPORATION

When the necessary documents have been filed with the Registrar alongwith the payment of requisite fee, the Registrar shall scrutinize these documents and if he is satisfied that (a) all the documents are in order and (b) all the requirements of the act in respect of registration have been duly complied with, he shall enter the name of the company in the Register of Companies and shall issue a certificate which is termed as 'Certificate of Incorporation.'

Note : If the Registrar is of the view that there are some minor defects in any document, he may require that the defects be rectified. But, if there are some material and substantial defects, the Registrar may refuse to register the company.

Contents of Certificate of Incorporation

The certificate of Incorporation contains:

> 1. the name of the company
> 2. the date of its issue
> 3. the signature of the Registrar with his real.

This certificate is literally the birth certificate of the company evidencing that the company is born with its name on the date mentioned in the certificate.

Note : A print of this certificate is to be a part of all copies of Memorandum and Articles of association.

Conclusiveness of Certificate of Incorporation

According to Sec 35 of the Companies Act,

(a) certificate of incorporation given by the Registrar of Companies in respect of any association shall be conclusive evidence that all the requirements of Companies Act have been complied with in respect of its registration as well as matters precedent and incidental thereto.

(b) the association is a company authorized to be registered and duly registered under the Act.

Certificate cannot be disputed on any ground whatsoever and nothing is required to be inquired into as to the regularity of the prior proceedings.

In view of the exclusiveness of its Certificate of Incorporation, irregularities relating to procedural matters pertaining to registration such as defects in the signatures of the subscribers, or other prescribed particulars will not affect the legal status or personality of the company though it does not prevent an aggrieved person presenting a claim against persons responsible for getting the company incorporated.

It should, however, be noted that the certificate of incorporation is not the conclusive proof with respect to the legality of the objective of the company, mentioned in the objects clause of the Memorandum of Association. As such, it a company has been registered whose objects are illegal, the incorporation does not validate the illegal objects. In such a case the only remedy available is to wind up the company.

EFFECTS OF REGISTRATION

1. From the date of incorporation, the original subscribers to the memorandum as well as the other persons who may, from time to time, become members of the company, shall constitute a body corporate by the name contained in the Memorandum of Association.

2. The body corporate shall be capable of exercising all the functions of an incorporated company.

3. The company shall have perpetual succession.

Perpetual Existence shows the properties of immortality. In other words, it means that a company's existence persists irrespective of the change in the composition of its membership. It continues to exist even if all its human members are dead. The company may be compared with a flowing river where water (members) keeps an changing continuously still the identity of the river (company) remain the same. Since it is created by law, it can be put to an end only by the process of law. Thus, a company shall continue to exist indefinitely till it is wound up in accordance with the provision of the Companies Act.

4. The company shall have a Common Seal.

    Common Seal means the official signatures of the company. Any document bearing the common seal of the company and duly witnessed by at least two directors will be legally binding on the company.

5. Members are liable to contribute to the assets of the company in the events of its being wound up to the extent of their contract or guarantee as the case may be.

6. The memorandum and articles when registered shall bind the company and members.

7. All money payable by any member to the company under Memorandum or Articles shall be a debt due from him to the company.

8. The subscribers of the memorandum of a company shall be deemed to have agreed to become members of the company and on its registration, shall be entered as members in its Register of Members.

9. A private company can commence its business immediately after obtaining the certificate of incorporation.

CERTIFICATE OF COMMENCEMENT OF BUSINESS

Meaning of Certificate of Commencement of Business

The certificate of commencement of business is a certificate which entitles a company to commence business or to exercise borrowing powers.

Companies not required to obtain certificate of commencement of business

Since a private company (whether or not having share capital) and a public company having no share capital can commence business immediately after its incorporation, such companies are not required to obtain certificate of commencement of business.

Company which is required to obtain certificate of commencement of business.

A public company having share capital is required to obtain certificate of commencement of business from the Registrar before it can commence its business or exercise borrowing powers.

Procedure for Obtaining the Certificate of Commencement of Business

I. If a public company, having share capital, has issued a prospectus, inviting the public to subscribe for its shares or debentures, it cannot commence any business or exercise borrowing powers unless —

(a) The company has allotted the shares upto the amount of minimum subscription

(b) Every director has paid to the company, in cash, the application and allotment money on the shares taken or contracted to be taken by him in the same proportion as public.

(c) No money is liable to be repaid to the applicants for failure to apply for or to obtain permission for the shares or debentures to be listed on any recognized stock exchange.

(d) Duly verified declaration in the prescribed Form No. 19 has been filed with the Registrar. The declaration must specify that clause (a), (b), and (c), as above have been complied with. The declaration must be verified by one of the directors or the Secretary of the Company. Where the Company has not appointed a Secretary, the declaration may be verified by a Secretary in whole time practice.

II. If the company has a share capital but does not issue a prospectus inviting the public to subscribe for its shares, the company cannot commence any business unless —

(a) The company files with the Registrar, a statement in lieu of prospectus, alongwith the report specified in Part II of Schedule III. The statement should be filed with the Registrar at least three days before the first allotment.

(b) Every director of the company has paid to the company, in cash, the application and allotment money on the shares taken or contracted to be taken by him.

(c) A duly verified declaration in the prescribed form has been filed with the Registrar at least three days before the first allotment is made. The declaration must specify that the above conditions have been complied with and must be verified by one of the directors or the Secretary of the Company. In case the company has not appointed a Secretary, the declaration may be verified by a Secretary in whole time practice.

When the above requirements are duly fulfilled, the Registrar shall issue a certificate known as 'certificate of commencement of business' . This document certifies that the company is entitled to commence business and is also a conclusive evidence of the fact that the company is so entitled. Any contract entered into will be binding on the company.

Consequences of Default

If any company commences business in contravention of these provisions, every person who is responsible for the default shall be punishable with fine which may extend to Rs 50,000 for every day during which the default continues.

Consequence of not commencing business

If any company does not commence its business within one year of its incorporation, it is liable to be wound up by the court under section 433.

MEMORANDUM OF ASSOCIATION – MEANING, PURPOSE, FORM, PRINTING, CONTENTS

Meaning of Memorandum of Association

According to Section 2(28) of The Companies Act, Memorandum means the memorandum of association of a company as originally framed or as altered from time to time in pursuance of any previous company law or of this Act. But this definition is not an exhaustive one.

The status and importance of memorandum of Association has been clearly brought out in many decided cases as follows:

1. "Memorandum of Association of a company contains the fundamental conditions upon which alone the company is allowed to be incorporated. They are conditions introduced for the benefit of the creditors and the outside public as well of the shareholders".

2. **Lord Cairns** observed Memorandum of Association of a company is its charter and defines the limitations on the powers of the company established under the Act, that it contains in it, both that which is affirmative and that which is negative and that it states affirmatively, the ambit and extent of vitality and power which by law are given to the corporation and it states negatively that nothing shall be done beyond that ambit".

3. Memorandum of Association defines its relations with the outside world and the scope of its activities. Its purpose is to enable the shareholders, creditors and those who deal with the company to know what is its permitted range of Activities.

To Sum up, Memorandum of Association is the constitution of the company which, lays down the fundamental conditions upon which alone the company is allowed to be formed. It defines as well as confines the powers of the company. It not only shows the objects of formation but also determines the utmost possible scope of its operations beyond which its action cannot go. If its enters into a contract which is beyond the powers conferred on it by the memorandum, such a contract will be ultra vires the company and hence void. Even the unanimous consent of the entire body of its members can not ratify such contract.

Thus, in this respect it is the company's charter defining its constitution and scope of the powers with which it has been established under the Act.

Purpose of Memorandum of Association

The memorandum of Association is a public document which is open for inspection by any member of the public on payment of prescribed fees [Sec 610]. Therefore every person who deals with the company is presumed to have the knowledge of its contents.

The purpose of Memorandum is two fold:

1. First, to enable the intending shareholders to know the purpose for which their money is going to be used and within what fields they are taking risk in making the investment.
2. Second, to enable the persons intending to deal with the company to know with certainty as to whether the contractual relationship which they intend to enter into with the company is within the corporate objects of the company or not.

Thus, Memorandum gives protection not only to the shareholders but also to persons who intend to deal with the company.

Form of Memorandum

According to Sec 14, the Memorandum of Association of a company must be in one of the forms given in Schedule I as may be applicable to the case of the company or in a firm as near there to as circumstances admit.

The Tables in Schedule I to the Act specify the following forms applicable to different types of companies as under:—

Table A : Memorandum of Association of a company Limited by Shares

Table B : Memorandum of Association of a company Limited by Guarantees and not having a share capital.

Table C : Memorandum of Association of a Company Limited by Guarantee and having a share capital.

Table D : Memorandum of Association of an Unlimited Company.

Printing and Signature of Memorandum

The memorandum must be —

(a) printed

(b) divided into paragraphs numbered consecutively, and

(c) signed by a least 7 persons in case of a public company and by at least 2 persons in case of a private company. The persons signing the Memorandum are known as **subscribers** to the Memorandum.

— Each subscriber must give his address, description and occupation (if any).

— The signature of each subscriber must be attested in the presence of at least one witness.

— The witness must aleast the signature and add his address, description and occupation (if any).

CONTENTS OF MEMORANDUM

The memorandum of association of a company must state the following clauses:—

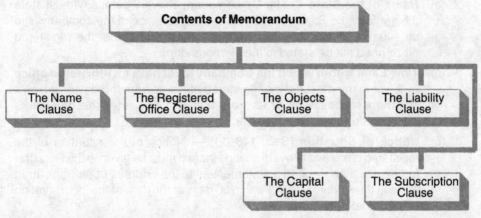

Let us know about each of the aforesaid clauses in detail.

1. **Name Clause**

   Legal Requirements:

   (a) **Last word** — The Memorandum of every company must state the name of the company with the word "Limited" as the last word of the name in the case of a public Limited company and with "Private Limited" as the last words of the name in the case of a private limited company.

   Exception in Case of Licensed Companies — The Central Government may be licence direct that a non-profit making association be registered as a company with limited liability without the addition of the word 'Limited' or the words 'Private limited'. A non-profit making association is an association which —

   (i) is formed for promoting commerce, art, science, religion, charity or any other useful object, and

   (ii) intends to apply its profits / income in promoting its objects

   (iii) prohibits the payment of any dividend to its members.

   (b) **Undesirable Names to be avoided** — The name must not be undesirable in the opinion of Central Government. The name shall be considered as undesirable if —

   (i) It is identical with or too resemble the name of an existing company.

   (ii) It is prohibited by the Emblems and Names (Prevention of Improper Use) Act 1950. This Act prohibits the use of the name and emblems of the United Nations and the World Health Organisation, the official seal and emblems of the Central and State Governments, the Indian National Flag, the name and pictorial representation of Mahatma Gandhi and the Prime Minister of India.

   (iii) It is in the contravention of the guidelines issued by the Department of Company Affairs (Govt. of India).

2. **Registered Office Clause**

   Legal Requirements:

   (a) **Name of the State** — The Memorandum of every company must state the name of the State in which the registered office of the company is to be situated. It may be noted that the exact address of the registered office need not be stated in the Memorandum.

   (b) **Time Limit within which the Company must have its registered office** — A company must have a registered office as from the day on which it commences business or as from the 30th day after the date of its incorporation whichever is earlier.

   (c) **Notice of Situation [Sec. 146 (2)]** — Notice of the situation of the registered office and of every change therein must be given to the Registrar (otherwise than through a statement as to the address of the registered office in the Annual Report) within 30 days of the date of the incorporation or of the date of change.

   Importance — All communications and notices are to be addressed to the registered office [Sec. 146(1)]. Every company must keep proper books of account at its registered office. [Sec. 209(1)]. The domicile and the nationality of the company and the jurisdiction of the Court is determined by the situation of its registered office.

3. **Objects Clause [Sec. 13]** — The Company registered after the commencement of the Companies (Amendment) Act 1965 must divide its object clause into two sub-clauses namely:

   (a) **Main Objects**

   This sub-clause covers the following two:

   (i) Main Objects of the Company to be pursued on its incorporation, and

   (ii) Objects incidental or ancillary to the attainment of the main objects

   (b) **Other Objects**

   This sub-clause covers the other objects which are not included in 'Main Objects'.

Restrictions on the Selection of objects

The subscribers to the memorandum may choose any 'objects' for the purposes of their company subject to the following restrictions:

(a) The objects must not include anything which is illegal or contrary to general law e.g. floating a company for dealing in lotteries.

(b) The objects must not include anything which is against public policy e.g. trading with alien enemies objects which are in restraint of trade

(c) The objects must not include anything which is prohibited by the Companies Act 1956.

Importance of Objects Clause

The objects clause is of fundamental importance to its members as well as its non-members. In the first place, it gives protection to subscribers (members) who learn from it the purposes to which their money can be applied. In the second place, it gives protection to outsiders dealing with the company who learn from it what its powers are and what is the range of its activities. The narrower the objects appended in the memorandum, the lesser is the subscribers' risk, the wider these objects, the greater is the security of those who transact business with the company.

4. **Liability Clause** — The liability clause states the nature of the liability of members. The legal requirements regarding this clause in respect of various types of companies are as under:

   (a) **In case of a Company limited by shares.**

   Liability clause must state that the liability of its members is limited. It means that liability of a member is limited to the nominal value of shares held by him. In case the shares are partly paid, then no member can be called upon to pay more than the amount that remains unpaid on his shares. Thus, a member is liable to pay only the unpaid amount on his shares and no further. For example, A shareholder holds a Rs. 10 share and has paid Rs. 8 on it so far. He can be called upon to pay Rs. 2 and nothing more. In this example, if he holds a fully paid-up share, then his liability is nil.

   (b) **In case of a Company limited by guarantee.**

   Liability clause must state that the liability of a member is limited to the amount which he has agreed to contribute to the assets of the company in the event of its being wound up.

5. **Capital Clause** — In case of limited companies by shares, this clause must state the amount of share capital with which the company is to be registered and the division thereof into shares of a fixed amount.

   Such capital is called 'Authorised' or 'Nominal' or 'Registered' capital. The fixed amount of a share is known as 'Par' or 'Nominal' value of a share. The amount of authorised capital should be sufficiently high considering the immediate needs of the business and possible expansion in the near future. The stamp duty and registration fee are payable on the basis of amount of authorised capital.

6. **Association or Subscription Clause**

   Legal Requirements:

   (a) Each of the subscribers must give in his own handwriting his name with surname, address, description (by the name of father, husband or wife as the case may be)

   (b) In case of a company having share capital, the each of the subscriber must also write in his own handwriting opposite his name, the number of shares agreed to be subscribed by him. Each subscriber must take at least one share.

   (c) That such declaration must be signed by at least 7 persons (in case of a public company) or 2 persons (in case of a private company).

(d) that an agent may sign the memorandum of association on behalf of subscriber if he is authorised by a power of attorney to do so.

(e) that each of the witnesses must give in his own handwriting, his name, with surname, the description & occupation if any.

(f) that the signatures of the subscribers must be attested by at least one witness who must not be from among the subscribers.

(g) such clauses must be strictly in accordance with the such one of formats given in Tables B, C, D & E of Schedule I as may be applicable to the case of company.

Specimen of Subscription Clause in case of memorandum of a company having a share capital.

"We the several persons whose names and addresses are subscribed, are desirous of being formed into a company in pursuance of the Memorandum of Association and we respectively agree to take the number of shares in the capital of the company set opposite our respective names".

ARTICLES OF ASSOCIATION – MEANING, FORM, PRINTING, CONTENTS

Meaning of Articles

Section 2(2) of the Companies Act defines Articles as the Articles of Association of a company as originally framed or as altered from time to time in pursuance of any previous companies law or of this Act. This definition is not sufficient to explain its meaning. Let us look at some of the observation made in judicial cases.

1. "The Articles of Association of a company are the internal rules and regulations to the management of its internal affairs."

2. "The articles play a part subsidiary to memorandum of association. They accept the memorandum of association as the charter of incorporation of the company and so accepting it, they proceed to define the duties, rights and powers of governing body as between themselves and the company at large and the mode and form in which the business of the company is to be carried on and the mode and form in which changes in the internal regulation of the company may from time to time be made."

Thus, the memorandum lays down the objects for which the company is formed, the articles lay down rules and regulations for the attainment of those objects.

Which companies are required to register its Articles

According to Sec. 26, the following companies are required to register its Articles alongwith the memorandum of association:

---

1. An Unlimited Company (Whether Public or Private)
2. A Company Limited by Guarantee (Whether Public or Private)
3. A Private Company Limited by Shares

Which company need not have its own Articles

A **public company limited by shares** need not necessarily have its own articles. A public company limited by shares may *either* have its own articles *or* it may adopt *either* wholly *or* partly Table A of Schedule I of the Companies Act. Even if it does register Articles of its own, Table A will still apply automatically unless it has been excluded or modified. In other words, there are three possible alternatives in which a public company limited by shares may adopt Articles of Association. These are:

(i)   It may adopt Table A in full; or

(ii) It may wholly exclude Table A and set out its Articles in full; or

(iii) It may set out its own Articles and adopt part of Table A.

If such a company goes in for the first alternative, then it is not necessary to get any Articles of Association registered. It has only to endorse on the face of the Memorandum of Association that it has adopted Table A as its Articles of Association. The advantage in adopting the regulations of Table A is that its provisions are legal beyond only doubt.

Specific Regulation Required in the Articles of Specific Companies

As per Sec. 27, the specific regulations required in the Articles of specific companies are given below:

Type of Company	Specific Regulation Required
1. **In case of an Unlimited Company**	Its Articles must state the number of members with which the company is to be registered and if it has a share capital, the amount of share capital with which it is to be registered **Note:** Its Articles must be in the Form given in Table E.
2. **In case of a company limited by guarantee but not having share capital**	its Articles must state the number of members with which it is to be registered. **Note:** Its Articles must be in the Form given in Table C.
3. **In case of a company limited by guarantee and having share capital**	Its Articles must state (a) the number of members (b) the amount of share capital with which it is to be registered. **Note:** Its Articles must be in the Form given in Table D.
4. **In case of a Private Company having share capital**	Its Articles must contain the following **four** restrictions as contained in Sec. 3(1) (iii) (a) Restricting the right to transfer its shares (b) limiting the number of its members to 50 excluding the past and present employees of the company.

		(c) prohibiting any invitation to the public to subscribe for any shares in or debentures of the company
		(d) prohibiting any invitation or acceptance of deposits from persons other than its members, directors or their relatives.
5.	**In case of a Private Company having no share capital**	Its Articles must contain the following three restrictions as contained in sub-clause (b) and (c) of Sec.3 (1)(iii):
		(a) limiting the number of its members to 50 excluding the past or present employees of the company.
		(b) prohibiting any invitation to the public to subscribe for any shares in or debentures of the company.
		(c) prohibiting any invitation or acceptance of deposits from persons other than its members, directors or their relatives.

Form of Articles

According to Sec. 29, the Articles of Association of a company must be in one of the forms given in Schedule I as may be applicable to the case of the company or in a form as near thereto as circumstances admit.

The Tables in Schedule I to the Act specify the following forms applicable to different types of Companies as under:

Table C :	Articles of Association of a company limited by guarantee and not having a share capital.
Table D :	Articles of Association of a company limited by guarantee and having a share capital.
Table E:	Articles of Association of an Unlimited Company

Note: Additional matters which are not inconsistent with the provisions contained in the form in any of the Tables C, D and E may be included in the Articles.

Printing and Signature of Articles

The Articles must be —
(a) printed
(b) divided into paragraphs numbered consecutively, and
(c) signed by at least 7 persons in case of a public company and by at least 2 persons in case of a private company. The person signing the Articles are known as 'Subscribers'. Each subscribers must give his address, description and occupation (if any). The signature of each subscriber must be attested in the presence of at least one witness. The witness must attest the signature and give his address description and occupation (if any).

Contents of Articles of Association

The Articles of Association may contain **any regulation** for the attainment of objects stated in the memorandum **subject to the following restrictions**:

(a) The Article must not include anything which is illegal or contrary to general law

(b) The Articles must not include anything which is against public policy.

(c) The Articles must not include anything which is prohibited by the Companies Act 1956.

Articles usually contain provisions relating to the following matters —

Examples of Matters Included in Articles

1. Share Capital & Right of Shareholders, Variation of these rights,
2. Allotment of Shares
3. Calls on Shares & Lien on Shares
4. Transfer of Shares
5. Transmission of Shares
6. Forfeiture of Shares
7. Conversion of Shares into Stock
8. Share warrants & Shares Certificates
9. Alteration of Capital
10. General Meeting & proceedings threat
11. Voting Rights, Voting & Poll & Proxies
12. Directors, their appointment, remuneration qualifications, powers & proceedings of Board of Directors
13. Manager / Secretary
14. Seal
15. Dividend & Reserves
16. Capitalisation of Profits
17. Accounts, Audit & borrowing powers
18. Winding up
19. The extent to which Table A of Schedule I of the Act is to apply or not to apply

DISTINCTION BETWEEN MEMORANDUM AND ARTICLES OF ASSOCIATION

The Memorandum of Association differs from the Articles of Association in the following respects:

Basis of Distinction	Memorandum of Association	Articles of Association
1. Contents	It contains the **fundamental conditions** upon which alone the company is allowed to be incorporated.	It contain the **internal rules and regulations** relating to management of internal affairs.
2. Fundamental / Subordinate document	It is a **fundamental** document.	It is **subordinate** to the Memorandum.
3. Compulsory or optional	Every company **must** have its own memorandum.	A public Company limited by shares **need not have** its own Articles. It may adopt Table A as its Articles.
4. Relationship defined	It defines the relationship **between the company and outsiders**.	It defines the relationship **between the company and its members** as members only and as members inter se.
5. Alteration whether easy or difficult	The memorandum **cannot** be so easily altered. The company has to follow the strict procedure for the alteration of its clauses. In some cases alteration requires the approval of the Company Law Board.	Articles **can** be **easily** altered by passing a special resolution.
6. Binding Effect of Ultra Vires Act	An act which is beyond the powers given in the Memorandum is ultra vires and **void and it cannot be ratified** even by the unanimous consent of all the members.	An act which is intra vires the Memorandum but ultra vires the Articles **may be ratified** by shareholders by passing a special resolution.
7. Outsiders' Remedy in case of ultra vires contacts	In case of the contracts ultra vires the memorandum, outsiders **have no remedy** against the company.	In case of contracts ultra vires the Articles, outsiders **can enforce** the contract against the company provided they had no knowledge of irregularity.

PROSPECTUS – MEANING, SIGNIFICANCE, CONTENTS

Meaning of Prospectus [Sec 2 (36)]

According to Sec 2 (36) prospectus means *"any document described or issued as prospectus and includes any notice, circular, advertisement or other document inviting deposits from the public or inviting offers from the public for the subscription or purchase of any shares in, or debentures of, a body corporate."* In simple words, the term 'Prospectus' means a document which invites deposits from the public invites offers from the public to subscribe or buy the shares or debentures of the company.

Thus, a prospectus is not an offer in itself but an invitation to make an offer. Application for making a deposit or for purchase of shares or debentures constitutes an offer by the applicant to the company. It is only on the acceptance of the offer, by the company, a binding contract comes into existence.

Significance of Prospectus

Prospectus is an important document because of the following reasons:

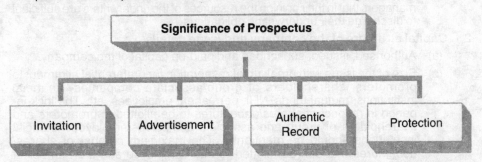

Let us discuss these reasons one by one.

1. **Invitation** — It serves as an invitation by the company to the public to invest through making deposit or subscribing shares or debentures.

2. **Advertisement** — It acts as a medium of advertisement since it informs the public about its present operations and future prospects.

3. **Authentic Record** — It serves as an authentic record of the terms & conditions of the issue of deposits, shares or debentures.

4. **Protection** — It protects the interests of the investors who invest on the faith of the prospectus since any mis-statement in the prospectus attracts both civil and criminal liability for persons who authorise the issue of prospectus.

MATTERS TO BE STATED IN THE PROSPECTUS

Keeping in view the requirements of Schedule II of The Companies Act, 1956 and the SEBI guidelines for disclosure and investor protection, the prospectus to be issued by companies should provide for the following matters:

1. **General information**
   (a) Name and address of registered office of the company;
   (b) Details of letter of intent/industrial licence obtained and disclaimer clause of SEBI about non-responsibility for financial soundness or correctness of statements;
   (c) Names of stock exchanges where listed (if applicable) and where listing applications have been made for the issue;
   (d) Provisions of Section 68A(1) of The Companies Act, 1956 regarding fictitious applications;
   (e) Declaration regarding minimum subscription and refund of application money in terms of Schedule II of The Companies Act, 1956 and SEBI guidelines;
   (f) Dates of opening, closing and earliest closing of the issue;
   (g) Names and addresses of lead managers, co-managers, trustees (if applicable), legal advisers to the company, auditors, bankers to the issue, brokers to the issue and the secretary.

(h) Whether or not credit rating from any other recognised agency has been obtained for the proposed debenture issue should be mentioned. If rating is obtained, it should be indicated, preferably with implications of the rating symbol. In terms of SEBI guidelines, rating of a credit agency is mandatory for debentures with maturity period of more than 18 months.

(i) Underwriting arrangements made for the issue, names of underwriters, amount underwritten and declaration by Board of directors and the lead managers that in their opinion the resources of the underwriters are sufficient to discharge their underwriting obligations.

2. **Capital structure of the company and issue details**

(a) Authorised, issued, subscribed and paid-up capital of the company.

(b) Size of the issue with break up of reservation for preferential allotment to promoters, shareholders of group/associate companies, financial institutions, mutual funds. NRI, permanent employees, etc. The lock-in-period in respect of shares/debentures to be allotted to promoters and shareholders of group and associate companies/employees/financial institutions should be mentioned. The maximum number of shares/debentures that can be allotted to each employee and the number of permanent employees in the company should be mentioned.

(c) Paid-up capital after the present issue and after conversion of debentures, if applicable.

3. **Details of the issue**

(a) Authority for the issue and details of resolutions passed for the issue.

(b) Terms of Payment:

The amount payable on application, allotment and on calls should be stated. Further, in case of premium issues, the appropriation of application, allotment and call money towards capital and premium should be indicated. For debenture issues with each debenture having several parts, the appropriation of application, allotment and call money towards each part of the debenture should be stated with further split between capital and premium.

(c) Rights of the instrument holders.

(d) Objects of the issue.

(e) Tax benefits available to the company and its shareholders.

(f) Justification for the premium on the issue, if any, disclosure of net asset value on the basis of the last audited results, and the premium eligibility on the basis of CCI guidelines.

4. **Details about the company management**

(a) History, main objects and present business of the company.

(b) Subsidiaries of the company.

(c) Promoters and their background.

(d) Names, addresses and occupation of manager, managing director and other directors including nominee directors, whole-time directors and their directorships in other companies.

5. **Details about the project**

(a) Cost of the project and means of financing

(b) Location of the project

(c) Plant and machinery for the project, technology adopted and process of manufacture

(d) Collaboration, performance guarantee or assistance in marketing by the

collaborators
- (e) Infrastructure facilities for raw materials
- (f) Utilities like water, power etc.
- (g) Schedule of implementation of the project, with separate details of land acquisition, civil work, installation of plant and machinery and the progress till the date of the prospectus
- (h) Expected date of trial production and commercial production
- (i) Nature of the products, consumer/industrial and end users and approach to marketing and proposed marketing set up
- (j) Export prospectus and export obligation
- (k) Expected capacity utilisation during the first 3 years from the date of commencement of production for each of the major product groups
- (l) Expected year when the company would be able to earn cash profits and net profits and the expected cash profits and net profits for the next 3 years.
- (m) High/Low equity prices of the shares/debentures of the company for each of the last 3 years and monthly high/low prices for the last 6 months (applicable to existing listed companies).

6. **Other information**
   - (a) In respect of any issue made by the company and other listed companies under the same management, the following details;
     - (i) Name of the company;
     - (ii) Year of issue;
     - (iii) Type of issue;
     - (iv) Amount of issue;
     - (v) Date of completion of delivery of share/debenture certificates/letters of allotment;
     - (vi) Date of completion of the project, where the object of the issue was for financing a project;
     - (vii) Rate of dividend paid.
   - (b) Declaration about the issue of allotment letter, refunds within a period of 10 weeks and liability to pay interest in case of delay in refund under Section 73 of Companies Act, 1956.
   - (c) Outstanding litigation pertaining to:
     - (i) matters likely to affect operation and finances of the company, including disputed tax liabilities;
     - (iii) criminal prosecution launched against the company and directors for alleged offences under the following statutes:

       The Indian Stamp Act, 1899

       The Central Excises Act, 1944

       The Imports and Export (Control) Act, 1951

       The Industries (Development and Regulation) Act, 1951

       The Prevention of Food Adulteration Act, 1954

       The Essential Commodities Act, 1955

       The Companies Act, 1956

       The Wealth-tax Act, 1957

       The Income-tax Act, 1961

       The Customs Act, 1962

       The Monopolies and Restrictive Trade Practices Act, 1969

       The Foreign Exchange Management Act, 1999.
   - (d) Particulars of default in meeting statutory dues, institutional dues, dues to holders of instruments like debentures, fixed deposits and arrears of

cumulative preference shares, pertaining to the company and/or other companies promoted by the same promoters, which are listed on stock exchanges.

(e) Any material development after the date of the last balance sheet and its impact on the performance and prospects of the company.

(f) Management's perception of risk factors relating to the project like exchange rate fluctuations, difficulty in availability of raw materials, or on marketing of products, cost and time over-run etc.

(g) Consent of directors, auditors, solicitors, managers to issue, registrar to issue, bankers, brokers to the issue to the company, bankers to the issue and experts.

(h) Changes in directors and auditors in the last three years, if any, and reason therefor.

(i) Procedure for making applications and availability of forms, prospectus and mode of payment.

(j) Procedure and time schedule for allotment and issue of certificates.

7. **Financial information**

A report from the auditors on:

(a) profits and losses of the company (where there is no subsidiary company) and the combined profits and losses of the subsidiaries or individual profits and losses of each subsidiary for each of the five financial years preceding the issue of prospectus (where there are subsidiaries);

(b) assets and liabilities of the company (where there is no subsidiary company) at the last date to which the accounts are made up and the combined assets and liabilities of the subsidiaries or individually with the assets and liabilities of each subsidiary (where there are subsidiaries);

(c) rates of the dividends paid by the company in respect of each class of shares for each of the five financial years preceding the issue of prospectus.

If no accounts have been made up in respect of any part of the period of five years ending three months before the date of issue of prospectus, the report should contain a statement of the fact. Further, a statement of accounts of the company should be made in respect of a part of the said period upto a date not earlier than six months of the date of issue of prospectus and the assets and liabilities position as at the end of that period. There should be a certificate from the auditors that such accounts have been examined and found correct by them.

The report should distinguish items of a non-recurring nature and indicate the nature of provisions or adjustments made or are yet to be made.

8. **Statutory and other information**

(a) Minimum subscription, as laid down in the SEBI guidelines.

(b) Expenses of the issue giving separately fees payable to advisers, registrars to the issue, managers to the issue and trustees for debenture holdes.

(c) Underwriting commission and brokerage.

(d) Previous issue for cash or consideration otherwise than for cash.

(e) Details of public or right issue during the last five years:

(i) Date of allotment and refund;

(ii) Date of listing on the stock exchange;

(iii) Amount of premium or discount, if applicable.

(f) Details of premium received in respect of any issue of shares made in the two years preceding the date of issue of prospectus or to be made stating the proposed date of the issue, the reasons for differentiation of premium for different categories, if applicable and the disposal of premia received or to be received.

(g) Commission or brokerage paid on previous issue.

(h) Debentures and redeemable preference shares and other instruments outstanding on the date of prospectus and the terms of their issue.

(i) Option to subscribe.

(j) Particulars of property purchased or proposed to be purchased from vendors to be paid for wholly or partly out of the proceeds of the issue and the interest of the promoters or directors in any transaction relating to the property within the last two years.

(k) Details of directors, proposed directors, whole-time directors, their remuneration, appointment and remuneration of the managing director(s).

(l) Interests of directors, their borrowing powers and qualification shares.

(m) Any amount or benefit paid or given within the two preceding years or intended to be paid or given to any promoter or officers and consideration for the payment or giving of the benefit.

(n) The dates of, parties to, and general nature of

  (i) every contract of appointment or remuneration of a managing director or manager;

  (ii) every other material contract, not being a contract entered into in the ordinary course of business of the company or entered into more than two years prior to the date of prospectus:

  Reasonable time and place for inspection of the contract should be provided for.

(o) Full particulars of the nature and extent of interest of every director or promoter:

  (i) in the promotion of the company; or

  (ii) in any property acquired by the company within two years of the date of the prospectus or proposed to be acquired by it.

(p) Rights of members regarding voting, dividend, lien on shares, modification of rights and forfeiture of shares/debentures.

(q) Restriction on transfer and transmission of shares/debentures and on consolidation/splitting.

(r) Revaluation of assets, if any, during the last 5 years.

STATEMENT IN LIEU OF PROSPECTUS

When required — When the public company having share capital decides to raise the capital privately (say from relatives and friends) without inviting offers from the public, it is required to issue a statement in lieu of prospectus.

Contents — The statement in lieu of prospectus shall contain the particulars and reports as set out in Schedule III to the Companies Act.

Signature — The statement to be delivered to the Registrar for registration must be signed by every person who is named in the statement as director or proposed director or his agent authorised in writing.

Delivery — The statement must be delivered to the Registrar for registration at least 3 days before the allotment of the shares or debentures.

Penalty for Default — The Company and every director of the company, who willfully authorises or permits contravention, shall be punishable with fine which may extend to Rs 10,000.

Liability for Mis-statement — The liability for any mis-statement in a Statement in lieu of Prospectus is the same as in case of a prospectus.

Is a Private Company required to issue Prospectus or Statement in lieu of Prospectus?

A private company is *neither* required to issue a prospectus nor a statement in lieu of prospectus since it can not invite public to subscribe for its shares or debentures as per restrictions of Sec 3 (1) (iii).

_____ EXERCISES _____

VERY SHORT ANSWERS QUESTIONS

1. What is meant by the term 'Promotion'?
2. Who is a promoter?
3. What are preliminary contracts?
4. What is 'Certificate of Incorporation'?
5. What is Statutory Declaration?
6. What is Memorandum of Association?
7. What is Articles of Association?
8. What is Prospectus?
9. Is a private company required to issue a prospectus or statement in lieu of prospectus?

SHORT ANSWER TYPE QUESTIONS

1. List the functions of promoters.
2. List the main documents to be filed for incorporating a company.
3. State the importance of Memorandum of Association.
4. List the clauses of Memorandum of Association.
5. State the importance of Articles of Association.
6. List the Five matters concerning the shares which are usually included in the Articles of Association.
7. List the five differences between the Memorandum and Articles of Association.
8. State the importance of prospectus.
9. List the five matters included in prospectus.
10. Write a short note on Statement in lieu of Prospectus.

LONG ANSWER TYPE QUESTIONS

1. What is meant by 'Promotion'? What are the functions of promoters?
2. Describe the steps involved in the formation of a company.
3. What is Memorandum of Association? State its purpose and contents.
4. What is Articles of Association? State its purpose and contents.
5. Distinguish between Memorandum and Articles of Association.
6. Define Prospectus. Discuss its significance. Give ten matters which are to be included in the prospectus.

Small Scale Business in India

8

MEANING OF SMALL SCALE UNITS

Small-scale and cottage industries are important parts of the structure and texture of Indian manufacturing sector. Small-scale industrial units are those which operate with a modest investment in fixed capital, relatively small-scale work force and which produce a relatively small volume of output of goods/services. They differ from large-scale industries with respect to size of capital, employment, production and management, flow of input and output and so on. They differ from cottage industries with respect to the degree of mechanisation of production, ratio of hired labour to family labour, geographic size of market, capital employed and so on.

The present Industrial policy of the Government of India has defined a small-scale industrial unit as a unit having investment upto Rs 1 crore in plant and machinery. In the case of an ancillary industrial unit, the limit is also Rs 1 crore.

CHARACTERISTICS OF SMALL SCALE UNITS

The main characteristics of small-scale units are as follows:

1. They are labour-intensive.
2. They are more broad-based and dispersed than large industrial units.
3. They have modest investment in fixed capital.
4. They have relatively small scale work force.
5. They produce relatively small volume of output of goods/services.
6. They are ancillary to large scale industries.

DISTINCTION BETWEEN SMALL SCALE AND COTTAGE INDUSTRIES

Small Scale industries differ from Cottage Industries in the following respects:

Basis of Distinction	Small Scale Industries	Basis of Distinction
1. Location	Small Scale industries are generally located in urban areas.	Cottage industries are generally located in rural areas.
2. Degree of Mechanisation	There is use of relatively high degree of mechanisation.	There is no or relatively less degree of machanisation.
3. Ratio of Hired Labour to Family Labour	The ratio of hired labour to family labour ratio in high.	The ratio of hired labour to family labour is low.
4. Geographic Size of Market	These units cover relatively large size of market.	These units cover relatively small size of market.

OBJECTIVES OF SMALL SCALE UNITS

The basic objectives behind development of small scale units, as outlined in the industrial policy announcement of 1980, and in the successive five-year plans, are as follows:

1. to create immediate employment opportunities with relatively low investment;
2. to make small industries export-oriented and help quality upgradation;
3. to remove regional disparities through a deliberate policy; and
4. encourage growth in villages and small towns.

Other Objectives

5. to reduce disparities in income, wealth and consumption;
6. to mobilise resources of capital and skills and their optimum utilisation;
7. to eliminate economic backwardness of rural and under-developed regions in the country;

8.   to provide steady source of income to the low-income groups living in rural and urban areas of the country;

9.   to provide substitutes for various industrial products now being imported into the country.

10.   to effect an integration of the activities of small business with the rural economy on the one hand and with the large-scale business on the other.

11.   to improve the quality of industrial products manufactured in the cottage industry sector and to enhance both production and exports, and

12.   to remove the problems created by urbanisation and consequent growth of big towns and cities.

13.   to attain self-reliance.

SIGNIFICANCE/RATIONALE OF SMALL-SCALE AND COTTAGE INDUSTRIES

Small scale and cottage industries occupy an important place in the Indian economy. The Government Industries Policy Resolution of 1956 outlines the rationale for small scale industries thus:

"They provide immediate large scale employment; they offer methods of ensuring a more equitable distribution of the income. They facilitate an effective mobilisation of resources, capital and skills which might otherwise remain unutilised. Some of the problems that unplanned urbanisation tend to create will be avoided by the establishment of small centres of industrial production all over the country".

Thus, the rationale for development and support for small industries may be outlined as follows:

1.   **Large Employment Opportunities** — They are labour-intensive and hence their employment creation potential per unit of investment is higher than that of larger industries. In countries like India which carry huge mass of unemployed, small industries are a boon.

2.   **Since there are more broad based and and dispersed than large industrial units, they facilitate —**

   (a)   decentralised regional development;

   (b)   reduction of extreme disparities in income and wealth;

   (c)   improvement of living standards of people; and

   (d)   removal of poverty.

3.   **Prevents concentration of Economic Power** — They facilitate the creation of a wider entrepreneurial base consisting of small industrial owners and operators. They represent a diffusion of economic power among a large number of small entrepreneurs rather than concentration of economic power among a small number of large entrepreneurs.

4.   **Mobilize Local Resources** — They permit an effective mopping up and mobilisation of small savings, scarce capital and local materials, human resources and skills.

5. **Development of some towns** — They help in development of small and medium-seized towns and cities which have more spread-effects on regional industrial development.

6. **Low Capital - Output Ratio** — Their capital resources are modest. They are more suitable for capital-scarce countries like India. The capital-output ratio for small industries is said to be lower than for large industries.

7. **Contribution to Industrial Growth** — They contribute substantialy to industrial production and industrial growth.

8. **Facilitate Development of Large Scale Industries** — They support the development of large industries by meeting their requirements of inputs of raw materials, intermediate goods, spare parts etc., and by utilising their output for further production. The productivity and capacity utilisation of large units depends to some extent upon the fulfillment of their specialised requirements by small scale units.

Small scale units play an important role in t he overall growth of the economy of the country. While the cost of investment in small scale units would be comparatively low, their potential for generation of employment as a sector is relatively high. Development of small scale units also results in dispersal of industries to backward, rural, and semi-urban areas, and this eventually leads to reduction of regional imbalances in growth. The small scale units also help the large industries off-load certain manufacturing activities on them, and they, thus, act as auxiliary or ancillary units to their larger counterparts. This helps the large industries reduce price and use capital in more advanced areas.

GOVERNMENT POLICY FOR DEVELOPMENT OF SMALL-SCALE INDUSTRY SECTOR

The basic policy for the small-scale sector was first enunciated in the Industrial Policy Resolution of 1956, which underwent changes in accordance with the course of industrial development in the country. The industrial policy announcement of 1980 recognised the need for growth of the small-scale sector, alongwith the growth of the medium and large sectors, for a rapid and balanced industrialisation of the country.

The Government has accorded fiscal concessions-like deductions and exemptions from duties and taxes on profit-to the small -scale units with a view to fostering generation of internal resources to make these units economically viable and self-reliant, to help competitive pricing of their products vis-a-vis those of large-scale manufacturers, and to enable them undertake modernisation and technological upgradation.

The Government's macro economic programme for promoting small scale industries has strongly focused on the following areas:

- Announcement of a Seven Point Action Plan for better credit flow to the SSI sector.

- Infrastructural suppport in rural and backward areas.

- Technology support for modernisation and improving quality.
- Upgrading entrepreneurship development programmes.
- Boosting special employment generation programmes.

Over the four decades since independence, the Government of India have taken a number of policy and other measures to boost and strengthen small-scale and village industries in India. They are summarized as follows:

1. In all the Industrial Policy Resolutions and Statements right from 1948, the Government of India underlined in very clear terms the significance of small-scale and cottage industries for overall economic development, reduction of poverty, more equitable distribution of wealth and income, balanced regional development and son on.

2. A number of institutions have been established by the Government to promote and co-ordinate the development of small and village industries, to meet their diverse needs and solve their problems, Under the Ministry of Industry, an organisation named 'Small Industries Development Corporation' (SIDC) was set up, which formulates, monitors and co-ordinates the development programmes in the field. It has a network of Small Industries Service Institutes, their branches and extension centres throughout the country through which it provides economic, technical and management consultancy services as also staff training and product testing facilities to small industrial units. Another Central Agency, National Small Industries Corporation, set up in 1955, provides machinery and equipment to small industrial units on hire-purchase basis. It also helps small units to procure raw materials inputs and to market their products. For development of traditional village and cottage industries, such All India organisations like Handloom Board, Khadi and Village Industries Commission, Central Handloom and Handicrafts Corporation, All-India Handicrafts Board, Central Silk Board and Coir Board have been established. The State have also established their own Directorates and Development Corporations for promotion of small and village indstries.

3. **Exemption from Industrial Licences** — Small industries units are exempted from obtaining industrial licences for manufacturing a wide range of items.

4. **Reservation of Items for Production** — A number of items have been exculsively reserved for production in the small-scale sector. For example, as many as 836 items had been reserved as at the end of December, 1996. Of these 23 have ben dereserved in 1997-98 and 1998-99. Infact, the Ninth Plan envisages dereservation of the items reserved for the small units. This is necessary in order to help small units in upgrading their technology, improving the quality of their products and boost their exports.

5. **Reservation of Items for Procurements** — About 410 items manufactured by small units have been exclusively reserved for procurement by the Government.

6. **Establishment of Industrial Estates** — A very large number of industrial Estates have been established all over India, with built factory sheds and premises (made available on rental basis) and other infrastructural facilities for setting up small industrial units.

7. **Setting-up of District Industries Centres** — District Industries Centres (DIC) were set up in about 400 districts for facilitating single-window clearance of a package of assistance and facilities such as credit, guidance, raw materials, training, marketing etc., to small and village industrial units.

8. **Long-term Financial Assistance** — Long-term short-term financial assistance for small and village industrial units is being provided by specialised institutional at State level, and by public sector banks and other scheduled banks at concessional rates of interest.

9. **Fiscal Concessions** — A wide range of fiscal and other concessions like exemption from excise duty, concessional excise duty, capital subsidy to units in backward areas, tax holiday for a specified number of years for new undertakings, investment allowance, allocation of scarce and essential indigenous imported materials, and so on, are available to small and village industrial units, to make them relatively viable and competitive.

10. **Introduction of Schemes** — With a view of further strengthening the provision of financial assistance to small scale sector, especially to the smaller amongst the small scale units, several schemes have been introduced in the recent past; the Small Industries Development Fund in 1986, National Equity Fund in 1987 and the Single Window Scheme in 1988. For meetings the long-standing demand of small scale industries a separate Apex Bank for providing assistance to them has been established. "The Small Industries Development Bank of India (SIDBI), has been established". SIDBI has two funds viz. Small Industries Development Fund and Small Industries Development Assistance Fund. 1998-99 Budget announced delinking of SIDBI from IDBI and making SIDBI more effective in providing credit to small units.

11. **Measures to ensure timely credit** — During 1993, on recommendation of the Nayak Committee, the RBI announced a special package of measure to ensure adequate timely credit to SSI Sector. The salient features of this package are:

    (a) Banks should give preference to village industries, tiny industries and other small scale units in that order, while meeting the credit requirements of the small scale sector;

    (b) The banks should set up the credit flow to meet the legitimate requirements of the SSI sector in full during the Eighth Plan;

    (c) An effective grievance redressal machinery within each bank which can be approached by the SSI in case of difficulties would be set up; and

    (d) Banks should adopt the single window clearance scheme of SIDBI for meeting the credit requirements of small scale units.

12. **Concessions** — Since 1994-95 in order to further strengthen the position of small-scale sector, many concessions have been provided. Important among these are:

    (a) A sceme of integrated infrastructural development was launched in 1994 to strengthen infrastructural facilities in rural and backward areas.

    (b) Quality certification scheme has been launched to improve SSI product quality.

(c) Seven point action has been initiated to improve credit flow to SSI sector.

(d) Scope of National Equity Plan has been enlarged to cover the whole country except metropolitan areas to support expansion, modernisation and technology upgradation.

(e) Technology development and modernisation fund scheme has been launched for modernisation and adoption of improved and updated technology.

13. **Credit Insurance Scheme** — In 1999-2000, a new Credit Insurance Scheme has been announced to improve flow of investment credit to SSI units.

14. **Increase in Working Capital Limit** — The working capital limit for SSI units stands enhanced as a result of increase in turnover limit from Rs 4 crores to Rs 5 crores.

15. **Rural Industrialisation** — A National Programme for Rural Industrialisation has been announced with a mission to set up 100 rural cluster every year.

16. **Information to SSI Association** — To co-ordinate the latest development with regard to World Trade Organisation, a cell has been set up to disseminate information to SSI Associations.

17. **Comprehensive Policy Package** — In August 2000, the Government announced a Comprehensive Policy Package to further encouarge the small scale sector. Under the policy, it raised the exemption limit for excise duty for small units, encouraged the small units to develop testing laboratories, raised the limits for composite loans, increased the coverage of integrated infrastructure Development Scheme and announced new schemes for addressing the problem of collaterals faced by the SSI units and to encourage technology upgradation.

In Addition to the above, various procedural simplifications, including new registration forms have been introduced. To ensure prompt payment to small scale units a new legislation has been enacted. A scheme has been formulated to train unemployed on non-technical graduates so as to augment the availability ot managers at affordable rates for the SSI sector and reduce educated unemployment.

PERFORMANCE AND CONTRIBUTION OF SMALL-SCALE AND COTTAGE INDUSTRIES

Since Independence, there has been an all-around development of small-scale and cottage industries in India. Their performance and contribution to the growth of the industrial economy of India has been quite remarkable. Which will be clear from the following points:

1. **Growth Rate in terms of Production** — The growth rate of small scale sector @ 9% per annum in term of production has been far faster than that of large scale since 1973. The production in small scale and cottage industries increased from Rs 13,600 crores in 1973-74 to more than Rs 5,78,000 crores in 1999-2000. It is estimated that they contribute about 40% of the gross value of output in the manufacturing sector.

2. **Growth in Numbers of Small Scale Sector** — The number of registered and unregistered small scale units which stood at 16,000 units in 1950 increased to 5.30 lakhs in 1981-82 and to 32.25 lakhs in 1999-2000.

3. **Growth in Employment in Small Scale Sector** — The small scale sector employed 178.5 lakhs persons in 1998-99 compared to 67 lakhs and 90 lakhs persons in 1979-80 and 1984-85 respectively. This represents about 60% of the total industrial employment. Employment in small scale and cottage industries is next only to that of agricultural sector.

4. **Growth in Exports from Small Scale Sector** — Exports from this sector increased from Rs 852 crores in 1973-74 to Rs 4,535 crores in 1998-89 and further to around more than Rs 54,000 crores in 1999-2000. It is estimated that this sector contributes over 45 percent of the manufacturing exports and 33 percent of the total exports.

5. **Growth in wide range of Product** — Small scale industrial units produce a very wide range of producer goods and consumer goods items needed by the economy. They include both simple and sophisiticated engineering products, electrical, electronics, chemicals plastics, steel, cement, textiles, paper, matches, ready made garments and so on.

6. Ancillary units contribute greatly and cater to the requirements of medium and large industrial units for materials, components, consumables and so on.

7. The traditional village and cottage industries which are generally clubbed with modern small-scale industries provide vital means of living to artisans, sustain the vitality and viability of countless number of villages and towns, enrich the quality of life in society by providing fine handicrafts and pieces of art and project the heritage of India.

8. A large number small-scale industries are engaged in the manufacture of consumer goods of mass consumption, thereby making them available in plenty which serves as a non-inflationary force.

9. The encouragement of small-scale and cottage industries with their higher output capital ratio and employment capital ratio has become a stabilising force in the Indian economy. With its factor endowments as they are, namely rich in manpower and poor in capital. The employment generating capacity per unit of capital of small and cottage industries was found to be atleast eight times greater than that of large industies while the output generating capacity per unit of capital was three times larger than that of large industries.

PROBLEMS OF SMALL SCALE SECTOR

V. Desai has summarised the problems as shown below:

External Problems	Internal Problems
Location	Choice of an idea
Power	Feeble structure

Water	Faulty Planning
Post Offices	Poor Project Implementation
Communication	Poor management
Capital	Poor Production
Working Capital	Quality
Long-term funds	Marketing
Recovery	Inadequate finance
Taxation	Labour problems
Raw materials	Capacity problems
Industrial & Financial Regulations	Lack of vertical and horizontal integration
Inspections	Inadequate training in skills
Technology	Poor and loose organisation
Government Policy and social attitude	Lack of strategies
Competitive and changing environement.	

1.   Small scale units are concentrated in more Industrised States and around urban conglomerates along with large scale units than in backward States and in medium and small scale towns. This is natural since several small scale units depend on large scale units and on large cities as sources of their markets. Their locations in developed States like Maharastra, Gujarat, Tamilnadu, Punjab etc. and large cities is beneficial from their point of view though not so for a balanced and decentralised development of industries in all States, small cities and towns. In a way, small-scale units have led to increased congestion of large metropolitan areas. While modern small-scale units concentrated in well-developed States and urban conglomerates have, by and large, prospered, traditional small, village and cottage industries which generally are found in small towns and villages have not flourished much. They do not get as much attention, public support and resources as modern small scale industries even though they have a more important role in ameliorating poverty, unemployment, misery and desolation in rural and small town areas and in arresting migration of people to large cities.

2.   A large number of small-scale units are said to be bogus and fictitious units. They exist only in name and in the register of government agencies, and not in reality. Unscrupulous individuals find it very easy to float small units (in view of few restrictions and requirements) and take advantage of concessional and liberalised allocation of import licences, scarce raw materials and finance only to divert them in the market to the highest bidder. This abuse is said to be very wide-spread in the small industry sector. Genuine small industrial units suffer thereby, because bogus units grab the cream.

3.   It is contended that employees and workers of small and cottage industries are less organised and united than those of large-scale industries and hence are more exploited by the ownership groups. Average salary and wage levels in small and cottage industries are only 50% of the levels which prevails in large industries. Employees and workers of small-scale units work longer hours and

in more shabby working conditions than their counterparts in large scale industries. Such employment conditions are fertile breeding grounds for strained industrial relations.

4. Opinion is sharply divided on the question of efficiency of small scale industrial units vis-a-vis large-scale units. Some studies as for example, by Dhar and Lydall, have found that small industries are less efficient in terms of capital and labour productivity than large scale industries, while other studies reached an opposite conclusion.

5. Doubts have been expressed about the entrepreneurial spirit of the owners of small enterprises. Small industry entrepreneurs are said to show more anxiety in availing of the liberal credit and other facilities offered by Government than in developing self-reliance and building up their own resources. Development of small industries would have been much less without government support, protection and patronage.

6. Evidence in favour of the above argument gets strengthened when the extent of industrial sickness and mortality in small industries are considered. Industrial sickness in small industries is far more chronic than in large industries. As many as 3.06 lakhs small scale units were reported to be sick as at the end of March, 99 in which the bank credit locked up was about Rs 4313 crores. There are reasons to believe that several thousands of unregistered small unit are sick or likely to be so. The resistance power of small units against sickness is low. The average life span of a large number of small industrial units is hardly two years.

7. As in large scale industries, small-scale industrial units suffer from serious under-utilisation of capacity, which has reached 50% in several units. Proliferation of units in the same industry, because of easy entry conditions, create more capacity than warranted by demand, small units sometimes indulge in unhealthy competition with each other under conditions of buyers' markets.

8. A few immature behavioural trends characterise small scale industrial units. Just to avoid the problems of compliance with a plethora of factory and labour laws, some small-scale units are said to resort to replacement of labour by capital and becomes more capital intensive, thereby undermining one of their major strong points, namely, labour intensity. Some other small scale units with a view to continue to enjoy the government support, protection, facilities and concessions, refuse to grow up once they reach the plant and machinery ceiling fixed by government in defining small scale units. They prefer to peg their operations and remain stagnant.

9. It is also stated that a few big business houses have indirectly spread their operations into small scale industrial units because of attractive concessions and facilities offered by government. If this is true, the distinction between small scale and large-scale industrial units, so far as owner-ship structure is concerned, tends to become confused.

10. Inspite of several protective and promotional measures adopted by the Central and State Governments, small scale and village industrial units still face problems in getting scarce raw materials, adequate credit, technical assistance,

marketing avenues and on.

11. In the case of a large number of small scale industries, the quality of products manufactured by them is not upto the desired standard. Several reasons account for this. Small industrial units lack the technical sophistication to make high quality products. For many products, there are no set standards of quality. There is not quality consciousness among some of the users of small industry products. There is no quality control system among many small industrial units.

12. Half of the country's machine tool manufacturers belong to the small scale industries (SSI) sector. They are involved in the production of spares, accessories and components.

Notwithstanding the impressive presence, the sector is plagued with policy and operational problems impeding its growth. Technical upgradation in the sector faces a problem of investment limitation since the permissible limit is Rs 1 crore.

The Indian Machine Tools Manufacturers Association (IMTMA) has urged the government to implement the Abid Hussain Committee recommendation to increase the investment limit to Rs 3 crores.

"Though the sector as a whole has demanded the investment capital of Rs 5 crores".

IMTMA functionaries point out that the strength of the small scale sector functions in an ancillary capacity.

"The fund limitation on Rs 1 crore in plant and machinery is extremely unreasonable, given the kind of work profile it has", president, IMTMA, added. According to association functionaries, as outsourcing by bigger companies like HMT and Godrej and Boyce are on an increase, prime importance should be given to the enhancement of the sector. Coupled with fund limitation, the sector also faces problems with technical upgradation due to unwillingness of banks and financial institutions to extend finances. According to industry observers, the clause of providing collaterals is prohibitive and, consequently, the sector is deprived of investments in fixed assets and operational machines.

The small scale sector significantly contributes to the prowess of the machine tool industry as it functions in an ancillary capacity.

Industry representatives say extending guarantees for repayment is difficult because of the long gestation of projects.

The high industry cost due to the policy implementation and the high input cost finder the growth of the sector. Goods procured by he small scale sector is not modvatable since they are non-exciseable.

IMTMA has submitted a representation to the finance ministry to make the inputs modavatable. The association also feels that the situation demands urgent attention since the industry is in a disadvantageous position in comparison to the big corporate players.

Moreover, the sector faces problems in sourcing customers and marketing its products due to resource crunch.

IMTMA says the relaxation of the investment levels coupled with modification of excise regulations will enable the sector to upgrade technically and fulfill important out-sourcing functions.

13. One of the main constraints is inadequacy of workig capital caused by delays in receiving payments for their supplies. It is well known that a large number of SSI units are managed by their promotors and/or persons with technical background who themselves find it difficult to provide attention continuously to the management of finances like receivables, including collection, accounting and follow-up. It is in this context SSI units can look upon the factoring.

14. With institutional credit not forthcoming, the small scale sector is now flooding the fleding Over-the-Counter Exchange of India (OTCEI) with request to go public for raising working capital.

All these units are in the small and medium sector and promoted by listed companies and well known groups.

However, while welcoming the present trend, experts say there exists greater scope for SSIs to hold public issues through the exchange. In fact, it is widely felt that if the government allows the large scale sector to hold up to 49 per cent stake in SSI units, it would further encourage investors to put their money in this sector.

These companies, on an average have a paid up capital base between Rs 35 lakhs to Rs 25 crores, while equity offered to the public is between Rs 80 lakhs to Rs 9 crores.

The equity itselt if being raised for a variety of projects in areas right from consumer goods, paper, machinery, ball bearings to fastners. While some companies are approaching the OTECI to raise money for expansion and diversification, most are raising working capital for new projects.

Interestingly, none of the SSI companies which have approached the OTCEI in Delhi has yet used the route offered by the Small Industries Development Bank of India (SIDBI) to get listed.

SIDBI, which became a member of the OTCEI in 1992, gives lines of credit to selected finance companies/merchant Bankers to enable them to provide equity finance to SSI units. Instead, the large scale promoters, with stake up to 24 per cent in the SSI unit, are finding it easy to convince merchant bankers of finance companies to sponsor each issue.

However, officials at the OTCEI would welcome more companies using the credit lines offered by SIDBI to raise equity finance.

There are some reasons why SSI units find it easy to approach the OTCEI first, the exchange offers a short-cut to SSI units, which are not widely known to investors, through its sponsorship operations and dealers networks.

Secondaly, a public issue through the OCTEI does not involve the heavy costs as in other exchanges. Besides, the Rs 8-10 lakhs mandatory expense of having a public issue in other exchanges, huge sums have to be spent on its publicity and brokerage. This would normally deter any SSI unit proposing to have an issue of about Rs 1.5 crores.

In the OTCEI, on the other hand, since it is the merchant banker sponsor who has to offer the equity to the public, the SSI unit saved publicity and brokerage costs.

The OTCEI is now approaching industry associations and individual promoters to spread greater awareness about the ways in which they can raise money, without waiting for fund starved financial institutions to step in.

EXERCISES

1. What is small scale business? State its main features.
2. State the objectives of small scale sector.
3. Discuss the role of small scale business in the economy of developing country.
4. State the problems of small scale business.

9 Insurance

NATURE AND CAUSES OF BUSINESS RISKS

Meaning — Business risks refer to the possibility of inadequate profits or even losses due to uncertainties or unexpected events which are beyond control. For instance, the demand for black & white TV has come down due to introduction of colour TV, the demand for Video Casette has come down due to cable facility, demand for 486 computer has come down due to Pentium Computers, heavy losses incurred in Gujarat due to earthquake on 26th Jan. 2001.

Causes — The important causes of business risks are the following:

(a) *Uncertainties* relating to —
(i) Demand for goods (e.g. decline due to change in fashion)
(ii) Prices
(iii) Competition (e.g. due to entry of more competitors)
(iv) Foreign exchange rates affecting the value of Imports & Exports (e.g.

placed order for import when $1 = Rs 35 but received delivery when $1 = Rs 50)

(v) Change in technology (e.g. Introduction of Pentium Computers)

(vi) Government Control (e.g. placed order for import when duty was 10% but received delivery when duty was 40%) or closure of industries from residential areas, closure of polluting industries)

(vii) Realisation of dues from customers (e.g. a customer who was declared insolvent, paid only 25%).

(b) **Unforeseen** *losses due to* —

 (i) fire

 (ii) theft

 (iii) flood

 (iv) earthquake etc.

(c) **Unexpected** *Events like* —

 (i) Damage of goods in transit

 (ii) Death or departure of a key employee

 (iii) Stoppage of work due to power failure

 (iv) Stoppage of work due to strike

(d) **Other Factors** *such as* —

 (i) Change in rates of interest on borrowed funds

 (ii) Change in rates of taxes (e.g. imposition of dividend tax, extra surcharge on Income Tax for Gujarat Earthquake, increase in Sales Tax Rate)

Insurance of Risks — Business risks may be insurable or non-insurable.

Insurable Risks — Insurable risks refer to those risks which can be covered by Insurance on payment of a nominal amount of premium for insurance. For example, Risks of loss due to fire, flood, theft, earthquake can be insured and the loss if any arising out of the risks can be recovered.

Risks covered by Insurance — 'Risk' is an unexpected happening of some future event. The various types of risks which can be insured may be grouped as follows:

Type of Insurance	Type of Risk
(a) Life Insurance	Risk of death or old age
(b) Fire Insurance	Risk of loss or damage to property due to fire
(c) Marine Insurance	Risk of loss or damage to ship or cargo or freight
(d) General Insurance	Risk of loss or damage due to theft, burglary in a premises, risk of loss or damage due to accidents.

Non-Insurable Risks — Non-insurable risks refer to those risks which can not be covered by insurance. For example, risk of loss due to decline in demand can not be insured. Similarly, risk of loss due to decline in price, can not be insured.

TERMS USED IN INSURANCE

In general, Insurance is an arrangement of pooling of risks under which a large number of people contribute to a fund out of which compensation is paid to the person suffering a particular type of loss.

Meaning of Insurance Contract — The *'Insurance contract'* refers to a contract in which the insurance company undertakes to indemnify the insured on the happening of certain event in consideration of a specified amount.

Meaning of Insurance Policy — The document which contains all the terms and conditions of insurance and risks covered under insurance is known as *'Insurance Policy'*.

Meaning of Insured — The person whose risk is insured is called *'Insured'*.

Meaning of Insurer — The person who insures is known as *'Insurer'*.

Meaning of Insurance Premium — The consideration in return for which the insurer agrees to make good the loss is known as *'Insurance Premium'*. This premium may be paid monthly, quarterly, half-yearly or annually.

Meaning of Sum Insured/Sum Assured — The amount for which the insurance policy is taken is called 'Sum Insured'. (in case of general insurance) or 'Sum Assured' (in case of life insurance).

Meaning of 'Term of Policy' — The period for which an insurance policy is taken is known as the *'Term of the policy'*.

Example — Mr X owns a car worth Rs. 3,00,000. He gets it insured with National Insurance Company Ltd. by paying Rs. 10,000. In this case —

Mr. X is known as **'Insured'**.

National Insurance Company Ltd. is known as **'Insurer'**

Rs. 3,00,000 is called **'Sum Insured'**

Rs. 10,000 is called **'Insurance Premium'**

The **document** containing the terms & conditions in writing is called **'Insurance Policy'**.

OBJECTIVES OF INSURANCE

The basic objective of insurance is to provide protection against risks of loss.

The different objectives of various types of insurance are as follows:

Type of Insurance	Objective of Insurance
1. Life Insurance	(a) To provide the pre-determined sum of money to the nominees of the insured in case of death of insured. (b) To encourage people to save and invest.
2. Fire Insurance	To indemnify the insured for any loss or damage caused by accidental fire.
3. Marine Insurance	To indemnify the insured for the actual loss to ship, cargo or freight due to perils of the sea.
4. Mediclaim Insurance or Health Insurance	To reimburse the expenditure on the medical treatment of the insured.
5. Employee's State Insurance	To insure industrial workers against various hazards of life and to protect them from economic insecurity.
6. Workmen's Compensation Insurance	To enable the employer to pay compensation to the workers.
7. Profits Insurance	To protect the insured against the risk of loss of profits arising due to closure of business due to fire.
8. Motor Car Insurance	To indemnify the insured for loss due to accidents, injury to death of any passengers or third party, loss by theft .
9. Burglary (Theft & Robbery Insurance)	To indemnify the insured against the risk of loss arising on account of burglary.
10. Fidelity Guarantee Insurance	To indemnify the insured against the risk of loss arising from the dishonesty of employees.
11. Personal Accidental Insurance	To indemnify the insured against the risk of personal accident causing permanent disability or death.

IMPORTANCE OF INSURANCE

The importance of insurance arises from the following benefits flowing from it:

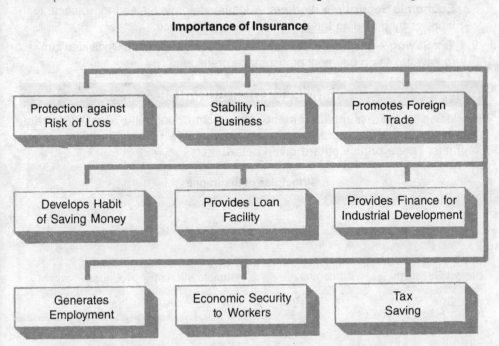

1. **Protection against Risk of Loss** — Insurance provides protection against the risks of loss. In case of life insurance, a sum is assured to be paid on the expiry of the policy or death of the insured whichever is earlier. In case of other insurances, insurance company compensates the insured for the actual loss suffered as per terms and conditions of the policy.

2. **Stability in Business** — Insurance leads to stability in the business by compensating the businessmen for the loss caused due to insured risks. Businessmen feel secure and free from all worries after getting their business insured.

3. **Promotes Foreign Trade** — Insurance promoter foreign trade by insuring against the risks of sea route. Since most of foreign trade is through sea routes.

4. **Develops Habit of Saving Money** — Insurance encourages the people to save and invest.

5. **Provides Loan Facility** — Insurance provides loan facility to the insured against the life insurance policy.

6. **Provides Finance for Industrial Development** — Insurance mobilises the savings of the public and invests in the shares and debentures of different companies and provides loans for the industrial development of the economy. Thus, insurance helps in the economic development of the country.

7. **Generates Employment** — Insurance generates employment since large number of people are required for carrying on the insurance business. Thus, insurance is helpful in solving the unemployment problems to that extent.

8. **Economic Security to Workers** — Insurance provides economic security to workers by providing the policies of social insurance.

9. **Tax Saving** — Insurance enables the individuals and Hindu Undivided families to save taxes on payment of insurance premiums.

PRINCIPLES OF INSURANCE

In addition to the essential elements required to constitute a valid contract, certain fundamental principles are also applicable to constitute insurance contracts. These principles are given below:

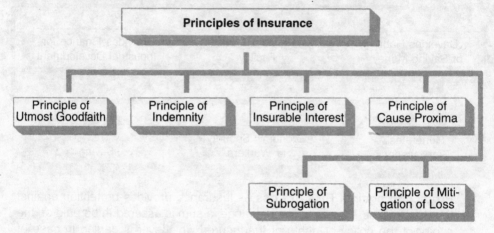

Let us discuss these principles one by one.

1. **Principle of Utmost Goodfaith** — Insurance contract is a contract of *uberrimae fidei* i.e. a contract of utmost good faith. This means that each of the parties to the contract is bound to disclose all material facts which may affect the decision of the other party to enter into such contract or the premium to be charged. There must be *neither* concealment *nor* mis-statement about the material facts. In case of concealment or mis-statement about the material facts, the insurance contract will not be valid.

2. **Principle of Indemnity** — A contract of insurance of (except contract of life Insurance) is a contract of indemnity. Under this contract, the insurer compensates the insured for the actual loss suffered by him. The insured is not permitted to make a profit out through the contract. A contract of life insurance is not a contract of indemnity because the insurer in this contract promises to pay a 'fixed amount' on the death of the 'insured' or on the expiry of the term of the policy whichever is earlier. The insurer does not compensate the actual loss in this case.

3. **Principle of Insurable Interest** — According to this principle, the insured must have insurable interest in the subject matter of the insurance. Insurable

interest is a pecuniary interest in the preservation of the subject matter of the insurance.

Who can have insurable interest?

One is said to have an insurable interest only when—

(a) one will derive monetary benefit from the preservation of the subject matter, *or*
(b) one will suffer monetary loss on the happening of the event insured.

Can non-owners have insurable interest?

The insured need not be the owner of the property. Even non-owner may have insurable interest. For example, legal heirs have insurable interest in the ancestral property. A creditor has insurable interest in the life of his debtor.

When the insured must have insurable interest

The point of time when the insured must have insurable interest differs from contract to contract.

Types of Insurance	Point of time when the insured must have the insurable interest
1. In Life Insurance	At the time of making the contract.
2. In Fire Insurance	Both at the time of making the contract and at the time of actual loss.
3. In Marine Insurance	At the time of Actual Loss.

4. **Principle of Cause Proxima** — According to the principle an insured can recover only that loss which is proximately caused by the risk insured against. When there is more than one cause of loss, the principle of proximate cause of loss is followed and the nearest cause of loss is considered. *For example*, where sugar is destroyed by sea water which enters, into the ship because of holes made in the bottom of the ship by rats. Making of holes by rats is a remote cause while sea water is a proximate or nearest cause. The insured can claim the loss because the sugar was insured against the risk of sea water.

5. **Principle of Subrogation** — The term 'subrogation' means substitution. According to this principle, the insurer steps into the shoes of the insured and becomes entitled to exercise all the rights of the insured regarding the subject matter of the insurance after the claim of the insured has finally settled. *For example*, in case of damage of property due to fire, the insurer will be entitled to dispose off the destroyed property after settling the claims of the insured.

6. **Principle of Mitigation of Loss** — According to this principle, an insured must take all reasonable steps which a man of ordinary prudence will take under those circumstances to reduce the loss.

TYPES OF INSURANCE

The important types of insurance are as follows:

1. Life Insurance
2. Fire Insurance
3. Marine Insurance

LIFE INSURANCE

What is Life Insurance?

Life Insurance is a contract for payment of a sum of money to the person assured (or failing him/her, to the person entitled to receive the same) on the happening of the event insured against. Usually the contract provides for the payment of an amount on the date of maturity or at specified dates at periodic intervals or at unfortunate death, if it occurs earlier. Among other things, the contract also provides for the payment of premium periodically to the Corporation by the assured. Life insurance is universally acknowledged to be an institution which eliminates 'risk', substituting certainty for uncertainty and comes to the timely aid of the family in the unfortunate event of the death of the breadwinner. By and large, life insurance is civilisation's partial solution to financial uncertainties caused by untimely death.

Life insurance, in short, is concerned with two hazards that stand across the life path of every person: that of dying prematurely leaving a dependent family to fend for itself and that of living to old age without visible means of support.

Thus, in a contract of life insurance, the insurer undertakes to pay a fixed amount on the death of the insured or on the expiry of the term of the policy whichever is earlier. Since a fixed amount is assured to be paid, life insurance is appropriately called 'Life Assurance'.

Insurance companies — Now, life insurance business is carried on not only by Life Insurance Corporation (LIC) but also by other companies in private sector like ICICI Prudential, OM KOTAK Mahindra, Max New York.

Why is it superior to other forms of Savings?

1. **Protection** — Savings through life insurance guarantee full protection against risk of death of the saver. In life insurance, on death, the full sum assured is payable (with bonuses wherever applicable) whereas in other savings schemes, only the amount saved (with interest) is payable.

2. **Aid to thrift** — Life insurance encourages 'thrift'. Long term saving can be made in a relatively 'painless' manner because of the 'easy instalment' facility built into the scheme (premiums can be paid through monthly, quarterly, half-yearly or yearly instalments). The Salary Savings Scheme, popularly known as SSS, provides a convenient method of paying premium each month through deduction from one's salary. The employer remits the deducted premium to the LIC. The Salary Savings Scheme can be introduced in an institution or establishment subject to specified terms and conditions.

3. **Liquidity** — Loans can be raised on the sole security of a policy which has acquired loan value. Besides, a life insurance policy is also generally accepted as security for even a commercial loan.

4. **Tax Relief** — Tax relief in Income Tax is available for amounts paid by way of premium for life insurance subject to the Income tax rates in force. Assesses can avail of provisions in the law for tax relief. In such cases the assured in effect pays a lower premium for his insurance than he would have to pay otherwise.

5. **Money when you need it** — A suitable insurance plan or a combination of different plans can be taken out to meet specific needs that are likely to arise in future, such as children's education, start-in-life or marriage provision or even periodical needs for cash over a predetermined stretch of time. Alternatively, policy moneys can be so arranged to be made available at the time of one's retirement from service to be used for any specific purpose, such as for the purchase of a house or for other investments. Subject to certain conditions, loans are granted to policyholders for house building or for purchase of flats.

Who can buy a Life Insurance Policy?

Any person who has attained majority and is eligible to enter into a valid contract can take out a life insurance policy for himself/herself and on those in whom he/she has insurable interest. Policies can also be taken out, subject to certain conditions, on the life of one's spouse or children. While underwriting proposals, factors such as the state of health of the life to be assured, the proponent's income and other relevant factors are considered by the Corporation.

Objectives of LIC

To spread Life Insurance widely and in particular to the rural areas and to the socially and economically backward classes with a view to reaching all insurable persons in the country and providing them adequate financial cover against death at a reasonable cost.

—   To maximise mobilisation of people's savings by making insurance-linked savings adequately attractive.
—   To bear in mind, in the investment of funds, the primary obligation to its policyholders, whose money it holds in trust, without losing sight of the interest of the community as a whole; the funds to be deployed to the best advantage of the investors as well as the community as a whole, keeping in view national priorities and obligations of attractive return.
—   To conduct business with utmost economy and with the full realisation that the moneys belong to the policyholders.
—   To act as trustees of the insured public in their individual and collective capacities.
—   To meet the various life insurance needs of the community that would arise in the changing social and economic environment.
—   To involve all people working in the Corporation to the best of their capability in furthering the interests of the insured public by providing efficient service with courtesy.
—   To promote amongst all agents and employees of the Corporation a sense of participation, pride and job satisfaction through discharge of their duties with dedication towards achievement of Corporate Objectives.

Types of Life Insurance Policies

There are various life insurance policies. The popular life insurance policies are discussed below:

1. **With Profit Policies** — Holder is entitled to receive the bonus at the declared rate. Traditionally bonus rate is expressed per thousand rupee of the sum assured. Bonus gets accumulated year after year but is paid at the time of maturity of the policy. Bonus is declared on sum assured and not on already accumulated bonus. *For example*, Mr X takes with profit life insurance policy for a sum assured of Rs. 1,00,000 for 5 years. If bonus is declared @ Rs. 70, Rs 71, Rs 72, Rs. 73, Rs. 74 for each of these 5 years. The amount to be received by Mr X at the time of maturity of the policy will be calculated as under:

A.	Sum Assured		Rs 1,00,000
B.	*Add:* Bonus		
	1st year [Rs 70 × Rs. 1,00,000/1000]	7,000	
	2nd year [Rs 71 × Rs. 1,00,000/1000]	7,100	
	3rd year [Rs 72 × Rs. 1,00,000/1000]	7,200	
	4th year [Rs 73 × Rs. 1,00,000/1000]	7,300	
	5th year [Rs 74 × Rs. 1,00,000/1000]	7,400	36,000
C.	Total Amount Receivable [A+B]		Rs 1,36,000

2. **Without Profit Policies** — Holder of Policy is not entitled to receive the bonus declared from time to time.

3. **With Accident Benefit Policies** — On payment of some extra premium, the holder is entitled to claim the accidental benefit. Under life insurance policies with accidental benefit, on death of the insured due to accident, either double or triple the sum assured is paid according to the type of policy taken.

4. **Without Accident Benefit Policies** — *Neither* extra premium is charged *nor* extra sum assured is paid.

Some of the popular life insurance policies are discussed below:

I. **Whole Life Policy** — Under this policy, the sum assured alongwith the bonuses (in case of with profits policies) is payable on attaining a specified age or death of insured whichever is earlier. For example, The following types of whole life policies are issued by Life Insurance Corporation of India.

II. **Endowment Policy** — Under this policy, the sum assured alongwith the bonuses (in case of with profit policies) is payable on the expiry of specified term of policy or death of insured whichever is earlier. *For example,* the following types of endowment policies are provided by Life Insurance Corporation of India.

Plan	Min. Age & Max. age	Minimum Sum Assured	Premium Paying term	Frequency of Premium Payment	Benefits: (Common to all)
Whole Life with Profit	15-60 years	Rs 25,000	Premiums are paid upto age 80 years or for 35 years whichever is more	Yearly, Hly, Qly, Mly, & Salary Saving Scheme	The Sum Assured along with the bonuses (For with profit policies only) payable on attaining age 80 years or on earlier death.
Limited Payment Whole Life — Without Profit — With Profit.	12-60 years	Rs 50,000 Rs 30,000	Premium payment term limited to 25 years 5 to 55 years depending on the age.	-do- -do-	Loan can be taken on policy if 3 years' premiums are paid. The accident benefit is available on payment of additional premium of Rs. 1 per thousand Sum Assured per year.
Convertible Whole Life Without Profit	12-45 years	Rs 50,000	10 to 55 years	-do-	
Whole Life Single Premium — Without Profit — With Profit	12-60 years	Rs. 50,000 Rs. 30,000	One time Payment -do-	Single -do-	
Endowment without profit and with profit	12 years to 65 years	Rs. 20,000	5 years to 55 years	Yly, Hly, Qly, Mly & Salary savings scheme	**On maturity or earlier death** —Full sum assured (*plus* bonus for with profit policies only)
Limited payment Endowment (with profit)	12 years to 60 years	Rs 50,000	15, 20 & 25 years	Yly, Hly, Qly, Mly Salary savings scheme & Single premium	**On maturity or earlier death** —Full sum assured (*plus* bonus for with profit policies only)

Double Endowment without profit	12 years to 55 years	Rs 25,000	10 to 40 years	Yly, Hly, Qly, Mly & Salary savings scheme	a) **On survival** -- Twice the sum assured. b) **On death** only sum assured
Jeevan Mitra double cover with profit	18 years to 50 years	Rs 25,000	15 years to 30 years	Yly, Hly, Qly, Mly & Salary savings scheme	a) **On maturity** Sum assured **plus** bonus b) **On death** Triple the sum assured **plus** bonus. c) **On death due to an accident** Four times the sum assured **plus** bonus.
Jeevan Mitra triple cover with profit	18 years to 50 years	Rs 25,000	15 years to 30 years	Yly, Hly, Qly, Mly & Salary savings scheme	a) **On maturity** Sum assured **plus** bonus b) **On death** triple the sum assured **plus** bonus. c) **On death due to accident** Four times the sum assured **plus** bonus.
Jeevan Saathi with profit (Ideal for married couple)	20 years to 50 years	Rs 25,000	15 years to 30 years	Yly, Hly, Qly, Mly & Salary savings scheme	a) **On survival of both the lives** Basic sum assured **plus** bonus.

					b) **On death of either of the lives:** 1) Future premiums waived. 2) Basic sum assured paid to survivor. 3) *On maturity* Sum assured paid to the survivor. 4) *In case of death due to accident*, Double the sum assured to the survivor.
Marriage Endowment/ Educational Annuity with profit	18 years to 60 years	Rs 25,000	5 years to 25 years	Yly, Hly, Qly, Mly & Salary savings scheme	a) Sum assured + bonus on maturity. b) Option to get the maturity benefit *Either* in lump sum *or* 10 yearly instalments.
Jeevan Chhaya with profit	18 years to 40 years	Rs 40,000	18 years to 25 years	Yly, Hly, Qly, Mly & Salary savings scheme	a) One fourth of the sum assured is available in each of the last four years of the term. b) Bonus on full sum assured at the end of the term. c) On death during the term one additional sum assured will become payable.

III.   **Term Policy** — Under this policy, the sum assured alongwith loyalty addition (if any) is payable on the death of the insured but sum equivalent to total amount of premiums paid (including accident premium but excluding other extras) alongwith loyalty addition (if any) is payable on the expiry of the specified term of the policy. For example, a BIMA KIRAN Policy has been provided by the Life Insurance Corporation of India.

Salient Features of BIMA KIRAN Policy:

Minimum & Maximum Age of Entry	18 to 45 years
Maximum Maturity Age	70 years
Minimum & Maximum Sum Assured	Rs 1,00,000 to Rs 5,00,000
Minimum & Maximum Term of Policy	15 to 25 years
Frequency of Premium Payment	Yly, Hly
Benefits	**On Death:** Sum Assured + Minimum Loyalty Additions (if any)
	On Survival: Total Premium paid (including accident premium but excluding extra premium) + Minimum Loyalty addition

IV.   **Joint Life Policy** — Under this policy, the lives of two or more persons are insured jointly. The sum assured is payable on the expiry of the specified term of the policy or death of any of the insured whichever is earlier. For example, LIC provides Jeevan Saathi Policy in this regard:

Salient Features of Jeevan Saathi Policy with Profit (Ideal for Married Couple)

Minimum & Maximum Age of Entry	20 to 50 years
Maximum Maturity Age	70 years
Minimum Sum Assured	Rs 25,000
Minimum & Maximum Term of Policy	15 to 30 years
Frequency of Premium Payment	Yly, Hly, Qly, Mly & Salary Saving Scheme
Benefits	(a) **On survival of both the lives:** Basic sum assured plus bonus.
	(b) **On death of either of the lives:**
	1. Future premium waived.
	2. Basic sum assured paid to survivor immediately
	3. On maturity sum assured with bonuses paid to the survivor.
	4. In case of death due to accident, double the sum assured to the survivor.

V. **Group Insurance Policy** — Under this policy, the sum assured is payable on the death of the insured but on survival only total premium paid alongwith loyalty addition (if any) is payable. This policy is usually taken on the lives of the employees of the organization.

VI. **Pension Plan** — Under this policy, pension is offered. The policyholder is given an option to select the pension plan in which he would like to receive the lumpsum amount and annuity. For example, LIC has provided New Jeevan Suraksha Policy in this regard:

Salient Features of New Jeevan Suraksha Policy:

Minimum & Maximum Age of Entry	18 to 65 years
Minimum & Maximum Vesting Age	50 to 79 years
Minimum & Maximum Deferment Period	2 to 35 years
Minimum Single Premium	Rs 10,000
Minimum Annual Premium	Rs 2,500
Minimum Annuity	Rs 250 p.m.
Minimum & Maximum Sum Assured	Rs 1,00,000 to 25,00,000 (for annual premium plan)
Minimum & Maximum Notional Cash Option [NCO]	Rs 50,000 to Rs 12,50,000 (for Annual Premium Plan)
Frequency of Premium Payment	Monthly, Qty., Half Yearly, Yearly, Single

Benefits: The benefits of NEW JEEVAN SURAKSHA are as follows:

1. Notional cash option together with reversionary Bonuses and final additional bonuses (if any) with or without 25% commutation will be compulsorily converted into annuity having the following options.
    Option 'A' — Annuity for life.
    Option 'B' — Annuity for life with guaranteed period of 5,10,15 and 20 years.
    Option 'C' — Joint life and last survivor annuity to the annuitant and his/her spouse, under which annuity payable to he spouse on death of the annuitant will be reduced to 50% of that payable to the annuitant.
    Option 'D' — Life annuity with annuity increasing at a simple rate of 3% p.a.
    Option 'E' — Life annuity with return of NCO.
2. Tax Benefits — Deduction, Under Section 80CCC (Maximum Rs 10,000)

FIRE INSURANCE

What is Fire Insurance?

In a contract of fire insurance, the insurer undertakes to compensate the insured for the actual loss suffered by him due to the damage or destruction of property by fire subject to the maximum limit of the sum insured. The insured is not allowed to make any profit out of this transaction. It may be noted that Fire Insurance Policies are always subject to **Average Clause**. Average clause is introduced to discourage under insurance. Average clause is applicable in case of under insurance (i.e. where the sum insured of policy is less than the value of the subject matter of the insurance). In such a case the actual claim is proportionately reduced as under:

Actual Claim according to Average Clause in case of Under Insurance

$$\text{Claim} = \text{Actual loss} \times \frac{\text{Sum Insured}}{\text{Sum Insurable}}$$

The calculation of claim can be understood with the help of the following example. *(the figures being in lakhs)*

Particulars	Case I	Case II	Case III	Case IV
A. Actual value of Property	1.00	1.00	1.00	1.00
B. Sum Insured	1.00	.50	.50	1.50
C. Actual Loss	.50	.60	.40	1.00
D. Amount of Claim	.50 [Being Actual Loss or Sum Insured whichever is lower]	.30 [60 × .50/1.00] *Note:* Average Clause applies in case of under insurance	.20 [40×.50/1.00] *Note:* Average Clause applies in case of under insurance	1.00 *Note:* Average Clause does not apply in case of over-insurance

Can the same property be got insured with different insurers?

Yes, the same property can be got insured with different insurers. In this case, all the insurers are jointly liable to bear the loss. But in no case, the total amount payable to the insured can exceed the amount of actual loss.

Types of Fire Insurance Policies

There are various types of fire insurance policies. The popular fire insurance policies are discussed as follows:

Types of Fire Insurance Policies	Meaning
1. **Specific Policy**	A policy in which the liability of the insurer is limited to a specified amount which is less than the value of the property insured.
2. **Valued Policy**	A policy in which the insurer agrees to pay a fixed amount in the event of loss irrespective of the actual loss suffered.
3. **Floating Policy**	A policy which is taken to insure the goods at different places and the quantity and value of which vary from time to time
4. **Replacement Policy**	A policy in which an insurer has option to pay the loss in cash or replace the property.
5. **Loss of Profit Policy**	A policy which protects the insured against loss of profit due to dislocation of business because of fire.
6. **Comprehensive Policy or Householders' Policy**	A policy which provides a cover against risks of loss due to various causes such as fire, riots, strike, earthquake, flood, storm, burglary, electric fluctuations, burning and overflowing of water tanks or pipes.

MARINE INSURANCE

What is Marine Insurance?

In a contract of marine insurance, the insurer undertakes to compensate the insured in return for the premium for the actual loss suffered by him due to perils of the sea.

Subject Matter of Marine Insurance — Marine Insurance may be in respect of ship, cargo, freight or any other subject connected with a marine voyage. The important three types of marine insurance are:

1. **Ship Insurance** — The ship owner takes the policy to cover the risk of loss or damage to the ship.

2. **Cargo Insurance** — The cargo owner takes the policy to cover the risk of loss of or damage to the cargo.

3. **Freight Insurance** — The transport company takes the policy to cover the risk of loss due to non-recovery of freight.

Marine Policy — The document which contains the terms and conditions, subject matters of insurance and the risks covered is called marine policy or sea policy.

Underwriter — The insurer who agrees to insure is called underwriter.

Types of Marine Insurance Policies

There are various marine insurance policies. The popular marine insurance policies are discussed below:

Types of Marine Insurance Policies	Meaning
1. **Voyage Policy**	A policy which insures the subject matter for a specified voyage.
2. **Time Policy**	A policy which insures the subject matter for a specified period of time. (usually not exceeding a year)
3. **Mixed Policy or Voyage cum Time Policy**	A policy which insures the subject matter on a specified voyage for a specified period of time. For example, a ship may be insured for a voyage between Mumbai and U.S.A. for a period of 6 months.
4. **Valued Policy**	A policy in which the insurer agrees to pay a fixed amount agreed at the time of taking a policy, in the event of loss irrespective of the actual loss suffered.
5. **Floating Policy**	A policy in which cargo owner gets the regular shipments of cargo automatically insured by making declaration about the value of cargo shipped. The total value of the policy goes on reducing by the amount of each declaration.
6. **Fleet Policy**	A policy which insures the whole fleet of liners *or* steamers.
7. **Port Policy**	A policy which insures the ship when it is anchored in a port.

COMPARATIVE STUDY OF LIFE INSURANCE, FIRE INSURANCE, MARINE INSURANCE

Basis of Comparison	Life Insurance	Fire Insurance	Marine Insurance
1. Risk covered	It covers the risk of **loss due to death** to the extent of sum assured.	It covers the risk of **loss due to fire.**	It covers the risks of **loss due to perils of sea.**
2. Certaining of Happening of event	The happening of event is **certain.** Both death of insured and maturity of the policy are certain.	The happening of event is **not certain.** Fire may or may not take place.	The happening of event **is not certain.** The sea risks may or may not arise.
3. Object	**To provide the predetermined sum** of money (alongwith bonus in case of with profits policy) to the nominees of the insured in case of death of insured.	**To indemnify** the insured for any loss or damage caused by accidental fire.	**To indemnify** the insured for any loss or damage caused by perils of sea.
4. Subject matter of Insurance	The subject matter of life insurance is **life.**	The subject matter of fire insurance is **property**.	The subject matter marine insurance is **ship, cargo and freight**.
5. Time when Insurable Interest is required	The insured must have the insurable interest **at the time of making the contact**.	The insured must have the insurable interest **both at the time of making the contract and at the time of actual loss.**	The insured must have the insurable interest **at the time of actual loss**.
6. Term of Policy	Life insurance policy is provided for a **longer period** say, 5, 10, 15, 20 years or even for the whole life.	Fire insurance policy is provided for **short period** generally a one year.	Marine insurance policy is provided for a **short period,** say for a particular voyage or one year.
7. Factors Determining Premium	Life insurance premium is determined according to the **age**	Fire insurance premium is determined according to the	Marine insurance premium is determined accordance to the

		nature and extent of risks involved.	nature and extent of risks involved.
	of the insured **and** the **term** of the policy.		
8. **Payment of Premium**	Premium is generally paid **in instalments (except in case of single premium policies).**	Premium is paid **in lumpsum.**	Premium is paid **in lumpsum.**
9. **Can Policy be surrendered?**	The policy **can be** surrendered before the expiry of the term of policy.	The policy **cannot** be surrendered.	The policy **cannot** be surrendered.
10. **Compensation**	Compensation is **only pre-determined sum** assured.	Compensation is the **actual loss** due to fire but not exceeding the sum insured.	Compensation is the **actual loss** due to perils of sea. It can be more than loss where some profit is added to actual loss.

EXERCISES

VERY SHORT ANSWER TYPE QUESTIONS

1. What is meant by the principle of *'uberrimae fidei'*?
2. What is meant by the principle of indemnity?
3. What is meant by 'Insurable Interest'?
4. Who can have insurable interest?
5. Can non-owners have insurable interest?
6. When must the insured have insurable interest?
7. What is meant by the principle of Cause Proxima?
8. What is meant by the principle of Subrogation?
9. What is meant by the principle of Mitigation of loss?
10. What is meant by the contract of life insurance?
11. What is meant by the contract of fire insurance?
12. What is meant by the contract of marine insurance?

SHORT ANSWER TYPE QUESTIONS

1. List the principles of insurance.
2. List the various types of insurance.
3. State the subject matter of marine insurance.

LONG ANSWER TYPE QUESTIONS

1. Explain the nature and causes of business risks.
2. Discuss the principles of insurance with example.

Channels of Distributions

10

MEANING OF CHANNEL OF DISTRIBUTION

The term **'channel of distribution'** is a network of institutions that perform a variety of interrelated and co-ordinated functions in the movement of goods from producers to consumers. In other words 'the channels of distribution' refer to the various intermediaries who help in moving the product from the producer to the consumer. These are a variety of middlemen and merchants who act as intermediaries between the producers and consumers.

FUNCTIONS OF CHANNELS OF DISTRIBUTION

The functions performed by channels of distribution are as follows:

1. **Transactional Functions** — The channels of distribution perform transactional functions which are necessary to a transaction of the goods. These transactional functions include buying, selling and risk bearing functions. For example, intermediaries buy goods from producers, sell goods to consumers and assume risk involved in buying and selling.

2. **Logistical Functions** — The channels of distribution perform logistical functions which are involved in the physical exchange of goods. These logistical functions include assembling, storage, grading, transportation.

3. **Facilitating Functions** — The channels of distribution perform facilitating functions like after sales service and maintenance, financing and market information etc. Traders provide necessary information about the product to buyers, financial assistance in the form of credit sales and after sales service. They also inform producers about the customers' opinions about the products.

4. **Create Place Utility** — The channels of distribution create place utility by facilitating the movement of goods from one place to another.

5. **Create Time Utility** — The channels of distribution create time utility by bringing the goods to the consumers when they want.

6. **Convenience Utility** — The channels of distribution create convenience utility by bringing goods to the consumers in a convenient shape, unit, size, style and package.

7. **Create Possession Utility** — The channels of distribution create possession utility by making it possible for the consumer to obtain goods at a price he is willing to pay and under conditions which bring him satisfaction and pride of ownership.

TYPES OF CHANNELS OF DISTRIBUTION

The channels of distribution can be grouped into the following two categories:

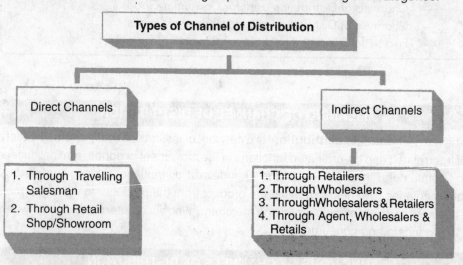

1. **Direct Channels** — When the producers sell their goods directly to the consumers, it is called a direct channel. No middlemen is present between the producer and the consumer. There can be two types of direct channels as follows:

    (a) **Through Travelling Salesmen** — The producers employ salesmen to book orders by contacting the potential users and supply goods out of the stock held by them. The main point in favour of this type of direct selling is the need:

    (i) to enlighten about the additional features of product and

    (ii) to educate the user about how to use the product.

Example — Direct selling of vacuum cleaners and water purifying equipment by Eureka Forbed Ltd. (EFL), a Mumbai based company. This direct channel can be shown below:

(b) **Through Retail Shop/Showroom** — The producers set up retail shops/showrooms is different localities and sell goods directly to the consumers. This direct channel can be shown below:

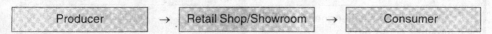

Example — Bata Shoes, Usha Sewing Machines, WIMPY, Mc-Donald, Raymonds.

2. **Indirect Channels** — When the producers sell their goods to consumers through middlemen, it is called indirect channel. There can be four types of indirect channels as follows:

(a) **Through Retailers** — The producers supply goods directly to retailers who in turn sell to the ultimate consumers. No wholesaler is involved. This indirect channel can be shown below:

(b) **Through Wholesalers** — The producers supply goods in bulk to the wholesalers who in turn directly sell the goods in small quantities to ultimate consumers. No retailer is involved. This indirect channel can be shown below:

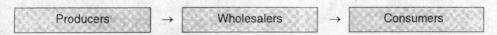

(c) **Through Wholesaler and Retailer** — The producers supply goods in bulk to the wholesalers who sell goods in small quantity to the retailers who in turn sell these goods to the ultimate consumers. Both wholesalers and retailers are involved. This indirect channel can be shown below:

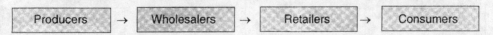

(d) **Through Agent, Wholesaler & Retailer** — The producers supply goods in bulk to the mercantile agent who in turn sell the goods to the wholesalers who in turn sell the goods to the retailers who in turn sell the goods to the ultimate consumers. In this channel, mercantile agent, wholesalers and retailers are involved. This indirect channel can be shown below:

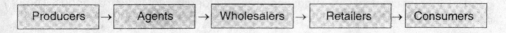

CHANNELS OF DISTRIBUTION USED FOR CONSUMER GOODS

The goods which are consumed by the household consumers are called consumer goods. Different channels of distribution are used for different consumer goods.

The different channels of distribution used for different consumer goods are given below:

Consumer Goods	Channels of Distribution Used
1. For durable Consumer goods like cars, furniture, shoes etc.	Showroom of manufacturers or dealers.
2. For consumer goods like auto spare parts, stereos etc.	Wholesalers and retailers.
3. For consumer goods of daily need like sugar, salt, soap, stationery.	Agent, wholesalers and retailers.

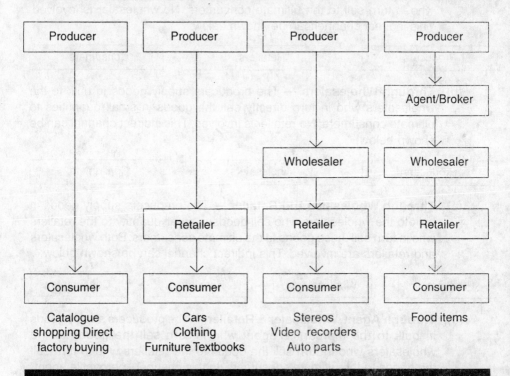

CHANNELS OF DISTRIBUTION USED FOR INDUSTRIAL GOODS

The goods which are consumed by industry for further production are called industrial goods. Different channels of distribution are used for different industrial goods. The different channels of distribution used for different industrial goods are given on next page:

Industrial Goods	Channels of Distribution Used
1. For high value industrial goods like computer, aircraft, heavy machinery etc.	Directly by manufacturers to consumers
2. For relatively less expensive items like trucks etc.	Through Distributors
3. For agricultural products like corn, coffee, soyabeans etc. for industrial consumption.	Through Agents

FACTORS INFLUENCING THE CHOICE OF CHANNEL OF DISTRIBUTION

The choice of the channel of distribution is influenced by the following factors:

1. **The Type of Product** — The nature of the product influence the choice of channel. *For example —*

Type of Product	Suitable Channel of Distribution
(a) For perishable products like eggs, milk, bread, butter, etc.	Short channels which facilitate quick movement from factory to consumers.
(b) For heavy and bulky products. (e.g., steel, cement)	Limited channels.
(c) For products requiring after sales service like television, air-conditioners, automobiles.	Seletive channels.
(d) For light weight and small size items like matchsticks, soap, toothpastes, hair oil, shampoos.	Long channels for intensive distribution.

2. **Nature and Extent of Market** — The nature and extent of market also influence the choice of channel of distribution. *For example —*

Nature of Customer	Suitable Channels of Distribution
(a) If the number of customers is large	Long and multiple channels for intensive distribution
(b) If the number of customer is small	Short and direct channels

3. **Buying Habits of Consumers** — The buying habits of consumers also influence the choice of channels of distribution. *For example* —

Buying Habits of Consumers	Suitable Channel of Distribution
(a) If customers purchase small quantities	Long and multiple channels for intensive distribution
(b) If customers purchase large quantities	Short and direct channels

4. **Number of Suppliers of Product** — The numbers of suppliers of product also influence the choice of channel of distribution. *For example* —

Number of Suppliers	Suitable Channel of Distribution
(a) If the number of suppliers is large in different regions	Long and multiple channels for intensive distribution.
(b) If the number of suppliers is small.	Short and direct channels

5. **Existing Channels used by Competitors** — The existing channels used by competitors also influence the choice of channels of distribution. Sometimes, producers use the same channel which is used by their competing producers. If any producer arranges exclusive distribution through a particular wholesaler, other producers also like to use the same.

6. **Cost involved in Distribution** — The cost involved in distribution also influence the choice of channels of distribution. Longer the channel of distribution, greater is its cost. Shorter the channel of distribution, lesser is its cost. A channel which is less expensive is normally preferred.

7. **Target volume of Sales** — The choice of channel also depends upon the target volume of sales. *For example* —

Target Volume of Sales	Suitable Channels of Distribution
(a) If target volume of sales is large	Long and multiple channels
(b) If taget volume of sales in small	Short and direct channels

8. **Characteristics of Middlemen** — The choice of channels of distribution is also influenced by the availability of middlemen. Efficiency of distribution depends upon the size, location and financing position of middlemen. It also depends upon the capability of middlemen to perform functions like standardisation, grading, packing etc. If the middlemen in a specific channel are dependable and efficient, that channel may be preferred by manufacturers.

9. **Future Market Conditions** — Future market conditions may also influence the choice of channels of distribution. If demand for a product is high and is likely to be increased in future also, the producers may decide to use long channels. If demand for a product is low and is likely to be decreased in future because of entry of competitors, the producers may decide to use short channels.

Conclusion — A rational decision regarding choice of channels of distribution should ensure —

> 1. Maximum geographical coverage of the market;
> 2. Maximum promotional efforts; and
> 3. Minimum cost;
> 4. Maximum satisfaction of consumers.

The task of manufacturer does not end after the channels have been selected. He has to review the services performed by the agencies involved at fairly frequent intervals, keep in close touch with the developments related to the distribution of his product and seek to improve his marketing methods constantly. He may also realise that what was the best channel when the product was introduced, may not be the most effective one when the product is established.

Criteria for Evaluation of Channel Members — The following criteria may be used for evaluation of channel members:

> 1. their sales performance;
> 2. their marketing capabilities;
> 3. their motivation to increase the volume of sales;
> 4. their growth prospects; and
> 5. the competition faced by them.

_____ **EXERCISES** _____

SHORT ANSWER TYPE QUESTIONS

1. What is meant by 'Channel of Distribution'?
2. What are the types of channels of distribution?
3. Enumerate the functions of channels of distribution.
4. Enumerate the types of channels of distribution.
5. Enumerate the factors determining the choice of channels of distribution.

LONG ANSWER TYPE QUESTIONS

1. Define channels of distribution. Explain the functions of channels of distribution.
2. Explain the direct channels of distribution.
3. Explain the indirect channels of distribution.
4. Briefly explain the various types of channels of distribution.
5. Discuss the factors influencing the choice of channel of distribution.
6. Explain the channels of distribution used for consumer goods.
7. Explain the channels of distribution used for industrial goods.

11 Internal Trade

MEANING OF TRADE

Trade is an important part of commerce. It refers to the sale, transfer or exchange of goods and services for a certain price. Trade establishes a link between producers and consumers through traders. Traders are involved in actual operation of purchase and sale of goods. They provide necessary support to producers and maintain smooth flow of goods for commerce. Traders not only buy the finished goods from producers but also supply raw-material, stores and spare parts, machinery & equipment to producers.

The interdependency between producers, traders and consumers has been shown below:

Thus, producers, traders and consumers are interdependent.

IMPORTANCE OF TRADE

Trade is of great significance for production as well as consumption of goods. Basically these are two barriers - one due to distance between place of production and place of consumption and another due to time lag between production and consumption. Trade removes these barriers by making the goods available to the consumer at right place and at right time. Its importance lies in its advantages which are given below:

1. It enables the producers to concentrate on their production activities by facilitating the sale of goods produced.

2. It enables the consumers to concentrate on their occupation by facilitating the availability of required goods at the required place and at required time.

3. It facilitates the specialization and large-scale production by facilitating the sale and purchase of goods not only within the country but also outside the country.

4. It increases the standard of living of people by making them available the goods of various kinds produced by different producers at required time.

5. It provides employment opportunities to various persons engaged in trade.

CLASSIFICATION OF TRADE

On geographical basis, Trade can be classified into two categories as follows:

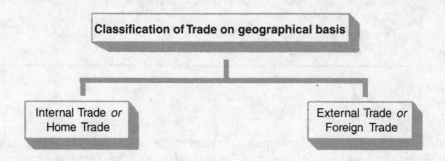

In this chapter, we will discuss internal trade and in the next chapter, we will discuss external trade.

INTERNAL TRADE OR HOME TRADE

Meaning of Internal Trade

Internal Trade *or* Home Trade refers to buying and selling of goods and services within a country. The main features of internal trade are as follows:

1. The buying and selling of goods and services take place within the boundaries of the same country.
2. The trade payments are made and received in the same home currency of the country.
3. Several modes of payment such as cash, cheque, draft, pay order etc. are available.
4. There are minimum legal and administrative formalities involved in organizing internal trade.
5. Several modes of transport such as Rickshaw, truck, rail, air etc. are available.

Classification of Internal Trade on the basis of scale of operations

Internal trade can be classified into two categories as follows:

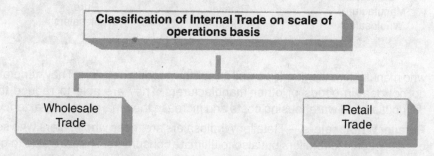

Let us discuss these categories of Internal Trade one by one.

WHOLESALE TRADE – MEANING, FEATURES, TYPES, FUNCTIONS, SERVICES

Meaning of Wholesale Trade

Wholesale trade refers to buying of goods in bulk from manufacturers or their agents and selling them to retailers and industrial users in relatively small quantities. Those who are engaged in wholesale trade are called wholesalers.

Features of Wholesale Trade

The main features of wholesale trade are given below:

1. Goods are bought directly from the manufacturers or their agents.
2. Goods are bought in bulk quantity.
3. Goods are sold to retailers and industrial users relatively in small quantities.
4. Wholesalers generally deal in one or few items only.

5. Wholesalers generally do not have direct link with ultimate consumers since they generally do not sell the production to ultimate consumers.

6. Wholesalers act as middle men between the manufacturers on the one hand and retailers and industrial users on the other.

Wholesalers solve the problems of both the manufacturers and retailers by placing large order with the manufacturers and by meeting the small orders of retailers.

Types of Wholesalers

Depending upon their activities the wholesalers may be classified into three categories:

Let us discuss these types of wholesalers one by one.

1. **Manufacturer Wholesalers** — Manufacturer Wholesalers are those wholesalers

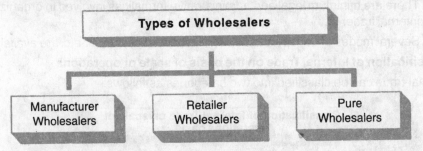

who manufacture the goods as well as sell the goods to retailers. They generally do not deal in goods of other manufacturers. They are able to reduce the distribution and warehousing costs and increase their margin to that extent.

2. **Retailer Wholesalers** — Retailer Wholesalers are those wholesalers who sell goods not only to retailers but also to ultimate consumers. They are able to get prompt and first hand information relating to the product directly from the ultimate consumers. They are also able to reduce the distribution costs and increase their margin to that extent.

3. **Pure Wholesalers** — Pure wholesalers are those who buy the goods in bulk from the manufacturers of goods and sell the goods only to retailers in relatively small quantities. They *neither* produce the goods *nor* sell the goods directly to the ultimate consumers. They are able to serve the manufacturers and retailers.

Functions of Wholesalers

Every wholesaler is required to perform the primary function of buying, storing and supplying goods. In addition to these primary functions, several others functions may also be performed by wholesalers. The various functions of wholesalers are given on next page:

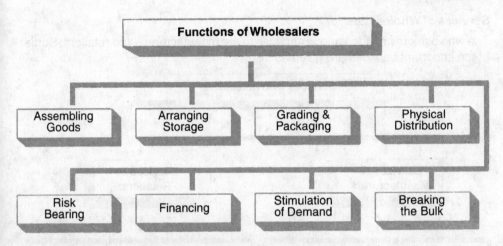

Let us discuss these functions of wholesalers one by one.

1. **Assembling Goods** — The wholesalers procure goods from manufacturers and hold adequate stock of these goods so as to make them available to the retailers as and when required.

2. **Arranging Storage** — The wholesalers make arrangement for holding stocks to meet the needs of retailers from time to time. By performing the function, they relieve the manufacturers and retailers of the burden of holding large stocks and providing storage space for the same.

3. **Grading and Packing** — The wholesalers sometimes perform grading functions i.e. sorting out the products according to their quality or size *or* others factors. After performing grading function, they perform packaging function by packing the goods in convenient lots so that they can be sold to the retailers.

4. **Physical Distribution** — The wholesalers facilitate the physical distribution of goods from the place of producers to the place of retailers.

5. **Risk Bearing** — The wholesalers have to bear the risk of loss which may be due to spoilage or damage of goods, changes in demand and prices in procuring and holding large stocks of goods till the time goods are sold.

6. **Financing** — The wholesalers perform financing function by providing credit facilities to the retailers and sometimes by providing advance money to the manufacturers.

7. **Stimulation of Demand** — The wholesalers sometimes undertake the activities like advertising, personal selling and sales promotion, to increase the demand for goods produced.

8. **Breaking the Bulk** — The wholesalers perform this function by buying goods in large quantities and selling them in relatively small quantities.

Services of Wholesalers

The wholesalers provide various services to the manufacturers and retailers. Some of the important services are given as follows:

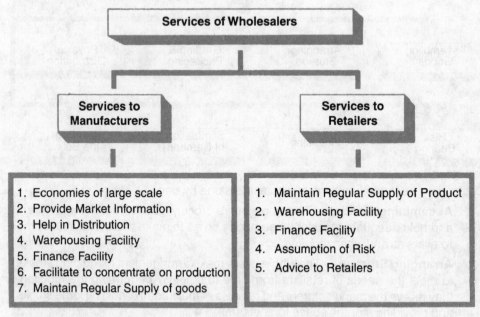

Let us discuss these services of wholesalers one by one.

Services to Manufacturers

1. **Economies of Large Scale** — The wholesalers enable the producers to take the advantages of economies of large scale by placing the order of large quantities.

2. **Provide Market Information** — The wholesalers enable the producers to develop the production plans in accordance with the changing market conditions by collecting important market information with respect to changes in demand, competition etc. from the retailers and passing on to the producers.

3. **Help in Distribution** — The wholesalers enable the producers to reach customers scattered over different geographical regions by distributing goods through retailers located in various regions.

4. **Warehousing Facility** — The wholesalers relieve the manufacturers from warehousing function by making arrangements for holding large stocks of goods in their own warehouse or hired warehouse.

5. **Finance Facility** — The wholesalers provide financial support to the producers by providing them advance money against bulk orders.

6. **Facilitate to Concentrate on Production** — The wholesalers enable the producers to concentrate on production activities by taking responsibility of distribution of goods.

7. **Maintaining Regular Supply of Production** — The wholesalers maintain regular supply of goods throughout the year by storing the goods both during season and off-season periods.

Services to Retailers

1. **Maintain Regular Supply of Products** — Wholesalers assure regular supply of production to the retailers by maintaining adequate stock of goods. This enables the retailers to buy goods in small quantities as and when required.

2. **Warehousing Facility** — Wholesalers relieve the retailers of the need for holding large stocks and making storage arrangements for the same by enabling the retailers to buy in small quantities.

3. **Finance Facility** — The wholesalers provide financial support to the retailers by supplying goods to them on credit.

4. **Assumption of Risk** — The wholesalers saves the retailers from assuming the risk of loss which may be due to spoilage or damage of goods, changes in demand and prices, in procuring and holding large stocks of goods since the retailers need not maintain large stock of goods.

5. **Advice to Retailers** — The wholesalers provide advice to the retailers regarding the quality, durability, price and timings of purchase of products. They also provide information about the new products to be introduced.

RETAIL TRADE – MEANING, FEATURES, FUNCTIONS, SERVICES, TYPES

Meaning of Retail Trade

Retail Trade refers to buying of goods from wholesalers or manufacturers and selling them directly to the ultimate consumers. Those who are engaged in retail trade are called retailers.

Features of Retail Trade

The main features of retail trade are given below:

1. Goods are bought from wholesalers or manufacturers.
2. Goods are bought in small quantity.
3. Goods are sold directly to the ultimate consumers.
4. Retailers generally deal in a variety of items.
5. Retailers generally do not have direct link with manufacturers since they generally purchase the products from wholesalers.
6. Retailers act as middlemen between the wholesalers on the one hand and ultimate consumers on the other.
7. Goods are generally bought on credit and sold for cash.
8. Retail trade is normally carried on near the place of ultimate consumers.

Distinction between Wholesale Trade and Retail Trade

The wholesale trade differs from the retail trade in the following respects:

Basis of Distinction	Wholesale Trade	Retail Trade
1. *Source of Purchase*	Goods are bought **from the manufacturers or their agents**.	Goods are bought **from the wholesalers** or sometimes manufacturers.
2. *To whom Goods Sold*	Goods are sold to the **retailers**.	Goods are sold to the ultimate **consumers**.
3. *Quantity of Goods*	Goods are bought in **large** quantity.	Goods are bought in **small** quantity.
4. *Number of items to be dealt with*	Wholesalers generally deal in **one or few items**.	Retailers generally deal in a **variety of items**.
5. *Middlemen*	Wholesalers act as middlemen **between manufacturer and retailer**.	Retailers act as middlemen **between wholesaler and ultimate consumer**.
6. *Location*	Wholesale Trade is normally carried on **in the same area where other wholesalers deal in similar products**.	Retail trade is normally carried on **near the place of ultimate consumers**.
7. *Display of Goods*	Goods **need** not be displayed.	Goods **need** to be displayed.
8. *Purpose of selling*	Goods are sold for **resale**.	Goods are sold for **consumption or ultimate use**.
9. *Amount of Capital required*	**Large** amount of Capital is required.	**Small** amount of Capital is required.

Functions of Retailers

A retailer acts an important middlemen between wholesalers and ultimate consumers. He performs a dual role in the sense that on one hand, he provides an outlet for the suppliers and on the other he facilitates the sale of 'goods to a large number of customers.

While performing this dual role, he performs the following functions:

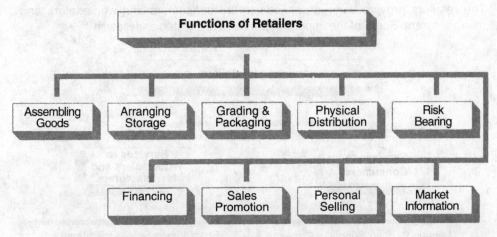

Let us discuss these functions of Retailers one by one.

1. **Assembling Goods** — The retailers procure different varieties of goods from wholesalers and hold adequate stock of these goods, so as to make them available to the ultimate consumers as and when required.

2. **Arranging Storage** — The retailers make arrangement for holding stocks to meet the needs of ultimate consumers from time to time.

3. **Grading and Packaging** — The retailers sometimes perform grading function (i.e. sorting out the production according to their quality or size or other factors). After performing grading function, they perform packaging function by packing the goods in convenient lots so that they can be sold to the ultimate consumers. For instance, fruit vendors purchase apples in containers (boxes), sort out on the basis of size and charge different rates for different sizes.

4. **Physical Distribution** — The retailers facilitate the physical distribution of goods from the place of wholesalers to the place of consumers.

5. **Risk Bearing** — The retailers have to bear the risk of loss which may be due to spoilage or damage of goods or deterioration of quality, in procuring and holding stock of goods till the time goods are sold.

6. **Financing** — The retailers perform financing functions by providing credit facilities to the regular customers.

7. **Sales Promotion** — The retailers perform sales promotion function through display of goods in attractive manner in window or shelf - to motivate the prospective consumers to buy.

8. **Personal Selling** — The retailers promote the sales through personal selling since they are in direct contact with the consumers. They can advise and guide the customers in the selection of goods and easily persuade them to buy the products.

9. **Market Information** — The retailers provide useful market information to the wholesalers and manufacturers regarding changes in tastes, fashion and preferences of the consumers, competing goods since they are in direct personal touch with the consumers.

Service of Retailers

The retailers provide various services to the consumers and wholesalers and manufacturers. Some of the important services are stated as follows:

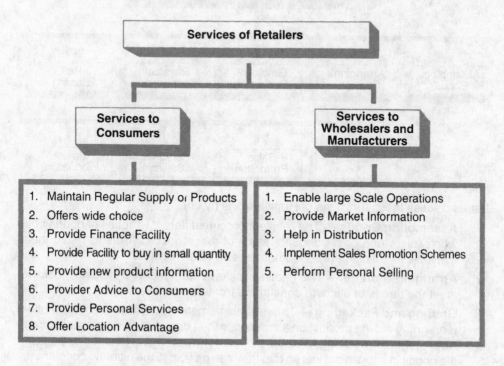

Let us discuss these services of Retailers one by one.

Services to Consumers

1. **Maintain Regular Supply of Production** — Retailers assure regular supply of goods to the consumers by maintaining adequate stock of goods. This enables the consumers to buy the goods as and when required according to their needs.

2. **Offer wide choice** — Retailers offer wide choice to customers by offering them different variety of goods manufactured by different manufacturers.

3. **Provide Finance Facility** — The retailers provide financial support to the regular customers by supplying goods to them on credit.

4. **Provide Facility to buy in small quantities** — The retailers provide their customers the facility of buying goods in small quantities as and when required according to their needs and ability to pay.

5. **Provide New Product Information** — The retailers provide information to their customers regarding new products through display of goods on shelves or in show-cases or through personal contract.

6. **Provide Advice to Consumers** — The retailers provide advice to the consumers regarding the quality, durability, price and timings of purchase of products.

7. **Provide Personal Services** — The retailers sometimes provide certain personal services like free home delivery, after sales service etc.

8. **Offer Location Advantage** — The retailers offer location advantage to the consumers by running their trade normally near the area of residential houses of ultimate consumers.

Services to Wholesalers & Manufacturers

1. **Enable large scale operations** — The retailers enable the wholesalers and manufacturers to carry on their operations on large scale by undertaking the sale of their products to the ultimate consumers.

2. **Provide Market Information** — The retailers enable the wholesalers and manufacturers to change their operations in accordance with changing market conditions by providing them useful information regarding changes in tastes, fashion, preferences of consumers, needs of customers, competing goods etc.

3. **Help in Distribution** — The retailers enable the wholesalers and manufacturers to reach the ultimate consumers who are scattered over different geographical regions by making goods available to consumers located in various regions.

4. **Employment Sales Promotion Schemes** — The retailers implement the sales promotion schemes (free gifts, coupons, contests etc.) introduced by the wholesalers and manufacturers.

5. **Perform Personal Selling** — The retailers promote sales through personal selling since they are in direct contact with the consumers. They can advise and guide the customers in the selection of goods and easily persuade them to buy the products. This is of course, a great help to the manufacturers and wholesalers.

Types of Retail Organizations

Retail organizations may be classified into two main categories (i) Itinerant Traders, and (ii) Fixed Shop Retailers. Further, Fixed Shop Retailers may be divided into two categories (a) Small Scale Retailers and (b) Large Scale Retailers.

The various types of retailers have been shown below:

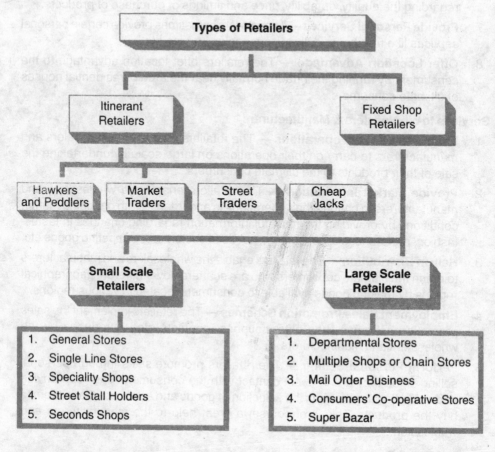

Let us these types of Retailers one by one.

ITINERANT RETAILERS – MEANING, TYPES

Meaning of Itinerant Retailers

Itinerant retailers are those who keep on moving from place to place to sell their goods. They do not have any fixed place of business. They deal in low priced consumer goods of regular use like toys, bangles, household utensils.

Types of Itinerant Retailers

Itinerant Retailers generally include hawkers, peddlers, market traders, street traders and cheap jacks.

(i)   **Hawkers and Peddlers** — Hawkers and Peddlers usually carry goods themselves in a basket or in shoulder bags or in push carts on wheels. They move about in residential areas and call out the names of articles they are selling. They also sell their wares in local trains and buses, in front of railway stations, at bus terminals and on roads crossings. They usually deal in goods of regular use such as vegetables, fruits, ice-cream, bangles. They normally do not carry different varieties of the same product.

(ii) **Market Traders** — Market Traders sell their goods at different places on fixed market dates. Weekly markets are usually held on different days of the week in different locations in many villages and towns. They move from one market to another in the neighbouring places on the particular days fixed for the market. They also include those retailers who set up stall, at 'melas' or fairs and exhibitions which are organized from time to time (say on Diwali festivals etc.)

(iii) **Street Traders/Pavement Traders** — Street Traders generally spread their goods on pavements at busy street corners or near railway stations or bus terminals. They generally deal in low priced products of regular use such as newspapers, magazines, stationery, footwear, fruits, vegetables etc. They sometimes put up temporary sheds or make shift platforms for display of goods.

(iv) **Cheap Jacks** — Cheap Jacks set up their place of business temporarily in a business locality and keep on shifting the location from one locality to another, depending upon the prospects of sale.

Services of Itinerant Retailers — They serve *either* at the consumers' door-step *or* in busy places through which consumers pass through. They save time and effort of customers in buying goods of ordinary use.

FIXED SHOP RETAILERS – MEANING, TYPES

Meaning of Fixed Shop Retailers
Fixed Shop Retailers are those who carry on their business in fixed shops where customers can easily reach and make their purchases.

Types of Fixed Shop Retailers
On the basis of scale of their operations, fixed shop retailers can be divided into two categories: (i) Small Scale Retailers (ii) Large Scale Retailers.

(i) **Small Scale Retailers** — Small Scale Retailers are those fixed shop retailers who carry on their business on a small scale and sell the goods in small quantities. They hold small stocks and carry on their business in fixed shops located in residential areas or market places. According to the nature of goods sold, the small retail shops may be divided into four categories as follows:

1. **General Stores** — These stores deal in different kinds of consumer goods of daily use. For example, provisions, bread, butter, milk, stationery, toothpaste, razors, blades, shaving Cream, bathing Soap, washing soap & powder. confectionary, soft-drink etc. Customers find it convenient to buy all their regulars requirements in one shop and save time and effort of going to different shops. These stores sometimes offer a facility of free home delivery or monthly credit to their regular customers.

2. **Single Line Stores** — These stores generally deal in a particular line of products such as ready-made garments (Children's, Men's and Ladies),

books (educational, general), medicines, shoes, stationery, electrical fittings, timber etc. They usually hold the stock of goods of different qualities, size, design etc. in the same product line. Customers find it convenient to buy their requirements from these stores due to the availability of different grades and sizes in the same product line.

3. **Speciality Stores** — These stores generally specialize in a single type of product instead of dealing in a line of products. For example, stores dealing in children's garments only, stores dealing in educational books only.

4. **Street Shops** —These shops are set up by fixing shelves on a wall or placing a table or making a platform or stand to display the goods. These shops are also known as 'street stalls'. Generally, low priced articles such as hosiery, pens, magazines etc are sold in these stalls. Usually they are located at street crossing or on main roads.

5. **Seconds Shops** — These shops sell second hand goods of different kinds like books, clothes, furniture etc. These shops enable the people who cannot afford to buy new things, to buy the required articles. Sometimes, rare articles such as old stamps, old books, are sold in these shops.

(ii) **Large Scale Retailers** — Large Scale Retailers are those fixed shop retailers who carry on their business on a large scale and sell the goods in small quantities. They hold large stocks of variety of goods. Large scale retailers include the following:

1. Departmental Stores
2. Multiple Shops *or* Chain Stores
3. Mail Order Business
4. Consumers' Co-operative Stores
5. Super Bazar

DEPARTMENTAL STORES – MEANING, OBJECTIVE, FEATURES, ADVANTAGES, LIMITATIONS

Meaning of a Departmental Store

A departmental store is a large scale retail store in which a wide variety of products are sold through separate departments under one roof. Each of the departments is like a separate shop which deals in a particular line of goods like garments, books, stationery, dress materials etc.

Objective of a Departmental Store

The objective of a departmental store is to provide a wide variety of goods to satisfy the requirements of the customers under one roof.

Features of a Departmental Store

A departmental store has the following features:

1. A wide variety of products are sold under one roof.
2. It has number of departments and each of the departments is like a separate shop which deals in a particular line of goods.
3. There is centralized selling but purchases may be made *either* centrally *or* by the departmental managers.
4. These are located in contral places so that they are within short distances of residential localities.
5. All departments are owned and centrolled by a single business organization.
6. These stores provide a number of services and facilities like telephone, toilets, rest rooms, crechés, credit facilities, home delivery facilities.
7. It requires huge investment since large stocks of varieties of products are maintained.

Advantages of A Departmental Store

The following are the advantages of a departmental store:

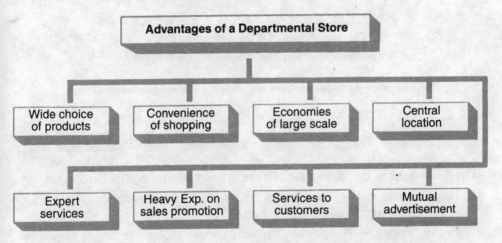

Let us discuss these advantages of a departmental store one by one.

1. **Wide choice of Products** — These stores enable the customers to have a wide choice of products since these stocks deal in a wide variety of products from different manufacturers.
2. **Convenience of Shopping** — These stores enable the customers to buy a large variety of goods under one roof and thus enable them to save the time and effort of making purchases at different places.
3. **Economies of Large Scale** — These stores are in position to take the advantages of large scale operations particularly in respect of purchase of goods since a large volume of goods are bought and sold in departmental stores.

4. **Central location** — These stores are in position to serve large number of customers during the day since these stores are located in central places so that they are within short distance of residential localities.

5. **Expert Services** — These stores are in position to employ specialization having expert knowledge of buying, sales promotion, cost control etc. because of their sound financial position.

6. **Heavy Expenditure on Sales Promotion** — These stores are in position to spend heavy expenditure on sales promotion because of their sound financial position.

7. **Services to Customers** — These stores provide a numbers of services like telephone, toilets, rest rooms, creches, credit facilities, home delivery facilities.

8. **Mutual Advertisement** — Each department of these stores acts as advertising media for other department since the customers who visit a particular department are often attracted by goods displayed in other departments and hence they may purchase items others than those they had originally in mind.

Disadvantages *or* Limitations of a Departmental Store

The following are the disadvantages *or* limitations of departmental stores:

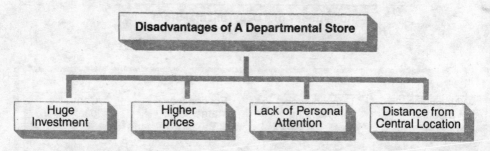

Let us discuss these disadvantages of a departmental store one by one.

1. **Huge Investment** — These stores require huge investment since large stocks of varieties of products are maintained.

2. **Higher Prices** — The prices charged by these stores are higher since the expenses of departmental stores on advertising, windows display, provision of facilities etc. make their operating cost relatively higher than small scale retail shops.

3. **Lack of Personal Attention** — There is lack of personal attention since it often becomes difficult to provide personal attention because of large scale operations.

4. **Distance from central location** — These stores are not suitable for those customers who are far away from the central location of these stores and who want to buy articles of daily use. They will prefer going to small retail shops situated in their residential areas.

MULTIPLE SHOPS (CHAIN STORES) – MEANING, FEATURES, ADVANTAGES, LIMITATIONS

Meaning of Multiple Shops or Chain Stores

Multiple Shops or Chain Stores refer to retail shops owned and controlled by a single organization and located in different parts of a city or throughout the country, which deal in similar products at uniform prices. In India, chain stores have been established by a numbers of manufacturers companies like Raymonds, Bata Shoes, McDonald, National Textile Corporation etc.

Objective of Multiple Shops or Chain Stores

The objective of multiple shops or chain stores is to provide similar products at uniform prices to various customers staying in different parts of a city or country.

Features of Multiple Shops or Chain Stores

The multiple shops or chain stores have the following features:

1. These shops are owned and controlled by a single organization.
2. These shops deal in a limited variety of products.
3. These shops deal in the uniform line of products.
4. The goods are centrally purchased or produced.
5. The goods are supplied to these shops by the central office.
6. The goods are sold at uniform prices fixed by the central office.
7. There is uniformity in the outward appearance and interior display of products at all these shops.
8. Goods are sold for cash only.

Advantages of Multiple Shops or Chain Stores

The following are the advantages of multiple shops or chain stores:

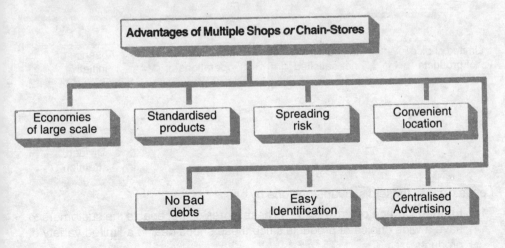

Let us discuss these advantages one by one.

1. **Economies of Large Scale** — These shops are in position to take the advantages of large scale operations particularly in respect of purchase/production of goods, since a large volume of goods are bought and sold in multiple shops.

2. **Standardised Products** — These shops assure the customers about the quality of the products since these shops deal in standardised products only.

3. **Spreading Risk** — The risk involved in business operations is minimized by spreading the risk over the different shops located in different areas. For instance, the product not in demand in a particular shop may be shifted to another shop, particular shop not doing well may be shifted or closed altogether.

4. **Convenient location** — These stores are in position to serve large number of customers during the day since these shops are located near the residential localities or in busy shopping centres.

5. **No Bad Debts** — These is no risk of any bad debt in such shops since the goods are sold for cash only.

6. **Easy Identification** — These shops are easily identifiable by the customers and others since there is uniformity in the outword appearance and interior display of products of all these shops.

7. **Centralised Advertising** — These shops are in position to take the advantages of large scale centralized advertising since most of the advertising for all these shops is done by the central office.

Disadvantages/Limitations of Multiple Shops or Chain Stores

The following are the disadvantages/limitations of the Multiple Shops *or* Chain Stores:

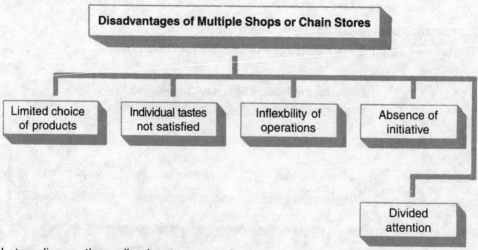

Let us discuss these disadvantages one by one.

1. **Limited Choice of Products** — These stores do not enable the customers to have a wide choice of products since these shops deal in a limited variety of products.

2. **Individual tastes not satisfied** — These stores are not in position to satisfy the individual tastes of the customers since these shops deal in standardized products only.

3. **Inflexibility of Operations** — These shops do not offer any inflexibility of operations to the shop managers since almost all decisions (e.g. Products to be produced/purchased, price, outward appearance, etc.) are taken by central office.

4. **Absence of Initiative** — The branch manager of a multiple shop do not have any initiative because he has to follow only the instructions given by central office.

5. **Divided Attention** — The organization which own and manage such shops may not be in position to carry out the function of production and retail distribution with equal efficiency since their attention is divided between production and distribution.

Distinction between Departmental Stores and Multiple Shops

The departmental stores differ from the multiple shops in the following respects:

Basis of Distinction	Departmental Stores	Multiple Shops
1. **Object**	The objective of these stores is to **provide a wide variety of goods** to satisfy the requirements of the consumers under one roof.	The objective of these stores is **to provide similar products at uniform price** to various consumers staying in different parts of a city or country.
2. **Variety of Products**	These stores deal in a **wide variety** of production.	These shops deal in a **limited variety** of products.
3. **Volume of Investments**	These stores require **huge** investment since large stocks of varieties of product are maintained.	These shops require relatively **small** investment since goods not in demand in one shop may be shifted to other shop.
4. **Cash Sales/Credit Sales**	These stores usuallly sell the goods on **credit** basis.	These shops sell the goods for **cash** only.
5. **Location**	These stores are located at **central places**.	These shops are located *near* **residential localities** or in busy markets.
6. **Prices**	The prices charged by these stores are **relatively higher** because of high operating cost.	The prices charged by these shops are **relatively lower** because of low operating cost.
7. **Centralisation of selling**	There is **centralised** selling of products.	There is **decentralised** selling of products.

8. **Centralisation of Purchase**	Purchases may be made **either centrally** *or* by the **departmental** managers.	There is **centralised** buying of products.
9. **Spreading of Risk**	Risk is **relatively greater** in departmental stores since its success depends on the prosperity of a particular location.	Risk is **relatively lower** in multiple shops since the risk is spread over the different shops located in different areas.
10. **Types of customers**	These stores attracts customer from **higher income** groups.	These stores attracts customers from **all categories** of income groups.

MAIL - ORDER BUSINESS (MOB) – MEANING, FEATURES, ADVANTAGES, LIMITATIONS, TYPES

Meaning of Mail Order Business (MOB)

Mail Order Business is one of the forms of retailing in which business transactions are made through postal communication without any personal contract with the buyers. It consists of receiving orders by mail and delivery of goods by parcel post. The sellers approach the prospective buyers through newspapers, magazines, televisions, circular letters, booklets etc. Customers are invited to send their orders by post to the address of the mail order house. After receipt of order, goods are properly packed and a parcel is delivered to the post office with the instruction that the same be delivered to the buyers on payment of the price. After the receipt of the price, price is remitted to the sender of goods. This service of the post office is known an 'Value Payable Post' (V.P.P.).

Thus, Mail Order Business consists of the following activities:

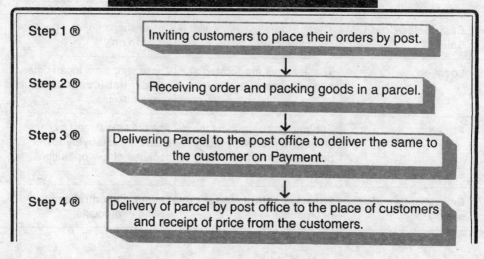

Activities Involved in Mail Order Business

Step 1 ® — Inviting customers to place their orders by post.

Step 2 ® — Receiving order and packing goods in a parcel.

Step 3 ® — Delivering Parcel to the post office to deliver the same to the customer on Payment.

Step 4 ® — Delivery of parcel by post office to the place of customers and receipt of price from the customers.

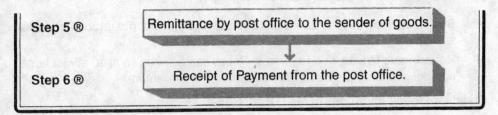

| Step 5 ® | Remittance by post office to the sender of goods. |
| Step 6 ® | Receipt of Payment from the post office. |

Features of Mail Order Business

Following are the features of Mail Order business:

1. Sales Orders are received by mail.
2. Goods are delivered by parcel post.
3. Payment for goods is received through post office.
4. Generally, standard consmer goods with trade names or brand names are dealt with by mail-order houses.

Advantages of Mail Order Business

Following are the advantages of Mail order Business:

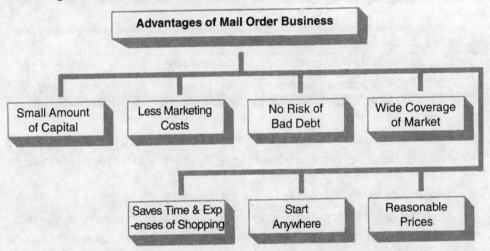

Let us discuss these advantages of Mail Order Business one by one.

1. **Small amount of capital** — Mail order business can be started with small amount of capital since investment in holding large stock is not required.
2. **Less Marketing Costs** — In Mail Order business, cost of marketing is least since no middlemen is involved.
3. **No Risk of Bad Debts** — There is no risk of bad debts since the delivery of goods is against the payment to Post office.
4. **Wide Coverage of Market** — In mail order business a wide market can be covered by means of postal communications.
5. **Saves time and Expenses of Shopping** — It saves the time and expenses of shopping since customers are able to get their requirements at their own place.

6. **Start Anywhere** — It can be started anywhere the postal services are available.

7. **Reasonable Prices** — Reasonable Prices can be fixed so as to attract large number of customers since overheads costs are minimum

Disadvantages/Limitations of Mail Order Business

Following are the disadvantages *or* limitations of mail order business:

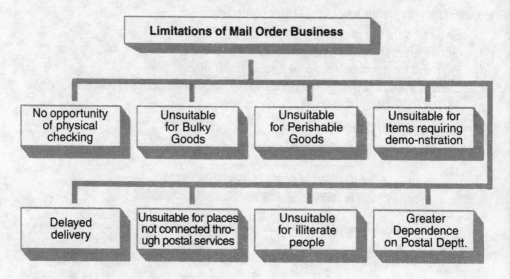

Let us discuss these limitations of Mail Orders Business one by one.

1. **No opportunity of physical checking** — The buyers do not have opportunity of physical checking of the goods.

2. **Unsuitable for Bulky Goods** — It is not suitable for bulky goods.

3. **Unsuitable for Perishable Goods** — It is not suitable for perishable goods.

4. **Unsuitable for Items requiring demonstration** — It is not suitable for those items which require demonstration before the buyers.

5. **Delayed delivery** — Customers do not get immediate delivery of goods since there is bound to be a delay in delivery through mail.

6. **Unsuitable for places not connected through postal services** — It is not suitable for those places which are not connected through postal services.

7. **Unsuitable for illiterate people** — It is not suitable for those who are illiterate.

8. **Greater Dependence on Postal Deptt.** — It is totally dependent on the postal department and hence bound to suffer in case of postal delays and postal strikes.

Types of Mail Order Houses

There are three types of mail order houses as follows:

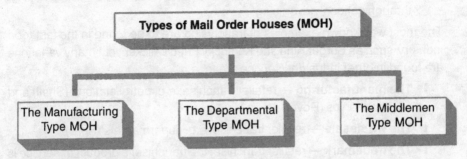

Let us discuss these types one by one.

1. **The Manufacturing Type MOH** — The manufacturing type mail order houses are those MOH where the manufacturers sell directly to the customers through mail.

2. **The Departmental Type MOH** — The departmental type mail order houses are those MOH where the departmental stores sell directly to the customers through mail, in addition to the selling through its different departments.

3. **The Middlemen Type MOH** — The middlemen type mail order houses are those MOH where the middlemen receive order by post and delivers the goods by post after buying from the manufacturers or wholesalers.

FRANCHISE

Modern Franchising originated in the United States

The first recorded business franchising was in the 1860s, during the American Civil War when Singer Sewing Machine Co developed a worldwide network to market their sewing machines. Today the franchise most well known throughout the world is McDonalds.

In 1977 eight firms, including the fast-food chain Wimpy, launched the British Franchise Association (BFA).

A typical franchise is when a company, for a fee, allows someone to sell its goods or services using its trademark (logo) and backup operation. Franchising is a method of marketing goods and services. The basic features of a typical franchising arrangement include:

1. The franchiser allowing the franchisee to use its name or brand,
2. The franchiser exercising continuing control over the franchisee,
3. The franchiser providing assistance to the franchisee, and
4. The franchisee making periodical payments to the franchiser.

    In franchising —

    ▌ A franchisee is the one who pays for the use of another company's name and the right to sell its products

I A franchiser is the firm that supplies the products, fits out the shop in the accepted company style and provides a wealth of marketing support, e.g. through national advertising.

The most well known examples of franchising are to be found in the fast food industry, such as Burger King and Kentucky Fried Chicken, but many variations are found in other industries/service areas, e.g.:

I **The manufacturing** — retailer franchise: e.g. petrol stations (Shell) and car dealerships (Rover)

I **The wholesale** — retailer franchise: e.g. supermarkets (Spar)

I **The trademark** — retailer franchise: the franchiser's product or service is marketed under a common trade name through outlets, e.g. Little Chef, Fast Frame, Body Shop.

Meaning of Franchise, Franchiser and Franchisee

A franchise arrangement is one in which a manufacturer grants someone the exclusive right to sell his product or services in specified areas subject to terms and conditions of an agreement.

The person who grants the franchise is called **'franchiser'**. The person to whom franchise is granted is called **'franchisee or franchise holder'**. The agreement between franchiser and franchisee is called **'franchise agreement'**.

Definition of A "Franchise"

Broadly, a franchise may be defined to include the following:

(a) where the franchisee is granted the right to operate a business according to a franchise system;

(b) where the franchisee has the right to use a trade mark, trade secret or any confidential information or intellectual property owned by the franchiser;

(c) where the franchiser has the right to administer continuous control over the franchise business;

(d) where the franchiser provides assistance in the form of provision of material, services, training, marketing and other business or technical assistance to the franchisee in the operation of his business

(e) where the franchisee operates the business separately from the franchiser and no relationship of partnership, service contract or agency exists between the parties; and

(f) in return for the grant of such rights, the franchisee is required to pay a fee, royalty or other form of consideration.

In this regard, labelling the business differently, such as "distributors" or "agents" will not assist if the nature of the business falls substantially within the definition of a "franchise" above. Examples of Franchise agreement include the following NIIT, APTECH, LCC, NIRULA'S.

Franchise Agreement

An agreement between franchiser and franchisee is called as "Franchise Agreement". Such agreement contains the various terms and conditions of franchise. The **examples** of some of these terms and conditions may be as under:

(a)   the franchise term must be for a minimum of 5 years

(b)   a compulsory renewal term in all franchise agreements subject to certain conditions

(c)   upon expiry, renewed franchise agreements to contain terms not less favourable than the original agreement

(d)   a compulsory cooling-off period of at least 7 working days in which time the franchisee can opt to terminate the agreement

(e)   to give an undertaking not to carry on a competing business during the term of the franchise and for 2 years after the expiration and/or termination of the Franchise Agreement

(f)   to give a written undertaking to the franchiser not to disclose confidential information pertaining to the franchise during the franchise term as well as 2 years after the expiration and/or termination of the Franchise Agreement

(g)   not to terminate the franchise agreement before its expiration date unless it is with "good cause".

Advantages of Franchising from the point of view of franchisee

1.   The franchisee is given support by the franchiser in respect of marketing and staff training.

2.   The franchisee may benefit from national advertising and being part of a well-known organization with an established name, format and product.

3.   The franchisee can expect support from the franchiser not only in the initial stages but also on a continuous basis.

4.   The initial outlay required by a franchisee will be less than that of a sole trader in the same field of business.

5.   A franchise allows people to start and run their own business with less risk. The chance of failure among new franchises is minimal as their product is a proven success and has a secure place in the market.

6.   Banks are usually more willing to lend money to a franchisee as there is documented information relating to the success of other franchisees with the same product.

7.   A franchisee keeps most of the profit.

Advantages of Franchising from the point of view of franchiser

1. The business can be expanded without having to invest large amounts of money on the many costs of expansion. The costs of new premises are met by the franchisee, who buys or leases premises from the franchiser. The cost of extra staff is met by the franchisee, who may also have to contribute to other costs, e.g. advertising.
2. A regular income is received through royalty payments from the franchisee.
3. Franchisers gain the economies of scale as a result of bulk buying from their suppliers.
4. They also make a profit on the supplies they sell to the franchisees.
5. Because franchisees have a financial stake in the success of the business they are likely to work very hard to make it succeed.
6. Most franchised businesses are profitable.
7. The franchiser retains control.

Disadvantages of Franchising from the point of view of franchisee

1. Franchisee has less independence than a sole trader. He may feel more like a manager than an owner.
2. He is required to make payment of royalties.
3. He may not be able to sell the business without the franchiser's approval, which is why it is important to have such aspects covered in the original contract.
4. Sometimes the franchisee is tied into buying all supplies from the franchiser when there may be a cheaper local alternative

Disadvantages of Franchising from the point of view of franchiser

1. The company's trade name and reputation can be tarnished if a franchisee does not maintain the standards.
2. There is an initial cost of the pilot operation, such as:
   (i) Getting specialist advice
   (ii) Setting up outlets in different locations and running them for at least 12 months to test the feasibility of going into full-scale franchising.
3. Ongoing costs of supporting the franchisee and national advertising.

Are there any risks involved in franchising?

Yes. The franchisee may not be capable of running its business properly, or it may not be sufficiently capitalised. In addition, the franchiser might fail to maintain a high quality level of continuing support services or it may make mistakes or policy decisions that may hurt the franchisee.

CONSUMER'S CO-OPERATIVE STORES – MEANING, OBJECTIVE, FEATURES, ADVANTAGES, LIMITATIONS

Meaning — Consumer's Co-operative Stores are retail stores run by Co-operative societies formed by consumers.

Objective — The objective of Consumers' Co-operative Store is to provide consumer goods at reasonable prices by eliminating middlemen in the distribution of products.

Features — The features of Consumer's Co-operative Stores are as under:

1. These stores are owned and managed by consumers.
2. These stores may deal in all types of consumer goods of daily use such as provisions, bread, butter, milk, stationery, medicine etc.
3. The goods are purchased from manufacturers or wholesalers.
4. The capital is raised by issue of shares to the members.
5. The management of the store is entrusted to an elected managing committee.
6. Each member has a single vote irrespective of the number of shares held by him.
7. These stores may sell goods to members as well as non-members.
8. Purchase Bonus is usually distributed to members on the basis of amount of purchases made by them.
9. Goods are usually sold for cash only.
10. Profit of the stores is distributed among the members by way of dividend.

Advantages — The advantages of consumers' co-operative stores are as follows:

1. **Reasonable Prices** — These stores provide consumer goods at reasonable prices since middlemen in the distribution are eliminated.
2. **Lower Marketing Costs** — The marketing costs of these stores are lower since no money is required to be spent on advertisement and other sales promotion activities.
3. **No Risk of Bad Debt** — These is no risk of bad debts since the goods are sold for cash only.
4. **Check on Monopolies & Wasteful Competition** — Monopolies & Wasteful Competition can be checked through such stores.
5. **Good Education of Co-operative Management** — These stores prove to be good education of co-operative management since such stores are managed on democratic style.

Limitations — The limitations of consumers' co-operative stores are as follows:

1. **Lack of Experience** — Usually the persons who manage such stores has lack of experience in managing business.
2. **Lack of Adequate Financial Resources** — The function of such stores is usually affected due to lack of adequate financial resources.
3. **Lack of Proper Warehousing Facilities** — The operation of such stores is usually affected due to lack of proper warehousing facilities.

4. **Greater Dependence in the Honorary Services** — The management of such stores is dependent on the honorary services of members.

SUPER BAZAR – MEANING, OBJECTIVE, FEATURES, ADVANTAGES, LIMITATIONS

Meaning — Super bazaars are large retail stores organized by co-operative societies which sell a wide variety of consumer goods under one roof.

Objective — The objective of super bazaar is to provide a wide variety of consumer goods under one roof at reasonable prices by eliminating middlemen in the distribution of the products.

Features — Super Bazar has the following features:

1. These stores are owned and managed by co-operative societies.
2. These stores deal in a wide variety of products under one roof.
3. The goods are purchased from manufacturers or wholesalers.
4. The capital is raised by issue of shares to the members.
5. The management of these bazaars is entrusted to an elected managing committee.
6. Each member has a single vote irrespective of the number of shares held by him.
7. These bazaars sell goods to members as well as non-members.
8. Goods are sold for cash only.
9. These stores are operated *either* on the principle of self-service *or* with separate counters served by salesman.
10. These stores are generally located at central places where large number of customers may reach.

Difference between Super Bazar and Super Market — Super Bazar is organized by a Co-operative society whereas the Super Market is generally established as a private sector organization.

Difference between Consumer Coperative store and Super Bazar — A consumer co-operative store is usually on a small scale whereas super bazaar is run on a large scale.

Advantages of Super Bazar — Following are the advantages of Super Bazar:

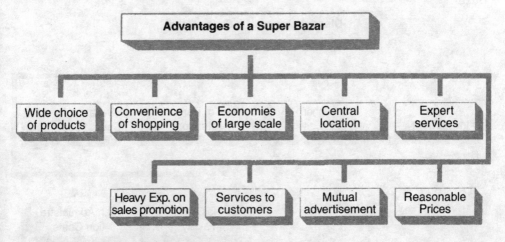

Let us discuss these advantages of Super Bazar one by one.

1. **Wide choice of Products** — These stores enable the customers to have a wide choice of products since these stocks deal in a wide variety of products from different manufacturers.

2. **Convenience of Shopping** — These stores enable the customers to buy a large variety of goods under one roof and thus enable them to save the time and effort of making purchases at different places.

3. **Economies of Large Scale** — These stores are in position to take the advantages of large scale operations particularly in respect of purchase of goods since a large volume of goods are bought and sold in departmental stores.

4. **Central location** — These stores are in position to serve large number of customers during the day since these stores are located in central places so that they are within short distance of residential localities.

5. **Expert Services** — These stores are in position to employ specialization having expert knowledge of buying, sales promotion, cost control etc. because of their sound financial position.

6. **Heavy Expenditure on Sales Promotion** — These stores are in position to spend heavy expenditure on sales promotion because of their sound financial position.

7. **Services to Customers** — These stores provide a numbers of services like telephone, toilets, rest rooms, creches, credit facilities, home delivery facilities.

8. **Mutual Advertisement** — Each department of these stores acts as advertising media for other department since the customers who visit a particular department are often attracted by goods displayed in other departments and hence they may purchase items others than those they had originally in mind.

9. **Reasonable Prices** — These stores provide consumers goods at reasonable prices since middleman in the distribution are eliminated.

Disadvantages/Limitations: Following are the disadvantages or limitations of Super Bazar:

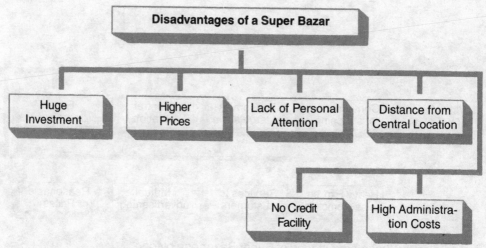

Let us discuss these disadvantages/limitations one by one.

1. **Huge Investment** — These stores require huge investment since large stocks of varieties of products are maintained.

2. **Higher Prices** — The prices charged by these stores are higher since the expenses on advertising, windows display, provision of facilities etc. make their operating cost relatively higher than small scale retail shops.

3. **Lack of Personal Attention** — There is lack of personal attention since it often becomes difficult to provide personal attention because of large scale operations.

4. **Distance from central location** — These stores are not suitable for those customers who are far away from the central location of these stores and who want to buy articles of daily use. They will prefer going to small retail shops situated in their residential areas.

5. **No Credit Facility** — These stores do not offer any credit facility since the goods are sold for cash.

6. **High Administration Costs** — Generally, the administration costs of such stores are high.

DIRECT MARKETING

Direct Marketing means marketing directly by manufacturers/wholesalers.

Direct Marketing can be done in various ways such as —

1. Through Mailing
2. Through own salesmen
3. Through owned managed shops
4. Through Telephone/Fax
5. Through Internet
6. Through Exhibitions/Fairs
7. Through Vending Machines

Retail sale of articles with the help of coin-operated automatic machines is known as automatic vending. Retailing on a large scale is possible in this way by placing machines at convenient locations like bus terminals, railway stations, airports, shopping centres, etc. This method of retail selling is very popular in western countries.

Cigarettes, razor blades, postage stamps, milk, ice-cream, soft drinks, soup, paperback books, newspapers, etc., are sold in cities through vending machines. Customers are required to insert necessary coins in a slot and press a button whereby the article is released automatically. The coins are collected from the machine periodically, and articles are put in as needed. Automatic vending facilitates buying of small items round the clock. There is no necessity of salesmen's services. However, the stocking capacity of machine is limited and there are risks of mechanical failures irritating the customers. Moreover, paper currency may not be used and coins of exact value are required to operate the machine.

In India, automatic vending has been used for limited purpose like selling postage stamps, flight insurance, milk, etc. It is not a popular retailing device in India due to the existence of a large number of small retail shops.

TELE-MARKETING

Tele shopping means shopping through Telephone. Under this arrangement information regarding the product and telephone number of marketers is provided to the public through television, directories, web-sites, hoardings, magazines and newspapers. In this case, the intending customer is required to dial the telephone number of the tele shop and to place the order. Tele marketer supplies the goods ordered at the place of the customer on receipt of the payment. In some cases, customers are given option to return the goods within prescribed time limit and to receive their money back if they are not satisfied with the product supplied.

For example:

Tele Brands
Worldwide
Ph. 1-600-11-8000 (For India)

INTERNET MARKETING

Internet Marketing means marketing through internet. Goods may purchased or sold using internet. E-commerce facilitates internet marketing.

───────────────── **EXERCISES** ─────────────────

VERY SHORT ANSWER TYPE QUESTIONS

1. State the meaning of 'Trade'
2. Name the categories of Trade on the basis of geographical limits of operation.
3. State the meaning of internal trade.
4. Name the categories of internal trade on the basis of scale of operations.
5. State the meaning of wholesale trade.
6. State the meaning of Retail Trade.
7. State the meaning Itinerant Retailers.
8. Define Departmental Store.
9. Define Multiple Shops.
10. What is meant by Mail Order Business?
11. Define Consumers' co-operative store.
12. Define Super Bazar.

SHORT ANSWER TYPE QUESTIONS

1. State the meaning and importance of trade.

2. What is internal trade? State its important features.
3. What is meant by wholesale trade? State its important features.
4. List the different types of wholesalers.
5. Briefly state the functions performed by a wholesaler.
6. Briefly state the services rendered by wholesalers to manufacturers.
7. Briefly state the services rendered by wholesalers to retailers.
8. What is meant by retail trade? State its important features.
9. Give three points of difference between wholesale trade and retail trade.
10. Briefly state the functions performed by a retailer.
11. Briefly state the services rendered by retailers to consumers.
12. Briefly state the services rendered by retailers to wholesalers/manufacturers.
13. List the various types of retail organizations.
14. List the various types of itinerant traders.
15. List the various types of fixed shop retailers.
16. List the various types of fixed shop retailers operating on small scale.
17. List the various types of fixed shop retailers operating on large scale.
18. Briefly explain the meaning and types of itinerant traders.
19. What is meant by Market Traders? How do they differ from Street Traders?
20. What is meant by speciality shops? How do they differ from single line stores?
21. What is Departmental Store? State its important features.
22. Give three advantages of a departmental store.
23. Give three disadvantages of a departmental store.
24. What is meant by 'Multiple Shops or Chain Stores'? State its important features.
25. Give three advantages of Multiple Shops.
26. Give three limitations of Multiple Shops.
27. Give three points of difference between Departmental Stores and Multiple Shops.
28. What is meant by 'Mail Orders Business'? State its important features.
29. Briefly explain the types of Mail Order Houses.
30. Define Consumers' Co-operative Stores. State its objective and important features.
31. Define Super Bazar. State its objective and important features.
32. State the basic difference between Super Bazar and Super Market.
33. State the basic difference between Super Bazar and Departmental Store.
34. Write short notes on:
    (a) Direct Marketing
    (b) Tele-Marketing
    (c) Internet Marketing
    (d) Franchise

LONG ANSWER TYPE QUESTIONS
1. Discuss the services rendered by wholesalers to manufacturers and retailers.
2. Distinguish between Wholesale Trade and Retail Trade.
3. Discuss the services rendered by retailers to consumers and wholesalers/manufacturers.
4. Discuss the various types of small scale retailers who run their fixed shops.
5. Explain the features, advantages and limitations of a departmental store.
6. Explain the features, advantages and limitations of Multiple Shops.
7. Distinguish between Departmental Store and Multiple Shops.
8. How is business transacted in mail order house? What are its advantages and limitations?
9. Explain the features, advantages and limitations of Consumers' Co-operative Store.
10. Explain the features, advantages and limitations of Super Bazar.
11. 'Consumers Co-operative stores, are formed to protect the consumers' common interests'. Discuss.

12 External Trade

MEANING OF EXTERNAL TRADE

External trade refers to buying and selling of goods and services between the nationals of different countries or trade between agencies of the governments of different countries. It is also known as foreign trade or international trade. It consist of export trade, import trade and entreport trade.

Export Trade — It involves the selling of goods and services to other countries. For example, when M/s. P.P. Jewellers, an Indian firm, exports gold plain jewellery to U.S.A., they are said to be involved in export trade.

Import Trade — It involves the purchasing of goods and services from other countries. For example, when M/s. Ratna Sagar, an Indian publisher, imports books from Frankfurt, they are said to be involved in import trade.

Entreport Trade — It involves importing the goods from one or more countries with the purpose of exporting them to some other country or countries. For example, when M/s Pustak Mahal, an Indian publisher imports some books from U.S.A. for the purpose of exporting them to Nepal, they are said to be involved in Entreport Trade. Singapore, Hongkong and Korea are important entrepot trade centres.

Visible Trade Vs. Invisible Trade

External trade may be visible trade or invisible trade.

Visible Trade — External trade in goods is referred to as *visible trade*. For example, when M/s. P.P. Jewellers, an Indian firm, exports gold plain jewellery to U.S. Jewellers, U.S.A. sales of goods would be regarded as visible exports and purchase of goods by U.S.A. firm would be regarded as visible imports.

Invisible Trade — External trade in services is referred to as *invisible trade*. For example, when M/s P.P. Jewellers avail of U.S. Shipping Services for transportation of goods, they have to pay for transport services. Purchase of services would be called invisible imports by India and sale of services would be called invisible exports by U.S.A.

Distinction between Home Trade and Foreign Trade

Home Trade differs from Foreign Trade in the following respects:

Basis of Distinction	Home Trade	Foreign Trade
1. **Where takes place**	Home Trade takes place **within a country**.	Foreign trade takes place **beyond the national boundaries of two or more countries**.
2. **People involved**	People involved in home trade are the **citizens of the same country**.	People involved in foreign trade are the **citizens of two or more countries**.
3. **Restrictions**	There is **little restriction** on home trade.	There are **many restrictions** on foreign trade.
4. **Currency to be used in payment**	Payment is made and received in the same **home currency**.	What the importer pays in his home currency has to be converted into **foreign currency** acceptable to the exporter.
5. **Mode of payment**	Payment can be made *either* in **cash** *or* by **cheque** on a national **bank** in case of home trade.	Payment can be made only **through the bank** in case of foreign trade.

IMPORTANCE OF FOREIGN TRADE

The differences in the quality and quantity of domestic resources available in different countries has given rise to foreign trade. The necessity of external trade arises mainly because no country is capable of producing everything equally efficiently for the consumption of its people and the development of its economy. This is due to the unequal distribution of resources and skills among different countries of the world on account of climate and geographical formation. Its importance lies in its advantages accruing to both the trading countries. The various advantages of foreign trade are given below:

Let us discuss these advantages of external trade one by one:

1. **Leads to Specialisation** — External trade enables each country to specialise in the production of those goods and services for which it has the greatest relative advantages as compared with other countries. The relative advantages arise because of the differences in the quantity and quality of resources available in countries on account of climate and geographical formation. Specialisation leads to increase in productivity and superior quality of goods and services. External trade facilitate the export of such specialised products. Thus, every country can derive the benefit of geographioal specialisations from external trade. For example, India has comparatively greater advantages for the production of agrobased products such as coffee, tea, sugar, textiles etc. Similarly some developed countries such as USA, Japan, Britain etc. have greater advantages for the production of industrial machinery, automobiles etc. Some gulf countries such as Iran, Libya, Iraq, Saudi Arabia etc. produce crude oil, petroleum etc. in abundance.

2. **Facilitates Economic Development** — External trade facilitates economic development of a country on the basis of import of those goods and services which it does not have and export of those goods and services which it can produce with relative advantages as compared with other countries. For

example, under-developed or developing countries can use the available natural resources with the help of imported machinery, equipments and technology from the developed countries like, UK, USA, Japan etc. It may be noted that external trade facilitates economic development not only of under-developed or developing countries but also of developed countries. It is on the basis of imports of raw-materials and export of manufactured goods that countries like UK, Japan etc. have achieved rapid economic development and growth.

3. **Equalises Prices** — External trade leads to equalisation of prices of commodities throughout the world markets after making allowances for transport and other costs. Whenever the prices of commodities tend to rise in a country, it can increase the level of its imports to check the rise in prices. Similarly, whenever prices of products decline, the trend may be counteracted by exporting the same. Thus, in the situation of surplus or shortage, the import and export of commodities often reduce violent fluctuations of the prices of those commodities.

4. **Facilitates the Development of Cultural Relations** — External trade facilitates the development of cultural relations since the people of a country when come in contract with people of other country, exchange their ideas, knowledge and skills. People develop not only business relations but also cultural relations among them.

5. **Generates Employment Opportunities** — External trade generates employment opportunities by facilitating the growth of agricultural and Industrial activities.

6. **Ensures Supplies in Case of Natural Calamities** — External trade ensures adequate supply of those commodities which are in short supply within the country due to natural calamities such as flood, drought, earthquake etc. For example, medicines and food can be imported from other countries during emergency.

7. **Improves Standard of Living** — External trade improves the standard of living of people in different countries by providing them through imports a variety of goods which can not be produced in the home country due to certain natural, physical or other limitations or can only be produced at a higher cost. Exchange of goods and consumption thereof leads to a higher standard of living of the people in the world.

DIFFICULTIES IN FOREIGN TRADE

The various difficulties which are faced by the parties involved in foreign trade are given below:

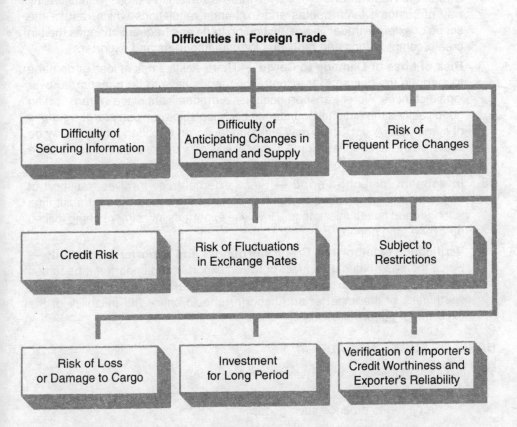

1. **Difficulty of Securing Information** — It is difficult to secure information about the suitability of products in the foreign market. This requires intensive market research on the potential sale of goods to be exported.

2. **Difficulty of Anticipating Changes in Demand and Supply** — It is difficult to anticipate changes in supply and demand conditions abroad. Such changes may be due to the entry of new competition, increased competition of local producers or changes in buyers' preferences etc.

3. **Risk of Frequent Price Changes** — There exists the risk of frequent price changes in the international market. Such changes may be due to the fluctuation in the exchange rates of the currencies of importing and exporting countries, changes in import duties or freight rates.

4. **Credit Risk** — The exporters often sell their products on credit and therefore have to bear the credit risk arising from the buyer's default, bankruptcy etc.

5. **Risk of Fluctuations in Exchange Rates** — The exporters and importers both are subject ot risk of fluctuations in exchange rates. The rate at which the

currency of importing country can be converted into the currency of exporter may cause losses to the exporter or importer. Devaluation of currency of importing country causes loss to importer and gain to exporter.

6. **Subject to Restrictions** — External trade is subject to various restrictions by way of customs tariff, quotas and exchange regulations which restrict the scope of external trade. The restriction on trade and frequent changes their in create complications and problems for both importers and exporters.

7. **Risk of Loss or Damage to Cargo** — There exists a risk of loss or damage to cargo in the course of transportation. goods have to be transported over long distances. Water transport occupies a predominant place in transporting goods across the national boundaries because ships can carry large volumes of cargo at low cost. Ships may sink due to storm or hidden rocks or may be captured by the enemies. Some of these risks may be covered through marine insurance but that also increases the cost of goods.

8. **Investment for Long Period** — Since external trade involves transport of goods over long distances except for neighbouring countries, the transit time is longer and hence this time gap involves exporter's investment being locked up over a long period.

9. **Verification of Importer's Credit Worthiness and Exporter's Reliability** — Since there is no direct contract between exporter and importer, it becomes necessary that the exporter must take adequate steps to verify the credit worthiness of the importer and importer should check the reliability of the exporter for supply of goods.

BASIS OF FOREIGN TRADE

The necessity of foreign trade arises mainly because:

(a) a country may not produce at all certain goods due to lack of resources required to produce such goods.

(b) a country may not produce certain goods as economically as other countries (In other words, if a country produces such goods, their cost will be relatively higher than that of other countries)

(c) a country may produce certain goods more economically than other countries (In other words, if a country produces such goods, their cost will be relatively lower than that of other countries)

The capability of a country to produce or not produce at relatively higher cost or lower cost depends upon the quality and quantity of domestic resources available in that country. Since no country is self sufficient and there are differences in the quality and quantity of domestic resources available in different countries, every country produces and exports only those goods in the production of which it has comparative cost advantage and imports only those goods which it can not produce at all or in the production of which it has comparative cost disadvantage. For example, India has comparatively greater advantages for the production of agrobased products such as coffee, tea, sugar, textiles, etc. and has become the exporter of these products. Japan has comparatively greater advantage for the production of electronic products and has become major exporter of these products.

The theory that explains the basis of foreign trade is called the theory of **'comparative cost advantages'**.

IMPORTANCE OF EXPORT TRADE

The importance of export trade lies in the fact that it is only through exports that a country can earn the foreign exchange which can be used in making payment for imports. The gap between imports and exports is called **'Balance of Trade'**. When imports are greater than exports, the balance of trade is said to be negative. Adverse balance of trade indicates the amount of foreign debt incurred by the importing country. Imports should be curtailed if foreign debt reaches beyond a reasonable limit.

MEANS OF EXPORT PROMOTION

. The following are the major means of Exports Promotion:

Let us discuss these means of export promotion one by one.

EXPORT PROMOTION THROUGH INSTITUTIONAL SUPPORT FOR EXPORTERS

A number of institutions in India are engaged in export promotion activities in their respective fields. Exporters should contact them for the necessary assistance.

1. **Export Promotion Councils (EPCs)** also known as registering authorities,

2. **Commodity Boards** assisting the exporters in the same manner as the Export Promotion Councils.

3. **Federation of Indian Export Organisations (FIEO),** Punjab Haryana Chamber Building, 4/2 Siri Fort Institutional Area, New Delhi 110016, is an apex organisation coordinating and supplementing the export promotional activities of various organisations and institutions.

4. **Indian Institute of Foreign Trade (IIFT),** B-21, Industrial Area, South of IIT, New Delhi 110016, develops and organises new training programmes, research and market studies in the field of foreign trade.

5. **Indian Institute of Packaging (IIP),** Plot No. 2, Marol Industrial Estate, P.B. 9432, Chakala Andheri (E), Mumbai 400093, for improving the standard of packaging for various benefits.

6. **Export Inspection Council (EIC),** 11th Floor, Pragati Tower, 26 Rajendra Place, New Delhi 10008, provides sound development of export trade through quality control and pre-shipment inspection.

7. **Indian Council of Arbitration (ICA),** Federation House, Tansen Marg, New Delhi 110001, promotes the use of commercial arbitration in India.

8. India Trade Promotion Organisation (ITPO), Pragati Bhawan, Pragati Maidan, New Delhi 110002 provides facilities concerning participation in fairs and exhibitions in India and abroad.

9. **Chambers of Commerce & Industry** help in issuing certificate of origin and taking up specific cases of exporters to the Govt.

10. **Bureau to Indian Standards (BIS),** 9, Manak Bhavan. Bhahdur Shah Zafar Marg, New Delhi 110002 is engaged in standard formulation, certification marking and laboratory testing.

11. **Export Directorate of Development Commissioner and Small Scale Industries.**

12. **Scope Shipping Standing Committee** functioning in the Ministry of Commerce, resolves the problems relating to quality, adequacy and cost of transportation problems faced by the exporters.

13. **Textiles Committee,** Textile Centre, Second Floor, 34 P D' Mello Road, Wadi Bandar, Mumbai 400 009, carries pre-shipment inspection of textiles and market research for textile yarns, textile machines etc.

14. **Marine Products Export Development Authority,** World Trade Centre, MG Road, Ernakulam South, Kochi 682016, helps in the development of marine products meant for export with special reference to processing, packaging, storage and marketing etc.

15. **India Investment Centre (IIC),** Jeevan Vihar, 4th floor, Parliament Street, New Delhi 110 001, advises and assists Indian businessmen for setting up of industrial or other joint ventures abroad.

16. **Freight Investigation Bureau** assists in solving problems relating to freight rates, shipping space and regular shipping facilities etc.

17. **Indian Govt. Trade Representative** at various important cities in foreign countries assist Indian exporters regarding promotion of Indian products to the World Market.

18. **Foreign Govt. Trade Missions** in India help in marketing Indian products to their markets.

19. **Directorate of Drawback** in the Ministry of Finance fixes drawback rates of items exported. It also formulates the procedure and documents required for claim of duty drawback.

20. **Board of Trade** in the Ministry of Commerce provides of forum for ensuring continuous dialogue with trade and industry in respect of major developments in the field of international trade.

21. **Office of the Director General of Foreign Trade (DGFT),** New Dehli is responsible for execution of the import and export policies of the Govt. of India. It has various subordinate offices in India.

22. **Director General of Commercial Intelligence and Statistics (DGCIS),** Council House Street, Kolkata 700001, is the primary agency for the collection, compliation and the publication of the foreign, inland and ancillary trade statistics and dissemination of various types of commercial information.

23. **State Liaison Officers** appointed by the State Governments develop export trade in goods produced in their States in consonance with the policies of the Central Government.

24. **Niryat Bandhus** are the nodal officers nominated by the States for export promotion work.

25. **Air Cargo Task Force** focuses attention and resolves problems faced by trade in the air freight industry.

26. **Export Facilitation Committee** set up by the Government, looks into the problems of generic nature faced by the exporters and which have not been resolved as a result of their interaction with the concerned agencies in the Ministry of Commerce or other Ministries/Departments.

FINANCIAL INCENTIVES FOR EXPORTS

The various financial incentives available to the exporters are as follows:

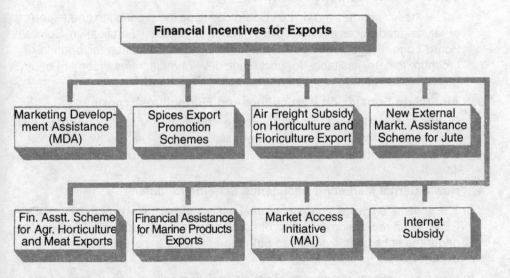

Let us discuss these financial incentives for exports one by one.

1. Marketing Development Assistance (MDA)

Assistance under Marketing Development Fund is provided by the Government for stimulating and diversifying the export trade. It is available in respect of the following purposes:

(i)   Market research, commodity research, area survey and research;

(ii) Export publicity and dissemination of information.

(iii) Participation in trade fairs and exhibitions;

(iv) Trade delegation and study teams;

(v)   Establishment of offices and branches in countries aborad; and

(vi) Grants in aid to Export Promotion Councils and other approved organisations.

The Federation of Indian Exporters Organisation (FIEO) disburses MDA grants for the following four activities on behalf of the Ministry of Commerce:

(i)   One person sale-cum-study tour(s) abroad;

(ii) Participation in fairs/exhibitions abroad;

(iii) Bringing out publications for use abroad; and

(iv) Adversiting in foreign media.

Export Promotion Councils/Commodity Boards/APEDA/MPEDA also grant MDA assistance for the above type of activities in conjunction with FIEO.

MDA for other activities like opening of foreign offices, setting up of warehouses and after sales services, installations abroad, research and development work on products etc. is disbursed directly by the Ministry of Commerce, Udyog Bhawan, New Delhi - 110 001.

2.   Spices Export Promotion Schemes

Under these schemes the Spices Board develops the production and exports of value added spices through spices through spice house certification, Spices Board Logo, Brand Promotion Scheme, Financial assistance for printing of brochure/folders, assitance for packaging development, reimbursement of air freight/courier charges for sending samples abroad etc.

3.   Air Freight Subsidy on Horticulture and Floriculture Exports

In order to make exports of horticulture (i.e. specified fresh fruits, and specified fresh vegetables) and floriculture products competitive in the world market, the Government grants air freight subsidy on selected fruits and floriculture items.

4.   New External Marketing Assistance Scheme for Jute

The scheme envisages grant of market assistance at the rate of 5-10% of the F.O.B. value realisation on export of specified diversified products. The benefit under the scheme is available to both manufacturer exporters and merchant exporters.

In order to promote the exports of agricultural, horticultural and meat products, Agricultural and Processed Food Products Export Development Authority (APEDA) provides financial assistance for the following purposes:

(i)   Feasibility surveys, consultancy and data base upgradation

(ii) Development of infrastructure

(iii) Export promotion and market development

(iv) Packaging development

(v) Quality control

(vi) Upgradation of meat plants

(vii) Organisation building and Human Resource Development

5. **Financial Assistance Scheme for Agricultural, Horticulture and Meat Exports**

The Agricultural Products Export Development Authority (APEDA) provides assistance upto 50 per cent of the cost of study subject to the ceiling of Rs 2 lakhs per beneficiary for undertaking feasibility studies and market surveys by growers, exporters and their organisations. The surveys may be conducted to find potential export markets/accessing market information and price trends, with respect to products, infrastructure requirements, etc. This assistance aims at encouraging exporters, growers and trade associations to develop their own market and information sources.

6. **Financial Assistance for Marine Products Exports**

There are a number of financial assistance schemes to promote export production and marketing of products of the fisheries sector. These schemes, inter *alia*, cover all stages or aspects like farming quality control, development of production infrastructure and equipment, transportation and air freighting of samples.

7. **Market Access Initiative (MAI)**

The Government would assist the industry in research & development, market research, specific market and product studies, warehousing and retail marketing infrastructure in select countries and direct market promotion activities through media advertising and buyer seller meets. A plan scheme has been evolved for this purpose.

8. **Internet Subsidy**

Export sector in India has also been given interest subsidy under which the working capital is made available by the banks to the export sector at a concessional or subsidised rates of interest. Under this scheme, working capital required for pre-shipment credit as well as post-shipment credit is provided to the export sector at cocessional rates of interest. This measure helps Indian exporters to reduce the working capital cost of export operation.

FISCAL INCENTIVES FOR EXPORTS

The following fiscal incentives accrue to the exporters:

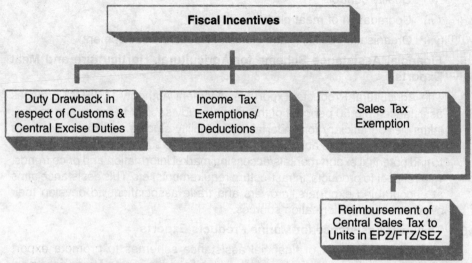

Let us discuss these fiscal incentives one by one.

1. Duty Drawback

Under the duty drawback scheme the export products get relief in respect of Customs and Excise Duties paid on raw materials and components used in their production. There are two types of rates of drawback.

(i) **All Industry Rates** are published in the form of notification by Govt. every year and are normally valid for one year.

The All Industry Rate is fixed on the basis of averaging principle. As such the All Industry Rate may not compensate different exporters fully for the Customs and Excise duties actually paid by them. Thus, Drawback Rules provide that where the All Industry Rate for any class of goods, is less than 4/5th of the duties actually paid in their manufacture, an application for fixation of Special Brand Rates may be made.

(ii) **Brand Rates** are fixed on the individual request of an exporter/manufacturer where the Govt. has not determined All Industry Rates in respect of any export product eligible for drawback or where the rate is not applicable because the manufacturer of the product has availed of certain duty free facilities but where sufficient duty paid inputs are also used. Fixation of brand rates is done under simplified procedure or normal procedures as may be aplicable.

Information on duty drawback rates is available from the concerned Export Promotion Council or from the Director (Drawback), Ministry of Finance, Jeevan Deep, Parliament Street, New Delhi - 110001.

How Payment of Drawback is made — For claiming the drawback on export of goods, the exporter is not required to file a separate application for granting the amount of drawback, as the drawback shipping bill itself treated as a claim and it is finalised after ensuring that the goods have been presented for examination by Customs and cleared for being put on board a vessel/air craft and ensuring that the necessary formalities to enable processing of claims are complied with. The payment of drawback claim is made directly by the Customs House/Central Excise Commissioner having jurisdiction over the port/airport/land customs stations through which the export is made.

2. Income Tax Exemptions & Deductions

The following exemptions and deductions at specified rates are available to the exporters and other foreign exchange earners under the Income Tax Act, 1961.

1. Deduction in respect of profits and gains from projects outside India[1] [Sec. 80HHB]

2. Deduction in respect of export turnover [Sec. 80HHC]

3. Deduction in respect of earnings in convertible foreign exchange [Sec. HHE]

4. Deduction in respect of export of Computer Software @ [Sec. 80HHE]

5. Deduction for export or transfer of Film Software etc. @ [Sec. 80HHF]

   @The Deductions under these provisions are being phased out with the deductible amount being reduced by 20% every year. No deduction under these provisions shall be allowed w.e.f. A.Y. 2005-06 onwards.

6. Ten Year Tax Holiday in respect of Newly Established Industrial undertaking in Free Trade Zones, Electronic Hardware Technology Parks and Software Technology Parks as well as Special Economic Zones, @ [Sec. 10A]

7. Ten Year Tax Holiday in respect of newly Established 100% Export Oriented Undertakings [EOUs] @ [Sec. 10B]

   @ Vide Finance Act, 2000 no deduction shall be allowed from A.Y. 2010-11 onwards.

3. Sales Tax Exemptions

(i) By virtue of section 5 of Central Sales Tax Act, any dealer who is registered with the Sales Tax authorities can claim the exemption from sales tax in respect of his sales made in the course of exports out of the territory of India.

(ii) The exporter may also buy the goods from dealer/manufacturer for the purpose of export trade without payment of sales tax by issuing Form H (where the selling dealer is in another state), to the selling dealer from whom he purchased goods for export. The basic condition to avail the sales tax exemption is that the exporter should be registered with the sales tax department.

After registration with the Sales Tax authorities, the exporter should apply in the prescribed proforma to the concerned sales tax officer for issuing Form H alongwith the prescribed documents. On receipt of the application, the sales tax officer issues Form H to the exporter. After the goods have been exported the exporter will fill in Form H in triplicate. One copy of the Form H will be retained by the exporter and remaining two copies will be given to dealer or manufacturer from whom the exporter has purchased the goods for export.

4. **Reimbursement of Central Sales Tax to units in Export Processing Zones (EPZs)/Free Trade Zones (FTZs)/Special Economic Zones (SEZs)**

   Units in Free Trade Zones/Export Processing Zones/Special Economic Zones are entitled to full reimbursement of Central Sales Tax paid by them on purchases made by them from Domestic Tariff Area (DTA) for utilisation in the production of goods for export. The supplies from DTA must be utilised for export production and may include raw materials, packing materials, consumables, capital goods etc. only against letter of authority issued by the Development Commissioner of the zone concerned.

PRICE QUOTATION AND TERMS OF SHIPMENT

In foreign trade, the terms of shipment are very important for concluding a contract to buy or sell goods. These terms reflect two aspects of the contract:

(i) Price Quotation or Sale Price

(ii) Terms of Shipment which determine the responsibility of the exporter to send goods to the importer.

Usually the following terms are used in foreign trade:

(a) **FOB Price** — FOB price indicates free on board. Under this price quotation, the exporter bears all cost of shipment till the goods are placed in the carrier—ship or aircraft.

(b) **C & F Price** — C & F indicates cost & freight. Under this price quotation, the exporter pays freight for carriage in addition to FOB cost. Therefore, C & F price = FOB price + Freight.

(c) **CIF Price** — CIF Price indicates cost, Insurance & Freight. Under this price quotation, the exporter pays insurance premium in addition to C & F price. Therefore, CIF = FOB + Freight + Insurance or CIF = C & F + Insurance. It may be noted that custom duty is levied on CIF Price after making adjustment for loading/unloading charges.

   Agreed Date of Shipment — The date by which goods must be shipped is known as '*agreed date of shipment*'. Export is required to ship the goods on or before this date of shipment. Importer is not legally bound to accept the consignment if goods are shipped after this date.

METHODS OF PAYMENT

The term of payment determine the manner of payment for goods by the importer. Depending upon the terms and conditions as agreed between the exporter and importer, the exporter can secure his payment in any one of the five methods given on next page:

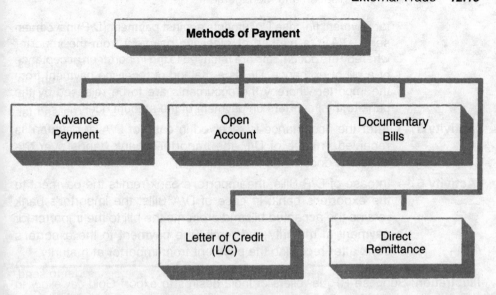

Let us discuss these methods of payment one by one.

1. **Advance Payment** — Under this method, exporter receives the payment *either* on signing of export contract *or* anytime before shipment is made by means of bank draft, mail / telegraphic transfer or international money order.

2. **Open Account** — Under this method, exporter receives the payment on periodic settlement of account. There exists risk in this method because there is no intermediary (i.e. Bank) to protect interest of the exporter.

3. **Documentary Bills Method** — Under this method, the payment by means of Bill of exchange is linked with the transfer of shipping documents. There may be two methods of receiving payment viz. D/A or D/P.

    (i) **D/A (or Documents Against Acceptance)** — It is a method of receiving payment from the importer whereby the documents are released on acceptance of a Bill of Exchange.

    (ii) **D/P (or Documents Against Payment)** — It is a method of receiving payment from the importer whereby the documents are released on payment of the Bill of Exchange.

Under this method the following activities are involved:

Activity 1	→	The exporter prepares a 'Bill of Exchange'. A bill of exchange is an order given by the exporter to the importer to pay the amount of sale value mentioned in it, generally through the bank.
Activity 2	→	The exporter hands over Bill of Exchange alongwith the other shipping documents to his bank.
Activity 3	→	The exporter's bank sends these documents to the importer's bank at the destination.
Activity 4	→	The importer's bank presents the Bill of exchange for acceptance [in case Documents against Acceptance (D/A) have been sent] or

for payment [in case Documents against payment (D/P) have been sent]. D/A is a method of receiving payment from the importer whereby the documents are released to the importer on acceptance of a bill of exchange. D/P is a method of receiving payment from the importer whereby the documents are to be released by the bank to the importers on payment of the amount due.

Activity 5 → After the acceptance is received in case of D/A or payment is received in case of D/P, the importer's bank hands over the transport documents to the importer.

Activity 6 → In case of D/P Bills, the importer's bank remits the payment to the exporter's bank. In case of D/A Bills, the importer's bank retains the accepted bill and presents the bill to the importer for payment at maturity and remits the payment to the exporter's bank after receiving the payment from importer at maturity.

Illustration: Suppose P.P. Jewellers of India desires to export Gold Jewellery to K.P. Jewellers of USA and decides to receive payment through Documentary Bills. The method of payment through documentary Bills operates in the following manner:

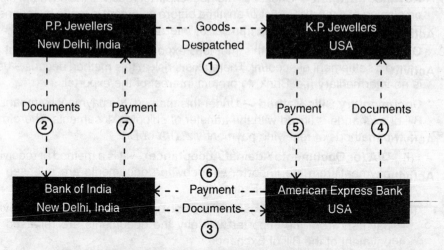

If the exporter wants to get the amount immediately, he can get the bill discounted with his bank. For this purpose, he has to issue a letter of hypothecation to the bank. A letter of hypothecation is a letter addressed to a bank alongwith the bill accepted by the importer. Through his letter of hypothecation, the exporter authorises the bank to sell the goods in case of dishonour of the bill by the importer. In the letter of hypothecation, it is also mentioned that if the sale proceeds of goods (after deducting expenses of selling the goods) exceeds the amount advanced, the exess will be returned to the exporter otherwise, short amount will be paid by the exporter to the Bank.

4. **Documentary Credit under Letter of Credit** — Documentary credit is a method of receiving payment from the importer whereby the importer arranges

for a bank to issue a letter of credit in favour of the exporter. A letter of credit is a document issued by importer's bank on behalf of the importer to authorise the negotiating bank to make payment of the amount stated therein to a party named therein or his order on presentation of documents mentioned in the letter of credit. There are four parties to a letter of credit as under:

(a) **Applicant:** Importer of goods

(b) **Issuing Bank:** Importer's bank who authorises negotiating bank to make payment

(c) **Advising and Negotiating Bank:** Exporter's Bank through which letter of credit is sent to the exporter.

(d) **Beneficiary:** Exporter of goods

Under this method, the following activities are involved:

Activity 1 →	The importer applies to his bank to issue a letter of credit in favour of exporter.
Activity 2 →	The importer's bank sends the letter of credit to its branch or negotiating bank in the exporting country.
Activity 3 →	The exporter hands over bill of exchange drawn upon importer alongwith the other shipping documents to his bank.
Activity 4 →	The exporter's bank scrutinises the documents and thereafter sends the documents to the importer's bank.
Activity 5 →	The importer's bank examines the documents with reference to requirement under the letter of credit and if finds them in order, sends the payment of Bill at sight or acceptance of the Bill after sight (i.e. date) to the exporter's bank.
Activity 6 →	The importer's bank debits the importer's account with the payment made and hands over the shipping documents to the importer.
Activity 7 →	The importer surrenders bill of lading/airway bill to the shipping company/ airline and gets the goods in return.

5. **Direct Remittance** — Under this method, the exporters sends both the goods and documents to title to the importer and the importer sends the payment to the exporter by means of bank draft, mail / telegraphic transfer or international money order. These exists risk in this method because there is no intermediary (i.e. Bank) to protect interest of the exporter.

EXPORT FINANCING BY BANKS

Banks provide financial assistance to the exporters at two stages viz. Pre-shipment stage and Post-shipment stage. Pre-shipment credit is given to the exporter to enable him to purchase raw materials, process them and convert them into finished goods for the purpose of export. Such credit is given on the basis of export order and letter of credit. Post-shipment credit is given to the exporters in the form of advances against bills of exchange or against shipping documents drawn under letter of credit.

EXIM Bank of India

Meaning — Export-Import Bank of India is a specialised financial institution for promoting foreign trade of India.

When Established — Exim Bank was established on Ist January 1982.

Objective — The main objective of Exim Bank is to coordinate the working of institutions engaged in financing of export and import.

Functions — The functions performed by Exim Bank include the following:

1. It provides export credit for medium-term and long-term where exporters have to offer sale on deferred credit basis.

2. It finances export of consultancy and related services.

3. It assists in setting up joint ventures in other countries and promotion of export oriented industries in India.

4. It undertakes export market studies.

5. It provides merchant banking services.

IMPORTANCE OF DOCUMENTS

The export-import trade cannot take place without certain documents such as Commercial Service, Bill of Lading / Airway Bill, Insurance Policy and Bill of Exchange. The importance of these documents lies in the fact that these documents protect the interests of both the exporter and importer. Through these documents, the importer is able to get the goods which he has ordered and the exporter is able to get the payment for goods exported.

SHIPPING DOCUMENTS

The main shipping documents are given below:

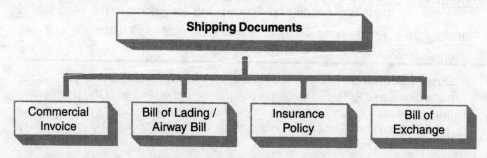

Let us discuss these shipping documents one by one.

1. Commercial Invoice

Who prepares — It is prepared by the exporter

Purpose — It enables the exporter to know what amount is due from importer and enables the importer to know what amount is due to exporter.

Contents — It contain the following information:

(a)   Name and Address of importer

(b)   Description of Goods

(c)   Number of packages

(d)   Weight and volume of packages

(e)   Per unit value of goods

(f)   Quantity of goods

(g)   Total Value

(h)   Terms of Shipment

(i)   Date of Shipment

(j)   Terms of Payment

(k)   Name of Ship / flight No

(l)   Export order no and date

2. Bill of Lading

Who Prepares — It is a document prepared by the shipping company when goods are sent by a ship.

Purpose — It is prepared to acknowledge the receipt of goods on board the ship at port of shipment and to the delivery the goods at port of destination on its surrender.

Contents — It contains the following information:

(a)   Name of Shipper (i.e. Exporter)

(b)   Name of Consignee (i.e. Importer)

(c)   Name of Notify party (i.e. the one whom information on arrival of the ship at the destination is to be sent by the shipping company)

(d)   Identification marks on packages

(e)   Description of Goods

(f)   Freight Charges

(g)   Number of Packages

(h)   Name of Ship

(i)   Weight and Volume of Goods

(j)   Port of Shipment

(k)   Port of Destination

(l)   Date of Shipment

(m)   Conditions of goods at the time of loading

Airway Bill

Who prepares — It is a document prepared by the Airlines when goods are sent by air.

Purpose — It is prepared to acknowledge the receipt of goods on airport of loading and to deliver the goods at airport of destination on its surrender.

Contents — It contain the following information:

(a)   Name and Address of Exporter

(b)   Name and Address Importer

(c)   Identification marks on packages

(d)   Description of Goods

(e)   Rate of freight and total freight

(f)   Number of packages

(g)   Weight and Volume of Goods

(h)   Airport of Loading

(i)   Airport of destination

(j)   Flight No.

(k)   Date of Departure

3. Insurance Policy

Who prepares — It is issued by the Insurance company.

Purpose — It is taken to cover the risks of loss or damage to goods in transit. In case of insurance, the loss can be recovered from the insurance company but in case of no insurance, the loss is to be borne by the owner (i.e. Exporter or Importer) depending upon the terms and conditions of contract of sale.

Who takes — Under CIF contract, insurance policy is taken by the exporter while under FOB contracts, insurance policy is generally taken by the importer.

Types -- There are different types of insurance policies to cover different types of risks in foreign trade.

4. Bill of Exchange

Who prepares — It is drawn by the exporter upon importer.

Purpose — In case of D/A, the purpose is to obtain the acceptance of the importer before the release of shipping documents and to receive payment at maturity date.

In case of D/P, the purpose is to obtain the payment from the importer before the release of shipping documents.

Contents — It contains the following information:

(a)   Name of Drawer (i.e. Exporter)

(b)   Name of Drawee (i.e. Importer)

(c)   Name of Payee

(d)   Date of Drawing

(e)   Term of Bill (At sight or after date)

(f)   Place of Payment

EXPORT TRADE PROCEDURE

When goods are exported to a foreign country, the exporter has to follow the procedure prescribed by the government of exporting country. Export trade procedure differs from country to country depending upon the existing policy of that country. The general procedure for exports from India involves the following stages:

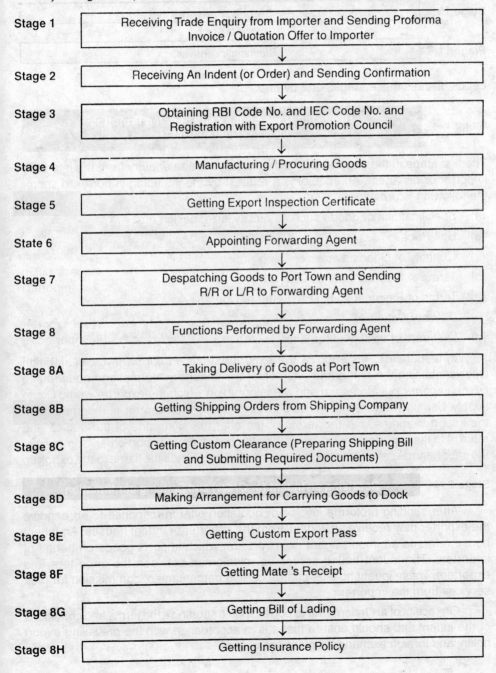

Stage 1	Receiving Trade Enquiry from Importer and Sending Proforma Invoice / Quotation Offer to Importer
Stage 2	Receiving An Indent (or Order) and Sending Confirmation
Stage 3	Obtaining RBI Code No. and IEC Code No. and Registration with Export Promotion Council
Stage 4	Manufacturing / Procuring Goods
Stage 5	Getting Export Inspection Certificate
State 6	Appointing Forwarding Agent
Stage 7	Despatching Goods to Port Town and Sending R/R or L/R to Forwarding Agent
Stage 8	Functions Performed by Forwarding Agent
Stage 8A	Taking Delivery of Goods at Port Town
Stage 8B	Getting Shipping Orders from Shipping Company
Stage 8C	Getting Custom Clearance (Preparing Shipping Bill and Submitting Required Documents)
Stage 8D	Making Arrangement for Carrying Goods to Dock
Stage 8E	Getting Custom Export Pass
Stage 8F	Getting Mate 's Receipt
Stage 8G	Getting Bill of Lading
Stage 8H	Getting Insurance Policy

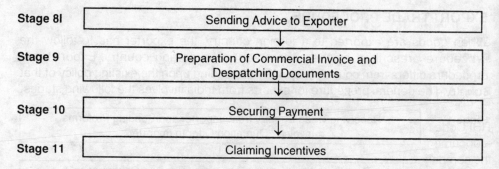

Stage 8|	Sending Advice to Exporter

↓

Stage 9	Preparation of Commercial Invoice and Despatching Documents

↓

Stage 10	Securing Payment

↓

Stage 11	Claiming Incentives

Let us discuss these stages one by one:

Stage 1 → **Receiving Trade Enquiry and Sending Proforma Invoice / Quotation Offer**

The first stage in the export trade is the receipt of trade enquiry from the intending importer or his agent. An enquiry is a request by the intending importer to supply the following information:

(a) Specifications of goods such as quality, size, design etc.

(b) Unit Price

(c) Quantity of Goods available

(d) Terms of Shipment (FOB, C&F, CIF)

(e) Terms of Payment (D/P, D/A, Letter of Credit)

(f) Delivery Schedule

(g) Last date of validity of the offer

In response to his enquiry, the exporter sends Proforma Invoice/Quotation Offer containing the name and address of the importer, information enquired into by the importer (as aforesaid) and the information which the exporter would like to supply. Usually three copies of the offer are sent by the exporter to the importer. If the importer agrees with the terms of the offer, he signs one of the copies and return it to the exporter. After signing, the offer becomes an export order. Sometimes, the importer makes out his own indent (or order) and sends the same to the exporter.

Stage 2 → **Receiving an Indent (or Order) and Sending confirmation**

After sending proforma invoice or quotation offer in response to an enquiry, the exporter may receive an 'Indent' from the importer or indent houses. An indent house refers to an import agent or import firm which imports goods on behalf of importers. The indent house serves as middlemen between the importers and exporters. These indent houses charge certain percentage of commission for their services from the importer.

On receipt of an 'Indent', the exporter should scrutinise the terms and conditions of the indent and should ensure that it is in accordance with the prevailing export policy and foreign exchange regulations of India.

If terms and conditions of the order are acceptable, a confirmation in writing giving the details of the order, terms and conditions etc. should be sent to the buyers at the earliest.

Stage 3 → **Obtaining RBI Code No. and IEC Code No. and Registration with export Promotion Council/Commodity Board**

RBI Code No. is allotted by the Reserve Bank of India on the basis of submission of a document called CNX form in duplicate alongwith a report of financial standing of the company given by the company's bankers. RBI co-ordinates the receipt of foreign exchange by the exporting companies and requires every companies to obtain RBI Code No. before entering into export business. RBI Code No. is required to be mentioned in different documents for obtaining permission from the custom authorities for shipment of goods. RBI Code No. is permanent and there is no need to renew it.

Importer Exporter Code number (IEC) is allotted by Joint Chief Controller of Imports and Exports (JCCI&E) on the basis of submission of a document called IEC Form in triplicate to the concerned office of JCCI&E. JCCI&E co-ordinates the grant of export and import licences. Such code number allotted to a person is valid for import of any commodity by that person subject to restrictions announced from time to time.

For obtaining export incentives (e.g. Cash compensatory Support, REP licence), an exporting company is required to get itself registered with the concerned Export Promotion Council/Commodity Board which looks after the export promotion of specified products. Export promotion agency issues a Registration-*cum*-Membership certificate (RCMC) on the basis of submission of a document called Registration-*cum*-membership certificate Form alongwith a certificate from the exporter's bank and membership fee. Such registration remains valid for four years. Registered exporters are required to submit quarterly reports about exports made by them.

Step 4 → **Manufacturing/Procuring Goods**

At this stage, the exporter manufacturers the goods or procures the goods from the market and get those goods packed strictly in accordance with the instructions given in the export order.

Step 5 → **Getting Export Inspection Certificate**

After the required goods have been manufactured/procured and packed in accordance prescribed specification, the exporter is required to make an application to export Inspection Agency to get Expert Inspection certification after the inspection of goods. An inspector is deputed by the Inspection Agency to inpect the export consignment. If the goods confirm to the prescribed specification, an Inspection Certificate is issued by the Inspection Agency.

Step 6 →

Appointing Forwarding Agents

After getting export inspection certificate, the exporter who does not want to complete the further formalities in this regard himself, appoints forwarding agents.

Stage 7 →

Despatching Goods to Port Down and sending the R/R or L/R to Forwarding Agent

The exporter sends the goods by rail or by road to the port town from where these are be shipped and receives Railway Receipt (RR) (in case goods are sent by rail) or Lorry Receipt (LR) (in case goods are sent by road). This receipt is sent to the Forwarding Agent after endorsing the same in his favour.

Stage 8 →

Functions Performed by Forwarding Agent

(i) **Taking delivery of goods at port town** — When the goods reach the port town, the agent takes the delivery of the consignment from the railway/truck on presentation of Railway receipt/Lorry receipt and arranges for its storage in the warehouse.

(ii) **Getting Shipping Order from shipping company** —To get the space reserved in the ship for loading goods, the agent signs an agreement with the shipping company for the issue of the shipping order which will enable him to put the goods on board the ship. The shipping order contains instructions to the captain of the ship to receive the specific quantity of goods from the exporter mentioned therein. If the consignment is very big, the exporter may charter a whole ship or major part of the ship. The agreement to hire the whole ship or major part of the ship is known as 'Charter Party'.

(iii) **Getting Custom Clearance** —To get custom clearance, the agent is required to—

(a) *Prepare three copies of shipping bill.*

Shipping bill contain the following information:

— Exporter's name and address

— Port of loading

— Port of Discharge

— Name of Ship

— Identification Marks on Packages

— Description of Goods

— Value of Goods

— Country of Destination

There are three types of shipping bills.

(i) White Shipping Bill	for duty free goods
(ii) Yellow Shipping Bill	for dutiable goods
(iii) Green Shipping Bill	for duty drawback goods

(b) *Submit the following documents to Custom Authorities :*

(i) Three copiers of Shipping Bill

(ii) AR-4 form (regarding excise duty payment)

(iii) G.R. form (declaring value of goods)

(iv) Original Order

(v) Letter of Credit

(vi) Commercial Invoice

(vii) Packing List (needed for inspection of goods)

(viii) Declaration form (a formal announcement by the exporter that the particulars entered in the shipping bill are in conformity with the export order)

(c) *Make Payment of Export Duty (in case of dutiable goods)*

(d) *Obtain the permission to bring the goods to the dock*

(iv) **Making Arrangement for carrying the goods to the dock** The agent makes arrangement for carrying the goods to the dock. To get the Dock Receipt, he is required to —

(a) *Prepare two copies of 'Dock Challan'*

(b) *Submit the following documents to the Dock Authorities*

— Two Copies of 'Dock Challan'

— One Copy of Shipping Bill

— One Copy of Shipping Order

(c) *Make Payment of Dock Charges.*

(v) **Getting Custom Export Pass or An endorsement 'Let Ship'** — After the goods have been carried to the dock but before the goods are actually loaded, the goods are physically examined by the custom office on the basis of declaration given in the Shipping Bill. If the custom officer is satisfied, he gives permission to load the goods on the ship by issuing a 'Custom Export Pass' or an endorsement 'Let Ship' on the duplicate copy of the shipping bill.

(vi) **Getting Mate's Receipt** — When goods are loaded on the ship, the mate (captain's assistant) of the ship issues a receipt in the acknowledgement of the goods after examining the packing and counting of the packages. This receipt is called the 'Mate's Receipt'. The mate issues a **clean receipt** if, he is satisfied with the packing of the goods *or* **foul receipt** if, he is not satisfied. The mate's remark on foul receipt is transferred to the bill of lading when the exporter gets it in exchange for the mate's receipt. Mate's receipt is very important document because it becomes the basis for the final transport document i.e. Bill of Lading.

(vii) **Getting Bill of Lading** — After getting Mate's Receipt, the agent goes to the office of the shipping company and gets the Bill of lading in exchange of Mate's Receipt. When the freight is paid in advance, the bill of lading is marked 'Freight paid'. When the freight is payable at the port of destination, the bill of lading is marked, 'Freight forward'. A bill of lading is a document by which the shipping company acknowledges the receipt of goods on board the ship. It contains the terms and conditions on which goods are to be delivered to the port of destination. It serves as an evidence of the terms of contract of afreightment between the sender of goods and the shipping company. It is a document of title to the goods without which goods can not be claimed. It can be enclosed to transfer the ownership of the goods to another. It may be noted that the bill of lading is **not a negotiable instrument** because the transferee's claim to the goods can never be better than the transferor's claim. If a bill were stolen and transferred to a third party, the third party could not claim legal right to the goods.

Distinction between Bill of Lading and Charter Party

Bill of Lading differs from Charter Party in the following respects:

Basis of Distinciton	Bill of Lading	Charter Party
1. Acknowledgement or Agreement	Bill of lading is an **acknowledgement** of the receipt of goods taken on board in the ship.	Charter Party is a **formal agreement** with the owner of the ship.
2. When issued?	It is issued only when entire **ship is not hired**.	It is issued only when entire **ship is hired**.
3. Whether can be Endorsed?	It **can be** endorsed in favour of a third party.	It **can not** *be endorsed* in favour of a third party.
4. Whether can be accepted as Security?	It **can be** accepted *as security* to avail of loan facility.	It **cannot** *be accepted as security* to avail of loan facility.
5. Loading Time	It does **not mention** loading time.	It **mentions** loading time.
6. Whether it is a Document of title of goods?	**It is** a document of title of the goods.	It is **not** a document of title of goods.
7. Whether it contains Terms?	It **may or may not** contain any term.	It **contains** all the terms of contract.

(viii) **Getting Insurance Policy** — Wherever required, the agent must get the goods insured for the various types of risks involved in transit and obtain insurance policy.

(ix) **Sending Advice to Exporter** — After the goods are placed an board, the agent informs the exporter about the shipment of goods and other related matters and sends the following documents alongwith a statement showing his expenses and remuneration to the exporter:

  (a) Bill of Lading or Charter Party

  (b) Copy of invoice duly attested by the Custom Authorities

  (c) Copies of the Shipping Bill

  (d) Duplicate copy of A R Form

  (e) Duplicate copy of G R Form

  (f) Original Export Order

  (g) Original Letter of Credit

Stage 9 →   **Preparing Commercial Invoice and Despatching Documents**

After receiving the necessary documents from the forwarding agent, the exporter prepares a Commercial Invoice also known as an export advice/foreign advice. It is prepared in triplicate according to the agreed terms and conditions of sale. Then, the exporter sends a shipment advice to the importer directly or through bank, alongwith the following documents:

  (a) Commercial Invoice

  (b) Bill of Exchange

  (c) Bill of Lading

  (d) Insurance Policy (if contract is on CIF basis)

  (e) Packing List

  (f) Any other document required by the importer.

Stage 10 →   **Securing Payment**

The exporter has to secure the payment of export dues either by means of documentary bills of exchange (D/P or D/A) or documentary credit under letter of credit.

Stage 11 →   **Claiming Incentives**

The last stage in export procedure is for the exporter to claim the export incentives (if any available). An exporter is entitled to claim export incentives offered by government to promote exports such as import replenishment, cash compensatory support, drawback of import duty and excise duty.

  (a) **Import Replenishment** refers to the issue of import licence to the exporters for import of raw materials required to produce export goods.

(b) **Cash compensation** is given to support the export of specified products.

(c) **Duty drawback**— The exporters are entitled to get refund of import duty paid on imported raw materials and excise duty on manufactured goods which are exported.

IMPORT TRADE PROCEDURE

When goods are imported from a foreign country, the importer has to follow the procedure prescribed by the government of importing country. Import trade procedure differs from country to country depending upon the existing policy of that country. The general procedure for import trade in India involves the following stages:

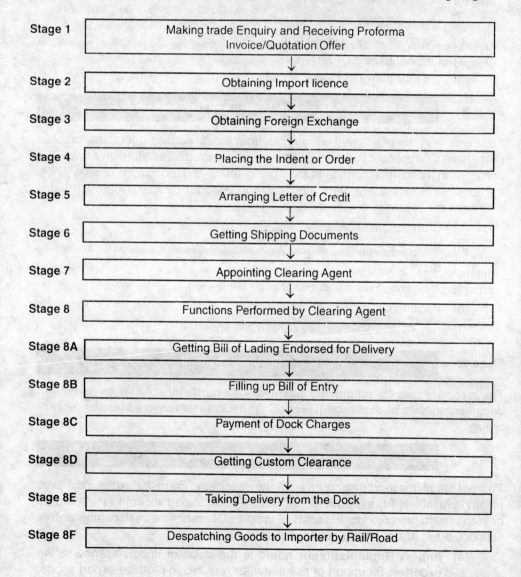

Stage 1	Making trade Enquiry and Receiving Proforma Invoice/Quotation Offer
Stage 2	Obtaining Import licence
Stage 3	Obtaining Foreign Exchange
Stage 4	Placing the Indent or Order
Stage 5	Arranging Letter of Credit
Stage 6	Getting Shipping Documents
Stage 7	Appointing Clearing Agent
Stage 8	Functions Performed by Clearing Agent
Stage 8A	Getting Bill of Lading Endorsed for Delivery
Stage 8B	Filling up Bill of Entry
Stage 8C	Payment of Dock Charges
Stage 8D	Getting Custom Clearance
Stage 8E	Taking Delivery from the Dock
Stage 8F	Despatching Goods to Importer by Rail/Road

Stage 8G	Sending Advice to the Importers

↓

Stage 9	Taking Delivery of goods from Railway/Carrier

↓

Stage 10	Making Payment

Let us discuss these stages one by one.

Stage 1 →

Making Trade Enquiry and Receiving proforma Invoice/Quotation offer

The first stage in the import trade is to make trade enquiry from the intending exporters or their agents. An enquiry is a request by the intending importer to supply the following information:

(a) Specification of goods such as quality, size, design etc.

(b) Unit Price

(c) Quantity of Goods available

(d) Terms of shipment (FOB, C & F, CIF)

(e) Terms of payment (D/P, D/A, Letter of credit)

(f) Delivery Schedule

(g) Last date of validity of the offer

In response to his enquiry, the importer may receive different proforma invoices/quotation offers, for different suppliers. After making a thorough comparison of different offers, the importer should decide about the supplier with whom the import order/indent should be placed.

Stage 2 →

Obtaining Import Licence

Where the importer wants to import an item for which import licence is required, he must first obtain import licence. To obtain an import licence, the intending importer makes an application in the prescribed form and submits it to the licensing authority along with the following documents:

(a) Treasury receipt for import licence fee,

(b) Certificate of the value of goods imported by the applicant in the previous year and

(c) Income tax verification certificate from Income tax-authorities

The licensing authority then issues the import licence in duplicate after examining the documents and satisfying itself about the claim of the applicant.

Stage 3 → | Obtaining Foreign Exchange

After obtaining the import licence, the intending importer makes an application in the prescribed form under the Foreign Exchange Management Act (FEMA) and submits it to the Exchange Control Department of RBI after getting it forwarded by his exchange bank. The RBI sanctions the release of the amount of foreign exchange to the importers after scrutinising the application. It may be noted that exchange is released and made available only for a specific transaction for which import order has been placed.

Stage 4 → | Placing the Indent or Order

After obtaining the import licence and requisite amount of foreign exchange, the importer should place the order directly or through 'Indent Houses'. An indent is an order sent abroad for the import of goods. An indent house refers to an import agent or import firm which imports goods on behalf of importers.

Stage 5 → | Arranging Letter of Credit

As per terms of payment if the importer is required to arrange a letter of credit, the importer instructs his bank to issue a letter of credit. Depending upon the deposit or credit worthiness of the importer, the importer's bank may issue a letter of credit. A letter of credit is a document issued by importer's bank on behalf of the importer to authorise the negotiating bank to make payment of the amount stated therein to a party named therein or his order on presentation of documents mentioned in the letter of credit.

Stage 6 → | Getting Shipping Documents

In case of D/A (Document against acceptance), importer gets the shipping documents on the acceptance of the bill.

In case of D/P (Documents against payment), Importer gets the shipping documents on the payment of the bill.

In case of letter of credit arrangement, importer gets the shipping documents from his bank.

Stage 7 → | Appointing Clearing Agent

After getting the shipping documents, the importer who does not want to complete further formalities in this regard himself, appoints clearing agent.

Stage 8 → | Functions Performed by the Clearing Agent

(i) **Getting Bill of Lading enclosed for delivery** — When the ship arrives at the port of destination, the agent gets the bill of lading endorsed by the shipping company in his favour after making the payment of freight if not paid earlier.

(ii) **Filling up Bill of Entry** — The agent is required to fill up three copies of 'Bill of Entry'. A bill of entry is a document which shows the details of goods imported and is used by custom authorities for determining import duty.

(iii) **Payment of Dock Charges** — The agent is required to fill up two copies of Port Trust Receipt and to submit these copies alongwith three copies of Bill of Entry and necessary dock changes, to the landing office at destination port. After receiving dock charges, the dock authority will return one copy of the Port Trust Receipt and two copies of the Bill of entry to the agent.

(iv) **Getting Custom Clearance** — The agent is required to submit one copy of Port Trust Receipt and two copies of the Bill of Entry alongwith other required documents to the Custom Authorities and make payment of import duty (in case of dutiable goods). He then gets the release order from the custom authorities.

(v) **Taking Delivery from the Dock** — The agent takes the delivery of the goods from the dock after submitting 'bill of lading', 'bill of entry', and Port Trust dues Receipt.

(vi) **Despatching Goods to Importer by Rail/Road** — After taking delivery of goods from the dock authority, the agent despatches goods to his principal by rail or by road and receives Railway Receipt (in case goods are sent by rail) or Lorry Receipt (in case goods are sent by road).

(vii) **Sending Advice to the Importer** — After despatch of the goods, the agent informs the importer about the despatch of goods other related matters and sends railway receipt / lorry receipt alongwith a statement showing his expenses and remuneration to the importer.

Stage 9 → **Taking Delivery of Goods from Railway / Carrier**

After receiving the advice from the clearing agent, the importer takes the delivery of goods from Railway / Carrier surrendering Railway Receipt/Lorry Receipt and carries them to his godown.

Stage 10 → **Making Payment**

The mode of payment for import depends upon the agreement between the importer and the exporter.

(a) In case of **Documents against Acceptance (D/A Bills)**, the importer gets the shipping documents on giving the acceptance of Bill of Exchange and makes the payment on the maturity date.

(b) In case of **Documents against Payment (D/P Bills)**, the importer gets the shipping documents on making payment of Bill of Exchange.

(c) In case of **letter of credit**, the importer gets the shipping documents after payment.

DOCUMENTS USED IN INTERNATIONAL TRADE

The list of main documents used in import trade and export trade is given as follows:

Documents used in Import Trade	Documents used in Export Trade
1. Indent (or Order) sent to exporter	1. Foreign Indent (or Order) received from Importer
2. Import Licence	2. Shipping Bill
3. Letter of Credit	3. Shipping Order
4. Bill of Lading	4. Dock Challan
5. Insurance Policy	5. Mate's Receipt
6. Bill of Exchange	6. Bill of Lading
7. Bill of Entry	7. Insurance Policy
	8. Export Invoice
	9. Letter of Credit
	10. Bill of Exchange

100% EXPORT ORIENTED UNITS [EOUs]

100% Export Oriented Units means an industrial unit offering for export its entire production excluding rejects and items otherwise specifically permitted to be supplied to the Domestic Tariff Area (DTA), 100% EOU may be set under the following schemes.

Schemes	Area where unit may be set up
1. **Export Oriented Unit (EOU) Scheme**	Any where in India subject to locational criteria.
2. **Export Processing Zones (EPZ) Scheme**	In specific areas separated from the Domestic Tariff Domestic Tariff Area by Physical barriers.
3. **Software Technology Park (STP) Scheme** The STP Scheme is a 100% EOU Scheme for units undertaking the development of software for export using data communication link or in the form of physical exports including export of Professional Services. A STP may be an independent unit or may be one of such units located in an area designated as STP complex by the Ministry of Information Technology.	In STP Complex
4. **Electronic Hardware Technology Park Scheme** EHTP Schme is primarily meant for manufacture and export of hardware, but the manufacture and export of software in an integrated manner, commonly known as systems software, is also allowed. However, units engaged exclusively in the manufacture	In EHTP Complex

of software are not permitted under this
scheme. It may be noted that the EHTP
may be a single unit by itself or one of
the such units located in an area
designated as an EHTP.

FREE TRADE AND EXPORT PROCESSING ZONES

So far following **nine** free trade and exort processing zones have been established.

1. Cochin Export Processing Zone (CEPZ), Kochi, Kerala.
2. Falta Export Processing Zone (FEPZ), West Bengal.
3. Kandla Free Trade Zone (KAFTZ), Gujarat.
4. Madras Export Processing Zone (MEPZ), Chennai.
5. Noida Export Processing Zone (NEPZ), Distt. Ghaziabad (U.P.)
6. Santacruz Electronics Export Processing Zone (SEEPZ), Mumbai
7. Vishakhapatnam Export Processing Zone, (VEPZ).
8. Surat Export Processing Zone.
9. Kay-foam Export Processing Zone, Kandivili, Mumbai

SOFTWARE TECHNOLOGY PARKS (STPS) SCHEME

Software Technology Parks (STPs) are 100% Export Oriented projects catering to the need of software development for 100% export.

No import licence is required for import of equipment into Techonology Park. All the imports into the Technology Park are completely free of duty. The Technology Parks are under the technical supervision of Deptt. of Electronics.

The Govt. of India has set up **seven** such parks at—

1. Pune
2. Bangalore
3. Bhubaneshwar
4. Hyderabad
5. Thiruvanan-thapuram
6. Gandinagar and
7. Noida

ELECTRONICS HARDWARE TECHNOLOGY PARKS (EHTPS) SCHEME

Under the Hardware Technology Park Scheme, an Electronic Hardware Technology Park may be set up by the Central Govt., State Governments, public or private sector undertakings. An EHTP may be an individual unit in itself or it may be one of such units located in an area designated as EHTP. The scheme is administered by the Deptt. of Electronics. An EHTP may import free of duty all types of goods including capital goods required by it for its production.

Facilities to 100% EOUs/EPZ/STP/EHTP Units

1. Proposals fulfilling certain conditions are granted automatic approvals within

15 days through the concerned Development Commissioner. In other cases, approvals are granted by Board of Approvals within 45 days.

2.   No import licence is required for import of capital goods, raw materials, consumables, etc.

3.   Such units may import free of duty all types of goods, including capital goods as defined in the EXIM Policy, required by it for the manufacture, services, trading, or in connection therewith provided they are not prohibited items of import in the ITC (HS).

4.   Exempted from payment of central excise duty on capital goods, components of raw materials etc. bought from the Domestic Tariff Area.

5.   Reimbursement of Central Sale Tax when supplies are made from the DTA to EOU/EPZ/EHTP/STP.

6.   Foreign equity participation upto 100% is permissible in the case of EOU/EPZ/EHTP/STP units.

7.   Procurement of raw materials and export of finished products shall be exempted from Central levies.

8.   Exempted from restrictions, if any, under Export Control Order on product manufactured and exported from EPZ/EOUs.

9.   Working credit facility for a period of 180 days is provided without production of firm export orders or letter of credit.

10. Remittance of profit and dividends earned by foreign investors allowed freely after payment of tax.

11. Telephone/telex connections released on priority basis.

12. Exports from EPZ/EOUs are exempted from the purview of Compulsory export Inspection.

13. Units in EPZs are offered concessional lease rent on pots/sheds for a maximum of initial three years, linked to commencement of production.

14. Import of second hand capital goods is permitted.

15. EPZ/EOUs/EHTPs/STPs/SEZs are eligible for complete tax holiday upto A.Y. 2009-10, subject to maximum of 10 consecutive assessment years. The exemption is not available from A. Y. 2010-11 and onwards.

16. Such units may import, without payment of duty, all types of goods for creating a Central facility for use by software development units in STP/EHTP/EPZ.

17. FOB value of export of an EOU/EPZ/EHTP/STP unit can be clubbed with the FOB value of exports of its parent economy in the DTA for the purpose of according status of Export House, Trading House. Star Trading House or Super Star Trading House for the latter.

18. Software Units may also be permitted to use the Computer System for training purpose (including commercial training) provided no computer terminal is installed outside the bonded premises for the purpose.

19. The EOUs are eligible for the Marketing Development Assistance (MDA) from confederation of 100% EOU, for their promotional activities.

20. EOU/EPZ units shall be issued automatially Green Card by the DC concerned after execution of legal undertaking. Green Card entitles the holders to avail following facilities:

    (a)   Automatic licensing.
    (b)   Automatic Customs Clearance for exports.
    (c)   Automatic Customs Clearance for imports related to exports.
    (d)   LUT facility for duty free imports and any such facility as may be specified from time to time.

21. Such units may sell 50% of the FOB value of exports in the DTA subject to the payment of applicable duties and fulfilement of minimum Net Foreign Exchange Earnings as a percentage of exports (NFEP) by the unit.

SPECIAL ECONOMIC ZONES (SEZs)

Exim Policy 1997-2002, April 2000 Ed. brought in the concept of establishment of Special Economic Zones, which are specially delineated.

Meaning of Special Economic Zones (SEZs)

Special Economic Zones [SEZs] are those zones which are specially delineated duty free enclaves and shall be deemd to be foreign territory for the purpose of trade operations and duties and tariffs.

Features of Special Economic Zones

1. Goods going into the SEZ area shall be treated as deemed exports.
2. Goods coming into Domestic Tariff Area (DTA) from the SEZ shall be treated as if the goods are being imported.

Setting up of Special Economic Zones

A SEZ may be set up in the public, private, joint sector or by State Govt. and also existing EPZ may be converted into SEZ, if so notified.

Minimum Investment to be made by a unit

The minimum investment in building, plant and machinery by a unit in SEZ shall be Rs 50.00 lakhs (not applicable to EPZ being converted into SEZ).

Facilities to Special Economic Zones (SEZs) Units

1. SEZ units may export goods and services including agro-products, partly processed jewellery, sub-assemblies and component. It may also export by-products, rejects, waste scrap arising out of the production process.
2. SEZ unit may import without payment of duty all types of goods, including capital goods, as defined in the Policy, whether new or second hand, required by it for its activities or in connection therewith, provided they are not prohibited items of imports in the ITC (HS). The units shall also be permitted to import goods required for the approved activity, including capital goods, free of cost or on loan from clients.

   SEZ units may procure goods required by it without payment of duty from bonded warehouses in the DTA set up under the policy.

   SEZ may import, without payment of duty, all types of goods for creating a central facility for use by software development units in SEZ. The central facility for software development can also be accessed by units in the DTA for export of software.

   Gem & Jewellery and Jewellery units may also source gold/silver/platinum through the nominated agencies.

   SEZ units may also import/procure from DTA specified goods without payment of duty and subject to such conditions, as may be notified by the Government, for setting up of units in the Zone.
3. SEZ unit may, on the basis of a firm contract between the parties, source the capital goods from a domestic/foreign leasing company. In such a case the SEZ unit and the domestic/foreign leasing company shall jointly file the documents to enable import/procurement of the capital goods without payment of duty.
4. SEZ unit shall be a positive net foreign exchange earner.
5. All activities of SEZ units, unless otherwise specified, shall be through self certification procedure.
6. The unit shall execute a legal undertaking with the Development Commissioner concerned and in the event of failure to achieve positive foreign exchange earning it shall be liable to penalty in terms of the legal undertaking or under any other law for the time being in force.

7. Goods imported/procured by an SEZ unit may be transferred or given on loan to another SEZ/EOU/EPZ/EHTP/STP unit which shall be duly accounted for, but not counted towards discharge of export performance.

   Transfers of goods within the same SEZ shall not require any permission but the unit shl! maintain proper accounts of the transaction.

8. SEZ unit, may subcontract a part of their production or production process through units in the DTA or through other SEZ/EOU/EPZ/EHTP/STP with the permission of the Customs authorities. Sub-contracting of part of production process may also be permitted abroad with the approval of the Board of Approval.

9. SEZ units may sell goods in the DTA on payment of applicable duties on the basis of self-certification.

10. Other Entitlements

    (i) Units set up in SEZs will be charged rent for lease of industrial plots and standard design factory buildings/sheds as per rates fixed from time to time.

    (ii) *Corporate tax:* SEZ units engaged in manufacturing and services will be eligible for entitlements in respect of payment of income tax as per the provisions of Income Tax Act.

    (iii) FOB Value of export of an SEZ unit can be clubbed with FOB value of export of its parent company in the DTA, or vice versa, for the purpose of according export House, Trading House, Star Trading House or Super Star Trading House status.

    (iv) Foreign Investment Foreign Equity up to 100% is permissible for all manufacturing activities in Special Economic Zones (SEZs), except for the following activities:

        (a) arms and amunition, explosives and allied items of defence equipment, defence aircraft and warships;

        (b) atomic substances;

        (c) narcotics and psychotropic substances and hazardous chemicals;

        (d) distillation and brewing of alcoholic drink; and

        (e) cigarettes/cigars and manufactured tobacco substitutes.

        Sectoral norms as notified by the Government shall apply to foreign investment in services.

    (v) SEZ units may retain 100% of their export proceeds in their EEFC account.

    (vi) Export value of goods and software by SEZ units may be realized and repartriated to India within 12 months from the date of export or within the time extended by Reserve Bank of India.

    (vii) Software units may, in additon, also be allowed to use the computer system for training purpose (including commercial training) subject to the condition that no computer terminal shall be installed outside the Zone premises for the purpose.

    (viii) Procurement of raw materials and export of finished products shall be exempted from Central levies.

    (ix) Exemption from industrial licensing for manufacture of items reserved for SSI sector.

    (x) Canalisation policy shall not apply to SEZ manufacturing units. Export of iron ore shall however be subject to the decision of the Government from time to time. Requirements of other conditions like minimum export price/export in consumer pack as per Exim Policy shall apply in case the raw materials are indigenous. Export of textile items shall be covered by bilateral agreements, if any.

(xi)   SEZ unit may install one fax machine at a place of its choice, outside the Zone, subject to intimation of its location to the concerned Customs/ Central excise authorities.

(xii) SEZ units may, temporarily take out of the Zone duty free laptop computers and video projection systems for working upon by persons authorised by unit.

(xiii) SEZ units may install personal computers not exceeding two in number imported/procure duty free in the registered/administrative office subject to the guidelines issued by Department of Revenue in this behalf.

(xiv) For IT and IT enabled services, persons authorized by the software units may access the facility installed in the SEZ unit through communication links.

——————— EXERCISES ———————

VERY SHORT ANSWER TYPE QUESTIONS

1. What is meant by 'External Trade'?
2. What is meant by 'Export Trade'?
3. What is meant by 'Import Trade'?
4. What is meant by 'Entreport Trade'?
5. What is meant by 'Visible Trade'?
6. What is meant by 'Invisible Trade'?
7. Give one example each of visible export and invisible import of India?
8. Name the theory that explains the basis of foreign trade.
9. What is FOB price?
10. What is C & F price?
11. What is CIF price?
12. What is meant by Documentary Bills?
13. What is meant by D/A?
14. What is meant by D/P?
15. What is meant by documentary letter of credit?
16. Name the parties to letter of credit.
17. What is meant by Letter of Hypothecation?
18. For what does the term 'Exim Bank' stand for?
19. What is commercial Invoice in external trade?
20. What is Bill of Loading?
21. What is Charter Party?
22. Name the party who takes insurance policy in external trade.
23. What is bill of exchange in external trade?
24. What is Trade enquiring in export trade?
25. What is Proforma Invoice / Quotation offer?
26. What is meant by 'Indent'?
27. Who is forwarding agent?
28. What is Shipping Bill?
29. What is Dock Challan?
30. What is Custom Export Pass?
31. What is Mate's Receipt?
32. What is Advice to Exporter?
33. What is 'Import Replenishment'?
34. What is Cash Compensation?
35. What is duty draw-pack?
36. What is Bill of Entry?
37. What is 'Advice to Importer'?

SHORT ANSWER TYPE QUESTIONS

1. Distinguish between Home Trade and Foreign Trade.
2. How does export trade lead to specialisation?
3. How does export trade facilitate economic development?
4. State the importance of export trade.
5. State two main advantages of foreign trade.
6. State two main difficulties faced by traders in foreign trade.
7. State the means of Export Promotion.
8. State any three institutions which are engaged in export promotion activities in India.
9. State any three financial incentives for exports.
10. State any three fiscal incentives for exports.
11. State the various terms of Price Quotations.
12. State the various terms of payment.
13. State the activities involved in Documentary Bills method of Payment.
14. State the activities involved in Document Credit under Letter of Credit method.
15. State the objective and function of Exim Bank of India.
16. State the importance of documents in external trade.
17. State the shipping documents used in external trade.
18. State the meaning, purpose and contents of Commercial Invoice.
19. State the meaning, purpose and contents of Bill of Loading.
20. State the meaning, purpose and contents of Airway Bill.
21. State the meaning and purpose of insurance Policy in external trade. Name the party who takes the insurance policy in external trade?
22. State the meaning, purpose and contents of Bill of exchange.
23. State three authorities with whom exporter is required to be registered.
24. State the functions performed by forwarding agent.
25. State the meaning, purpose and contents of Shipping Bill.
26. Distinguish between Bill of lading and Charter's Party.
27. Distinguish between Bill of lading and Shipping Bill.
28. Name any four documents used in export trade.
29. Name any four documents used in import trade.
30. Name any three documents used both in export and import trade.
31. Name any three export incentives.
32. State the functions pursued by clearing agent in import trade.
33. State the schemes under which 100%. EOU may be set up in India.
34. State any three free trade & export processing zones.
35. State any three Software Technology parts set up in India.
36. What is meant by Special Economic Zones?

LONG ANSWER TYPE QUESTIONS

1. What is meant by external trade? Explain its advantages.
2. What are the difficulties which may be faced in external trade by the traders? Discuss.
3. Explain fully the basis of external trade with reference to the theory of Comparative Cost Advantage.
4. Describe briefly the following methods of payment in export import operation:
   (i) Documentary Bills
   (ii) Documentary letter of credit
5. Explain the procedure for exporting goods to USA from India by sea route.
6. Describe the procedure of importing goods into India by sea route.
7. Explain in brief the means of export promotion.
8. Explain in brief the schemes under which 100% EOU may be set up in India.

13 Advertising and Salesmanship

MEANING OF ADVERTISING

Meaning of Advertising

Advertising may be defined as any paid form of non-personal presentation or promotion of ideas, goods or services by an identified sponsor.

Advertising is the dissemination of or spreading the information concerning an idea, product, or service to induce action in accordance with the intent and purpose of the advertiser.

Advertising makes the product/idea/service known to the people. It attracts and holds their attention, creates and sustains demands and wins their confidence.

What is advertised is the sales message which is known as advertisement.

FEATURES OF ADVERTISING

The main features of advertising are shown below:

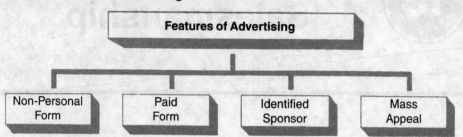

Let us discuss the features of advertising one by one.

1. **Non-Personal Form** — It is a non-personal form of presentation of ideas, goods or services because there is no face to face contract with the customer.

2. **Paid Form** — It is a paid form of communication. The advertiser has to pay for the space or time used by him for advertising.

3. **Identified Sponsor** — It is done by a sponsor- who can be identified in the advertisement. Thus, the public knows who is behind the advertising in the advertisement itself.

4. **Mass Appeal** — It has mass appeal. It can influence large section of people.

PURPOSES OF ADVERTISING

The purposes of advertising are shown below:

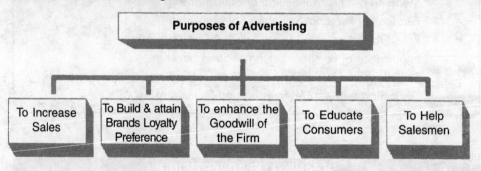

Let us discuss the purposes of advertising one by one.

1. **To Increase Sales** — The main purpose of advertising is to increase sales. Advertising creates and sustains demand for a product/service and expand the market.

2. **To Build and Retain Brands Loyalty** — One of the purposes of advertising is to build and retain brand loyalty. Proper advertising emphasises the recognition and identification of brands of a product. It is through advertising that people recognise a product by its brand, names or trade mark such as MAGGI Noodles, BPL Washing Machines, LG Airconditioners, SONY TV's.

3. **To Enhance the Goodwill of the Firm** — One of the purposes of advertising is to enhance reputation of the firm. Advertisements which highlight the

achievement of the firm, information about new discoveries, customer services etc. create good image of the firm.

For example — An advertisement highlights the 9th continuous Export Performance Award by M/s P.P. Jewellers, free pollution check by M/s VIKAS MOTORS, an authorised dealer of Maruti.

4. **To Educate Consumers** — One of the purposes of advertising is to educate consumers. Advertising explains the various features and uses of a Product.

5. **To Help Salesmen** — One of the purposes of advertising is to help salesmen. It supports salesmanship in the sense that the customer is already aware and informed about the product. The salesmen are required to give some more detailed information about the product and to execute the sales.

IMPORTANCE OF ADVERTISING

The importance of advertising has increased in the modern era of large scale production and tough competition in the market. Advertising is needed not only to the manufacturers and traders but also to the customers and society. The importance of advertising arises from the benefits to manufacturers, customers and society in general.

I. Benefits to Manufacturers

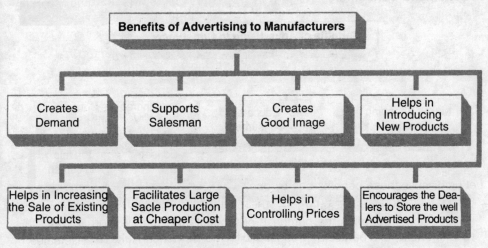

Let us discuss these benefits one by one.

1. **Creates Demand** — Advertising helps in creating steady demand of the products. For example, Glucone-D, a product of Glaxo Laboratories, is sold during summers and winters both through different advertisements. In summers, it is advertised as a useful drink necessary to fight tiredness caused by heat. In winter, it is advertised as an essential drink to gain more energy to fight cold.

2. **Supports Salesmen** — Advertising supports personal selling since the consumer is already familiar with the product.

3. **Creates Good Image** — Advertising helps in creating good image of the firm and reputation of its products.

4. **Helps in Introducing New Products** — Advertising helps in introducing new products in competitive market since repeated advertisements through popular media create awareness among consumers.

5. **Helps in Increasing the Sale of Existing Products** — Advertising helps in increasing the sale of existing products by entering into new markets and attracting new customers.

6. **Facilitates Large Scale Production at Cheaper Cost** — Advertising facilitates large-scale production at cheaper cost because (i) It creates new demand and maintains existing demand. (ii) Middlemen are eliminated because of direct appeal to the consumers and hence the cost of distribution is reduced.

7. **Helps in Controlling Prices** — Advertising helps them in controlling prices by labelling or announcing the maximum retail price for the consumers. Hence, the dealers are not in a position to charge high prices.

8. **Encourages the Dealers to Store the Well Advertised Products** — Advertising encourages the dealers to store the well-advertised products because there is no need for them to make extra efforts in selling the products as they are backed by advertising.

II. Benefits to Consumers

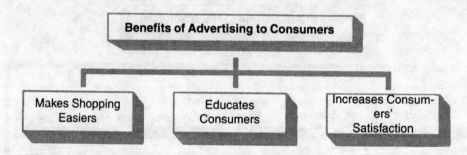

Let us discuss these benefits one by one.

1. **Makes Shopping Easiers** — Advertising helps the consumers in making decisions regarding the purchase of products because it informs about the superiority of a particular product and the consumer can take a quick decision as to which product he should buy.

2. **Educates Consumers** — Advertising educates consumers about the existence, features, uses and prices of old and new products.

3. **Increases, Consumers' Satisfaction** — Advertising increases consumer's satisfaction by ensuring better quality of products at cheaper prices.

III. Benefits to the Society

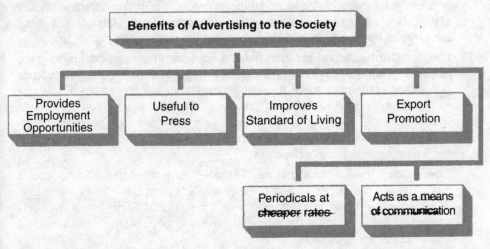

Let us discuss these benefits one by one.

1. **Provides Employment Opportunities** — Advertising provides employment opportunities to a large number of people engaged in writing, designing, producing and issuing advertisements. Thus, persons like photographers, singers, musicians, artists etc. have benefited by the development of advertising.

2. **Useful to Press** — Advertising provides an important source of income to the press, radio and television.

3. **Improves Standard of Living** — Advertising improves standard of living of the people by making them available a variety of high quality goods.

4. **Export Promotion** — Advertising is helpful in finding customers in the international market which is essential for earning foreign exchange.

5. **Periodicals at Cheaper Rates** — Advertising benefits the customers because they get newspapers and magazines at cheaper rates.

6. **Acts as a Means of Communication** — Advertising acts as a means of communication for different sections of the society. Different people express their views, thoughts, opinions and requirements. For example, in classified advertisements, there are separate advertisements for vacancies for jobs vacant, jobs wanted, marriage, birth, death, lost, change in name etc.

OBJECTIONS TO ADVERTISING

Some people feel that advertising is a social waste and they raise the following objections to advertising:

1. **Promotes materialism** — Advertising promotes materialism and hence it is becoming a main source of discontentment. People feel discontented when they are not in a position to get all the products which are advertised. Everyone wants to have more and more.

2. **Encourages Inferior Goods** — Some critics of advertising feel that it encourages the sale of inferior and dubious products by giving attractive display of the product. Manufacturers through advertisements make false claims about the utility of the products and thereby cheat the customers.

3. **Creates Confusion rather than help** — Advertising creates confusion in the minds of people by providing numbers of products which make their choice difficult and sometimes there are wasteful expenditure. For example, it is difficult to choose among Ariel washing powder or Wheel washing powder or VIM washing powder. Although some cheaper varieties of washing powders (which are not advertised) are available in the market, yet the choice is made out of the well advertised costly powders.

4. **Some Advertisements are in bad Taste** — Sometimes the advertisements are prepared without considering the people's tastes. Sometimes the matter of advertisement has no relationship with the products. Some advertisements are in bad taste. Whether the advertisement is in good taste or bad taste is a matter of personal opinion.

5. **Increases the Cost** — Advertising adds to the cost of the product. The customer is required to pay more on account of the cost incurred on advertisement since no manufacturer pays for the advertisement costs out of his own pocket.

6. **Multiplies Wants** — Advertising multiplies wants of the customers by encouraging them to buy those products which they do not require. Such purchases may make life of the people miserable by bringing about wastage of individual and social resources.

7. **Creates Monopoly of Brand** — Advertising may lead to the monopoly of a particular brand or trade mark. Big manufacturers who can afford to invest large amount of money for advertising can create brand monopoly and thereby eliminate smaller producers. Brand monopoly may lead to malpractices which may be followed by the monopolist. Smaller producers find it difficult to compete with the established brands which have acquired their status due to heavy advertising over a number of years.

8. **Undermines the ethical values** — Advertising undermines the ethical values. It encourages wines, cigarettes, pan masala etc. which are harmful to human beings. Advertisements which use indecent language, action and photographs to advertise their products, adversely affect the culture and behaviour of the people.

9. **Wasteful Expenditure** — Advertising which does not create/ increase the demand or which merely shifts demand from one brand to another is wasteful expenditure.

The above criticisms are not always true especially in those cases where the advertising, by increasing the demand for a product, has led to large-scale production and enabled the manufacturers to produce goods at a lower cost per unit and accordingly sell at a lower price.

Reconciliation — Advertising is beneficial if above ill points are avoided. Most of the above mentioned criticisms are ill-founded.

Increase in cost of sales is compensated by increase in sales thus enabling the enterprise to have the benefits of large scale production. Consumers, being rational human beings, can judge their needs accordingly. Advertising makes buying easier for consumers and educates them about new products and their uses.

MEDIA OF ADVERTISING

Meaning of Media of Advertising

Media is the plural of medium. Advertising media are the means to communicate the message of the advertiser to the customers. Manufacturers communicate information about their products to their present and prospective customers through advertising media. Basically, the need for advertising media arises because of the large number of persons to be informed and their location in different areas and regions.

Types of Advertising Media

The various types of advertising media are shown below:

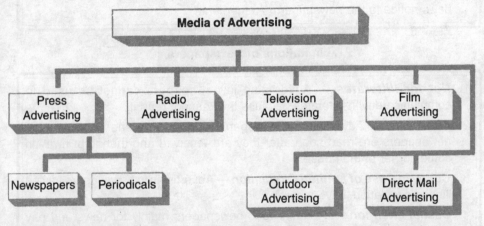

Let us discuss the media of advertising one by one.

1. Press Advertising

Press advertising mainly includes advertising in newspapers and periodicals.

(i) Newspapers

It is one of the most common media of advertising. Newspapers are published in Hindi (e.g., Navbharat Times, Hindustan, Janasatta, Punjab Kesari, Rashtriya Sahara etc.) or English (e.g., Times of India, The Hindustan Times, Indian Express) or regional languages (e.g., Gujarati Samachat). Newspapers may be of local or state or national level. The choice of a particular newspaper for advertising depends upon its circulation, the geographical region in which it is popular, the class of readers it serves, the cost of space, and general reputation of the newspaper. This media is used to reach literate and educated people. The advantages and limitations of advertising in newspapers are discussed below:

Advantages of Newspapers

1. *Wide Coverage* — A newspaper has a wide circulation. A single advertisement in a newspaper can quickly reach a large number of people.
2. *Economical* — The cost of advertisement per reader is relatively low because of wide circulation.
3. *Benefit of Continuity* — Advertising in newspapers has the benefit of continuity in the sense that the same advertisement can be repeated a number of times to remind the readers about the product.
4. *Benefit of Selectivity* — Advertising in newspapers has a benefit of selectivity in the sense that they provide greater choice to the advertisers because the desired market or regions can be approached through local or regional newspapers.
5. *Benefit of Flexibility* — Advertising in newspapers has a benefit of flexibility in the sense that it can be quickly started or stopped or changed on even a day's notice to the newspaper management.

Limitations of Newspapers

1. *Not for Illiterates* — Advertising in newspapers cannot be used to communicate with illiterates because they cannot read it.
2. *Short Life* — Advertising in newspapers has a very short life because newspapers are read soon after they are received and then kept away in some corner of the house.
3. *Costly in Case of Limited Circulation* — Advertising in newspapers having limited circulation, is very costly.
4. *Casual attention* — Readers read newspapers mainly for news and pay only casual attention to advertisements in newspapers.

(ii) Periodicals (or Magazines or Journals)

Periodicals are another form of printed media of advertising. Periodicals may be in the form of magazines or journals. Magazines are published weekly (e.g., Illustrated Weekly, India Today), fortnightly (e.g., Sarita) or monthly. Journals are generally published monthly, quarterly or bi-annually. Magazines may be general or special. General magazines (e.g., India Today, Sarita) cater to reading habits of general people and hence useful for advertising products of general use. Special magazines (e.g., Business India, Capital Markets) cater to the reading habits of specific people and hence are useful for advertising products of specific use. For example, capital market magazine is useful for advertisers like banks, share brokers, sub-brokers, finance company, investment companies, journals of special interest such as Indian Law Digest, Medical Journal, The Chartered Accountant, The Company Secretary are useful for advertising the product meant for that particular profession. For example, Medical Journal is useful for advertising medicines and drugs.

Examples — The following types of magazines and journals can be used for specified product messages.

Product-related message	Examples of Appropriate Magazines and Journals
1. Products of common use	*Magazines of general interest such as — Illustrated weekly, India Today, Caravan.*
2. Household goods, fashion, garments, cosmetics	*Eve's Weekly, Filmfare, Femina, Sarita, Griha Shobha*
3. Sports goods	*Sports Week, Sports Star*
4. Medicines and diseases	*Medical Journal*
5. Books on taxation	*— Income Tax Reporter* *— Taxation* *— The Chartered Accountant* *— The Chartered Secretary*
6. Books on company law	*— The Chartered Accountant* *— The Chartered Secretary* *— Company Law Reporter*
7. Books on accountancy	*— The Chartered Accountant* *— The Chartered Secretary* *— The Management Accountant* *— The Accountant*

This media facilitates the selective appeal to specific segments.

The advantages and limitations of advertising in periodicals are discussed on below:

Advantages of Periodicals

1. *Longer Life* — The life of advertisement in periodicals is longer because periodicals are preserved for a longer period of time. People can go through the advertisements again and again.

2. *Careful attention* — There is lesser chance of the advertisement escaping the attention of the readers because periodicals are read more carefully and at great leisure.

3. *Benefit of Selectivity* — Advertising in periodicals has the benefit of selectivity in the sense that periodicals may be selected for giving advertisement having regard to the nature of the product and its users. Special magazines reduce the chances of wastage because advertisement is directed towards target customers and towards all types of customers. **For example,** medical appliances should be advertised in medical journals and not in sports journals.

4. *Attractive Appeal* — Advertisement in periodicals can lie in colour, therefore it is more attractive to the eyes and hence more appealing. It helps the customers in identifying the products at the time of purchase.

Limitations of Periodicals

1. **Lacks Flexibility** — The message in periodical advertising cannot be changed or repeated daily because the copy of advertisement has to be prepared and sent well in advance for publication. It is difficult to make last minute changes in the advertisement.
2. **Costlier** — The cost of advertisement per reader is relatively high because of small circulation of periodicals in comparison to newspapers.
3. **Not Useful for Retail Advertising** — Periodical advertising is not useful for retail advertising. Retailers prefer a medium which will allow them to give information as and when required. They prefer newspapers as compared to periodicals.

(b) Radio Advertising

Radio advertising refers to the transmission of product-related message through radio. In this medium, messages are sent from transmitting stations and are picked up by the receiving sets owned by the public. In India, there is a special channel known as Vividh Bharti for commercial broadcasting.

Advantages of Radio Advertising

1. **Wider Appeal** — Radio advertising has a wider appeal because it can reach all types of people whether they live in urban areas or rural areas, whether they are literate or illiterate, whether they are old or young or even children. People can listen to advertisements during leisure time or even while working.
2. **Benefit of Selectivity** — Radio advertising has the benefits of selectivity in the sense that different types of radio programmes could be used for different product messages. For example, in the programmes meant for farmers advertisements for seeds, fertilisers, pesticides etc. can be given.
3. **Benefit of Flexibility** — Radio advertising has the benefit of flexibility in the sense that the same advertisement can be repeated in different programmes to communicate with different types of people.

Limitations of Radio Advertising

1. **Short Life** — Radio advertising has a short life because the advertiser has to pay for the advertisement in accordance with the time taken on radio. Because of short duration of the radio advertisements, it becomes difficult to communicate all the particulars of the product. Besides this, sometimes the radio advertisement may not be fully understood by the listener.
2. **Costlier** — The cost of radio advertisement per listener is relatively high in comparison to press advertising.
3. **Less Impact** — The impact of radio advertising is relatively less as compared to that of television and cinema because people can only listen to the message and cannot see the product advertised.

(c) Television Advertising

Television advertising refers to the transmission of product-related messages through television. Television was first introduced in India in 1959. Television advertising started on 1st January 1976. Nowadays, it has become a powerful advertising medium. The advantages and limitations of television advertising are discussed below:

Advantages of Television Advertising

1. *Greater Impact* — The impact of television advertising is relatively greater as compared to radio advertising because the viewers can both see the product as well as listen to the product message.

2. *Appropriate for Illiterates* — Television advertising is an appropriate medium to communicate information to illiterate people because they can receive the product message by seeing the picture through eyes and listen through ears.

3. *Attractive and Attentive Appeal* — Television advertising has an attentive appeal because most advertisements appear during the leisure time when people are watching a film, a serial or a music programme. It has an attractive appeal because film stars and famous models are associated with the advertisements on television.

Limitations of Television Advertising

1. *Costly Medium* — Television advertising is a very costly medium. Due to its high cost, small business units cannot advertise their products on television. Only big business enterprises can use it.

2. *Limited Appeal* — Television advertising has a limited appeal because television sets are owned only by a very small number of people in India.

3. *Short Life and Duration* — Television advertising being costly, is of short duration. Because of short duration, it becomes difficult to communicate all the particulars of the product. The message is not available for reference purposes unless it is repeated.

4. *Lack of Flexibility* — No immediate change can be made because advertisement are to be prepared well in advance.

(d) Film Advertising

Film advertising refers to the transmission of product-related message through short films or slides shown before the regular shows start or during the intermission. Cinema is a popular form of entertainment and a large number of people go to cinema houses for recreation. The advantages and limitations of film advertising are discussed on next page:

1. *Greater Impact* — The impact of film advertising is greater because the viewers can both see the product as well as listen to the product message.
2. *Appropriate for Illiterates* — It is an appropriate medium to communicate information to illiterate people because they can see the picture through eyes and listen to the product message through ears.
3. *Attractive and Attentive Appeal* — It has an attentive appeal because viewers view the advertisement during the leisure time. It has an attractive appeal because film stars and famous models are associated with the advertisements.
4. *Wider Appeal* — It has a wider appeal because a large number of people from all walks of life go to cinema houses for entertainment.
5. *Benefit of Selectivity* — It has a benefit of selectivity in the sense that advertisement can be shown in those areas where a businessman wants to sell his products.

Limitations of Film Advertising

1. *Costly Medium* — It is a costly medium. Due to high cost, small units cannot advertise their products on film. Only big business enterprises can use it.
2. *Lacks Flexibility* — It lacks flexibility. No immediate change can be made because films are to be prepared well in advance.
3. *Short Life and Duration* — Film advertisements are of a short duration and have a temporary effect on the people.
4. *Not Interested* — People may not take interest in advertisements because they go to cinema houses to see films for entertainment.

(e) Outdoor Advertising

Outdoor advertising refers to the transmission of product-related messages through posters, hoardings, billboards and the like. It is the oldest medium of advertising and is still popular in spite of the emergence of many new media.

Posters are pasted on the walls to transmit the message to the people who pass through that area. Billboards contain the painted advertisements and are fixed at busy and prominent crossings and remain in use for a relatively longer period of time.

Electric displays include the use of electrical lights and neontubes to attract attention particularly at night and are put at the centre of heavy traffic on top of a building and at road crossing and railway stations.

Transport advertising include advertisements painted or pasted on buses, cars, railway stations and airports.

Handbills are the advertisements printed on small sheets of paper and distributed either directly to people or through newspaper hawkers. The advantages and limitations of outdoor advertising are discussed as under:

Advantages of Outdoor Advertising

1. *Wide Appeal* — It has a wide appeal. It demands little time and reading effort from the customers. It attracts attention quickly.

2. *Wastage Avoided* — Wastage can be avoided by placing the advertisements at appropriate locations.

3. *Flexibility* — It is flexible in the sense that outdoor advertisements can be made bigger or smaller depending upon the nature of the product to be advertised and the information to be passed on to the customers.

4. *Economical* — It is economical in the sense that the same copy can be seen by thousands of people. Hence, the cost of advertisement per unit is very low.

5. *Selectivity* — It has the benefit of selectivity in the sense that different types of matters can be displayed in different types of outdoor advertising to communicate a series of product messages to potential customers.

Limitations of Outdoor Advertising

1. *Not a Major Medium* — It cannot be a major medium of advertising because the advertisements in outdoor advertising cannot be placed in all parts of the country.

2. *Against Public Opinion* — Public opinion is not favourable to this type of advertising because posters and paintings disfigure walls and other public places and may divert attention of the people causing accidents.

3. *Short Message* — The message has to be short since it is on a running vehicle and has to be read as fast as possible.

4. *Segmentation* — The message reaches only that segment of people who travel frequently on that route or area.

(f) Direct Mail Advertising

Direct mail advertising refers to the transmission of product-related messages through sales letters, folders, pamphlets, booklets, catalogues and the like. The advertiser prepares the list of potential customers (known as mailing list) and sends information to them at regular intervals of time or as and when desired. This list is revised from time to time to make it up to date.

Advantages of Direct Mail Adversiting

1. *Benefits of Selectivity* — It has the benefit of selectivity in the sense that the advertisement can be mailed to selected people (i.e., the persons who are likely to buy the product).

2. *Economical* — It is economical in the sense that the message is sent to the selected people only. Hence, the cost of advertisement per unit is low.

3. *Secrecy* — It ensures secrecy in the sense that the information contained in the message is not easily available to the competitors.

4. *Personal Touch* — It gives a personal touch to the message because it is sent directly in the name of the person who is likely to buy/recommend the product and is addressed to the customers in the same way as talking to them.

5. *Flexibility* — It is flexible in the sense that the message can be changed to suit the particular situation whenever necessary.

6. *Detailed Information* — The advertiser can give the detailed information about his product because there is no limitation of time or place as in newspapers, periodicals, television etc.

Limitations of Direct Mail Advertising

1. *Not a Major Medium* — It cannot be a major medium of advertising because individual letters cannot be sent to all customers.

2. *Difficult to Prepare Mailing List* — If goods are to consumed on a large scale, it becomes difficult to have a complete list of present and prospective customers, further, it is difficult to update it due to continuous changes.

3. *Not Suitable for all Types of Products* — It is not suitable for all types of products particularly for non-standardised products.

FACTORS DETERMINING THE CHOICE OF ADVERTISING MEDIA

The choice of advertising media is made keeping in view the requirements of each individual situation. The factors to be kept in mind before selecting a particular medium of advertising are shown on next page:

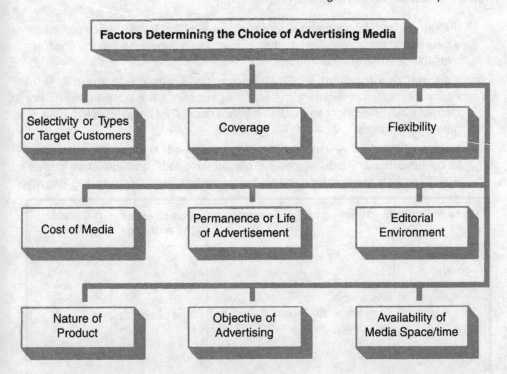

Let us discuss these factors one by one.

1. **Selectivity or Type of Target Customers** — Selectivity refers to the ability of a medium to reach a particular audience. Selection of media also depends upon the type of target customers to be approached. If the advertiser has to convey the message to illiterate people, he has to depend upon television, radio and film advertising and not upon newspapers and magazines. If he has to convey the message to educated people, newspapers and magazines can be used.

2. **Coverage** — Coverage refers to the size of audience a particular medium can reach. For example, a local general and provision store should advertise in the local newspapers or slides in cinema to inform the local residents of that area.

3. **Flexibility** — Flexibility in advertising refers to speed and care with which changes that can be made from time to time. TV and film media are less flexible as compared to posters, hoardings or newspapers.

4. **Cost of Media** — Selection of media depends upon the amount of funds available as per advertising budget. The companies having sufficiently large advertising budget (e.g., Pepsi Cola, Proctor and Gamble, Hindustan Lever) can advertise their products in any medium they like. They can use expensive media like television and cinema. The small business houses have to depend upon less costly media of advertising like newspapers, radio, outdoor media.

5. **Permanence or Life of Advertisement** — Permanence refers to the durability of the medium. Life of advertisement refers to the availability of advertising message for reference or rereading purposes. The messages transmitted

through radio, television and cinema are not available for reference purposes, whereas the messages transmitted through newspapers and magazines are available for reference purposes.

6. **Editorial Environment** — Editorial environment refers to the nature of information or entertainment material that surrounds the advertisement. For example, advertisement for industrial goods should not be given in a magazine meant for females.

7. **Nature of Product** — The choice of media depends upon nature of product to be advertised. Products can be consumer goods and industrial goods. Which media is suitable for each type of goods has been discussed as follows:

Types of Goods	Meaning	Examples	Objectives of Advertising	Suitable Media
I. **Consumer goods** (a) *Convenience goods*	These include all non-durable items which are frequently bought by people.	Bread, butter, tea, toilet soaps, hair oil, washing powder, soft drinks	To popularize the product, its brand name.	Radio and television
(b) *Shopping goods*	These include all those consumer durables which are bought after consi-dering suitabilities, quality and other considerations.	Television sets, radio set, watches, refrigerators, heaters	To give detailed information about utility and safety of product.	Newspapers and magazine
(c) *Speciality goods*	These include all those consumer durables for which buyers are willing to make special purchasing efforts.	Jewellery, music system, fancy dress, antiques	To develop brand preference and popularize the shop	Radio, television, newspapers, magazines, direct mail advertising
II. **Industrial goods**	These include those goods which are used by businessmen in the production of goods or in the rendering of services.	Raw materials, machinery, component parts, tools, equipments	To give a detailed information about the product and to popularize the name of the manufacturer	Radio, television, newspapers, trade journals, profess-ional journals

8. **Objective of Advertising** — The objective of advertising affects the selection of media to a great extent. There may be various objectives of advertising (e.g., to introduce a new product, to prevent loss of sale due to competitive advertising, to sell an existing product at reduced price. Some of the examples are illustrated below:

Objective of Advertising	Advertising Media to be Selected
(i) To introduce a new product	Heavy advertising through Press/ Radio/ TV
(ii) To sell existing product at reduced prices	Handbills, local newspapers of the area in which sale at reduced prices is to be offered
(iii) To prevent loss of sale due to competitive advertising	Same medium which is used by the competitors to advertise their products

9. **Availability of Media Space or Time** — Availability of space in newspapers and magazines and time in television, cinema and radio also affects the selection of advertising media. The advertiser who has to transmit detailed information about the product has to depend on some other media to convey the product message to target customers.

On the basis of above discussion, the relative suitability of different advertising media is given in the following table:

Table showing the examples of products for different advertising media.

Types of Media	Examples of Products
(i) **Newspapers and general magazines**	Shopping goods like furniture, watches, television sets, radio sets Speciality goods like jewellery, camera, music systems etc.
(ii) **Specialised magazines**	Sports magazines for sports goods; Medical Journal for medical equipments and Drugs Law Journal for Law Book;. Industrial journals for industrial goods
(iii) **Radio and television**	Convenience goods like washing powders, washing machines, razor blades, shaving creams aftershave lotions, toilet soaps, soft drinks, hairoils, toothpastes/tooth powders, shampoos
(iv) **Cinema**	Goods meant for local consumption, local restaurants, local beauty parlours, local sweet shops, local tailors, local provision store and local furniture houses, gensral stores

(v) **Outdoor Advertising**	Films, fancy shows, beauty contests, cellular phones
(vi) **Direct Mail**	For law books to advocates and other professionals
	For medical books to doctors
	For accountancy books to chartered accountants
	For text books to professors, teachers and lecturers
	For management books to managers
	For industrial goods to industrial houses, trading houses

Illustration 1 *Suppose you are the marketing manager of an organisation, selling heavy machinery for producing specialised product. Which media would you choose for advertising the product and why ? What other promotional methods would you recommend ?*

Ans.: Being a marketing manager one should prefer to advertise through magazines, journals and direct mailing.

Magazines and journals relating to industry and business are most suitable as they are read by the concerned users and prospective buyers.

Direct mailing to the members of that particular industry is another very good and effective advertising media for heavy machinery. As the approach of advertising is direct, it is easy to send detailed trade advertising material containing technical data to the members of the industry.

Other promotional methods:

(i) Free demonstration;

(ii) Participation in trade fairs and exhibitions.

Illustration 2 X Ltd. is engaged in marketing ladies garments. The sales manager is to select either newspapers or magazines as medium of advertising. Which one of these media will you recommend as more suitable and why?

Ans.: Magazines are the best media of advertising ladies garments for the following reasons:

(i) Effective presentation and longer life;

(ii) Wide circulation.

Illustration 3 An organisation produces refined sunflower oil used in cooking. Which medium should it choose for advertising the product and why?

Ans.: Television will be the best medium for advertising sunflower oil for the following reasons:

(i) Wider coverage;

(ii) Better presentation;

(iii)   Longer·life;

(iv)   Suitable in case of illiterate consumers also.

PUBLICITY

Meaning — Publicity refers to the communication of any non-sponsored commercially significant information about the organisation or its product or service to the public through non-personal media (e.g. Radio, Television, Newspaper, Magazines) without any financial charge to the organisation.

Objective — The objective of publicity is to form public opinion about the organisation and its products or services.

Functions — The publicity has a vital role in disseminating information regarding—

1. New Products;
2. Warranty terms;
3. Product Replacement Services;
4. Customer Service arrangements;
5. New R & D Findings;
6. Contributions made to promotion of sports, culture, and technology, employees' welfare;
7. Dealers' Training;
8. Promotion Activities;
9. Membership of top and senior employees in government and international bodies;
10. Community Development Programmes;
11. Promotion of Company Trade Mark and Slogans;
12. Issues of Public Interest and Welfare.

Distinction between Publicity and Advertisement

Publicity differs from Advertisement in the following respects:

Basis of Distinction	Publicity	Advertisement
1. **What it is?**	Publicity is non-sponsored and non-paid form of non-personal presentation of ideas, goods or services by the media voluntarily.	Advertisement is a paid form of non-personal presentation of ideas, goods or services by an identified sponsor.
2. **Object**	Its object is to form a public opinion (e.g., regarding Govt. policy, nation-wide activities, etc.)	Its object is to stimulate and create demand for goods and services.
3. **Commercial Value**	It may or may not have any economic or commercial value.	It is intended to have commercial or economic value.
4. **Sponsor**	There is no identifiable sponsor.	There is identifiable sponsor.
5. **Payment**	The organisation is not required to make any payment to the media.	The organisation is required to make payment to the media.

MEANING OF PERSONAL SELLING OR SALESMANSHIP

Salesmanship or Personal selling is face to face oral communication with the potential customers for persuading (or convincing) them to buy certain goods or services for mutual advantage.

Salesmanship is a process of persuasion that influences people to buy goods & services.

Personal selling may be defined as the process whereby the seller personally or through his representative ascertains and activates the needs or wants of the buyer and satisfies the needs or wants to the mutual advantage of both the buyer and the seller.

According to the National Association of Marketing Teachers of America, *"The salesmanship is the ability to persuade people to buy goods and services at a profit to the seller and benefit to the buyer."*

FEATURES OF PERSONAL SELLING OR SALESMANSHIP

The essential features of personal selling are as follows:

1. Personal selling **involves direct and personal communication** between the seller (or his representative) and the buyer.
2. Personal selling **relies on oral messages** only.
3. Personal selling implies **contract with limited number** of people.
4. Personal selling has a **feature of feedback** in the sense that salesman can give clarification about the doubts and reply to the objections raised by customers on the spot.
5. Personal selling is **mutually advantageous** to both sellers and buyers in the sense that sellers are able to sell goods at profits and buyers are able to satisfy their needs.

ROLE/OBJECTIVES OF PERSONAL SELLING OR SALESMANSHIP

The role of personal selling in sales promotion is discussed below:

1. Personal selling **facilitates the transmission of product related messages** in a personal way.
2. Personal selling enables the salesman to **identify the prospective customers**.
3. Personal selling enables the salesman **to make sales representation** in a quicker way.
4. Personal selling enables the salesman **to demonstrate** how his product is superior to other products available in the market.
5. Personal selling enables the salesman **to convince the customers** and win their confidence.
6. Personal selling enables the salesman **to receive the order** on the spot.
7. Personal selling enables the salesman **to provide feedback** to the management about the tastes, attitudes and behaviour of customers.

IMPORTANCE OF PERSONAL SELLING OR SALESMANSHIP

Personal selling is an important technique of sales promotion. The success of business depends upon the sales revenue which in turn depends upon the efficiency of the salesmen. Thus, the success of a business house depends upon the successful salesmanship. The importance of personal selling arises from the benefits discussed below that are available to consumers, businessmen and the society:

I. Benefits to Consumers

Salesman helps the consumer in a number of ways such as:

1. He **informs** him of **new uses** of the existing products and the new products.
2. He **demonstrates how** his **product is superior** to other products available in the market.
3. He **assists** the consumer **in selecting products** which match his needs and income.
4. He **guides** the consumer **in purchasing products** which will give him maximum satisfaction.

II. Benefits to Businessmen

Salesman helps businessmen in a number of ways such as:

1. He helps him **in identifying the prospective customers**.
2. He helps him **in creating the demand** for new products.
3. He helps him **in maintaining demand** for the existing products.
4. He helps him **in designing and developing the products** according to the needs of the customers.
5. He helps him **in acquiring information about the tastes**, attitudes and behaviour of customers.

III. Benefits to Society

Salesman helps society in a number of ways such as:

1. He helps society by way of **increased employment** opportunities and income through increase in sales.
2. He **performs other functions** such as after sales service, attending complaints, delivering goods, collecting payments etc.
3. He **helps in raising the standard of living** of people by convincing them to buy new products.
4. He helps in **greater utilization of resources** through increase in demand for goods.

STEPS INVOLVED IN THE PROCESS OF PERSONAL SELLING

The steps involved in the process of personal selling are enumerated as follows:

Step 1 → Presale Preparation: A salesperson should know—

(a) the products he will be selling,

(b) the customers (i.e., customer types, buying motives and buying process) to whom he will be selling;

(c) the competitors against whom he will be selling, and

(d) the philosophy, policies and range of products of his organisation.

Step 2 → Prospecting and Qualifying

Prospecting — A salesperson should locate and prepare a list of prospective customers. Prospects can be located through.

1. identifying the potential of buying more in the existing customers,
2. recommendations of existing customers,
3. winning back lost customers,
4. attracting competitor's customers,
5. customers' information request from advertisement,
6. newspaper announcements,
7. public records,
8. directories like telephone, trade association etc.
9. other salesmen,
10. references from friends, neighbours and business associates, and
11. cold canvassing, that is, going from door-to-door.

Qualifying — The qualifying of prospects is the process of separating the prospects from the suspects. The located prospects should first be qualified broadly in terms of —

1. whether they want the product and how intense their want is,
2. whether they have the adequate purchasing power, and
3. whether and who possesses the power or authorisation to purchase and spend the required money.

It is worth-mentioning here that the ability to search prospect is the most essential ability of a successful salesperson. A good salesperson keeps examining, weeding out the already tapped prospects and updating his lists of prospects, and remains in constant search of new prospects.

Step 3 → Pre-approach — The salesperson should possess detailed information relating to the prospects in terms of existing products consumed, their scale of operation, product range, their buying size, frequency, budget and the process, etc. In short, obtain customer orientation. The sources of information for the purpose include company annual reports, other salespersons, other suppliers to the prospects, census of manufacturers, professional journals, newspapers and market intelligence. The availability of the above information in as detailed a manner as possible will help the salesperson in ranking the prospect in terms of their priority to the company. Good salespersons use the above information in classifying the prospects in A, B and C categories in terms of the priortories of the attention to be given to them.

Step 4 → Approach — 'First impression counts'. As such, this step needs to be carefully planned. This step has two distinct parts — **One,** to meet the customer after fixing an appointment with a positive set of mind, and the **Second,** to make an impact on him. For the latter the salesperson should equip himself with the key benefit to be emphasised, samples or new literature to be handed over, etc. Sales persons should create awareness by presenting and demonstrating the product.

Step 5 → Sales Presentation — The sales presentation should generally go according to the AIDA — Attention, Interest, Desire, and Action approach. Use of key benefit or a problem solver, or a unique act of the salesperson results in gaining attention.

The presentation should proceed in a straightforward manner to help the prospect know that you understand his problem and that is the reason of your being there. To convince the prospect as early as possible, the salesperson should offer evidence through demonstration of the product, use of exhibits, models, sharing of acts, citing examples of its successful applications/usage, showing testimonials, etc. A sales person should convince the customer with regard to the quality and durability of the product. He should correlate the utility and benefits of his products with the needs and requirements of the customer. The overall approach should be to build credibility and confidence in the supplying organisation, its products, and also in its competence to render specialised type of service to the complete satisfaction of its customers.

Step 6 → Handling Objections — A salesperson should clarify all doubts and objections raised by the customer without entering into controversy with the customer.

These doubts or objections should be welcome and they should be answered with confidence. There is certainly no doubt that the prospect has to be thoroughly convinced that the product would satisfy his need.

The golden rules for handling objections are:

1.   Welcome the objection and show respect to the prospect, and

2.   Do not argue with the prospect.

3.   Even when the objections raised are half-backed or trivial in nature, the salesperson should handle the situation tactfully.

4.   Only in extreme necessity, a salesperson should ask the prospect to adequately explain his problem faced. Even under these circumstances courtesy should not be lost sight of, and while the discussion is on. the salesperson should start recounting the benefits of the product agreed upon, and lead the prospect to make a favourable decision. It should be remembered that handling objections sharpens the selling skills of the salespersons.

Step 7 → Closing the Sale — Closing is that aspect of the selling process in which the salesperson asks the prospect to buy the product. There is a critical point during each presentation when the salesperson should ask for the order. Pending the location of the critical point, as the objections are being met, the salesperson should help reduce the choice of options, summarise the benefits of buying, and the consequences of not buying, and if need be, make use of the big idea appeal of buying 'now' at that moment.

The salesperson should have the ability of catching the buying signals given by the prospect and should act on them fast. Some such signals are changing the sitting/standing position and moving closer to the product; reading the instructions on the product; pursuing the testimonials; showing hesitation in being able to afford; asking for another demonstration, if applicable; checking the warranty or asking questions relating to warranty terms. These signals, show that the time is ripe to start taking the order.

Step 8 → Post-sale Follow-up — The selling process does not come to an end by writing the order. A few repetitions reassuring the benefits of the product keep the customer sold. Follow-up provides an opportunity to ensure that the product is being rightly used, and if necessary to re-explain the method of using, handling, and storing of the product when not in use. This builds favourable feelings and nurtures strong buyer-seller relationships. Post-sale follow-up not only reinforces the customer's confidence in the salesperson and his company but also tends to keep competition out. This also helps generate repeat business and valuable word-of-mouth publicity. The following-up is a good source of feedback too.

Conclusion — Although the eight steps of the selling process are essential in spirit, these may not always be followed. **For examples,** When the customer walks walks into the store for buying a product, (2) In case of the expertise of the salesperson (such that he can ignore or assume some information), or (3) the seller's market of the product where customers generally queue up for the product.

Let us also look at the findings of a study by Robertson and Chase on the subject. They point out that:

1. The more closely matched the physical, social and personal characteristics of the customer and salesperson, the more likely is the sale.
2. The more believable and trustworthy the customer, perceives a salesperson to be, the more likely is the sale.
3. The more persuadable a customer is, the more likely is a sale.
4. The more a salesperson can make prospective buyers view themselves favourably, the more likely a sale is.

QUALITIES OF A SALESMAN

The qualities of a good and successful salesman are shown below:

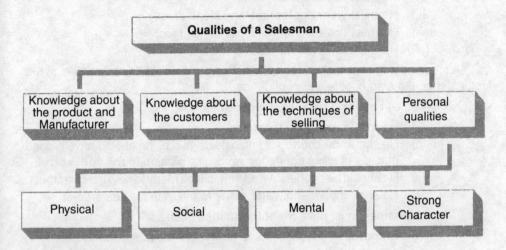

Let us discuss the qualities of a salesman one by one.

1. **Knowledge about the Product and Manufacturer** — In order to answer the questions of the customers, the salesman must have complete knowledge about the product and its manufacturer. He must be in position to answer the various relevant questions of the customers such as:

   (i) What is this product?
   (ii) What are the main uses of this product?
   (iii) What are the other uses of this product?
   (iv) What is the price of this product?
   (v) What is the life of this product?
   (vi) What are the different sizes and varieties of this product?
   (vii) How is this product superior to other products available in the market?
   (viii) What are the terms and conditions of sale?
   (ix) What are the after sales services?
   (x) What is the annual maintenance contract (AMC)?

2. **Knowledge about the Customers** — A salesman must have sufficient knowledge about the customers to whom he is to sell. He must try to understand their nature, types, habits, buying motives, and preferences.

3. **Knowledge about the Selling Techniques** — A salesman must have knowledge about the selling techniques and must be able to distinguish which selling technique is appropriate to be used in a given situation. He must use the appropriate selling technique to create a desire in the mind of prospective customers to possess the goods.

4. **Personal Qualities** — Some of the personal qualities of a salesman are discussed below:

    I. A salesman must have requisite **physical qualities** such as:

        (i)   He must have sound health;
        (ii) He must wear appropriate and clean dress;
        (iii) He must have a cheerful smile on his face;
        (iv) He must have an impressive voice.

    A pleasing and charming personality not only impresses the customers in the first instance but also boosts self-confidence.

    II. A salesman must have **social qualities** such as:

        (i)   He must have good manners;
        (ii) He should be courteous in his dealings (i.e., he should have a good practice of using courteous words like **please, thank you, sorry**);
        (iii) He should be cooperative and should be ready to help his customers;
        (iv) He should be friendly and ready to mix with his customers.

    III. A salesman must have **mental qualities** such as:

        (i)   **Empathy** — He must have ability to understand the problems of customers;
        (ii) He must now a good power of observation;
        (iii) He must have presence of mind;
        (iv) He must have sharp memory;
        (v)   He must have the powers to take quick decisions;
        (vi) He should be tactful in his dealing with the customers. It means that he must have ability to say the proper thing and do the right think without offending others;
        (vii) He must be able to recognize customers, their buying motives and adjust his sales talk accordingly.

    IV. A salesman must have **strong character** such as:

        (i)   **Honest** — He must be honest in his dealings. It means that he should not try to win the customers through false and misleading representation;
        (ii) **Loyal** — He must be loyal both to the employer and the customer;
        (iii) **Dependable** — He must be dependable;
        (iv) **Ego Drive** — He must have a personal passion (or need) to make sale as a measure of recognition and personal success and not just for money.

DISTINCTION BETWEEN ADVERTISING AND SALESMANSHIP

Advertising differs from salesmanship in the following respects:

Basis of Distinction	Advertising	Salesmanship
1. **Meaning**	It may be defined as any paid form of non-personal presentation or promotion of ideas, goods or services by an identified sponsor.	It is the face to face communication between a seller and a buyer.
2. **Interpersonal communication**	It **does not involve** inter-personal communication.	It **involves** interpersonal communication.
3. **Number of persons contacted**	It implies contact with a **large** number of people.	It implies contact with a **limited** number of people.
4. **Feature of feedback**	It **does not have** a feature of feedback.	It **has** a feature of feedback in the sense that the salesman can give clarification about the doubts and can reply to the objections raised by customers on the spot.
5. **Receipt of order on the spot**	It is **not possible** to receive an order on the spot.	It **enables** the salesman **to receive** an order on the spot.
6. **Identification of prospects**	Prospects of product, service or idea **cannot be identified**.	It **enables** the salesman **to identify** the prospects.
7. **Support/Use**	It **supports personal selling**.	It **makes use of advertising**.

_____ EXERCISES _____

SHORT ANSWER TYPE QUESTIONS

Advertising

1. What is advertising?
2. Explain briefly the advantages of advertising to manufacturers.
3. Explain briefly the advantages of advertising to the customers.

4. Enumerate the objections to advertising.
5. Enumerate any six media of advertising.
6. What are the advantages of newspaper advertising of products?
7. What are the advantages and limitations of periodical advertising?
8. What are the advantages and limitations of radio advertising?
9. What are the advantages and limitations of television advertising?
10. What are the advantages and limitations of film advertising?
11. What are the advantages and limitations of outdoor advertising?
12. What are the advantages and limitations of direct mail advertising?
13. Suggest at least two media of advertising for each of the following products:
    (a) Watches
    (b) Gold jewellery
    (c) Medical equipments
    (d) Textbook of business studies
    (e) Films
    (f) Industrial goods
    (g) Local restaurant
    (h) Refined sunflower oil
    (i) Toys
    (j) Heavy machinery
14. Suggest at least two products for each of, the following media of advertising:
    (a) Newspapers
    (b) Medical journals
    (c) Radio
    (d) Television
    (e) Outdoor advertising
    (f) Direct mail advertising
15. An organisation produces refined sunflower oil used in cooking. Which media should it choose for advertising the product and why?
16. Suppose you are the manager in charge of advertising of an organisation manufacturing toys. Which media would you choose for advertising your product and why?
17. Suppose you are the marketing manager of an organisation selling heavy machinery for producing specialised products. Which media would you choose for advertising the product and why? What other promotion methods would you recommend?
18. Enumerate the steps involved in the procedure of advertising.

Personal Selling or Salesmanship

19. What is meant by personal selling?

20. State the role of personal selling in sales promotion.
21. Enumerate the essential qualities of a good salesman.
22. Enumerate the basic principles of salesmanship which every salesman should bear in mind with regard to dealing with customer.
23. Distinguish between advertising and personal selling.

LONG ANSWER TYPE QUESTIONS
Advertising
24. What is advertising? Explain its objectives.
25. What is advertising? Explain the importance of advertising for manufacturers, consumers and the society.
26. "It pays to advertise." Explain.
27. Is advertising socially undesirable? Explain briefly with examples.
28. "All advertising is a social waste." Explain.
29. Explain briefly the functions of advertising.
30. Explain briefly the factors that you will keep in mind while selecting a suitable medium of advertisement.
31. "Advertising is unnecessary and wasteful." Do you agree with this statement? Give reasons for your answer.
32. "Money spent in advertisement is a waste." Explain.
33. Explain briefly the advantages and limitations of press advertising.
34. Explain in brief the steps involved in the procedure of advertising.
35. "Outdoor advertisement is the best medium of advertising." Comment.

Personal Selling or Salesmanship
36. What is personal selling? What are its essential features? Explain the role of personal selling in sales promotion.
37. Describe the various qualities of a successful salesmen.
38. Explain what is meant by 'personal selling'. Discuss the steps in the process of personal selling.
39. Explain personal selling and state advantages of personal selling.
40. What is personal selling? Explain briefly the qualities of a good salesman.

Financial Planning and Capital Structure

FINANCIAL PLANNING

MEANING OF FINANCIAL PLANNING

Broadly speaking, financial planning is the process of determining the objectives, policies, procedures, programmes and budgets to deal with the financial activities of an enterprise. It is the responsibility of top level management. It includes the following aspects:

1. **Estimating the Amount of Capital to be raised**

Basically, the amount of capital required depends upon the nature and scale of business and future expansion programmes. For this purpose, Budgets have to be drawn up to estimate its fixed and working capital requirements. Capital Expenditure Budgets are prepared to estimate the requirements of fixed assets. Cash Budgets and other short-term budgets are prepared to estimate the requirements of working capital.

2. **Determining the form and proportionate Amount of Securities to be issued.**

After estimating the requirements of total capital, decision is to be taken on the type of securities to be issued and the relative proportion between them. Following decisions are to be taken.

   (a) Whether funds to be raised through Owners' Funds (equity) or Borrowed Funds (Debt);

   (b) How much funds to be raised through Owners' Funds (equity) — Equity share, Preference Shares;

   (c) How much funds to be raised through Borrowed Funds (Debt) — Debentures, Long-term loans.

The aforesaie decisions should be taken keeing in mind three factors viz. Cost, risk and control. There should be a proper mix of various sources in such a manner that the funds are procured at optimum cost with the least risk and the least dilution of control of the present owners.

3. **Formulation of Financial Policies for the Administration of Capital** — The second step in financial planning is to formulate the policies which will guide all actions for achieving the firm's primary objectives. These policies cover the areas of procuring, administering and distributing the funds of the organisation. Some of the examples of financial policies are: fixed asset management policy, capital structure policy, working capital management policy, Inventory Management Policy, Debtors Management Policy, Cash Management Policy, Dividend Policy.

4. **Formulation of Financial Procedures** — The third step in financial planning is to formulate the procedures which will help in the practical implementation of the firm's financial policies. Each procedure should be detailed enough to ensure consistency in action. Each person involved in the process should know what he is supposed to do. In developing financial procedures, the financial manager will decide about the control system, develop standards of performance, evaluate the performance and then compare the activities with the standards. To ensure

the best possible use of funds, the finance manager may employ the techniques of capital budgeting, financial forecasting and financial analysis like ratios, budgeting control etc.

OBJECTIVES OF FINANCIAL PLANNING

The objectives of financial planning may be described as follows:

1. **To provide adequate funds** so that enterprise may employ other resources at the optimum level and ensure sufficient profit.

2. **To raise funds at minimum cost** and at most advantageous terms.

3. To balance costs and risks with a view **to protect owner from the risk of loss of control** over management of the enterprise.

4. **To co-ordinate** different functional areas eliminating wastage of resources.

5. **To provide adequate flexibility** so as to enable the enterprise to adjust its capital structure to changing conditions.

IMPORTANCE OF FINANCIAL PLANNING

The importance of financial planning in financial management arises from the following benefits which flow from it:

1. **Prevents the situation of Surplus or Shortage** — Financial planning helps in preventing the situation of surplus or shortage of funds by estimating the current and future capital requirements in a proper manner.

2. **Ensures Co-ordination** — It ensures co-ordination among different functional areas in the business by allocating funds for various activities in accordance with the financial objectives, policies and procedures.

3. **Facilitates Financial Control** — It facilitates financial control by specifying standards of performance, evaluating the performance and comparing the activities with the standards.

4. **Eliminates Wastage** — It helps in elimination of wastage of resources.

CAPITAL STRUCTURE

MEANING OF CAPITAL STRUCTURE

Capital structure (*also known as financial structure*) refers to the composition of long-term funds such as debentures, long-term borrowings, preference shares, equity shares (including retained earnings) in the capitalization of a company. The essence of capital structure decision is to determine the relative proportion of equity and debt. Equity here in broader sense means owners' funds which can be raised by issue of equity shares and preference shares and by retaining earnings. Debt can be raised by issuing debentures/ bonds or by taking long-term borrowings.

The capital structure decision is a significant financial decision because it affects the shareholders' return and risk and, consequently, the market value of shares. The use of the sources of funds with fixed cost such as debt and preference share capital along with the owner's equity capital in the capital structure is described as financial leverage or trading on equity. The use of the term 'trading on equity' is derived from the fact that it is the owner's equity that is used as a basis to raise debt, that is, the equity that is traded upon.

MEANING OF AN OPTIMUM CAPITAL STRUCTURE

Theoretically speaking, the financial manager should plan the 'optimum capital structure' for his company. The optimum capital structure is obtained when the market value per share is maximum in the long run. This value will be maximised when the marginal real cost of each source of funds is the same.

Practically speaking, the determination of the optimum capital structure is a difficult task because a number of factors influence the capital structure decision. That's why different industries follow different capital structures and, within an industry, different companies follow different capital structures.

FEATURES OF AN APPROPRIATE CAPITAL STRUCTURE

While developing an appropriate capital structure for his company, the financial manager should aim at maximising the long-term market price of equity shares. A sound or appropriate capital structure should have the following features:

1. **Profitability** — The capital structure of the company should be most advantageous. Within the constraints, maximum use of the leverage at a minimum cost should be made so as to obtain maximum advantage of trading on equity at minimum cost.

2. **Solvency** — The capital structure should involve minimum risk of financial insolvency. The use of excessive debt threatens the solvency. of the company.

3. **Flexibility** — The capital structure should be flexible to meet the changing conditions. It should also be possible for the company to provide funds whenever needed to finance its profitable activities.

4. **Conservatism** — The capital structure should be conservative in the sense that the debt capacity of the company should not be exceeded. The debt capacity of a company depends on its ability to generate cash flows. It should have enough cash to pay the fixed periodic charges (e.g., interest) and the principal sum on maturity.

5. **Control** — The capital structure should involve minimum risk of loss of control of the company.

The relative importance of each of these features may differ from company to company. For example, a company may give more importance to flexibility than control while another company may be more concerned about solvency than any other requirement. Furthermore, the relative importance of these requirements may change with changing conditions.

FACTORS DETERMINING THE CAPITAL STRUCTURE

A variety of factors are to be considered while determining the capital structure. These factors are shown below:

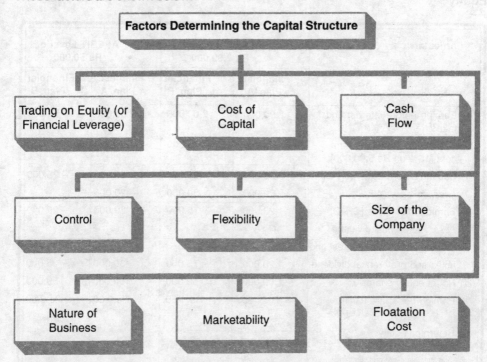

Let us discuss the factors determining the capital structure one by one.

1. **Trading on Equity (or Leverage or EBIT-EPS Analysis)** — The use of the sources of funds with fixed cost, such as debt and preference share capital along with the owner's equity capital in the capital structure is known as 'financial leverage' or 'trading on equity'. The use of the term 'trading on equity' is derived from the fact that it is the owner's equity that is used as a basis to raise debt, that is the equity that is traded upon.

    To examine the impact of leverage on the EPS (i.e., earning per share), EBIT-EPS analysis should be considered. EBIT-EPS analysis shows the impact of various financing alternatives on EPS at various levels of EBIT. Let us consider the effect of financial leverage on EPS by considering two alternative plans.

Example:

Total Funds required	–	Rs 10,00,000
Financial Plan 'A'	–	100% equity shares of Rs 100 each
Financial Plan 'B'	–	50% equity shares of Rs 50 each, and
		50%, 15% debt.
Tax Rate	–	40%

Level of earning before interest and taxes (EBIT) situation (a) Rs 2,00,000, situation (b) Rs 50,000.

Solution:

Statement Showing the Effect of Financial Leverage on EPS and Return on Equity

Particulars	At EBIT Level of Rs 2,00,000		At EBIT Level of Rs 50,000	
	Financial Plan 'A'	Financial Plan 'B'	Financial Plan 'A'	Financial Plan 'B'
(A) Earning before interest and taxes	2,00,000	2,00,000	50,000	50,000
(B) *Less:* Interest on long term debt [15% on Rs 5,00,000]	–	75,000	–	75,000
(C) Earning before taxes [A – B]	2,00,000	1,25,000	50,000	– 25,000
(D) *Less:* Taxes @ 40%	80,000	50,000	20,000	
(E) Earning after taxes [C – D]	1,20,000	75,000	30,000	– 25,000
(F) *Less:* Preferential dividend	–	–	–	
(G) Earning after equity interest and taxes and preferential dividend	1,20,000	75,000	30,000	– 25,000
(H) No. of equity shares	1,00,000	50,000	100,000	50,000
(I) Earning per share [G/H]	Rs 1.20	Rs 1.50	Re 0.30	– Re 0.50
(J) Return on equity $= \dfrac{\text{Earning after interest \& pref. dividend}}{\text{Equity shareholders' funds}} \times 100$	$= \dfrac{120,000}{1,000,000} \times 100$ = 12%	$= \dfrac{75,000}{500,000} \times 100$ = 15%	$= \dfrac{30,000}{1,000,000} \times 100$ = 3%	$= \dfrac{-25,000}{500,000} \times 100$ = – 5%

Analysis

I. At EBIT level of Rs 200,000, Plan B is the most attractive because EPS of Rs 1.50 is higher than EPS of Rs 1.20 as under plan 'A'. This is because of the following two reasons:

    (a) Use of debt in financial plan 'B', and

    (b) Return on total assets $\left(20\% \text{ i.e., } \dfrac{2,00,000}{10,00,000} \times 100\right)$ exceeds the interest cost of debt [i.e., 15% (before tax cost) and 9% (after tax cost)]

II. At EBIT level of Rs 50,000, plan 'A' is the most attractive because EPS of 30 paise is higher than negative EPS of 50 paise as under plan 'B'. This is because of the following two reasons:

    (a) Use of debt in financial plan 'B', and

    (b) Return on total assets $\left(5\% \text{ i.e., } \dfrac{50,000}{10,00,000} \times 100\right)$ less than the interest cost of debt [i.e., 15% (before tax cost) and 9% (after tax cost)].

Thus, the financial leverage is a double-edged sword because on the one hand, it increases shareholders' return and, on the other hand, it increases their risk. It will have a favourable impact on EPS (earning per share) and ROE (return on equity) if return on assets exceeds the interest cost of debt but it will have an unfavourable impact if return on assets is less than the cost of debt. The advantage of debt is that it saves taxes since interest is a deductible expense. The disadvantage is that it can cause financial distress. Financial distress becomes costly when the firm finds it difficult to pay interest and capital.

A firm can avoid financial risk altogether if it does not use any debt in its capital structure. But when no debt is used in the capital structure, the shareholders will be deprived of the benefit of increases in EPS arising from financial leverage (a trading on equity). Therefore, a firm should employ debt to the extent the financial risk perceived by the shareholders does not exceed the benefit of increased EPS. It can be shown as follows:

Case	If ROI> Cost of Debt		If ROI < Cost of Debt	
	Effect on EPS	Effect on Financial Risk	Effect on EPS	Effect on Financial Risk
I. Use of more debt in capital structure	Increases	Increases	Decreases — even if it may lead to negative EPS.	Increases — threat of insolvency
II. Use of less debt in capital structure	Relatively less increases	Relatively less increases	Relatively less decreases	Relatively less increases

2. **Cost of Capital** — The cost of a source of finance is the minimum return expected by its suppliers. The expected return depends on the degree of risk assumed by investors. Higher the degree of risk assumed, the higher will be the return expected by the suppliers of funds. The degree of risk assumed and return expected by suppliers of funds are shown below:

Source of Fund	Degree of Risk Assumed	Return Expected
1. Debt	Lower than any other source of fund	Lower than any other source of fund
2. Preference share capital	Higher than debt but lower than equity share capital	Higher than debt but lower than equity share capital
3. Equity share capital	Higher than any other source of fund	Higher than any other source of fund

The cost of equity includes the cost of new issue of shares and the cost of retained earning. The cost of retained earnings is !ess than the cost of new issues because the company does not have to pay tax on profits distributed as dividend and also no floatation costs are incurred. Thus,

Cost of Debt	<	Cost of Preference Shares	<	Cost of New Issue of Equity Shares	<	Cost of Retained Earnings

Though the cost of debt is cheaper than the cost of shares, it does not mean that a company can minimise its overall cost of capital by employing debt because, after a certain point, the debt becomes more expensive because of the increased risk of excessive debt to creditors and shareholders. Thus, the company should continue to use debt upto the point the overall cost of capital decreases but should not use debt beyond that point when the overall cost of capital starts increasing. Theoretically, the optimal debt equity mix for the company is at a point where the overall cost of capital is minimum.

Example — The cost of debt and of equity capital at various levels of debt-equity mix are estimated as follows:

Debt (%)	Equity (%)	Cost of Debt (%)	Cost ot Equity (%)
0	100	10	14
20	80	10	14
40	60	11	16
50	50	12	18
60	40	13	20

Let us determine the optimal debt-equity mix.

A	B	C = A × B	D	E	F = D × E	G = C + F
Debt	Cost of Debt %	Total Cost of Debt	Equity	Cost of Equity (%)	Total Cost of Equity	Average Cost of Capital
0	10	0	1.00	14	14.00	14.00
.20	10	2.0	.80	14	11.20	13.20
.40	11	4.4	.60	16	9.60	14.00
.50	12	6.0	.50	18	9.00	15.00
.60	13	7.8	.40	20	8.00	15.80

Conclusion: A mix of 20% debt and 80% equity will make the capital structure optimal because it gives the minimum overall cost of capital.

3. **Cash Flow** — The ability of a business to discharge its fixed obligations (e.g., payment. of interest on debt, payment of the principal amount of debt) depends on the availability of liquid cash. The firm may earn sufficient profits to cover

the fixed charges arising out of debt but the firm may not have sufficient cash to pay as the profits get continually invested in the form of more inventory, book debts or even purchase of equipment particularly if it is a growing concern. If a company is not able to generate enough cash to meet its fixed obligations, it may have to face financial insolvency. Hence, besides profitability, it is necessary to estimate the cash flows before deciding on the proportion of debt in the capital structure.

4.   **Control** — The existing management group in order to retain its control over the company, may prefer to raise additional finance through the issue of preference shares or raising debt instead of issuing equity shares. This is because the equity shareholders have rights to elect directors and to participate in the management of the company whereas the suppliers of debt and preference shareholders do not have such rights. The risk of loss of control involved in raising finance through the issue of new equity shares can almost be avoided by distributing shares widely (e.g., by allotting shares to applicants of different regions instead of allotting maximum shares to the applicants of a particular region) and in small lots (i.e., by allotting minimum number of shares (say, in lots of 100 shares) to each applicant. That's why the risk of loss of control is an important consideration in case of a closely held company (i.e., the company in which majority of the shares are held by a few members) instead of a widely held company (i.e., the company in which majority of shares are widely scattered). In case of a widely held company most of the shareholders hold shares in small lots and are widely scattered. They are simply interested in dividend, bonus and appreciation in the price of shares. They are not interested in taking active part in the company's management.

To avoid the loss of control, the company should not use the excessive debt because the restrictions imposed by the suppliers of large amount of debt may curtail the freedom of the management to run the business and it (excessive debt) may also cause bankruptcy which means a complete loss of control.

5.   **Flexibility** — Flexibility means the firm's ability to adapt its capital structure to the needs of the changing conditions. The capital structure of a company is considered to be flexible when the company has ability to change the composition of the capital structure. The company should be in a position to raise funds whenever needed and to redeem its redeemable preference shares or debt whenever required.

6.   **Size of the Company** — The size of a company as well as its credit standing greatly influence the availability of funds from different sources. A small company has to depend on owner's funds (i.e., capital and retained earnings) because it is often difficult for it to raise long-term loans. A large company can obtain long-term loans on easy terms and can also issue equity shares, preference shares and debentures to the public. Similarly, the company enjoying high credit standing among investors and lenders is in a better position to raise funds from various sources as compared to a company enjoying low credit standing. A company should make the best use of its size in planning the capital structure.

7. **Nature of Business** — The nature of business of a company also determines the extent to which equity or debt capital should be raised. If a company is engaged in business activities in which sales are subject to wide fluctuations, it is desirable to have a smaller proportion of borrowed funds because it may face financial distress during lean business due to its inability to discharge the fixed obligations. But if a company is engaged in business activities in which sales and earnings are almost stable, it may have larger proportion of borrowed funds. Similarly, the companies operating in competitive industry (e.g., readymade garments) should rely less on debt capital and more on equity capital.

8. **Market Conditions or Marketability** — Marketability here means the ability of the company to sell or market a particular type of security in a particular period of time. It depends upon the readiness of the investors to buy the security. Due to the changing market sentiments, the company has to decide whether to raise funds through equity shares or through debt. During the boom period in the share market, the company should raise funds through the issue of shares instead of debentures. During the lean period, the company should raise funds through the issue of debentures instead of shares.

9. **Floatation Costs** — Floatation costs here mean the costs incurred by retaining earnings. Floatation costs may be an important factor influencing the capital structure of a company especially in case of small companies which are interested in raising a small amount of funds through the capital market.

CAPITALIZATION

MEANING OF SHARE CAPITAL

The term 'share capital' is used only in relation to corporate form of organisation. Share capital means the capital raised by the issue of shares. The amounts invested by the shareholders towards the face value of shares are collectively known as 'share capital' which is quite distinct from the capital put in by individual shareholders. The persons who contribute money through shares are called 'shareholders'. Under the existing provisions of Section 86 of the Companies Act, 1956, now only two kinds of shares may be issued viz., preference shares and equity shares. Thus, the term 'share capital' is the sum total of paid-up value of equity share capital and preference share capital. In the form of an equation, share capital may be shown below:

Share capital = Paid-up equity share capital + Paid-up preference share capital

MEANING OF CAPITAL

The term 'capital' is used in relation to sole proprietorship or partnership firms, companies and other forms of organisations. In relation to corporate form of organisation, the term 'capital' represents the total funds (long-term or short-term) invested in a business in the form of various assets. In the form of equations, capital may be shown as under:

Equation I	: Capital	= Total funds
Equation II	: Capital	= Long-term funds + short-term funds
Equation III	: Capital	= [Shareholders' funds + long-term debt] + short-term funds
Equation IV	: Capital	= [(share capital + net reserves and surplus) + long-term debt] + short-term funds
Equation V	: Capital	= Net fixed assets + investments + current assets

MEANING OF CAPITALIZATION

The term 'capitalization' is used only in relation to corporate form of organisation. Capitalization is the sum total of all long-term funds available to a company and the surplus earnings not meant for distribution. Capitalization is the valuation of the capital of an enterprise. The valuation of capital depends upon the earnings of a company. The amount of capitalization which a company should have is closely connected with the earning capacity of the business. The total capital invested in the business should be justified by its earnings. Every business is expected to earn at least that much which similar businesses in the same industry are earning. In the form of equations, capitalization may be presented as under:

Equation I	: Capital	= Total funds
Equation I	: Capitalization	= Shareholders' funds + long-term debt
Equation II	: Capitalization	= [Equity shareholders' funds + preference share capital] + long-term debt
Equation III	: Capitalization	= [(Equity share capital + net reserves and surplus + preference share capital] + long-term debt

There may be one of three situations as follows:

Type of Capitalization	Condition
1. Fair or Normal Capitalization	If Actual Rate of Return = Average Rate of Earnings of on Capital Employed an Industry *or* $$\text{Actual Capitalization} = \frac{\text{Actual Earnings} \times 100}{\text{Average Rate of Earnings of an Industry}}$$
2. Over Capitalization	If Actual Rate of Return < Average Rate of Earnings of on Capital Employed an Industry *or* $$\text{Actual Capitalization} > \frac{\text{Actual Earnings} \times 100}{\text{Average Rate of Earnings of an Industry}}$$

3. **Under Capitalization** on Capital Employed	If Actual Rate of Return > Average Rate of Earnings of an Industry
	or
	Actual Capitalization < $\dfrac{\text{Actual Earnings} \times 100}{\text{Average Rate of Earnings of an Industry}}$

Example — Average Rate of Earnings of an Industry   = 10%

Actual Earnings of X Ltd.   = Rs 1,00,000

State the position of X Ltd. if it has invested (a) Rs 10,00,000, (b) Rs 12,00,000, (c) Rs 8,00,000.

Situation	Actual Rate of Return	Average Rate of Return	Capitalisation
(a) If invested Rs 10,00,000	$= \dfrac{\text{Rs } 1,00,000}{\text{Rs } 10,00,000} \times 100 = 10\%$	10%	Normal
(b) If invested Rs 12,00,000	$= \dfrac{\text{Rs } 1,00,000}{\text{Rs } 12,00,000} \times 100 = 8.33\%$	10%	Over
(c) If invested Rs 8,00,000	$= \dfrac{\text{Rs } 1,00,000}{\text{Rs } 8,00,000} \times 100 = 12.5\%$	10%	Under

DISTINCTION AMONG CAPITALIZATION, CAPITAL AND SHARE CAPITAL

The distinction among capitalization, capital and share capital could be presented in the form of statement shown below:

	Rs
(A) Fixed Assets [*net of depreciation*]	xxx
(B) Investments	xxx
(C) Current Assets	xxx
(D) Total Capital [A + B + C]	xxx
(E) *Less:* Current Liabilities	xxx
(F) Capitalization [D – E]	xxx
(G) *Less:* Long-term Debts	xxx
(H) Shareholders' Funds [F – G]	xxx
(I) *Less:* Net Reserves and Surplus	xxx
(J) Share Capital [H – I]	xxx

The distinction among capitalization, capital and share capital can be shown in the below:

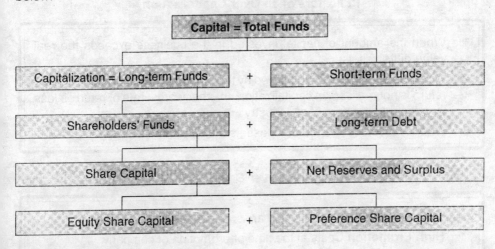

Capitalization and Capital Structure

Capitalization deals with the **quantitative** aspect of financing i.e., it shows the total amount of capital requirement, while capital structure covers both **qualitative** and **quantitative aspects** of financing i.e., it shows the amount and relative importance of different securities in the capitalisation.

OVER-CAPITALIZATION

MEANING OF OVER-CAPITALIZATION

A company is said to be over-capitalized when its long-term funds are more than the amount of proper capitalization as justified by its requirements. It is chiefly ascertained on the basis of rate of return actually earned by a company. In case of over-capitalization, the actual rate of return is very low in relation to rate of return enjoyed by similar companies belonging to the same industry. *For Example —*

A company earns Rs 6,00,000 p.a. after tax and investors consider 10% to be the proper after tax rate of return, then the amount of proper capitalization should be Rs 60,00,000 (Rs 600,000 × 100/10).

If the company has actually Rs 75,00,000 as capitalization, its profit of Rs 6,00,000 will generate a rate of return of 8% [i.e., (Rs 6,00,000/Rs 75,00,000) × 100] which is less than the expected rate of return. It is a case of over-capitalization since the company has an actual capitalization of Rs 75 lakh which is more than the proper capitalization of Rs 60 lakh. [i.e., Rs 6,00,000 × 100/10]

Thus, There are three indicators of an over-capitalised company as follows:

Indicators of an Over-Capitalisation

1. When the amount of capital invested in the business exceeds the real value of its assets;
2. When the earnings are not justified by the amount of capitalization i.e. a fair return is not realised on capitalization. In other words, rate of return is less than the rate of return of an industry;
3. When a business has more net assets than it requires.

Causes of Over-Capitalization

The causes of over-capitalization are stated below:

1. **High Promotion** Costs at the time of promotion of company.
2. **Unduly high price paid for assets** — Acquisition of fixed assets and other assets (particularly goodwill) at a much higher value than that warranted by the service which the assets could render.
3. **Inflationary Conditions during a Boom Period** — Fall in the market price of assets subsequent to their purchases which was the condition of several companies after the World War I when the prices of plants and machinery purchased during the war period slumped in the post-war period.
4. **Inadequate Provision of Depreciation** — Showing the fixed assets without providing adequate depreciation. It may be mentioned that provisions regarding depreciation under Section 205(1) of the Companies Act, 1956, have been included only to prevent recurrence of such a state of affairs.
5. **Existing idle assets** which the company is unable to utilise fully.
6. **Existence of idle funds** which the company is unable to use profitably.

In short, over-capitalization takes place when the company has idle funds or the company's funds have been lost but the same has not been given effect in the books of accounts.

Effects of Over-Capitalisation on the Company

Effects of over-Capitalisation on the company are enumerated as follows:

1. The market value of the shares of the company falls drastically. This affects the marketability of its shares.
2. As the credit standing of the company is adversely affected, it becomes very difficult for the company to raise loans or issue fresh capital from the market.
3. The company is forced to cut down the expenditure on maintenance, replacement of assets and adequate provision for depreciation.
4. The company may be involved in the manipulation of accounts to show higher profits.
5. Because of low profitability, reputation or goodwill of the company is lowered. Company may have to opt for capital reorganisation.

Effects of Over-Capitalisation on the Shareholders

The effects of over-capitalisation on the shareholders are enumerated as follows:

1. Earning per share (EPS) is lower.
2. Shareholders suffer losses due to drastic fall in the market value of the shares.
3. Earnings of company become uncertain and irregular and thus, it results in reduction and uncertainty in dividends.
4. The shares of these companies are not accepted as securities for the purpose of taking loan.
5. In case of capital reorganisation of the company, shareholders have to suffer the most because the face value of their shares is brought down.

Effects of Over-Capitalisation on the Society

The effects of over-capitalisation on the society are enumerated as follows:

1. Company may follow the tactics of increase in prices and decline in the quality of products to increase its profit. Sufferers in this case are the consumers.
2. There is a possibility of labour unrest and strikes in case expenses on wages are curtailed.
3. Creditors of the company may suffer due to irregular payment of interest.
4. Over-capitalized companies become a drain on the resources of society because of their inability to earn adequate return on capital.

Remedies to Overcome the Situation of Over-Capitalization

The remedies to overcome the situation of over-capitalization are summarised as under:

Type of Over-Capitalization	Remedy
(a) When the company has idle funds	To find out profitable investment opportunities or to reduce the surplus capital by paying off loan or redeeming redeemable preference shares under Section 80 of the Companies Act, 1956, or reducing paid-up capital by paying off surplus capital under Sections 100-105 or by buying back of equity shares under sec. 80A.
(b) When the company's funds have been lost but the same have not been given effect in the books of accounts	To write off the artificial values of the assets and to introduce fresh capital to the extent necessary by preparing and implementing the scheme of Internal Reconstruction.

UNDER-CAPITALIZATION

MEANING OF UNDER-CAPITALIZATION

A company is said to be under-capitalized when its long-term funds are less than the amount of proper capitalization as justified by its requirements. It is chiefly ascertained on the basis of rate of return earned by a company. In case of under-capitalization, the **actual rate of return** is very **high** in relation to the rate of return enjoyed by similar companies belonging to the same industry. For example, a company earns Rs 6,00,000 p.a. after tax and investors consider 10% to be proper after tax rate of return, then the amount of proper capitalization should be Rs 60 lakh (i.e., Rs 6,00,000 × 100/10). If the company has actually Rs 50 lakh, its profits of Rs 6,00,000 will generate a rate of return of 12% [i.e., Rs (6,00,000/ Rs 50,00,000) × 100] which is more than the expected rate of return. It is a case of under-capitalization since the company has an actual capitalization of Rs 50 lakh which is less than the proper capitalization of Rs 60 lakh.

Causes of Under-Capitalisation

The causes of under-capitalisation are explained as follows:

1. **Under estimation of Earnings** — At the time of financial planning, a company has underestimated the earnings.
2. **Floatation of a company during depression** — The company was promoted or it acquired fixed assets during depression or when the economy was recovering. This might result in increase in earnings disproportionately to the capital employed during boom.
3. **Conservative Dividend Policy** — The company has followed conservative dividend policy and retained profits for the purpose of creating reserves. This has resulted in higher earnings on capital employed and hence the company is said to be under-capitalised.
4. **High Efficiency** — There is high degree of efficiency in the company due to proper use and maintenance of assets and use of improved technology.
5. **Large amount of Secret Resources** — The company may have large secret reserves due to which its profitability is higher and may, therefore, result in under capitalisation. Secret reserves may be the result of excessive depreciation charges, price level changes etc.

Effects of Under-Capitalisation on the Company

The effects of under-capitalisation on the company are enumerated as follows:

1. Earning Per Share (EPS) is higher.
2. The market value of the shares of a company will be very high.
3. It will be easy for the company to raise loans as the credit standing of the company will be very good.
4. Secret reserves may be built by the company.
5. On seeing higher rate of profit, workers may be tempted to demand higher rate of wages and bonus. This may result in dissatisfaction and labour disputes.
6. This may induce competitors to enter the same line of business. That will result in more competition and less margin of profit to the company.
7. Exceptionally high rate of profit may also induce the government to impose heavy tax.

Effects of Under-Capitalisation on the Shareholders

The effects of under-capitalisation on shareholders are enumerated as follows:
1. Shareholders gain due to increase in the market value of the shares.
2. Earnings of the shareholders become high, certain and regular due to higher rate of dividend and more bonus.
3. The shares of these companies are readily accepted as securities for the purpose of taking loan.

Effects of Under-Capitalisation on the Society

Effects of under-capitalisation on the society are enumerated as follows:
1. Because of higher profits, customers may feel exploited. They may feel that due to higher pricing policy, company is earning very much.
2. Workers are looked after properly.
3. Creditors of the company will get their payment and interest regularly in time.
4. Under-capitalisation results in increase in market price of its shares. This encourages unhealthy speculation in stock exchange and affects the investment climate adversely.

Remedy to Overcome the Situation of Under-Capitalization

The real remedy for an under-capitalized company lies in the introduction of more fresh capital to the extent necessary.

DISTINCTION BETWEEN OVER-CAPITALIZATION AND UNDER-CAPITALIZATION

Over-capitalization and under-capitalization can be distinguished as follows:

Basis of Distinction	Over-Capitalization	Under-Capitalization
1. **Meaning**	A company is said to be over-capitalized when the amount of actual capitalization is more than the amount of proper capitali-zation as justified by its by requirements.	A company is said to be under-capitalized when the amount of actual capitalization at less than the amount of proper capitalization as justified by its requirements.
2. **Earning per share (EPS)**	EPS is **lower**.	EPS is **higher**.

3.	Certainty about periodic income	Periodic income is **uncertain** and irregular.	Periodic income is **certain** and regular.
4.	Market value of share	Market value of share is **reduced**.	Market value of share is **increased**.
5.	Credit-worthiness	Creditworthiness is reduced.	Creditworthiness is **Increased**
6.	Investor's opinion	Investors do **not** have **good** opinion about the company.	Investors have a **good** opinion about the company.
7.	Increased competition	Lower rate of earnings does **not invite** increased competition.	Higher rate of earnings **invites** increased competition.
8.	Agitation for higher bonus and wages	Lower rate of earning **does not tempt employees to agitate** for higher wages and bonus.	Higher rate of earnings **tempts employees to agitate** for higher wages and bonus.
9.	Feeling in customer	Lower rate of earnings does **not create** a feeling in customers that they are being exploited.	Higher rate of earnings may create a feeling in customers that they are being exploited.
10.	Unfair practice	It forces the management to adopt unfair practices to hide the adverse situation and inflate profits artificially.	It does not force the management to adopt unfair practices.
11.	Capital turnover ratio	The capital turnover ratio is **low**.	The capital turnover ratio is **high**.
12.	Current ratio	The current ratio is **high**.	The current ratio is **low**.
13.	Working capital	The working capital is **higher**.	The working capital is **lower.** Because of lower working capital the company **fails**: (a) to have adequate inventory; (b) to extend requisite credit to its customers; (c) to have adequate cash and bank balance to exploit profitable

		opportunities (e.g., losing quantity discount, cash discount); (d) to utilise fixed assets economically; (e) to incur certain essential expenditure such as repairs and maintenance, advertising etc.; (f) to spend money on research and development activities and such other activities as are essential for growth of the company on continuous basis.

Both under capitalization and over capitalization are evils but under capitalization is a lesser evil because the company may have to go in for a complete reorganization in case of an over-capitalized company.

EXERCISES

SHORT ANSWER TYPE QUESTIONS

1. What is meant by 'financial planning'?
2. State any three objectives and aspects of financial planning.
3. Explain the importance of financial planning.
4. Explain the role of financial planning in corporate financial management.
5. Enumerate the important decisions taken under financial planning.
6. What are the various aspects of financial planning?
7. State any three factors affecting financial planning.
8. What is meant by 'capital structure'?
9. What is meant by 'the optimum capital structure'?
10. State any four features of an appropriate capital structure of a company.
11. State any four factors which affect the capital structure of a company.
12. What is meant by 'share capital'?
13. What is meant by 'capital'?
14. Explain the term 'capitalization'.
15. What do you understand by the term 'capitalization'? What is the difference between capitalization and share capital of a company set?

16. Explain the term over-capitalization.
17. State any three causes of over-capitalization.
18. Explain any three effects of over-capitalization on shareholders.
19. Explain any four effects of over-capitalization on society.
20. Explain the term 'under-capitalization'.
21. State any three causes of 'under-capitalization'.
22. Explain any three effects of under-capitalization on a company.
23. Explain any three effects of under-capitalization on shareholders.
24. Distinguish between over-capitalization and under-capitalization.
25. Compare the effects of over-capitalization and under capitalization on the working of a company.
26. Compare the effects of over-capitalization and under-capitalization on shareholders.
27. Distinguish between capitalization and capital structure.
28. State the remedies to overcome the situation of over capitalization.
29. State the remedies to overcome the situation of under capitalization.

LONG ANSWER TYPE QUESTIONS

1. What is meant by financial planning? Explain briefly the steps involved and the role of financial planning in financial management?
2. State briefly the elements included in financial planning and the role played by it in the financial management.
3. What is meant by financial planning? Discuss the various aspects of financial planning. What is its significance in financial management?
4. What is meant by financial planning? What factors should be kept in mind while formulating a financial plan?
5. Explain 'financial planning' and discuss the essentials of a sound financial plan.
6. Explain briefly the characteristics of a sound financial plan.
7. Explain briefly three limitations of financial planning.
8. "Financial planning does not serve any useful purpose." Comment.
9. "Financial planning restricts the discretion and creativity of a financial manager." Comment.
10. What is meant by capital structure? State briefly the essentials of an ideal capital structure.
11. What is meant by capital structure? Explain briefly the factors affecting the capital structure of a company.
12. What is meant by the term 'capitalization'? How does it differ from capital structure and capital?
13. Explain the term 'over-capitalization and under-capitalization'. State the effects of over-capitalization and under capitalization on the company and shareholders.
14. Explain the term 'under-capitalization'. How will you identify an under-capitalized company?

Sources of Business Finance

15

MEANING OF FINANCE

Money used for any activity is known as finance. Every activity whether economic or non-economic, requires money to run it. Some of the examples of economic and non-economic activities which require finance are given below:

Non-economic Activities requiring finance	Economic Activities requiring finance
1. To buy kitchen utensils by a household.	1. To manufacture kitchen utensils.
2. To buy TV by a household.	2. To manufacture TV's by a TV manufacturer.
3. To pay for children's books.	3. To publish educational books by a publisher.
4. To pay house rent	4. To construct residential flats by a builder.
5. To meet expenses on marriage	5. To construct Banquet Hall for marriages & parties

Finance is required in every type of organization whether a profit-seeking organization (e.g., TISCO) or a non-profit-seeking organization (e.g., Red Cross Society) or a political organization (e.g., Bharatiya Janata Party) or a large size organization (e.g., Steel Authority of India Ltd.) or a small size organization (e.g., a hawker selling bananas).

MEANING OF BUSINESS FINANCE

Business finance refers to money and credit employed in business. It involves procurement and utilization of funds for business purposes. The following characteristics of business finance will make its meaning more clear:

1. **Includes All Types of Funds** — Business Finance includes all types of funds used in business. (e.g. Owners' Funds, Borrowed Funds)

2. **Required Everywhere** — Business finance is required in all types of organizations whether large or small, manufacturing or trading.

3. **Amount varies according to nature & size of operations** — The amount of business finance differs according to the nature and size of business operations. For example, smaller the size of business operations, smaller will be the amount of business finance required, larger the size of business operations, larger will be the amount of business finance required.

4. **Amount varies from time to time** — The amount of business finance varies from time to time.

5. **Involves Estimation etc.** — It involves estimation, procurement, utilisation and investment of funds.

6. **Required on continuous basis** — It is required on continuous basis during the life of the business organisation.

SIGNIFICANCE OF BUSINESS FINANCE

Business finance is required for the establishment of every business organization. Finance is required not only to start the business but also to operate it, to expand or modernize its operations and to secure stable growth. The importance of business finance arises basically to bridge the time gap. Manufacturers require business finance to bridge the time gap between the production and recovery of sales. Traders require finance to bridge the time gap between the purchase and recovery of sales of goods.

The need for business finance arises for the following purposes:

1. **To acquire Fixed Assets** — Every business organization whether manufacturing or trading need finance to acquire some fixed assets. Manufacturers need finance to acquire land & building, plant & machinery, furniture etc. Traders need finance to acquire shops for sale of goods, godown for storage of goods and vehicles for distribution of goods.

2. **To purchase raw-materials/goods** — Manufacturers need finance to acquire raw-materials and consumable stores for production. Traders need finance to acquire goods for distribution.

3. **To acquire services of human being** — Manufacturers need finance to pay their workers, supervisors, managers and other staff employed by them. Traders need finance to pay their staff employed by them.

4. **To meet other operating expenses** — Every organization need finance to meet day to day other operating expenses like payment for electricity bills, water bills, telephone bills, travelling & conveyance of staff, postage & telegram expenses & so on.

5. **To adopt Modern Technology** — With fast changing technology, business organization need finance to modernize their plants & machineries, production methods and distribution methods. An enterprise may decide to replace outdated and obsolete assets with new assets to operate more economically.

6. **To meet contingencies** — Every organization needs finance to meet the ups and downs of business and unforeseen problems.

7. **To expand existing operations** — Every organization needs finance to expand its existing operations. For example, a company manufacturing audio cassettes at a rate of 10,000 per day needs finance to increase its plant capacity to manufacture 20,000 cassettes per day.

8. **To diversify** — Every organization which decides to diversify, needs finance to add new products to the existing line. For example, the company manufacturing audio-cassettes needs finance to add new products say Ganga Water.

9. **To avail of business opportunities** — Finance is required to avail of business opportunities. For example, where raw-materials are available at heavy cash discounts, the enterprises need finance to avail of this opportunity.

Finance is said to be life blood of business. It is required not only at the fine of setting up of business but at every stage during the existence of business. It must be available at the time when it is needed. It must also be adequate for the purpose for which it is needed.

Thus, finance is required to bring a business into existence, to keep it alive and to see it growing. Men, materials, machinery and managers can be brought together and engaged in business when adequate finance is available. Many business firms are known to have failed mainly due to shortage of finance. The importance of finance has increased in modern times for two reasons viz., (i) the business activities are now undertaken on a much larger scale than in the past, and (ii) the manufacturing process has become more complex than it used to be. With the growth in size and volume of business and with the increasing complexity of production and trade, there is growing need for finance.

Without adequate finance no business can survive and without efficient financial management no business can earn profits and grow. The survival and growth of a firm is possible if it utilizes its funds in an effective manner. **Collin Brooks** says, *"Bad production management and bad sales management have slain their hundreds but faulty finance has slain its thousands."* If a firm ignores finance it does so at its own peril. A proper financial management provides a strong motivation to work in the right direction.

TYPES OF BUSINESS FINANCE

The types of finance required by business organizations may broadly be divided into the following categories:

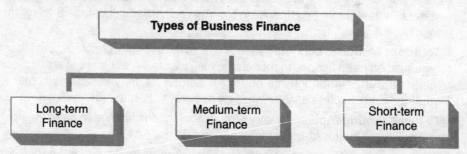

Let us discuss these types of finance one by one.

LONG-TERM FINANCE – MEANING, PURPOSE, FACTORS AFFECTING

Meaning of Long-term Finance or Fixed Capital

Long-term finance refers to the funds required to be invested in the business for a long period of time (say more than 5 years). It is also known as long-term capital or fixed capital.

Purpose of Long-term Finance or Fixed Capital

Long-term Finance is required to acquire fixed assets like land, building, plant, machinery, furniture etc. and to finance permanent working capital (i.e. that part of working capital which is permanently required to hold a minimum level of current assets irrespective of the level of operations).

Factors Affecting the amount of Fixed Capital or Long-term Finance required

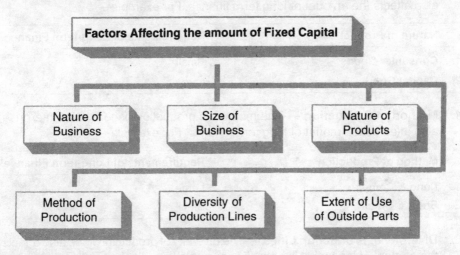

Let us discuss these factors one by one.

1. **Nature of Business** — The nature of the business generally determines the amount of long term finance. Some of the examples are given below:

Nature of Business	Requirement of Long-term Finance
1. **Public Utilities (e.g. electricity generation and supply, water supply)**	Large
2. **Hotels, restaurants and eating houses**	Large
3. **Heavy Engineering Industries like Automobiles, Iron & Steel**	Large
4. **Trading**	Lesser as compared to manufacturing business

2. **Size of Business** — The size of business also affects the amount of long term finance. Size may be measured in terms of the scale of operations. Larger the scale of operations, larger will be the requirements of long term funds, smaller the scale of operations, smaller will be the requirements of long term funds. For example—

Size of Business	Requirement of Long-term Finance
1. **Large Scale Manufacturing enterprises**	Large
2. **Small Scale Manufacturing enterprises**	Small
3. **Large Scale Trading enterprises**	Large but relatively less as compared to manufacturing Enterprises
4. **Small Scale Trading enterprises**	Small but relatively less as compared to manufacturing Enterprises

3. **Nature of Products** — The nature of product manufactured by the enterprise also affects the amount of long term finance. For example—

	Nature of Product	Requirements of Long-term Finance
1.	Consumer Goods	Small
2.	Capital Goods	Large

4. **Method of Production** — The method of production used by the enterprise also affects the amount of long term finance. For example—

	Method of Production	Requirements of Long-term Finance
1.	Long & Complex	Large
2.	Short & Small	Small

5. **Diversity of Production Lines** — The diversity of production lines also affects the amount of long term finance. For example—

	Number of Products	Requirements of Long-term Finance
1.	Multi-Products	Large
2.	Single Product	Small

6. **Extent of Use of Outside Parts** — The extent of use of parts manufactured by outside parties also affects the requirements of funds. For Example—

	Extent of use of Outside Parts	Requirement of Long-term Finance
1.	Nil i.e. each part is manufactured by the enterprise itself.	Small
2.	More use of parts manufactured by outside parties.	Large

Why should Fixed Assets be financed out of long-term finance?

Fixed assets should be financed out of long term finance because investment in fixed assets involves a commitment for a longer period of time and the funds once invested in fixed assets cannot be withdrawn and put to some other use, so long as the enterprise is a going concern.

Sources of Long-term Finance

The various sources of long-term finance include the following:

I. **Ownership Capital**
   1. Equity Shareholders' Funds
      (a) Equity Share Capital
      (b) Retained Earnings

2. Preference Share Capital

II. Borrowed Capital
1. Issue of Debentures
2. Raising of Long-term Loans

MEDIUM-TERM FINANCE – MEANING, PURPOSE, FACTORS AFFECTING

Meaning of Medium-term Finance

Medium-term finance refers to the funds required to be invested in the business for a medium period (say exceeding 1 year but not exceeding 5 years). It is also known as medium-term capital.

Purpose of Medium-term Finance

Medium-term finance is required to meet expenses on modernization of plant & machinery, heavy advertisement campaign, adoption of new methods of production or distribution, renovation of building.

Factors affecting the amount of Medium-term Finance required

The nature of the purpose generally determine the amount of medium-term finance.

Factors affecting the need for medium-term finance

The need for medium term finance generally arises on account of changes in technology or increasing competition.

Sources of Medium-term Finance

The various sources of medium-term financial include the following:
1. Loans from Commercial Banks
2. Public Deposits
3. Retained Profits
4. Redeemable Debentures
5. Redeemable Preference Shares
6. Loans from financial institutions

SHORT-TERM FINANCE – MEANING, PURPOSE, FACTORS AFFECTING

Meaning of Short-term Finance or Working Capital

Short-term finance refers to funds required to be invested in the business for a short period usually upto one year. It is also known as short-term capital or circulating capital or working capital.

Purpose of Short-term Finance or Working Capital

Short-term finance is required to meet day to day operating expenses and for holding stocks of raw-materials, spare parts, consumable, work in progress and finished goods and book debts (i.e. debtors balances and bills receivable). More specifically, working capital is needed:

1. to hold the stock of raw materials for such a period so as to facilitate an uninterrupted supply of raw material to production process;
2. to hold the stock of work-in-progress for process period (i.e., the time duration needed to convert the raw materials into finished products);
3. to hold the stock of finished goods for such a period so as to meet the demands of customers on continuous basis and sudden demand from some customers;
4. to grant credit to its customers for marketing and competitive reasons;
5. to hold cash balances to meet the manufacturing, office and administrative, selling and distribution expenses, taxes etc.

Need for Short-term Finance or Working Capital

Basically, working capital is needed because of the existence of operating cycle.

Operating cycle in a trading firm is the length of time required:

1. to convert cash into inventory of finished goods;
2. to convert inventory of finished goods into receivables;
3. to convert receivables into cash;

Operating Cycle in a Trading Firm is shown below.

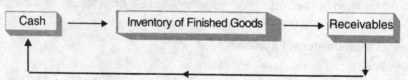

Fig. Operating Cycle in a Trading Firm Selling Goods on Credit

Operating Cycle in a Manufacturing Firm is the length of time required:

1. to convert cash into inventory of raw materials;
2. to convert inventory of raw materials into work-in-progress;
3. to convert inventory of work-in-progress into finished goods;
4. to convert inventory of finished goods into receivables;
5. to convert receivables into cash.

The **Operating Cycle in a Manufacturing Firm** is shown below:

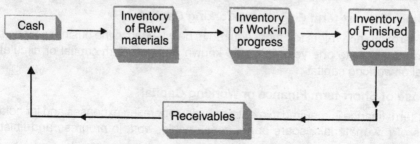

Fig. Operating Cycle in a Manufacturing Firm

Why is Working Capital called as Circulating Capital *or* Revolving Capital?

Working capital is sometimes known as circulating capital or revolving capital because funds invested in current assets are continuously recovered through the realization of cash and again reinvested in current assets. Thus, the amount keeps on circulating or revolving from cash to current assets and back again to cash.

Concepts of Working Capital

There are two concepts of working capital, namely, gross concept and net concept.

(a)   **Gross Working Capital** — It refers to the firm's investment in current assets. Current assets refer to the assets which are held for their conversion into cash within an operating cycle *i.e.*, time duration between the conversion of cash into inventory items (raw-materials in case of a manufacturing firm and finished goods in case of a trading firm) and their conversion into cash.

(b)   **Net Working Capital** — It refers to the difference between current assets and current liabilities. Current liabilities refer to those claims of outsiders which are expected to mature for payment within an operating cycle and include creditors, bills payable, outstanding expenses, bank overdraft. It can be positive or negative. A positive net working capital occurs when current assets exceed current liabilities and a negative net working capital occurs when current liabilities exceed current assets.

In the form of an equation, gross working capital can be shown below:

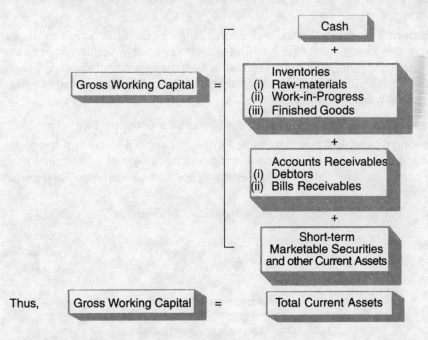

Net working capital is a qualitative concept which indicates:

(a)   Liquidity position of the firm as it represents safety margin available to short-term creditors so as to discharge their obligations within an operating cycle.

(b)   The part of the current assets which should be financed with long-term funds such as equity share capital, preference share capital, debentures, long-term borrowings.

In the form of an equation, net working capital has been shown below:

Net Working Capital	=	Gross Working Capital *or* Current Assets
		less
		Current Liabilities

Permanent and Temporary Working Capital

Permanent Working Capital — It refers to a certain minimum level of current assets which is essentially for the firm to carry on its business irrespective of the level of operations. This is the irreducible minimum amount necessary for maintaining the circulation of the current assets. This minimum level of investment in current assets is permanently locked up in business and is, therefore, referred to as **permanent** or **fixed** or **hardcore working capital**. It is permanent in the same way as investment in firm's fixed assets is. This amount of working capital should be financed with long-term funds.

Temporary Working Capital — It refers to the amount of working capital over and above the fixed minimum amount of working capital, which is required to meet seasonal and other temporary requirements. It may keep on fluctuating from period to period depending upon several factors. It is also called **fluctuating** or **variable** or **seasonal working capital**.

Working Capital in Case of a Stable Firm and a Growing Firm

Working Capital in Case of a Stable Firm — In case of a stable firm, the permanent working capital is stable over time and takes the shape of a horizontal line while temporary working capital is fluctuating — sometimes increasing and sometimes decreasing.

Both these kinds of working capital are shown below:

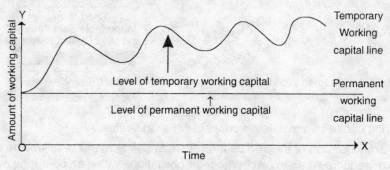

Fig.   Working Capital in case of Stable Firm

Working Capital in Case of a Growing Firm: In case of a growing firm, the permanent working capital may also keep on increasing over time to support a rising level of activity and hence permanent working capital line may not always be horizontal.

Both these kinds of working capital are shown below:

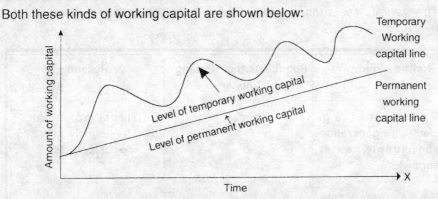

Fig. Working Capital in case of a Growing Firm

Importance of Working Capital Management

The management of working capital is an integral part of the overall financial management and ultimately of the overall corporate management. Neglect of management of working capital may result in technical insolvency and even liquidation of a business unit. Inefficient working capital management may cause *either* inadequate *or* excessive working capital which is dangerous.

Factors Determining the Working Capital

The working capital requirements of an enterprise depends on a variety of factors. These factors affect different enterprises differently and vary from time to time. These factors are shown below:

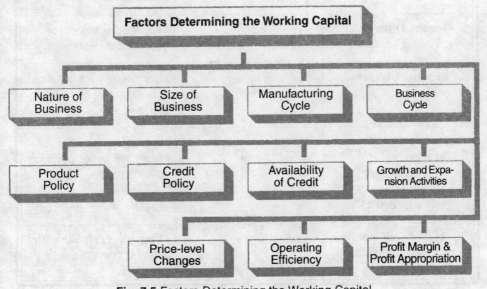

Fig. 7.5 Factors Determining the Working Capital

Let us discuss these factors which determine the working capital one by one:

1. **Nature of Business —** The working capital needs are basically influenced by the nature of business. The proportion of current assets to total assets measures the relative requirements of working capital of various industries. The various researches conducted in India have shown the following results:

Nature of Firm	Requirement of Working Capital	Reason
1. **Public utilities (e.g. electricity generation and supply, water supply)**	Small	(a) They have cash sales. (b) They supply services and not products.
2. **Hotels, restaurants and eating houses**	Small	They mostly have cash sales and only small amount of debtors' balances.
3. **Trading firms**	Large	(a) They require large quantities of goods to be held in stock. (b) They carry large debtors' balances.
4. **Financial firms**	Large	They carry large debtors balances.
5. **Tobacco firm**	Large	They require large quantities of inventories.
6. **Construction firm**	Large	They require large quantities of raw material and work-in-progress.
7. **Manufacturing firm** (a) **Heavy engineering industry (e.g., BHEL)**	Large	They have larger period of operating cycle.
(b) **Rice mill/cotton spinning mill/ steel rolling mill**	Small	They have smaller and period of operating cycle.

2. **Size of Business** — The size of business also affects the working capital needs. Size may be measured in terms of the scale of operations. Larger the scale of operations, larger will be the firm's working capital requirements, smaller the scale of operations, smaller will be the firm's working capital requirements.

3. **Manufacturing Cycle** — Manufacturing cycle also affects the working capital needs. Manufacturing cycle refers to the time gap between the purchase of raw materials and the production of finished goods. Larger the manufacturing cycle, larger will be the firm's working capital requirements. Shorter the manufacturing cycle, smaller will be the firm's working capital requirements. For example, a distillery, which has long manufacturing cycle due to ageing process, requires heavy investment in inventory, whereas a bakery having shorter manufacturing cycle, requires low investment in inventories.

4. **Business Cycle** — Seasonal and cyclical fluctuations in demand for a product affect the working capital requirements, especially the temporary working capital requirements. It has been shown below:

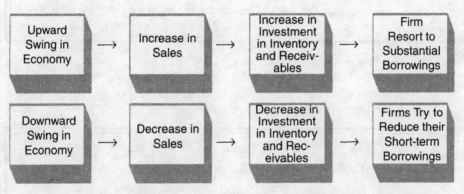

Fig. Effect of Business Cycle on Working Capital

To avoid the production problems arising due to seasonal fluctuations, the firm may follow a policy of steady production in all seasons to utilize its resources to the fullest extent which means accumulation of inventories in off-season and their quick disposal in peak season. Since seasonal fluctuations generally conform to a steady pattern, financial arrangements for seasonal working capital requirements should be made in advance.

5. **Production Policy** — The production policy of the firm affects the working capital by influencing the level of inventories. A firm engaged in manufacture of products the demand of which is seasonal, may follow any of the following three production polices:

Production Policy	Effect
(1) **Seasonal production policy (i.e., production during peak period only)**	(a) Increasing production during peak period may be expensive due to increased costs of materials, labour and other expenses.

	(b) The firm will have to sustain its working force and physical facilities.
	(c) The working capital requirements will be large during peak period and small during slack period.
(2) **Steady production policy**	(a) Resources are utilized to the fullest extent.
	(b) Accumulation of inventories during off-season and their quick disposal during the peak season.
	(c) Firm will be exposed to greater inventory costs and risks.
	(d) The working capital requirements will follow a steady pattern.
(3) **Diversified production policy**	(a) Manufacturing of original product during the peak period.
	(b) Manufacturing of other product during slack period to utilize physical resources and working force.
	(c) The working capital requirements will vary according to the nature of the product.

6. **Credit Policy** — The credit policy of the firm affects working capital by influencing the level of book debts. The credit policy of a firm depends upon industry practice, current economic conditions and the management's attitude. Its effect on working capital is shown below:

Credit Policy	Effects
(a) Liberal credit policy	Higher credit sales, higher book debts, higher working capital.
(b) Tight credit policy	Lower credit sales, lower book debts, lower working capital.

7. **Availability of Credit from suppliers** — The working capital requirements are also determined by the credit terms available to the firm from its creditors. A firm will need less working capital if liberal credit terms are available to it. A firm will need more working capital if no credit or tight credit terms are available to it.

8. **Growth and Expansion Activities** — Growing firm requires more working capital than those that are static. As a company grows, logically larger amount of working capital will be needed. It is difficult to determine precisely the relationship between growth in the volume of a company and its working capital needs. It is also important to note that the need for increased working capital funds precedes the growth in volume of business, rather than follow it. In other words, the need for working capital arises before the growth takes place. That is why an advance planning of working capital is to be made for a growing firm on continuous basis.

9. **Price Level Changes** — Changes in the price level also affect the working capital requirements. However, the effects of changes in the price level may be felt differently by different prices. Generally, rising price level requires a higher investment in working capital because increased investment is required to maintain the same level of current assets. However, the firm which can immediately revise prices of their products upwards may not face a severe working capital problem in periods of rising price levels.

10. **Operating Efficiency** — The operating efficiency means the optimum utilization of resources at minimum costs. The operating efficiency of management also affects the level of working capital. It is shown below:

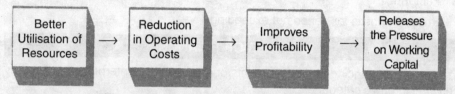

Fig. Effect of Operating Efficiency on Working Capital

11. **Profit Margin and Profit Appropriation** — Profit margin also affects the level of working capital. A high net profit margin contributes towards the working capital pool. The net profit is a source of working capital to the extent it has been earned in cash. Cash from operations can be found out by adjusting non-cash items such as depreciation, losses written off etc.

The availability of internal funds for working capital requirements is determined not merely by the profit margin but also by the manner of appropriation of profits. The availability of cash generated from operations depends upon taxation, dividend policy, depreciation policy, reserves. It can be observed from the figure shown below:

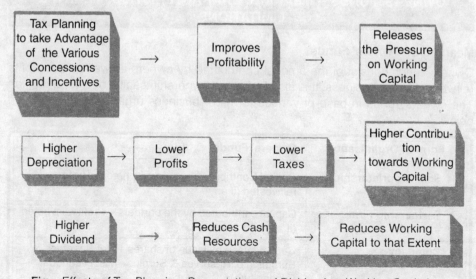

Fig. Effects of Tax Planning, Depreciation and Dividend on Working Capital.

Sources of Short term Finance

The various sources of short-term finance include the following:

1. Trade Credit from suppliers
2. Advances from customers
3. Discounting Bills of Exchange
4. Bank Overdraft
5. Cash Credit
6. Factoring
7. Public Deposits for period not exceeding 1 year

SOURCES OF FINANCE

The sources of financing the requirements of any business enterprise may broadly be divided into two categories:

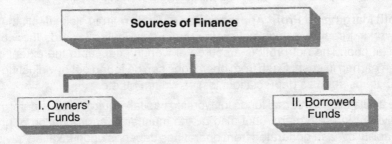

Let us discuss these sources one by one.

OWNERS' FUNDS – MEANING, CHARACTERISTICS, MERITS & LIMITATIONS

Meaning of Owners' Funds

Owners' funds consist of the amount contributed by owners as well as the profits reinvested in the business. It is also known as ownership capital or owned capital. The owners' funds in case of various forms of business organizations are given below:

Form of Organisation	Owners' Funds
1. **Sole-Proprietorship**	Capital Contributed by sole-proprietor + Profit reinvested (if any)
2. **Partnership Firm**	Capital contributed by the partners + Profit reinvested (if any)
3. **Company**	Capital raised by issue of shares + Net Reserves & Surplus (i.e. Reserves & Surplus - Miscellaneous Expenditure)

Characteristics of Owners' Funds

The main characteristics of owners' funds are as follows:

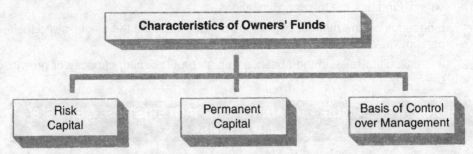

Let us discuss these Characteristics of Owners' Funds one by one.

1. **Risk Capital** — Owners' funds provide risk capital. It is known as risk capital because every business runs the risk of loss or low profits and it is the owners who bear the risk. The effects of risk of loss or low profits are shown below:

Type of Risk	Effect
1. **Risk of low profits**	Owners get low return on their investment.
2. **Risk of loss**	Owners do not get any return on their investment. They may not recover even their original investment if losses continue.

Why owners contribute Risk Capital — The owners contribute risk capital in the hope that the value of the enterprise will appreciate as a result of higher earnings and growth in the size of the enterprise.

2. **Permanent Capital** — Owners' Funds provide permanent capital. It is known as permanent capital because it remains permanently invested in the business and is not refundable like borrowed funds. These funds are used to finance fixed assets and permanent working capital (e.g. minimum level of current assets which is permanently locked up in business)

3. **Basis of Control over Management** -— Owners' funds provide the basis on which they acquire their right of control over the management. Owners can never be ignored by the managers of the business. Who controls where can be seen below:

Merits of Owners' Fund

The owners' fund has the following advantages:

1. It provides **risk capital**.
2. It provides **permanent capital**.
3. It provides the **basis** on which owners acquire their right of control over management.

    Note : In case of a company, after the commencement of The Companies (Amendment) Act, 2000, the equity shares issued without voting rights shall not enjoy this advantage.

4.   It does **not require security** of assets to be offered to raise ownership capital.

Limitations of Owners' Fund

The owners' fund has the following limitations:

1.   It depends on the number of persons prepared to take the risk involved their personal savings.

2.   It is difficult to raise in the absence of high profit earning capacity or growth prospects.

BORROWED FUNDS – MEANING, CHARACTERISTICS, MERITS & LIMITATIONS

Meaning of Borrowed Funds

Borrowed funds consists of the amount raised by way of loans or credit. It is also known as borrowed capital. The borrowed funds in case of various forms of business organizations are given below:

Form of Organistion	Borrowed Funds
1. **Sole-Proprietorship**	Loans raised by the proprietor on his personal security or on the security of his existing assets.
2. **Partnership Firm**	Loan raised by the firm on the personal security of the partners or the security of the assets.
3. **Company**	Borrowings raised by issue of debentures, through loans or credit

Characteristics of Borrowed Funds

The main characteristics of borrowed funds are as follows:

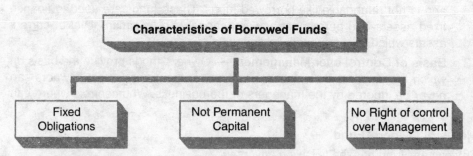

Let us discuss these Characteristics of Borrowed Funds one by one.

1.   **Fixed Obligations** — Borrowed Capital involves the following two fixed obligations:

 (a)   Interest is payable at half yearly or yearly intervals. Interest is payable as a charge against the profits irrespective of the fact whether there are profits or losses.

(b) The principal amount is payable as and when due.

2. **Not Permanent Capital** — Borrowed capital is not a permanent capital in the sense that it can not be used permanently by any business because it is available for a specified period and is repayable at the end of the specified period or after stated intervals in certain instalments according to the terms & conditions of loan agreement.

3. **No Right of control over management** — Lenders and creditors normally do not have any right of control over the management of the borrowing organization.

Merits of Borrowed Funds

The borrowed funds have the following advantages:

1. **Tax Advantage — Interest** is a **tax deductible expense**. In other words, interest is charged as an expense against profits and as a result profits get reduced thereby and consequently, the tax liability gets reduced. An example to illustrate this point is given below:

Particulars	If ownership capital is used	If borrowed capital is used
A. Earnings before interest & tax	1,00,000	1,00,000
B. *Less:* Interest	—	30,000
C. Earning after interest	1,00,000	70,000
D. *Less:* Tax @ 40%	40,000	28,000
	60,000	42,000

2. **Advantage of Trading on Equity** — The borrower has an **advantage of trading on equity** if the rate of return on investment exceeds the rate of interest payable on borrowings. In this case owners get higher rate of return on their investment. An **example** to illustrate this point is given below:

Particulars	If ownership capital is used	If borrowed capital is used
A. Earning before Interest & Taxes [@ 20% on Rs. 10,00,000]	2,00,000	2,00,000
B. *Less:* Interest [@ 15% on Rs. 5,00,000]	—	75,000
C. Earning before tax [A–B]	2,00,000	1,25,000
D. *Less:* Taxes @ 40%	80,000	50,000
E. Earnings after tax [C–D]	1,20,000	75,000
F. Return on owners' Investment	$\frac{1,20,000}{10,00,000} \times 100 = 12\%$	$\frac{75,000}{5,00,000} \times 100 = 15\%$

3. **No Risk of Loss of Control** — There does **not exist any risk of loss of control** as the lenders and creditors normally can not participate in the management of the company.

4. **Lower Cost of Debt** — The **cost of debts** is **lower** than the cost of ownership capital because of the following two reasons.

   (a) Lenders expect low rates of interest as they assume low degree of risk

   (b) Interest is tax deductible expense.

Limitations of Borrowed Funds

The borrowed funds have the following limitations :

1. It **involves fixed obligations** to pay interest and principal amount.

2. It **requires adequate security** to be offered against loans.

3. There **exists the risk of insolvency** because of the following two reasons:

    (a) Interest is a charge against the profits and is to be paid even if there are losses

    (b) Borrowings are to be repaid as and when due.

    The use of debt can cause financial distress when the firm finds it difficult to pay interest and principal.

4. The use of debt **increases the risk of owners** because it will have unfavourable impact if return on assets is less than the cost of debt.

DISTINCTION BETWEEN OWNERS' FUND AND BORROWED FUND

Ownership capital differs from borrowed capital in the following respects:

Basis of Distinction	Owners' Fund	Borrowed Fund
1. **Risk Capital**	It **provides** risk capital.	It does **not provide** risk capital.
2. **Permanent Capital**	It **provides** permanent capital.	It does **not provide** permanent capital.
3. **Basis of Control**	It **provides** the basis on which owners acquire their right of control over management.	It does **not affect** the owners' control over management.
4. **Security of Assets**	It does **not require** security of assets to be offered to raise ownership capital.	It **requires** security of assets to be offered to raise borrowed capital.
5. **Reward**	Reward for ownership capital is an **appropriation** out of profits and is given if there are profits.	Reward for borrowed capital is a **charge** against the profits and is payable even if there are losses.

6. Reward Whether Tax Deductible	Reward for ownership capital is **not tax deductible**.	Reward for borrowed capital is **tax deductible**.
7. Higher Rate of Return in case of high profits	Its owners **enjoy higher** *rate* of return in case the overall rate of return on investment exceeds rate of interest on borrowed capital.	Lenders get **only fixed** *rate* of interest even if profits are high.
8. Fixed Obligations	It does **not involve** any fixed obligation.	It **involves** fixed obligations to pay interest and to repay principal.
9. Priority as to payment of reward	Reward for ownership capital **does not get priority** over the payment of interest.	Payment of interest on borrowed capital **gets priority** over the payment of reward for ownership capital.
10. Priority as to repayment of principal during winding up	Payment of ownership capital is made **after** the repayment of borrowed capital.	Payment of borrowed capital is made **before** the payment of ownership capital.
11. Rate of return - Fixed or Fluctuating	The rate of return on ownership capital is **fluctuating** since it may vary from year to year.	The rate of interest on borrowed capital is **fixed**.

COMPARATIVE STUDY OF SOURCES OF RAISING FUNDS IN CASE OF A COMPANY

A company needs funds to meet its different types of financial needs. A basic principle is that short-term financial needs should be met from short-term sources, medium-term financial needs from medium-term sources and long-term financial needs from long-term sources. Accordingly, the method of raising the funds is to be decided with reference to the period for which funds are required.

The purpose, period and sources of various finances available in India are summarised as under:

Basis of Distinction	Short-term Sources	Medium-term Sources	Long-term Sources
1. *Purpose*	To finance temporary working capital	To finance deferred revenue expenditure (e.g., have publicity and advertisement campaign)	To finance fixed assets and hard core (permanent) working capital

2. *Period for which funds are required (Note: distinction is arbitrary)*	Normally not exceeding one year	Exceeding one year but normally not exceeding five years	Exceeding five years
3. *Sources*	(i) Trade credit from suppliers (ii) Advances from customers (iii) Bill discounting facility (iv) Overdraft (v) Cash credit (vi) Factoring (vii) Public deposits for a period not exceeding one year	(i) Commercial banks (ii) Public deposits (iii) Retained Profits (iv) Redeemable debentures (v) Redeemable preference shares (vi) Loan from financial institutions	(i) Equity shares (ii) Preference shares (iii) Debentures (iv) Loans from financial institutions (v) Retained Profits

SOURCES OF LONG-TERM FINANCE

To finance fixed assets and permanent part of working capital (also known as hard core working capital), long-term capital is required for a long period (normally exceeding 5 years but not exceeding 25 years). The principal sources of raising long-term capital in case of a company are shown below:

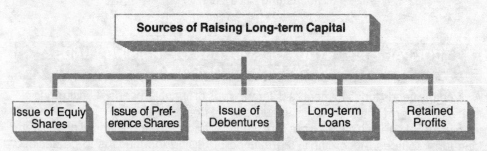

Let us discuss the sources of raising long-term capital one by one.

ISSUE OF EQUITY SHARES – MEANING, FEATURES, MERITS, LIMITATIONS

Meaning of An Equity Share

An equity share is a share which is not a preference share. In other words, it is a share which does not carry two preferential rights (viz., right to receive dividend and right to receive repayment of capital) attached to a preference share. The capital raised through equity shares is called equity share capital and the persons who contribute money through equity shares are called equity shareholders.

The main features of these shares are discussed below:

1. The equity shareholders generally enjoy voting rights. They have right to elect directors and to participate in the management.

    Note: After the commencement of The Companies (Amendment) Act, 2000, the company can issue equity shares without voting rights or with disproportionate voting rights.

2. The rate of equity dividend is not fixed and may vary from year to year depending upon the profits available and the decision of directors (at board meeting) and members (at annual general meeting).

3. The equity share capital is generally not redeemable during the life of the company unless the company decides to buy back its shares.

    The merits and limitations equity share capital from the point of view of both the company and the shareholders are discussed below:

Merits of Equity Share Capital from the Point of View of Company

The merits of equity share capital from the point of view of company are given below:

1. **Permanent Capital** — Equity share capital is the permanent capital because it is not generally redeemable during the life of the company unless the company decides to buy back its shares.

2. **No Fixed Obligation** — There is no fixed obligation to pay equity dividend because the rate of equity dividend depends on the profits available, and the decision of directors and members.

3. **No Security** — Equity shares are issued without any charge (security) on assets.

4. **Enhances the Capacity of Raise Further Debt** — Equity share capital raises the capacity of the company to raise further debt.

5. **No Risk of Financial Insolvency** — There does not exist any risk of financial insolvency as there is not fixed obligation.

Limitations of Equity Share Capital from the Point of View of Company

The limitations of equity share capital from the point of view of company are given below:

1. **Highest Cost** — The cost of equity shares is highest because of the following four reasons:

    (i) Equity shareholders expect high rates of dividends as they assume higher degree of risk.

    (ii) Dividends are not tax deductible as dividend is treated as an appropriation out of profits and not as a charge against the profits.

    (iii) Flotation cost of new issue of equity shares is higher than that of other sources of funds

2. **Risk of Loss of Control** — There exists the risk of loss of control as the equity shareholders having voting rights may vote against the existing management group of the company.

3. **No Advantage of Trading on Equity** — Exclusive dependence on equity share capital does not permit the company to take advantage of trading on equity.

4. **Not Attracts Many Investors** — Issue of equity does not attract many investors because of risk of fluctuation in the rate of dividend and market value of shares.

Merits of Equity Share Capital from the Point of View of Shareholders

The merits of equity share capital from the point of view of shareholders are given below:

1. **Voting Rights** — They enjoy voting rights. They have rights to elect directors and to participate in the management of the company.

2. **High Dividend** — They may get high rates of dividend in profitable years.

3. **Bonus Shares** — They may get bonus shares in profitable years.

4. **Capital Appreciation** — They may get capital appreciation in the value of their shares.

5. **High Liquidity** — They may sell shares in the share market to get liquid funds.

Limitations of Equity Share Capital from the Point of View of Shareholders

The limitations of equity share capital from the point of view of shareholders are discussed below:

1. **Uncertainty of Earnings** —They bear high degree of risk associated with uncertainty of earnings of the company. They may not get any dividend in the years of losses or lesser profits.

2. **High Risks** — They bear high degree of risk associated with the fluctuation in the market prices of their shares.

3. **Inability to Participate in the Management** — In case of widely held company, they are practically not in a position to participate in the management of the company as they are usually scattered and hold shares in small lots.

4. **No Security** — They may get less or nothing at the time of liquidation because they are repaid at the last only and that their shares are not secured against any asset.

5. **No Control Over Increase in Rate of Dividend** — They cannot increase the rates of equity dividend as proposed by the board of directors.

ISSUE OF PREFERENCE SHARES – MEANING, KINDS, MERITS & LIMITATIONS

Meaning of Preference Share

According to Section 85 of the Companies Act, 1956, a preference share is one which carries the following two rights:

1. **A right to receive dividend** at a stipulated rate or of a fixed amount before any dividend is paid on equity shares; and

2. **A right to receive repayment of capital** on winding up of the company, before the capital of equity shareholders is returned.

Kinds of Preference Shares

In addition to the aforesaid two preferential rights, a preference share may carry some other rights. On the basis of additional rights, preference shares can be classified into seven types as under:

1. **Cumulative preference share** is the share on which arrears of dividend accumulate. Unless stated otherwise, a preference share is always deemed to be a cumulative share.

2. **Non-cumulative preference share** is the share on which, arrears of dividend do not accumulate as per the express provision in the articles of association.

3. **Participating Preference Share** is that share which, in addition to two basic preferential rights, also carries one or more of the following rights as per the articles of association:

   (i) a right to participate in the surplus profits left after paying dividend to equity shareholders; and

   (ii) a right to participate in the surplus assets left after the repayment of capital to equity shareholders on the winding up of the company.

4. **Non-participating preference share** is the share which is not a participating share. Unless stated otherwise, a preference share is always deemed to be a non-participating preference share.

5. **Convertible preference share** is the share which confers on its holder a right of conversion into equity share.

6. **Non-convertible preference share** is the share which does not confer on its holder a right of conversion into equity share. Unless stated otherwise, a preference share is always deemed to be a non-convertible share.

7. **Redeemable preference share** is the share which is redeemable in accordance with the provisions of Sections 80 And 80A of the Companies Act, 1956. After the commencement of the Companies (Amendment) Act, 1988, no company limited by shares can issue any preference share which is irredeemable.

The merits and limitations of preference share capital from the point of view of company and shareholders are discussed below:

Merits of Preference Share Capital from the Point of View of Company

The merits of preference share capital from the point of view of company are discussed below:

1. **Dividend Not Charge** — Preference dividend is payable at a **fixed rate** and is payable as an appropriation and not as a charge. In other words, it is payable only if there are profits.

2. **No Risk of Loss of Control** — There does not exist any risk of loss of control as the preference shareholders do not have any voting rights (except at their class meetings) and they cannot participate in the management of the company.

3. **No Security** — Preference shares are issued without any charge (security) on assets.

4. **No Risk of Financing Insolvency** — There does not exist any risk of financial insolvency in relation to payment of preference dividend because preference dividend is an appropriation out of profits and not a charge against the profits.

5. **Low Cost** — The cost of preference share is lower than the cost of equity shares.

6. **Advantage of Trading on Equity** — The Company has an advantage of trading on equity if the rate of return on investment exceeds the rate of preference dividend. In this case, equity shareholders get higher rate of return on their investment. An example to illustrate this point is given below:

Statement showing the Effect of Use of Preference Share Capital on Return on Equity Share Capital

Particulars	If Equity Share Capital (Rs. 10,00,000 alone is used)	If Equity Share Capital (Rs. 5,00,000) alongwith Preference Share Capital (Rs. 5,00,000) is used
A. Earning After Tax	2,00,000	2,00,000
B. *Less:* Pref. Dividend @ 15%	—	75,000
C. Earning available for Equity Shareholders	2,00,000	1,25,000
D. Return on Equity Share Capital	$\frac{2,00,000}{10,00,000} \times 100 = 20\%$	$\frac{1,25,000}{5,00,000} \times 100 = 25\%$

Limitations of Preference Share Capital from the Point of View of Company

The limitations of preference share capital from the point of view of company are discussed below:

1. **Cost Higher than that of Debt** — The cost of preference share is higher than the cost of debt because of the following four reasons:
   (i) Preference shareholders **expect high rates of return** in comparison to suppliers of debt.
   (ii) Dividends are **not tax deductible** as dividend is treated as an appropriation out of profits and not as a charge against the profits.
   (iii) **Flotation cost** of new issue of preference share is **higher** than that of issue of debentures.

2. **Not Permanent Capital** — Preference share capital is not a permanent capital because it is to be redeemed within a period which can never exceed 10 years.

3. **Not Attracts many investors** — Issue of preference shares does not attract many investors because of risk of no dividend in case of losses or inadequate profits.

Merits of Preference Share Capital from the Point of View of Shareholders

The merits of preference share capital from the point of view of shareholders are discussed below:

1. **Preferential right as to the payment of dividend** — They enjoy preferential right as to the payment of dividend as the payment of preference dividend is made before the payment of equity dividend.

2. **Preferential right as to the repayment of capital** — They enjoy preferential right as to the repayment of preference share capital as the repayment of preference share capital is made before the repayment of equity share capital.

3. **No Reduction in Dividend** — The rate of preference dividend cannot be reduced as it is already fixed.

4. **Accumulation of Dividend** — In case of cumulative preference shares, the arrears of dividend also accumulate.

5. **Redeemable** — The shares are redeemable during the life time of the company.

Limitations of Preference Share Capital from the Point of View of Shareholders

The limitations of preference share capital from the point of view of shareholders are discussed below:

1. **No Voting Rights** — Shareholders do not have any voting rights except at their class meetings. They do not have right to appoint directors and to participate in the management of the company.

2. **No Capital Appreciation** — Shareholders do not get any capital appreciation in the value of their shares as in the case with equity shares.

3. **No Increase in Dividend** — Shareholders do not get increased rates of dividend in the years of high profits as the rate of preference dividend is fixed.

DISTINCTION BETWEEN AN EQUITY SHARE AND A PREFERENCE SHARE

An equity share and a preference share can be distinguished as follows:

Basis of Distinction	An Equity Share	A Preference Share
1. **Preferential right as to the payment of dividend**	Payment of equity dividend is made **after** the payment of preference dividend.	Payment of preference dividend is made **before** the payment of equity dividend.
2. **Preferential right as to the repayment of capital**	Repayment of equity share capital is made **after** the repayment of preference share capital.	Repayment of preference share capital is made **before** the repayment of equity share capital.
3. **Rate of dividend - Fixed or Fluctuating**	The rate of equity dividend **may fluctuate** from year to year depending upon the decision of directors and members.	The rate of preference dividend is **fixed**.
4. **Arrears of dividend**	In case of an equity share, arrears of dividend **cannot accumulate** in any case.	In case of preference shares, arrears of dividend **may accumulate**.
5. **Convertibility**	It **cannot be** convertible.	It **may be** convertible.
6. **Redeemability**	It is **not redeemable** during the lifetime of the company **unless** the company decides to **buy-back** its shares.	It is **redeemable** during the lifetime of the company.
7. **Right to receive premium on redemption**	It **cannot carry** a right to receive premium on redemption.	It **may carry** a right to receive premium on redemption.
8. **Voting rights**	Equity shareholders **generally enjoy** voting rights.	Preference share holders **do not** have any voting rights except at their class meetings.
9. **Fluctuation in market Value**	Its market value **fluctuates**.	Its market value **usually does not fluctuate**.

ISSUE OF DEBENTURES – MEANING, FEATURES, KINDS, MERITS & LIMITATIONS

Meaning of Debenture

A debenture is a written instrument acknowledging a debt and containing provisions as regards the repayment of principal and the payment of interest at a fixed rate. According to Sec. 2 (12) of The Companies Act, 1956, debenture includes debentures, stock, bonds and any other securities of a company whether constituting a charge on the assets of the company or not. Debenture represents a debt. The persons who contribute money through debentures are called debentureholders. The main features of the debentures are discussed below:

1. **Fixed Interest** — The rate of interest payable on debentures is fixed and is payable on the face value of the debentures.

2. **No Voting Rights** — The debentureholders do not enjoy voting rights except at their class meetings. They do not have rights to elect directors and to participate in the management.

3. **Redeemable** — The debentures are redeemable during the life of the company.

Kinds of Debentures

Depending upon the terms and conditions of the issue and redemption, the debentures may of the various types as given below:

1. **Naked Debentures or Unsecured Debentures** are those which are not secured on any asset. The holders of these debentures are treated as ordinary creditors.

2. **Secured Debentures** are those which are secured either on a particular asset or on all the assets of the company in general. According to SEBI Guidelines, non-convertible debentures for a term exceeding 18 months must be secured.

3. **First Mortgage Debentures** are those which have a first claim on the assets charged.

4. **Second Mortgage Debentures** are those which have a second claim on the assets charged.

5. **Redeemable Debentures** are those which are repayable after a specified period in lumpsum or by instalments during the life time of the company

6. **Irredeemable Debentures (or Perpetual Debentures)** are those which are not redeemable during the life time of the company.

7. **Registered Debentures** are those which are payable to the persons whose names appear in the Register of Debenture-holders. These can be transferred only by executing a transfer deed. Interest is paid to the registered holder.

8. **Bearer Debentures** are those which are payable to bearer thereof. These can be transferred merely by delivery. Interest is paid to the person who produces the interest coupon attached to such debentures.

9. **Convertible Debentures** are those, the holders of which have a right to convert them into shares.

A convertible debenture is one which entitles its holder a right of conversion into share. The portion of debenture which is fully convertible into shares is termed as FCD (i.e. Fully Convertible Debenture) portion and the remaining portion which is not convertible into shares is termed as NCD (i.e. Non-convertible Debenture) portion. The worth noting points in this regard are as follows:

(i) Conversion takes place as per the terms of issue.

(ii) Conversion can take place —

— at a specified date (e.g. at 31st Dec. 2005)

— after a specified period (e.g. on the expiry of 6 months from the date of allotment)

— Within a specified period (e.g. after the expiry of 3 years but within years from the date of allotment).

(iii) Conversion can take place even before the expiry of the specified period after passing the necessary resolution at the meeting of debenture-holders e.g., Convertible Debenture (Part III) of Reliance Petrochemicals Ltd. were converted before the expiry of specified period of 5 years. However, in such a case conversion is optional.

10. **Non-convertible (NCD)** are those, the holders of which do not have a right to convert them into shares. Unless otherwise stated, the debentures are deemed to be non-convertible debentures.

Merits of Debentures from the Point of View of the Company

The merits of debentures from the point of view of the company are discussed below:

1. **Low Cost** — The **cost** of debt is **lower** than the cost of share because of the following reasons:

   (i) Debenture holders expect low rates of interest as they assume low degree of risk.

   (ii) Interest is **tax deductible** expense. In other words, interest is allowed as deduction while computing total income on which tax liability is calculated. As a result, tax liability is reduced.

2. **No Risk of Loss of Control** — There does not exist any risk of loss of control as the debenture holders do not have any voting rights (except at their class meeting) and cannot participate in the management of the company.

3. **Advantage of Trading on Equity** — The company has an advantage of trading on equity if the rate of return on investment exceeds the rate of interest payable on debentures. In this case, equity shareholders get higher rate of return on their investment. An example to illustrate this point is given below:

Statement showing the Advantage of Use of Debt

Particulars	If Company has Issued equity shares of Rs. 10,00,000	If the company has issued equity shares of Rs. 5,00,000 & 15% debentures of Rs. 5,00,000
A. Earning before Interest & taxes [20% on Rs. 10,00,000]	2,00,000	2,00,000
B. *Less:* Interest	—	75,000
C. Earnings before tax [A-B]	2,00,000	1,25,000
D. *Less:* Tax @ 40%	80,000	50,000
E. Earnings after tax [C-D]	1,20,000	75,000
F. Return on Equity Capital	$\frac{1,20,000}{10,00,000} \times 100 = 12\%$	$\frac{75,000}{5,00,000} \times 100 = 15\%$

Limitations of Debentures from the Point of View of the Company

The limitations of debentures from the point of view of the company are discussed below:

1. **Risk of Financial Insolvency** — There exists the risk of financial insolvency because of the following two reasons:

   (i) Interest on debentures is a charge against the profits and is to be paid even if the company suffers losses.

   (ii) Debentures are to be redeemed at the scheduled time of redemption during the life time of the company.

   The use of debt can cause financial distress when the firm finds it difficult to pay interest and principal.

2. **Security** — Non-convertible debentures (NCD) for a term exceeding 18 months are to be secured against assets.

3. **Increases Risk of Shareholders** — The use of debt increases the risk of shareholders because it will have unfavourable impact if return on assets is less than the cost of debt.

DISTINCTION BETWEEN A SHARE AND A DEBENTURE

A share and debenture can be distinguished as follows:

Basis of Distinction	A Share	A Debenture
1. **Capital *vs* Loan**	Share is a part of **owned** capital.	Debenture constitutes a loan.
2. **Reward for investment**	Reward is the payment of dividend.	Reward is the payment of interest.

3. **Rate of interest and dividend-Fluctuating or Fixed**	The rate of dividend **may fluctuate** from year to year depending upon the profit, decisions of directors and members.	The rate of interest is **fixed**.
4. **Charge *vs* Appropriation**	Payment of dividend is an **appropriation** out of profit and this cannot be made if there is no profit.	Payment of interest is a **charge** against profits and is to be made even if there is no profit.
5. **Priority as to payment of interest/dividend**	Payment of **dividend gets no priority** over the payment of interest.	Payment of **interest gets priority** over the payment of dividend.
6. **Priority as to repayment of principal during winding up**	Payment of share capital is made **after** the repayment of debentures.	Payment of debentures is made **before** the payment of share capital.
7. **Secured by charge**	Shares are **not secured** by any charge.	Non-convertible debentures for a term exceeding 18 months are always **secured** by a charge.
8. **Restriction on issue at discount**	Sec. 79 of the Companies Act, 1956, imposes certain **restrictions** on issue of shares at discount.	**No restriction** is imposed on the issue of debentures at discount.
9. **Voting rights**	Shareholders generally **enjoy** voting rights.	Debentureholders **do not have** any voting rights (except at their class meetings).
10. **Convertibility**	Equity shares can **never be convertible**.	Debentures **can be convertible**.
11. **Trust Deed**	Share Trust Deed is **not required** to be executed.	Debenture trust deed is **required** to be executed.

LONG-TERM LOAN – MEANING, MERITS AND LIMITATIONS

Meaning of Long-Term Loans

Long-term loans are raised by the companies from financial institutions like the Industrial Development Bank of India (IDBI), Industrial Credit and Investment Corporation of India (ICICI) etc.

The merits and limitations of long-term loans from the point of view of the company are discussed below:

Merits of Long-Term Loans

The merits of long-term loans from the point of view of the company are given below:

1. **Low Cost** — The cost of term loans is lower than the cost of equity or preference share capital because interest is a tax deductible expense and the rate of interest is lower than the rate of dividend.

2. **Advantage of Trading on Equity** — The company has an advantage of trading on equity if the Rate of Return on Investment (ROI) exceeds the rate of interest payable on term loan.

Limitations of Long-Term Loans

The limitations of long-term loans from the point of view of the company are given below:

1. **Risk of Financial Insolvency** — There exists the risk of financial insolvency because of the following two reasons:

   (i) Interest on term loan is a charge against the profits and is to be paid even if the company is suffering losses.

   (ii) Term loans are to be repaid at the scheduled time during the life time of the company.

2. **Security** — The term loans are to be secured by securities by way of mortgage, hypothecation etc.

3. **Increases the Risk of Shareholders** — The use of term loan increases the risk of shareholders because it will have unfavourable impact if return on assets is less than the cost of debt.

4. **Interference with management** — Usually the financial institutions nominate one or two directors to have some degree of control over the functioning of the company. These nominee directors may interfere the management of the affairs of the company.

5. **Restrictive Clauses** — The loan agreement may also provide for conversion of loans into equity capital after a stated period of the lending institution so desires. The loan agreement may impose restriction an dividend payments to shareholders or may prevent the company from taking additional loans.

6. **Long Processing Time** — The lending institutions usually take a long time in sanctioning loans.

RETAINED PROFITS – MEANING, ADVANTAGES AND LIMITATIONS

Meaning of Retained Profits

That portion of the profits which is not distributed but is retained and reinvested in the business is known as retained profits. The retained profit is an internal source of finance. This method of financing is also known as *reinvestment of profits* or *ploughing back of profits* or *self-financing* or *internal financing*.

Creation — Under this method of financing, a certain proportion of profits is transferred to reserves which are shown under the head **'Reserves & Surplus'**.

Part of Shareholders' funds — Since retained profits actually belong to the shareholders of the company, these are treated as part of shareholders' funds.

Use — The retained profits may be used to meet long-term, medium-term and short-term financial needs.

Advantages of Using Retained Profits

The main advantages of using retained profits as a source of financing are as follows:

1. **No Explicit Cost** — It does not involve any explicit cost in term of flotation costs (e.g. expenses on printing, advertisement and distribution of prospectus, brokerage, underwriting commission). Hence, it is cheaper than issue of shares.

2. **More Dependable** — It is more dependable than external sources since it is not required to depend upon external investors who may or may not subscribe the issue.

3. **No Fixed Obligation** — It does not involve any fixed obligation to pay any dividend on profits reinvested.

4. **Not Affect Control** — Its use does not affect the control over the management of the company since there is no addition to the number of shareholders.

5. **No Security** — It does not require the security of assets to be offered.

6. **Increases Capacity to Raise Debt** — It increases the capacity of the company to raise further debt.

7. **Increases Financial Strength** — Accumulation of reserves increases financial strength to the company.

8. **Source for Bonus Shares** — It acts as a source of issuing Bonus Shares.

Limitations of Using Retained Profits

The main limitations of using retained profits as a source of financing are as follows:

1. **Available only to Profitable companies** — This source of financing is available only to profitable companies.

2. **Concentration of Economic Power** — Growth of companies through accumulation of reserves leads to concentration of economic power.

3. **Involves Opportunity Cost** — It involves opportunity cost (i.e. the return which the shareholders could have earned if the profits were distributed). The management sometimes does not consider this cost while declaring dividend to equity share holders.

4. **Danger of Over-capitalisation** — There is always a danger of over-capitalization if the company retains profits on continuous basis year after year without requirements of funds for profitable investments.

SOURCES OF MEDIUM-TERM FINANCE

To finance deferred revenue expenditure (e.g., heavy advertising, renovation of building, modernisation of plant and machinery) medium-term capital is required for a medium period (normally exceeding one year but not exceeding five years). The principal sources of raising medium-term capital in case of a company are shown below:

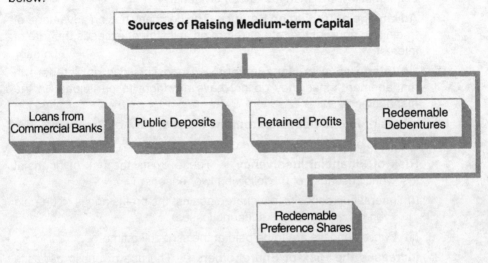

Fig. Sources of Raising Medium-term Capital

Let us discuss the sources of raising medium-term capital one by one.

(a) **Loans from Commercial Banks** — Medium-term loans are raised by companies from commercial banks against the security of assets. The banks do not interfere with the management of the company. Such loans can be repaid in parts and interest can be saved to that extent.

(b) **Public Deposits** — Public deposits are raised by companies by inviting their shareholders, employees and the general public to deposit their savings with the companies. It may be noted that a private company cannot invite general public to deposit their savings with the company. Such deposits can be accepted for a period not less than six months but not exceeding three years at a time. Thus, public deposits can be raised by companies to meet their short-term and medium-term financial needs.

The merits and limitations of public deposits are discussed below:

Merits of Public Deposits From the Point of View of Company

The merits of public deposits are discussed below:

1. **No Security** — The deposits are not required to be covered by securities by way of mortgage, hypothecation etc.

2. **Easy Invitation** — The deposits can be easily invited by offering a rate of interest higher than the interest on bank deposits.

3. **Less Flotation Costs** — The flotation costs relating to raising of public deposits are less than those relating to other external sources of financing.

4. **Flexible Source** — Public deposits is a flexible source since the public deposits can be raised when needed and refunded when not required.

5. **Low Cost** — The cost of public deposits is lower than that of equity or preference share capital because interest is a tax deductible and the rate of interest is lower than the rate of dividend.

6. **Advantage of Trading on Equity** — The company has an advantage of trading on equity if the rate of return on investment exceeds the rate of interest.

7. **No Interference in Management** — Depositors can not interfere in management since they do not have any right to participate in the management.

Limitations of Public Deposits from the Point of View of Company

The limitations of public deposits are discussed below:

1. **Risk of Financial Insolvency** — These exists the risk of financial insolvency because of the following two reasons:

    (i) Interest on deposits is a charge against the profits and is to be paid even if the company is suffering losses.

    (ii) Public deposits are to be paid at the scheduled time.

2. **Increases the Risk of Shareholders** — The use of public deposits increases the risk of shareholders because it will have unfavourable impact if return on assets is less than the cost of deposits.

3. **Unsuitable for Long Term Financing** — Public deposits are not suitable for long-term financing since these are available for a maximum period of 3 years.

4. **Uncertain Source** — Public deposits are uncertain specially in the period of depression. The company may or may not get public deposits.

5. **Unsuitable for New Companies** — New companies may not get public deposits due to lack of sound credit standing.

6. **Maximum Limit** — The aggregate of all outstanding deposits cannot exceed 25% of the paid-up capital and free reserves of the company.

7. **Maximum Rate of Interest** — Interest to be allowed on public deposits cannot exceed the maximum rate fixed by the government (i.e., 14% p.a. for a manufacturing company).

8. **Liqulity Norms** — At the beginning of each year, at least 10% of the deposits maturing during that year are required to be deposited in a bank or to be invested in approved securities.

9. **Return to be filed** — A return or statement containing all information relating to the deposits is required to be filed every year with the Registrar.

(c) **Retained Profits** — *Refer to page 8.33.*

(d) **Redeemable Debentures** — *Refer to Page 8.29.*

(e) **Redeemable Preference Shares** — *Refer to page 8.25.*

SOURCES OF SHORT-TERM FINANCE

To finance temporary working capital, short-term capital is required for a short period (normally not exceeding one year).

The principal sources of raising short-term capital in case of a company are shown below:

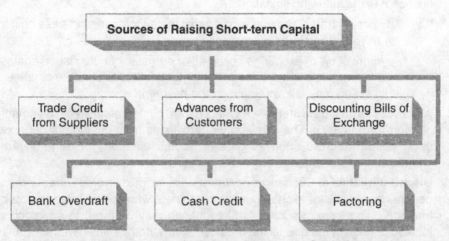

Fig. Sources of Raising Short-term Capital

Let us discuss the sources of raising short-term capital one by one:

1. **Trade Credit** — Trade credit refers to an arrangement whereby the supplies of raw materials, components, stores and spare parts, finished goods, allow the customers to pay their outstanding balances within the credit period allowed by them. Generally, suppliers grant credit for a period of three to six months and thus provide short-term funds to finance current assets. The availability of trade credit depends upon various factors such as nature and size of the firm, status of the firm (i.e., credit worthiness), activity level of the firm, policy of trade credit suppliers, prevailing economic conditions etc. Trade credit may be allowed in the shape of open account of bills payable. The major advantages of trade credit include ready availability, absence of issue formalities etc. The major limitation of trade credit is that it involves loss of cash discount which could be earned if payments were made within seven to ten days from the date of purchase. This loss is regarded as the cost of trade credit.

   Does trade credit have any cost? Initially cost of trade credit may be absorbed by supplier but in the long run, he may try to pass it on to the buyer in the shape of increased prices depending upon the type of goods and elasticity of demand. In such circumstances buyer should find out alternate sources of supply to avoid costs loaded by supplier to the extent possible. It does not have any explicit cost if buyer pays the bills within normal credit period.

Merits of Trade Credit — The trade credit as a source of short-term finance has the following advantages:

1. Trade credit is readily available according to the prevailing customs.

2. Trade credit is a flexible source of finance which can be easily adjusted to the changing needs for purchases.

3. Trade creditors generally adjust the time of payment in view of past dealings.

4. Trade credit does not involve any flotation costs.

Limitations of Trade Credit — The trade credit as a source of short term finance has the following limitations:

1. The cost of trade credit may increase if the supplier tries to pass on it to the buyer in the shape of increased prices.

2. Payment of bill of exchange accepted or promissory note issued against credit is required to be made at the maturity of the bill or note otherwise legal action may follow to recover the payment.

2. **Advances from Customers** — Advances from customers also act as source of short-term finance. The availability of advances from customers depends upon various factors such as type of goods, elasticity of demand and creditworthiness of supplier etc.

3. **Discounting Bills of Exchange** — When goods are sold on credit, the suppliers generally draw bills of exchange upon customers who are required to accept the same. The term of such bills of exchange may be three to six months. Instead of holding the bills till the date of maturity, companies generally prefer to get them discounted with the bank. Discounting bills of exchange refers to an act of selling of a bill to obtain payment for it before its maturity. The bank charges discount in terms of interest for the unexpired term of the bill (i.e., period from the date of discounting to the date of maturity of the bill). The bank credits the net proceeds (i.e., amount of bill *less* discount charges) to the account of the customer. On date of maturity of the bill, the bank presents the bill before the acceptor of the bill for payment and receives the full amount of the bill. If the bank does not receive the payment from the acceptor, it is known as dishonour of a bill. The bank returns the dishonoured bill to the company and debits to the account of the company. The cost of raising finance by this method is the discount charged by the bank.

4. **Bank Overdraft** — Bank overdraft refers to an arrangement whereby the bank allows the customers to overdraw from its current deposit account within a specified limit. The overdraft facility is granted against the securities of assets or personal security as in case of cash credit. Interest is charged only on the amount actually overdrawn (i.e., debit balance) for the actual period of use (i.e., for the period the debit balance in current deposit account remains outstanding). The cost of raising finance by this method is the interest charged by the bank.

5. **Cash Credit** — Cash credit refers to an arrangement whereby the bank allows the borrower to draw money from time to time within a specified limit (known as cash credit limit). The cash credit facility is granted against the pledge or hypothecation of stock or pledge of marketable instruments etc. or personal security. During the period of credit, the borrow can draw, repay and again draw amounts within the sanctioned limit. Interest is charged only on the amount actually withdrawn for the actual period of use. The cost of raising finance by this method is the interest charged by the bank. The advantage of this source of finance is that the amount can be adjusted according to the needs of finance.

6. **Factoring** — Factoring refers to an arrangement whereby the book debts (i.e., trade debtors) are assigned to bank and the payment is received against the debtors' balances in advance from the bank. The bank provides this facility on a payment of specified charges. The bank keeps a margin for non-realisation of debts while calculating the amount to be advanced against debtors' balances. The major disadvantage of factoring is that customers who are in genuine difficulty do not get the facility of delaying payment which they might have otherwise got from the company. The bank charge payable for the purpose is treated as the cost of raising funds.

INTERNATIONAL FINANCING

The essence of financial management is to raise and utilise the funds effectively. This also holds goods for the procurement of funds in the international capital markets, for a multi-national organisation in any any currency. There are various avenues for a multi-national organisation to raise funds either though internal or external sources. Internal funds comprise share capital, loans from parent company and retained earnings. Now a days external funds can be raised from a number of **sources,** as follows:—

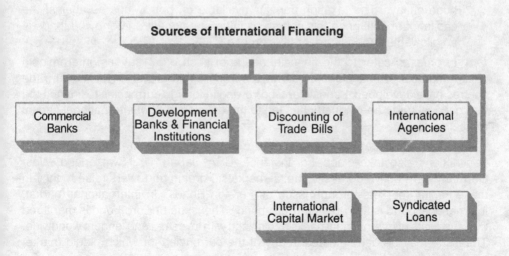

1. **Commercial Banks** — Like domestic loans, commercial banks all over the world extend foreign currency loans also for international operations. These banks also provide facility to overdraw, over and above the loan amount. Interest is also changed on overdrawn amount.

2. **Development Banks and Financial Institutions** — In almost all the countries development banks offer long and medium term loans including foreign currency component. Many agencies at the national level offer a number of concessions to foreign companies to invest within their country and to finance exports from their countries. Examples in this respect may be quoted of EXIM Bank of United States of America which offers loans to buyers outside USA for purchasing US manufactured goods. Similarly the EXIM Bank of India also performs a similar role by providing a number of facilities to Indian businessmen and foreign importers.

3. **Discounting of trade bills** — Discounting of trade bills is used as short term financing method. This method is widely used in Europe and Asian countries to finance both domestic and international business. In this arrangements,, companies holding bills of exchange, get the bills discounted by commercial banks before their maturity.

4. **International Agencies** — A number of international agencies have emerged during the recent years to finance international trade and business. The International Finance Corporation (IFC), the International Bank for Reconstruction and Development (IBRD), the Asian Development Bank (ADB), the International Monetary Fund (IMF), the Aid India Club etc. are some of the agencies which may be quoted in this respect. These agencies finance projects both in public and private sectors.

5. **International Capital Market** — It is well known today that modern organisations including multinationals largely depend upon sizable borrowings in rupees as well as in foreign currencies to finance their projects involving huge outlays. The taxation benefits available on borrowings as against the capital often influence this course as interest payment on borrowed funds is an allowable expenditure for tax purpose.

In order to cater to the financial needs of such organisations, international capital markets of financial centres have sprung up wherever international trade centres have developed. Lending and borrowing in foreign currencies to finance the international trade and industry has led to the development of international capital market.

In domestic capital markets of various countries, international capital transactions also take place. For instance, USA, Japan, UK, Switzerland, West Germany have active domestic capital markets. Foreign borrowers raise money in these capital markets through issue of 'Foreign Bonds'. In international market, international bond is known as a "Euro-bond". The issue of Euro-bond is managed by a syndicate of international banks and placed with investors and lenders worldwide. The issue may be denominated in any of the currencies for which liquid market exist.

In international capital market, the availability of foreign currency is assured under the four main systems viz. (1) Euro-currency market; (2) Export Credit Facilities; (3) Bonds issues, and (4) Financial Institutions. Euro-Currency market was originated with dollar dominated bank deposits and provide loans in Europe particularly, in London. Euro-dollar deposits form the main ingredient of Euro-currency market. Euro-dollar deposits are dollar denominated time deposits available at foreign branches of US banks and at some foreign banks. These deposits are acquired by these banks from foreign Governments and various firms and individuals who want to hold dollars outside USA. Banks based in Europe accept dollar denominated deposits and make dollar denominated loans to the customers. This forms the basis of Euro-currency market spread over various parts of the world. In Euro-currency market, (funds are made available as loans through syndicated Euro-credit or instruments known as Floating Rate Notes PRNs/FRCDs (Certificates of deposits). London has remained as the main centre for Euro-currency credit.

The creditors however insist on bank guarantees. Several multinational banks of Japanese, American, British, German and French origin, operate all over the world, extending financial assistance for trade and projects. Several multinational banks like Citi Bank, ANZ Grindlays bank, Standard Chartered bank, American Express, Bank of America, etc. are aggressive players in India and they issue specific bank guarantees to facilitate business transactions between various parties, including government agencies. Commercial borrowings as well as Exim Bank finance however, constitute major part.

6. **Syndicated Loans** — The borrower should obtain a good credit rating from the rating agencies. Large loans can be obtained in a reasonably short period with few formalities. Duration of the loan is generally 5 to 10 years, interest rate is based on LIBOR plus spread depending upon rating. Some convenants are laid down by the lending institutions like maintenance of key financial rates.

FINANCIAL INSTRUMENT IN INTERNATIONAL MARKET

The liberalised measures have boosted the confidence of foreign investors and also provided an opportunity to Indian companies to explore the possibility of tapping the European market for their financial requirements, where the resources are raised through the mechanism of Euro-issues i.e. Global Depository Receipts (GDRs) and Euro-bonds.

Euro-issues — The term Euro-issue, in the Indian context, denotes that the issue is listed on a European Stock Exchange. However, subscription can come from any part of the world except India. Finance can be raised by Global Depository Receipts (GDRs) Foreign Currency Convertible Bond(FCCBs) and pure debt bonds. However, GDRs and FCCBs are more popular instruments. These instruments have been described as follows:—

GLOBAL DEPOSITORY RECEIPTS (GDRs)

Meaning of Global Depository Receipts (GDRs) — A depository receipt is basically a negotiable certificate, denominated in US dollars, that represents a non US company's publicly-traded local currency (Indian rupee) equity shares. In theory, though a depository receipt can also represent a debt instrument, in practice it rarely does. DRs(depository receipts) are created when the local currency shares of an Indian company are delivered to the depository's local custodian bank, against which the Depository bank (such as the Bank of New York) issues depository receipts in US dollars. These depository receipts may trade freely in the overseas markets-like any other dollar-denominated security, either on a foreign stock exchange, or in the over-the-counter market, or among a restricted group such as Qualified Institutional Buyers(QIBs). Indian issues have taken the form of GDRs to reflect the fact that they are marketed globally, rather than in a specific country or market. Rule 144A of the Securities and Exchange Commission of U.S.A. permits companies from outside USA to offer their GDRs to certain institutional buyers. These are known as Qualified Institutional Buyers (QIBs). There are institutions in USA which, in the aggregate, own and invest on a discretionary basis at least US $ 100 million in eligible securities.

Legal Definition as per Issue of Foreign Currency Convertible Bonds and Ordinary Shares (Through Depository Receipt Mechanism) Scheme, 1993

"**Global Depository Receipts**" means any instrument in the form of a depository receipt or certificate *[by whatever name it is called]* created by the Overseas Depository Bank outside India and issued to non-resident investors against the issue of ordinary shares of Foreign Currency Convertible Bonds of issuing company;

"**Issuing Company**" means an Indian company permitted to issue Foreign Currency Convertible Bonds or ordinary shares of that company against Global Depository Receipts;

"**Overseas Depository Bank**" means a bank authorised by the issuing company to issue global depository receipts against issue of Foreign Currency Convertible bonds or ordinary shares of the issuing company;

Characteristics of GDRs

1. Holders of GDRS participate in the economic benefits of being ordinary shareholders, though they do not have voting rights.
2. GDRs are settled through CEDEL & Euro-clear international book entry systems.
3. GDRs are listed on the Luxemberg stock exchange.
4. Trading takes place between professional market makers on an OTC (over the counter) basis.
5. As far as the case of liquidation of GDRs is concerned, an investor may get the GDR cancelled any time after a cooling off period of 45 days.

Mechanism of GDRs

The mechanism of a GDR issue may be described with the help of following diagram.

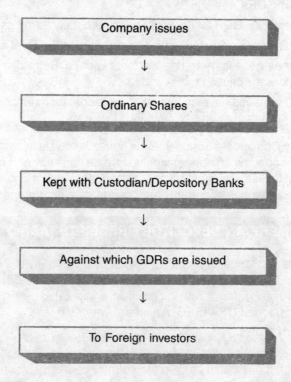

Company issues

↓

Ordinary Shares

↓

Kept with Custodian/Depository Banks

↓

Against which GDRs are issued

↓

To Foreign investors

Markets of GDR's

1. GDR's are sold primarily to institutional investors.
2. Demand is likely to be dominated by emerging market funds.
3. Switching by foreign institutional investors from ordinary shares into GDRs is likely.
4. Major demand is also in UK, USA (Qualified Institutional Buyers), South East Asia. (Hongkong, Singapore), and to some extent continental Europe (principally France and Switzerland).

Advantages of GDRs to Investors:

1. GDRs are usually quoted in dollars, and interest and dividend payments are also in dollars.
2. GDRs overcome obstacles that mutual funds, pension funds and other institutions may have in purchasing and holding securities outside their domestic markets.
3. Global custodians/safe-keeping charges are eliminated, saving GDR investors 30 to 60 basis points annually.
4. GDRs are as liquid as the underlying securities because the two are interchargeable.

5. GDRs are negotiable.

6. GDRs overcome foreign investment restrictions.

Disadvantages of GDRs

1. As straight equity a GDR issue would be immediately earnings dilutive.

2. Pricing of GDRs are expected to be at a discount to the local market price.

3. It is sometimes necessary to use warrants with GDRs to disguise discount, which can increase dilution.

4. In India, GDRs issues have an uneven track record for international investors.

Foreign Currency Convertible Bond (FCCBs)

"Foreign Currency Convertible Bonds" means bonds issued in accordance with this scheme and subscribed by an non-resident in foreign currency and convertible into ordinary shares of the issuing company in any manner, either in whole, or in part, on the basis of any equity related warrants attached to debt instruments,

AMERICAN DEPOSITORY RECEIPTS (ADRs)

Meaning of ADRs — Depository receipts issued by a company in the United State of America (USA) is known as American Depository Receipts (ADRs). Such receipts have to be issued in accordance with the provisions stipulated by the Securities and Exchange Commission of USA (SEC) which are very stringent.

Characteristics of ADRs

1. An ADR is generally created by deposit of the securities of a non-United States company with a custodian bank in the country of incorporation of the issuing company. The Custodian bank informs the depository in the United States that the ADRs can be issued.

2. ADRs are United States dollar denominated and are traded in the same way as are the securities of United State companies.

3. The ADR holder is entitled to the same rights and advantages as owners of underlying securities in the home country.

   Several variations of ADRs have developed over time to meet more specialized demands in different markets. One such variations is the GDRs which are identical in structure to an ADR, the only difference being that they can be traded in more than one currency and within as well as outside the United States.

Advantages of ADRs

1. The major advantage of ADRs of the investor is that dividends are paid promptly and in United States dollars.

2. The facilities are registered in the United States so that some assurance is provided to the investor with respect to the protection of ownership rights.

3. These instruments also obviate the need to transport physically securities between markets.

4. Communications services are also provided by the depository, including provisios of periodic reports on the issuing company (in English) in a format familiar to United States investors. Important information pertinent to the issuing company is transmitted to the investor by the depository.

5. In general, ADRs increase access to United States capital markets by lowering the costs of investing in the securities of non-United States companies and by providing the benefits of a convenient, familiar and well regulated trading environment.

6. Issues of ADRs can increase the liquidity of an emerging market issuer's shares, and can potentially lower the future cost of raising equity capital by raising the company's visibility and international familiarity with the company's name, and by increasing the size of the potential investor base.

Disadvantages of ADRs

1. High costs of meeting the partial or full reporting requirements of the Securities and Exchange Commission, As per the estimates, the cost of preparing and filing US GAAP account only ranges from $5,00,000 to $ 10,00,000 with the ongoing cost of $ 1,50,000 to $ 2,00,000 per annum. Because of the additional work involved, legal fees are considerably higher for a US listing, which ranges between $ 2,50,000 to $ 3,50,000 for the underwriters, to be reimbursed by the issuer.

2. The initial Securities Exchange Commission registration fees which are based on a percentage of the issue size as well as 'blue sky' registration costs (permitting the securities to be offered in all States of the US) are required to be met.

3. It has further been observed that while implied legal responsibility lies on a company's directors for the information contained in the offering document as required by any stock exchange, the US is widely recognised as the 'most litigious market in the world'. Accordingly, the broader the target investor base in the US (such as retail investors), the higher the potential legal liability.

FOREIGN DIRECT INVESTMENT (FDI)

International Investment is one of the most important vehicle, of global operations. Economic growth and development of countries depend to a large extent on adequate capital and technological inputs. Most often, these inputs are not sufficiently available in a number of countries. So importation of these inputs is made to supplement domestic resources that enhance investment as well as productivity. Foreign capital can come to countries seeking it in various forms. It can be a loan capital, direct investment and also portfolio investment, etc.

The growing international production and trade require increased amount of international investment. As a result, the flow of international investment has been increasing. The country requires international investment for enhancing the production, trade and distribution, capabilities. The need for international investment is more pronounced in the developing countries where the capital is in scarce. World

Investment Report, 1999 has advocated the need of foreign investment. It says that the development priorities of developing countries include achieving sustained income growth for their economies by raising investment rates, strengthening technological capacities and skills, and improving the competitiveness of their exports in world markets, distributing the benefits of growth equitably by creating more and better employment opportunities, and protecting and conserving the physical environment for future generations. The international investment play an important role in the above effort of the developing countries. There are two major types of international investment. They are Foreign direct Investment and Portfolio Investment. Let us first learn about them.

Meaning of Foreign Direct Investment

Foreign Direct Investment occurs when an investor based in one country (the home country) acquires as asset in another country (one host country) with the interest to manage the asset. The company investing in this country also transfers assets such as technology, management and marketing. Further, the investing company also seeks the power to exercise control over decision-making in a foreign enterprise - the extent of which has to vary according to its equity participation. Foreign Direct Investment also includes reinvested earnings which comprise the direct investor's share of earnings not distributed as dividends by affiliates or earnings not remitted to the direct investor. Such retained profits of affiliates of foreign enterprise are reinvested.

Characteristics of FDI

There are four main characteristic features of growth of foreign direct investment. These are:

1. The bulk of FDI flows is among the developed countries.
2. The growth of FDI has been substantial.
3. The developing countries have increasingly become recipients of FDI.
4. The flow of FDI to developing countries, however, is concentrated in approximately ten countries.

Advantages of FDI

FDI helps in the development of the host countries. FDI helps in accelerating the rate of economic growth of the host country.

In specific term, the major advantages are discussed as follows:

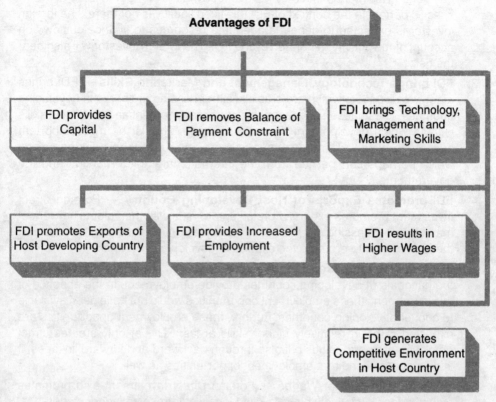

Let us discuss these Advantages of FDI one by one.

1. **FDI provides Capital** — Foreign Direct Investment is expected to bring needed capital to developing countries. The developing countries need higher investment to achieve increased targets of growth in national income. Since they cannot normally have adequate savings, there is need to supplement savings of these countries from foreign savings. This can be done either through external borrowings or through permitting and encouraging Foreign Direct Investment. Foreign Direct Investment is an effective source of this additional capital and comes with its own risks.

2. **FDI removes Balance of Payments Constraint** — FDI provides inflow of foreign exchange resource and removes the constraints on balance of payment. It can be seen that a large number of developing countries suffer from balance of payments deficits for their demand on foreign exchange which is normally far in excess of their ability to earn. FDI inflows by providing foreign exchange resources remove the constraint of developing countries seeking higher growth rates.

    FDI has a distinct advantage over the external borrowings considered from the balance of payments point of view. Loans create fixed liability. The governments or corporations have to repay. The resulting international debt of the government and the corporation parts a fixed liability on balance of payments. This means that they have to repay loans along with interest over a specific period. In the context of FDI this fixed liability is not there. The foreign investor is expected to generate adequate resources to finance outflows on account of the activity generated by the FDI. The foreign investor will also bear the risk.

3. **FDI brings Technology, Management and Marketing Skills** — FDI brings along with it assets which are crucially either missing or scarce in developing countries. These assets are technology and management and marketing skills without which development cannot take place. This is the most important advantage of FDI. This advantage is more important than bringing capital which perhaps can be had from the international capital markets and the governments.

4. **FDI promotes Exports of Host Developing Country** — Foreign direct investment promotes exports. Foreign enterprises with their global network of marketing, possessing marketing information are in a unique position to exploit these strengths to promote the exports of developing countries.

5. **FDI provides Increased Employment** — Foreign enterprises by employing the nationals of developing countries provide employment. In the absence of this investment, these employment opportunities would not have been available to a lot of developing countries. Further, these employment opportunities are expected to be in relatively higher skills areas. FDI not only creates direct employment opportunities but also through backward and forward linkages, it is able generate indirect employment opportunities as well.

6. **FDI results in Higher Wages** — Foreign Direct Investment also promotes higher wages. Relatively higher skilled jobs would receive higher wages.

7. **FDI generates Competitive Environment in Host Country** — Entry of foreign enterprises in domestic market creates a competitive environment compelling national enterprises to compete with the foreign enterprises operating in the domestic market. This leads to higher efficiency and better products and services. The Consumer may have a wider Choice.

Limitations of FDI

Besides, these favourable impact of FDI, there are some limitations which have been discussed as follows.

1. **Foreign Enterprises depend on Domestic Capital** — Very often foreign enterprise brings very limited capital. It takes recourse to borrowing from domestic capital markets and banks. It has been the experience of a number of developing countries where foreign enterprises have depended to a large extent on domestic capital markets and have heavily borrowed from the national financial institutions. Thus, they compete effectively with the national firms for scarce capital available domestically. Very often they deprive national firms of the needed capital. Thus, the argument that they bring sufficient capital is spurious.

2. **FDI need not necessarily remove Balance of Payments Constraint in the Long Run** — While FDI may remove balance of payments constraint in the

initial stages, the outflows generated in the form of dividend, royalty and technical management fees may be far in excess of equity inflows in the early stages. Further, many foreign enterprises take recourse to loan finance rather than equity finance. This obviously is a fixed liability on the enterprises as well as fixed commitment for the balance of payments.

Over and above this, when enterprises want to move their capital out of the country, the repatriation may create balance of payments crisis.

3. **FDI does not Transfer Technology Effectively** — Foreign enterprise very often keeps control of technology. Therefore, effective transfer of technology and management skill does not take place. What it does is to transfer technology relating to adaptation to local conditions otherwise one has to deal with trouble shooting technologies. Fundamental aspects of technology are strictly kept with the parent company. Thus, the host economy, especially the developing countries, may not have effective transfer of technology arising out of FDI.

4. **FDI is not a provider of Additional Employment** — It is argued that this will arise when FDI does not substitute national investment. When FDI substitutes national investment, what exactly happens is that it replaces employment opportunities that could have been created by the national enterprises. Thus the net employment opportunities generated will be insignificant. Further, there are no effective backward linkages fo the Transnational Corporations. The operations of TNCs would depend on imports for getting their supplies rather than depending on domestic sources of supply of host countries.

5. **FDI does not create Higher Wages** — Most often FDI indulge in exploiting the wages in host developing countries. Hence the argument that they generate higher wages is not correct. Further, the employment of local personnel in high paid jobs is less because it is very often taken by foreign nationals.

6. **FDI does not create Additional Exports** — Most often FDI comes to exploit the domestic market. Barring a few export processing zones, the foreign enterprises most often exploit the domestic market.

7. **FDI does not create Competitive Environment** — The TNCs through their market power always create oligopolistic or monopolistic market conditions. Three or four TNCs control the market.

The present consensus has been despite this debate, the FDI has a net positive impact on the development of developing countries. It may, however, be noted here that for growth and development of an economy it is not necessary to depend on FDI flows.

FINANCIAL INSTITUTIONS

Meaning of Financial Institution

Financial institutions refer to those institutions which provide financial assistance.

Types of Financial Institution

All financial institutions may broadly be divided into the following two categories:

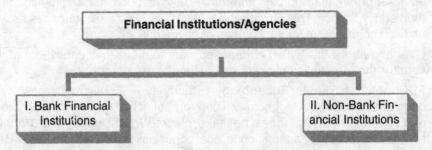

I.   **Bank financial Institutions** — These institutions accepts the deposits from the public repayable on demand and lend the money. For example, Commercial Banks

II. **Non-Bank Financial Institutions** — These Institutions generally pay back the money taken from the public only after a specified time and not on demand. They provide not only financial assistance but also promotional assistance to the industries. These non-bank financial institutions can broadly be classified into the following three categories:

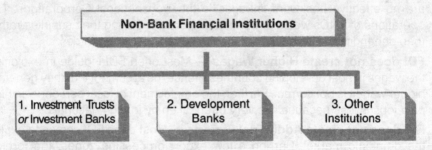

Let us discuss these non-bank financial institutions one by one.

1.   **Investment Trusts** — These institutions are also known as investment banks. They mobilise the savings of scattered masses and channelise them to productive uses. They invest their excess money in various securities in addition to the provision of long-term loans. They also undertake merchant banking activities including underwriting of securities. This type of institutions include the Life Insurance Corporation of India (LIC), General Insurance Corporation of India (GICI) and the Unit Trust of India (UTI).

2.   **Development Banks** — These institutions are also known as special Financial Institutions. They provide long-term financial assistance to industrial undertakings in various forms. Since they also undertake many promotional functions, they are known as development banks. These institutions include Industrial Finance Corporation of India (IFCI), Industrial Credit and Investment Corporation of India (ICICI) and Industrial Development Bank of India (IDBI) at national level while the State Financial Corporations (SFCs) and State Industrial Development Corporations (SIDCs) exist at the State level.

3. **Other Institutions** — Generally some institutions do not provide financial assistance. They mainly undertake promotional activities and provide various services to entrepreneurs. These institutions include National Small Industries Development Corporation (NSIC), State Small Industries Development Corporations (SSIDCs) and Technical Consultancy Organisations (TCOs).

SPECIALISED FINANCIAL INSTITUTIONS

Meaning of Specialised Financial Institutions

Specialised financial institutions are the institutions which provide mainly the long-term financial assistance to industrial undertakings in various forms.

Now, these institutions are also known as **'development banks'** or **'development financial institutions'** since these institutions also undertake promotional functions such as —

1. Undertaking potential industrial surveys
2. Identifying growth projects
3. Providing technical, managerial and other assistance to interested entrepreneurs rights from the stage of project formulation to the commissioning and operation of the project.

Thus, development bank is a special kind of institutions which performs the functions of both finance corporation and development corporation and thus provides three basic ingredients to industry.

1. Capital,
2. Knowledge, and
3. Entrepreneurship.

Functions of Specialised Financial Institutions

The following are the functions of specialised financial institutions or development banks:

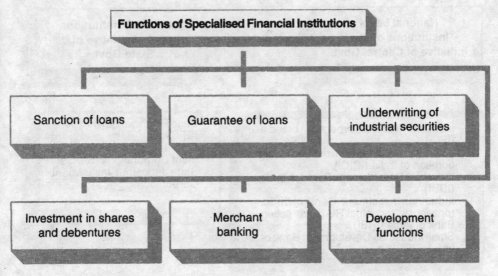

1. **Sanction of loans:** The important function of the most of the development banks is to provide long-term and medium term loans to industrial concerns. Certain development banks grant loans in foreign currencies also.

2. **Guarantee of loans:** They also provide guarantees for loans raised by business concerns from other sources. They extend guarantees for deferred payments for purchase of capital goods from abroad.

3. **Underwriting of industrial securities:** Another important function of development banks is to underwrite the issue of shares, bonds or debentures of industrial concerns.

4. **Investment in shares and debentures:** In addition to underwriting, the development banks also directly invest in industrial undertakings by subscribing to their shares and debentures.

5. **Merchant banking:** In the recent past, some development banks have established subsidiary companies, for undertaking various merchant banking activities.

6. **Development functions:** Special financial institutions not only act as term lending institutions but also as development banks. They formulate projects, conduct techno-economic surveys, provide training and consultancy to entrepreneurs, and improve management of industrial units.

Types of Specialised Financial Institutions

Some Special Financial Institutions have been set upon the initiative of the Central Government and others have been set up in different states on the initiative of the concerned State Governments.

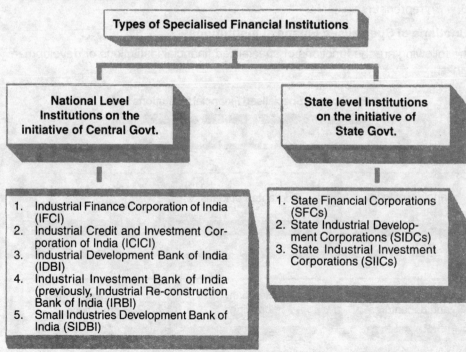

Let us discuss these financial institutions one by one.

INDUSTRIAL FINANCE CORPORATION OF INDIA (IFCI)

Establishment of IFCI

Industrial Finance Corporation of India (IFCI) is the first development Bank established in India. It was established as a statutory corporation on 1st. July, 1948 by The Special Act of the Parliament, IFCI Act 1948. It was converted into a public limited company on 1st July 1993 to ensure greater flexibility and to have an access to the capital market.

Objectives of IFCI

The primary object of the formation of the Corporation was to make medium and long-term credit facilities easily available to the industrial concerns especially in the areas, where normal banking facilities are inappropriate or recourse to capital issue method is impracticable. It provides financial assistance to those companies or Co-operating societies that have been registered in the Country and are concerned with manufacturing, mining, shipping, hotel etc. It does not provide finance to small scale industries and unregistered companies. More specifically the objectives are:

1. To grant loans and advances to industrial concerns
2. To subscribe to debentures floated by them which are repayable within 25 years.
3. To guarantee the loans raised by industrial concerns in the open market or from scheduled banks and cooperative banks.
4. To underwrite the issue of shares, debentures and bonds by industrial concerns. But it is required to dispose of these securities within 7 years.

Resources of IFCI

The resources of IFCI consist of the following:

1. Share Capital
2. Reserves
3. Loan from Government of India
4. Loan from RBI
5. Issue of Bonds
6. Commercial Borrowings in International Capital Markets
7. Lines of Credit from foreign lending agencies.

Management of Organisation of IFCI

Industrial Finance Corporation of India (IFCI) is managed by a Board of Directors, which consists of partly elected and partly nominated directors. The Central Government appoints the whole-time Chairman of the Board in consultation with the Industrial Development Bank of India (IDBI).

The Board consists of the following.

One Chairman	—	appointed by the Central Government
Two Directors	—	nominated by the Central Government
One Director	—	nominated by the Reserve Bank of India
Three Directors	—	nominated by Industrial Development Bank of India (IDBI)
Two Directors	—	elected by Insurance Concerns, Investment Trusts, etc.
Two Directors	—	elected by Co-operative Banks.

Functions of IFCI

Following are the important functions of Industrial Finance Corporation of India:

1. **Direct Subscription** — It subscribes directly to the shares issued by industrial concerns.

2. **Granting Loan** — It grants loans and advances to industrial concerns and subscribing to debentures floated by them which are repayable within 25 years.

3. **Guaranteeing Loans** — It guarantees the loans raised by industrial concerns in the open market or from scheduled banks and cooperative banks.

4. **Guaranteeing Foreign Currency Loans** — It guarantees loan in foreign currency raised by industrial concerns from any bank or institutions in a foreign country. However, prior approval of the Central Government is required for the purpose.

5. **Guaranteeing Credit Purchase of Capital Goods** — It guarantees credit purchase of capital goods from foreign manufacturers. With the approval of the Central Government, the IFCI can guarantee the loans raised in foreign currency from foreign institutions.

6. **Underwriting** — It underwrites the issue of shares, debentures and bonds by industrial concerns. But it is required to dispose of these securities within 7 years.

7. **Acting as Agent** — It acts as an agent for the Central Government and for the World Bank with regard to loans sanctioned by them to industrial concerns in India.

8. **Providing Assistance** — It provides assistance under the soft loan scheme to selected industries such as cement, cotton textiles, jute, engineering, etc, the expedite modernisation, replacement and renovation of their plant and machinery.

9. **Undertaking Promotional Activities** — It undertakes various promotional activities financed out of its benevolent Reserve Fund and allocations of Interest Differential funds received from the Government. The corporation has been emphasising the development of backward areas and the helping and the developing of small and medium scale industrial entrepreneurs. It has been providing them with the needed guidance for the establishment and management of these units.

10. **Merchant Banking** — It provides merchant banking services.
11. **Lease Finance** — It provides lease finance.

Present Structure

Now, IFCI is offering a wide range of financial servies through setting up of many specialised companies which include the following.

1. IFCI Financial Services Ltd. for merchant banking, stock broking etc.
2. IFCI Custodian Services Ltd. for providing custodian services.
3. IFCI Investor Services for Register & Transfer Services.

INDUSTRIAL CREDIT AND INVESTMENT CORPORATION OF INDIA (ICICI)

Establishment of ICICI

Industrial Credit and Investment Corporation of India (ICICI) was the second all India level financial institution established in India on Jan. 5, 1955. It was established as a public limited company under The Indian Companies Act, 1955. Unlike other development banks in India, this is a privately owned and operated corporation. The World Bank played a crucial role in the establishment of corporation.

Objectives of ICICI

The following are the objectives of the ICICI.

1. To provide financial resources to industrial concerns for their promotion, development and modernisation.
2. To encourage inflow and participation of foreign capital in the private sector units.
3. To encourage private ownership in industrial investment and
4. To increase the scope of investment market.

Resources of ICICI

The resources of ICICI consist of the following:

1. Share Capital
2. Reserves
3. Borrowings from Government of India
4. Foreign Currency borrowings from World Bank
5. Rupee Loan from IDBI
6. Borrowings from RBI
7. Bonds Issues in Indian and Foregin Capital Markets
8. Issue of shares to Indian Public

Management of ICICI

Ownership and management of ICICI is vested in the hands of a Board of Directors consisting 12 directors. The Chairman and a managing director are appointed by Government of India after consulting Industrial Development Bank of India.

Long-term Functions of ICICI

The following are the functions of ICICI.

1. **Providing Long-term Loans** — It provides loans repayable over a period of 15 years.
2. **Subscription** — It provides finance through equity participation.
3. **Underwriting** — It sponsors and underwrites new issues of shares and other securities.
4. **Makes Funds Investments** — It makes funds available for investment by revolving investment as quickly as possible.
5. **Guaranteeing Loans from Pvt. Sources** — It guarantees loans from private investment sources including deferred payment.
6. **Granting Loans in Foreign Currency** — It provides loans in foreign currency to import capital equipment.
7. **Providing Managerial etc. Services** — It furnishes managerial, technical and administrative services to the industry.
8. **Promotional Actitivities** — It undertakes promotional activities with a view to fostering growth in the backward areas.
9. **Merchant Banking** — Promoting other It provides merchant banking services.
10. **Promoting other Institutions** — It promotes the other financial institutions.
11. **Credit Rating Services** — It provides credit rating services to the corporate sector.

Present Structure — Now ICICI is offering a wide range of financial servies through the setting up of many specialised companies which include the following:

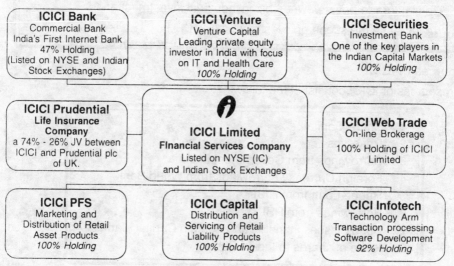

Recently, ICICI has merged with ICICI Bank.

INDUSTRIAL DEVELOPMENT BANK OF INDIA (IDBI)

Establishment of IDBI

Industrial Development Bank of India was set up as a wholly owned subsidiary of the Reserve Bank of India in July 1964 by an Act of Parliament. Since 16th February, 1976, it has been delinked from the RBI and made an autonomous corporation. This was done mainly to enlarge its role as an apex financial institutions to achieve effective coordination among all the financial institutions in the country.

Objectives of IDBI

The principal objectives of setting up the IDBI was to make a coordinated effort to achieve maximum industrial growth. The overall activities of the Bank may be classified into three broad categories namely, coordination, financing and promotion. The objectives of the bank are summarised below:

1. To serve as an apex institution for term finance for industry.
2. To coordinate working of institutions engaged in financing, promoting or developing industries and to assist the development of these institutions.
3. To provide term finance to industry.
4. To plan, promote and develop industries to fill gaps in the industrial structure of the country.
5. To provide technical and administrative assistance for promotion and expansion of industry.
6. To undertake market and investment research and surveys as also technical and economic studies in connection with the development of industry.
7. To act as lender of last resort to finance projects that are in conformity with national priorities.

Resources of IDBI

The resources of IDBI consist of the following:

1. Share Capital
2. Reserves
3. Loans from Central Government
4. Loans from RBI
5. Loans from Foreign Sources
6. Bonds & Share Issues in India

Management of IDBI

The management of the IDBI is vested in a Board of Directors consisting of 22 directors including a full-time Chairman-*cum*-Managing Director appointed by the Central Government. The other Board member comprise a representative of the Reserve Bank of India, two officials of the Central Government, 5 representatives of financial institutions, 6 representatives of public sector banks and SFCs, 2 employees of financial institutions, and 5 persons with special knowledge and professional experience, nominated by the Government of India.

The Board has constituted an Executive Committee consisting of ten directors including the Chairman and Managing Director. The Board of Directors deal with the overall policy matters and the Executive Committee deals with proposals for the sanction of financial assistance and other matters.

The central office of the bank is located in Mumbai. It has five regional offices at Kolkata, Delhi, Chennai, Mumbai, and Ahmedabad. Besides these regional offices, the IDBI has eleven branches at Bangalore, Bhopal, Bhubaneshwar, Chandigarh, Kochi, Hyderabad, Jaipur, Jammu, Kanpur, Patna and Simla.

Functions of IDBI

The following are the functions of IDBI:

1. **Direct financing** — It provides direct financial assistance to industrial concerns by giving them long-term loans and advances.

2. **Guaranteeing of loans** — It guarantees loans raised by industrial concerns in the open market or from banks or other financial institutions.

3. **Acceptance and discounting of bills** — It accepts, discounts and rediscounts bills of exchange, promissory notes, hundis, etc. of industrial concerns.

4. **Direct subscriptions and underwriting** — It subscribes to shares, bonds, and debentures issued by industrial concerns. It also underwrites such issues.

5. **Refinancing** — It provides refinancing facilities to scheduled banks and other financial institutions. Its refinances include:

    (i) loans between 3 to 25 years granted by IFCI, SFCs or any other financial institutions,

    (ii) loans between 3 to 10 years granted by a scheduled or a cooperative bank to any industrial concern,

    (iii) Export loans between 6 months to 10 years given by a scheduled bank or a co-operative bank or any other financial institutions.

6. **Promotional activities** — It provides and arranges technical and managerial assistance for an industrial concern (or person) for promotion, management or expansion of any industry. It is also entrusted with the responsibility of planning, promoting and developing industries with a view to filling gaps in the industrial structure. It also takes up entrepreneurship development, technology development etc.

7. **Other functions** — It undertakes research and surveys in the field of marketing and investment. It may establish subsidiaries to carryout its functions and undertake any business which the central government may ask it to undertake.

Present Structure

Now, IDBI is offering a wide range of financial services through the setting up of many specialised companies which include the following:

1. IDBI Bank Ltd.
2. IDBI Capital Market Services Ltd.
3. IDBI Mutual Fund
4. SIDBI

INDUSTRIAL RECONSTRUCTION BANK OF INDIA (IRBI)

Establishment of IRBI

The Industrial Reconstruction Bank of India (IRBI) was established as a statutory corporation on 20th March, 1985 to take over the operations of the Industrial Reconstruction Corporation of India (IRCI).

Objectives of IRBI

The following are the main **objectives of IDBI**:

1. To function as the principal credit and reconstruction agency for the revival of sick industries.
2. To bring coordination among various agencies working for the revival of such units.

Management of IRBI

Its management is vested in the hands of Board of Directors with one Chairman and Managing Directors and 12 directors. All of them are appointed by Government of India.

Resources of IRBI

Its authorised capital was Rs 200 crore, while its paid up capital was Rs 98 crore as on June 1988. It has the privilege to receive interest free loans from Central Government to the tune of Rs 80 crore every year. It can also raise foreign loans guaranteed by Government of India.

Functions of IRBI

The following are the functions of IRBI:

1. **Taking over Management of Sick Units** — It takes over the management of sick industrial units, leases them out, sells them as running concerns or prepares schemes for reconstruction by scaling down the liabilities.
2. **Promoting Industrial Development** — It assists and promotes industrial development by granting loans and advances and also by subscription and underwriting of shares and debentures.
3. **Range of Activities Undertaken** — Its range of activities also includes services like provision of infrastructure facilities, consultancy, managerial and merchant banking activities.
4. **Provides Lease Finance** — It provides lease finance and hire purchase credit.

SMALL INDUSTRIES DEVELOPMENT BANK OF INDIA (SIDBI)

Establishment of SIDBI

Small Industries Development Bank of India (SIDBI) was set up as a wholly-owned subsidiary of IDBI under the Small Industries Development Bank of India Act, 1990 and has takeover from IDBI the responsibility of administering the Small Industries Development Fund and the National Equity Fund. It commenced its operations on April 2, 1990.

Objectives of SIDBI

The following are the objectives of SIDBI:

1. To promote, finance and developed small scale industries.
2. To co-ordinate the functions of existing institutions engaged in similar activities.
3. To initiate steps for technological upgradation and modernisation of existing small units.
4. To expand channels for marketing of SSI sector products in India and abroad.
5. To promote employment oriented industries in semi-urban areas and to check migration of populations to big cities.

Functions of SIDBI

The following are the functions of SIDBI:

1. **Discounting/Re-discounting Bills** — It discounts and rediscounts bills arising from the sale of machinery to small units.
2. **Provides Seed Capital** — It extends seed capital/staff loan assistance through National Equity Fund and through seed capital schemes of specialised lending institutions.
3. **Refinances Loans** — It refinances loans.
4. **Factoring, Leasing Services etc.** — It provides services like factoring, leasing and so on.

NEED FOR STATE LEVEL TERM-LENDING INSTITUTIONS

Industrial Finance Corporation of India (IFCI) was established in 1948 at all India level to provide finance exclusively to large scale industrial units. Financial needs of medium and small size industries were not covered by IFCI. The government, therefore, felt the need for starting development banks at the regional level to provide assistance to small scale industries. Consequently, State Financial Corporations, (SFCs) and State Industrial Development Corporations (SIDCs) were established in all the states.

Now let us study the functions, types of assistance provided and the working of two important term lending money State Financial. Corporations (SFCs) and State Industrial Development Corporations (SIDCs).

STATE FINANCIAL CORPORATIONS (SFCs)

Establishment of SFCs

State Financial Corporations Act, 1951 was brought into force to enable all State Governments (except Jammu and Kashmir) to set up State Financial Corporations as regional development banks. They are to meet the financial requirements of small and medium size industrial units in the respective States. The first State Financial Corporation was established in Punjab in 1953. Subsequently Andhra Pradesh and Bihar State Government took the lead to set up SFCs in 1960 followed by Uttar Pradesh, Karnataka, Gujarat, Maharashtra and Orissa. At present, there are 18 SFCs operating in different States and Union Territories in the country.

Objectives of SFCs

State level development banks were established with the following objectives:

1. To provide financial assistance to industrial units particularly small scale units in the State.
2. For establishing and managing the industrial estates.
3. To concentrate on the development of less developed parts of the State, through provision of infrastructure facilities like roads, electricity, drainage and water supply.
4. To establish institutes to provide training to the middle and high level technicians.
5. To decentralise the development banking activities and take them to semi-urban areas in the State.
6. To provide better access to the borrowers and client.
7. To have through knowledge about the local conditions and problems.
8. To overcome the problem of language and communication.

Resources of SFCs

The resources of SFCs consist of the following:

1. Share Capital
2. Reserves
3. Loans from State Government
4. Loans from RBI
5. Loans from IDBI
6. Refinance from RBI & IDBI
7. Fixed Deposits from State Govts., Local Authorities, Public
8. Foreign Currency line of credit from IDBI

Management of SFCs

Every SFC is managed by a 12 member Board of Directors. The State Government concerned appoints the Chairman and the Managing Director, and nominates three directors. IFCI and IDBI nominate one director each. Three directors are elected by financial institutions. The rest will be chosen on the basis of one each from schedule banks, cooperative banks and other financial institutions. One director is elected by non-institutional shareholders.

Functions of SFCs

The following are the functions of SFCs:

1. To grant long-term loans to industries for the purchase of land, buildings and machinery.
2. To guarantee payment on behalf of the entrepreneur for purchasing machinery on deferred payments from suppliers within India.
3. To underwrite issue of shares, bonds and debentures of industrial concerns.
4. To guarantee loans raised by industrial concerns for a period not exceeding 20 years.
5. To guarantee loans raised by industries from commercial bank or co-operative banks for acquiring fixed assets.
6. To subscribe debentures of industrial units.
7. To provide foreign exchange loans to industries under the World Bank line of credit.
8. To provide Special capital assistance upto Rs 2 lakhs.
9. To provide Loans to industries in collaboration with the central financial institutions like the IDBI, the IFCI and the ICICI, and joint financing of projects along with the SIDCs and the commercial banks.
10. To act as an agent of the State or Central Government or any other finance institutions notified on this behalf by the Central Government.

Organisation Eligible for Financial Assistance

Industrial concerns under any form of ownership viz., a proprietary concern, joint Hindu family, registered co-operative society, private of public limited company engaged in or proposed to engage in one or more of the following activities are eligible for financial assistance.

1. Manufacture of goods
2. Preservation of goods
3. Processing of goods
4. Mining
5. Hotel industry
6. Development of industrial estates
7. Generation and distribution of electricity or any other form of power
8. Transport industry
9. Assembling, repairing or packing any article with the aid of machinery or power
10. Fishing or providing shore facilities for fishing or maintenance thereof
11. Providing special or technical knowledge or other services for the promotion of industrial growth.

STATE INDUSTRIAL DEVELOPMENT CORPORATIONS (SIDCs)

Since 1960, many States and Union Territories started State Industrial Development Corporations (SIDCs) for accelerating industrial development in their respective States. In certain States these are called State Industrial Investment corporations. Andhra Pradesh and Bihar were the first to set up such corporations in 1960 followed by Uttar Pradesh and Kerala in 1961 and Maharashtra, Gujarat and Orissa in 1962. By the year 1988 there were 28 SIDCs spread all over the country.

Objectives of SIDCs

The objectives of SIDCs are as follows:

1. To promote rapid industrialisation
2. To bring about balanced regional development by assisting backward areas in particular.

Resources of SIDCs

The resources of SIDCs consist of the following:

1. Paid-up Capital
2. Reserves
3. Loans from State Governments,
4. Issues of bonds and debentures
5. Refinance from IDBI

Management of SIDCs

The SIDCs function under the guidance of respective State governments. Except for one nominee of the IDBI, all other members of their Boards of Directors are nominated by State government. The boards constitute special committees as and when they feel necessary. Those committees advise the board on various issues relating to the business. Managing Director is the Chief Executive of an SIDC. He looks after its day-to-day management.

Functions of SIDCs

The following are the functions of State Industrial Development Corporations:

1. They promote industrial activities such as project identification, preparation of feasibility reports, identifying entrepreneurs and assisting them in project implementation.
2. They set up of medium and large industrial projects either in joint sector or as wholly-owned subsidiaries.
3. They provide infrastructural facilities and market intelligence services.
4. They grant financial assistance by way of term loans/bridge loans and underwriting or subscription of equity and preference shares.
5. They act as agent of State and Central Governments in respect of granting subsidies, incentives, etc.

6. They operate the seed capital scheme on behalf of Small Industries Development Bank of India.

7. They provide risk capital by way of equity participation.

8. They develop industrial areas, plots, sheds and estates.

UNIT TRUST OF INDIA (UTI)

Establishment of UTI

The Unit Trust of India was established under the UTI Act, 1963. It started its operations on 1st July 1964. The UTI is an investment institution which offers the small investor a share in the India's industrial growth and productive investment with a minimum risk and reasonable returns.

Nature of UTI

The Unit Trust of India (UTI) is an investment trust/investment bank and not a development bank. Unit trust is comparable to Mutual Funds in the USA. It mobilises the savings of people through sale of units and channelises them to productive uses.

Objectives of UTI

The primary objective of UTI is to encourage and mobilize savings of the community. It channelises them into productive corporate investments so as to promote the growth and diversification of the country's economy. Specifically, the objectives of the Trust are the following:

1. It mobilizes the savings of the community and channelises them into productive investment. By promising savers the triple benefits of **safety**, **liquidity** and **profitability** of their investments, the Trust encourages individuals to save.

2. It gives every one a chance to indirectly own shares and securities in a large number of select companies and enables the investors to share in the widening prosperity consequent on industrial growth.

Resources of UTI

Initial Capital — The initial capital of the UTI was statutorily fixed at Rs. 5 crore. It was to be contributed by the Reserve bank of India (Rs. 2.5 crore), the Life Insurance Corporation of India (Rs. 0.75 crore), the State Bank of India and its subsidiaries (Rs. 0.75 crore) and other financial institutions including banks (Rs. 1.0 crore). In 1976 the initial capital held by the Reserve Bank of India was transferred to the IDBI and thus the UTI became an associate institution of the latter.

Unit Capital — The main source of the funds of the UTI is the unit capital which is raised from the sale of units to public under various schemes. The bulk of the funds obtained in this form are under the Unit Scheme, 1964 and Capital Gains Units Scheme, 1983. These two schemes presently account for more than two-thirds of the collections from the sale of units. The Unit Scheme, 1964 was the first scheme to be introduced by the UTI and has always been popular with the investors. The units sold under this scheme are of the face value of Rs. 10 each. However their market price is periodically determined and is higher than the face value. The basis for determining the market price of units under this scheme is the market valuation of the aggregate investments of the UTI over the previous period. The purchase price is kept lower than the sale price and between the two there has been always margin of 30 paise or more.

Investment Policy of UTI

The investment policy of the UTI attempts to strike a balance between security of principal and return on capital. From the point of view of the security of capital, the securities in which investments are made must be of proven soundness and should be easily marketable. This implies that in the choice of securities safe and liquid securities should be preferred. Often these securities also ensure reasonable return on capital together with fair prospects of capital appreciation.

The UTI is not constrained like the LIC and banks to invest a certain proportion of its funds in government and other approved securities. It has the freedom to decide where it wants to invest its funds. However there are certain guidelines in this regard which suggest that the investment by the UTI in any one company should not exceed 5% of its (the UTI's) total invisible funds or 15% of the value of the securities issued and outstanding of such a company. Moreover, investment in the initial issues of securities of new industrial undertakings should in any case be less than 5% of the UTI's total invisible fund. The purpose of laying down these guiding principles for making investment by the UTI is to ensure that there is a reasonable amount of diversification of the investment portfolio.

Working Methodology of UTI

1. UTI offers 'units' to the public under various schemes.
2. It invests its funds in shares and debentures of different organisations.
3. It receives interest and dividend on securities held by it.
4. It distributes at least 90% of its income after meeting its management expenses among the unit holders of the scheme.
5. It buys back its own units at the purchase price fixed by it from time to time.

Advantages to the Unit Holders

The investors derive the following advantages by investing in the units of Unit Trust of India.

1. **Safety of Investment** — The investment made in the units of UTI is quite safe. The UTI reinvests this money in wide range of securities covering risk and return. Hence the investors are assured safety for their investment.
2. **Steady and Reasonable return on Investment** — As per the statutory guidelines, the UTI has to distribute not less than 90% of its total income among the unit holders. It means that the unit holders are assured of a steady and reasonable rate of return on their investment.
3. **Liquidity** — The unit holders can easily convert their units into cash. The UTI repurchases the units anytime at the prices fixed by it. Further, the unit holders can transfer their units to third parties or can get loan from banks by putting units as security.

LIFE INSURANCE CORPORATION OF INDIA (LIC)

Establishment of LIC

The Life Insurance Corporation of India (LIC) was constituted under the LIC Act, 1956 as a wholly-owned government corporation by nationalizing 245 private companies operating from 97 centres in India.

Objectives of LIC

The following are the specific **objectives of LIC**:

1. To spread Life Insurance widely and in particular to the rural areas and to the socially and economically backward classes with a view to reaching all insurable persons in the country and providing them adequate financial cover against death at a reasonable cost.
2. To maximise mobilisaiton of people's savings by making insurance-linked saving adequately attractive.
3. To bear in mind, in the investment of funds, the primary obligation to its policyholders, whose money it holds in trust, without losing sight of the interest of the community as a whole; the funds to be deployed to the best advantage of the investors as well as the community as a whole, keeping in view national priorities and obligations of attractive return.
4. To conduct business with utmost economy and with the full realisation that the moneys belong to the policyholders.
5. To act as trustees of the insured public in their individual and collective capacities.
6. To meet the various life insurance needs of the community that would arise in the changing social and economic environment.
7. To involve all people working in the Corporation to the best of their capability in furthering the interests of the insured public by providing efficient service with courtesy.
8. To promote amongst all agents and employees of the Corporation a sense of participation, pride and and job satisfaction through discharge of their duties with dedication towards achievement of Corporate Objectives.

Resources of LIC

When the LIC was nationalized, an initial capital of Rs. 50 crore was provided by the Government of India. Premiums paid by the policy holders are the principal source of funds of the LIC. Besides, the LIC receives interest, dividends, repayments and redemptions which add upto its investible resources.

Investment Policy of LIC

The LIC is essentially an investment institution. Its investment policy has been designed taking into account the cardinal principles of safety of the principal amount. Diversification of funds in terms of various types of securities, number and types of enterprises, maturity and regions. The corporation is supposed to function on business principles and its investment policy is guided by the consideration of the interest of its policy-holders unless it is in the larger interest of the country.

The pattern of investment policy of the LIC until recently was governed by Section 27 A of the Insurance Act. 1938 which was amended in April 1975. The following are the general guidelines relating to the investment policy of LIC:

1. The keynote of the corporation's investment policy is that it should invest its funds in such a manner as to safeguard and promote, to the maximum extent possible, the interest of the policyholders. The larger interest of the country should not however be ignored.

2. Investment should be dispersed over different classes of securities, industries and regions. The Corporation's policy has been not to acquire more than 30% of the outstanding equity shares of a company.

3. The corporation should act purely as an investor. It should not assume the role of an operator or speculator in order to take advantage of temporary fluctuations in the market prices of securities.

4. The Corporation should underwrite security issues after a careful investigation of the project from financial, economic, technical, managerial and social angles.

5. The Corporation should review its investment portfolio from time to time and make such changes in its composition as may be warranted under the circumstances.

6. The Corporation should not acquire control of or participate in the management of any concern in which it has an interest as an investor, unless exceptional circumstances warrant such participation.

Present Structure

Now LIC is offering a wide range of financial servies through setting up of many specialised companies which include the following:

1. LIC Housing Finance Ltd.
2. LIC Mutual Fund
3. LIC (International) E.C.
4. Jeevan Bima Sahyog Asset Management Company Ltd.

MUTUAL FUND

Mutual Fund Industry — An Overview

The mutual fund industry in India began with the setting up of the Unit Trust In India (UTI) in 1964 by the Government of India. During the last 36 years, UTI has grown to be a dominant player in the industry with assets of over Rs. 76,547 Crores as of March 31, 2000. The UTI is governed by a special legislation, the Unit Trust of India Act, 1963. In 1987 public sector banks and insurance companies were permitted to set up mutual funds and accordingly since 1987, 6 public sector banks have set up mutual funds. Also the two Insurance companies LIC and GIC established mutual funds. Securities Exchange Board of India (SEBI) formulated the Mutual Fund (Regulation) 1993, which for the first time established a comprehensive regulatory framework for the mutual fund industry. Since then several mutual funds have been set up by the private and joint sectors.

Meaning of Mutual Fund

A Mutual Fund is a trust that pools the savings of a number of investors who share a common financial goal. The money thus collected this then invested in capital market instruments such as shares, debentures and other securities. The income earned through these investments and the capital appreciation realised and shared by its unit holders in proportion to the number of units owned by them. Thus a Mutual Fund is the most suitable investment for the common man as it offers an opportunity to invest in a diversified, professionally managed basket of securities at a relatively low cost.

Working of a Mutual Fund

The flow chart below describes broadly the working of a mutual fund:

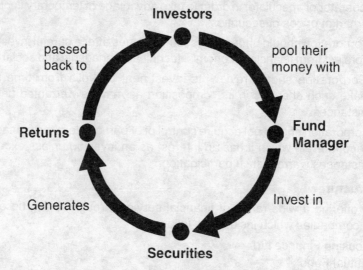

Organisation of a Mutual Fund

There are many entities involved and the diagram below illustrates the organisational set up of a mutual fund:

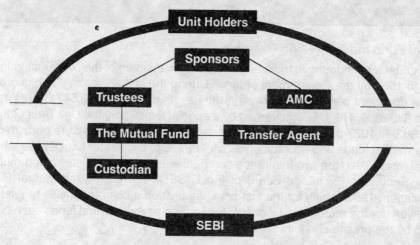

Organisation of a Mutual Fund

There are many entities involved and the diagram below illustrates the organisational set up of a mutual fund:

1. **Sponsor** — The sponsor is a company registered under The Companies Act, 1956. This company must have a sound track record, general reputation and fairness in all their business transactions. The major responsibilities of sponsor include:

    (a) To create the Mutual Fund Trust

    (b) To submit the Trust Deed to SEBI for prior approval

2. **Mutual Fund Trust** — Mutual Fund proposed by a sponsor has to be set up as a trust under the Indian Trusts Act, 1882 (and not as a company under the Companies Act, 1956). The major responsibilities of Mutual Fund Trust include:

    (a) To float one or several different schemes under which units are to be issued to the investors;

    (b) To make arrangement for periodic reporting to the unit holders of Mutual Fund.

    (c) To ensure the compliance with the guidelines.

3. **Asset Management Company (AMC)** — Asset Management Company (AMC) is appointed by the Mutual Trust to manage the assets of the Mutual Fund. The major responsibilities of AMC include:

    (a) To prepare a prospectus/letter of offer for each scheme and to get it vetted by SEBI.

    (b) To conduct necessary equity research.

    (c) To invest directly in primary market or through brokers in a secondary market.

    (d) To submit quarterly report on the functioning of the mutual fund to the trustees.

    (e) To make necessary arrangement for transfer of units, settlement of accounts, payment of dividend etc.

4. **Registrars and Transfer Agents** — Their major responsibilities include:

    (a) Receiving and processing the application form of investors.

    (b) Issuing of Unit/Share Certificates on behalf of Mutual Fund.

    (c) Maintain detailed records of Unit holders transactions.

    (d) Purchasing, selling, transferring and redeeming the Unit/Shares Certificates.

    (e) Issuing of income/dividend Warrants, broker Cheques etc.

    (f) Creating security interest on Units/Certificates for allowing loans against them

5. **Advertiser** — Major responsibilities of an advertiser include:

    (a) Helping mutual funds organisers to prepare a media plan for marketing the fund.

(b) Issuing/buying the space in newspapers and other electronic media for advertising the various features of a fund.

(c) Arranging for hoardings at public places.

6. **Advisor/manager** — It is generally a corporate entity who does the following jobs:

(a) Professional advice on the Fund's Investments.

(b) Advice on Asset Management Services.

7. **Custodian** — A custodian which is again a corporate body does the following functions:

(a) Holds securities

(b) Receives and delivers securities

(c) Collects income/interest/ dividends on the securities

(d) Holds and processes cash

Besides the above, other players are as under;

(a) Fund administrator;

(b) Fund Accounting Services;

(c) Legal Advisors;

(d) Fund Officers;

(e) Underwriters/Distributors;

(f) Legal Advisors.

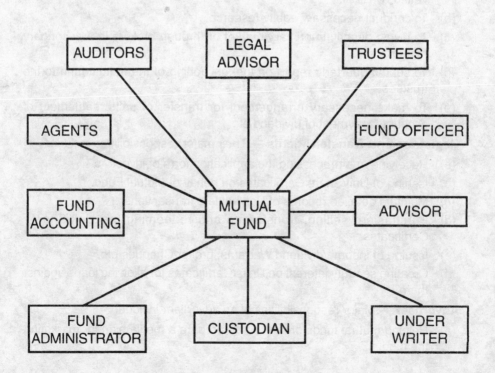

All the above agencies play a major role in any mutual fund organised as they are separate agencies/corporations independent of the mutual fund. However, in India so far mutual funds have taken the services of the following outside agencies.

(a) Registrars and Transfer Agents

(b) Advertisers

(c) Legal Advisors

(d) Custodians

Other services are organised inhouse and a Trustee's job is undertaken by the bank who promotes the mutual funds. Figure shows important players who help to organise and operate a mutual fund.

Advantages of Mutual Funds

The advantages of investing in a Mutual Fund are:

1. **Professional Management** — The advantages of professional management are available since mutual funds are managed by expert professional funds managers.

2. **Diversification** — The funds are invested in different industries and different companies and hence it reduces the risk of reliance on a particular industry or company.

3. **Return Potential** — Mutual funds have the potential to provide higher return than that from bank deposits.

4. **Low Costs** — The cost of investing in a mutual fund is less than the cost of investing in the securities of secondary market since no brokerage is involved.

5. **Liquidity** — Buy-back arrangements or listing on some stock exchanges offer high liquidity to investors.

6. **Transparency** — The figures of Net Asset Value, Sale Price, Repurchase Price etc. are readily available in the offices of Mutual Funds, Newspapers and on Internet.

7. **Operational Flexibility** — Mutual funds provide operational flexibility by providing systematise investment plan, withdrawal plan.

8. **Choice of Schemes** — Mutual funds offers variety of schemes such as Growth Schemes, Income Schemes, Growth Plus Income Schemes, Tax Planning Scheme etc.

9. **Tax Benefits** — Investments made in Tax Planning Schemes of Mutual Funds carry tax reliefs such as —

(a) Tax Rebate u/s 88 on Investment made.

(b) Exemption of Income from Units of Mutual Fund.

10. **Well regulated** — Mutual Funds are regulated by Mutual Funds (Regulation) 1993 which provides a comprehensive regulatory framework for the mutual fund industry.

11. **Facility of Re-investment** — Mutual Fund schemes enable the investor to re-invest the dividend or capital gain. Even the smallest dividend or capital gain gets re-invested, thus effective return enhances.

Types of Mutual Fund Schemes

Wide variety of Mutual Fund Schemes exists to cater to the needs such as financial position, risk tolerance and return expectations etc. The various types of schemes in the Industry are as follows:

1. **Open-ended Mutual Fund Schemes** — Under these schemes, the units are sold and repurchased everyday on the basis of that day's Net Asset Value (NAV). NAV is calculated as under:

$$NAV = \frac{\text{Total Market Value of Assets} - \text{Liabilities}}{\text{Number of Units Outstanding}}$$

Normally, sale price and repurchase price differ due to sales load and repurchase load to be charged from the investor.

Examples of Open-Ended Schemes — US-1964, ULIP 1971 of UTI.

Features of Open-Ended Schemes

The main features of these schemes are as follows:

(a) **Flexible Size** — The size of the corpus and the number of units of the fund is flexible.

(b) **No Fixed Subscription Period** — There is no fixed period within which the units are to be subscribed.

(c) **No Fixed Redemption Period** — There is no fixed redemption date.

(d) **No Listing Requirement** — The units of these schemes need not be listed on the stock exchange.

(e) **Greater Liquidity** — These schemes offer greater liquidity to the investors who can sell their units to the mutual fund as and when they so decide.

2. **Close-ended Mutual Fund Schemes** — Under these schemes, the units can be subscribed for only during the fixed period when the issue is open for subscription.

Examples of Close-ended Mutual Fund Schemes — Master Share, Master Gain Schemes of UTI.

Features of Close-Ended Schemes

The main features of these schemes are as follows:

(a) **Fixed Size** — The size of the corpus and the number of units of the fund is fixed.

(b) **Fixed Subscription Period** — The period within which the units are to be subscribed is fixed.

(c) **Fixed Redemption Period** — The period after the expiry of which, units are to be redeemed or repurchased is fixed.

(d) **Listing Requirement** — The units of these schemes are to listed on the stock exchange.

(e) **Lower Liquidity** — These schemes do not offer greater liquidity to the investor who can not sell their units to the mutual fund before the expiry of fixed period.

3. **Income Fund Schemes** — These schemes offer high returns on regular basis to investors. The pattern of investment is oriented towards fixed income yielding securities like non-convertible debentures of consistently good dividend paying

companies. For example, US-64 Scheme of UTI.

4. **Growth Fund Schemes** — These schemes offer high capital appreciation in the long run. The pattern of investment is oriented towards shares of high growth companies. For example, Master Share, Master Share Plus, Master Gain Schemes of UTI.

5. **Growth *Plus* Income Funds or Balanced Funds Schemes** — These schemes offer reasonable regular return and capital appreciation in the long run. The pattern of investment is oriented towards both fixed income yielding securities and shares with growth potential. For example, PNB Premium Plus-91 Scheme of PNB Mutual Fund, Master Share, Master Share Plus, Master Gain Schemes of UTI.

6. **Tax Relief Funds Schemes** — These schemes offer tax relief to the investors. The investors can claim tax rebate u/s 88 of the Income Tax Act, 1961, by investing in the these schemes.

7. **Industry Funds or Specialised Funds Schemes** — These scheme offer opportunities and threats attached to a particular industry. These funds carry high risks with them as the entire fund is exposed to a particular industry such as Software, Infrastructure, Power etc.

8. **Domestic Mutual Funds Schemes** — These schemes provide offers to domestic investors to invest their funds. For example, SBI Mutual Fund, LIC Mutual Fund etc.

9. **Overseas or Off Share or Foreign Mutual Funds Schemes** — These schemes provide offers to foreign investors to invest their funds in the country of the issuing company. For example, India Growth Fund and India Fund raised in the US and UK respectively.

10. **Index Fund Schemes** — These funds invest their resources only in a portfolio of script included in a select index. In India, they can be operated either through SENSEX or NSE-Index or BSE Index. For example, Access Fund (based on NSE-Index) of UTI, Equity Fund (based on NSE & SENSEX) of UTI.

11. **Venture Capital Funds** — These funds invest their funds in venture capital companies. These are meant primarily for institutional investors.

Growth of Mutual Funds

The Indian Mutual Fund has passed through three phases. The first phase was between 1964 and 1987 and the only player was the Unit Trust of India, which had a total asset of Rs 6,700/- crores at the end of 1988. The second phase is between 1987 and 1993 during which period 8 funds were established (6 by banks and one each by LIC and GIC). The total assets under management had grown to Rs 61,028/- crores at the end of 1994 and the number of schemes were 167.

The third phase began with the entry of private and foreign sectors in the Mutual Fund industry in 1993. Kothari Pioneer Mutual Fund was the first fund to be established by the private sector in association with a foreign fund.

As at the end of financial year 2000 (31st March) 32 funds were functioning with Rs 1,13,005 crores as total assets under management. As on August end 2000, there were 33 funds with 391 schemes and assets under management with Rs 1,02,849 crores.

The Securities and Exchange Board of India (SEBI) came out with comprehensive regulation in 1993 which defined the structure of Mutual Fund and Asset Management Companies for the first time.

Several private sectors Mutual Funds were launched in 1993 and 1994. The shares of the private players has been risen rapidly since then.

Currently there are 34 Mutual Fund organisations in India managing over Rs 1,02,000/- crores.

MUTUAL FUNDS IN INDIA

(A) Unit Trust of India

(B) Bank Sponsored
   a. BOB Asset Management Co. Ltd.
   b. BOI Asset Management Co. Ltd.
   c. Canbank Investment Management Services Ltd.
   d. PNB Asset Management Co. Ltd.
   e. SBI Funds Management Ltd.
   f. Indfund Management Ltd.

(C) Institutions
   a. GIC Asset Management Co. Ltd.
   b. IDBI Principal Asset Management Co. Ltd.
   c. IL & FS Asset Management Co. Ltd.
   d. Jeevan Bima Sahyog Asset Management Co. Ltd.

(D) Private Sector

1. Indian
   a. Bench Mark Asset Management Co. Ltd.
   b. Kotak Mahindra Asset Management Co. Ltd.
   c. Shriram Asset Management Co. Ltd.
   d. Reliance Capital Asset Management Ltd.
   e. J.M. Capital Management Ltd.
   f. Escorts Asset Management Ltd.

2. Joint Ventures — Predominantly Indian
   a. Birla Sun Life Asset Management Pvt. Co. Ltd.
   b. Cholamandalam Cazenove Asset Management Co. Ltd.
   c. DSP Merrill Lynch Investment Managers (India) Ltd.
   d. First Indian Asset Management Private Ltd.
   e. HDFC Asset Management Company Ltd.
   f. Sundaram Newton Asset Management Company
   g. Pioneer ITI AMC Ltd.
   h. Tata TD Waterhouse Asset Management Private Ltd.
   i. Credit Capital Asset Management Co. Ltd.

3. Joint Ventures — Predominantly Foreign
   a. Alliance Capital Asset Management (India) Pvt. Ltd.
   b. Standard Chartered Asset Mgmt. Co. Pvt. Ltd.
   c. Dundee Investment Management & Research (Pvt.) Ltd.
   d. ING Investment Management (India) Pvt. Ltd.
   e. JF Asset Management (India) Pvt. Ltd.
   f. Morgan Stanley Investment Management Pvt. Ltd.
   g. Prudential ICICI Management Co. Ltd.
   h. Sun F & C Asset Management (I) Pvt. Ltd.
   i. Templeton Asset Management (India) Pvt. Ltd.
   j. Jurich India Asset Management Corpn. Ltd.

EXERCISES

VERY SHORT ANSWER TYPE QUESTIONS

1. What is meant by finance?
2. Is finance required for both economic and non-economic activities?
3. What is meant by business finance?
4. What is meant by long-term finance?
5. What is the purpose of long-term finance?
6. What is meant by medium-term finance?
7. What is the purpose of medium-term finance?
8. (a) What is meant by short-term finance?
   (b) What is circulating capital?
   (c) What is working capital?
9. What is the purpose of short-term finance?
10. What is an operating cycle in a trading firm?
11. What is an operating cycle in a manufacturing firm?
12. What is meant by 'Owners Funds'/Ownership Capital?
13. What is meant by 'Borrowed Funds'/Borrowed Capital?
14. What is meant by Equity Shares?
15. (a) What is meant by Preference Shares?
    (b) Why are preference shares so called?
16. What is meant by 'Cumulative Preference Shares'?
17. What is meant by 'Non-Cumulative Preference Shares'?
18. What is meant by 'Participating Preference Shares'?
19. What is meant by 'Non-Participating Preference Shares'?
20. What is meant by 'Convertible Preference Shares'?
21. What is meant by 'Non-Convertible Preference Shares'?
22. What is meant by 'Debentures'?
23. What is meant by 'Unsecured Debentures'?
24. What is meant by 'Secured Debentures'?
25. What is meant by 'First Mortgage Debentures'?
26. What is meant by 'Second Mortgage Debentures'?
27. What is meant by 'Redeemable Debentures'?
28. What is meant by 'Perpetual Debentures'?
29. What is meant by 'Registered Debentures'?
30. What is meant by 'Bearer Debentures'?
31. What is meant by 'Convertible Debentures'?
32. What is meant by 'Non-Convertible Debentures'?
33. What is meant by 'Self-financing or internal financing or ploughing back of profits?
34. What is meant by 'Public Deposits'?
35. What is meant by 'Trade Credit'?
36. What is meant by 'Factoring'?
37. What is meant by 'Discounting Bill of exchange'?
38. What is meant by 'Cash Credit'?

39. What is meant by 'Bank Overdraft'?
40. What is meant by 'Development Banks'?
41. For what does 'IFCI' Stand for?
42. For what does 'IDBI' Stand for?
43. For what does 'ICICI' stand for?
44. For what does 'SIDBI' stand for?
45. For What ADRs stand for?
46. For what GDRs stand for?
47. For what FDI stand for?

SHORT ANSWER TYPE QUESTIONS

1. List any five purposes for which the need for business arises.
2. List the types of business finance.
3. Enumerate any two major factors which determine the amount of long-term finance required.
4. Why should fixed assets be financed out of long-term finance?
5. Enumerate the sources of long-term finance.
6. Enumerate the sources of medium-term finance.
7. Why does the need for short term-finance arise?
8. Why is working capital called a 'Circulating Capital' or 'Revolving Capital'?
9. (a) Enumerate two factors which bring out the importance of working capital in a business.
   (b) List the factors which determine the amount of working capital required?
10. (a) Enumerate the sources of short-term finance.
    (b) Identify two sources of variable working capital.
11. List the types of business finance on the basis of ownership.
12. List the main characteristics of owners funds.
13. Why is ownership capital called risk capital?
14. Why is ownership capital called permanent capital?
15. Give any three merits of ownership capital.
16. Give any two limitations of ownership capital.
17. List the main characteristics of borrowed capital.
18. Give any three merits of borrowed capital.
19. Give any three limitations of borrowed capital.
20. Give any four points of difference between ownership capital and borrowed capital.
21. Briefly state the methods of issuing securities.
22. What is meant by 'Trading on Equity'? State the conditions under which the benefit of trading on equity is available.
23. What are the characteristics of equity shares?
24. State any four merits of equity share capital from the point of view of a company.
25. State any three limitations of equity share capital from the point of view of a company.
26. State any four merits of equity share capital from the point of view of shareholders.

27. State any four limitations of equity share capital from the point of view of shareholders.
28. (a) What are the characteristics of preference shares?
    (b) What is the advantage of participating preference shares over other preference shares?
29. State any four merits of preference share capital from the point of view of a company.
30. State any two limitations of preference share capital from the point of view of company.
31. State any four merits of preference share capital from the point of view of shareholders.
32. State any two limitations of preference share capital from the point of view of shareholders.
33. Give four point of difference between an Equity Share and Preference Share.
34. What are the main features of debentures?
35. State any three merits of debentures from the point of view of a company.
36. State any two limitations of debentures from the point of view of a company.
37. Give four points of difference between a share and a debenture.
38. State any two merits of term loan from the point of view of a company.
39. State any four limitations of term loan from the point of view of a company.
40. Give two advantages of retained profits or ploughing back of profits.
41. Give two limitations of retained profits.
42. State any three sources of medium-term finance in a company.
43. State the merits and limitations of public deposits.
44. State any four sources of short-term finance.
45. State any three merits of trade credit.
46. State of two limitations of trade credit.
47. Give two points of difference between fixed capital and working capital.
48. Give two functions of a commercial bank.
49. Mention two types of deposits accepted by commercial banks.
50. Mention two ancilliary services rendered by commercial banks.
51. Give the main forms in which financial assistance from a bank may be available.
52. Write a short note on underwriting of shares.
53. Name any two mutual funds.
54. Name any two advantages of mutual funds.
55. Name any two schemes of mutual funds.
56. Name three national level Financial Institutions.
57. Name three state level financial institutions.
58. Mention the main objective of ICICI.
59. State the purpose for which the State Finance Corporations (SFCs) were set up.
60. Mention the main objective of IFCI.
61. Mention the main objective of IDBI.
62. Mention the main objective of IRBI.

63. Mention the main objective of SIDCs.
64. Mention the main Characteristics of GDRs.
65. Mention the main Characteristics of ADRs.
66. Mention the main Characteristics of FDI.

LONG ANSWER TYPE QUESTIONS

1. Explain the importance of finance in modern business.
2. Explain the meaning, purpose and sources of various types of finance.
3. Explain the meaning, characteristics, merits and limitations of ownership capital.
4. Explain the meaning, characteristics, merits and limitations of borrowed capital.
5. Distinguish between owned capital and borrowed capital.
6. Describe the advantages of borrowed capital as compared with those of ownership capital.
7. Describe the meaning, characteristics, merits and limitations of equity shares.
8. Describe the meaning, characteristics, types, merits and limitations of preference shares.
9. Distinguish between an Equity Share and a Preference Share.
10. Describe the meaning, features, types, merits and limitations of debentures.
11. Distinguish between Share and Debenture.
12. Explain the meaning, advantages and limitations of retained profits.
13. Explain the meaning, advantages and limitations of public deposits.
14. Explain the various sources of short-term finance.
15. Discuss briefly the objectives, resources, management and functions of IFCI.
16. Discuss briefly the objectives, resources, management and functions of ICICI.
17. Discuss briefly the objectives, resources, management and functions of IDBI.
18. Discuss briefly the objectives, resources, management and functions of IRBI.
19. Discuss briefly objectives, resources, management and functions of State Financial Corporations (SFCs).
20. Discuss briefly objectives, resources, management and functions of State Industrial Corporations (SIDCs).
21. Discuss the factors which influence the determination of fixed capital of a business.
22. Define working capital. Give the factors determining the amount of wroking capital of an organisation.
23. Discuss the role of working capital in a business concern.
24. Discuss the main advantages of obtaining funds from specialised financial institutions.
25. Explain the meaning, Characteristics and Advantages of GDRs, ADRs and Foreign Direct Investments.

Part B   Management

16 Nature and Significance of Management

INTRODUCTION

Generally the term 'management' is used to mean the group of persons who manage the organisation. Management is needed everywhere in every activity at every time. Management is not confined merely to business organisations. It is also needed in other organisations such as government, religious, charitable bodies etc. In this chapter, we shall study the meaning, nature, levels, objectives, importance and functions of management.

MEANING OF MANAGEMENT

Let us look at the traditional and modern views of management.

Traditional Definition

According to traditional view "*Management is getting things done through others.*" This definition is incomplete and misleading because it treats the employees as mere means to certain ends. People are not cogs in the wheel, so they should not be treated as a commodity. Needs and aspirations of the people working in an organisation should not be overlooked. They must be satisfied so as to obtain and sustain consistent efforts from them towards organisational objectives.

Modern Definition

According to one modern view, the term 'management' may be defined as "*creating the internal environment of an enterprise where individuals working together in groups can perform sufficiently and effectively towards the attainment of group goals*". On the basis of this definition, the two important features of management are as under:

(a) Management is goal oriented in the sense that its purpose is to achieve group goals.

(b) Management involves creating an internal environment or conditions so that the people are able to perform their tasks efficiently.

According to George R. Terry, "*Management is a distinct process consisting of planning, organising, activating and controlling, performed to determine and accomplish the objectives by the use of people and resources.*" On the basis of this definition, the three important features of management are as under:

(a) Management is a distinct process.

(b) It consists of planning, organising, activating and controlling.

(c) It is meant to accomplish predetermined objectives by the use of people and resources.

DIFFERENT SCHOOLS OF THOUGHT

Different schools of thought have defined management differently. According to them the word 'management' may be interpreted as a process, activity, discipline, an economic resource, a system of authority and as a class or elite. Let us discuss the different interpretations as follows:

1. MANAGEMENT AS A PROCESS

Management is regarded as a process because it includes a series of interrelated managerial actions. The management process consists of setting objectives for an enterprise and of taking steps to ensure that these objectives are achieved. The steps include functions like planning, organising, staffing, directing and controlling. This process is social, integrating and continuous. Let us know why it is called so.

(i)   Why is management regarded as a social process?

Management is regarded as a social process because the activities involved in the achievement of organisational goals are carried out when organisational participants interact with one another.

The resources which are handled by the management are to be used in such a manner that the needs of the society are satisfied efficiently and effectively. Every manager is required to use various skills of human relations to achieve good relations with the various groups of society like shareholders, workers, consumers, government, suppliers etc.

(ii)   Why is management regarded as an integrating process?

Management is regarded as an integrating process because management integrates human efforts with non-human resources like material, machines, technology, financial resources etc. by their concerted and well thought of efforts. Management undertakes in bringing together the human, physical and financial resources so that there is harmony among them.

(iii)   Why is management regarded as a continuous process?

Management is regarded as a continuous process because it involves continuous handling and integrating human and non-human resources. In other words, it is not a one-time process which is required at a particular point of time. Rather it is an ongoing continuous process which is required at all points of time. Management is concerned with constantly identifying the problems and solving them by taking appropriate actions.

2. MANAGEMENT AS AN ACTIVITY

Management as an activity means what managers do in the process of management. This includes the following activities:

(i)   **Informational activities** i.e., activities relating to receiving and giving information. Managers constantly communicate with their subordinates as well as superiors.

(ii)   **Decisional activities** i.e., activities relating to developing and choosing from among alternatives. Managers constantly perform decisional activities to make decisions of various kinds in various situations. These decisions become the bases of actions to follow.

(iii)   **Inter-personal activities** i.e., activities relating to developing and maintaining relations with people. Management involves achieving goals through people. Managers constantly interact with their superiors and subordinates to achieve goals.

3. MANAGEMENT AS A DISCIPLINE

Management as a discipline refers to the systematised body of knowledge and as a separate field of study. Management is regarded as a discipline because it satisfies all the requirements of a separate field as given on next page:

(i) There should be scholars and thinkers who communicate the relevant knowledge through research and publications. (Scholars are doing research on the principles and practice of management.)

(ii) There should be efforts to formally impart the knowledge so generated to others. (The findings of scholars and researchers are published in books and magazines specializing in management and can be learnt through instructions and teaching.)

4. MANAGEMENT AS A GROUP

The term 'management as a group' may be interpreted in two ways as under:

(i) **Technically**, this term is used to indicate all the people who carry out managerial activities. Under this interpretation, all the managers from the chief executive to the first line supervisors are collectively addressed as management.

(ii) **Practically**, this term is used to indicate only the top management of the organisation *(e.g.,* board of directors of a company) which normally has the authority for making important decisions like whether to the introduce a particular product or not.

Management is a field of study of the principles and practice of management. It may be studied either to know what role a manager may play in our society or to specialise in any area of functional management like production, marketing, personnel, finance etc. It is a multidisciplinary approach as it has taken a number of things from economics, sociology, psychology, anthropology etc.

NATURE OF MANAGEMENT

The main characteristics which reveal the nature of management are shown below:

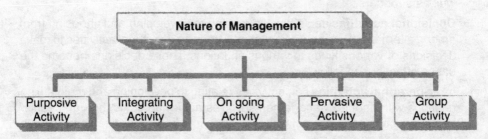

Let us discuss these characteristics one by one as follows:

1. **Purposive Activity** — Management is a purposive activity in the sense that its purpose is always to achieve certain predetermined objectives. The tasks of management are directed towards effectiveness (i.e., attainment of organi-sational goals) and efficiency *(i.e.,* attainment of goal with economy of resource use).

2. **Integrating Activity** — Management is an integrating activity in the sense that it integrates human efforts with non-human resources like material, machines, technology, financial resources etc.

3. **On going Activity** — Management is a on going or continuous activity in the sense that the cycle of management continues to operate so long as there is organisation or organised activity for the achievement of organisational goals.

4. **Pervasive** — Management is pervasive in the sense that it is relevant for all organisations irrespective of the size (small or large), nature (economic, social or political) and location (in India or abroad or in rural or urban areas).

5. **Group Activity** — Management is a group activity in the sense that it co-ordinates the efforts of organisational members so as to achieve the predetermined objectives of the organisation.

The nature of management can be further understood by examining whether it is a science or an art.

MANAGEMENT AS A SCIENCE

To decide whether management can be regarded as science, one must answer the following two questions:

(a)   What is science? What are the features of science?

(b)   Whether the management has all the features of science or not?

Let us answer the aforesaid questions.

(a) What is science? What are the features of science?

Science refers to a systematic body of knowledge acquired through observation and experimentation which is capable of verification. The main features of science are discussed below:

1. *Existence of systematised body of knowledge* — Science is systematised in the sense that it is based on cause and effect relationship.

2. *Use of scientific methods of observation* — Science uses the scientific methods of observation which are unbiased and objective.

3. *Principles based on experiments* — Scientific principles are first developed through observations and then tested by repeated experimentation.

4. *Universal validity of principles* — Scientific principles have universal validity and application.

(b) Whether management has all the features of science or not?

Let us compare the features of science with those of management as follows:

Science	Management
1. Existence of systematised body of knowledge.	1. Existence of systematised body of knowledge.
2. Use of scientific methods of observation which are unbiased and objective.	2. Methods of observation followed by management are not cent per cent objective since the management deals with the human beings whose behaviour cannot be predicted on the basis of absolute laws and experimentations.
3. Principles based on experiments.	3. Principles of management are evolved on the basis of repeated experimentation in various types of organisations.
4. Universal validity of principles.	4. Management principles do not have universal applicability since their application and use has to be modified according to given situations.

Like other social sciences, management is also related with human beings and it is not an exact science like physics or chemistry. Though inexact, management, like social sciences, is based on a systematised body of knowledge; its practice depends on cause and effect relations, and not the personal likes and dislikes of managers. Principles of management, as in the case of sciences, are also derived from observations and experiments in different types of organisations.

Conclusion—Management may be regarded as an inexact science because it has some of the characteristics of science but not all. Management being a social science deals with people and their behaviour but human behaviour cannot be subjected to laboratory experiments as is possible in natural sciences like physics and chemistry. It is not possible to predict human behaviour with complete accuracy but it is possible in natural sciences.

MANAGEMENT AS AN ART

To decide whether management can be regarded as an art, one must answer the following two questions:

(a)   What is an 'art'? What are the features of an 'art'?

(b)   Whether the management has all the features of 'art' or not?

Let us answer the aforesaid questions.

(a) What is an art? What are the features of an 'art'?

Art refers to the application of skill and knowledge to attain the desired results. The main features of an 'art' are discussed below:

1. *Existence of theoretical knowledge* — Art presupposes the existence of theoretical knowledge.

2. *Personalised application* — The application of skill and knowledge is personalised in the sense that the manner of application differs from practitioner to practitioner.

3. *Practice and creativity* — Art involves practice of the basic principles and then infusing creativity and developing own style of doing.

(b) Whether management has all the features of 'art' or not?

Management can be regarded as an art because it has all its features as under:

1. There exist general principles for managing various aspects of business.

2. Application to principles of management is personalised in the sense that every manager has his own approach to problem solving and depends upon his experience and skill.

3. Management involves practice and creativity. Each manager learns the principles of management but applies them differently depending on how much he has practised them and how much creative he is. Management is creative in the sense that it is the function of creating and producing situations needed for further improvements.

MANAGEMENT BOTH SCIENCE AND ART

Management can be regarded as both science and art because it combines the features of both of them. Management as a science provides the systematised body of knowledge which can be used to train the prospective and present managers. It is because of this that an old saying **'Managers are born' has been replaced by 'Managers are made'**. Management as an art involves personal practice and creativity. To become a successful manager, one must use theoretical knowledge along with personal practice and creativity and develop one's own style of managing.

In fact, science and art are not mutually exclusive but complementary to each other.

Knowledge (science) without skill (art) is useless and dangerous and skill (art) without knowledge (science) means stagnancy and inability to pass on learning. Like a doctor, a manager too is required to know not only principles of management, but also possess the skill to put his knowledge into practice. Improvement in one facilitates the other.

MANAGEMENT AS A PROFESSION

To decide whether management is a profession or not, one must-

(a) know the meaning and features of profession, and

(b) compare the features of management with those of profession.

(a) Meaning and Features of Profession

Profession is a specialised field which has the following features:

1. *Well defined body of knowledge* — Every profession has a systematised body of knowledge which can be learnt through instructions.

2. *Restricted entry* — Every profession has restricted entry on the basis of examination or education.

3. *Professional association* — Every profession has professional association of which membership is essential. Such association regulates the entry in the profession, grants certificate of practice, formulates and enforces code of conduct.

4. *Service to others* — Every profession has dominance of service motive. True professionals serve their clients' interests through dedication and commitment.

(b) Comparison between Profession and Management

To know whether management has all the features of a profession, let us compare the features of both.

Profession	Management
(a) Existence of systematised body of knowledge	Existence of systematised body of knowledge
(b) Entry to the field of specialisation requires prior requirements to be fulfilled.	Entry to this field does not require any prior requirement to be fulfilled.
(c) Existence of professional association (e.g. Bar Council, Medical Council) of which membership is essential	No existence of professional association of which membership is essential for practising managers
(d) Service motive of profession	At present, service is not the only goal of management. It is fast moving in this direction since there is growing concern for social responsibility.
(e) Formal training is necessary	Formal training may or may not be necessary.
(f) Members are regulated by formal code of conduct enforceable by regulating authority like Bar Council or Medical Council	Managers are not regulated by formal code of conduct.

Conclusion — At present, management cannot be regarded as a profession in all respects because it has only some of the characteristics of profession but not all. It may also be noted that though there is growing awareness in the society to employ properly educated and trained people for managing business enterprises, still self-made managers cannot altogether be eliminated. Management of today is becoming creative rather than adaptive being conscious of its ethical and social responsibilities. It indicates that now management is moving in the direction of profession.

GENERAL OBJECTIVES OF MANAGEMENT

The specific objectives of management may differ from one organisation to another but the general objectives of management remain the same for each organisation. The general objectives of management are shown below:

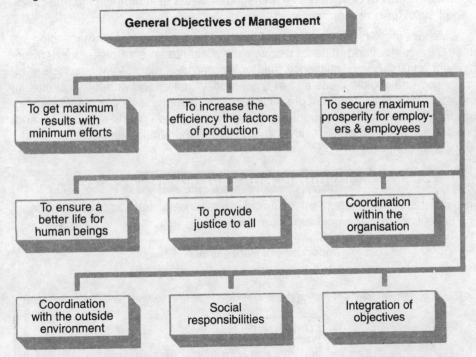

Let us discuss them one by one.

1. **To Get Maximum Results with Minimum Efforts or Optimum and Economical use of resources** — It is the general objective of every management to secure maximum results with minimum efforts and resources. As a result of fulfillment of this objective, the cost of production is reduced.

2. **To Increase the Efficiency of the Factors of Production** — Every management aims at utilizing the factors of production (like labour and capital) properly. As a result of fulfillment of this objective, wastage of resources is reduced and productivity of resources is increased.

3. **To Secure Maximum Prosperity for Employers and Employees** — Management secures maximum prosperity for employers by earning high

profits at minimum costs and for employees by providing adequate remuneration and other benefits for their services.

4. **To Ensure a Better Life for Human Beings** — Management ensures a better life for human beings by increasing productivity and employment.

5. **To Provide Justice to All** — Management provides justice to all by following its policies on a uniform basis.

6. **Coordination Within the Organisation** — Management coordinates the efforts of all factors of production and of different departments and workers.

7. **Coordination with the outside environment** — Management coordinates the enterprises and outside world.

8. **Social responsibilities** — Management ensures that the enterprise should fulfil its social responsibilities.

9. **Integration of objectives** — Management aims at integrating the objectives of individuals and organisation.

Management plays an important role in the success of an organisation by utilising the human and material resources available to an enterprises for deriving the best results; brings efficiency through proper utilisation of various factors of production and avoiding wastage of time, money and efforts and thus increasing the productivity of all factors of production; brings soundness by aiming at securing maximum prosperity for the employees by generating high profits at least cost and thus satisfying the employees through adequate remuneration and benefits for the efforts they put in.

IMPORTANCE OF MANAGEMENT

The importance of management arises out of the benefits attached to management. The benefits of management are shown on below:

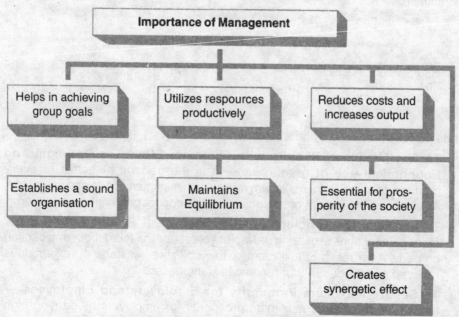

Let us discuss them one by one.

1. **Helps in Achieving Group Goals** — Management helps in achieving group goals by directing the activities of the managers towards attainment of group goals of the organisation.

2. **Optimum Utilization of Resources** — Management utilizes human and non-human resources productively and as a result wastage is eliminated and efficiency is increased.

3. **Reduces Costs and Increases Output** — An efficient management leads to reduced costs and increased output through a better planning, organising, controlling and the use of various techniques of cost control and cost reduction.

4. **Establishes a Sound Organisation** — Management establishes a sound organisation by dividing the total work into specific jobs, grouping jobs into departments and establishing clear-cut authority relationships among the positions held by people.

5. **Maintains Equilibrium** — An efficient management enables an organisation to adjust to the complex and ever changing external environment. That is why the management is held responsible for survival and stable growth of an organisation.

6. **Essential for Prosperity of the Society** — Management improves the standard of living of the people by providing them useful new products manufactured with the use of latest technology. By adopting latest technology and producing new products, management provides maximum satisfaction of consumers needs in society.

7. **Creates Synergetic Effect** — Management creates synergetic effect by producing results which are more than the sum of individual efforts of the group members.

MANAGEMENT AND ADMINISTRATION

Meaning of Administration

There are different views on the usage of the terms-Management and Administration. One view treats 'Management as part of Administration' but another view treats 'Administration' as part of 'Management'. Let us see the different views as follows:

According to Haimann, 'Administration' means:

(a)   overall determination of policies,

(b)   the setting of major objectives,

(c)   the identification of general purposes, and

(d)   the laying out of broad programmes, major projects, and so forth.

Thus, administration is concerned with policy making to attain given objectives.

According to American school of thought, "administration is a thinking function or a top-level function. It sets objectives which management strives to realise and lays down policies under which management operates". This school emphasizes that administration is a broader concept than management.

According to British school of thought, *"administration handles the current problems which arise in carrying out the policies laid down by the management"*. This school emphasises that management is a wider concept than administration.

According to reconciling school of thought, *"management is categorized as administrative and operative. Administrative management is top management incharge of planning function. Operative management is middle and lower managements responsible for execution of the plans"*.

The element of administration increases as one progresses to higher ranks (or positions) and the element of management increases as one proceeds to lower ranks. This may be observed from the diagram given below:

Diagram showing the elements of administration and management at various levels of management

Higher the rank of a manager, greater is his role in making policies, setting general organisational objectives and formulating plans and programmes. In fact, top management is mainly concerned with performing administrative activities, whereas managers at lower levels are mainly concerned with executive functions.

DISTINCTION BETWEEN MANAGEMENT AND ADMINISTRATION

The management and administration can be distinguished as follows:

Basis of Distinction	Administration	Management
1. Meaning	It means overall determination of policies, the setting of major objectives, the identification of general purposes, the laying out of broad programmes.	It means creating the internal environment of an enterprise where individuals working together in groups can perform efficiently towards the attainment of group goals.
2. Type of function performed	It performs a **decision-making function** since it determines the policies to be executed by management.	It performs an **executive function** since it executes the policies determined by administration.
3. Decision	It decides what is to be done and when it is be done	It decides who should do it and how should he do it.
4. Nature of function performed	It is a **thinking function**.	It is a **doing function**.
5. Relative importance	The element of administration **increases as one progresses to higher** levels of management.	The element of management **increases as one descends to lower** levels of management.
6. Factors influencing the decision-making	Decisions are influenced by the forces of **public opinion, government policies, religious and social customs.**	Decisions are influenced by the **opinions, beliefs** and **values of managers.**
7. Owners/Employees	It represents the **owners** of the enterprise who receive profits in the form of dividend.	It represents the **employees** of the enterprise who are paid remuneration in the form of salaries and some times also a share in profits.
8. Use of the term	It is generally used in **non-business institutions** like government offices, military, social, cultural and religious organisations.	It is generally used in **business enterprises**.

LEVELS OF MANAGEMENT

Meaning

A series of managerial positions from top to bottom is called levels of management. A level of management determines the amount of authority and status enjoyed by any managerial position. The chain of command consisting of a series of managerial positions is also known as 'management hierarchy'.

Classification

The levels of management can be classified into three as follows:

Level of Management	Who are regarded	Main functions
1. **Top level**	(a) Board of directors, (b) Chief executive, and (c) The departmental heads.	1. To establish overall long-term goals 2. To establish the ways of attaining the long-term goals 3. To relate the organisation to the external environment. 4. To laydown overall policies 5. To provide direction and leadership to the organisation as a whole
2. **Middle-level management**	Departmental managers and branch managers like purchase managers, production managers, personnel managers, finance managers, marketing managers etc.	1. To link the top and supervi-sory levels of management 2. To transmit orders, suggestions, policy deci- sions and detailed instructions downwards 3. To carry the problems and suggestions upwards 4. To inspire operating managers towards better performance
3. **Supervisory or Operating management** i.e. those executives whose work has to be largely with personal	First line supervisors like superintendents, section officers, foremen etc.	1. To assign jobs and tasks to subordinates 2. To arrange machinery and tools 3. To assist and advise the subordinates by explaining the work and procedures

oversight and direction of operative employees.		4. To supervise the work of operatives to ensure the work of requisite quantity and of required quality 5. To report the problems faced and suggestions made by workers to the middle-level management

Importance of Classification

The important implication of analysing levels of management is for managerial training through which skills are imparted to meet the specific needs of managers of each level of management.

FUNCTIONS OF MANAGEMENT

Meaning of Functions of Management

The functions of management refer to those activities which are required to be undertaken for the creation of an environment for the achievement of organisational goals.

Functions of Management

Luther Gullick made a list of managerial functions under the word PODSCRBM taking the first letters of the functions like:

P — Planning
O — Organising
D — Directing
S — Staffing

C — Co-ordinating
R — Reporting
B — Budgeting
M — Motivating

The functions may be grouped into the following categories:

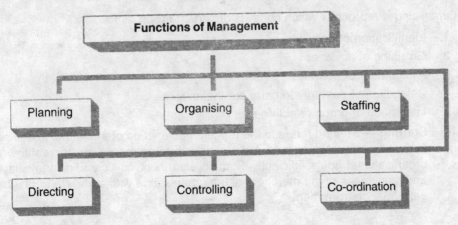

Let us discuss these functions of management one by one.

(a) **Planning** — Planning is the process of **thinking before doing**. It involves determination of goals as well as the activities required to be undertaken to achieve the goals. More specifically, planning consists of deciding in advance —

   (i) **What** is to be done in the future [*i.e.*, determination of future objectives];

   (ii) **How** it is to be done [*i.e.*, determination of means to achieve future objectives];

   (iii) **Where** it is to be done;

   (iv) **When** it is to be done;

   (v) **By whom** it is to be don

Planning is a process which consists of certain **steps** as follows:

1. Forecasting after the appraisal of internal and external environment
2. Establishment of the planning premises
3. Development of alternative courses of action
4. Evaluation of alternative courses of action
5. Making choice from among the alternatives
6. Formulation of medium-range and short-range plans
7. Making arrangements for effective implementation of plans
8. Review of existing plans

(b) **Organising** — As a function of management, the term 'organising' refers to the process of —

   (i) bringing together human and non-human resources (e.g., materials, machines, money), and

   (ii) defining and establishing the authority-responsibility relationships for the achievement of organisational goals.

The outcome of organising process is the creation of 'organisation structure'.

The purpose of organising is to relate organisational people to each other and to work for the achievement of organisational goals.

Organising is a process which consists of certain **steps** as follows:

1. Identification of activities
2. Grouping of activities
3. Assignment of activities
4. Delegation of authority to carry out the activities
5. Integration of group of activities

(c) **Staffing** — Staffing refers to the managerial function of attracting, acquiring, activating, developing and maintaining human resources for achieving organisational goals efficiently. Staffing also involves upgrading the quality and usefulness of the members of the organisation with a view to get higher performance from them.

Just like the other managerial functions, the function of staffing may be viewed as a process consisting of certain well-recognised **activities** as follows:

1. Human resource planning
2. Recruitment
3. Selection
4. Placement and orientation
5. Training
6. Development
7. Performance appraisal
8. Promotion and transfer
9. Remuneration

(d) **Directing** — Directing as a function of management is the process of instructing, guiding, supervising, motivating and leading the subordinates to contribute to the best of their capability for the achievement of organisational objectives.

More specifically, *directing is telling the subordinates what to do and how to do and seeing that they do it to the best of their ability.*

Directing comprises:

(i) **issuing orders and instructions** by a superior to his subordinates;

(ii) **motivating** subordinates to contribute to the best of their capability for the achievement of organisational objectives;

(iii) providing **leadership** to subordinates to influence group activities towards the achievement of certain goals;

(iv) **observing** the subordinates at work to ensure that they are working according to plans and policies of the organisation and helping subordinates to resolve their work problems.

(e) **Controlling** — Control is the process of verifying whether actual performance is in conformity with planned performance and taking corrective action where necessary.

More specifically, ***control involves:***

(i) knowing what work is to be done as to quantity, quality and time available;

(ii) verifying whether work has been or is being carried out in accordance with the plan;

(iii) analysing deviations (*i.e.,* difference between planned performance and actual performance) so as to ascertain the causes thereof;

(iv) adopting remedial measures to correct the deviations; and

(v) suggesting revision of plans, if necessary.

(f) **Co-ordination** — Co-ordination may be defined as *"the orderly arrangement of group efforts to provide unity of action in the realisation of a common* *purpose."* In other words, it refers to the task of integrating the activities of separate units of an organisation to accomplish the organisational goals efficiently.

CO-ORDINATION

Management has to procure and make the best use of resources like men, material, money and machines to succeed in achieving business objectives. The resources are at the disposal of managers for different types of functions and operations which are interrelated. Thus, to attain the objectives of the organisation efficiently, different activities and efforts must be planned, organised and carried out in an orderly manner.

The various activities of a business organisation are grouped and carried out in different departments. Within each department again there is division and sub-division of operations according to the nature of tasks involved. Activities of such divisions, sub-divisions and departments are to be monitored by harmonising individual and group efforts. This can be achieved through co-ordination only.

You must have seen that in an orchestra, its conductor directs activities of the group in such a manner that it produces harmony and melody in music. Similarly, in an enterprise a manager (conductor) must also direct the activities of the group in such a manner that it brings harmonious and united action to ach.eve the common goal.

In every organisation, division and sub-division of activities become necessary to derive the benefits of specialisation and smooth operation. Individuals and members of groups are expected to contribute maximum efforts in the performance of their tasks. But, to ensure that their efforts are not in conflict with each other, individual and group activities are to be harmonised so that there is unity of action. **The process by which a manager brings unity of action in an organisation is co-ordination**. Thus, managers at all levels are required to co-ordinate the efforts of their subordinates.

Definition of Co-ordination

Co-ordination refers to the orderly arrangement of individual and group efforts to ensure unity of action in the realisation of common objectives. It involves synchronisation of different actions or efforts of the various units of an organisation to provide the requisite amount, quality, timing and sequence of efforts so that the planned objectives may be achieved with minimum of conflict.

According to Brech, *"Co-ordination is balancing and keeping together the team by ensuring suitable allocation of tasks to the various members and seeing that the tasks are performed with harmony among the members themselves."*

According to McFarland, *"Co-ordination is the process whereby an executive develops an orderly pattern of group efforts among his subordinates and secures unity of action in the pursuit of common purpose."*

According to Theo Haimann, *"Co-ordination is the orderly synchronising of efforts of the subordinates to provide proper amount, timing and quality of execution* *so that their united efforts lead to the stated objectives, namely, the common purpose of the enterprise ."*

From the above definitions we can infer that co-ordination is a conscious process of assembling and synchronising various kinds of activities with a view to achieve specific objectives.

Nature of Co-ordination

The aforesaid definition highlights the nature of co-ordination as under:

1. **Harmonises group efforts** — It is through co-ordination that the group efforts are synchronised to ensure proper timing and quality of execution so that the organisational objectives are realised.

2. **Ensures unity of action** — Its purpose is to secure unity of action in realisation of common purpose.

3. **Pursuit of common purpose** — It is through co-ordination that the manager persuades individuals and groups to work for a common purpose while achieving their own objectives as well as resolving the conflict, if any, in attaining personal and organisational goals.

4. **Continuous process** — Co-ordination is not a one-time function but a continuous process. It starts with the very first action in the process of establishment of business and runs through until its closure. It is a continuous process for achieving unity of purpose in the organisation.

5. **Pervasive** — Co-ordination is needed at all levels of management *due to the interdependent nature of activities assigned to various departments and units, and to different individuals.* Work of the different departments like purchase, production, and sales should be properly co-ordinated to achieve the common objectives of the organisation. Foreman must ensure that the performance of his subordinates taken together contributes to the daily or weekly output of the workshop in conformity with the planned output. Work assigned to different departments, units and individuals must be co-ordinated by all managers at various levels at a regular function, *without harmony and integration of activities, overlapping and even chaos may be in the organisation.* Therefore, co-ordination is needed at all levels of management.

6. **Every manager's responsibility** — Co-ordination is the most important responsibility of every manager in the organisation as he tries to synchronise the efforts of his subordinates with others.

Importance of Co-ordination

Co-ordination is not a separate function of management, but is the very essence of management. *For performing any function of management efficiently and effectively, co-ordination must be there in one form or the other.* **Koontz and O'Donnel** rightly say, *"Like a thread in garland, co-ordination is part of all management functions. "* Let us see how co-ordination is required in performing every function of management.

1. In **planning,** co-ordination is required:

    (i) between overall plan of the organisation and the departmental plans;

      (ii)   between objectives and available physical and human resources; and

      (iii) among different functional managers.

2.   In **organising,** co-ordination is required:

      (i)   between resources of an enterprise and activities to be performed: and

      (ii)   among authority, responsibility and accountability.

3.   In **staffing**, co-ordination is required:

      (i)   between skills of workers and jobs assigned to them;

      (ii)   between efficiency of workers and compensation;

      (iii) between training and technology of production; and

      (iv) between efficiency and promotion.

4.   In **directing,** co-ordination is required:

      (i)   among orders, instructions, guidelines, suggestions, coaching etc.;

      (ii)   between superior and subordinates;

      (iii) between efficiency and motivation; and

      (iv) between past and present communication.

5.   In **controlling,** co-ordination is required:

      (i)   between standards fixed and actual performance;

      (ii)   between correction of deviation and achievement of objectives; and

      (iii) between planning and controlling.

To conclude, **Mary Parker** rightly say:

"Co-ordination starts from the very first stage of management function, i.e., planning, and goes systematically with all the functions, i.e., organisation, direction, policy implementation and motivation.

Co-ordination versus Co-operation

The terms 'co-ordination' and 'co-operation' cannot be used interchangeably. Co-operation refers to the collective efforts of people who associate voluntarily to achieve specified objectives. Co-operation indicates the willingness of people to help each other, while co-ordination is much more inclusive requiring more than the desire and willingness to co-operate. Co-ordination is an organisational effort while co-operation is individual.

Co-ordination is an orderly arrangement of group efforts to provide unity of action in the pursuit of common objectives. It requires deliberate effort on the part of management. Existence of co-operation among members of the group facilitates co-ordination but it does not mean that co-ordination originates automatically from the voluntary efforts of the group members.

Co-ordination has to be achieved through conscious and deliberate efforts of the manager. For example, when a dozen persons are required to shift a heavy object from its present position to another position, their willingness to co-operate with one another for the common purpose may not be successful unless one of them co-ordinates their efforts. He must give proper direction to all members of the group to apply the right type of effort at the right time and the right place. Co-operation is a necessary but not a sufficient condition of co-ordination. Co-ordination without co-operation and co-operation without co-ordination are detrimental to the organisation. To be effective, an organisation requires both co-operation and co-ordination.

Distinction between Co-ordination and Co-operation

1. Co-operation is the result of voluntary attitudes on the part of people in an organisation while co-ordination is a state of affairs which an executive brings about through deliberate action on his part.

2. Co-operation is necessary for successful co-ordination, while co-ordination is necessary for the success of the organisation as a whole. Co-ordination is a broader concept.

3. Co-operation has no elements like time, quality or direction, whereas co-ordination is the concerted effort of requisite quantity and quality arranged at the proper time.

EXERCISES

SHORT ANSWER TYPE QUESTIONS

1. What is meant by management?
2. Why is management regarded as a process?
3. Why is management regarded as a social process?
4. Why is management regarded as an integrating process?
5. Why is management regarded as a continuous process?
6. Define management as an activity.
7. Define management as a group.
8. Define management as a discipline.
9. Why is management regarded as a discipline?
10. Explain the nature of management.
11. 'Management is an inexact science.' Explain.
12. Why is management regarded as an art? Explain.
13. Can management be regarded as both science and art?
14. Why is management regarded as a profession? Explain.
15. What is meant by 'management hierarchy'?
16. What is meant by levels of management?
17. Who are regarded as the top management in a business organisation?
18. Who are regarded as the middle management in a business organisation?
19. Who are considered to be the operating management in a business organisation?
20. Name any two activities undertaken at the top level management.
21. State any three functions of middle level management.
22. State any three functions of lower level management.

23. State briefly the functions of operating management.
24. Name any two designations given to the first line managers.
25. Name the levels of management engaged in: (a) overseeing the activities of the workers (b) taking key decisions.
26. State any two objectives of management.
27. What is meant by administration?
28. Define 'co-ordination'.
29. Write short notes on the following:
    (a) Management as a process   (b) Management as an activity
    (c) Management as a group   (d) Management as a discipline
    (e) Management as a science   (f) Management as an art
    (g) Management as a profession   (h) Levels of management

LONG ANSWER TYPE QUESTIONS

1. *"Management is an activity concerned with guiding human and physical resources in such a manner that organisational goals are achieved efficiently."* Explain.
2. *"Management is concerned with ideas, things and people."* Comment.
3. *"Management is personnel administration."* Comment.
4. *"Function of management is to manage work and workers."* Comment.
5. *"Management may be understood as a discipline, a group or a process."* Explain the statement.
6. Explain whether management is an art or science.
7. *"Management is a trinity of art, science and profession."* In the light of this statement, explain the nature of management.
8. *"Management is both a science and an art."* In the light of this statement, explain the nature of management.
9. What is meant by levels of management? Briefly explain the various levels of management.
10. Explain the general objectives of management.
11. Explain the importance of management.
12. *"Management is the art of getting things done through other people."* Explain the importance of management in the light of this statement.
13. Distinguish between administration and management.
14. Why is management not considered to be a profession?
15. Explain briefly the objectives of management.
16. Describe briefly the important functions of management.
17. State the meaning and nature of co-ordination.
18. *'Co-ordination is an essence of management.'* Explain.
19. *'Co-ordination is needed at all levels of management.'* Explain the statement with examples.
20. *'Co-ordination is the orderly arrangement of group efforts to provide unity of action in the pursuit of a common purpose.'* In the light of this statement, explain the nature of co-ordination.

Principles of Management

17

MEANING OF MANAGEMENT PRINCIPLES

Management principles are statements of fundamental truth which provide guidelines for managerial decision-making and action. In other words, the principles of management act as guides for the practice of management. These principles are helpful in predicting and understanding the results of managerial actions.

HOW MANAGEMENT PRINCIPLES ARE DERIVED?

The management principles are derived on the basis of the following methods:

1. **Observation Method** — Under this method, a manager observes certain events in actual practice and analyses them to get experience which may be used in future as a guide.

2. **Experimental Method** — Under this method, a researcher with field of management may conduct empirical studies to define the principles and to test their validity. For example, if he wishes to conduct an experiment to confirm the

validity of principle of unity of command that states that every person should receive orders from only one superior, he may take two groups: one under the direct supervision of a single boss and the other under the supervision of two or more superiors. After sometime, he can measure and compare the performance of both and can find out the results.

NATURE OF MANAGEMENT PRINCIPLES

The main characteristics which highlight the nature of management principles are given below:

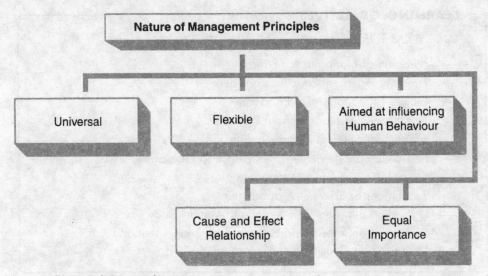

Let us discuss them one by one:

1. **Universal** — Management principles are universal in the sense that these can be applied to all managerial situations irrespective of the size (small or large) and nature (business, government or social organisation). Universality of management principles also implies that managerial skills are transferable and managers can be trained and developed.

2. **Flexible** — Management principles are flexible in the sense that these can be used in different situations with modifications.

3. **Aimed at Influencing Human Behaviour** — Management principles are directed towards regulating human behaviour so that the members of the organisation give their best to the organisation.

4. **Cause and Effect Relationship** — Management principles indicate cause and effect relationship. For instance, the principle of unity of command states that presence of a single boss avoids confusion, here the presence of unity of command is the cause and avoidance of confusion is the effect.

5. **Equal Importance** — All the management principles have equal importance, for example, one cannot say that unity of command is more important than division of labour.

SIGNIFICANCE OF MANAGEMENT PRINCIPLES

The need and importance of management principles arise from the benefits shown below:

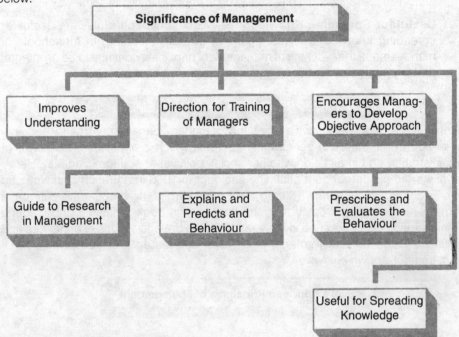

Let us discuss them one by one.

1. **Improves Understanding** — Management principles provide a means of organising knowledge and experience in management. They help in improving the art of management by suggesting how things should be done to get good results in an efficient manner.

2. **Direction for Training of Managers** — The management principles are helpful in identifying the areas of management in which existing and future managers should be trained.

3. **Encourages Managers to Develop Objective Approach** — Knowledge of principles is helpful in encouraging managers to develop an objective and mature approach to planning, problem-solving and decision-making. They help managers in getting away from guess work, trial and error, hit or miss methods of doing things.

4. **Guide to Research in Management** — The network of management principles represents a key area for conducting research studies (*whether pure or applied*) to identify the conditions under which specific management principles would become applicable and effective.

5. **Explains and Predicts the Behaviour** — Descriptive principles not only bring out and clarify the underlying facts and factors of any situation but also help in predicting the likely outcomes of a particular course of action.

6. **Prescribes and Evaluates the Behaviour** — Normative principles attempt to prescribe and evaluate the behaviour of the members of the organisation. These principles prescribe what one should do to improve things in some way.

7. **Useful for Spreading Knowledge** — Management principles are useful for spreading knowledge of management through teaching. In all schools of management, the teaching of management principles continue to be an integral part of management education.

FAYOL'S PRINCIPLES OF MANAGEMENT

Henry Fayol is popularly known as the father of modern management theory because he laid down the theory of general management which is applicable to all kinds of administration and in all fields whether social, political or economic equally. Henry Fayol started his career as a coalmine engineer in 1860 in a French coalmine and was its chief executive from 1898 to 1916 during which he brought the enterprise from the verge of bankruptcy to high success. His book Industrial and General Administration was published in the year 1916. On the basis of his experiences and foresight in the field of management, Fayol suggested fourteen principles of management, shown below:

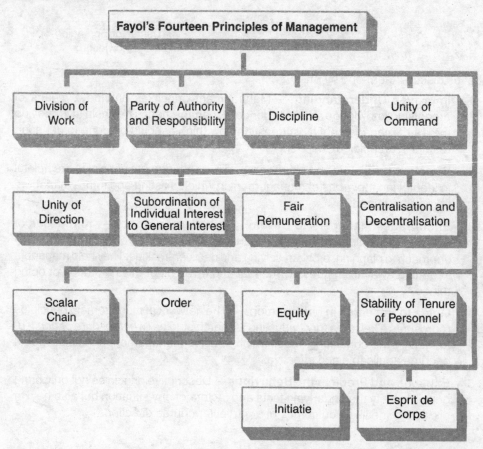

Fayol's Fourteen Principles of Management

- Division of Work
- Parity of Authority and Responsibility
- Discipline
- Unity of Command
- Unity of Direction
- Subordination of Individual Interest to General Interest
- Fair Remuneration
- Centralisation and Decentralisation
- Scalar Chain
- Order
- Equity
- Stability of Tenure of Personnel
- Initiatie
- Esprit de Corps

Let us discuss these principles one by one.

1. **Division of Work** — Division of work implies dividing the work into compact jobs and allocating these compact jobs to different individuals. When an individual does the same job on repetitive basis, he specialises in his task and thus acquires speed and accuracy in the performance. As a result, the efficiency of every individual and of the whole organisation improves. Thus, division of labour facilitates specialisation and improves efficiency. It may be noted that this principle applies to both managerial work and non-managerial work (i.e., technical).

2. **Parity of Authority and Responsibility** — Authority of an individual refers to his official right to take decisions on the tasks assigned to him and to manage people and other resources of organisation for the accomplishment of tasks assigned. Responsibility is the obligation of an individual to complete the tasks assigned to him and to give account of the result achieved in terms of the standard of performance laid down.

    According to the principle of parity of authority and responsibility, there must be parity between authority and responsibility. If a person is given authority without corresponding responsibility, there may be arbitrary and unmindful use of authority. Similarly, if a person is given some responsibility without adequate authority, such person will be ineffective.

3. **Discipline** — Discipline means obedience, proper conduct in relation to other members of organisation and complying with the rules and regulations of the organisation. It is required for the smooth running of the organisation. It must be enforced throughout the organisation. Discipline requires good supervisors at all levels, clarity of rules and regulations and provision of penalties to prevent its violation. Discipline can best be maintained by —

    (a) having good supervision at all levels;

    (b) entering into clear and fair agreements with individuals or with the union; and

    (c) ensuring that penalties are judiciously imposed.

4. **Unity of Command**

    Meaning — According to this principle, a subordinate should receive order from one superior only and should be accountable to that superior from whom he received order. In other words, every employee should have only one boss.

    Necessity — Unity of Command principle is necessary —

    (a) to avoid conflict among superiors regarding how the work should be accomplished;

    (b) to avoid confusion among subordinates regarding whose instructions should be followed;

    (c) to fix responsibility for mistakes;

    (d) to maintain discipline.

Diagram — Unity and multiplicity of command and subordinate relationships have been shown below:

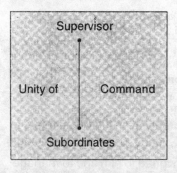
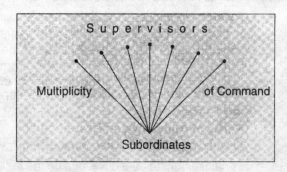

Benefits — Adoption of this principle results in the following benefits:

(a)   Subordinates will get exact orders and instructions.

(b)   Fixing of responsibility will be easier.

(c)   Orders and instructions of every superior will be honoured.

(d)   It avoids conflict among superiors regarding how the work should be accomplished.

(e)   It avoids confusion among subordinates regarding whose instructions should be followed.

5.   **Unity of Direction** — According to this principle, there should be one head and one plan for a group of activities having the same objectives. This principle emphasises the importance of common goals being pursued by all in a group activity under the direction of one head. This principle promotes smooth co-ordination of activities, efforts and resources.

The violation of this principle leads to the following consequences:

(a)   Wastage.

(b)   Over expenditure.

(c)   Useless competition in the same organisation.

6.   **Subordination of Individual Interest to General Interest** — According to this principle, individual interests of members of an organisation must be subordinated to the overall interests of the organisation. It means that the selfish attitude of an individual should be surrendered if it affects the interests of the enterprise. This is essential for the welfare of the organisation and its members.

7.   **Fair Remuneration** — Remuneration and the methods of payment in an organisation should be fair. It should bring about high productivity for the organisation and satisfaction to the personnel.

8.   **Centralisation and Decentralisation** — Centralisation of authority refers to relative concentration of authority for decision-making especially at top managerial level. Decentralisation of authority refers to relative dispersal of authority especially among the lower managerial levels to facilitate operational decision-making. There should be proper combination and balance between centralisation and decentralisation in an organisation based on consideration

of several factors such as experience of the superior, ability of the subordinate, size of the organisation etc. The degrees of centralisation and decentralisation are shown:

Complete
Centralisation
↓

Complete
Decentralisation
↓

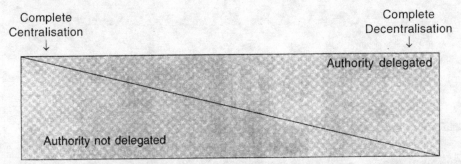

Authority delegated

Authority not delegated

Nowadays the question is not whether decentralisation is necessary rather the question is to what extent the centralisation is necessary. In other words, centralisation and decentralisation are relative concepts depicting proportions. Neither complete centralisation nor complete decentralisation is desirable.

9. **Scalar Chain** — Scalar chain implies the chain of superiors ranging from the top to the lowest ranks in management. Each manager is superior to the manager below him but he is also subordinate to his own superior.

When authority relationships are said to be scalar

Authority relationships are said to be scalar when subordinates report to their immediate superiors and when their superiors report directly as subordinates to their superiors.

What functions does the scalar chain perform?

Scalar chain performs several functions such as:

1. **Determines Line of Authority** — It determines the clear line of authority from top to bottom linking managers at all levels;

2. **Server as a Chain of Command** — It serves as a chain of command because orders or instructions issued at higher levels flow through middle levels before reaching lower levels;

3. **Server as a Chain of Communication** — It serves as a chain of communication because all communications are required to flow through the chain in the hierarchy.

    Gang Plank — The concept of gang plank allows two employees at the same level to communicate directly with each other. But each one of them must inform his superior. The use of the concept of gang plank avoids the delays in communication through scalar chain.

Let us look at the following:

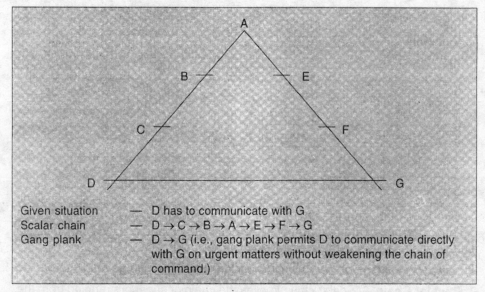

Given situation	— D has to communicate with G
Scalar chain	— D→C→B→A→E→F→G
Gang plank	— D → G (i.e., gang plank permits D to communicate directly with G on urgent matters without weakening the chain of command.)

Why Fayol introduced the concept of 'Gang Plank' — Principle of scalar chain requires that all communications should flow through the chain of hierarchy.

Communication through scalar chain sometimes involves delays as there is a set line of authority through which employees and managers communicate with each other.

Communication is required to flow through the chain at the same level in the hierarchy.

To avoid delays Fayol suggested the concept of 'gang plank' which enables two subordinates or employees at the same level to communicate directly with each other.

10. **Order** — Order refers to a systematic arrangement of materials (i.e., material order) and placement of people (i.e., social order) in the organisation. Material order requires that there should be specific place for each material and each material must be in its allotted place. Social order requires that there should be specific place of work for each employee and each employee must be in his assigned place of work. This principle stresses upon the proper utilization of physical and human resources. For example, production manager may be allotted an office room in the factory, the typist a particular table, the foreman to supervise a workshop.

11. **Equity** — Equity refers to fair treatment to all workers in an organisation. Fair treatment involves kindness and justice on the part of superiors while dealing with their subordinates delay with their subordinates. In other words, it means that similar treatment should be assured to people in similar positions. For example, workers performing similar jobs should be paid the same wage rate. Equity promotes friendly atmosphere between superiors and subordinates and brings loyalty.

12. **Stability of Tenure of Personnel** — Organisations should make efforts to achieve relative stability and continuity of tenure of their personnel. This could be achieved by providing attractive remuneration and honourable treatment to employees. Stability and continuity of personnel promote teamwork, loyalty and economy and minimise employees' turnover. No employee possessing the requisite abilities should be removed within a short time because time is required for an employee to get used to new work and succeed in doing it well.

13. **Initiative** — Initiative means eagerness to initiate action in work related matters without being asked to do so. An organisation should encourage desire and initiative among its managers and employees by extending opportunities and freedom to contribute their best. This principle states that —

   (a) Subordinates should be given an opportunity to take initiative in making and executing the plans.

   (b) Subordinates with initiative should be encouraged within the limits of authority and discipline.

14. **Esprit de Corps** — It refers to team spirit. Managers must take steps to develop a sense of belonging among the members of a work group. This principle emphasises the need for teamwork. It facilitates the development of an atmosphere of mutual trust and understanding among employees and minimises the need to use penalties for default. This principle states that the unity is the strength and the managers should infuse the spirit of teamwork in their subordinates.

SCIENTIFIC MANAGEMENT

Meaning of Scientific Management

Scientific Management refers to application of scientific methods in decision-making for solving management problems rather than depending on rule of thumb or trial and error methods for the purpose. F. W. Taylor is regarded as the father of scientific management which was started in the Midvale Steel Company in USA in the early twentieth century and widely adopted in Western European countries. More specifically, scientific management consists of the following Activities:

Activities covered under Scientific Management

1. observation and analysis of each task;
2. determination of the standard of work;
3. selecting and training men to perform their jobs; and
4. ensuring that work is done in the most efficient manner.

Main Objective of Scientific Management

The main objective of scientific management is to increase the productive efficiency of individual workers at the shop-floor level.

PRINCIPLES OF SCIENTIFIC MANAGEMENT

On the basis of his observations and experiments, Taylor formulated the principles of scientific management which are shown below:

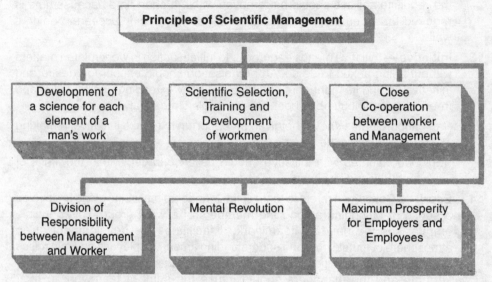

Let us discuss the principles of scientific management one by one.

1. **Development of a Science for each Element of a Man's Work** — This principle suggests the development and use of scientific methods for the following purposes:

   (i) to determine time normally required to perform a job;

   (ii) to determine a fair day's work for the workmen;

   (iii) to determine the best way of doing work;

   (iv) to set work standards (e.g., selecting standard tools and equipment, maintaining standard working conditions).

2. **Scientific Selection, Training and Development of Workmen** — This principle suggests that the skills and experience of the workers must be properly matched with the requirements of the respective jobs which they have to perform. This principle requires that:

   (i) workers should be selected on the basis of tests and interviews;

   (ii) workers so selected should be given training to learn how to perform the specific tasks assigned;

   (iii) workers' capabilities for future managerial tasks should also be developed for maximum efficiency.

3. **Close Cooperation between Workers and Management** — This principle suggests to secure cooperation of workers. It is only through cooperation with workmen that managers can ensure that work is carried out in accordance with plans and standard of performance.

4. **Division of Responsibility between Management and Worker** — This principle suggests separation of planning from doing. In other words, there should be clear cut division of work and responsibility between management and workers as follows:

Work	Responsibility
Planning of work	Responsibility of managers
Execution of planned work	Responsibility of workers

This principle enables the worker to perform at his best and earn accordingly.

5. **Mental Revolution** — This principle requires that there should be a complete change of outlook of workers and management with respect to their mutual relations and work efforts. Mental revolution on the part of workers and management may be stated as follows:

Mental revolution on the part of management	Management should create suitable working conditions and resolve all problems scientifically.
Mental revolution on the part of workers	Workers should perform their works with utmost devotion and should utilise the resources very efficiently.

This principle is necessary to derive the benefits of scientific management through harmony and co-operation rather than individualism and discord. The great revolution that takes place in the mental attitude of the two parties under scientific management is that both sides take their eyes off the division of the surplus as the all-important matter and together turn their attention towards increasing the size of the surplus.

Implications of Mental Revaluation — **According to F. W. Taylor,** mental revolution has three following implications:

(i) Creating the spirit of mutual trust and confidence.

(ii) Generating the scientific attitude towards problems.

(iii) Directing all efforts for increasing the production.

6. **Maximum Prosperity for Employers and Employees** — This principle requires that the aim of management should be to secure maximum prosperity for the employers along with maximum welfare of employees.

TECHNIQUES OF SCIENTIFIC MANAGEMENT

The techniques of scientific management refer to the mechanism which facilitates application of the principle of management. These techniques are shown below:

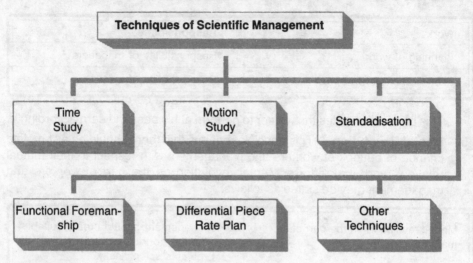

1. **Time Study**

   Meaning — Time study is a technique which is used to measure the time that may be taken by a workman of reasonable skills and ability to perform various elements of the tasks in a job.

   Purpose — The purpose of time study is to determine —

   (i)   time normally required to perform a certain job, and

   (ii) a fair day's work for the workman.

   Tools — Time study is conducted with the help of stopwatch.

2. **Motion Study**

   Meaning — Motion study is a technique which involves close observation of the movements of body and limbs required to perform a job.

   Purpose — The purpose of motion study is —

   (i)   to eliminate wasteful motions, and

   (ii) to determine the best way of doing a job.

   Tools — Time study is conducted with the help of a movie camera connected with micro-chronometer (i.e., a kind of clock).

DISTINCTION BETWEEN TIME STUDY AND MOTION STUDY

Time study and motion study can be distinguished as under:

Basis of Distinction	Time Study	Motion Study
1. **Meaning**	It is a technique which is used to measure the time that may be taken by a workman of reasonable skills and ability to perform various elements of the tasks in a job.	It is a technique which involves close observation of the movements of the body and limbs required to perform a job.
2. **Purpose**	Its purpose is to determine time normally required to perform a certain job and a fair day's work for the workman.	Its purpose is to detect and eliminate wasteful motions and determine the best way of doing a job.
3. **Tools of study**	It is conducted with the help of stopwatch.	It is conducted with the help of a movie camera connected with micro-chronometer (i.e., a kind of clock).

3. **Standardisation**

   Meaning — Standardisation is a technique which involves the methods of —

   (i) selecting standard tools and equipments for use by workers, and

   (ii) maintaining standard working conditions at the workplace.

   Purpose — The purpose of standardisation is to attain the efficient performance of jobs.

4. **Functional Foremanship**

   Meaning — Functional foremanship is a technique which involves supervision of a worker by several specialist foremen. This concept is the opposite of the principle of unity of command propounded by Herry Fayol.

   Example — Under functional foremanship, matters relating to speed of work and repairs are supervised by speed boss and repair boss respectively.

   Purpose — The purpose of functional foremanship is to improve the quality of supervision of workers by employing specialist foremen. Taylor believed that a single foreman may not be competent to supervise all functional matters.

   Usefulness — Functional foremanship is useful for the production department.

Diagram — Functional foremanship is shown below:

Functional Foremanship

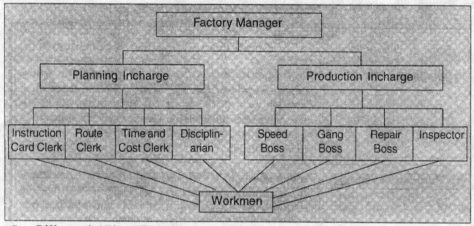

5. Differential Piece Rate Plan

Meaning — Differential piece rate plan is a method of wage payment in which efficient and inefficient workers are paid at different rates viz., higher rate per piece for a worker who produces equal to or more than a certain number of pieces and lower rate per piece for a worker who produces less than a certain number of pieces.

Purpose — The purpose of differential piece rate plan is to distinguish between an efficient worker and an inefficient worker by linking rewards with performance. This plan motivates workers to produce more and earn more.

6. Other Techniques

Other techniques include use of graphs, charts, manuals, slide rules, instruction cards for planning and standardising the tasks.

Taylor's Techniques of Management whether universally applicable?

Taylor's techniques of management are most specific and, therefore are not universally applicable. Following techniques may not be universally applicable.

1. **Differential Piece Rate Plan** — Taylor's different piece rate plan is not applied universally. The purpose of differential piece rate plan is to motivate the workers for achieving higher standards of efficiency. This purpose may be achieved by various other methods of incentive wage payment.

2. **Functional Foremanship** — Since functional foremanship lacks unity of command, it may not be applied by many organisations.

3. **Standardisation** — Most of the employers do not set the standard task before wage fixation.

DISTINCTION BETWEEN TAYLOR'S SCIENTIFIC MANAGEMENT AND HENRY FAYOL'S PRINCIPLES OF MANAGEMENT

Taylor's scientific management and Henry Fayol's general principles of management can be distinguished as under:

Basis of Distinction	Taylor's Scientific Management	Henry Fayol's Principles of Management
1. **Beginning**	Taylor began from the lowest workers and moved upwards.	Fayol began from top management and proceeded downwards.
2. **Level of management emphasised**	Operating level	Top level
3. **Subject matter emphasised**	Efficiency of workers and managers in actual production	Functions of management as a whole and principles involved therein
4. **Purpose**	To increase the productivity of workers and eliminate all types of wastes	To develop general theory of administration
5. **Outcome**	Taylor developed certain principles (like development of a science for each element of a man's work, scientific selection, training and development) and certain techniques to facilitate the applications of principles of scientific management (such as time study, motion study, standardisation, functional foremanship, differential piece rate plan).	Fayol developed 14 principles of management (such as division of labour, unity of command, unity of direction, scalar chain and esprit de corps).
6. **Rigidity**	Taylor's approach was relatively rigid.	Fayol's principles were flexible in nature.

Taylor's Principles and Fayol's Principles whether Mutually Complementary?

Yes. Although, Taylor and Fayol belonged to different schools of management thought, their approaches are mutually complementary. It is clear from the following:

1. Taylor's principles and techniques were suggested with bottom upward approach whereas Fayol's principles are based on top downward approach.
2. Taylor's principles and techniques are relevant mainly with respect to production activities whereas Fayol's principles have wider relevance in all functional areas.

3. Taylor's techniques are more specific whereas Fayol's principles are more general in nature having input of flexibility.

4. Taylor's principles and techniques are focussed on worker's efficiency while Fayol's principles are focussed on managerial efficiency.

5. Taylor's principles of functionalisation provides for multiple accountability of workmen. Fayol's principle of unity of command provides for single accountability.

_____ Exercises _____

SHORT ANSWER TYPE QUESTIONS

1. What is meant by management principles?
2. How are the management principles derived?
3. State any two characteristics of the principles of management.
4. What is meant by 'universality of management principles'?
5. Enumerate Fayol's principles of management.
6. Explain the principle of division of work.
7. What is meant by 'parity of authority and responsibility'?
8. What is meant by 'principle of discipline'?
9. Explain the meaning and necessity of unity of command principle.
10. "One head one plan." Which principle is based on this idea? What is meant by this principle?
11. Explain the meaning and necessity of unity of direction principle.
12. Which principle of management is violated if a subordinate is asked to receive orders from two superiors? Name any adverse effect that may take place due to this violation.
13. What is meant by subordination of individual interest to general interest?
14. Define scalar chain.
15. What functions does the scalar chain perform?
16. Explain the concept of gang plank with the help of a diagram.
17. Why did Fayol suggest the idea of 'gang plank'? What light does this idea throw on the nature of Fayol's principles?
18. Explain the principle of 'order'.
19. Explain the principle of 'equity'.
20. How can Fayol's principle of equity and order be applied in a work?
21. What is meant by 'stability of tenure of personnel'?
22. Explain the principle of 'initiative'.
23. Explain the principle of 'esprit de corps'.
24. What is meant by 'scientific management'?

25. What is the main objective of 'scientific management'?
26. Explain the 'development and use of scientific methods' principle of scientific management.
27. What is meant by 'mental revolution' in scientific management?
28. Enumerate the principles of scientific management.
29. Enumerate the techniques of scientific management.
30. Explain the meaning, purpose and tools of time study.
31. Explain the meaning, purpose and tools of motion study.
32. How do the techniques of time study and motion study help in improving workers' efficiency?
33. Explain the meaning and purpose of 'standardisation'.
34. Explain the concept of 'functional foremanship' with the help of a diagram. Is it different from function of management?
35. What is meant by 'differential piece rate plan'?
36. Distinguish between the following:
    (a) Unity of command and unity of direction.
    (b) Unity of command and functional foremanship.
    (c) Time study and motion study.
    (d) Taylor's scientific management and Henry Fayol's principles of management.

LONG ANSWER TYPE QUESTIONS

1. Explain the nature of principles of management.
2. Explain briefly the characteristics of the principles of management.
3. Explain the need and importance of principles of management.
4. Explain the principles of scientific management.
5. Explain briefly the techniques of scientific management.
6. Describe Taylor's principle of 'replacing rule of thumb with science'.
7. Explain the purposes of time study and motion study.
8. What is the principle of 'scalar chain'? Explain briefly the utility of 'gang plank' with the help of a diagram.

18 Planning

MEANING OF PLANNING

Planning is the process of thinking before doing. It involves determination of goals as well as the activities required to be undertaken to achieve the goals. More specifically, planning consists of deciding in advance —

1. **What** is to be done in the future [i.e., determination of future objectives];
2. **How** it is to be done [i.e., determination of means to achieve future objectives];
3. **Where** it is to be done;
4. **When** it is to be done; and
5. **By whom** it is to be done.

In other words, the gap between current status and future image is filled up by planning. It is shown below:

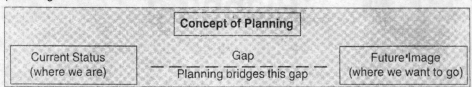

Concept of Planning		
Current Status (where we are)	Gap — — — — — — — — — Planning bridges this gap	Future Image (where we want to go)

Example: Mr X has just completed his graduation. His father is in service. He wants to start his own business. His current status is having no business and his future image is to do business. In order to achieve this goal, he has to take various decisions such as —

1. whether to do manufacturing or trading;
2. if he decides to do manufacturing, whether to manufacture jewellery, chemicals, garments, etc;
3. if he decides to manufacture jewellery, whether to manufacture real jewellery or artificial jewellery;
4. if he decides to manufacture real jewellery, whether to manufacture diamond jewellery, gold jewellery or silver jewellery;
5. if he decides to manufacture gold jewellery, whether to manufacture KDM jewellery (i.e., jewellery in which joints are made of gold) or non-KDM jewellery;
6. if he decides to manufacture KDM jewellery, whether to get it manufactured in house or on contract basis, and whether to sell it in inland market or export market, and so on.

FEATURES OF PLANNING

The various features of planning, which reflect the nature of planning, are shown below:

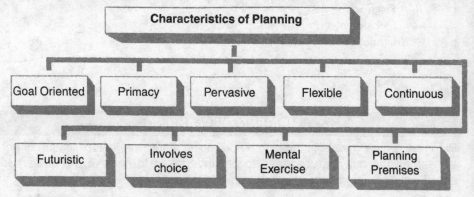

Characteristics of Planning

Goal Oriented — Primacy — Pervasive — Flexible — Continuous

Futuristic — Involves choice — Mental Exercise — Planning Premises

Let us discuss the features of planning one by one:

1. **Goal Oriented** — Planning is purposeful in the sense that its purpose is always to determine the goals to be achieved and the activities required to be undertaken to achieve those goals. Planning is the exercise of creative thinking in the solution of various problems. The purpose of every plan and all derivative plans is to facilitate the accomplishment of organizational objectives.

2. **Primacy** — Primacy of planning means that planning precedes all other managerial functions. It is a primary function in the sense that it provides the basis for the other functions of organising, staffing, directing and controlling. It is correctly said that planning is the basic function and the structure of all other functions depends on it.

3. **Pervasive** — Planning is a pervasive function in the sense that it is required—

   (i)   at all levels of management (top, middle or lower),

   (ii) in all departments of an organisation (purchase, production, personnel, finance or research development),

   (iii) in all types of organisations (small, large, economic, social, religious or political).

However, the nature and scope of planning differs from level to level. To understand this, let us look at the following table:

Level of Management	Relevant Type of Planning
1. **Top level of management**	Top management is basically concerned with the following types of planning- (a) Strategic planning (which refers to the process of formulating strategies in the light of environmental changes and internal resources) (b) Long-range planning (which refers to the process of formulating the long-range objectives and of determining the ways and means of achieving such objectives)
2. **Middle and lower levels of management**	Middle and lower levels of management are basically concerned with the following types of planning — (a) Tactical planning (which refers to the process of formulating more specific functional sub-plans to implement the strategic plan) (b) Short-range planning (which refers to the process of formulating short-range objectives and determining the ways and means of achieving such objectives). It is carried out within the framework of long-range planning and for achieving long-range objectives.

Thus, planning is the function to be performed by all managers at all levels in all types of organisations.

4. **Flexible** — Planning is a dynamic process in the sense that it prepares the organisation to adjust its activities in response to changes taking place in the external environment by revising the existing plans of the organisation. Plans are drawn on the basis of forecast. Since the future is uncertain, planning must cope with changes in future conditions.

5. **Continuous** — Planning is a continuous activity in the sense that the planning cycle continues to operate so long as there is an organisation. Continuity of planning is related with planning cycle. Planning cycle has been demonstrated below:

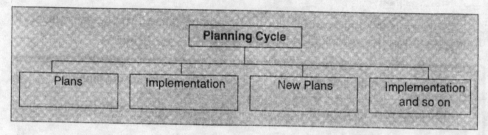

Planning is a dynamic function and plans need continuous review.

6. **Futuristic** — Planning is futuristic in the sense that it essentially involves looking ahead into the future and making provision to tackle future events and situations. Planning is intended to cope with future uncertainties and unknowns. Of course, while planning for the future, managers consider the relevant events and situations of the past and present within and outside the organisation.

7. **Involves Choice** — Planning involves problem solving and decision-making. It is demonstrated below:

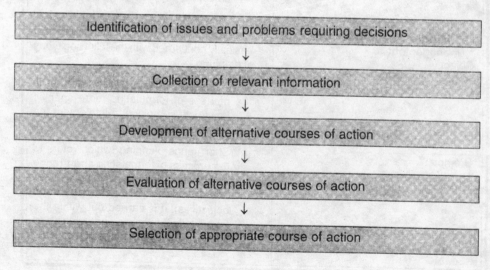

Thus, planning is a choosing process as it essentially involves choice from among various alternative courses of action.

8. **Mental Exercise** — Planning is an intellectual process in the sense that it requires certain conceptual and analytical skills for the following purposes:

   (i) to look ahead into the future;

   (ii) to anticipate opportunities and threats in the environment;

   (iii) to develop alternative courses of action;

   (iv) to evaluate alternative courses of action;

   (v) to choose the appropriate course of action.

9. **Planning Premises** — Planning is based on planning premises. Planning premises refer to certain assumptions and estimates about the future behaviour of events and situations in the environment which are likely to have effect on achievement of goals. Some important planning premises include market demand for goods, cost of raw-materials, state of technology, intensity of competition, government policies etc. Planning premises are derived through the process of forecasting. Planning premises are required to have a sense of security and certainty in the midst of grave uncertainties and complexities of the environment. There can be no planning without planning premises are determined.

IMPORTANCE OF PLANNING

The importance of planning arises from the following benefits shown below:.

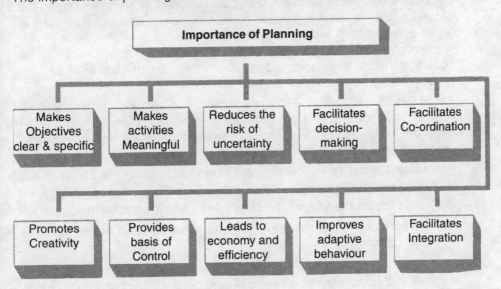

Let us discuss these benefits one by one.

1. **Makes Objectives Clear and Specific** — Planning provides a clear sense of direction to the activities of the organisation and to the job behaviour of managers and others.

The planning provides such direction —

(i) by making the objectives clear and specific; and

(ii) by formulating the policies and programmes for achieving those objectives.

2. **Makes Activities Meaningful** — Planning makes the activities meaningful in the sense that it enables the manager and others to know how their activities relate to organisational goals and encourages them to put their efforts to achieve them.

3. **Reduces the Risk of Uncertainty** — Planning reduces the risk of uncertainty by anticipating future events and making provision to tackle them. Observe the following example.

Present status of the day — cloudy

How does planning reduce the risk of uncertainty —

(i) It anticipates uncertain future event i.e., rain.

(ii) It anticipates the risk of future event i.e., risk of getting wet.

(iii) It makes provision to reduce the risk of uncertainty by providing for an umbrella.

Thus, stepping out of home on a cloudy day with an umbrella in hand is the way to cover the risk of getting wet against the anticipated but uncertain future rain which may or may not be there. Thus, planning minimises the effect of uncertainities of the future.

4. **Facilitates decision-making** — Planning facilitates decision-making in the sense that on the basis of planned objectives various alternative courses of action are developed and then evaluated on the basis of merits, demerits and consequences of each alternative course of action and, finally, an appropriate choice is made from among the alternatives on the basis of certain predetermined selection criteria.

5. **Facilitates Co-ordination** — Planning facilitates co-ordination of departmental operations by establishing common goals. By drawing plans of production department, on the basis of plans of sales department, the activities of production and sales departments can be co-ordinated.

6. **Promotes Creativity** — Planning promotes creativity in the sense that it stimulates management —

(i) to anticipate the future crises and threats and to ward them off;

(ii) to perceive future opportunities and to seize them ahead of other competitors;

(iii) to gain a competitive lead over others.

As a result of creative thinking, new ideas are developed, which lead to growth and prosperity of the business.

7. **Provides Basis of Control** — Planning provides the basis of control in the sense that it provides the standards against which actual performance is compared. For example, sales targets become the standards against which

actual sale is measured. There can be no control without planning because actual performance cannot be compared in the absence of any standards.

8. **Leads to Economy and Efficiency** — Planning helps managers to allocate the organisation's limited resources in the most efficient manner to achieve the organisational goals by specifying what is to be done, how it is to be done and when it is to be done.

   Planning prompts managers to close gaps, to plug loopholes, to reduce wastage and leakage of human efforts and skill and non-human resources so as to bring about an overall improvement in the utilization of available resources.

9. **Improves Adaptive Behaviour** — Planning tends to improve the ability of the organisation to adapt effectively and adjust its activities in response to changes in the external environment.

10. **Facilitates Integration** — Planning brings about effective integration of the diverse decisions and activities of the managers not only at a point of time but also over a period of time. Planning enables orderly functioning in the sense that it involves logical thinking and decision-making as to what is to be done, how it is to be done, when it is to be done and by whom it is to be done. It projects a course of action for future through consistent and co-ordinated actions.

ORGANISATIONAL PLANS

Meaning of Plan

The term **'plan'** may be defined as a course of action determined in advance by the management. A plan has a time frame, whether it is explicit or implied. It is a commitment to action and commitment of resources. It is also a package of decisions on intended efforts to achieve some results. It is a relatively static picture or blue print of action which is partly a means of mechanism of planning and partly an end product of the planning process. Plans may be single use plans and standing plans.

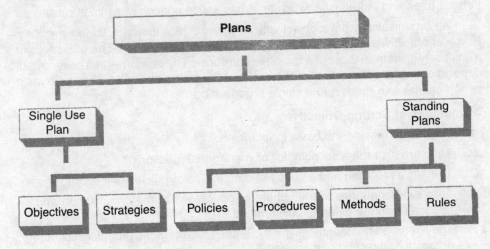

SINGLE USE PLAN

A single use plan is one which is specific to a particular situation of a non-repetitive nature. It may not have use for different situations. It becomes obsolete once its purpose is over. Examples of single use plans are objectives, strategies, projects, programmes, schedules, budgets and so on. Let us say a business firm sets a target to achieve 15% increase in its sales volume for the year 20X1-20X2. Once this objective is achieved this plan ceases to exist.

However, some objectives, like the objective of continuous updating of modern technology, continue to remain relevant. Such objectives may perhaps be regarded as policies. The other examples of single use plans, such as strategies, projects, budgets etc. are 'tailor made' to specific needs of the organisation. For example each project is unique in respect of its environment, resource requirements, completion time and so on.

OBJECTIVES

Mening of Objectives

The term 'objectives' may be defined as a **planned target of performance or the desired end result of an activity which one attempts to realise**. It provides meaning and purpose to the organisation. It has definite scope and direction. It is a commitment to a course of action. It is to be followed by determining the ways and means of achievement. Often, a time frame is determined for its achievement. In other words, objectives may be of a time bound nature. Objectives are variously termed as purposes, goals, missions aims, ends and so on. These terms are often used interchangeably. However, it is possible to distinguish among them. Thus, purpose is the basic reason for the existence of an entity, whether it is a human being or a human organisation. The purpose of an educational institution is to systematically spread knowledge. Goal is viewed as a milestone along the path towards the objective. It is a part of an objective. Mission is the specific and well-defined roles and activities in which an organisation concentrates its efforts.

All organisations have objectives, whether or not they are stated explicitly. However objectives may differ from organisation to organisation. The objectives of a university differ from those of a business enterprise. The objectives of a government department differ from those of a hospital. Objectives may also change over a period of time with respect to a single organisation.

Advantages of Setting Objectives

1. Objectives provide the basis for planning.
2. They are also the focal point for all managerial functions.
3. They give meaning and a sense of direction to organisational efforts.
4. They set boundaries in the sphere of operations of the organisation and its relations with the external environment.
5. They serve as the foundation for the entire management, process of planning, organising, direction and control .

6. They provide the framework for formulation of strategies, policies, programmes, procedures and so on.

7. Objectives serve as criteria and constraints for managerial decision making on acquisition and utilisation of resources.

8. They are the rallying points for the motivation of members of the organisation.

9. They provide a foundation for the standards of organisational performance and the evaluation of performance.

Single vs. multiple objectives

An organisation may have a single objective or more than one objective. It is often stated that the only objective of a business firm is to maximise its profits and that all its activitive focus on this single objective. This may or may not be true. In general, an organisation has more than one objective. For example, a business enterprise not only aims at profit making but is also concerned with healthy growth of its activities, customer service, employee welfare, efficient operations and upgradation of its technology. Organisations establish objectives in all key areas of their activities. For example, a large business enterprise needs to formulate its objectives with respect of its various functions like manufacturing, purchasing, finance, marketing personnel and so on. However, it is necessary that the multiple objectives of the organization are related to each other in some way.

Classification of objectives

With respect to a single organisation, we may think of its objectives from several perspectives which provide a basis for their classification along the following lines:

1. Broad organisation-wide objectives such as services, rapid growth, profitable operations, public image and so on, and sub-corporate objectives applicable to its various departments, divisions and functions.

2. Long-range objectives and short range objectives.

3. Primary objectives and secondary objectives. For example, survival and stability are primary objectives while social responsibility is a secondary objective.

4. Economic, commercial objectives and non-economic social objectives. Profit is an economic commercial objective while concern for environmental safety is a social objective.

5. Quantifiable and Qualitative objectives. Achieving a market share of 40% is a quantifiable objective while gaining reputation as a clean and honest enterprise is a qualitative objective.

Nature and importance of objectives

Organisations differ not only in their objectives but also in the priorities which they accord to them. One enterprise may give priority to stability while the second enterprise may emphasise rapid growth of its business. In some situations conflict among two or more objectives is possible. For example, the objective of bringing down the cost of doing business clashes with the objectives of satisfying the needs and demands of employees. Organisations have to be sensitive to such conflicts and devise ways and means of resolving them to the extent possible. The basic major objectives of an organisation are generally set by its top management, after taking into careful consideration of the purpose and the function of the organisation. In setting objectives, the values of top management and the availability of its resources also play a significant role. Basic or major objectives have to be operationalised into subsidiary and derivative objectives at middle and lower organisational levels. The latter are set through processes of formal or informal consultation and discussion with middle and lower level managers in the organisation.

With the above discussion the importance of objectives may be listed as below.

1. Objectives provide direction to the individual efforts and activities of an organisation.

2. They provide the basis for determining policies, procedures, strategies, programmes, budgets and other plans.

3. They serve as a means for achieving personal goals.

4. They help in effective delegation of authority.

5. They serve as standard for the evaluation of actual performance.

6. They help in coordinating the efforts of the people.

STRATEGIES

Meaning of Strategies or Strategic Plans

Anthony defines strategies as resulting from *"the process of deciding on objectives of the organisation, on changes in these objectives, on the resources used to attain these objectives, and on the policies that are to govern the acquisition, use and disposition of these resources."*

Chandler defines a strategy as *"the determination of the basic long-term goals and objectives of an enterprise, and the adoption of courses of action and the allocation of resources necessary to carry out these goals."*

Strategic plans or strategies are derived from the process of strategic planning. The term **'strategy'** may be defined as a unified, integrated and comprehensive plan of action to achieve an objective or set of objectives. It is a plan prepared for meeting the challenge posed by the environmental forces. It is concerned with the ways and means of coping and gaining command over the complex external problems, threats and opportunities by mobilising internal organisational efforts, resources and strengths.

It addresses the **'how' aspects** of achieving an objective. As a student one of your objectives is to pass the examination. In order to achieve this, you may evolve a strategy of continuous hardwork along with discussion of relevant issues with your friends and teachers. Similarly, an objective of a business enterprise may be to achieve a sales volume of Rs. 50 crores over the next two years from the present level of Rs 25 crores. The enterprise may evolve a composite strategy of product improvement, introduction of one or two new products, aggressive advertising, expansion of marketing channels and so on. These are the ways and means of achieving the objective. Strategy is thus closely related to objective. It should be consistent with the objective. It is to be 'tailormade' to achieve the objective. It is to be formulated with reference to relevant internal and external factors.

Features — The main features of strategies are as follows:

1. **Generally Long range** — It is generally long range in nature, though it is valid for short range situations also and has short range implications.

2. **Action oriented** — It is action oriented and is more specific than objectives.

3. **Integrated** — It is multipronged and integrated.

4. **Dynamic** — It is flexible and dynamic.

5. **To cope with challenges** — It is generally meant to cope with a competitive and complex setting.

6. **Translates goals & objectives into realities** — It flows out of the goals and objectives of the enterprise and is meant to translate them into realities.

7. **Concerned with External Forces** — It is concerned with perceiving opportunities and threats and siezing initiatives to cope with them. It is also concerned with deployment of limited organisational resources in the best possible manner.

8. **Formulation at Top Level** — It is formulated at the top management level, though middle and lower level managers are associated in their formulation and in designing sub-strategies.

9. It provides unified criteria for managers in their function of decision making.

10. It gives importance to the combination, sequence, timing, direction and depth of various moves and action initiatives taken by managers to handle environmental uncertainities and complexities.

Need for Strategies

Strageties are needed —

1. To guide the future direction of managerial moves and decisions for handling major specific, unique, and novel problems.

2. To spell out priorities of the enterprise in specific terms, indicate the combination of moves and countermoves to be devised by the enterprise to cope with external situations.

3. To identify the areas over which the enterprise has to concentrate and the points from which to launch assault with a view to gain command. For example, when a rival enterprise operating in a competitive environment reduces its price to secure higher sales, the options available to the other enterprises in the industry are to match the price cut, to keep the price intact and improve quality and service, to make bargain offers in some other form, to launch an aggressive advertising compaign or to design a new product for offering at the reduced price and so on.

In business and other organisations, strategies are needed for managing the achievement of objectives especially in the context of growing competition and other complexities. Corporate and business strategies are necessary for survival, growth, diversification, market dominance, competitive standing, technological dynamism etc. so as to accomplish relevant objectives. There are also occasions for strategies for management development and succession, acquisition of scarce raw materials, and other resources, negotiations with labour unions, changing the structure of the organisation and so on.

Steps involved in the Formulation of a Strategy

Following steps are involved in the formulation of a strategy:

Step 1 → Evaluating the current status of the enterprise—its range of activities, its physical, financial, and man power resources, its technology, information control etc.

Step 2 → Spelling out Business Mission and Purpose in terms of a set of goals and objectives such as growth, profitability, market share, technology, human resources development, social obligations.

Step 3 → Appraising of External Environment — Opportunities and threats which the enterprise encounters therein and the implications of such opportunities and threats. Setting up systems for monitoring, forecasting and evaluating the state of its external environment on a continuous basis.

Step 4 → Identifying strategic decision Issues and problems after relating the insights drawn from external environment appraisal to the profile of internal strengths and weaknesses.

Step 5 → Development of Alternative Strategies to bridge strategic gap.

Step 6 → Evaluation of alternative strategies against some predetermined but flexible criteria.

Step 7 → Making choice from among alternative strategies through a process of progressive elimination

Components of Strategies

A strategy consists of at least three factors: 1. a course of action, 2. a commitment of resources, and 3. a detailed blue print for consistent combination of moves, initiatives, responses with an eye on their timing. It is a master plan of moving the organisation towards its objectives through the complex and volatile environment. It attempts to relate the organisations capabilities with external opportunities. A strategic plan must accurately state objectives, define the policies which are to be pursued, underline the assumptions regarding the internal and external forces, and outline the courses of action and the means of mobilising resources. It must also specify the possible alternative courses open if the expected conditions change. So development of contingency plans for handling a range of situational changes is also a plan of strategic action plan.

Classification of Strategies

Strategies may also be classified on the following basis.

1.	**On the basis of scope**	Master or grand strategies, programme strategies and substrategies.
2.	**On the basis of organisational level**	Corporate headquarter strategies and divisional strategies.
3.	**On the basis of purpose**	Growth strategy, survival strategy, market development strategy, acquisition strategy and so on.
4.	**On the basis of function**	Marketing strategy, manufacturing strategy, financial strategy, and so on.

Importance of Strategy

The importance of strategies arises due to the following benefits arising from them.

1. Strategies provide basic and integrated frame of reference to managers to take advantage of external opportunities, to cope with challenges and threats, and to deploy organisational resources and efforts in an intelligent manner.
2. They help management in relating the present state of the organisation with its desired future state and tackle them together.
3. Strategic decisions and actions replace impulsive and hasty ones.
4. They offer a technique and discipline to manage and cope with changes in the internal and external environment.
5. They increase the prospect of efficient and effective resource mobilisation and utilisation.
6. They provide a framework for making integrated decisions by managers at the top management and lower levels.
7. Strategies provide directions for the achievement of organizational goals
8. They help the organization in meeting the demands of a difficult situation.
9. They give meaning to other plans.
10. They help in relating an organization to its external environment.

How to Evaluate Strategy

Seymour Tiles suggested the following six criteria for evaluating the appropriateness of a business strategies:

1. **Internal consistency** with other strategies and also its goals, policies and plans.
2. **Consistency with environment** so as to enhance the confidence and capability of the enterprise to manage and adapt with or gain command over the environmental forces.

3. **Appropriateness in the light of available resources** to ensure that the enterprise's resources are not over-stretched or over-strained on one hand and to utilize the existing /commandable resources in the best possible manner on the other.

4. **Acceptable Degree of Risk** to ensure the risk inherent in a strategy within the bearable capability of the enterprise and proper match between risk and return financial and otherwise.

5. **Appropriate Time Horizon of Strategy** to ensure some flexibility and to avoid the problem of forecasting.

6. **Workability** to ensure feasibility of the strategy to produce desired results withiin the constraints and parameters known to management.

STANDING PLANS

Meaning of Standing Plans

Standing Plans are those which are of a relatively long standing by nature. They are meant to serve as standing guidelines, criteria and constraints on managerial decision making an action. A standing plan can be repeatedly used over a period of time for tackling a range of frequently recurring and related problems and issues. Policies, procedures, rules and methods are generally categorised as standing plans. For example, an enterprise's policy of selling its products and services only on cash terms provides a standing guideline and constraint to managers in concluding sales deals with customers. A procedure on purchase of materials and components will continue to be useful over a period of time for a range of actions on purchases of such items. Thus. Standing plans are meant for ready guidance, steady observance and repeated reference for managers and others for their decision making and action behaviour.

Importance of Standing Plans

1. Standing plans are designed to guide managerial decisions and actions on a range of recurring problems and issues.

2. They are meant to be continuously useful and to cover a variety of repetitive situations.

3. They represent a progressive translation of organisational managerial intents into actionable packages.

4. They facilitate the task of processing problems and activities in a programmed manner at managerial and other levels.

5. They are means or methods of co-ordination to the extent that they are meant to ensure unity, consistency, continuity and orderliness in organisational decisions and activities at a point of time and over a period of time among the various organisational sub-systems.

6. They facilitate delegation of authority and tasks to the successively lower managerial levels without loss of control at progressively higher managerial levels.

7. They help in economising the time and efforts of managers and others to the extent that these people do not have to get themselves into confusion on what is to be done whenever they come across a situation for decision and action.

8. They are thus labour saving devices.

9. Standing plans also insulate the organisational decisions and actions from the personal biases and whims of managers and others.

10. The performance of managers and others can be evaluated on the basis of how effectively they are able to understand, apply and observe the spirit of standing plans, especially organisational policies.

POLICIES

Meaning of Policies

Policies are general statements or understandings which guide or channel thinking and action in decision making. They are concerned with the administrative action. They serve as a principle for conduct. They are routes to the realisation of objectives. According to **Harold Koontz** *"Policy is a means of encouraging discretion and initiative but within units."* They are predetermined decision rules applicable for a range of managerial decisions and action. Moreover, policies are aids to the managers on how objectives are to be achieved.

Managers are required to make decisions and handle action situations on a wide range of matters. For this purpose, a policy framework is needed so that the functioning of manager takes place in a coordinated and consistent manner. Policies lay down the broad scope and limits within which managers are allowed to commit the organisation to specific decisions and actions. However, policies *neither* offer readymade decisions or solutions *nor* specify how exactly managers should make decisions and handle events. They only indicate to managers the broad considerations to be kept in mind while making decisions. They also set constraints and outer-boundaries for managerial discretion and judgment in decision-making. To be sure, policies leave sufficient discretion and freedom to managers within the set boundaries and constraints, so that managers will be in a position to handle decision situations in a pragmatic manner.

For example, it is the policy of the firm to promptly attend to customer complaints by replacing the defective product, if it is within 3 months from the date of sale.

In short policies tend to predecide issues and avoid repeated analysis and give a unified structure to the organisation. Major policies covering the entire organisation are formulated by the top managenent. They are often translated into derivative policies at the level of middle and subordinate managers.

Examples of Policies

1. Product policy regarding the products to be manufactured,
2. Pricing Policy regarding prices to be charged,
3. Marketing Policy regarding the markets to be served,

4. Purchasing Policy
5. Quality Control Policy,
6. Inventory Management Policy,
7. Depreciation Policy,
8. Sales Promotion Policy
9. Distribution Policy,
10. Unemployment and service matters of employees and workers,
11. Production Technology Policy.
12. Debtors Management Policy
13. Working Capital Management Policy
14. Dividend Policy
15. Personnel Management Policy

Form of Policies

Policies may be in written form or may take the form of implied, unwritten practices, precedents, principles, and conventions. It is generally believed that written policies tend to minimise the scope for confusion and misinterpetation and tend to promote unified thinking for decision-making and action purposes. However, there is a danger that written policies may become useless and theoretical postulates may be divorced from organisational realities. They may be ignored by managers in their day-to-day work behaviour.

Distinction between Plans and Policies

The term **'plan'** is a more comprehensive concept covering not only policy but also several other predetermined courses of action. In this sense plans and policies are different concepts but they are not distinctly different. Well-formulated policies are a key to the success of any plan. The implementation of any plan requires policy guidelines. Organisations plans are based on established policies. Thus, planning and policy-making go together as important functions of management.

Importance of Polices

Organisational policies serve a range of important purposes which are given below:

1. They are among the most important standing plans to guide and direct the future course of managerial action in specific areas of activity.
2. They clarify and crystallize the real values and intentions of top management.
3. They facilitate delegation of authority among the various managerial levels, by defining the decision-making authority and the constraints on its exercise.
4. They contribute to the organisations evolution as an orderly system of goal-oriented activity.
5. They facilitate uniformity of action and coordination of effort.
6. They minimise the destruction of decision-making process.
7. They indicate to outsiders the general attitudes and approaches of the organisation on specific matters of common interest and concern.
8. They provide guideance, a sense of direction and understanding to managers in their action.

9. They provide conceptual and pragmatic guidelines to managers on how objectives are to be achieved and what is to be done to convert objectives into realities.

10. They minimize the possibility of bringing manager's personal prejudicies in decision and decisions in adhoc, arbitrary, haphazard manner.

Types of Policies

Policies may be classified into four types as follows:

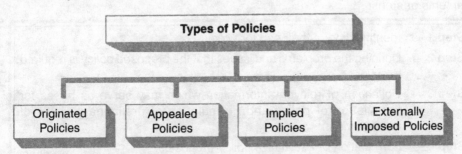

Let us discuss these types of policies one by one.

1. **Originated Policies** — Originated policies are deliberately formulated by top managers on their own initiative in order to guide the actions of their subordinates. Top management formulates, its policies in consultation with the middle and lower level management. These policies are corporate in nature. **For example,** personnel policies, financial policies, marketing policies etc. They may or may not be in writing.

2. **Appealed Policies** — Appealed Policies are those which are formulated at higher managerial levels in response to appeals or reference made by lower level managers. At times managers at lower levels experience policy gaps or vacuum in their areas of activity. They may find themselves unable to make decisions on particular issues or problems because of the absence of clear-cut policies. In such cases, they refer the matters to higher level managers who might pronounce their stand on the same, whereupon it takes the form of a policy. Appealed policies can originate at any level but are common at middle and lower levels. They generally tend to be unwritten.

3. **Implied Policies** — Implied Policies evolve themselves when a series of decisions on related matters are made by managers over a period of time. They emerge when managers do not have the will or time to formulate formal or explicit policies. They exist in an unwritten form. They are set by precedents and conventions. A series of relatively consistent decisions on particular matters form themselves as implied policies which are unstated and unwritten. Implied policies are pervasive in a large number of organisations, as for example for employee selection, promotions and transfers, product quality, customer service, social responsibility and so on.

4. **Externally Imposed Policies** — Externally Imposed Policies are those which are imposed upon the organisation directly or indirectly by external agencies

such as government, labour unions, trade associations etc. The organisation has little option but to incorporate the dictates of the external agencies into its own policy framework which may be in such areas as personnel, marketing, purchasing, quality control, social responsibility, and so on.

Step involved in the Process of Policy Formulation

Policy formulation is an important function of managers especially at the top level of the organisation. It is also a process, just like planning, consisting of the following elements or steps:

Step 1 → Identification of the need for policy.

Step 2 → Defining the problems and issues that the proposed policy is required to cover.

Step 3 → Collection of relevant information which may serve as bases for formulation of policy and Formulation of preliminary views of management.

Step 4 → Formulation of alternative policy proposals.

Step 5 → Evaluation of Alternative Policy Proposals thorough discussion of the proposals at all relevant managerial levels.

Step 6 → Making choice from among alternative policies through a process of progressive elimination.

Step 7 → Testing the policy in action and removing 'bugs' *if any.*

Step 8 → Incorporation of policy in the Policy Mannual.

The above steps are only suggestive. In general the objectives and strategies of the organisation provide the framework for policies. Organisational policies have to be consistent with and contribute to the smooth accomplishment of organisational objectives.

Factors Influencing Formulation of Policy

The various internal and external factors determine and influence the process of policy formulation. Some of these factors are given below:

Internal Factors	External Factors
1. Organisational Goals and Strategies;	1. Social – Political Factors such Government Policy on environment.
2. Manager's own system of personal values, perceptions and preferences;	2. Product Market Factors such as nature of demand and competition, type of customers, structure of industry.
3. Organisational Resources such as Manpower, Finance, Physical Equipment and Facilities;	3. Resource Market Factors such conditions of labour market, conditions of capital market.
4. Organisational Structure;	
5. Organisational Politics such internal power, dynamics, rivalry for authority, status, vested interests.	

It is desirable that policy proposals are extensively discussed at relevant managery levels. Once policies are finalised at the relevant managerial level, they should be formally or informally communicated to the managers and others at lower levels for their information and compliance. Steps are also to be taken to ensure that policies are followed by managers on a consistent basis while making decisions.

Features of a Good Policy

A good policy should have the following features:

1. Policy should conform to certain general requirements.
2. There should be clear and definitive policies to govern all the major areas of organisational functioning.
3. All policies must be communicated to the relevant managerial and other personnel.
4. They should clearly focus on achievement of organisational objectives and should be consistent with them.
5. They should also be internally consistent with each other.
6. Policies should be pragmatic, actionable and understandable to those who have to those who have to follow them.
7. They should be stable over a period of time and should also be flexible.
8. Basic and major policies have to be operationalised by sub-policies and derivative policies.
9. They should be legally valid, socially responsible and ethically sound.
10. They should be periodically reviewed and recast as circumstances warrant.

Distinction between Policies and Objectives

Both objectives and policies belong to the category of strategic postulates of an organisation but they differ in the following respects:

Basis of Distinction	Objectives	Policies
1. **Types of Plans**	Objectives are single use plans	Policies fall into the category of standing plans.
2. **Time Limit**	Objectives have often got a time frame within which they are to be achieved;	Policies have no such time limits.
3. **Basic to Existence**	Objectives are basic and critical to the very existence of an organisation. One cannot think of an organisation without any objective.	Policies are not that basic to the existence of an organisation. It is possible for an organisation to function without policies. For example, several

			small and medium-sized organisations are managed in a rather opportunistic and adhoc manner without any policy framework
4.	**Purpose**	Objectives are meant to be achieved	Policies are meant to be observed as guidelines.
5.	**Place**	In the machinery of organisational plans, objectives occupy a higher place than policies.	Policies occupy a lower place than Objectives.
6.	**Means/Ends**	Objectives are ends.	Policies are means to achieve ends. Policies focus on objectives and throw light on how the latter are to be achieved.
7.	**Vague/specific**	Objectives are vague and abstract. They take the form of ideals, expectations, aspirations, and content.	Policies are more specific and clear. They are meant to operationlise the objectives into realities. They give meaning and content to objectives. They spell out the implications of objectives.
8.	**Official goals/Real Goals**	Objectives are regarded as official goals and are often meant to remain on paper.	They give meaning and content to the objectives. It is often stated that policies reflect the real intents and character of an organisation.

Relationship between Policies and Strategies — As regards the relationship between policies and strategies, both reinforce each other and jointly contribute as the means of achievement of organisational objectives. Also, the formation of strategies has to be done within a policy framework. Managers need policy guidelines for design of organisational strategies. Policies may be truly regarded as part of strategic plans of the organisation; they have significant strategic content.

Distinction between Policies and Strategies

Following are the differences between policies and strategies:

Basis of Distinction	Policies	Strategies
1. **Type of Plan**	Policies are **standing plans** valid for handling range of decision problems in a subject matter.	Strategies are **single use plans** like objectives in the sense that its applicability is confined to a specific use in a specific situation to reach a specific goal.
2. **Purpose**	Policies are formulated **to deal with specific problems.**	Strategies are formulated **to meet environmental threats and opportunities.**
3. **Concerned with**	Policies are concerned with the **organisation as a whole or particular departments.**	Strategies are concerned with the **organisation as a whole.**
4. **Closeness to objectives**	Policies are **not so closer** to objectives than strategies.	Strategies are **closer** to objectives as the means of achieving them than policies.
5. **What indicates?**	Policy indicates the **parameters and constraints** which managers have to observe while making decsions concerning the achievements of objectives.	Strategy maps out **how an organisation plans to get where it wants to go.**
6. **Nexus**	Policy seeks to provide a nexus **between organisational intent and action.** In other words, policy serves to interpret and clarify organisational intents on specific subject matters of decisions-making.	Strategy relates the firm's distinctive strengths and weaknesses to the relevant environmental opportunities and threats. It attempts to provide a fit **between organisational intents and goals with its programmes and perormance.**

7.	Role	The role of policy is **to indicate the direction and degree of emphasis to be laid on different aspects of strategy.** It helps to establish a predicatable pattern of decisions on the implementation of strategy. The implications of strategy are explained in policy.	The role of strategy is to provide a firm but flexible sense of direction to the organisation on **how to cope with major problems** in the course of achievement of its objectives.
8.	Place	Many policies are derived from objectives and policy is a **supportive instrument** of stragegy.	In the hierarcy of organistional plans, strategy occupies a **higher place than policy.** Strategy is generally more abstract than policy
9.	Terminology	Policy is a **civilian term** and is meant to infuse some structure and pattern in managerial decision-making and action.	The term 'Strategy' belongs to **military terminology** and has the connotation of where, when and how to attack the enemy, what size and combination of forces and resources to be deployed.

PROCEDURES

Meaning of Procedures

The term '**Procedure'** is defined as a set of sequential steps determined in advance and standardised for initiating, carrying through and completing a certain routine and repetitive activity. Examples of such activities include recruitment and selection of Man Power, purchase of raw materials for the manufacturing department, passing vendors' bills for payment, settlement of workers' grievances, hiring manpower for the office, sanctioning earned leave. and so on. A procedure specifies the tasks to be done sequentially for completing a piece of work. It **lays down the process of doing routine and repetitive activity,** for the guidance of those who are to carry out such activity. In other words, a procedure may be regarded as a guide to action how a sequence of steps should be performed. **For example,** the procedure of an admission of students in a university is —

Step 1 →	Candidates should apply in advance on the prescribed application form and furnish the required information and documents
Step 2 →	The university office receives and records the applications received before the last date
Step 3 →	The applications will be screened by the appropriate committee to ensure that all the requirements are satisfied
Step 4 →	The applicants will be ranked according to their merit and depending on the number of seats available, candidates will be selected and offered admission.

It is clear from the above that a procedure outlines the sequence of actions or steps be taken in performing specific jobs of a repetitive nature. The series of steps or action are mostly administrative/clerical in nature. The formulation of procedure is a managerial function. Managers at relevant levels lay down and specify the procedure to be followed by the subordinate administrative and clerical personnel for carrying out the myriad of routine activities in organisations. A large number of standard operations or procedures are to be found in almost all business and other organisation for facilitating smooth, orderly and expeditious work flow in administration and related areas.

Characteristics of a Good Procedures

The characteristics of a good procedure include the following:

1. It should be **purposeful and functional**.
2. It should be in a **written form**.
3. It should be **simple and clear**.
4. It should really serve as a **guide** to those who have to follow it.
5. It should **not** be overly **rigid**.
6. It should be **exposed to periodic review** and reform.

Importance of Procedures

Procedures serve several useful purposes as given below:

1. Procedure provide a basis for operators to know how to process the activity without leaving loose ends in the best interests of the organisation.
2. Procedures help in structuring, standardising, streamlining and smoothing the day-to-day activity in organisations and in creating a 'management by system'.
3. A standard set of operating procedurs promote tidy working habit patterns in the various units of the organisation.
4. They are the means of implementing organisational decisions and policies.
5. They help reduce or remove administrative bottlenecks in the work flow on a day to day basis.
6. They also help expedite and accelerate clerical and paper work without duplication and waste motion.

7. A coherent set of procedures governing administrative action enables personnel to actively involve themselves in work without feeling confused and harassed.

8. Procedures lubricate the channels of information flow and thereby help management in timely decision making, control and coordination.

9. Procedure-based activities can easily be delegated to lower administrative and clerical level, thereby conserving managerial time for more important non-routine activities.

10. Procedure-based action on the part of managers and others has the merit of contributing to the evolution of organisational procedures and an overly rigid observance of procedures are often regarded as inimical to dynamic management. Procedures which are means to ends should not be mistaken as ends in themselves.

11. Procedures provide guidance and instruction to administrative and other personnel on how to carry out specific activities in a systematic manner. They aid in simplifying, routinising and standardising the day-to-day paper work in organisations.

12. Procedures facilitate smooth, effective and orderly flow of activity in organisations and thus promote 'management by system' Procedures also permit consistency of action in various departments or sections at a point of time and over a period of time

13. They serve as tools of supervision, control and coordination in the hands of managers with regard to the task performance of their subordinates.

14. Since procedures are laid down by mangers after careful thinking they represent the correct and proper ways of doing work.

15. Procedures save clerical and administrative time. They also safeguard the interests of those who have to carry out work or are affected by them in some way. If employees faithfully follow standard procedures, they will be saved from harassment by their superiors, colleagues and outsiders.

Distinction between Policies and Procedures

The formulation of procedure takes place within the framework of policies. In fact, procedures are partly meant to subserve and implement policies. Hence procedures are to be consistent with policies. For example "it is the policy of the company that every employee is entitled to a safe and congenial working environment and every effort should be made to prevent accidents in any phase of operation". In order to implement the above policy a procedure is laid down on maintenance of machinery and equipment. A part of the procedure is specified as follows for illustrative purposes:

Each maintenance person assigned to work on a job will look out the machine properly and disconnect it with his own safety lock and keep the key in his possession. If he does not finish the job before the shift change, he will remove his lock and put a seal on the disconnect. He will hang a danger tap on the control station, stating why the equipment is shut down.

Although policies and procedures belong to the category of standing plans and are closely related yet they differ in the following respects.

Basis of Distinction	Policies	Procedures
1. **Guidelines**	Policies are guidelines **to decision making.**	Procedures are guidelines **for sequential action.**
2. **Scope for discretion**	Policies are relatively flexible and leave **some** latitude and **discretion** to managers while deciding upon relevant issues.	Procedures are more detailed and deterministic with **little scope for discretion** and deviation.
3. **Strategic/Tool**	Policies form **part of the basic strategic postures** of the organisation in combination with objectives and strategies to cope with complex environmental conditions.	Procedures are **operational and tactical tools** to the efficient guidance of routine internal organisational activity.
4. **Formulation**	Policies in general are formulated **at top management level.**	Procedures are laid down at **a somewhat lower managerial level.**
5. **Bridge**	Policies serve as bridges **between organisational purpose and performance.**	Procedures serve as bridges **between activities and outcomes.**
6. **Treatment**	A policy centred thinking on the part of managers is **considered as a healthy sign** and hence is encouraged in organisations.	A procedures centred thinking is **considered bureaucratic, rigid and self-defeating.** Some procedures may even stifle and slow-down organisational work flow.

The distinction between policies and procedures can be indicated by means of an example. An enterprise may adopt a policy of making all recruitment and selection through the personnel department. The personnel department may then chalk out the procedure of recruitment. The procedure may consist of steps like application blanks (forms), preliminary interviews, aptitude tests, trade tests, employment interview, verification of references, medical examination and approval by the supervisor. To take one of these steps, it may be laid down that the employment intrreview will be conducted by a board of five persons from within the organisation.

The above example suggests that **policies** have **broad areas** of application while **procedures specify how and when to do things**. Both are important for orderly and consistent functioning of organisations.

STANDARD METHOD

A method is a prescribed process in which a particular operation or a task is performed. It specifies in a detailed and guidance-oriented manner the one best efficient and expeditious way of performing each step or segment of a task. It defines the technology of individual operations in a work situation. Methods are viewed as scientific, objective, rational and logical means of ensuring standardisation, systematisation and simplification of work. In organisational settings, methods of work in physical and other task situations are standardized by experts after detailed experimental studies and analyses. One of the gains of the scientific management movement of Frederick Taylor was the determination of standardised, simplified and efficient methods of performing physical tasks by operatives. In the modern 'Organisation & Methods (O&M) areas of activity, much attention is devoted to develop and refine the methods of carrying out clerical, administrative and managerial tasks. In modern computer systems also, standard methods are generated to instruct the computer on the operations it has to perform in processing data.

RULES

Rules are prescriptive directives to people in organisations and elsewhere to do or not to do things, to behave or not to behave in particular ways. They are almost in the nature of commandments, cautions, taboos and norms to discipline, to structure, standardize and restrain individual and group behavirour and task performance. They are generally formalised in writing and are impersonal in nature. They are meant for strict observance. No Smoking is a rule in some work areas and other places. Similarly, organisations formulate service rules and work rules on recruitment, promotion, leave, transfer, discipline, administration of benefits, safety, retirement and so on. Rules also govern behaviour and performance of people in functional and other areas, as for example, purchase rules.

Purpose of Rule

Rules are meant for strict observance. The observance of rules is mandatory on all, irrespective of personalities involved. Of course there may be exceptions to rules under certain conditions. But exceptions are limited. Otherwise, the credibility of rules gets undermined.

Importance of Rules

1. People in work situations gain a sense of safety and security if they go by rules in a strict manner.
2. Rules define minimum acceptable behaviour of people by providing guidelines on what is expected behaviour.
3. Rules reduce the need for close supervision in certain respects since observance of known rules is all that is needed.
4. Rules are generally precise and clear so that there is little room for confusion.

Demerits of Rules

1. Rules tend to strait-jacket human behaviour and even to mechanise it.
2. Issues and matters are treated according to rules and not according to individual needs and situations.

3. Rules are often associated with tyranny, coercion, conformism and blind loyalty at the cost of individual freedom, situational demands and, functional needs.

4. In a rule ridden situation, individual initiative, imagination and innovation are discouraged.

Can a Policy take form of Rules?

Some simple policies may take the form of rules. For example, recruitment of clerical staff only through employment exchanges is at once a policy and a rule followed by some organisations. Sometimes, a set of rules systematically tied together may add up to a procedure, a standard method or even a policy. The existence and enforcement of a set of rules facilitates the process of management and control of people and events in an indirect manner, since they sharply define and delimit the areas and aspects of compliance in a uniform manner. They legitimise punishment and other disciplinary measures in organisations.

Distinction betwen Methods and Rules

Methods differ from Rules in the following respects:

Basis of Distinciton	Methods	Rules
1. **Purpose**	Methods are meant **for efficient performance** of physical tasks.	Rules are meant **for strict observance.** Rules generally relate to individuals and group behaviour and have little to do with efficiency in general.
2. **Standardisation**	Standardisation of methods also **calls for standardisation of related working conditions** within which tasks are performed, to facilitate adherence to and application of methods.	**No such standardisation** is **called for** in the case of rules.
3. **Formulation**	Formulation of Methods involves much scietific research and analysis. It is not a simple or routine task.	Rules are formulated **on the basis of legal requirements, corporate objectives, managerial values and common sense.**
4. **Penalty for Deviation**	In general deviation from methods **does not attract penalty.**	Deviation from Rules **attract penalty.**
5. **Backed by**	Methods are backed by **knowledge.**	Rules are generally backed by **managerial authority and prerogative.**
6. **Enforcement**	There is **no formal enforcement** in the cases of methods.	Rules are sought **to be enforced.**

SCHEDULES

Meaning of Schedules

The term '**Schedule**' is defined as a plan of action which focuses on the '**when**' aspects of initiating and completing operations regarding specific jobs. In manufacturing operations, machines and manpower are to be optionally utilised for production of concerned products and components have to be systematically planned in advance. For this purpose time schedules are prepared for the starting and completion of the whole operation. While preparing such a schedule, managers at the operational level take into consideration several factors like delivery schedules of the completed products/ components, the plant capacity, the machine work loads already committed but are pending to be executed, availability of labour, position regarding availability of materials and other inputs and so on.

Distinction between Procedures and Schedules

Following are the differences between procedures and schedules:

Basis of Distinciton	Procedures	Schedule
1. What lays down	Procedures lay down the **sequence of operations** to be done for completing a particular piece of work or job.	Schedules lay down the **starting time for each operation and the length of time required for completing that operation.**
2. Nature	Procedures are generally **administrative aids and tools.**	Schedules are largely concerned with **technical operation**.
3. Degree of Co-ordination Synchronization and balancing	In the case of procedures, **no such problems** are generally experienced.	**Very high degree of coordination, synchronization and balancing is needed** in working out schedules for different operations and for different procedures especially when production facilities are common for them.

BUDGETS

Budgets is single-use plan containing expected results in numberical terms. Budgets may be expressed in time, money, materials or other suitable units capable of numberical expression. Income and expense budget, for example, projects the expected revenues and expenses for a given period. Since budget is an important control device it is often thought of in connection with controlling alone. However, budget making is primarily a planning process whereas its administration is part of controlling.

Meaning of the term 'Budget'

According to C.I.M.A., London. *"A budget is a financial and/or quantitative statement, prepared and approved prior to a defined period of time, of the policy to be pursued during that period for the purpose of attaining a given objective. It may include income, expenditure and the employment of capital."* A budget is a plan covering phases and operations for a definite period in the future. It is the form of quantitative expression of policies, plans, objectives and goals laid down in advance by top management for the concern as a whole and for each sub-division thereof.

The main **characteristics of a budget** are:

1. **Prepared in Advance** — It is prepared in advance and is derived from the long-term strategy of the organisation.

2. **Relates to Future** — It is related to future period for which objectives or goals have already been laid down

3. **Expressed in Quantitative/Financial Terms** — It is expressed in quantitative form, physical or monetary units, or both.

Meaning of Budgeting

Budgeting is the art of building budgets.

Objectives of Budgets

The objectives of Budgets are given below:

1. To determine targets of performance for each section or department of the business for the budget period.

2. To lay down the responsibilities of each of the executives and other personnel so that every one knows what is expected of him and how he will be judged.

3. To provide a basis for the comparison of actual performance with the predetermined targets.

4. To ascertain the variance (i.e., differences between actual performance and budgeted performance) and analyse the reasons therefor.

5. To take the necessary corrective action.

6. To provide a basis for revision of current & future policies.

7. To draw up long-range plans with a fair measure of accuracy.

8. To ensure the best use of all available resources to maximise profit or production subject to the budget (or limiting) factors.

9. To co-ordinate the various activities of the business.

10. To centralise control.

11. To decentralise responsibility to each manager.

12. To show the management where action is needed to remedy a situation.

13. To act as a guide for management decisions when unforeseeable conditions affect the budget.

14. To engender a spirit of careful forethought, assessment of what is possible and an attempt at it. It leads to dynamism without recklessness.

15. To plan and control income and expenditure of manufacturing or training operations so that the most practicable profits are obtained.

16. To plan and control capital expenditure in the most profitable direction.

17. To plan and control the financing of the business so that adequate working capital, including liquid resources are available for carrying out the policy of the business.

18. To plan and control expenditure on research and development.

19. To combine the ideas of all levels of management in the preparation of the firm's plans.

Step involved in the preparation of Budgets

The following steps are involved in the preparation of budgets:

Step 1 → Appointment of Budget Controller

Although the Chief Executive is finally responsible for the budget programme, it is better if a large part of the supervisory responsibility is delegated to a special official designated as Budget Controller or Budget Director. Such a person should have knowledge of the technical details of the business and should report directly to the President or the Chief Executive of the organisation.

Step 2 → Formulation of Budget Committee

The Budget Controller is assisted in his work by the Budget Committee. The Committee consists of all the Heads of various departments, viz., Production, Sales, Finance, Personnel, Purchase, etc. with the Managing Director as its Chairman. It is generally the responsibility of the Budget Committee to submit, discuss and finally approve the budget figures. Each head of the department should have his own Sub-committee with executives working under him as its members.

Each member will prepare his own budget which will be discussed at the committee meeting before a final shape is given for co-ordinated action. The important function of a budget committee are as follows:

(a) To define general policies of the management;

(b) To receive and review budget estimates;

(c) To approve budget estimates;

(d) To analyse variances and recommend corrective action where necessary; and

(e) To co-ordinate budget programme.

Step 3 → **Fixation of Budget period**

The period covered by a budget is known as budget period. There is no general rule governing the selection of the budget period. The length of the budget period depends upon the nature of the plan and circumstances of the business. **For example,** industries which are subject to fashion change use short budget period whereas industries involving long-term expenditure with relatively little change in product design use long budget periods. **For example,** (i) a shoe industry uses short-term budgets and (ii) a telephone manufacturing company uses long-term budgets. Normally, one year is a normal period for budget because it coincides with the accounting year. A common practice however, is to have a series of budget periods. Thus, sales budget may cover the next five years while production and cost budgets may cover only one year. The capital expenditure budget may cover even 5 to 10 years; the yearly budgets may also be broken down into monthly periods. Long-term budgets may be supplemented by short term budgets. Thus, **For example,** a long-term budget for three to five years may be supplemented by short-term budgets for one year or less.

For control purposes, the budget period may be divided into shorter periods. The period of time covered by a budget and the resulting comparative statement of actual and budgeted expenditure should be largely determined by the requirements and outlook of the persons whose activities are planned in the budget. **For example,** a foreman may need a weekly budget and report on certain costs because he exercises day-to-day control over such expenditure. The departmental manager with a broader outlook, may not be interested in short-term fluctuations. Normally, the control period covers a month.

Step 4 → **Identification of Budget factor (or Key factor or limiting Factor)**

The factor which sets a limit to the total activity is known as budget factor, key factor or limiting factor. **For example,** if production can not be increased inspite of heavy demand, due to non-availability of raw-material/power, raw-material/power is called here key factor. The key factors should be correctly identified and their extent of influence must first be carefully assessed.

Examples of Principal Budget Factors (or Key Factors)

Item	Budget Factor (or Key Factor)
(a) Materials:	(i) Availability of supplies. (ii) Restrictions imposed by the Government like, quotas.
(b) Labour:	(i) Shortage in certain key processes.
(c) Plant and machinery:	(i) Insufficient capacity for lack of space. (ii) Bottlenecks in certain key processes.
(d) Sales:	(i) Low market demand. (ii) Insufficient advertising due to lack of funds.
(e) Finance:	(i) Long-term finance. (ii) Short-term funds.
(f) Management:	(i) Lack of managerial time for additional work.

It would be desirable to prepare first the budget relating to this particular factor, and then prepare the other budgets. An illustrative list of key factors in certain industries is given below:

Examples of Key Factor in Specific Industries

Industry	Key Factor
Motor Car	Sales demand
Aluminium	Power
Petroleum Refinery	Supply of crude oil
Electro-optics	Skilled technicians
Hydro power generation	Monsoon

A key factor is not necessarily a permanent factor. It is often a temporary one. In the long run, it may be possible for the management to overcome the limitations imposed by a factor by raising funds necessary to finance capital expenditure, finding alternative sources of raw material or substitutes for raw materials; in the short run by working overtime, hiring equipment, etc. Thus, the aim of locating limitations is to seek harmony among the various factors of production from the beginning and to maintain it throughout the budget period.

Step 5 → **Identification of Budget Centers**

It is a well known saying that "costs are the best controlled at the point of incurrence." Thus, for example, in the case of production cost the point of control will be at the supervisor or operator level. In this way, suitable areas of control have to be selected. These areas should not be too large because the span of control should be limited. Normally, the areas chosen should conform to the natural responsibilities of executives. Such areas are known as budget centres. A budget which refers to a budget centre is a department budget. A budget centre may again consist of a number of cost centres representing different groups of machines.

Step 6 → **Preparation of Budget Manual**

The budget manual is a schedule, document or booklet which shows, in written forms budgeting organisation and procedures. The manual should be well written and indexed, a copy thereof may be given to each departmental head for guidance.

Contents of Budgets Manual — Budget Manual should include the following matters:

1. Introduction: A brief explanation of the principle of budgetary control system, its objectives and benefits.

2. Procedure to be adopted in operating the system. For example, 'distribution instruction', will specify as to whom various budget schedules are to be sent.

3. Definition of duties and responsibilities of (a) operational executives, (b) budget committee and (c) budget controller.

4. Nature, type and specimen forms of various reports. It also specifies the persons responsible for the preparation of the reports and the programme of distribution of the reports to the various officers.

5. The account code and classification used by the company.

6. The budget calendar showing the dates for completion of each part of the budget and submission of reports.

7. The budget periods and control periods.

8. The follow-up procedures.

Advantages of Budget Manual — The following are the advantages of Budget Manual:

1. An overall well co-ordinated plan, provided by budgetary control system, shows what role each manager is expected to play in maximising the profits.

2. Any problem arising from the operation of a budgetary control system can be settled through the manual.

3. New employees get acquainted with the procedure involved in the operation of the system by referring to manual.

4. Methods and procedures become standardised.

5. Since co-ordination is maintained, there is no overlapping of instructions. There

is in other words synchronisation of all efforts which leads to the attainment of the objectives with minimum of friction.

Types of Budgets

Budgets may be classified on various basis as follows:

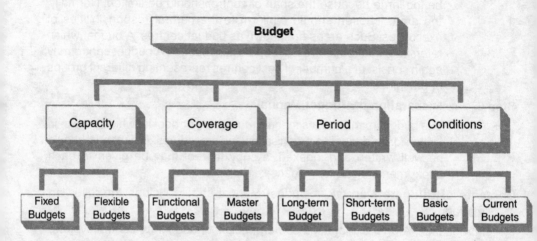

Let us discuss these types of Budgets one by one.

1. **Fixed Budget — According to C.I.M.A. London** *"a fixed budget is a budget designed to remain unchanged irrespective of the level of activity actually attained".* Fixed Budget is used as an effective tool of cost control. In case, the level of activity attained is different from the level of activity for budgeting purposes, the fixed budget becomes ineffective because it does not give due consideration to cost behaviour at different levels of activity. Such as budget is quite suitable for fixed expenses. The main features of a fixed budget are as follows:

   1. It is prepared for one fixed level of activity.
   2. It does not change with the change in the level of activity.
   3. Expenses are not classified into fixed, variable and semi-variable.

2. **Flexible Budget — According to C.I.M.A., London** *"a flexible budget is a budget which, by recognising the difference between fixed, semi-variable and variable costs is designed to change in relation to the level of activity attained."* In a flexible budgetary control system, a series of budgets are prepared one for each of a number of alternative production levels or volumes. Flexible budgets represent the amount of expenses that is reasonably necessary to achieve each level of output specified. In other words, the allowances given under flexible budgetary control system serve as a standard of what costs should be at each level of output. It is more realistic and practicable because it gives due consideration to cost behaviour at different levels of activity. The main features of flexible budget are as follows:

   1. It is prepared for different levels of activity.

2. It changes with the change in the level of activity.

3. Expenses are classified into fixed, variable and semi-variable. Semi-variable expenses are further segregated into fixed and variable expenses.

Need: The need for preparation of flexible budgets arises in the following circumstances:

(i) In case of industries where there are seasonal fluctuations in sales and/or production-for example, in soft drinks industry;

(ii) In case of a company which keeps on introducing new products or make changes in the design of its products frequently;

(iii) In case of industries engaged in make-to-order business like ship-building;

(iv) In case of an industry which is influenced by changes in fashion; and

(v) When there are general changes in sales.

(vi) In the case of new business venture due to its typical nature it may be difficult to forecast the demand of a product accurately.

(vii) Where the business is dependent upon the mercy of nature, e.g., a person dealing in wool trade may have enough market if temperature goes below the freezing point.

(viii) In the case of labour intensive industry where the production of the concern is dependent upon the availability of labour.

Distinction between Fixed Budget and Flexible Budget

Fixed Budget differs from Flexible Budget in the following respects:

Basis of Distinction	Fixed Budget	Flexible Budget
1. **Change with activity**	It does not change with actual volume of activity achieved. Thus, it is known as **rigid or inflexible budget.**	It can be recasted on the basis of activity level to be achieved. Thus, it is **not rigid.**
2. **One level or different levels of activity**	It op**erates on one level of activity** and under one set of conditions. It assumes that there will be no change in the prevailing conditions, which is unrealistic.	It consists of various budgets for **different levels of activity.**
3. **Utility of variance analysis**	Since all costs like-fixed, variable and semi-variable are related to only one level of activity, variance analysis **does not give useful information.**	Here analysis of variance **provides useful information** as each cost is analysed according to its behaviour.
4. **Decision making**	If the budgeted and actual activity levels differ significantly, then the aspects like **cost**	Flexible budgeting at different levels of activity, **facilitates the decision - making** regarding

	ascertainment and price fixation do not give a correct picture.	ascertainment of cost, fixation of selling price and tendering of quotations.
5. Basis of Comparison	Comparison of actual performance with budgeted targets **will be meaningless specially when there is a difference between the two activity levels**.	It provides a meaningful basis of comparison of the actual performance with the budgeted targets.

3. **Functional Budgets** — Budgets which relate to the individual functions in an organization are known as Functional Budgets. **For example,** purchase budget; sales budget; production budget; plant-utilisation budget and cash budget.

4. **Master Budget** — It is a consolidated summary of the various functional budgets. It serves as the basis upon which budgeted P & L A/c and forecasted Balance Sheet are built up.

5. **Long-term Budgets** — The budgets which are prepared for periods longer than a year are called long-term budgets. Such budgets are helpful in business forecasting and forward planning. Capital expenditure budget and Research and Development budget are examples of long-term budgets.

6. **Short-term Budgets** — Budgets which are prepared for period less than a year are known as short-term budgets. Cash budget is an example of short-term budget. Such type of budgets are prepared in cases where a specific action has to be immediately taken to bring any variation under control, as in cash budgets.

7. **Basic Budgets** — A budget which remains unaltered over a long period of time is called basic budget.

8. **Current Budgets** — A budget which is established for use over a short period of time and is related to the current conditions is called current budget.

PROGRAMME

Programme refers to the outline of plans of work to be carried out in proper sequence for the purpose of achieving specific objectives. Thus, a company might embark upon an expansion programme increasing its size by, say, seventy per cent. And to implement this programme, management must lay down certain policies, procedures, methods, rules and other assignments properly related and co-ordinated for its successful implementation. Programme is frequently supported by capital, revenue and expense budgets. Thus, programme is a complex structure of policies, procedures, methods, rules, budgets and other assignments.

Programme can originate at any level in the organisation and can be a major programme or a minor one. Basic or major programmes usually call for establishing a number of derivative programmes.

STEPS INVOLVED IN THE PLANNING PROCESS

Planning is a process which consists of various steps which have been demonstrated in the following diagram:

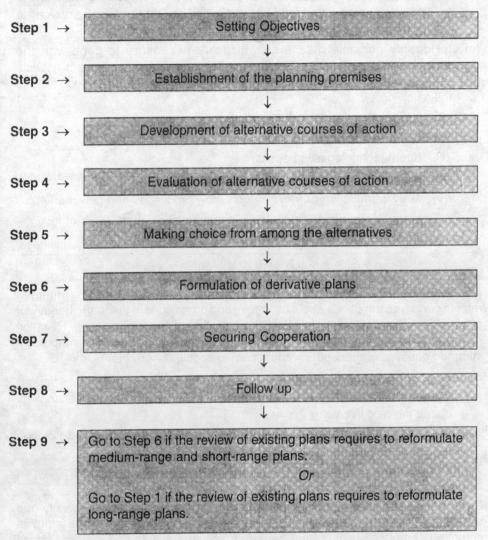

Step 1 → Setting Objectives
↓
Step 2 → Establishment of the planning premises
↓
Step 3 → Development of alternative courses of action
↓
Step 4 → Evaluation of alternative courses of action
↓
Step 5 → Making choice from among the alternatives
↓
Step 6 → Formulation of derivative plans
↓
Step 7 → Securing Cooperation
↓
Step 8 → Follow up
↓
Step 9 → Go to Step 6 if the review of existing plans requires to reformulate medium-range and short-range plans.
Or
Go to Step 1 if the review of existing plans requires to reformulate long-range plans.

Let us discuss these steps involved in the planning process one by one.

Step 1 → Setting Objectives

Forecasting is a process of predicting the future behaviour of variables which are likely to affect the activities of the organisation. Forecasting provides vital clues to managers on what the future problems and prospects are likely to be for the organisation. Before forecasting, management is required —

(a) to make analysis of internal environment (i.e., existing plans, products, processes, activities, performance levels, human and non-human resources), achievements and problems, to review the specific strengths and weaknesses of the organisation;

(b)   to make analysis of external environment (i.e., elements and events in the world outside the organisation which affect its present and future functioning), to identify the present and future opportunities and threats which are likely to help or hinder the performance and progress of the organisation;

(c)   to identify possible measures which are necessary to cope with the environmental opportunities and threats. Through forecasting, several aspects of future trends should be understood. The examples of future trends include the following:

  (i)   future sales trends of the products;

  (ii)   future trends of profitability;

  (iii)   future technological changes;

  (iv)   general economic and industrial trends;

  (v)   likely introduction of new products, new processes and new markets;

  (vi)   probable changes in population characteristics, their levels of income, life styles and buying habits.

Step 2 → Establishment of the planning premises

After forecasting, the next step is to establish 'planning premises'. Planning premises refer to certain assumptions about estimates and projections of the future behaviour of variables which are likely to affect the activities of the organisation. Planning premises form the foundation of organisational plans. They are in the nature of informed guesses of managers with respect to specific future trends.

Examples of planning premises —

(a)   There will be revolutionary developments in mass communication technology during the next five years.

(b)   There will be future liberalisation in the economic, industrial and taxation policies of government.

Types of planning premises — The planning premises may be of different types as under:

Note: Future forecasts and planning premises do not reduce the complexity and uncertainty of the future but only aid managers in understanding the state of complexity and uncertainty of the behaviour of future events and in going ahead with confidence to cope with them.

Types of Premises	Meaning	Examples of Premises
(a) **Internal Premises**	These relate to the activities of the organisation.	Cost of products, profitability etc.
(b) **External premises**	These relate to general economic and business conditions, social, political, technological and other trends.	Liberalised economic and industrial policies of government.
(c) **Tangible premises**	These refer to those premises which can be quantified in terms of rupees, working days, man days, unity of production etc.	Sales volume of Rs 100 crore, production of 100 crore units.
(d) **Intangible premises**	These refer to those premises which cannot be quantified in numerical terms.	Goodwill, competence and character of managerial personnel.
(e) **Controllable premises**	These refer to those premises which can be controlled by the organisation.	Expenditure on advertisement.
(f) **Uncontrollable premises**	These refer to those premises which are beyond the control of organisation.	Government policies, fire in the plant.

Step 3 → Development of alternative courses of action

After the establishment of planning premises, the next step is to develop alternative courses of action. At this stage, managers are required to apply their creative and innovative skills to develop alternative courses of actions. For example, the objective of improving the economic power and profitability can be achieved by any one or a combination of the following courses of action:

1. by increasing the sales of its existing products in the existing markets;
2. by exploring new markets;
3. by introducing new products;
4. by introducing new processes of production;
5. by acquiring other organisations.

Step 4 → Evaluation of alternative courses of action

After the development of alternative courses of action, the next step is to evaluate them. At this stage, the managers are required to examine the merits, demerits and consequences of each alternative course of action.

Step 5 → Making choice from among alternatives

After the evaluation of alternative courses of action, the next step is to make choice from among alternatives. At this stage, managers are required to make choices from among the alternatives on the basis of certain predetermined selection criteria. These choices reflect the long-range plans of the organisation for a specified period of time.

Step 6 → Formulation of Derivative Plans

After the formulation of long-range plans the next step is to formulate medium-range and short-range plans. Medium-range plans generally have a duration of more than one year but up to three years. Short-range plans generally have a duration of less than one year. These plans are known as **derivative plans or operational plans**. These plans generally relate to functional activities such as manufacturing, marketing, purchase, personnel, finance, research, development, and so on. These plans must indicate the time schedule and sequence of accomplishing various tasks. These plans are further converted into detailed sectional plans which indicate the time schedule and sequence of accomplishing various tasks.

Step 7 → Securing Co-operation of Employees

After the formulation of medium-range and short-range plans, the next step is to make the necessary arrangements for effective implementation of plans and securing the maximum co-operation of employees.

At this stage, the management takes the necessary steps to secure the co-operation, participation and commitment of the members of organisation. These steps include proper communication of plans in details.

Step 8 → Follow up

After implementation of the plan, the next step is to review the existing plans periodically to ensure their relevance and effectiveness.

On the basis of review of existing plans, the long-range, medium-range or short-range plans may be revised.

LIMITATIONS OF PLANNING

Though planning is a primary and pervasive function of management, yet it is subject to certain limitations shown below:

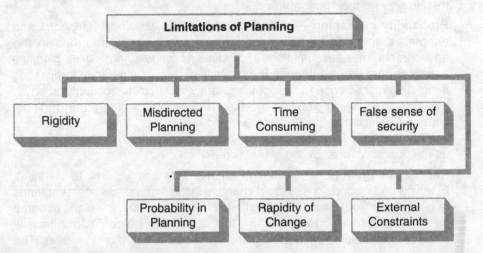

Let us discuss the limitations of planning one by one.

1. **Rigidity** — Plans tend to introduce rigidity into the functioning of the organisation when the managers and others become more concerned with observance of policies, procedures and rules as specified in the plan rather than achieving the organisational goals.

   Effects of rigidity —

   (i) The managers become reluctant to deviate from the plans.

   (ii) The managers lose much of their initiative.

   (iii) The adaptation of plans in response to changes taking place in external environment becomes difficult.

   (iv) Sometimes new opportunities and better options forego.

2. **Misdirected Planning** — Planning may not serve any useful purpose when it is directed towards meeting individual goals ignoring the achievement of organisational goals.

3. **Time Consuming** — Planning is a time consuming process because thinking and deciding are somewhat slow intellectual exercises. As a result, action is likely to be delayed. When timely action is not taken particularly during the emergencies and crises, when quick decisions are needed, the organisation is bound to suffer due to delayed action. Thus, planning is useful only in normal circumstances and not in abnormal circumstances.

   Planning is very costly in the sense that it takes a lot of time, and cost of planning is directly proportionate to the time spent for planning. When cost of planning exceeds the value of benefits derived from it, it is uneconomical and unpurposeful to plan.

4. **False Sense of Security** — Planning sometimes creates a false sense of security among the managers and others when they assume that as long as work goes on according to plans, it is satisfactory. As a result, they become more concerned with the fulfilment of the requirements of specific plans rather than improving their performance.

5. **Probability in Planing** — Planning is based on certain assumptions and estimates about the future behaviour of events and situations in the environment. These assumptions and estimates *(popularly known as 'planning premises')* are derived through the process of forecasting. Since forecasting is not an exact science to predict the future with absolute accuracy, such an assumption on which planning is based is always subject to an error. Thus, plans are as accurate as the forecasts. More distant the future, less accurate are likely to be the forecasts. Thus, the degree of inaccuracy in plans increases as the period covered by the plans increases.

6. **Rapidity of Change** — Rapidity of change sets another limit to planning. Planning under conditions of rapid changes in the external environment tends to be a difficult job. Under the conditions of rapid changes, the plans become outdated and irrelevant even before they are implemented. Though flexible plans may be helpful, yet flexible plans are also subject to certain limits. The existence of a plan puts managerial activities in a rigid framework in the sense that the existing plans are strictly adhered to irrespective of changes in environmental factors. This may prevent managers from taking initiative and from doing innovative thinking.

7. **External Constraints** — External constraints also set limit to planning because management has very little or no control at all. For example, personnel policies and decisions may be limited by considerations of labour union pressures particularly when union is organised on national basis and also by legal provisions as laid down by government from time to time. Similarly, government policies (regarding taxation, import, export etc.), technological changes, competition etc. act as limits to planning.

Examples of limitations of planning which are beyond the control of an organisation.

(i) Natural calamities

Example: Flood, cyclone

(ii) Change in economic policies

Example: Increase in sales tax or excise duty.

(iii) Change in technology

Example: Use of computers, use of CD's. Use of movable hard-disk.

(iv) Change in fashion, taste etc.

Example: Jean in place of trousers, use of fast food etc.

(v) Strategies of competitors.

Example: Introduction of improved mode of existing product.

Key Elements in the concept of Planning.

Following are the key elements in the concept of planning:

1. **Setting objectives** — The first element is the setting objectives. Objectives provide the rational for undertaking various activities and point to the end result of planning.

2. **Identifying alternative programmes** — Having determined objectives, the next element is to ascertain the various alternative programmes to achieve desired results.

3. **Selecting the best programme** — There will be more than one way to achieve a particular objective. Each alternative should be closely examined and the best programme should be selected.

_____ **EXERCISES** _____

SHORT ANSWER TYPE QUESTIONS

1. What do you mean by the planning function of management?
2. Give any three features of planning.
3. Explain the term 'primacy of planning'.
4. Why is planning regarded as a pervasive function?
5. "Planning is futuristic." Explain.
6. Why is planning regarded as forward looking function?
7. "Planning involves choice." Explain.
8. "Planning is a mental exercise." Explain.
9. How does planning provide the basis of control?
10. How does planning facilitate decision-making?
11. How does planning help co-ordination?
12. How does planning promote creativity?
13. How does planning lead to economy and efficiency?
14. "Planning reduces the risk of uncertainty." Comment.
15. Why are plans considered to be probabilistic?
16. "Planning leads to rigidity." Explain.
17. "Planning is a time consuming process." Explain.
18. How does planning create a false sense of security?
19. State the limitations of planning.
20. Enumerate the steps involved in the planning process.
21. Why are derivative plans so called?
22. Why are derivative plans formulated? Justify with a suitable example.
23. Define the term 'planning premises'.

24. Explain the meaning of objectives. State the advantages of setting objectives.
25. Explain the meaning of strategies. State their main features.
26. Why are strategies needed?
27. Enumerate the steps involved in the formulation of strategies.
28. Explain the importance of stretegy.
29. Explain the meaning and importance of standing plans.
30. Explain the meaning and importance of policies.
31. Enumerate the steps involved in the process of formulation of policies.
32. State the features of good policy.
33. Explain the meaning, characteristics and importance of procedures.
34. Explain the meaning, importance and demerits of rules. Can a policy take form of rules?
35. Distinguish between the following:
    (a) Plans and Policies
    (b) Objectives and Policies
    (c) Policies and Strategies
    (d) Policies and Procedures
    (e) Methods and Rules
    (g) Procedures and Schedules
    (h) Budget and Programme
36. Write short notes on the following:
    (a) Role of Standing Plans
    (b) Role of Organisational Objectives
    (c) Procedures
    (d) Standard Method
    (e) Rules
    (f) Schedules
    (g) Budgets
    (h) Programmes
    (i) Means-end-Chain

LONG ANSWER TYPE QUESTIONS

1. What is meant by planning? Explain briefly its features.
2. "Planning is looking ahead." Explain the statement and state any five features of planning.
3. Explain briefly the importance of planning for a large business enterprise.
4. Explain briefly the benefits of planning to an organisation.
5. "Planning is of vital importance in the managerial process." Explain.
6. "Planning facilitates decision-making and co-ordination." Explain.
7. Define planning. Illustrate with example how planning offsets the uncertainties of future and how it facilitates control.
8. How does planning help co-ordination, facilitate decision-making and promote creativity?

9. How does planning reduce the risk of uncertainty, provide the basis of control and lead to economy?

10. Why is planning necessary for effective management? Give six reasons.

11. Explain briefly the limitations of planning.

12. Briefly explain the various external limitations of planning.

13. What is planning? How can government policies and technological changes create problems in planning?

14. Why does planning sometimes fail inspite of the best efforts of management?

15. Explain in brief the steps involved in planning process.

16. Explain briefly the process of planning.

17. "Planning involves a choice between the alternative courses of action." Comment.

18. "Planning is the basis of control, action its essence, delegation its key and information is its guide." Comment.

19. What is meant by single use plan? Explain any two single use plans.

20. What is meant by standing plan? Explain any two standing plans.

19   Organising

MEANING OF ORGANISING

In general sense, the term 'organising' means systematic arrangement of activities.

In the context of organisation, the term 'organising' refers to the way in which the work of a group of people is arranged and distributed among group members to achieve the objectives of an organisation.

The term *'organising'* should not be confused with the term *'organisation'* because organising is a function of management while organisation refers to a group of persons who have come together to achieve some common objectives.

As a function of management, the term *'organising'* refers to the process of —

(a) bringing together human and non-human resources (e.g., materials, machines, money), and

(b) defining and establishing the authority-responsibility relationships, for the achievement of organisational goals.

Outcome of organising process —The outcome of organising process is the creation of formal relationship known as 'organisation structure'.

Purpose of organising process —The purpose of organising process is to relate organisational people to each other and to work for the achievement of organisational goals.

IMPORTANCE OF ORGANISING PROCESS AND ORGANISATION STRUCTURE

The importance of the process of organising and the structure of organisation arises from the benefits listed below:

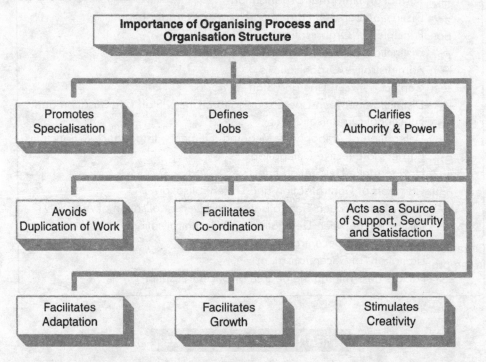

Let us discuss the importance of organising process and organisation structure as under:

1. **Promotes Specialisation** — The process of organising promotes specialisation in the sense that the various organisational activities are divided,

sub-divided and then grouped into units which lead to specialisation of work. Specialisation permits the optimum use of human efforts and brings about internal economies in the business.

2. **Defines the Jobs** — The process of organising clearly defines the jobs of managers and non-managers. This enables them to know what is expected of them as members of the group. This facilitates the process of fitting the right person to the right job.

3. **Clarifies Authority & Power** — The process of organising clarifies the authority of the managers of different departments. This minimises the conflict and confusion about the powers of managers.

4. **Avoids Duplication of Work** — The process of organising avoids duplication of work and overlapping in responsibilities among various organisational members and work units by assigning specific jobs to individuals and work units.

5. **Facilitates Co-ordination** — The organisation structure facilitates co-ordination in the sense that it clearly shows who can exercise authority over whom to bring harmony of work and unity of efforts of people.

6. **Acts as a Source of Support, Security and Satisfaction** — Organisation structure acts as a source of support, security and satisfaction to managers and non-managers in the sense that it shows their definite statuses and positions and also their relative positions in relation to others.

7. **Facilitates Adaptation** — Flexible organisation structure facilitates adaptation in the sense that it ensures the ability to adapt and adjust the activities in response to the changes taking place in the external environment with respect to technology, market, product, process etc.

8. **Facilitates Growth** — A flexible organisation structure facilitates growth of the organisation by increasing its capacity to handle increased level of activity.

9. **Stimulates Creativity** — A sound organisation structure stimulates creative thinking and initiative among organisational members by providing well-defined patterns of authority.

STEPS IN THE PROCESS OF ORGANISING

Organising is a process which consists of certain steps. The various steps involved in the organising process have been demonstrated in the following diagram:

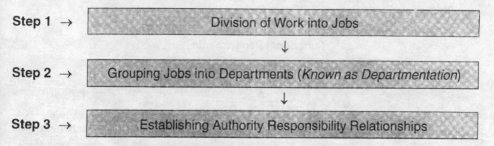

Step 1 → Division of Work into Jobs

↓

Step 2 → Grouping Jobs into Departments (*Known as Departmentation*)

↓

Step 3 → Establishing Authority Responsibility Relationships

Let us discuss these steps in detail one by one:

Step 1 → Division of Work into Jobs

On the basis of principle of division of labour, the total activities of an organisation are divided into major functional activities, and each such functional activity is further sub-divided into specific jobs. Each job consists of certain related tasks which can be carried out by an individual. This division and sub-division of activities goes on till individual positions have been created for performing all types of work in an organisation. The reasons of dividing and sub-dividing activities are given below.

1. The total work may be so large that it cannot be done by a singe individual or by a few persons.
2. After dividing the work into smaller units, it becomes easy to assign work to individuals who have necessary skill and knowledge to perform the work efficiently.
3. Division of work facilitates specialisation which in turn leads to efficiency and quality.

   Thus, at this stage, specific jobs are created for managers and subordinates.

Step 2 → Grouping Jobs into Departments (Known as Departmentation)

After the identification of activities, the next step is to group activities on certain well-defined basis (such as function, product, territory, customer, process or project). This grouping process is called *'departmentation'*. The necessity of departmentation arises because of the anxiety on the part of management to achieve the organisational goals through co-ordinated efforts of the individuals working in the organisation.

The departmentation helps in achieving the benefits of specialisation, administrative control, fixation of responsibility, freedom or autonomy and development of managers.

Bases of Departmentation — Departmentation can be done on the bases of function, product, territory, customers, process or project. These bases have been discussed as follows:

(i) *Function* — Under this basis of departmentation, the departments are created on the basis of function of activities of an organisation. This type of departmentation is followed almost in every organisation. This has been shown below.

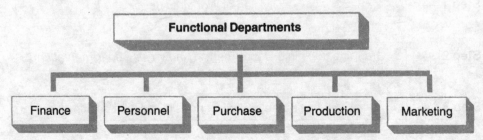

(ii) **Product** — Under this basis of departmentation, the departments are created on the basis of products of an organisation. This type of departmentation is followed in those organisations where manufacturing and marketing characteristics of the product are of primary concern. This has been shown below.

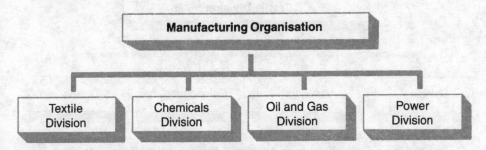

(iii) **Territory** — Under this basis of departmentation, the divisions are created on the basis of their geographical location. This basis is adopted where the activities of an organisation cover a wide geographical area. This type of departmentation is usually followed in service organisations such as banks, insurance and transport companies. This has been shown below.

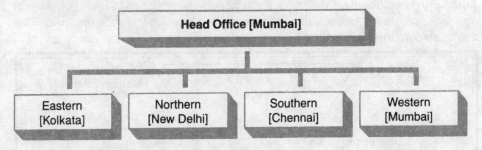

(iv) **Customers** — Under this basis of departmentation, the departments are created to serve the needs of particular customers. This type of departmentation is followed where marketing services are of primary concern. This has been shown below.

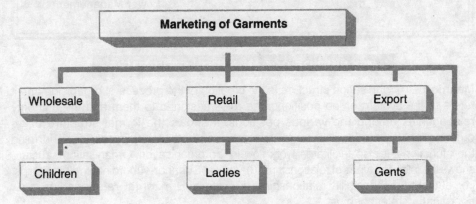

(v) ***Process of Equipment*** — Under this basis of departmentation, the departments are created on the basis of manufacturing processes. This type of departmentation is followed where the manufacturing of products involves different processes. This has been shown below.

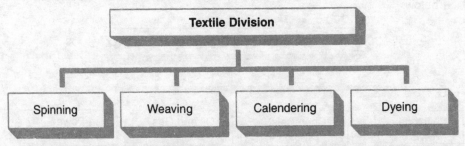

Step 3 → Establishing Authority Responsibility Relationship

After the grouping of activities, the next step is to establish authority-responsibility relationships among the various members of the organisation who perform the jobs. At this stage, *hierarchy of authority* (i.e., a definite ranking order of managerial position) is created by granting different degrees of authority to different positions.

Authority flows downwards from the top managerial positions to lower managerial positions in a graded manner and, as a result, its content decreases gradually. This has been demonstrated below:

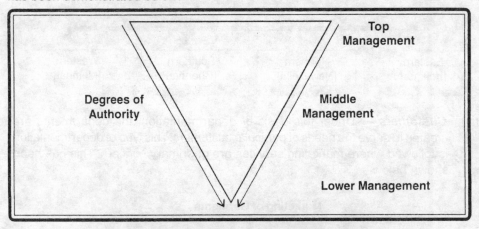

MEANING OF ORGANISATION STRUCTURE

Meaning — Organisation structure is the creation of the process of organising and it refers to the system of job positions, the roles assigned to them and the authority relationships among the various positions. It shows the formal structure of an organisation. It provides a basis for managers and other employees for performing their functions. It also facilitates work flow in the organisation. Organisation structure shows the following types of relationships: (i) Vertical/Superior-subordinate relationships, i.e., authority-responsibility relationships. (ii) Lateral/Horizontal relationships, i.e., coordinating relationships.

Chart — It can be shown in a chart. It looks like a pyramid with a narrow top and a broad bottom. The organisation structure of a manufacturing unit has been demonstrated below:

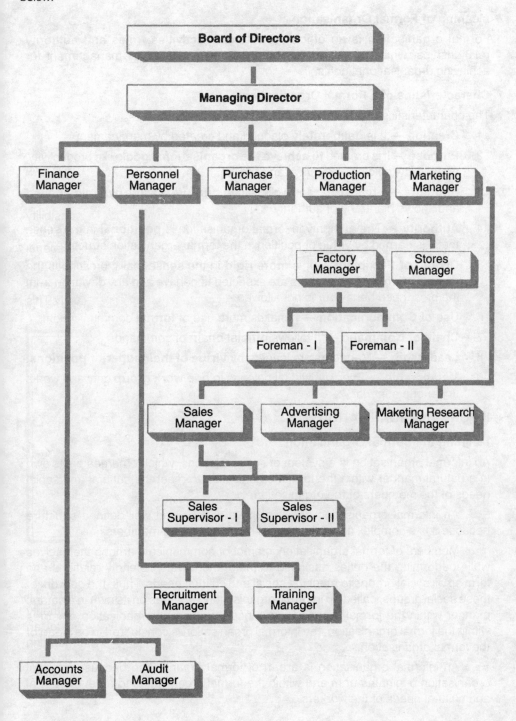

FORMAL AND INFORMAL ORGANISATION

FORMAL ORGANISATION

Meaning of Formal Organisation

Formal organisation is an official structure of activities, roles and authority relationships, which is deliberately planned and executed by management for achieving organisational goals.

Characteristics of a Formal Organisation

The characteristics of a formal organisation are as follows:

1. **Creation** — It is **deliberately** planned and created by management.
2. **Purpose** — It is created **to achieve the organisational goals** like productivity, profitability, efficiency, survival and growth.
3. **Structure** — It has a clear and well-defined structure which is **pyramid-shaped** and shows hierarchy of authority.
4. **Authority** — The authority in formal organisation is **positional** in the sense that it is earned by virtue of position in the formal organisation structure.
5. **Degree of Flexibility** — It is **more rigid** in the sense that it prescribes the manner in which the members are expected to behave and any deviation from the prescribed behaviour is not allowed.
6. **Use of Communication** — It makes more use of **formal** communication.
7. **Chain of Command** — It follows **official chain** of command.
8. **Leadership** — Managers are leaders **by virtue of their superior positions**.
9. **Membership** — Every individual belongs to **one work group** only and works under one superior.

INFORMAL ORGANISATION

Meaning of Informal Organisation

An informal organisation is a system of social relations, which emerges on its own in a natural manner within the formal organisation to meet the cultural and social needs of the members of the organisation.

An informal organisation does not have a clear and well-defined structure because it is a complex network of social relations among members.

Members of formal organisation interact or communicate among themselves while performing the duties assigned to them and develop friendly relations and form small social groups to meet the social and cultural needs. Thus, the network of these social groups, called an informal organisation, emerges on its own in a natural manner within the formal organisation. Since the informal organisation emerges within the formal organisation, the informal organisation is considered to be a part of the formal organisation.

An informal organisation is a part of formal organisation because informal organisation originates from and within the formal organisation to meet the social and cultural needs of the workers.

An organisation is *neither* totally formal *nor* totally informal but a combination of both the aspects. Both the formal and the informal organisations co-exist together. One cannot be separated from the other since both are related to each other. Both the types of organisation affect and are affected by each other.

Characteristics of an Informal Organisation

The characteristics of an informal organisation are as follows:

1. **Creation** — It emerges **on its own** in a natural manner as a result of social interactions among people.

2. **Purpose** — It emerges **to meet the social and cultural needs** of the members of the organisation.

3. **Structure** — It does **not have** a clear and **well-defined structure** because it is a complex network of social relations among the members.

4. **Authority** — The authority in an informal organisation is **personal** and is given by group members.

5. **Degree of Flexibility** — It is **more flexible** in the sense that standards of behaviour are not officially prescribed but are evolved by mutual consent of group members. Deviation from the mutually agreed behaviour is allowed to some extent.

6. **Use of Grapevine** — It makes more use of **informal channels** of communication (which are popularly known as 'Grapevine'). Informal communication is faster than formal communication but the greatest danger is that it may give rise to rumours. Rumours may prove to be detrimental to the interests of the organisation.

7. **Chain of Command** — It **may or may not follow official chain** of command.

8. **Leadership** — Leaders are **chosen voluntarily** by the group members. An informal leader may or may not be the superior under whom the group members are working.

9. **Membership** — An individual **can be** a member **of more than one group** according to his choice. He may be a leader in one group and a follower in another.

Why does informal organisation exist within the framework of formal organisation?

Informal organisation exist within the framework of formal organisation because of the following reasons:

1. Informal organsiation arises due to natural desires of organisation members.

2. Informal organisation originates from within the formal organisation to meet the cultural needs.

3. Informal organisation satisfies social needs. Organisational members have need for friendships and for social interactions which give them social satisfaction.

4. Formal organisation does not always provide an opportunity to members to exchange personal views and experiences. Informal organisation emerge to exchange personal views and experiences.

5. Informal organisation is a source of getting feedback.

DISTINCTION BETWEEN FORMAL AND INFORMAL ORGANISATION

Formal organisation and informal organisation can be distinguished as follows:

Basis of Distinction	Formal Organisation	Informal Organisation
1. Meaning	It is an **official structure** of activities, roles and authority relationship which is deliberately planned and executed by management for achieving organisational goals.	It is a **system of social relations** which emerges on its own in a natural manner within the formal organisation to meet the social and cultural needs of the members of the organisation.
2. Formation	It is created **deliberately**.	It emerges **on its own** as a result of social interactions among people.
3. Purpose	It is created **to achieve organisational goals**.	It emerges **to meet the social and cultural** needs of the members of the organisation.
4. Regidity vs flexibility	It is **more rigid** in the sense that deviation from standard behaviour is not allowed.	It is **more flexible** in the sense that deviation from the mutually agreed behaviour is allowed to some extent.
5. Structure	It **has a clear and well-defined** structure which is pyramid shaped.	It does **not have a clear and well-defined structure** because it is a complex network of social relations among the members.
6. Standards of behaviour and performance	Standards of behaviour and performance are **prescribed by management**.	Standards of behaviour and performance are **evolved by mutual consent** among members.
7. Use of communication	It makes more use of **formal** communication.	It makes more use of **informal** communication which is very fast but the greatest danger is that it may give rise to rumours.

8. Leadership	Managers are leaders **by virtue of** their superior **positions**.	Leaders are **chosen voluntarily** by the members of organisation. An informal leader may or may not be the superior.
9. **Authority**	The authority in formal organisation is **positional**.	The authority in an informal organisation is **personal**.
10. **Part of each other**	It is **not a part** of informal organisation.	It is a **part of** formal organisation.
11. **Official Chain of command**	It **follows** official chain of command.	It **may or may not** follow official chain of command.
12. **Membership**	Every individual belongs to **one work group** only and works under one superior only.	An individual can be a member of **more than one group** according to his choice. He may be a leader in one group and a follower in another group.

Illustration Name the type of organisation in which:

(a) Friendly relationships exist among the members.

(b) Official relationships exist among the members.

(c) Unplanned relationships exist among the members.

(d) Officially, hierarchy relationships exist among the members.

(e) Managers are leaders by virtue of their superior positions.

(f) Leaders are chosen voluntarily by members.

(g) Unity of command is strictly followed.

(h) Unity of command is not observed in general.

Ans. (a) Informal organisation, (b) Formal orgnisation, (c) Informal organisation, (d) Formal organisation, (e) Formal organisation, (f) Informal organisation, (h) Formal organisation, (i) Informal organisation.

PRINCIPLES OF ORGANISATION

Principles of organisation are the guidelines for planning an efficient organisation structure. Management principles are the guidelines for the managers for performing their managerial functions of planning, organising, directing and controlling in an effective manner. The management thinkers such as Henry Fayol, Frederick Taylor, Lyndall Urwick have suggested various principles of organisation. The important principles of organisation have been shown below:

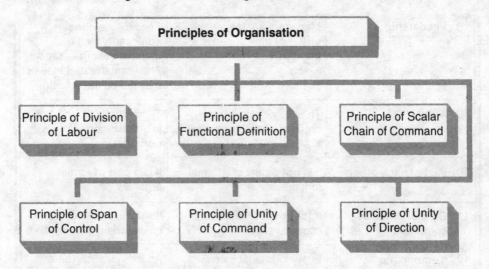

Let us discuss the principles of organisation one by one:

1. **Principle of Division of Labour** — According to this principle, the entire work in the organisation should be divided into specific jobs and a specific job should be given to an individual. Such an individual specialises in the specific job assigned by performing that job on repetitive basis. Such specialisation brings about internal economies in the business such as increase in productivity and quality. This principle is applicable to both managerial and non-managerial work. Over specialisation should be avoided because it may result in loss of motivation among the personnel when the jobs become monotonous and boring.

2. **Principle of Functional Definition** — According to this principle, the functions which are required to be performed by an individual, should be so well defined that there is no overlapping of functions. More specifically, this principle enables to know what is expected from them as members of the group.

3. **Principle of Scalar Chain of Command (or Scalar Principle)** — Scalar chain of command means a stepwise chain of authority. Authority is the right to decide, direct and co-ordinate. According to this principle, *"there must be an unbroken chain of authority running from the top to the bottom of the organisation."* Authority relationships are said to be scalar when subordinates (e.g., supervisors) report to their immediate superiors (e.g., departmental managers) who report as subordinates to their superiors (e.g., production manager). Thus, each manager is superior to a manager below him but he is subordinate to his own superior. This has been demonstrated below:

Scalar Chain of Command ↓ Superior subordinate relationship →	Superior to . . .	Subordinate to . . .
Chief Executive	Marketing Manager	Board of Directors
Marketing Manager	Sales Manager	Chief Executive
Sales Manager	Sales Officer	Marketing Manager
Sales Officer	Salesman	Sales Manager
Salesman	—	Sales Officer

4. **Principle of Span of Control** — The term 'span of control' is also known as 'span of management' or 'span of supervision'. It refers to the number of subordinates which a manager can effectively supervise. According to the principle of span of control 'the number of subordinates directly reporting to a superior should be limited so as to make supervision and control effective'. In other words, no manager should be required to supervise more candidates than he can effectively manage within the limits of available time and his ability.

Narrow span versus wide span — The span of control should *neither* be too narrow *nor* too wide. An ideal span must be selected after considering the merits and demerits of narrow and wide spans.

Narrow span — In a narrow span, there are only a limited number of subordinates under the manager. It permits more effective and close supervision of subordinates. It results in multiple levels of management. The process of communication takes larger time because it has to pass through a larger number of levels of management. A narrow span has been demonstrated below:

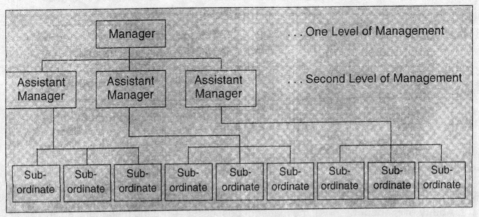

Explanation — A manager instead of directly supervising subordinates, is supervising only three assistant managers who in turn are supervising three subordinates each.

Wide span — In a wide span, there are larger number of subordinates under the manager. It permits only general supervision due to larger number of subordinates under the manager. It results in fewer levels of management. The process of communication takes shorter time because it has to pass through a fewer number of levels of management. The wide span has been demonstrated below:

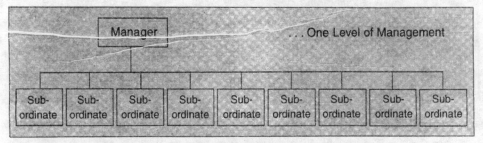

Explanation — One manager is directly supervising nine subordinates.

DISTINCTION BETWEEN NARROW SPAN AND WIDE SPAN

Narrow span and wide span can be distinguished as follows:

Basis of Distinction	Narrow Span	Wide Span
1. **No. of subordinates**	There are only a **limited number** of subordinates under a manager.	There are a **larger number** of subordinates under manager.
2. **Supervision**	It permits **close** supervision.	It permits only a **general** supervision.
3. **Level of management**	It results in **multiple** levels of management.	It results in **fewer** levels of management.
4. **Process of communication**	The process of communication **takes longer time**.	The process of communication **takes shorter time**.

Ideal span of control — Theoretically, a limit of four at higher levels and eight to twelve subordinates at lower levels was used to be considered as an ideal span of control but practically an ideal span depends on a number of factors. Some important factors are discussed below:

Factors	Conditions Suitable for Wide Span	Conditions Suitable for Narrow Span
1. **Nature of work**	If the work is simple and of repetitive nature	If the work requires close supervision
2. **Ability of manager**	If the manager possesses leadership qualities, decision-making ability and communication skill in greater degree	If the manager's ability to supervise is limited

3. **Ability of subordinates**	If the subordinates are trained persons who have acquired experience in the job and have sense of obligation and good judgement	If the subordinates are fresh or less trained persons
4. **Availability of time**	If the manager (e.g., middle or lower manager) have sufficient time for supervision	If the manager (e.g., top manager) have less time for supervision

5. **Principle of Unity of Command** — According to this principle, a subordinate should receive order from one superior only and should be accountable to that superior from whom he receives order. In other words, every employee should have only one boss. This principle enables everyone to know from whom he has to receive the instructions and to whom he has to give instructions.

Objectives — The adjectives of Unity of Command principle are as follows:

(i)   to avoid conflict among supervisors regarding who should give the instructions;

(ii)   to avoid confusion among subordinates regarding whose instructions should be followed;

(iii) to fix responsibility for mistakes.

Diagram — Unity and multiplicity of command and subordinate relationship have been shown below:

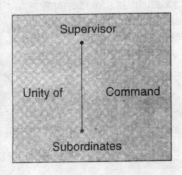

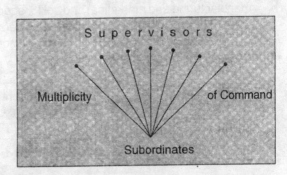

6. **Principle of Unity of Direction** — According to this principle, there should be one head and one plan for a group of activities having the same objectives. This principle emphasises the importance of common goals being pursued by all in a group activity under the direction of one head. This principle promotes smooth co-ordination of activities, efforts and resources.

In addition to the above six principles of organisation, there are a few more principles which have been discussed in the latter part of this chapter.

ADMINISTRATIVE ORGANISATIONS

Meaning of an Administrative Organisation

An administrative organisation refers to an organisation in which the tasks or functions to be carried out in order to achieve its goals, the roles of various managerial positions, and the authority relationships among them are clearly laid down at all levels of management. It may be noted that an administrative organisation refers to the overall structure of an organisation and not of any particular unit or department within it.

Types of Administrative Organisations

Broadly, all administrative organisations are classified under the following three categories:

Let us discuss t

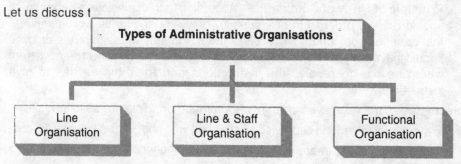

(a) **Line Organisations** — The line organisation refers to an organisation in which only one form of authority (viz. line authority) exists. Line authority refers to the direct authority of a manager over his subordinates. Under this form of organisation, departments are created only for basic activities (like manufacturing and marketing) and not for specialised activities (like recruitment, selection, training and development of personnel, accounting, legal, public relations). Line organisation has been demonstrated below:

Features — Following are the main features of a line organisation:

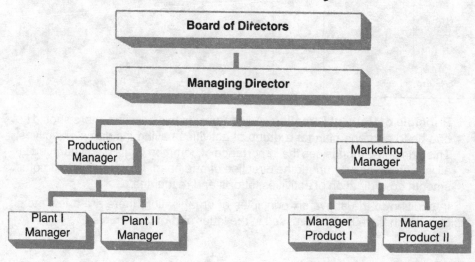

1.   *Simplicity* — It is a **simple** type of organisation.

2.   *Form of authority* — In line organisation, only **one** form of authority(i . e . , line authority) exists.

3.   *Creation of departments* — Departments are created only for **basic activities** like manufacturing and marketing.

4.   *Degree of specialisation* — There is **low** degree of specialisation because the specialised activities are not specifically recognised.

5.   *Workload of manager* — The workload of managers is **higher** because each line manager has to handle both basic activities and specialised activities.

6.   *Principle of unity of command* — Principle of unity of command is strictly **observed** in line organisation.

7.   *Economy* — It is **economical** to operate and maintain because managers employed are generalists.

Merits of Line Organisation — Following are the merits of Line Organisation:

1.   *Simplicity* — It is a **simple** type of organisation.

2.   *Principle of unity of command* — Principle of unity of command is strictly **observed** in line organisation.

3.   *Economy* — It is **economical** to operate and maintain because managers employed are generalists.

Demerits of Line Organisation — Following are the demerits of Line Organisation:

1.   *Degree of specialisation* — There is **low** degree of specialisation because the specialised activities are not specifically recognised.

2.   *Workload of manager* — The workload of managers is **higher** because each line manager has to handle both basic activities and specialised activities.

(b)   **Line and Staff Organisation** — The line and staff organisation refers to an organisation in which two forms of authority (viz. line authority and advisory authority) co-exist. Advisory authority means an authority to advise, to support and to serve. Under this form of organisation, departments are created for basic activities as well as specialised activities. However, the role of staff of advisory authority is generally confined to making recommendations and render advice on matters of line management and not to make decisions relating to organisational operations and activities. Line and staff organisation has been demonstrated below:

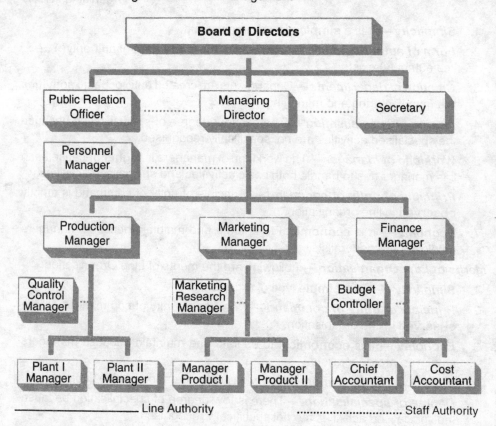

_____ Line Authority   .... Staff Authority

Features — Following are the features of a line and staff organisation:

1. **Complexity** — It is a **more complex** type of organisation than a line organisation.

2. **Forms of authority** — **Two** forms of authority i.e. line authority and advisory authority co exist.

3. **Creation of departments** — Departments are created **both for basic activities and specialised activities**.

4. **Degree of specialisation** — There is **moderate** degree of specialisation because the specialised activities are specifically recognised.

5. **Workload of managers** — The workload of managers is **moderate** because each manager has to handle *either* basic activities *or* specialised activities.

6. **Principle of unity of command** — The principle of unity of command is **observed to a great extent**.

7. **Economy** — It is **expensive** to operate and maintain because of employment of specialists.

Merits of Line & Staff Organisation — The merits of Line & Staff Organisation are as under:

1. **Degree of specialisation** — There is **moderate** degree of specialisation because the specialised activities are specifically recognised.

2. *Workload of managers* — The workload of managers is **moderate** because each manager has to handle *either* basic activities *or* specialised activities.

3. *Principle of unity of command* — The principle of unity of command is **observed to a great extent**.

Demerits of Line & Staff Organisation — The demerits of Line & Staff Organisation are as under:

1. *Complexity* — It is a **more complex** type of organisation than a line organisation.

2. *Expensive* — It is **expensive** to operate and maintain because of employment of specialists.

CONFLICT BETWEEN LINE AND STAFF

The main drawback of line and staff organisation is the conflict between line and staff. The important causes of line and staff conflict as reported by linemen and staff men are discussed below:

Causes of Conflict Reported by Linemen	Causes of Conflict Reported by Staff Men
1. Staff men encroach upon linemen's authority and try to tell them how to do their work.	1. Linemen do not make a proper use of staff men's services.
2. Staff men recommend a cause of action which is not practical.	2. Linemen lack authority to implement their ideas.
3. Staff men have the tendency to take credit for the decisions which prove successful.	3. Linemen generally resist new ideas given by staff men.
4. Staff men have the tendency to lay the blame on linemen for the decisions which do not prove successful.	4. Linemen feel that asking for the advice is admitting defeat.

How to remove the conflict between Line and Staff

The following steps are suggested to remove the conflict between line and staff:

1. The limits of line and staff authority should be laid down clearly.
2. Linemen should be made responsible for the implementation of various decisions.
3. Staff men should be made responsible only for providing advice and service to the linemen.
4. Linemen should state reasons for not accepting the advice of staff men.
5. Staff men should not consider it as a prestige issue if sometimes their advice is not followed.
6. Staff men should try to appreciate the practical difficulties in implementing their new ideas.

(c) **Functional Organisation** — The functional organisation refers to an organisation in which line authority, staff authority and functional authority exist together. Functional authority is a limited form of line authority given to a manager over certain specific specialised activities under the normal supervision of managers belonging to other departments. For example, in a functional organisation, personnel manager is given a limited line authority to ensure that personnel policies are observed in all the departments throughout the organisation. This limited line authority is known as functional authority.

Under functional organisations various activities of the organisation are classified according to certain functions (like production, marketing, finance, personnel) and are put under the charge of functional specialists. The subordinates receive instructions not from one superior but from several functional specialists. Thus, subordinates are accountable to different functional specialists for the performance of different functions. A functional organisation has been demonstrated below:

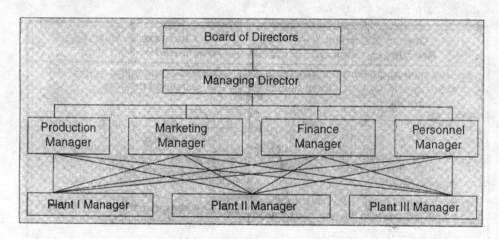

Explanation — The line of authority is diagonal because each functional manager has authority over his function wherever it is performed.

Features — Following are the main features of functional organisation:

1. *Complexity* — It is a **more complex** type of organisation than the line organisation and the line and staff organisation.

2. ***Forms of authority*** — **Three** forms of authority (i.e., line authority, advisory authority and functional authority) exist together.

3. ***Creation of departments*** — Departments are created. **for basic and specialised activities**.

4. ***Degree of specialisation*** — There is **high** degree of specialisation because staff specialists in addition to their advisory authority are also entrusted with a limited line authority.

5. ***Workload of manager*** — The workload is **more** for those managers who are entrusted with functional authority in **addition** to their respective authority and less for those managers who have **only line authority or advisory authority**.

6. ***Principle of unity of command*** — This principle is **not** generally **followed** because the subordinates may get instructions not only from his immediate boss but also from bosses in other departments.

7. ***Economy*** — It is very **expensive** to operate and maintain because of employment of those specialists who can exercise functional authority in effective manner.

8. ***Suitability*** — It is suitable **for large enterprises**.

Merits of Functional Organisation — The merits of Functional Organisation are as under:

1. ***Degree of specialisation*** — There is **high** degree of specialisation because staff specialists in addition to their advisory authority are also entrusted with a limited line authority.

2. ***Suitability*** — It is suitable **for large enterprises**.

Demerits of Functional Organisation — The demerits of Functional Organisation are as under:

1. ***Complexity*** — It is a **more complex** type of organisation than the line organisation and the line and staff organisation.

2. ***Workload of manager*** — The workload is **more** for those managers who are entrusted with functional authority in **addition** to their respective authority and less for those managers who have **only line authority or advisory authority**.

3. ***Principle of unity of command*** — This principle is **not** generally **followed** because the subordinates may get instructions not only from his immediate boss but also from bosses in other departments.

4. ***Expensive*** — It is very **expensive** to operate and maintain because of employment of those specialists who can exercise functional authority in effective manner.

DISTINCTION AMONG LINE ORGANISATION, LINE AND STAFF ORGANISATION AND FUNCTIONAL ORGANISATION

Basis of Comparison	Line Organisation	Line and Staff Organisation	Functional Organisation
1. **Simplicity**	It is a **simple** type of organisation.	It is **relatively more complex** type of organisation than line organisation and relatively less complex than the functional organisation.	It is a **more complex** type of organisation than the line organisation and the line and staff organisation.
2. **Suitability**	It is suitable **for** relatively **small enterprises**.	It is suitable **for medium enterprises**.	It is suitable **for large enterprises**.
3. **Degree of specialisation**	There is **low** degree of specialisation since the specialised activities are not specifically recognised.	There is **moderate** degree of specialisation since the specialised activities are specifically recognised.	There is **high** degree of specialisation since staff specialists in addition to their advisory authority are entrusted with a limited line authority.
4. **Workload of managers**	The workload of managers is **higher** because each line manager has to handle both basic and specialised activities.	The workload of managers is **moderate** because each manager has to handle either basic activities or specialised activities.	The workload is **more** for those managers who are entrusted with functional authority in addition to their respective authority and **less** for those managers who have only line authority or advisory authority.
5. **Principle of unity of command**	This principle is **strictly observed**.	This principle is **observed to a great extent**.	This principle is **not generally observed** because one may

			get instructions not only from his immediate boss but also from bosses in other departments.
6. **Economy as to operation and maintenance**	It is **economical** to operate and maintain because of generalist managers.	It is **expensive** to operate and maintain because of employment of specialists.	It is **very expensive** to operate and maintain because of employment of specialists who can exercise functional authority in effective manner.
7. **Forms of authority**	Only **one** form of authority (viz. line authority) exists.	**Two** forms of authority (viz. line authority and advisory authority) co-exist.	**Three** forms of authority (viz. line authority, advisory authority and functional authority) exist together.
8. **Creation of departments**	Departments are created only **for basic activities**.	Departments are created **both for basic and specialised activities**.	Departments are created **both for basic and specialised activities**.

The line organisation, line and staff organisation and functional organisation can be distinguished as under:

Illustration Name the type of organisation in which

(a)   the principle of unity of command is strictly followed;

(b)   the principle of unity of command does not hold good;

(c)   the workload of some managers is more and of some others less;

(d)   the workload for all mangers is more;

(e)   it is very expensive to operate;

(f)   it is economical to operate.

Ans.: (a) Line oganisation, (b) Functional organisation, (c) Functional organisation, (d) Line organisation, (e) Functional organisation, (f) Line organisation.

Illustration Which type of organisation is more suitable in the following cases:

(a)   when the work is of routine nature;

(b)   when the business is carried at a large scale;

(c)   when the subordinates and operations are less in numbers;

(d)   when a high degree of specialisation is required.

Ans.: (a) Line organisation, (b) Line and staff/functional organisation, (c) Line organisation, (d) Line and staff/functional organisation.

Illustration The owner of a small factory producing simple toys for children, has decided to expand his business by setting up a medium scale unit now to produce mechanical toys and subsequently having a large production unit for complex electronic play things. He wants you to suggest what type of administrative organisation will be most suitable for his present and proposed units of production and why?

Ans.: For present unit, line organisation is most suitable. It is so because the factory is small and produces simple toys and the nature of operations must be simple. Line organisation is the most suitable when nature of operations is simple and number of operations are limited.

For proposed unit, line and staff organisation will be most suitable. It is so because in the proposed unit production will be on large scale and more complex. Line and staff organisation has two types of managers — line managers and staff managers. Line managers get the benefit of specialised knowledge of staff managers who are experts and specialists. Line and staff organisation provides greater scope for the growth and expansion of business in future.

DELEGATION OF AUTHORITY

Meaning of Delegation of Authority

As an organisation grows in size and the manager's job increases beyond his personal capacity, it becomes impossible for the manager to exercise all the authority for making decisions in an effective manner. The only way the manager can achieve more is through delegation. The concept of delegation is based on the principle of division of labour.

To delegate means to grant or confer.

What is granted or conferred — It is the authority which is granted or conferred. Authority is the sum of powers and rights to perform the tasks assigned.

Delegator — The person who grants authority is known as *'delegator or superior or manager'*.

Delegatee — The person to whom the authority is granted is known as *'delegatee or subordinate'*.

Thus, delegation is a superior's act of assigning formal authority and responsibility to his subordinate to perform the tasks assigned. Delegation enables subordinates to function independently without reference to the supervisor but within the limits set by the supervisor and the normal framework of the organisational objectives, policies, rules, and procedures. The manager's success lies in his ability to multiply himself by training his subordinates and sharing his authority and responsibility with them. Each manager derives authority granted by his superior and grants authority to his subordinates. This has been demonstrated shown below:

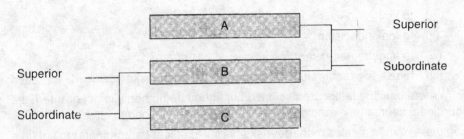

Distinction between Delegation and Work Assignment

Delegation differs from work assignment. Delegation constitutes a master-agent relationship while work assignment constitutes a master-servant relationship. An employee's work assignment may be reflected in his job description while delegated duties may not form the part of the employee's normal duties.

Time when the Authority must be Delegated

There is a limit to the number of persons a manager can effectively supervise. Once this limit is passed, the manager must delegate authority to his subordinates who will make decisions within the areas of their assigned duties.

ELEMENTS OF DELEGATION

There are three elements of delegation shown below:

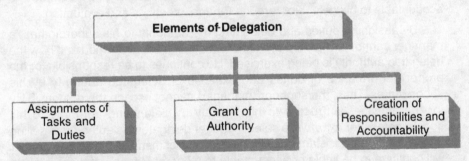

Let us discuss the elements of delegation one by one:

1. **Assignment of Tasks or Duties** — the first step in delegation is to assign the tasks to the subordinates. Before the tasks are assigned, the delegator (superior) must —

    (i) determine the results expected from subordinates;

    (ii) identify the tasks to be assigned;

    (iii) define the tasks to be assigned.

Example — A sales manager asks his sales Officer (subordinate) to set up a sales office. Here, the sales manager must explain the objectives, the sales territory etc.

2. **Grant of Authority** — The second step in delegation is to grant the necessary authority to subordinates to perform the tasks assigned to them. Authority is the sum of powers and rights to perform the tasks assigned. Grant of authority implies giving the right to subordinates —

    (i)   to act;

    (ii) to make decision;

    (iii) to acquire necessary resources;

    (iv) to use the resources, for the performance of tasks assigned.

Where only the tasks are assigned but adequate authority is not granted, the subordinate cannot be expected to perform the task assigned to him.

Example — When a sales manager asks his sales officer (subordinate) to set up a sales office. Here, the sales manager must give him the right to acquire and use necessary resources for setting up a sales office.

3.   **Creation of Responsibility and Accountability** — Once the tasks are assigned and authority is granted to subordinates, the delegator creates responsibility and accountability. Responsibility arises out of authority and implies obligation of subordinate to exercise the authority and to complete the tasks assigned to him by his superior. Accountability arises out of responsibility and implies the obligation of subordinate to render an account of the results achieved and bear responsibility in terms of the standards of performance specified. Since the responsibility is fixed to the position, it can *neither* be delegated *nor* shifted to another person. This is also known as the principle of absoluteness of responsibility. The subordinate is always answerable to the superior for the task assigned to him. Thus, the superior can control the performance of his subordinate through accountability. The delegatee is accountable to his delegator through reports, meetings and evaluation.

      By assigning duties and delegating the authority to his subordinates, a manager cannot turn a blind eye to how the duties are performed and how the delegated authority is being exercised. He continues to be responsible for the proper performance of duties and exercise of delegated authority by his subordinates. Thus, the superior (manager) cannot escape the responsibility for the activities entrusted to him merely by delegating authority to his subordinates. *For example*, a sales manager delegates his authority of selling goods to different assistant sales managers or salesmen. But the sales manager will continue to be liable or accountable to General Manager if there is short fall in sales.

Comparison and Contrast among Authority, Responsibility and Accountability

Authority, responsibility and accountability can be compared as under:

1.   Authority is delegated but responsibility is created and accountability is imposed.

2.   Authority flows downwards but responsibility and accountability flow upwards.

3.   Responsibility arises out of authority while accountability arises out of responsibility.

4.   Authority can be delegated but responsibility and accountability cannot be delegated.

The relationship between authority, responsibility and accountability can be viewed as under:

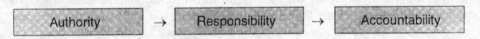

Authority → Responsibility → Accountability

IMPORTANCE OF DELEGATION

The importance of delegation of authority arises from the benefits shown below:

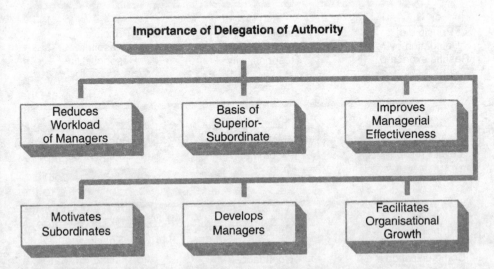

Let us discuss the benefits of delegation of authority one by one:

1. **Reduces workload of Managers** — Delegation reduces the workload of managers because managers share their workload with their subordinates through delegation.

2. **Basis of superior-subordinate relations** — Delegation of authority provides a basis of superior-subordinate relations. The flow of authority from top level to lower level is directed and resulted by the process of delegation.

3. **Improves managerial effectiveness** — Delegation improves managerial effectiveness because delegation of authority for routine works leaves the manager free to concentrate on important matters which need his attention.

4. **Motivates subordinates** — Delegation motivates subordinates to utilise their abilities and skill to do work assigned to them.

5. **Develops Managers** — Delegation acts as a source of development of managers because through delegation subordinates can be developed and trained to take up higher responsibilities.

6. **Facilitates organisational growth** — Delegation facilitates organisational growth because additional workload due to expansion and growth is assumed by creating more managerial jobs through delegation.

PRINCIPLES OF DELEGATION

There are certain principles which may be followed as guidelines for effective delegation. These principles have been shown below:

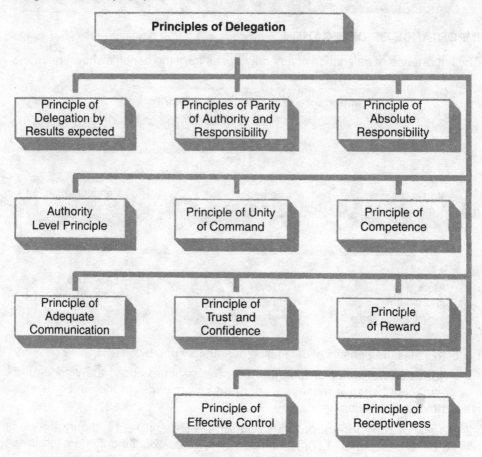

Let us discuss the principles of delegation one by one:

1. **Principle of delegation by results expected** — According to this principle, the delegated authority must be in accordance with the results expected from subordinates. In other words, the delegator must determine the results expected from subordinates, identify the tasks to be assigned, define the tasks to be assigned, communicate the results expected and tasks to the delegatee and must ensure that the delegatee has understood the results expected and tasks.

2. **Principle of parity of authority and responsibility** — According to this principle, the authority delegated to a subordinate must be equal to his responsibility. In other words, one must not be greater than the other.

3. **Principle of absolute responsibility** — According to this principle, responsibility can *neither* be delegated *nor* be shifted to another person. In

other words, the responsibility of the subordinate to his superior for performance of the delegated duties is absolute and cannot be shifted. A superior cannot escape from his responsibility for any default on the part of his subordinates.

4. **Authority level principle** — According to this principle, the managers should consider only those matters on which they have authority to take decisions at their levels and should refer to their superiors all matters on which they do not have authority to take decisions and, at the same time, should not unduly interfere with the decision-making authority of subordinates.

5. **Principle of unity of command** — According to this principle, each subordinate should have only one boss to whom he should be accountable to avoid confusion and conflict.

6. **Principle of competence** — According to this principle, the person selected as a delegatee must be competent for the tasks assigned to him.

7. **Principle of adequate communication** — According to this principle, there should be free flow of information between superior and subordinate to enable the latter to understand correctly the nature of the tasks assigned and authority delegated and to take decisions.

8. **Principle of trust and confidence** — According to this principle, there must be a feeling of trust and confidence between the delegator and delegatee.

9. **Principle of reward** — According to this principle, effective delegation and proper exercise of authority should be rewarded. A rational system of reward would act as an incentive to the subordinate to willingly assume authority and responsibility.

10. **Principle of effective control** — According to this principle, the delegator should develop and use effective control system to ensure that the authority delegated is properly used.

11. **Principle of receptiveness** — According to this principle, the delegator must be receptive enough to accommodate the ideas of his subordinates.

Illustration The production manager asks the foreman to achieve a target production of 200 units per day. But he does not give him the adequate authority to requisition tools and materials from the stores department. Can the production manager blame the foreman if he is not able to achieve the desired target? Explain briefly the principle relating to the situation.

Ans.: Decision: No, the production manager cannot blame the foreman if he is not able to achieve the desired target.

The relevant principle is the 'principle of parity of authority and responsibility'.

This principle states that adequate authority should be granted by the superior to the subordinate to complete the work assigned.

Illustration The marketing manager of an organisation has been asked to achieve target sales of 100 generators per day. He delegates the tasks to 10 sales managers working under him. Two of them could not achieve their respective targets. Is the marketing manager responsible? Briefly explain the relevant principle in support of your answer.

Ans.: Decision: The marketing manager is responsible for the failure of two sales managers to achieve their respective target.

Principle relating to situation — The relevant principle applicable in the case is the '**principle of absolute responsibility**'.

This principle states that while a manager delegates his authority to his subordinate, he cannot delegate the responsibility. Responsibility is absolute and he cannot escape it.

BARRIERS TO EFFECTIVE DELEGATION

The reluctance of the superior to delegate and the reluctance or avoidance of the subordinates to accept delegation are the major barriers to delegation. These barriers have been shown below:

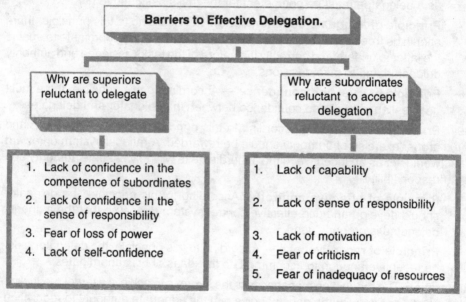

Let us discuss the barriers to effective delegation one by one:

Why are Superiors Reluctant to Delegate

Superiors are something reluctant to delegate authority due to the following reasons.

1. **Lack of confidence in the competence of subordinates** — A superior is reluctant to delegate authority when he does not have confidence in the capability and competence of subordinates and considers that he himself can do the job better.

2. **Lack of confidence in the sense of responsibility of subordinates** — A superior is reluctant to delegate authority when he does not have confidence in the sense of responsibility of his subordinates.

3. **Fear of loss of power** — A superior is reluctant to delegate authority when he feels insecure and fears that if the subordinates perform well he may lose his powers.

4. **Lack of self-confidence** — A superior is often reluctant to delegate if he lacks self-confidence.

Why are Subordinates Reluctant to Accept Delegation

Subordinates are reluctant to accept delegation due to the following reasons:

1. **Lack of capability** — A subordinate is reluctant to accept delegation when he does not have capability to perform the task to be assigned.

2. **Lack of sense of responsibility** — A subordinate is reluctant to accept delegation when he feels that he lacks sense of responsibility.

3. **Lack of motivation** — A subordinate is reluctant to accept delegation when there is lack of motivation to assume authority and responsibility.

4. **Fear of criticism** — A subordinate is reluctant to accept delegation when there is fear of criticism for inefficiency or mistakes.

5. **Fear of inadequacy of resources** — A subordinate is reluctant to accept delegation when there is fear of inadequacy of necessary resources for completion of the task and uncooperative attitude of the delegator.

HOW TO MAKE DELEGATION EFFECTIVE

Delegation is only a technique of management. It is a part of the attitude of business itself. As such, what is necessary is the atmosphere of giving and taking responsibility in the organization by creating an atmosphere of mutual trust and confidence. Effectiveness of delegation is governed largely by the general attitude of business which depends on various factors like management policies, professional outlook and willingness on the part of superior to delegate authority and the competence as well as willingness of the subordinates to accept delegation. The delegation may be made effective by taking the various measures shown below:

Let us discuss the measures to make delegation effective one by one:

1. **Create proper organizational climate** — An atmosphere of giving and taking responsibility in the organization should be created to make delegation effective.

2. **Create mutual trust and confidence** — An atmosphere of mutual trust and confidence between superior and subordinate should be created to make delegation effective.

3. **Provide necessary training** — The necessary training should be provided to the subordinates to perform the tasks to be assigned and to use the authority to be delegated.

4. **Motivate subordinate** — The subordinate should be motivated to assume authority and responsibility.

5. **Define objectives** — The delegator should establish clear objectives so that the delegatee may know what is expected from him. In other words, delegatee should know what he has to achieve.

6. **Define authority and responsibility** — The delegator should grant the adequate authority (e.g., to act, to make decisions, to acquire and use necessary resources), to the subordinates to perform the tasks assigned to them. It must be ensured that authority is equal to the responsibility. In other words, one must not be greater than the other.

7. **Improve communication** — There should be free flow of information between the superior and the subordinate to enable the latter to take decisions and understand the nature of task to be completed and authority to be used.

8. **Establish adequate controls** — An adequate system of control should be established to enable the delegator to maintain accountability.

CONCEPT OF CENTRALISATION AND DECENTRALISATION

Meaning of Centralisation of Authority

Centralisation of authority means concentration or retention of authority for decision-making at higher or top level of management. An organisation is said to be highly centralised if top management retains absolute authority for making almost all decisions on the functioning of the organisation. According to Henry Fayol, "Everything that goes to reduce the importance of the subordinates' role in the organisation is the centralisation." In centralisation, power and discretion are concentrated in a few executives. Absolute centralisation is untenable because it would mean that subordinates have no duties, power or authority. Centralisation may be essential in small organisations to survive in a highly competitive world. But as the organisation grows in size and complexity, there arises the need to reduce the burden of the top executives or, in other words, the need for decentralisation arises.

Meaning of Decentralisation of Authority

Decentralisation of authority refers to systematic delegation or dispersal of authority at all levels of management and in all departments of the organisation. An organisation is said to be decentralised if top management retains authority for taking major decisions and framing policies and for overall control and coordination of the organisation. At the same time the middle and lower managements are entrusted with operating authority for taking decisions on tasks assigned to them.

According to Henry Fayol, "Everything that goes to increase the importance of the subordinates' role in the organisation is decentralisation." Decentralisation is basically the transference of decisionmaking authority from a higher level to a lower level.

Example: Consider an organisation where all leave applications are processed by G. M. He feels over-burdened and transfers this authority of leave processing to Purchase Manager. This is an example of Delegation of Authority.

If the Purchase Manager also feel over-burdened and requests the G. M. to give him some relief, G.M. may disperse this authority to various heads throughout the organisation and instruct them to process the leave applications of their respective departmental subordinates. This is an example of how delegated authority may be extended to decentralised authority.

DISTINCTION BETWEEN CENTRALISATION AND DECENTRALISATION OF AUTHORITY

Centralisation and Decentralisation can be distinguished as under:

Bases of Distinction	Centralisation	Decentralisation
1. Meaning	It refers to centralisation or retention of authority for decision-making at higher or top level of management.	It refers to the systematic delegation or dispersal of authority at all levels of management and in all departments of organisation.
2. Authority of top management	Top management retains absolute authority for making almost all decisions on the functioning of organisation.	Top management retains authority for making major decisions and framing major policies and for overall control and co-ordination of the organisation.
3. Authority of middle and lower management	Middle and lower management is not entrusted with operational authority for taking decisions on the tasks assigned to them.	Middle and lower management is entrusted with operational authority for taking decisions on the tasks assigned to them.
4. Freedom of action	Managers have less freedom of action since they are kept under close supervision by their supervisors.	Managers have more freedom of action since they are not kept under close supervision by their supervisors.
5. Flexibility	It does not provide greater flexibility to tackle problems quickly and competently.	It provides greater flexibility to tackle problems quickly and competently.
6. Significance	It loses its significance in case of expansion of activities, coping with complexities of changes in technological competitive and other conditions in the environment.	It is necessary to prepare the organisation for handling major expansion of its activities and to cope with complexities of changes in the technological, competitive and other conditions in the environment.

DISTINCTION BETWEEN DELEGATION AND DECENTRALISATION

Although decentralisation is closely related to delegation, still delegation of authority is different from decentralisation of authority in the following respects:

Bases of Distinction	Delegation of Authority	Decentralisation of Authority
1. **Scope**	It involves entrusting the authority by a manager to his immediate subordinates in a work unit.	It involves systematic delegation of authority at all levels and in all functions of the organisation. It is an extension of delegation to the lowest level in the organisation. Thus, it is **wider** in scope and consequence than delegation.
2. **Significance**	It is a **routine** act of managing to get things done through subordinates.	It is a **vital decision** with a view to prepare the organisation for handling major expansion of its activities and for coping with changing conditions of environment.
3. **Freedom of action**	Subordinates have **less** freedom of action since they are kept under close supervision by their superiors.	Managers have **greater** freedom of action since they are not kept under close supervision by their superiors.
4. **Necessity**	It is an **essential** feature of organising and managing since an organisation cannot function without delegation of authority.	It is **not** an **essential** feature of organising and managing since an organisation can function without decentralisation.

IMPORTANCE OF DECENTRALISATION

The importance of decentralisation arises due to the following benefits:

1. **Reduces the burden of managers** — Decentralisation is required to reduce the burden of managers when it increases due to increase in the size and complexity of the organisation.

2. **Facilitates growing and complex organisation** — Decentralisation is needed when the organisation grows in size and becomes complex.

3. **Facilitates diversification** — Decentralisation is needed when organisation wants to diversify its activities.

4. **Facilitates quick decision-making** — Decentralisation facilitates quick decision-making at the action centres.

5. **Facilitates democratic management** — Decentralisation facilitates democratic management where each individual is respected for his inherent worth and constitution.

LIMITATIONS OF DECENTRALISATION

The limitations of decentralisation are discussed below:

1. **Conflict** — Decentralisation encourages the departmental managers to become more department conscious. As a result there may be interdepartmental competition within the organisation, which may result in inter-divisional conflict.

2. **Disintegration** — Decentralisation leads to disintegration of the organisation. Disintegration may bring about the diseconomy of scale with the increase in the overhead expenses of each decentralisation unit.

3. **Not required for specialised services** — Decentralisation is not required for specialised services like research and development, accounting, personnel etc.

4. **Not required for central key areas** — Decentralisation is not required for central key areas like overall organisation objectives, long-term planning, formulation of overall organisation policy, etc.

FACTORS DETERMINING THE DEGREE OF DECENTRALISATION

The degree of decentralisation is determined by several factors discussed below:

1. **Top management philosophy** — The extent to which the authority is to be decentralised depends upon the attitude and philosophy of top management.

2. **Size of organisation** — As the organisation grows in size and complexity, the need for decentralisation tends to increase.

3. **Costs and risk of decentralisation** — The high cost and high risk decisions may be taken at the top level but routine decisions involving low cost and low risk can be taken at lower levels. Thus, decentralisation is influenced by the costs and risk involved in decision-making.

4. **Availability of managerial resources** — The extent to which the authority is to be decentralised depends upon the availability of trained and competent managerial personnel.

5. **External environment** — The degree of decentralisation is also influenced by external environmental factors like tax policies, government controls, unionism, and labour laws.

Degrees of Centralisation and Decentralisation

Decentralisation is a correlate of delegation. To the extent the authority is delegated, the organisation is said to be decentralised. To the extent the authority is not delegated, the organisation is said to be centralised. The degrees of centralisation and decentralisation are shown below:

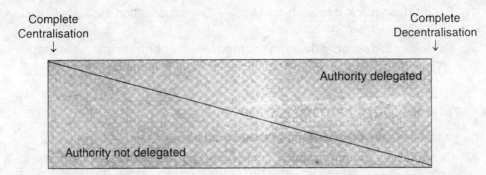

Complete
Centralisation
↓

Complete
Decentralisation
↓

Authority delegated

Authority not delegated

Absolute centralisation is undesirable because it would mean that subordinates have no duties, power or authority. Absolute decentralisation is not possible because managers cannot delegate all their authority. If they do so, their status as managers would cease and their positions could be eliminated.

Neither complete centralisation *nor* complete decentralisation is desirable. What is required is the optimum balance between centralisation and decentralisation. The question before managers is not whether an organisation should be decentralised but to what extent it should remain centralised.

EXERCISES

SHORT ANSWER TYPE QUESTIONS

1. Explain briefly the meaning of 'organising'.
2. Enumerate the steps in the process of organising.
3. What is meant by 'departmentation'?
4. Enumerate the basis of departmentation.
5. Explain briefly the meaning of 'organisational structure'.
6. Give a chart showing organisational structure of a large business enterprise.
7. What is a formal organisation?
8. What is an informal organisation?
9. (a) Enumerate the principles of organisation.
   (b) What is Span of Control?
10. What is meant by an administrative organisation?
11. State the main features of a line organisation.
12. Give any three merits of a line organisation.
13. Give any three demerits of a line organisation.
14. Draw a chart of a line organisation.
15. Give any three merits of a line and staff organisation.
16. Give any three demerits of a line and staff organisation.
17. Draw a chart of a line and staff organisation.

18. Give any three merits of a functional organisation.
19. Give any three demerits of a functional organisation.
20. Draw a chart of a functional organisation.
21. What is delegation of authority?
22. What is centralisation of authority?
23. What is decentralisation of authority?

LONG ANSWER TYPE QUESTIONS

1. Explain briefly the steps in the process of organising.
2. Explain the importance of organising as a function of management.
3. What is a formal organisation? State its essential features.
4. What is an informal organisation? State its essential features.
5. Distinguish between a formal and an informal organisation.
6. Distinguish between formal and informal organisation on the basis of purpose, behaviour of members and communication.
7. Distinguish between formal organisation and informal organisation on the basis of relationship among members, flow of communication and purpose.
8. Differentiate between formal and informal organisation on the basis of formation, purpose, structure and communication.
9. Distinguish between formal and informal organisation on the basis of purpose, mutual relationship among members, flow of authority and flexibility.
10. Briefly describe the principles of organisation.
11. What is span of control? Distinguish between narrow span and wide span. State the conditions suitable for wide span and narrow span.
12. What is meant by a line organisation? State its main characteristics.
13. Explain in brief the merits and demerits of a line organisation.
14. State the circumstances in which the line organisation is more suitable.
15. What is meant by a line and staff organisation? State its main features.
16. In a line and staff organisation, what kind of authority does the legal adviser have? Explain.
17. Describe 'line and staff organisation'. Why is it considered better than line organisation?
18. State the features of line and staff organisation. Mention two of its advantages.
19. Explain in brief the merits and demerits of a line and staff organisation .
20. Distinguish between line organisation and line and staff organisation on the basis of authority, type of personnel, nature and specialisation. Give diagrams also.
21. Distinguish between 'line' and 'line and staff' organisation.
22. What is functional organisation? State its essential features.
23. Explain in brief the merits and demerits of functional organisation.
24. State the circumstances in which functional organisation is more suitable.

25. Why does the principle of command not hold good in the case of functional organisation?

26. Distinguish between line organisation and functional organisation.

27. Distinguish between line organisation and functional organisation on the basis of suitability, specialisation, unity of command and economy.

28. How does functional organisation differ from line and staff organisation?

29. Distinguish between line organisation, line and staff organisation and functional organisation.

30. Briefly explain the elements of delegation.

31. "Delegation of authority is based on the elementary principle of division of work." Explain.

32. "Authority can be delegated but not responsibility." Explain.

33. Explain briefly the principles of delegation.

34. Give the meaning and importance of delegation of authority.

35. Why is it necessary to delegate authority?

36. Why is delegation of authority essential but decentralisation not?

37. Explain the meaning of delegation of authority. How is delegation different from decentralisation?

38. What is delegation of authority? What are the requirements of an effective delegation?

39. What is meant by decentralisation of authority? How is it different from delegation of authority?

40. How are responsibility and authority related?

41. "The concepts of centralisation and decentralisation are related to the concept of delegation." Explain.

42. The marketing manager of an organisation has been asked to achieve a target sales of 100 generators per day. He delegates the task to 10 sales managers working under him. Two of them could not achieve their respective targets. Is the marketing manager responsible? Briefly explain the relevant principle in support of your answer.

43. The production manager asked the foreman to achieve a target production of 200 units per day. But he does not give him the authority to requisition tools and materials from the stores department. Can the production manager blame the foreman if he is not able to achieve the desired target? Explain briefly the principle relating to the situation.

44. Distinguish between decentralisation and delegation on the basis of nature, control, need and responsibility.

45. Distinguish between delegation and decentralisation of authority on the basis of purpose, parties involved and withdrawal of authority.

46. "Line and staff is an obsolete concept." Comment.

47. "Both absolute centralisation and absolute decentralisation are hypothetical concepts." Comment.

48. "Centralisation and decentralisation are mutually dependent." Comment.

20 Staffing

MEANING OF STAFFING FUNCTION

Staffing refers to the managerial function of attracting, acquiring, activating, developing and maintaining human resources for achieving organisational goals efficiently. Staffing also involves upgrading the quality and usefulness of the members of the organisation with a view to get higher performance from them. All types of organisations irrespective of size have to perform staffing function. In small organisations, this function is performed by the members themselves whereas in case of large organisations, this function is performed by 'personnel department' headed by personnel manager to look after human resource planning, recruitment, selection, placement, training etc.

NATURE OF STAFFING FUNCTION

The main characteristics which highlight the nature of staffing function are shown below:

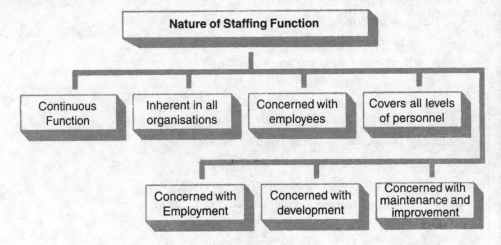

1. **Continuous Function** — Staffing is a continuous function of management and not a one-time function because the organisation's need to retain and maintain its personnel is a never-ending process. Managers have to keep a regular watch on the size and composition of personnel needed by the organisation. They have also to take care of the additional staffing needs when the organisation expands its activities. At any point of time, some people will be leaving, retiring, getting promotions or transferred. The vacancies thus caused have to be filled up.

2. **Inherent in all Organisations** — Staffing function is required in every type of organisation whether it is profit organisation, non-profit organisation, government organisation, non-government organisation, small organisation or large organisation.

3. **Concerned with Employees** — Staffing function is concerned with employees both as individuals and as a group.

4. **Covers all Levels of Personnel** — Staffing function covers all levels of personnel whether blue-collared employees like foreman, craftsman or white-collared employees like officials, managers.

5. **Concerned with Employment** — Staffing function is concerned with employing the right person for the right job.

6. **Concerned with Development of Employees** — Staffing function is concerned with developing the required personnel.

7. **Concerned with Maintenance and Improvement** — Staffing function is concerned with maintaining and improving the competence and performance of the personnel.

IMPORTANCE OF STAFFING FUNCTION

The staffing function derives its importance from the benefits which flow from it. These are discussed below:

1. **Key to Effectiveness of other Functions** — The functions of planning, organising, directing and controlling become non-starters without a manager and other members of the organisation. The effectiveness of the other managerial functions depends on the efficiency with which the staffing function is carried out.

2. **Aids in Building Sound and Strong Organisation** — An organisation is strong to the extent that its members are strong in their abilities, skills and efforts to do things and to get things done.

   Staffing aids in building sound and strong organisation by —

   (a) identifying right people

   (b) including right people to join the organisation and

   (c) creating conditions for their continued association with the organisation.

3. **Avoids Conversion of Human Assets into Human Liabilities** — Staffing function avoids the conversion of human assets into human liabilities by developing, preserving and utilising human resources effectively for the achievement of organisational goals. If human assets are not effectively utilised, they will become burden for the organisation.

4. **Activates Organisation** — Without people or personnel, organisations are empty entities which cannot move a bit towards the achievement of their objectives. It is the staffing function which injects life and action into the organisation and makes its functioning possible. Human resources are considered as the most valuable resources of an enterprise because all the physical factors or assets are of no use and remain idle or inactive unless and until there is competent force of personnel to operate efficiently and effectively.

5. **Facilitates to take Advantage of Opportunities of Growth** — Staffing function facilitates to take advantage of opportunities of growth by hiring, retaining and developing the right quality of people.

STAFFING AS A PART OF HUMAN RESOURCE MANAGEMENT

Staffing is a part of human resource management because staffing is one of the major areas of human resource management.

Meaning of Human Resource Management

Human Resource management is that part of general management which is specifically concerned with the human resources in an organisation. Without human resources, non-human resources (e.g., materials, machines, money) remain idle. To activate non-human resources, the use of human resources is essential. Human Resource management may be defined as the art of procuring, developing and maintaining competent workforce to achieve organisational goals efficiently. Human Resource management aims at relating the people at work with the activities necessary to achieve the organisational goals.

Areas of Human Resource Management

The areas of Human Resource Management can be divided into six major categories as follow:

1. **Planning** — The Human Resource Manager is responsible for determining the quantity and quality of manpower required in different departments and at different levels. This determination is done through a systematic process. For example, man hours required to perform an activity are determined through the techniques of time study, motion study and fatigue study.

2. **Staffing** — The Human Resource Manager is also responsible for recruiting and selecting the prospective employees with the requisite skills, abilities, knowledge and experience to perform the job.

3. **Employee Development** — The Human Resource Manager is also responsible for the training and development of managers and non-managers at all levels. Training is essential for upgrading human knowledge and skills. Training is imported at two stages —

    (a) Pre-Employment; (b) Post-Employment;

    (a) **Pre-Employment Training** — Such training is required to impart specific job skills in order to ensure a proper 'Job Fit'.

    (b) **Post-Employment Training** — Such training is required to upgrade knowledge and skills of employees in term of changing skill requirements, expanding knowledge.

    An organisation will not be able to compete if it does not have a sound training and development programmes.

4. **Employees Maintenance** — The Human Resource Manager also responsible for maintaining an effective work force. He is required to plan and develop the personnel programmes covering the various aspects as given on next page:

Aspects to be covered	Subject Matter of Aspects
1. Safety Aspect	Measures to prevent physical injuries so as to provide safe working conditions
2. Health Aspect	Measure to provide healthy conditions
3. Welfare Aspect	Measures to provide amenities such as housing, canteen, recreation facilities.
4. Industrial Relations Aspect	Measures to negotiate with trade unions, to settle disputes between labour and management.
5. Resolving Aspect	Measures to reduce conflicts among the employees e.g. through effective communication, counselling and guidance.

5. **Formulating Personnel Policies** — The Human Resource Manager is also responsible for formulating personnel policies regarding different issues related to personnel. Such policies should be formulated after taking into consideration the interests of the management and workers.

6. **Providing Specialised Services** — The Human Resource Manager is also responsible for providing specialised services by understanding job evaluation, merit rating and performance evaluation which require specialised knowledge and skill. Job evaluation is the evaluation or rating of jobs to determine the relative job worth (i.e., the position of a job in the job hierarchy) for the purpose of establishing consistent wage rate differentials by objective means. Performance appraisal is a systematic and objective way of judging the relative worth or ability of an employee in performing his task.

RESPONSIBILITY FOR STAFFING

Every organization whether small or large sized has a staffing function to perform. When an organization grows and reaches a certain size, staffing as a separate function takes a distinct shape.

Who perform staffing function?

(a) **In case of Small Organisations** — The responsibility for staffing rests upon the members of the organisation. Staffing function is performed by the concerned manager looking after a specialised function. But it does not mean that line managers do not play any role in personnel function.

(b) **In case of Large Organisations** — Both line managers and staff managers perform staffing function.

   (i) **Line Managers** — Personnel requirements are initiated at the line level. They identify the quantity and quality of the work force required in their specific departments communicate personnel requirements to the personnel department.

They also share the role of Human Resource Department in so far as the maintenance and utilization of the organisation's human resources are concerned.

(ii) **Human Resource Department** — Human Resource department provides specialized staff services to line departments by under taking —

(a) Manpower planning;

(b) Recruitment;

(c) Selection;

(d) Placement;

(e) Training;

(f) Induction/Orientation;

(g) Job Evaluation;

(h) Compensation;

(i) Performance Appraisal;

(j) Labour Relations.

When an organization grows in size, the line managers need the assistance, specialized knowledge and advice of the personnel staff. Human Resource department merely assists, guides and directs the line in the staffing functions. Human Resource department can get the desired results through line departments only when all levels of line management accept their full responsibility and utilize properly the specialized staff services available to them.

Thus, the staffing function is best handled as a shared responsibility between operating (i.e., line) and staff managers.

STEPS INVOLVED IN STAFFING PROCESS

Just like the other managerial functions, the function of staffing may be viewed as a process consisting of certain well-recognised activities. These activities are also called elements. All these elements when arranged sequentially may be regarded as the steps or phases of the staffing process. The activities which make up the process of staffing are shown below:

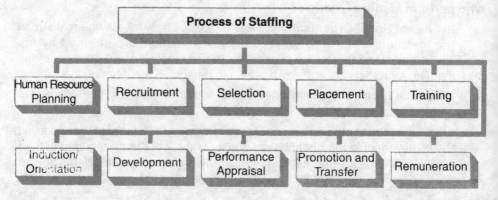

Let us discuss the activities in the process of staffing function in detail.

HUMAN RESOURCE PLANNING

Meaning of Human Resource Planning

Human Resource planning is the process by which an organisation ensures that it has the right number and right quality of people at the right place and at the right time. Two basic human resource planning strategies are staffing and employee development.

Human Resource planning may be defined as the process of forecasting the future manpower requirements, analysing the present manpower resources to determine their adequacy both quantitatively and qualitatively and planning the necessary programmes of recruitment, selection, training, development, motivation and compensation to meet the future human resource requirements.

It is essentially the process of securing the services of qualified people for various positions in the organisation at the right time.

There are two aspects of Human Resource planning which are as follows:

(a) **Quantitative Aspect** — Quantitative analysis is required to determine the quantitative needs of the organisation, i.e., how many people will be needed in the future. Its objective is to ensure a fair number of personnel in each department and at each level. There should not be too high staff or too low staff leading to over-staffing on under-staffing respectively.

(b) **Qualitative Aspect** — Qualitative analysis is required to determine what qualities and characteristics are required for performing a job. Its objective is to get a proper balance between the job requirement and requirement on the part of personnel in terms of qualification, experience and personality orientation.

Thus, qualitative aspect involves job analysis which involves two major aspects — Job Description and Job Specification.

Job Analysis

Meaning — Job analysis is a process of gathering, analysing and synthesizing information regarding the operations, duties and responsibilities of a specific job. There are two major aspects of job analysis — Job Description and Job Specification.

Uses — Job analysis is helpful in various ways under:

(a) It is helpful in human resource planning, recruitment, selection and placement.
(b) It is helpful in developing training programmer.
(c) It is helpful in job evaluation.
(d) It is helpful in performance appraisal.

Job Description

Meaning — Job description is a statement of the duties and responsibilities of a specific job. It contains information —

(a) What is to be done;

(b)   How is to be done;

(c)   Why is to be done.

Basically, it is a summary of contents of a job itself without any reference to names of workers to be associated with the job or the work to be assigned to a particular individual.

Uses — Job description is helpful in various ways as under:

(a)   It provides as basis for assigning work and for guiding and monitoring individual performance.

(b)   It is helpful in human resource planning, recruitment, selection and placement.

(c)   It is helpful in job evaluation.

(d)   It is helpful in developing training and development programme.

(e)   It is helpful in carrying out performance appraisal.

(f)   It is helpful for job specification.

Job Specification

Meaning — Job specification is a statement of minimum qualities which a person should possess to perform the job effectively. The job specification may relate to —

(a)   Aptitude and abilities.

(b)   Personality and related characteristics

(c)   Educational qualification and training

(d)   Experience

(e)   Physical and mental requirements

(f)   Decision making and judgement

Job description provides basis for job specification.

Uses — Job specification is helpful in various ways as under:

(a)   It provides information needed to formulate the application.

(b)   It helps in placing the right employee in the right job according to his/her qualification and experience.

(c)   It provides supervisors with a basis for counselling employees during performance appraisal.

Major Elements or Activities of Human Resource Planning

The major elements or activities involved in human resource planning include the following:

1.   **Forecasting Future Human Resources Needs** — The management has to forecast the future manpower requirements at various levels with different skills on the basis of past experience and specific future plans of the company.

2.   **Assessing Current Manpower Situation** — The management has to prepare a man power inventory of present manpower resources, which is a detailed statement of the number of people working in the organisation with their relative positions, salaries, skills, qualification etc. This helps in determining quantity and quality of the existing human resources.

3. **Analysing** — The management has to analyse the degree to which the present manpower resources are utilised optimally.

4. **Anticipating** — The management has to anticipate the man-power problems by projecting present resources into the future. Projections are to be made about the likely retirements, termination of services, promotions and transfers of its present personnel.

5. **Planning** — The management has to prepare the necessary programmes of recruitment, selection, training, development, motivation and compensation to meet the future manpower requirements.

Need for Human Resource Planning

The need for human resource planning arises due to the following reasons:

1. Organisation need human resource planning to meet the demand of changing job requirements due to a rapidly changing technology. For example, an introduction of new equipment, products or process results in changes in job design and organization structure.

2. Technological changes create demand for new professionals who specialise in high skilled jobs. Planning is essential to train existing employees to acquire new skills or to recruit new employees with specialized skills.

3. Certain new types of human resources may be required due to changes in/ introduction of new legislative measures. For example, the demand for air and water pollution control specialists has increased after the government has passed certain legislation on environment policy.

4. Human resource planning provide a competitive edge to employees and organisations.

5. Human resource planing is needed to meet the demand of changing job requirements due to anticipated expansion and diversification.

Objectives of Human Resource Planning

The objectives of human resource planning are summarised as under:

1. To forecast the future manpower requirements.

2. To ensure the optimum use of present human resources employed.

3. To ensure the availability of the necessary human resources of required quantity and requisite quality as and when required on a continuous basis.

Factors affecting the Human Resource Requirements

The factors which are required to be considered while determining human resource requirements include the following:

1. Future plans of expansion of operations, products, services, facilities;

2. Changes in organisational structure (e.g., likely extent of decentralisation, creation of new staff units);

3. Changes in technology to be adopted for production activities e.g., extent of mechanisation and automation;

4. Likely turnover of present human resource;
5. Likely retirement and termination of services;
6. Likely promotions and transfers of its present personnel;
7. Current status of present human resource (e.g. their positions, qualifications, skills, experience, age).

Human resource flows in and out of an organisation due to a variety of reasons as shown below:

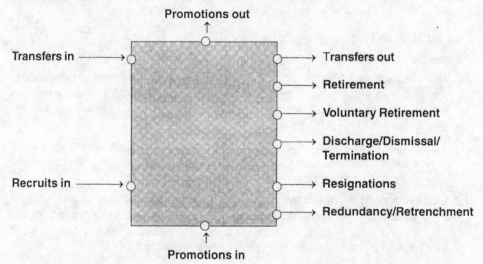

Human resource requirements of an organisation can be estimated by carrying out 'work load' and 'work force' analysis.

Total human resource needs of an organisation can be built up from projections made for specific segments of their work force. Different work groups relate differently to various predicators and thus have different productivity ratios. In each case the following process is followed:

(a) find the appropriate business factor;
(b) draw up the historical record of that factor in relation to human resource employed;
(c) compute the productivity ratios;
(d) determine the trend;
(e) make the necessary adjustments in the trend, past and future, and project to the target year.

Some firms develop the total projection for the work force at the operating level and work out the projections at various responsibility levels in each job/skill group by means of ratios.

Importance of Human Resource Planning

The need and importance of human resource planning arises from the following benefits which flow from it:

1. It forecasts the future human resource requirements.

2. It helps in obtaining and retaining human resources of required quantity and of requisite quality as and when required on a continuous basis.

3. **Prevents the situation of Shortage/Surplus** — It anticipates the situations of surplus and shortage of human resources at any point of time and helps in preventing such situations.

4. **Internal Planning** — It provides the basis for the subsequent staffing functions of recruitment, selection, training, development, promotion etc. Since a large number of persons have to be replaced from time to time due to retirement of death etc. of existing employees, there is constant need for planning such replacements.

5. **Copes with the changes** — It enables the organisation to cope with internal and external changes. Changes in market conditions, technology, product etc. often require changes to be made in job content, skill requirements, accounting and quality of personnel.

6. It determines the skill and expertise required to achieve the organisational and departmental objectives.

7. It keeps the investment and expenditure on staff at a reasonable level.

8. It develops action plans to optimise the contribution and satisfaction of the present human resources.

9. It develops action plans to meet anticipated human resource needs.

Steps Involved in Human Resource Planning

The human resource planning involves the following six steps:

Step 1 → Assessing Current Manpower Situation

The first step in the human resource planning process is to assess current human resource situation. This assessment is done by preparing a human resource inventory. Human resource inventory is a comprehensive statement of the number of employees working in the organisation with their relative positions, salaries, designations, qualifications, skills, jobs etc. This statement facilitates to determine the quantity and quality of the present human resources. In addition the management analyses the degree to which present human resources are utilized optimally.

Step 2 → Forecasting Future Human Resource Needs

After assessing current human resource situation, the next step is to forecast the future human resource requirements at various levels with different skills on the basis of past experience and specific future plans of the company. For example where the organisation has plans to expand and diversify its activities, then more human resource may be required.

Step 3 → Projecting Supply of Future Human Resources

After forecasting future human resource needs, the next step is to project the supply of future human resources. Projections are the estimates of the number and kinds of employees that can be expected to constitute the total work force of an organisation at a particular point of time in future. Such projections are made on the basis of:

(a) Current Human Resource Supply; and

(b) likely movement of an employee through an organisation over a period of time.

For the above purpose, the requirements of data are more comprehensive than for other purposes because the planners have to estimate availability of future skills. Usually the information collected for this purposes include the following:

(a) Personnel Data;

(b) Work History Data;

(c) Training and Development;

(d) Skill Inventory Data for current jobs;

(e) Aggregate data such as total number of employees and their age distribution.

Step 4 → **Comparison of forecast needs with projected supply to determine net employees requirements.**

After projecting supply of future human resources, the next step is to compare the forecast needs for human resources with the projected supply of internal human resources. Such comparison is required to determine the net employees requirements.

For example:

Forecast needs for supervision	50
Projected internal supply for supervision	30
Net employees requirements	20

Such net employees requirements should be determined for each job in each department and for the whole organisation.

Step 5 → **Planning policies and programmes to meet human resources needs**

After determining the net employees requirements, the next step is to formulate human resource policies and programmes designed to handle anticipated shortages and surpluses.

Step 6 → **Evaluating Human Resource Planning Effectiveness**

After formulating the human resource policies and programmes, the next step is to evaluate human resource planning in order to determine its effectiveness.

For example, if large number of jobs remaining, vacant for a long period of time, it indicates organisation's failure to plan effectively for its human resource needs.

RECRUITMENT

Meaning of Recruitment — Recruitment is the process of identifying the sources for prospective candidates and encouraging them to apply for a particular job or jobs in an organisation. It involves placing right person on the right job. It aims at stimulating and attracting job applicants for positions in the organisation. It requires careful planning especially when unusual jobs are to be filled.

Purpose of Recruitment — Its purpose is to provide a sufficiently large group of eligible candidates in order to have wide choice for the organisation in the selection of the most suitable candidate. The aim of recruitment is to develop and maintain adequate human resource upon which an organisation can depend. It involves seeking and attracting a pool of people from which qualified candidate for job vacancies can be chosen. Accordingly, the purpose of recruitment is to locate sources of human resource to meet job requirements and job specification.

Nature of Recruitment Activity — It is a positive activity because it encourages people to apply. For this purpose, the organisation is to locate the sources and publicise the specific personnel needs so as to inform and induce the people to apply for the job in the organisation.

When does the process of recruitment begin — The process of recruitment begins after human resource requirements are determined in terms of quality through job analysis and quantity through forecasting and planning.

Sources of Recruitment

There are basically two sources of recruitment—internal and external. The various sources of recruitment have been shown below:

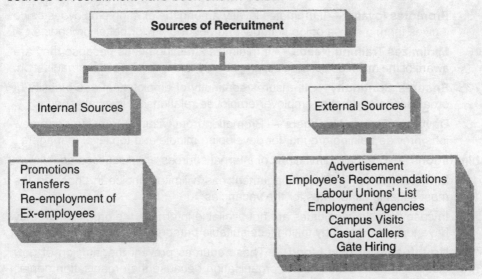

Let us discuss these sources of recruitment in detail.

INTERNAL SOURCES OF RECRUITMENT

Meaning — Internal sources of recruitment include personnel already on the payroll of the organisation. Recruitment out of internal sources refers to the recruitment for jobs from within the organisation. The major internal sources include the following:

1. **Promotion** refers to moving the employees to positions of higher authority and responsibility. Promotion may be based on employee's seniority or merit.

2. **Transfer** refers to moving the employees to similar positions in other work unit. It may involve a promotion or demotion or no change in the responsibility. The transfers may be helpful in avoiding replacement, layoff, job enrichment, shift change and removing individual grievance etc.

3. **Re-employment of Ex-employees** — It refers to employing the employees who have left the organisation. It may be on a temporary or permanent basis.

Advantages — The major advantages of internal sources of recruitment are discussed as follows:

1. **Familiarity** — The organisation and its employees are familiar to each other.

2. **Better utilisation of internal talent** — Internal recruitment enables the organisation to make best use of the talent of its employees and to develop them further.

3. **Less expensive method** — The process of internal recruitment does not involve any expense in the form of advertising for vacancies, recruiting etc.

4. **Source of motivation** — The employees are motivated to do their jobs well so as to earn the desired promotion. Since the opportunity of promotion is implicit in internal recruitment, internal recruitment acts as a source of motivation for employees to improve their career and income levels. It is also a means of attracting and retaining competent employees.

5. **Promotes loyalty** — It promotes loyalty among the existing employees since it gives them a sense of job security and opportunity for better prospects.

6. **Minimizes Training Needs** — It minimizes training needs because they are aware of the major goals, policies, procedures and functions of the organisation.

7. **Ensures Continuity** — It ensures continuity of employment and stability of organisation and better employer-employee relationship is established.

8. **Develops Future Managers** — Promotion from within or transferring to new jobs provide training ground, for developing middle and top level managers.

Limitations — The major limitations of internal sources are discussed as follows:

1. **Limited choice** — The management has a limited choice in choosing the most suitable candidates for the vacancies.

   In case suitable candidates are not available internally, the organisation may have to compromise by taking less suitable persons from internal sources.

2. **No infusion of new blood** — These sources prevent the infusion of new blood and new ideas into the organisation because the organisation denies itself fresh talent from outside.

3. **Absence of competition** — Internal employees may lose the drive for proving their worth since they may expect automatic promotion by seniority and sure prospect.

4. **Conflict among employees** — These may cause dissatisfaction and frustration among those employees who aspire for promotion but are not promoted.

5. **Stagnation of skills** — In the long run, the skill of internal employees may become stagnant or obsolete which may decrease the productivity and efficiency of the organisation.

6. **Encourages Favourtism and Nepotism** — It may encourage favouritism and nepotism, i.e., appointment may be restricted to their kith or kin.

EXTERNAL SOURCES OF RECRUITMENT

Meaning — External sources of recruitment include personnel outside the organisation. Recruitment from external sources refers to the recruitment of candidates outside the organisation. The major external sources include the following:

1. **Advertisements** — The organisation advertises its vacancies through newspapers, trade journals, professional journals, magazines, radio, television, internet on computers. The contents and design of the advertisements should be prepared in such a manner that (a) unsuitable candidates may not apply, and (b) suitable candidates should have courage to apply. Only particular types of posts should be advertised in the professional journals. The media where the advertisement is placed is often determined by the level of job. Higher the position, more widely dispersed the advertisement is and lower the position, less widely dispersed the advertisement is. **For example,** the advertisement for the part of a top executive may be in national daily and advertisement for post of blue-collar jobs may be confined to the local daily newspapers. Some of the posts and some suitable professional journals to advertise them are given below:

Post	Professional Journal
1. Controller of Finance, Finance Manager, Manager Taxation, Manager Accounts, Chief Accountant, Manager Audit	**The Chartered Accountant** published by the Institute of Chartered Accountants of India, New Delhi.
2. Cost Accountant	**The Management Accountant** published by the Institute of Cost & Works Accountants, Kolkata.
3. Company Secretary, Manager Company Law	**The Chartered Secretary** published by the Institute of Chartered Secretaries of India, New Delhi.

2. **Employee's recommendation** — The candidates who are recommended by an employee of an organisation are also a good source of external recruitment. An employee rarely recommands someone unless he believes that the individual is suitable for the job since reputation of recommender is at stake.

3. **Labour union's list** — Labour union's list of candidates seeking employment in the company also acts as one of the sources of external recruitment. Labour

unions operate placement services for the benefit of their members and employees. This helps in saving recruitment costs.

4. **Employment Agencies** — The organisation intimates the employment exchange about the number, nature, and type of vacancies. The employment exchange (i.e., an agency which maintains records of persons who need jobs, their qualifications, experiences etc.) provides the list of candidates to the organisation.

    Employment agencies may be of three types:

    (a) **Public or State Agencies** — These public agencies operate to help both the job seekers by providing them the suitable employment and the employers by providing them suitable workers. The public agencies tend to attract and place predominantly semi-skilled, blue-collared workers. Only few individuals with high skills place their names with public agencies and few employers seeking individuals with high skills approach state agencies.

    (b) **Private Employment Agencies** — These agencies (like ABC Consultants Ltd.) bring together the employers and suitable persons available for a job. To meet the needs of employees, these agencies provide a list of suitable candidates. Private employment agencies advertise the vacancies and screen the applicants against the criteria specified by the employer. Their fees can be absorbed by *either* the employee *or* employer or partly by employee and partly by employer. The major difference between the public and private agencies is their image.

    (c) **Management consultants** — The management consulting firms specialize in the placement of executives at middle level and top level. These are basically executive search agencies. **For example,** ABC consultants Ltd. These agencies differ from the private employment agencies in the following respects.

        1. The level at which they operate;
        2. The charge which is quite substantial;
        3. Their national wide contracts;
        4. The thoroughness of their investigation.

5. **Campus Visits** — In order to fill up entry level positions, the organisation conducts interviews of the students directly from their schools, colleges and professional and technical institutes (like IITs, IIMs). This is popularly known as campus interviews or campus selection. Many educational institutions operate placement services where prospective employers can review credentials and interview candidates.

6. **Casual callers** — The unsolicited applicants (i.e., those who visit the organisation without any announcement of vacancy to find out if jobs are available) also provide a source of external recruitment.

7. **Gate hiring** —This source of recruitment is usually followed by the production department of the organisation to fill up vacancies at the lower levels. The employer selects the required number of workers out of those who present themselves at the factory gate.

Advantages — The major advantages of external sources of recruitment are discussed as under:

1. **Wide choice** — The management has a wide choice in choosing the most suitable candidates for the vacancies.

2. **Infusion of new blood** — These sources permit the infusion of new blood and new ideas into the organisation.

3. **Presence of competition** — Internal employees do not lose the drive for proving their worth since they have to compete with outside candidates.

Limitations — The major limitations of external sources of recruitment are discussed as under:

1. **Conflict among the employees** — These may cause dissatisfaction and frustration among those employees who aspire for promotion but are not selected. There is greater deterioration in the employer-employee relationship which may result in industrial strike and unrest, and lockouts.

2. **More expensive method** — The process of external recruitment involves considerable expenses in the form of advertising for vacancies, screening, selection etc.

3. **Time consuming** — The process of external recruitment takes more time than the internal recruitment. The process of orienting external candidates into the organisation is also time consuming.

4. **No certainty** — There is no certainty as to whether the selected candidates from outside will come out to be good or bad, will stay or not.

5. **No familiarity** — The external candidates being new to the organisation are not familiar with the job and internal conditions of the organisation. The organisation is also not familiar with the strengths and weaknesses of the external candidates. The personnel selected from outside may suffer from the danger of adjustment to new work environment.

6. **Discourage the existing employees** — Since the existing employees are not sure to get promotion, they feel discouraged from working hard. As a result, the productivity and efficiency of the organisation decrease. The existing employees lose their sense of security and tend to develop indifference towards the organisation.

Distinction Between Internal and External Sources of Recruitment

Internal sources differ from external sources of recruitment in the following respects:

Basis of Distinction	Internal Sources	External Sources
1. **Familiarity**	Employees are **familiar** to the organisation.	Outsiders are **not familiar** to the organisation.
2. **Choice**	The management has a **limited choice** in choosing the most suitable candidates for the vacancies.	The management has a **wide choice** in choosing the most suitable candidates for the vacancies.
3. **Infusion of new blood**	These sources **prevent** the infusion of new blood and new ideas into the organisation.	These sources **permit** the infusion of new blood and new ideas into the organisation.
4. **Competition**	Internal employees may lose the drive for proving their worth since they expect automatic promotion by seniority and sure prospects.	Internal employees do not lose the drive for proving their worth since they have to compete with outside candidates.
5. **Economy**	The process of internal recruitment is **less expensive** as it does not involve expenses in the form of advertising for vacancies etc.	The process of external recruitment is **more expensive** as it involves considerable expenses in the form of advertisement for vacancies etc.
6. **Motivation vs. conflict**	Internal recruitment acts as a **source of motivation** since opportunity for promotion is inherent in internal recruitments.	External recruitment acts as a **source of conflict**, dissatisfaction and fraustration for those who aspire promotion but are not selected.
7. **Time consuming**	It is **less time consuming**.	It is **more time consuming**.
8. **Quality**	It may **not involve quality** of recruitment since it restricts the option and freedom in choosing the candidates.	It may **involve quality** of recruitment since a large number applicants are available.

SELECTION

Meaning of Selection — Selection is the process of choosing the most suitable candidates from among the applicants for jobs after carefully screening the candidates who offer themselves for appointment.

Purpose of Selection — The purpose of selection is to select the most suitable candidates from among the applicants keeping in view the job analysis information.

Nature of Selection Process — The nature of selection process is negative in the sense that it involves rejection of unsuitable or less suitable applicants.

Pre-conditions for Selection Process — The selection process can not be operated effectively untill the following three steps have been taken:

(a) Requirements of the job to be filled have been specified;

(b) Qualifications and experience required have been specified;

(c) Adequate response to the recruitment effort has been received.

Steps In Selection Process — Selection process differs from one organisation to another. Usually 'successive hurdle technique' is adopted in selection process. An applicant is required to cross the successive hurdles. These hurdles are created to eliminate the unsuitable applicant at any stage in the selection process. An applicant who qualifies a hurdle goes to the next one and the one who does not qualify it is dropped out. These hurdles need not necessarily be placed in the same order. The arrangement of these hurdles may differ from one organisation to another. These successive hurdles may also be termed as steps involved in the selection process. These steps or hurdles involved in the selection process are shown below:

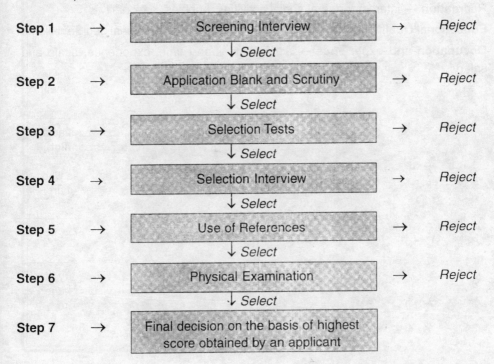

Let us discuss these hurdles or steps in the selective process in detail as under:

Step 1 → Screening Interview

Meaning — This is a sorting process in which organisation gives the necessary information about the job requirements to the prospective applicants and collects the necessary information from the candidates about their education, experience, skills, salary expected etc. If a candidate is found suitable, an application form is given to him to fill in and submit.

Purpose — The purpose of screening interview is to eliminate the unsuitable candidate in the beginning itself.

Precaution — Due care should be taken so that suitable candidates are not turned down in a hurry.

Step 2 → Application Blank and Scrutiny

Application blank is a very common tool of selection. Its design and proforma differs from organisation to organisation. The most commonly sought information in application blank are the following.

Biographical details — name, age, sex, parentage, height, marital status,

Recreation — interest, general social activities, hobbies, nationality,

Educational Qualifications — secondary, university or professional degree/diploma

Occupation and experience — Jobs full-time/part time, experience, scale and salary.

SPECIMEN OF APPLICATION BLANK

1. NAME (IN BLOCK LETTERS)
    SURNAME _____ MIDDLE NAME _____ FIRST NAME _____
2. FATHER'S NAME _____
3. PERMANENT ADDRESS _____
4. PRESENT CORRESPONDENCE ADDRESS _____
5. TELEPHONE NUMBER — OFFICE _____ RESIDENCE _____
6. E-MAIL ADDRESS _____
7. DATE OF BIRTH (MM/DD/YY) _____ PLACE OF BIRTH _____
8. NATIONALITY _____
9. SEX (MALE/FEMALE) _____
10. PHYSICAL DETAILS: WEIGHT _____ HEIGHT _____
11. MARITAL STATUS (SINGLE/MARRIED) _____
12. NUMBER OF DEPENDENTS (IF ANY) _____
13. **EDUCATIONAL QUALIFICATIONS:**

YEAR	COURSE	BOARD/UNIVERSITY	% MARKS	DISTINCTION/POSITION

14. **PRESENT STATUS:** PRESENT POST _____ PRESENT EMPLOYER _____
    PRESENT SALARY _____
15. **PREVIOUS EXPERIENCE:**

INSTITUTION	POST	DURATION	MAIN ACTIVITIES	REASON FOR LEAVING

16. NAMES OF TWO REFERENCES: 1 _____ 2 _____
17. INTERESTS _____
18. EXPECTED SALARY _____

_____
APPLICANT'S SIGNATURE

Purposes for Which the Information Given in the Application Blank can be Used

The information given in the application blank can be used —

1. to provide data for permanent employee record to the company;
2. to indicate that the applicant has consistently progressed to better jobs or not;
3. to see the logical pattern of the education and occupational experience of the candidate;
4. to provide interviewer the basis and point of departure from interview; and
5. to provide information for reference checking etc.

Scrutiny of Application Blank

Meaning — This is a sorting process in which applicants who do not meet the relevant eligibility criteria are outrightly rejected.

Purposes — The purposes of scrutiny of Application Blank are as follows:

(a) To find out suitable candidates who can be put to next hurdle (i.e., selection tests).

(b) To find out unsuitable candidates who should be dropped out at this stage.

Step 3 → Selection Tests

Meaning — A test implies a comparision with a given standard. Test is means of evaluating the skill, knowledge, experience, aptitude, personality and interest of the applicant.

Objectives — Tests are conducted:

1. To provide more objective and authentic means of measuring the competence of job applicants for job suitability.

2. To uncover talent that would not be detected by interviews.

3. To eliminate the possibility of prejudice or subjectivity of interviewer in the selection decision.

Validity and Reliability of Test — The test must be validated in the sense that the results of the tests must be compared with some criterion of performance such as success in examination, measures of output or assessment of performances. The test must be reliable in the sense that it should be given with standard instructions in a standard time. A test which is reliable and which predicts performance is a useful instrument.

Classification of Tests — Selection tests include the following categories of tests:

1. **Aptitude Tests or Potential Ability Tests**

   These tests measure the latent ability of an applicant to learn a new job or skill. There are two types of aptitude tests —

   (a) Cognitive tests measure mental and intellectual aptitudes.

   (b) Motor tests measure physical dimensions such as manual dexterity or hand-eye co-ordination.

2. **Achievement or Trade or Intelligence or Proficiency Tests**

   These tests measure the job knowledge and skills acquired through training or job experience. **For example,** test conducted for electricians measure knowledge of electrical devices, circuits , wiring and so on.

3. **Motivation or Internal Tests**

   These tests measure the motivation, interest and job preference of the applicant.

4. **Situational or Personality Tests**

   These tests measure the applicant's ability to react to stressful but realistic real life situations. Under such types of tests, the applicants are presented with a problem which requires group co-operation and observation and the observers observe how applicants are reacting to such problems.

Step 4 → Selection Interview

Meaning — An interview is a personal face to face conversation between one person on one side and another person or persons on the other. An interview should cover all important aspects of personality. Marks should be allotted to each of these aspects. The total of all these will determine the final position of an applicant at the interview.

Objectives — The objectives of the interview are as follows:

1. To measure the mental ability and work competence of the applicants against the specific requirements of the job.
2. To decide whether they will be good for the jobs.
3. To allow the applicant to ask questions about the jobs and organisation.
4. To motivate the satisfactory applicant to want to work.

Benefits — The benefits of interviews are as follows:

1. It provides a valid sample of the applicant's behaviour.
2. It can uncover clues to the applicant's motivation and his attitudes towards himself and to the kind of situation he finds troublesome.
3. Interviewer can guide the applicant into explaining why certain jobs appeal to him.
4. The interviewer can assess the applicant's level of aspiration.

Limitations — The limitations of interviews are as follows:

1. The interviewing process is both expensive and time consuming.
2. The unskillful interviewer can easily evaluate the performance of the applicant in accordance with his own prejudices.
3. The validity of technique is also affected by the personality of the interviewer.
4. The conversation lags causes embarrassment and the procedure is stressful for both interviewers and the candidate.
5. Candidates react very differently depending upon who is interviewing them and how the candidate is being handled.

Step 5 → Use of References

Meaning — References check mean asking the persons whose references have been given by the applicant in the application. The usefulness of references depends upon the speed and promptness with which they are attended to.

Objective — The objective of using references is to obtain frank opinion about the candidate either on specified points or in general.

Limitation — Generally references give a positive report about the candidates and do not mention their weaknesses. To overcome this limitation, now a days organisation have started sending structured forms on which the refreeze are expected to give their responses about the suitability of the candidates.

Step 6 → Physical examination

Meaning — It is an examination of physical health of an applicant. An applicant who gets over the previous hurdles is sent for physical examination either to the organisation's physicians or to a medical officer approved for this purpose.

Purposes — The purposes of physical examination are as follows:

(a) To discover the physical fitness of a candidate for the job concerned.

(b) To discover and record existing disabilities which may be helpful in deciding the settlement of workmen compensation claims.

Step 7 → Final Decision

All those applicants who cross all the hurdles are finally considered. On the basis of their scores in the tests and interviews, a final setting of short-listed candidates is often made. If there are more such candidates than the number required for a job, those with the highest scores are finally selected.

DISTINCTION BETWEEN RECRUITMENT AND SELECTION

Recruitment and selection can be distinguished as under:

Basis of Distinction	Recruitment	Selection
1. **Meaning**	It is the process of searching for prospective candidates and encouraging them to apply for jobs in an organisation.	It is the process of choosing the suitable candidates from among the applicants for the jobs.
2. **Objective**	Its objective is **to provide a sufficiently large group** of qualified candidates.	Its objective is **to eliminate the unsuitable or less suitable candidates** and find out the suitable candidates.
3. **Process**	Its process is **simple** and candidates are not required to cross several hurdles.	Its process is **complex** and candidates are required to cross several hurdles created by management deliberately.
4. **Nature of activity**	It is a **positive** activity because it encourages people to apply.	It is a **negative** activity because it rejects a good proportion of applicants.

PLACEMENT

Meaning of Placement — Placement is a process of placing the right person on the right job. In some cases when two or more alternative positions are to be filled, the placement may be tentative in some cases and the final placement may be done after the candidate is tested on alternative jobs.

Purpose of Placement — The objective of placement is to place the selected candidates in the jobs for which they are most suited.

Benefits of Placement — A proper placement reduces employee turnover. absenteeism and accident rates and improves morale.

ORIENTATION/INDUCTION

Meaning of Orientation — Orientation is the process of introducing the new employee to the job and the organisation. It is also a process of socialising the new employee with his fellow employees, superiors and subordinates.

Purpose of Orientation — The purpose of orientation is to introduce the new employee to the job and the organisation.

Orientation Programme — An orientation programme consists of the following types of orientation:

Type	Purpose
(a) **General orientation by the staff**	To enable the new employee to know about the history and the operations of the organisation.
(b) **Specific orientation by the job supervisor**	To enable the new employee to know the job requirements, his place of work, the location of facilities, under whom and with whom he should work, hours of work, and so on.
(c) **Follow-up orientation by the personnel department**	To find out whether the employee is reasonably well satisfied with his job, supervisor and so on.

Benefits — Proper orientation of the new employees is likely to reduce their anxieties on how to cope with the job requirements, how to become acceptable to the work group, how to become a part of the organisation, how to adjust with his work and environment. The initial problems of adjustment with the organisation during the first few critical weeks are minimised.

TRAINING

Meaning of Training — Training is a service function, which provides management with professional support in meeting the organisational's objectives. Training is an act of imparting or improving or updating the knowledge and skills of an employee (whether existing or new) for performing a particular job in an effective manner. In other words, training is the process of helping employees to acquire more knowledge of the job and to learn or sharpen the needed skills, attitudes and values associated with efficient performance of their jobs. Training is undertaken to fulfil three important needs as follows:

1. Training of new employees;
2. Training of the present employees;
3. Training for a long-term purpose aimed at giving proper personality development.

Objectives of Training — The important objectives of training are discussed as follows:

1. **To impart job knowledge and skills to new employees** — Training is essential to impart the required job knowledge and skill to newly recruited employees.

2. **To improve and update the existing job knowledge and skills of existing employees** — Training is essential to improve and update the existing job knowledge and skills of existing employees so that they may cope with the complex and changing conditions of their environment.

3. **To prepare employees for their promotion** — Training is also essential to prepare existing employees for their promotion and for assuming higher job responsibilities. In addition, training is also necessary when a person has to move from one job to another because of transfer or demotion.

4. **To improve the attitudes and behaviour of employees** — Training is also essential to improve the attitudes and behaviour of employees in such matters as discipline, good relations with superiors, subordinates, co-employees, careful use of equipment, materials, facilities, regular attendance and so on.

Need and Importance of Training — The need and importance of training arises from the following benefits which flow from it:

Benefits of Training to Employees

1. **Acquisition of new job skills** — Training enables the newly recruited employees to acquire the required job knowledge and skills.

2. **Improving existing job skills** — Training enables the existing employees to improve and update their existing job knowledge and skills.

3. **Prepares for promotion** — Training prepares the existing employees for their promotion and for assuming higher job responsibilities.

4. **Improves attitude** — Training improves the attitudes and behaviour of employees in such matters as discipline, good relation with superiors, subordinates and co-employees, and so on.

5. **Improves motivation** — Training improves the level of motivation and job satisfaction of employees.

6. **Raises moral** — Training raises the employees' morale because the employees who receive training feel that they are being taken care of by the management.

7. **Broadens the prospective** — Training broadens the perspectives and problem-solving abilities of employees.

8. **Improves the quality** — Training improves the quality of employees and the quality of their working life.

9. **Prepares to cope with environment** — Training makes the employees more competent, confident and adaptive so as to cope with the complex and changing conditions of their environment.

Benefits of Training to Organisation

1. **Economic operation** — Training results in better and economical use of facilities because a well-trained employee knows how to use the available facilities in an efficient manner. As a result, machine breakage and maintenance cost is reduced.

2. **Increases productivity** — Training results in higher productivity because a well-trained employee performs his job in an efficient manner. As a result, quality and quantity of output improve and cost of output per unit decreases.

3. **Reduces the need for supervision** — Training reduces the need for supervision because an intensive supervision is not required in case of well-trained employees. Trained employees become capable of self-direction and self-control. With reduced supervision, a manager can widen his span of control and spend greater time on more non-routine matters.

4. **Standardisation of position procedure** — Training helps in standardisation of procedures by teaching the standardised procedures to all the employees.

5. **Raises high morale** — Training helps in raising the employees' morale. A good training programme moulds employee's attitudes towards work. As a result, he can perform his work in a confident manner. Moreover, employee's who receive training feel that they are being taken care of by the management and this results in raising their morale.

6. **Reduces rate of labour turnover** — Training helps in reducing employees absenteeism and turnover.

7. **Reduces Manpower Obsolescence** — Training helps in reducing manpower obsolescence.

8. **Prepares prospective managers** — Training prepares and develops future managers by imparting training to employees with exceptional talent, creativity and initiative, for higher positions.

Requirements of Training

The major requirements of training are discussed below:

1. The objectives of each training programme should be clearly specified.

2. Training programmes should be prepared so as to meet the needs of jobs, job holders and organisation.

3. Training should be functional and practically useful to employees who undergo it.

4. Training programmes should be reviewed and evaluated at periodic intervals to ascertain the extent of their effect on the job behaviour and performance of those who have undergone training.

5. The cost of training should be kept within reasonable limits having regard to the benefits thereof.

METHODS OF TRAINING

There are several methods of imparting training suitable to different categories of employees and to different training needs. Training can be imparted through (I) on the job-methods or (II) off the job-methods.

I. On the Job Methods of Training

Under these methods, the principle of learning by doing is adopted and the employees are trained on the job, at their workplace and under the same working conditions under which they will be required to work in the normal course. The techniques of on the job-methods include the following:

1. **Vestibule training** — It involves classroom training imparted with the help of equipment and machines identical to those in use at place of work. Theoretical training is given in the classroom while practical training is given on the actual production line. It is generally used to train clerks, bank tellers, inspectors, machine operators etc. It is particularly suitable where a large number of employees are to be trained at the same time for the same kind of work. The emphasis is on learning new skills rather than performing the actual job.

2. **Coaching** — A trainee is placed in a new job and is told how it is to be performed. Coaching and instruction are given by experienced workers, first line supervisors, or by special training instructors. Supervisor familiarises him with the tools, equipments, materials etc. The learner or trainee picks up the skill and speed gradually. Gradually, supervision is reduced by the trainer and trainee starts functioning independently.

3. **Apprenticeship** — It is a technique of training under which a major part of training time is spent on the productive job work and each apprentice is given a programme of assignments according to a predetermined schedule which provides for efficient training and acquisition of trade skills. This method is appropriate for training in crafts, trades and technical areas e.g., job of a craftsman, a printer, a toolmaker, a pattern designer etc.

   Experienced workers, first line supervisors and specially qualified instructors serve as trainers in on the job training. It helps trainees to learn things by doing and quickens the process of self-learning and self-correction. It requires trainees to learn under job pressure.

4. **Under study** — Under this technique, specific individuals are trained to assume at a future time the full duties and responsibilities during managers' long absence or illness or their retirements, transfers or promotions.

5. **Creation of 'assistant to' positions** — Under the technique, a trainee works as an 'assistant to' a senior manager. Senior manager provides job-related experience to the trainee. The objective is to develop the abilities of the trainee and to train him to assume full responsibilities of the job held by the senior manager.

6. **Job rotation** — It is a technique of training under which trainees are periodically rotated on different but related assignments. Job rotation can be in non-supervisory work situations, managerial training positions, middle level positions. Job rotation enables the employees to get experience of different jobs in the organisation. **For example,** in case of banks, job rotation technique is very popular.

7. **Simulation** — It is an extension of vestibule training. Under this technique, a trainee works in closely duplicated real job conditions. This is essential in cases in which actual on the job training is expensive or it might result in serious injury or destruction of valuable resources, e.g., in aeronautical industry.

8. **Demonstration** — It is a technique of training under which a trainee demonstrates how to do a certain work and gives step by step explanation of 'why', 'how' and 'what' of what he is doing. The emphasis under this technique is on know-how.

Distinction between 'Job Rotation' and 'Under Study' as Methods of Employee's Training

1. In job rotation, training is imparted to newly recruited employees, whereas in under study, training is given to those employees who are promoted.

2. In job rotation, training is provided on the job itself, whereas in case of under study, training is imparted in such a manner that person should be in a position to take up the responsibilities with the executives.

II. Off the Job Methods of Training

Under these methods, the principle of learning by acquiring knowledge rather than by doing is adopted and the employees are trained away from the actual workplace so that they may be free from the job pressure and job demands during training period. The techniques of off the job training include the following:

1. **Conferences** — Under this technique of training, employees of the same organisation or of different organisations come together to discuss various aspects of a particular subject. Participants exchange their ideas and experiences to arrive at better methods of dealing with the given problem. The participants come to teach each other and to learn together. This technique is ideally suited for analysing problems and issues, and examining them from different viewpoints. Participants often develop an analytical frame of mind and a questioning attitude. The chairman is a key figure in the conference. He is responsible for summing up and controlling the proceedings.

2. **Seminar** — The term 'seminar' is derived from the latin word 'seed-plot'. Under this technique, the trainees learn through discussion of a paper on a selected subject in depth. This paper is written by one or more specialists and is distributed in advance to all participants. The most common seminar is a conference on a smaller scale but incorporates a larger number of members.

3. **Discussions** — Under this method, the subject matter and related issues are discussed and clarified. The discussion leader requires skill in planning and careful preparation in encouraging the involvement of individuals. The objectives of a discussion should be clearly specified in advance.

4. **Case study** — Under this technique, a real (or hypothetical) business problem is presented to the trainees who are required to identify the problems involved, to suggest various alternatives to solve them, to analyse each of such alternatives, to find out their comparative suitability and to decide the best solution. This technique promotes analytical thinking and problem-solving ability. It encourages open-mindedness, patient listening, respecting others' views and integrating the knowledge obtained from different basic disciplines. This method is extensively used in professional schools of law, and management and in supervisory and executive training programmes in industry. Bridge is provided to fill up the gap between theoretical knowledge and practical application.

5. **Role playing** — This technique is also called 'role reversal', 'socio-drama' or 'psycho-drama'. It is a technique of training which imparts practical orientation to a given role in the enterprise. It brings into sharp focus the interdependencies and interactions involved in different roles and positions. Thus, inter-dependency and in-built contradictions are sought to be highlighted by assigning roles to the trainees so that they are able to develop a more realistic perspective about the complexities involved in various roles and positions. Under this technique, two or more trainees are assigned roles in a given situation which is explained to the group. The role players have to quickly respond to the situation that is ever changing and to react to it as they would in the real one. It is a method of interaction which involves realistic behaviour in an imaginary or hypothetical situation.

   For example — One trainee may be assigned the role of a 'salesman' and another trainee may be assigned the role of a 'consumer'. Trainee in the role of salesman may be required to explain the main features of a product, say, International Surf Ultra and to respond the enquiries made by consumer and trainee in the role of consumer may be required to make enquiries about the product from different angles.

6. **Sensitivity training** — Under this technique, trainees are brought together in a free and open environment in which they get the opportunity to express their ideas, beliefs and attitudes. The trainees function as catalysts or facilitators. The objectives of this training are —

   (i) to make the trainees understand their own behaviour, self-awareness, and how others perceive them;

   (ii) to develop their sensitivity to the views, feelings and reactions of others;

   (iii) to improve their listening skills, openness of mind, tolerance for differences, conflict-resolution skills, their capacity to absorb tensions and stresses, and their understanding of group processes.

7. **Special courses** — Under this technique of training, an organisation conducts some special courses through their own departments or outside agencies. A series of lectures are given to the trainees. Lectures are formally organised talks by an instructor on specific topics. The lectures can be used for a large group of persons to be trained in a short time. This method is useful when concepts, attitudes, theories have to be discussed.

Usually, the academicians, professionals and technicians from outside agencies serve as trainers in off the job training. It helps trainees to learn things in a steady and systematic manner without any job pressure. It does not quicken the process of self-learning and self-correction.

Distinction between 'Role Playing' and 'Sensitivity Analysis' as Methods of Training Employees

'Role playing' is a method of training which imparts practical orientation to a given role in the enterprise. The purpose is to bring into sharp focus the contradictions and interdependencies which are involved in different positions and roles.

Whereas the purpose of sensitivity training is to enable the trainees to have self-realisation and to understand and tolerate the views of others, this training is given to an unstructured group.

DISTINCTION BETWEEN ON THE JOB TRAINING AND OFF THE JOB TRAINING

On the job training differs from off the job training in the following respects:

Basis of Distinction	On the Job Training	Off the Job Training
1. **Principle adopted**	The principle of **learning** *by* **doing** is adopted.	The training of **learning** *by* **acquiring knowledge** is adopted.
2. **Place of training**	The employees are trained on the job at their **workplace**.	The employees are trained **away from** their actual **workplaces**.
3. **Techniques of training**	The techniques of on the job training include: (a) coaching, (b) under study or working as an assistant, (c) job rotation, (d) vestibule training, (e) simulation training, (f) demonstration and examples, (g) apprenticeship.	The techniques of off the job training include: (a) classroom lectures, (b) conferences, (c) case studies, (d) discussions, (e) seminars, (f) role playing, (g) programmed instructions, (h) sensitivity training.
4. **Trainers**	Experienced workers, first line supervisors and specially qualified instructors serve as trainers in on the job training.	Usually, the academicians, professionals and technicians from outside agencies serve as trainers in off the job training.
5. **Merit**	It helps trainees to learn things by doing and quickens the process of self-learning and self-correction.	It helps trainees to learn things in a steady and systematic manner without any job pressure.
6. **Demerit**	It requires trainees to learn under job pressure.	It does not quicken the process of self-learning and self-correction.

Factors to be Considered at the Time of Choosing a Method of Training

The factors to be considered at the time of choosing a method of training are enumerated as follows:

1. Cost involved in conducting training;
2. Time Available for training;
3. The number of personnel to be trained;
4. The background of trainee personnel;
5. The type of knowledge and skills to be provided;
6. Interest of workers.

DEVELOPMENT

Development is a long-term educational process of improving the overall personality of an employee. It is career oriented. The purpose of development is to have long-term development of personnel by providing philosophical, conceptual and theoretical knowledge. Both training and development programmes are necessary for any organisation.

Meaning of Management Development Programmes — The methods and techniques of training for development of its managers at various levels of an organisation are referred to as management development programmes. The emphasis of these programmes is not on skills but on handling of situations, people and managerial problems.

Objectives of Management Development Programmes — The major objectives of management development programmes are discussed below:

1. To sustain good performance of managers throughout their careers.
2. To improve the existing performance of managers at all levels.
3. To encourage existing managers to increase their capacity to assume and handle greater responsibility.
4. To enable the organisation to have the availability of required number of managers with the required skills to meet the present and anticipated (future) needs of the organisation.

Requirements of Management Development Programmes — The major requirements of management development programmes are as under:

1. These must relate to all managers at all levels in the organisation.
2. These must lead to growth and self-development of the organisation.
3. These must be dynamic and qualitative rather than static replacement based on mechanical rotation.
4. The focus of these programmes must be on the future requirements rather than those of today.
5. These programmes must be definite, comprehensive and co-ordinated.
6. These programmes should preferably be drawn after consultation with the people concerned.

7. These programmes must be communicated to all the persons concerned.

8. These programmes must begin with the top management so as to set an example for other levels of management.

DISTINCTION BETWEEN TRAINING, EDUCATION AND DEVELOPMENT

Basis of Distinction	Training	Education	Development
1. **Meaning**	It is an act of imparting, improving or updating the knowledge and skills of an employee for performing a particular job.	It is concerned with improving the general knowledge and understanding of the employees' total environment.	It is the process by which employees acquire not only skills and competency in their present jobs but also capabilities for future managerial tasks of increasing difficulty and scope.
2. **Orientation**	It is **job-oriented**.	It is **knowledge-oriented**.	It is **career-oriented**.

COMPENSATION

After determining the relative worth of jobs, the next step is to assign wages and salary rates to each job.

Meaning of Compensation

Compensation refers to the reward (monetary or non-monetary or both) paid by an organisation to an employee for work performed. Monetary award may be regarded as direct compensation and non-monetary award may be regarded as indirect compensation. Job Evaluation is the most important basis for determining the level of compensation of individual employees.

The objective of a compensation system is to create a system of reward which is equitable to the employers and employees alike so that the employee is attracted to the work and motivated to do a good job.

Meaning of 'Equitable Compensation'

In any organisation, the compensation payable should be equitable so as to—

(i) attract capable employees;

(ii) motivate the employees towards better performance; and

(iii) retain the employees' service over an extended period of time.

Who are responsible for compensation Decision?

Compensation decisions are the joint responsibility of operating executives (line managers), supervisors and personnel specialists.

Financial Elements of Income

The financial elements are evolved to meet different employees' need or different organisation objectives. The financial elements of income are as follows:

(a) **Salaries & Wages**	These represent the periodic pay which is received by an employee.
(b) **Bonus**	It is an amount which represents extra income. It is given to employees when the additional profits are earned by the organisation.
(c) **Long-term Income**	It is a lumpsum award earned over a long period of time, which dramatically changes an employees' life style. For example, increase in prices of shares of his organisation purchased by an employee.
(d) **Benefits**	These represent economic protection such as Group Insurance Schemes, Earned Leave, Re-imbursement of medical expenses and other fringe benefits.
(e) **Estate Building Plans**	There are plans which enable employees to accumulate or manage savings. From these savings, advance for house building can be granted.

Purpose of Wage and Salary Programme

The objectives of wage and salary programme are as follows:

1. To attract competent applicants
2. To motivate employees towards better performance
3. To retain employees for a longer period of time.
4. To provide a sense of fair pay and justice to the employees by developing pay scales through a systematic process of job evaluation.

INCENTIVES — MONETARY AND NON-MONETARY

After determining the needs of the people working under him, the manager should provide an environment in which appropriate incentives are available for their need satisfaction.

Meaning of Incentives

Any act or promise which induces an individual to respond in a desired manner is called an incentive. It stimulates a person towards some goal. Incentives may be *either* positive *or* negative.

Need of Incentives

The need of incentives arises because of the following benefits:

(a) Incentives induce the employees to respond in a desired manner.

(b) Incentives encourage the employees to put in their maximum efforts.

(c) Incentives help in increasing employees' productivity and efficiency.

(d) Incentives help in boosting employees' morale.

(e) Incentives help in minimising the conflicts between management and workers.

(f) Incentives help the employees to be directed towards achievement of organisational goals.

Meaning of Positive Incentives

Positive Incentives arise out of positive motivation which refers to the process of influencing employees' behaviour through the possibility of reward. Positive incentives provide a positive assurance of fulfilling needs. Example of positive incentives are: recognition and appreciation of employees' contribution towards achievement of organisational goals, delegation of the authority.

Meaning of Negative Incentives

Negative incentives arise out of negative motivation which refers to the process of influencing employees' behaviour through the fear of punishment. Negative incentives aim at correcting an individual for defaults or undesirable behaviour. Examples of negative incentives are : demotion, lay off.

Forms of Incentives — Monetary Incentives vs. Non-Monetary Incentives

To satisfy varying needs of employees, the manager should provide different forms of incentives. Since some of the needs can be satisfied by money while others cannot, the manager should provide both the monetary incentives and non-monetary incentives to the people working under him. A comparative analysis of monetary incentives and non-monetary incentives is given below:

Bases of Comparison	Monetary Incentives	Non-Monetary Incentives
1. **Meaning**	These refer to those incentives which are directly or indirectly associated with **monetary** benefits.	These refer to those incentives which are **not measurable in** terms of **money**.
2. **Purpose**	The purpose of these incentives is **to satisfy the physiological, security and social needs**.	The purpose of these incentives is **to satisfy the esteem and self-actualisation needs**.

3. **Role**	These incentives play a significant role in case of employees **at** comparatively **lower levels** of management.	These incentives play a significant role in case of employees **at** comparatively **higher levels** of management.
4. **Examples**	These incentives include wages, salaries, bonus, leave with pay, LIC premiums, medical reimbursement, free house, free car, free servant etc.	These incentives include grant of higher status, recognition, assignment of challenging jobs, workers' participation in management, suggestion system, opportunities for growth etc.

Conclusion — From the above discussion, it can be said that money is not always a motivator because people are motivated by money only up to the stage they are struggling for satisfying their physiological and security needs. After satisfaction of physiological and security needs, people are motivated by non-monetary incentives to satisfy their needs such as esteem, self-actualisation. Thus, it can be said that money is not the only motivator.

METHODS OF WAGE PAYMENT

The two principal methods of wage payment are as under:

(a) Time rate method,   (b) Piece rate method

TIME RATE METHOD

Meaning — Under this method, a worker is paid a fixed rate per hour or per day or per month for the time devoted by a worker. The time rate may be fixed with reference to rate prevailing in the industry. But it must be noted that this rate must not be less than the minimum wages fixed under the Minimum Wages Act or any other Act for the time being in force. In this method, output produced by the worker is not relevant for calculating wages.

Computation of Wages — Under this method, the wages are computed as under:

Wages = Actual time devoted × Time rate

For example — Mr X, a worker, gets Rs 10 per hour. If he works for 8 hours, he will get Rs 80 (i.e., 8 × Rs 10).

Usefulness — This method is useful in the following circumstances:

1. Where a worker has to do a variety of dissimilar jobs.
2. Where tasks cannot be readily measured, inspected and counted.
3. Where quality of work is especially important.
4. Where supervision is good and supervisors know what constitutes a fair day's work.

5. Where work delays are frequent and beyond the control of employees.
6. Where employees have little control over the quantity of output.

Advantages — The major advantages of this method include the following:

1. This method is **easy to understand**.
2. This method is **easy to compute**.
3. This method is readily acceptable to labour unions as it takes care of the interest of an **average worker**.
4. Workers concentrate on the **quality** rather than the quantity of job.
5. This method is **good for learners and apprentices**.
6. This method serves as the only method of wage payment **where quantum of work cannot be computed** (e.g., in case of repairs and maintenance work).
7. There is **reduced damage** or rough handling of machines, tools and equipments due to slow and steady pace of the workers.
8. It provides a **constant and stable income** to the employees.

Disadvantages — The major disadvantages of this method include the following:

1. There is **no linkage between performance and reward**. Both efficient and inefficient workers get the same amount of wages as long as they spend equal time on the job.
2. **High degree of supervision** is required to secure a fair day's work.
3. There develops a **tendency to go slow** during the normal working hours in the hope of getting overtime wages. This tendency arises where the practice of overtime wages is prevailing.
4. There is no incentive to improve methods and procedures.

PIECE RATE METHOD

There are basically two types of piece-rates — Straight Piece Rate and Differential Piece Rate

Meaning of Straight Piece Rate — Under this method, a worker is paid at a fixed rate per unit produced or job completed. In this method, time spent on job is not considered for calculating wages.

Computation of Wages — Under this method, the wages are computed as under:

Wages = Number of units produced x Piece rate per unit

For example — Mr *Y*, a worker, gets Rs 5 per piece. If he produces 20 pieces, he will get Rs 100 (i.e., 20 x Rs 5).

Usefulness — This method is useful in the following circumstances:

1. Where a worker has to do the jobs of repetitive or standard nature.
2. Where tasks can be readily measured, inspected and counted.
3. Where the quality consideration is less important than quantity of output.
4. Where high degree of supervision is not required.

Advantages — The major advantages of this method include the following:

1. The **linkage between performance and reward** motivates the employee to produce more and earn more.
2. **Low degree of supervision** is required because the workers themselves take care of the time and output.
3. **Cost ascertainment is simple** because labour cost for each unit is available.

Disadvantages — The major disadvantages of this method include the following:

1. This method is not useful where quality is more important than quantity because employees tend to increase the quantity ignoring the quality thereof.
2. This method does not reward the employees for seniority or merit.
3. The calculation of piece rate is more difficult than time rate.
4. Workers feel insecure in the absence of any guaranteed wages as in case of time rate method.
5. Earnings tend to fluctuate since the employee may not produce equally over all periods of time.

Differential Piece Rate

Features

The main features of this system are:

1. It offers a higher piece rate to workers beyond a defined level of output;
2. It distinguishes between workers through two types of piece rates: (i) a lower rate for sub-standard performance (say 80% of piece rate), and (ii) a higher rate for standard and above standard performance, which is much more than time wages (say 120% of piece rate)
3. It acts a an additional incentive to expert workers towards maximization of production; and
4. It ignores any form of guaranteed day wages.

Method of Computation

Total earnings of a worker whose performance is below standard
= Number of units produced × Piece rate per unit × 80%
Total earning of a worker whose performance is standard or above standard
= Number of units produced × Piece rate unit × 120%

Illustration

Standard Time allowed   10 units per hour
Normal Piece Rate   Rs 5 for 10 units
Differential Piece Rate:
80% of Piece Rate for output below standard
120% of Piece Rate for output at or above standard

A produces 75 units in a day of 8 hours
B produces 100 units in a day of 8 hours

Required — Compute wages of A and B under Differential Piece Rate System

Solution

Piece Rate will be 5 ÷ 10 = Re 0.50 per unit
Standard Output in 8 hours is = 8 × 10 = 80 units
So A's performance is below standard and B's above standard.
Earnings of A = 75 × 0.50 × 80% = Rs 30
Earning of B = 100 × 0.50 × 120% = Rs 60

DISTINCTION BETWEEN TIME RATE OF WAGES AND PIECE RATE OF WAGES

Time rate of wages and piece rate of wages can be distinguished as follows:

Basis of Distinction	Time Rate of Wages	Piece Rate of Wages
1. **Basis of payment**	A worker is paid at a fixed rate **per hour**, per day or per month for the time devoted by a worker.	A worker is paid at a fixed rate **per unit** produced or job completed.
2. **Linkage between performance and reward**	There is **no linkage** between performance and reward. Both efficient and inefficient workers get the same amount of wages as long as they spend equal time on the job.	The **linkage** between performance and reward motivates the people to produce more and earn more.
3. **Degree of supervision**	Workers need to be controlled through constant and **close** supervision to secure reasonable contribution from the workers in terms of quantity of the product.	Workers *need not be* controlled through **constant and close** supervision as the workers themselves take care of the time and output.
4. **Usefulness**	This method is useful where a worker has to do a variety of **dissimilar jobs** or where tasks cannot be readily measured, inspected and counted.	This method is useful where a worker has to do the jobs of a **repetitive nature** or where tasks can be readily measured, inspected and counted.
5. **Adoption**	This method is adopted for compensating **clerical staff**, managers and operatives employed in jobs which do not require much skill.	This method is adopted *for* compensating **skilled and official workers** who can increase their earning by working to their full capacity.
6. **Assurance**	A worker is **assured** of his wages for work period irrespective of his output.	**No** such **assurance** is given.

Which method of wage payment-time rate or piece rate would you adopt in the following situations and why?

1. When a collective effort of a group of individuals is necessary for completion of a job?
2. When skilled personnel is engaged in tasks requiring high quality workmanship?
3. Where quantity of work can be readily measured, inspected and counted?
4. Where the work is of a repetitive nature and there is a need to increase the production?
5. Where the nature of work requires close supervision?

Ans.

Situation	Suitable Wage Rate Method	Reason
(a)	Time Rate	Because this system is more suitable when it is difficult to measure precisely the output of individual workers.
(b)	Time Rate	Because high quality work is required, i.e., workers are not in a hurry to complete their work to get more wages.
(c)	Piece Rate	Because quantity of work is measurable and it is easy to differentiate between efficient and non-efficient workers.
(d)	Piece Rate	Because there is a need to increase the production and work is of a repetitive nature and no supervision and no skilled personnel is required. Further, quality is not so important.
(e)	Time Rate	Because quality is more important than quantity and the nature of work requires close supervision.

INCENTIVE PLANS

Meaning of incentive plans

Wages are paid to labour on time rate or piece rate. But individual performance must also receive attention in a structure of wages so that an appreciable difference is maintained between a good worker, an average worker and a bad worker. Since, efficiency of labour usually saves time and cost, it would be justified that a portion of the benefit which goes to the organization through labour efficiency is also shared by those who generate this benefit. **Incentive plans are used to compensate the efficiency of labour for his extra efforts used in minimizing the time or cost.** It may be in the form of a bonus or premium. Incentive plans are devised to compensate the worker through an additional payment over and above their guaranteed wages. The plans also aim at keeping efficient workers satisfied with their employment. The standard time and standard performance are determined in advance so as to judge individual contribution. In case there is a gain on time saved, it is distributed between the employers and workers.

The **main features** of most incentive plans are:

1. The standard time and standard performance are determined in advance.
2. Time wages are guaranteed to all workers.
3. Efficient workers are given incentive by way of bonus for the time saved.
4. Wages per hour increase but not in the same proportion as the output.
5. Labour cost per unit of output decreases. The employer also shares the benefit of efficiency which induced him to improve the methods and equipment.

Lets us discuss the various incentive plans as under:

Halsey Premium Plan

Features of Halsey Premium Plan

The main features of Halsey Premium Plan as a method of incentive to efficient workers are as follows:

1. Standard time and standard work are prescribed in advance.
2. Workers are paid for the actual time they take to complete the job as per the time rate.
3. If a worker complete the job in less than the pre-determined standard time, he is given a bonus for the time saved. This is in addition to his wages for the actual time spent on the job.
4. A bonus equal to 50 per cent of the wages of time saved is paid to the worker as a reward to his good work.
5. Workers who fail to reach the prescribed standard get the time wage.

Merits of Halsey Premium Plan

1. It is a simple system to operate.
2. It guarantees the hourly wages to workers for the actual time.

Demerits of Halsey Premium Plan

1. Fixation of standard time is a difficult process.
2. Workers however, feel that they do not get the full benefit for the time saved under this system.

Method of Computation of Halsey Premium Plan

Total Earnings of the worker = Time Rate Wages + Bonus
= (Time Rate × Actual Time taken)
$+ \frac{1}{2} \times$ Time Saved × Time Rate

or,
$= (AH \times R) + \frac{1}{2} \times (SH - AH) \times R$

Where, SH = Standard time
AH = Actual time taken
R = Rate of Wages per hour

Illustration The standard Hours for a Job = 8 hours, Actual Hours = 6 hours, Wage Rate per Hour = Rs 7. Calculate earnings according to Halsey Plan.

Solution. Time rate wages = AH × R = 6 × Rs 7 = 42

$$\text{Bonus} = \frac{1}{2} \times (SH - AH) \times R = \frac{1}{2}(8-6) \times Rs\ 7 = Rs\ 7$$

Total earnings of the worker = Time Rate Wages + Bonus

= Rs 42 + Rs7 = Rs 49

Average rate of actual earnings per hour

$$= \frac{\text{Total Earnings}}{\text{Actual Hours}} = \frac{Rs\ 49}{6} = Rs\ 8.167 \text{ per hour}$$

Rowan Premium Plan

Features of Rowan Premium Plan

Rowan Premium Plan is similar to Halsey Plan. The main features of Rowan Plan are:

1. Workers are paid for the actual time taken by them in completing the job on the basis of time rate.
2. They are paid a bonus for the time saved, i.e., for the difference between the standard time and actual time.
3. Bonus under this method is calculated as a proportion of the time wages as time saved bears to the standard time.

Merits of Rowan Premium Plan

1. It is a simple system to operate.
2. It guarantees the hourly wages to workers for the actual time.
3. The worker is not induced to rush through the work because if time saved is more than 50 per cent of the standard time, the bonus will decrease.

Demerits of Rowan Premium Plan

1. Fixation of standard time is a difficult process.
2. Workers however, feel that they do not get the full benefit for the time saved under this system
3. The calculation of bonus is complicated.

Method of Computation of Rowan Premium Plan

Total Earning = Time Rate Wages + Bonus

$$= (AH \times R) + \frac{AH}{SH} \times (SH - AH) \times R$$

Illustration Standard Hours for a Job 8 Hours, Actual Hours 6 Hours, Wage Rate per Hour Rs 7. Calculate earnings according to Rowan Plan.

Solution. Time Rate Wages = AH × R = 6 × Rs 7= Rs 42

$$\text{Bonus} = \frac{AH}{SH}(SH - AH) \times R = \frac{6}{8}(8-6) \times Rs\ 7 = Rs\ 10.50$$

Total earnings of the worker $\quad$ = Time Rate Wages + Bonus

$$= Rs\ 42 + Rs\ 10.50 = Rs\ 52.50$$

$$\text{Average rate of actual earnings per hour} = \frac{\text{Total Earnings}}{\text{Actual Hours}} = \frac{Rs\ 52.50}{6}$$

$$= Rs\ 8.75 \text{ per hour}$$

Illustration The standard time allowed to complete a job is 100 hours and the hourly rate of wage payment is Rs 5. The actual time taken by the worker to complete the job is 80 hours. Calculate the total wages of the worker on the basis of

(i)　Time Rate

(ii)　Piece Rate

(iii)　Halsey Plan

(iv)　Rowan Plan

Also compare the effective earnings per hour under the above methods.

Solution

(i)　**Time Rate Wages**

　　Total Wages = 80 × Rs 5 = Rs 400

(ii)　**Piece Rate Wages**

　　Total Wages = 100 × Rs 5 = Rs 500

(iii)　**Halsey Plan**

Time Rate Wages for 80 hours at Rs 5 per hour= Rs 400

$$\text{Bonus} = \frac{1}{2} \times (SH - AH) \times R$$

$$= \frac{1}{2} \times (100 - 80) \times Rs\ 5 = Rs\ 50$$

Total Wages = Time Rate Wages + Bonus = Rs 400 + Rs 50 = Rs 450

(iv)　**Rowan Plan**

Time Rate Wages for 80 hours @ Rs 5 per hour= Rs 400

$$\text{Bonus for Time Saved} = \frac{AH}{SH}(SH - AH) \times R = \frac{80}{100} \times (100 - 80) \times Rs\ 5 = Rs\ 80$$

Total Wages = Rs 400 + Rs 80 = Rs 480

Comparative Earnings per Hour

Time Rate = Rs 400 ÷ 80 = Rs 5

Piece Wage = Rs 500 ÷ 80 = Rs 6.25

Halsey Plan = Rs 450 ÷ 80 = Rs 5.625

Rowan Plan = Rs 480 ÷ 80 = Rs.6

Illustration A worker completes a job in 6 hours as against the standard time of 8 hours. If the hourly wage rate is Rs 5, how much bonus will be given to him under Hasley plan and Rowan Plan? As a manager of the organization, which plan will you prefer and why?

Solution

Bonus under Halsey Plan $= \dfrac{1}{2} (SH - AH) \times R = \dfrac{1}{2} (8 - 6) \times Rs.5 = Rs.5$

Bonus under Rowan Plan $= \dfrac{AH}{SH} \times (SH - AH) \times R$

$= \dfrac{6}{8} \times (8 - 6) \times Rs\ 5 = Rs\ 7.50$

It is evident that Halsey Plan is economical but workers are exploited and quality of goods is affected. But under Rowan Plan beside assurance of minimum wages of workers, they are *neither* exploited *nor* overburdened. Quality of goods is comparatively maintained.

Hence, Rowan Plan is better than Halsey Plan.

Gantt Task Bonus Plan

This system combines the (a) Time Wage, (b) Piece Wage, and (c) Bonus Plan. It mainly follows a differential piece rate basis of remuneration with the following method of computation:

1. Output below standard to be paid at Guaranteed Time Rate
2. Output at standard to be paid at 120% of Time Rate
3. Output above standard to be paid at high piece rate (i.e., 120% of Ordinary Piece Rate) on the entire output of the worker.

Gantt System, therefore, offers an incentive to efficient workers for increased production. It means lesser the time consumed in completing the job, higher the earnings per hour. The standard output within a specified period is pre-determined. Bonus is paid at the rate of 20% for 100% efficiency. Those workers who complete their job in the standard time are treated as 100 per cent efficient. They get wages for time taken plus bonus at a fixed percentage of wages. If a worker completes his job in less than the standard time, he gets wages for standard time *plus* bonus at a fixed percentage of wages earned (which is usually 20%). Slow workers, however, still get the guaranteed wage of the day.

Illustration

Standard Rate = Rs 5 per hour

Standard Hours for the Job = 8 hours

Bonus = 20% of Standard Time

Worker A completes the work in 10 hours

Worker B completes the work in 8 hours

Worker C completes the work in 6 hours

Required — Compute the earnings of A, B and C under Gantt Task Bonus Plan.

Solution. The comparative earnings per hour of the three workers will be computed as follows:

A: Wages for 10 hours at Rs 5 per hour = Rs 50

B: Wages for 8 hours at Rs 5 per hour = Rs 40 + 20% of 8 hours' wages

= Rs 40 + 8 = Rs 48

C: Wages for 6 hours = Wages of 8 hours at Rs 5 per hour

= Rs 40 + 20% of 8 hours' wages=Rs 48

A's earnings per hour = Rs $\dfrac{50}{10}$ = Rs 5

B's earnings per hour = Rs $\dfrac{48}{8}$ = Rs 6

C's earnings per hour = $\dfrac{48}{6}$ = Rs 8

EXERCISES

SHORT ANSWER TYPE QUESTIONS

Staffing

1. What is meant by staffing as a function of management?
2. Explain the nature of staffing.
3. "Staffing is a continuous function." Explain.
4. "Staffing is a basic function of every manager." Explain.
5. Why is the staffing function considered to be the key of other managerial function?
6. "Staffing is the responsibility of managers and not of the personnel." Explain.

Manpower Planning

7. State the need for human resource planning? Why is manpower planning necessary? Give three reasons.
8. Why do present day organisations undertake systematic human resources planning?
9. Enumerate the elements involved in human resource.

Recruitment and Selection

10. What is meant by recruitment of employees?
11. Distinguish between recruitment and selection.

12. What is the difference between the aim of recruitment and that of selection of employees?

13. (a) State the internal sources of recruitment.

    (b) Write a short note on 'Promotions and Transfers.'

14. Briefly explain any three advantages of recruiting employees from internal sources.

15. State the external sources of recruitment.

16. Briefly explain any three advantages of recruiting employees from external sources.

17. What is preliminary screening of candidates for employment?

Training

18. State the meaning of training.

19. State the objectives of training.

20. State the importance of training.

21. Describe the benefits of training to an organisation.

22. State the requirements of training.

23. Enumerate the various methods of training. Enumerate the need for training.

24. What is job rotation?

25. What is coaching method of training?

26. What is vestibule training?

27. What is apprenticeship training?

28. What is Internship?

29. State the methods used for the training of workers.

30. What is meant by on the job training?

31. What is meant by off the job training?

32. Explain any four off the job methods of training.

33. Explain any two on the job methods of training.

34. What is case study method of training?

35. What is conference method of training?

36. What is seminar method of training?

37. What is role playing method of training?

38. What is sensitivity training?

39. Distinguish between 'on the job training' and 'off the job training'.

Development

40. What is meant by 'employees' development'?

41. Distinguish between training and development with reference to personnel management.

42. Distinguish between training and development on the basis of level of trainees and scope of learning.

43. Compare and contrast among training, education and development.

Compensation

44. Define the term 'compensation' in personnel management?
45. What is meant by 'equitable compensation' in personnel management?
46. Give the financial elements of income. State the methods of wage payment.
47. What is time rate wage method?
48. State the circumstances under which time rate wage method is suitable.
49. State any four advantages of time rate wage method.
50. State any four disadvantages (or limitations) of time rate wage method.
51. What is piece rate wage method?
52. State the circumstances under which piece rate wage method is suitable.
53. State any two advantages of piece rate wage method.
54. State any two disadvantages of piece rate wage method.
55. What is differential Piece Rate Method?
56. What is Halsey Plan?
57. What is Rown Plan?
58. What is Gant Task Bonus Plant?
59. Which method of wage payment-time rate or piece rate would you prefer in the following situations?
    (a) when production process is complicated and requires high degree of skill
    (b) when quantity of output is more important than its quality
    (c) when job is of a repetitive nature and output can easily be measured
    (d) when collective efforts of a group of workers are required for the performance of work
    (e) when workers have no control over the rate of output
    (f) when work and work methods are of a standardised nature
    (g) when workers are to be remunerated on a group basis
    (h) when quality of output is more important than its quantity
    (i) when machines used are delicate and expensive
60. Why are human resources considered as the most valuable resources of an enterprise?
61. Enumerate the steps involved in the process of staffing.
62. What is meant by 'manpower planning'?
63. Enumerate the steps involved in 'manpower planning'.
64. What is meant by 'job analysis'?
65. What is meant by 'job description'?
66. What is meant by 'job specification'?
67. What is meant by 'job evaluation'?
68. State the meaning of 'recruitment'.

69. Enumerate the external sources of recruitment.
70. Enumerate the internal sources of recruitment.
71. Why is recruitment considered to be positive process?
72. What is meant by 'selection'?
73. Why is selection considered to be negative process?
74. Enumerate the steps involved in the selection procedure.
75. State the meaning of placement as a staffing function.
76. State the meaning of training.
77. What is meant by orientation of employees?
78. In a small organisation who performs the staffing function?

LONG ANSWER TYPE QUESTIONS

Staffing

1. What is meant by staffing? Explain briefly its needs and importance.
2. Explain the meaning and nature of staffing. What are the various elements in the process of staffing?
3. What is staffing? Briefly discuss the steps in the process of staffing.
4. 'Human Resource Management is an extension of the staffing function'. Discuss.
5. Explain the role and responsibility of staffing in a large organisation.

Human Resources Planning

6. What is manpower planning? How will you assess the manpower requirements of a business enterprise?
7. What is meant by manpower planning? Why is it important?
8. What is human resource planning? Explain briefly the steps involved in the human resource planning.
9. What is recruitment? Explain briefly the various external sources of recruitment of employees.
10. What is selection? Explain briefly the steps involved in the selection procedure.

Recruitment and Selection

11. Describe the two sources of supply of manpower.
12. Describe briefly the advantages and disadvantages of internal sources of recruitment.
13. Describe briefly the advantages and disadvantages of external sources of recruitment.
14. Briefly describe the steps taken in the selection of personnel.
15. How are candidates short-listed through preliminary and selection interview?
16. Explain the process of selection in a modern business organisation.
17. Describe the benefits and limitations of conducting interviews?

Training

18. What is the meaning of training? What are its chief objectives?

19. State the factors which give rise to the need for training of employees.

17. Explain the benefits of training as an effective tool in increasing the efficiency of a firm.

20. What do you mean by on the job training? Explain the various methods of on the job training.

21. What is meant by off the job training? State and explain any three methods of off the job training.

22. Discuss the major off the job training methods meant to train the managers.

23. Briefly explain the job training methods.

24. "Training increases job-skill while development shapes attitudes." In the light of this statement explain the nature of relationship between training and development.

Compensation

25. What is meant by 'time rate wage method'? Describe its suitability, advantages and disadvantages.

26. What is meant by 'piece rate wage method'? Describe its suitability, benefits and limitations.

27. Distinguish between time wage method and piece wage method.

28. Distinguish between Monetary and Non-Monetary Incentives.

29. Name the concepts which relate to the following:
    (i) Determining the competence of an employee
    (ii) Calculating the worth of a job

30. Discuss the benefits and limitations of piece-wage incentive plan.

31. Explain the Halsey Plan with the help of an example.

32. Explain the Rown Incentive Plan with the help of an example.

33. Explain the Gantt Task Bonus Plan with the help of an example.

21 Directing— Supervision

┌─ **LEARNING OBJECTIVES** ─────────────────────┐

After studying this chapter, you should be able to know —

— Meaning of Direction
— Features of Directing Function
— Importance of Direction
— Elements of Direction
— Meaning of Supervision
— Meaning of Supervisor
— Role of Supervisor
— Functions of a Supervisor
— Distinction between Direction and Supervision

└──┘

MEANING OF DIRECTION

Directing as a function of management is the process of instructing, guiding, supervising, motivating and leading the subordinates to contribute to the best of their capabilities for the achievement of organisational objectives.

More specifically, directing is telling the subordinates what to do, how to do and seeing that they do it to the best of their abilities.

Directing comprises—

1. issuing orders and instructions by a superior to his subordinates;

2. motivating subordinates to contribute to the best of their capabilities for the achievement of organisational objectives;

3. providing leadership to subordinates to influence group activities towards the achievement of certain goals;

4. observing the subordinates at work to ensure that they are working according to plans and policies of the organisation and helping subordinates to resolve their work problems.

FEATURES OF DIRECTING FUNCTION

The main features of directing function are shown below:

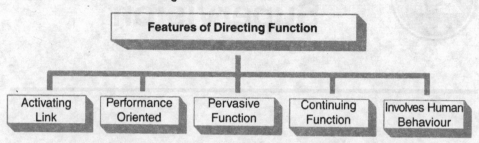

Let us discuss the features of directing function one by one.

1. **Activating Link** — It is a connecting and activating link among all the managerial functions. Direction may also be regarded as the heart of management process. It is a process around which all performance revolves. Planning, organising and staffing are preparatory functions whereas controlling is a continuous checking process. It is the direction function which helps in coordinating all these functions for the achievement of organisational objectives.

   Planning, organising and staffing functions are concerned with creating the preconditions for taking appropriate action to accomplish the organisational goals whereas the directing function is concerned with making actual use of these preconditions. It converts plans into results and provides the basis for control.

2. **Performance-Oriented** — Direction is a performance-oriented function in the sense that it converts plans into performance. It is a creative function that makes things happen.

3. **Pervasive Function** — Direction is a pervasive function in the sense that it exists at every level, location and operation throughout the organisation.

4. **Continuing Function** — Direction is a continuing function in the sense that it is required on continuous basis. The techniques and methods of direction have to be changed with changing organisational conditions.

5. **Involves Human Behaviour** — Direction involves the management of human behaviour. A superior is required to understand the needs, aspirations and expectations of his subordinates in order to manage them effectively. Directing concerns the total manner in which a manager influences his subordinates.

IMPORTANCE OF DIRECTION

Direction is the heart, the essence, of the management process in the sense that it works as a nucleus around which all other management functions like planning, organisating, staffing revolve.

The importance of direction arises due to the following benefits which flow from it.

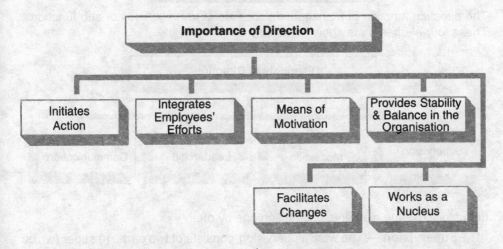

1. **Initiates Action** — It makes use of the preconditions created by planning, organising and staffing and initiates action by issuing instructions to subordinates and by supervising their work. Thus, without direction, other managerial activities like planning, organising and staffing remain ineffective.

2. **Integrates Employees' Efforts** — It is the integrating function of management in the sense that it integrates the individual and group goals with organisational objectives. It integrates the efforts of employees by supervising, guiding and counselling.

3. **Means of Motivation** — It motivates the employees to contribute to the best of their abilities for the achievement of organisational objectives.

4. **Provides Stability & Balance in the Organisation** — It brings about stability and balance in the organisation through interpersonal communication, effective leadership and motivation.

5. **Facilitates Changes** — It enables the organisation to cope with the changing conditions of the environment through effective communication and persuasive leadership. Resistance to change is human behaviour. Before the change is introduced, the employees may be informed about the nature of changes and the benefits that are likely to follow and they may be taken into confidence through persuasive leadership and information sharing.

6. **Works as a Nucleus** — It works as a nucleus around which all other management functions revolve.

ELEMENTS OF DIRECTION

The directing function of management consists of four elements or sub-functions. These four elements are shown on below:

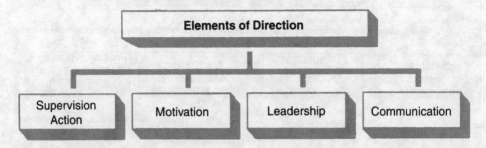

Let us discuss the elements of direction one by one.

1. **Supervision** — The word 'supervision' consists of two parts: (i) super (which means over and above) and (ii) vision (which is the art of seeing objects or viewing mental images or looking over). In management, the term 'supervision' means overseeing the subordinates at work by their superiors.

2. **Motivation** — It may be defined as the process of stimulating people to action to accomplish desired goals.

3. **Leadership** — It may be defined as the process of influencing the behaviour of other members of the group to attain organisational objectives.

4. **Communication** — It may be defined as the process of sending a message to another and ensuring that the receiver has understood it in the same sense as intended by the sender.

SUPERVISION

MEANING OF SUPERVISION

The word **'supervision'** consists of two parts:

(i) **super** (which means over and above) and

(ii) **vision** (which is the art of seeing objects or viewing mental images or looking over). In management, the term **'supervision'** means overseeing the subordinates at work by their superiors.

In other words, supervision means observing the subordinates at work to ensure that they are working according to the plans and schedules and to help them in solving their work problems.

Pervasiveness of supervision — Supervision exists at every level, location and operation throughout the organisation. Top management supervises the work of middle level managers who in turn supervise the work of first line managers who in turn supervise the employees engaged in basic operations. This has been shown on next page:

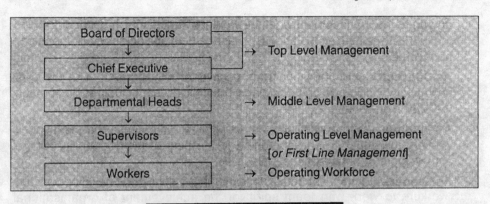

MEANING OF SUPERVISOR

The term 'supervisor' refers to a person who assigns work to subordinates and oversees their activities and performance. In management, the first line managers at operating level management are called 'supervisors' because it is the primary or basic duty of first line managers to supervise the employees engaged in the basic operations (also called operating workforce). The first line manager may also be designated as 'foreman', 'chargeman', 'overseer', 'section incharge' and' superintendent'.

ROLE OF SUPERVISOR

The role of a supervisor in an organisation has been shown below:

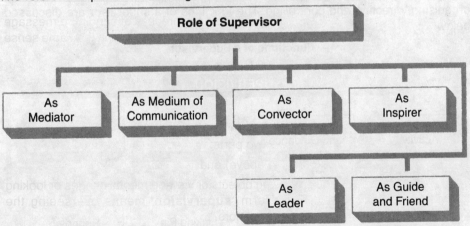

Let us discuss the role of supervisor one by one.

1. **As Mediator** — Supervisor acts as a mediator between higher level management and the workers.

2. **As Medium of Communication** — Supervisor acts as a medium of communication between higher level managers and workers. He explains management policies to the workers and conveys the workers' attitudes, opinions, grievances and problems to higher level management. In other words, he communicates (i) to the workers what the management expects from them

and (ii) to the management what the workers want. Thus, supervisor bridges the gap between the expectations of management and demands of operatives and workers.

3. **As Convector** — Supervisor acts as a convertor in the sense that he occupies such a key position which turns plans and policies into actual results through the efforts of workers.

4. **As Inspirer** — Supervisor acts as an inspirer in the sense that he inspires workers to cooperate and contribute to the best of their capability for the achievement of organisational objectives.

5. **As Leader** — Supervisor acts as a leader in the sense that he influences the workers to work with team spirit for the achievement of organisational objectives. He also provides a cohesive force which holds the group intact and develops a spirit of cooperation and discipline among the employees.

6. **As Guide and Friend** — Supervisor acts as a guide and friend in the sense that he educates and trains the workers, creates friendly environment and solves the disputes of the workers. In this way, he ensures team spirit, co-operation and discipline amongst the members.

Thus, the supervisor is expected to secure not only the efficiency of operations but also the team spirit, co-operation and discipline among the employees.

FUNCTIONS OF A SUPERVISOR

Supervisors perform all the basic functions of management, namely, planning, organising, directing and controlling. The functions of a supervisor are discussed below:

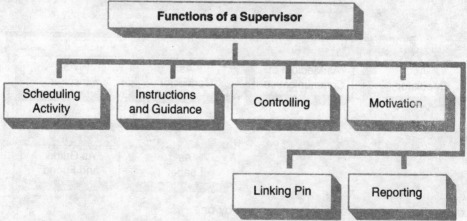

Let us discuss the functions of a supervisor one by one.

1. **Scheduling Activity** — The supervisor prepares the schedule of activities of the work group under his supervision to ensure that each work is completed according to schedule.

2. **Instructions and Guidance** — The supervisor issues orders and instructions to subordinates, guides them and resolves their problems.

3. **Controlling** — The supervisor controls the work and work group. He regulates the performance of workers and takes remedial action whenever necessary.

4. **Motivation** — The supervisor inspires and directs behaviour towards better performance.

5. **Linking Pin** — The supervisor acts as a linking pin between management and operatives. On the one hand, he communicates management decisions to the workers and implements plans and policies of the management and, on the other hand, as a representative of the operatives, he conveys their suggestions and complaints to higher level management.

6. **Reporting** —The supervisor prepares periodic reports —

   (i)   on the progress of work entrusted to him,

   (ii) on the fulfillment of planned tasks, and

   (iii) on the performance of his work team.

He sends the consolidated report to the top management at Periodic intervals of a week, a month or quarter.

DISTINCTION BETWEEN DIRECTION AND SUPERVISION

Direction and supervision can be distinguished as follows:

1. Direction is a wider term than supervision. Supervision is one of the elements of direction.

2. Direction is given by the top level management whereas supervision is done by the operative level management.

3. Direction as a function of management is performed at all levels of management whereas supervisory function is preformed at selective levels of management in the organisation.

4. Direction is the process of issuing orders and instructions for guiding and inspiring the human behaviour in the enterprise while supervision is the process of checking and comparing the performance of personnel in the organisation.

———————— EXERCISES ————————

SHORT ANSWER TYPE QUESTIONS

1. State the meaning of 'direction'.
2. Explain in brief the nature (or features) of directing function of management.
3. Give any three elements of directing.
4. State in brief the elements of directing.
5. What is meant by the term 'supervision' in management?
6. What is meant by pervasiveness of supervision?
7. Explain the meaning of 'supervisor'.
8. Explain briefly any four functions of a supervisor.

9. Give two functions of a supervisor.
10. Distinguish between direction and supervision.

LONG ANSWER TYPE QUESTIONS

1. Explain the importance of directing as a function of management.
2. "Directing is the essence of management." Explain.
3. "Directing is the heart of the management process." Explain.
4. Explain in brief the nature of direction.
5. Explain in brief the role and functions of a supervisor in an organisation.
6. Explain in brief the functions of a supervisor.

22 Directing— Motivation

LEARNING OBJECTIVES

After studying this chapter, you should be able to know —

— Meaning of Motivation
— Nature of Motivation
— Process of Motivation
— Importance of Motivation
— Maslow's Need Hierarchy — Proposition, Merits, Criticism
— McGreger's Theory X and Theory Y
  • Assumptions about the Nature of People at Work
  • Approaches to Manage the people at work under Theory X and Theory Y
  • Characteristics of Theory X and Theory Y Oriented Organisation
  • Criticism of Theory X and Theory Y
— Herzberg's Motivation–Hygiene Theory
  • Comparative Study of Maintenance Factors and Motivational Factors
  • Some other observations of Herzberg's Theory
  • Criticism of Herzberg's Theory
  • Advantages of Herzberg's Theory
— Comparison of between Herzberg's and Maslow's Theories
— Relationship between Herzberg's and Maslow's Theories
— Incentives — Meaning, Need, Positive, Negative, Monetary, Non-Monetary

INTRODUCTION

In any organisation, some employees are found to be more efficient than others. The difference in their performance can be due to differences *either* in their abilities *or* in their willingness to perform as best as possible. The performance of an individual is considered as a product function of two different variables as follows:

1. An individual's ability/capacity to perform the work;
2. An individual's willingness to use his ability to perform the work.

In algebric terms, if **P** stands for performance, **C** stands for capacity to perform work and **M** stands for willingness to use capacity to perform the work, then **P** may be expressed as follows:

> Performance = Capacity to perform work × Willingness to use capacity to perform the work
>
> $$P = C \times M$$

Thus, given the ability, it is the willingness of employees which determines whether they will be more efficient or less. Similarly, given the willingness, it is the ability of empoyees which determine whether they will be more efficient or less.

How to make people work more or work better is an issue that requires an understanding of what motivates people to do so.

MEANING OF MOTIVATION

The term 'motivation' is derived from the word 'motive'. Motive may be defined as needs, wants, drives or impulses within the individual,

Need — A need is a requirement of a person for operational adjustment to the environmental. **For example,** need for food, need for shelter.

Want — Want is similar to need but implies that the object is social, not merely physiological.

Drive — A drive is a physiological condition that moves the person to satisfy needs. It is not specifically directed to some object. **For example,** the hunger drive moves a hungary person to satisfy a need for food but not towards a specific type of food.

Motive — A motive is an inner psychological state of an individual which activates, directs, sustains or stops his behaviour towads some goal.

Motives are expressions of a person's needs and hence they are personal and internal. Need here means something within an individual that prompts him to action. Motives or needs are 'whys' of behaviour. Motives are the primary energisers of behaviour which prompt people to action. Motives give direction to human behaviour because they are directed towards achievement of certain 'goals'.

Thus, motivation refers to the process by which human needs direct and control the behaviour of a human being. Motivation may also be defined as the process which inspires the people at work to contribute to the best of their capability for the achievement of organisational objectives. In other words, motivation may be defined as the process of stimulating people to action to accomplish desired goals. In simple terms, creation of a will to work or to work more or better is motivation.

NATURE OF MOTIVATION

The characteristics of motives highlight the nature of motivation.

1. **Personal and Internal** — Motives are personal, internal and invisible because these are expressions of a person's needs. Motives are the energising forces within us. Motivation is a psychological phenomenon which arises from the feeling of needs and wants of individuals.

2. **Differ from Individual to Individual** — Motives differ from individual to individual because every individual has his own set of needs at a particular point of time.

3. **Differ from Time to Time** — Motives energising us differ from time to time. Motives come and go. A motive need not have the same energy potential at all points of time.

4. **Different Behaviour from same Motive** — One motive may result in many different behaviours.

5. **Same Behaviour from Different Motives** — The same behaviour may result from many different motives. That's why a motive cannot be identified from any specific behaviour.

6. **Continuous Process** — Motivation is a continuous process because human needs are unlimited and fulfillment of one set of needs gives rise to another set of needs.

7. **Pervasive Function** — Motivation is required in all types of organisation (commercial, social, religious, political, small or large) and at all levels of management. However, its ways, methods, forms and types may differ at different levels of management as also in different organisations.

8. **Behaviour for Estimating Motives** — Repeated behaviour can be used as an estimate of an individual's motives. It is possible to get repeated observations of one individual's behaviour and then make an estimate of the cause of that behaviour.

9. **Operate in Harmony or in Conflict** — Motives can operate in harmony or in conflict. For example, a student may want to get high marks in school while also wanting to help his father in the business.

10. **Interact with the Environment** — Motives interact with the environment.

11. **Causes Goal-Directed Behaviour** — Motives cause goaldirected behaviour.

PROCESS OF MOTIVATION

The elements of the process of motivation are:

(1) motives, (2) behaviour, (3) goal, (4) feedback. The process of motivation has been shown below:

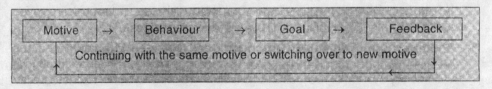

Motive → Behaviour → Goal → Feedback

Continuing with the same motive or switching over to new motive

1. **Motive** — Motive may also be termed as need, drive or want. Motives prompt people to action. Motives determine the general direction of an individual's behaviour.

2. **Behaviour** — Behaviour is a series of activities of an individual. It is generally motivated by a desire to achieve a goal.

3. **Goal** — Motives are directed towards goals. Goals are the ends which provide satisfaction of human wants.

4. **Feedback** — Feedback may be in the form of reduction or increase in tension.

IMPORTANCE OF MOTIVATION

Motivation is the core of management. The importance of motivation arises from the benefits which flow from it. These benefits are shown below:

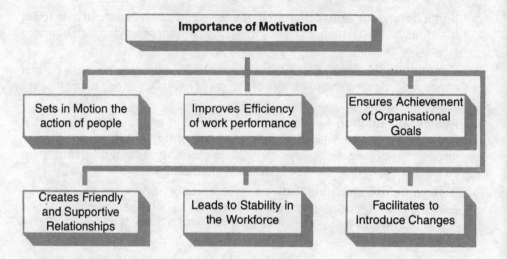

Let us discuss the benefits arising out of motivation one by one.

1. **Sets in Motion the Action of People** — Motivation activates human resources by creating the will to work among human beings. Unless the human resources are activated, the other resources (physical and financial) will remain idle because it is the human resource which activates other resources.

2. **Improves Efficiency of Work Performance** — Motivation improves the efficiency of work performance by bridging the gap between the ability and willingness to work. As a result, quantity and quality of production is increased and cost of operations is reduced. The level of performance of employees depends not only on individual's abilities but also on his willingness to achieve a high level of performance. Given the ability, it is the motive of employee which determines whether he will be more efficient or less.

3. **Ensures Achievement of Organisational Goals** — Motivation ensures achievement of organisational goals by meeting individual needs through a satisfactory system of rewards and by inspiring people at work to contribute to the best of their capabilities for the achievement of organisational goals.

4. **Creates Friendly and Supportive Relationships** — Motivation creates friendly and supportive relationships between the employer and the employees by satisfying them through monetary and non-monetary incentives. When the industrial relations become better, industrial disputes are reduced.

5. **Leads to Stability in the Workforce** — Higher motivation leads to job satisfaction of the workers which reduces absenteeism, labour turnover and labour unrest. Given opportunities in the organisation for need satisfaction, workers will be more committed to the organisation and better workforce will be willing to join the organisation and the loyalty of the employees to work will increase. This results in maintaining stable workforce.

6. **Facilitates to Introduce Changes** — Motivation helps the management in introducing changes in the organisation and to overcome resistance to change because motivated employees support all changes that are in the interest of the organisation as they anticipate their own advancement after the introduction of change.

MASLOW'S NEED HIERARCHY

To get work done with the cooperation of people for the attainment of organisational objectives every manager must study the behaviour of people working under him, determine their needs and provide an environment in which appropriate incentives are available for their need satisfaction. Human needs serve as driving force in human behaviour.

Abraham Maslow explained how needs influence human behaviour through his 'Need Hierarchy Theory of Motivation' in 1943.

1. **Five Types of Human Needs** — He identified five broad types of human needs as follows:

Need	Meaning	Examples
1. **Physiological needs**	These needs relate to the survival and maintenance of human life.	Need for food, clothing, shelter, air, water
2. **Security needs or Safety Needs**	These needs relate to the economic and physical security.	Security of source of income, personal security, provision for old-age insurance against risks.
3. **Social or Affiliation or Acceptance Needs**	These needs relate to social interaction. There are the desires to belong and be socially accepted, to love and be loved, as a social animal. Socialising is one of those reasons why many individuals (especially older people) go to work, and why people generally work better in small groups where they	Need for love, affection, affiliation, acceptance belongingness.

	can develop affiliations that are important to them.	
4. **Esteem or Ego Needs**	These needs relate to the awareness of self-importance and recognition from others.	Need for self-image, self-confidence, self-respect, status, recognition prestiage, attention, and respect from others.
5. **Self-Actualisation or Self-Fulfilment needs**	These needs relate to self-fulfillment. These are the desires to realize one's own full creative potential through creativity, self-expression and self-development to become what one is capable of becoming.	Need to grow, sense of fulfillment, maximum self-development, personal achievement.

2. **Hierarchy of Human Needs** — He proposed that human needs can be arranged in a particular order (i.e., hierarchy) of their importance or prepotency) from the lower to the higher level needs. Physiological needs are placed at the lowest level of hierarchy of needs. Then safety needs, social needs and esteem needs are positioned in ascending order. Self-actualisation needs are placed at the highest level of hierarchy of needs.

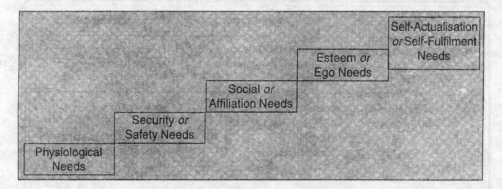

3. **Tendency to satisfy the needs in order** — People tend to satisfy their needs by giving more importance to lower level needs first and then proceeding to higher order needs in a sequential, step by step manner. For example, a hungry man thinks of food and not of security of income. The second need (i.e. security of income) does not dominate unless the first need (i.e., food) is reasonably satisfied.

4. **Satisfaction of a need gives rise to next need** — Reasonable satisfaction of needs at a particular level gives rise to the next higher level needs and is the precondition for activation of the next higher level need. At every level, the

desire to satisfy the felt needs influences human behaviour and motivates people to do something and not to do something to satisfy their needs. Thus, only unsatisfied needs act as a motivator of behaviour. For example, if physiological needs of a person are reasonably satisfied, his need for safety will arise.

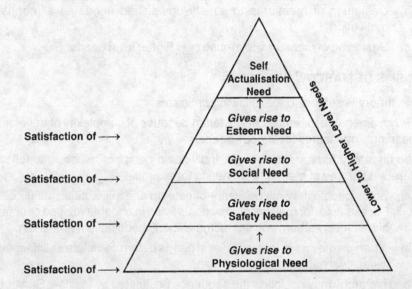

5. **Satisfied need being no longer a motivator** — A satisfied need is no longer a motivator of behaviour. Once a need is satisfied, it no longer motivates behaviour. For example, if a person is assured of his job security, his need for safety is satisfied, he takes job security for granted and hence does not feel aroused to do as good job or do better. He looks for fulfillment of some other unsatisfied need which motivates his behaviour.

6. **Lower Level Needs Finite and Higher Level Needs Infinite** — The physiological and security needs are finite, but the needs of higher order are sufficiently infinite and are likely to be dominant in persons at higher levels in the organisation. Studies have also revealed that those needs which are thought to be most important like social needs, ego needs and self-realisation needs are also the best satisfiers.

MERITS OF MASLOW'S NEED HIERARCHY

Following are the merits of Maslow's Need Hierarchy:

1. It is simple to understand and has an intuitive appeal.

2. It is a general theory of human motivation, broadly applicable to a wide range of cultures.

3. It recognizes the spectrum of human needs and indicates how humans are motivated in their work behaviour.

4. Its basic proposition that deprivation of a need dominates behaviours, seems to be sensible.

5. It provides some guidance to managers on —

    (a) Identification of unfulfilled needs among the various individuals and groups at different levels in organisations

    (b) Designing of measures to satisfy unsatisfied needs as a means of motivation

    (c) Designing of measures to arouse new higher level needs.

CRITICISMS OF MASLOW'S THEORY

Maslow's theory is subject to the following criticisms:

1. It is not amenable for empirical validation because of complexity of developing meaningful measures for various needs.

2. The hierarchy appears to be rigid. Individuals need not necessarily follow a step-by-step way of meeting their needs for example—

    (a) Some people may not be aware of esteem and self-actualisation needs. For example, for majority of individuals living in underdeveloped countries, higher level esteem and self-actualisation needs have no meaning.

    (b) A person may go in for higher level needs before complete satisfaction of lower level needs.

    Need hierarchy may not follow the sequence postulated by Maslow. Surveys in continental European countries and Japan have shown that the model does not apply very well to their managers. The degree of satisfaction of needs does not vary according to the need priority model. For example, workers in Spain and Belgium felt that their esteem needs are better satisfied than their security and social needs. Apparently, cultural differences are an important cause of these differences.

3. It is doubtful whether Self-actualisation is a need or not. it is merely a philosophical and ethical aspiration. It is based on wishes and dreams of what one should be than on What one can be or one is.

4. There is direct link between needs and motivation. Different people may adopt different practices to fulfil the same type of needs. Different types of needs may be gratified by similar methods.

5. It fails to capture the complexity of human needs and motivation since the individuals differ—

    (a) in awareness of their needs;

    (b) in the extent and depth of their needs;

    (c) in their willingness to fulfil their needs;

    (d) in their ability to fulfil their needs;

    (e) in ordering their needs on a preference scale;

    (f) in choosing ways and means to fulfil their needs;

    (g) in the degree of gratification which they desire from meeting their needs.

For example, for some people in need for self-esteem seems to be more prominent than that of love. There are also creative people in whom the drive for creativeness seems to be more important. In certain people, the level of motivation may be permanently lower. For instance, a person who has experienced chronic unemployment may continue to be satisfied for the rest of his life if only he can get enough food. Another cause of reversal of need hierarchy is that when a need has been satisfied for a long time it may be under-evaluated.

6.   Need not necessarily be the only factor which influences an individual's behaviour at a particular point of time. There may be other factors which may affect the behaviour at that time.

7.   It is also doubtful —

   (a)   whether deprivation of a need dominates behaviour at all. It may not motivate the individual in a undirectional positive manner. It may even lead to his depression, diversion, frustration and inaction.

   (b)   Whether relative gratification of needs at a particular level triggers the individuals to move to next higher level needs.

   (c)   Whether a satisfied need causes to motivate. He may remain at that level and continue to seek need fulfillment in a routine manner. Several needs recur in cycles, short or long, and hence satisfaction could not be a permanent or one time affair.

   (d)   one need is satisfied at one time. The phenomenon of multiple motivation is of great practical importance in understanding the behaviour of man. Man's behaviour at any time is mostly guided by multiplicity of motives. However, one or two motives in any situation may be predominant while others may be of secondary importance. Moreover, at different levels of needs, the motivation will be different.

MCGREGER'S THEORY X AND THEORY Y

Douglar McGreger formulated Theories *X* and *Y* as two alternative sets of (1) assumptions about the nature of people at work and (2) approaches to manage the people at work.

Let us study the Assumptions of Theory *X* and Theory *Y* about the nature of people at work, Approaches to Manage the People at work and the Characteristics of Theory *X* and Theory *Y* oriented organisations.

ASSUMPTIONS OF THEORY *X* AND THEORY *Y* ABOUT THE NATURE OF PEOPLE AT WORK

Basis of Assumption	Assumption of Theory X	Assumption of Theory Y
1. **Attitude towards work**	Average human being has **inherent dislike for work.**	Average human being has **not inherent dislike for the work**. Rather he treats engaging in physical and mental efforts **as natural as play or rest.**
2. **Inner Personality**	He is **lazy, dull, self-centred** and simplistic person.	He is **active, intelligence, sociable** and shrewd person.
3. **Capacity to excercise self-direction & self control**	He is **not competent** to excercise self-direction and self-control. External control and the threat are the only means of directing efforts towards organisational efforts. He prefers to be led and directed by others.	He is **competent** to excercise self-direction and self-control. External Control and the threat of punishment are not the only means of directing efforts towards organisational efforts.
4. **Rewards**	Direct result of his efforts towards organisation objectives is the reward in the form **satisfaction of physiological & security needs.**	Direct result of his efforts towards organisation objectives is the reward in the form of **satisfaction of not only physiological, security & social needs but also ego and self-actualisation needs.**
5. **Attitude towards Responsibility**	He **avoids** responsibility.	Average human being learn under proper conditions **not only to accept but to seek responsibility.** Avoidance of responsibility, lack of ambition and emphasis on security are generally consequences of experience and not inherent characteristics.

6.	Capacity to excercise high degree of imagination etc.	The capacity to excercise a high degree of imagination, ingenuity and creativity is **narrowly distributed** in the population and hence, **average human** being **does not have** such capacity.	The capacity to excercise a high degree of imagination, ingenuity and creativity is **widely distributed in the population** and hence, average human being **has such capacity**.
7.	Intellectual Potentialities	He **does not have** intellectual potentialities at all.	Under conditions of modern industrial life, the intellectual potentialities of the average human being are **only partially utilised**.
8.	Attitude towards Achievement	He is **not achievement oriented**.	He is **ambitious and achievement oriented**.
9.	Attitude towards change & challenge	He **resists** change and challenge.	He **accepts** change and challenge.
10.	Range of Needs	He has very **limited** set of needs.	He has a **wide** range of needs, both economic & non-economic.
11.	Static/Dynamic	He is **static** in his attitude towards fulfillment of needs.	He is **dynamic** in his attitude towards fulfillment of needs.
12.	Attitude towards organisational needs	He is **indifferent** to organisational needs.	He is **very much concerned** with organisational needs and wants his organisation to succeed.
13.	Attitude towards decision-making	He is **not competent** to make decision and hence **avoids** making decision.	He is **competent** to make decision and hence **makes** decision within his commitment.

APPROACHES TO MANAGE THE PEOPLE AT WORK UNDER THEORY X AND THEORY Y

Under Theory *X*	Under Theory *Y*
The management has — 1. To assume full responsibility for achieving organisational goals by getting things done through people in a disciplined and structured setting. 2. To guide, direct, control and coerce employees in a strict manner. 3. To administer appropriate rewards and penalities so as to cope with their modest needs and fears. 4. to clearly specify their roles and responsibilities	The management has to design conducive organisational structures and processes so as to enable people— 1. To realise their potential 2. To release their energies 3. To contribute their best to the goals of the organisation. 4. To fulfil their own personal needs.

CHARACTERISTICS OF THEORY X & THEORY Y ORIENTED ORGANISATION

Characteristic	Theory X Oriented Organisation	Theory Y Oriented Organisation
1. **Nature of Organisational Structure**	**Rigid, bureaucratic,** hierarchical, rule-ridden structure exists.	**Flexible and democratic** structure exists.
2. **Degree of Centralisation of Authority**	There is **over centralisation** of Authority.	There is **decentralisation** of authority.
3. **Attitude of Manager**	The Attitude of Manager is **autocratic.**	The attitude of manager is **democratic.**
4. **Communication**	There exists **one way** communication.	There exists a **two-way** communication.
5. **Span of Control**	There exists **narrow** span of control which permits close and coercive supervision.	There exists a **wide** span of control which permits self-direction & self control.
6. **Emphasis on Incentive**	There is over-emphasis on **monetary** incentives.	There is over-emphasis on **non-monetary** incentives.

7.	Nature of Relations between superiors & subordinates	There exists **formal** relations between superiors and subordinates.	There exist **informal** relations between superiors and subordinates.
8.	**Opportunities for initiative etc.**	There are **no opportunities** for initiative, creativity and innovation.	There are **opportunities** for incentives, creativity and innovations.
9.	**Participative Management**	There exists **autocratic** management.	There exists **participative** management.
10.	**Conflict between the organisational goals and individual goals**	There **exists** conflict between the organisational goals and individual goals.	There **does not exist** conflict between the organisational goals and individual goals.
11.	**Usefulness**	These organisations are useful **where people at work are not self-motivated, self controlled, mature and responsible.**	These organisational are useful where **self-motivated, self-controlled, mature and responsible people work.**

CRITICISM OF THEORY *X* AND THEORY *Y*

1. **Not theories at all** — Theory *X* and Theory *Y* were not based on any empirical research but were mere formulations of certain untested propositions and assumptions. They are not theories about human nature for the simple reason that it is too little known to be captured into any theory.

2. **No Average Employee** — There is no 'average' employee as described in Theories *X* and *Y*.

3. **Changing behaviour of Humans** — Human display different behaviour at different times and circumstances. The same human may display —

    (a) stupid behaviour at one time and intelligent behaviour at another time.

    (b) lazy behaviour at one time and hard working behaviour at another time.

    (c) resistant behaviour at one time and acceptance behaviour at another time.

    (d) static behaviour at one time and dynamic behaviour at another time.

    (e) sickness at one time and healthyness at another time.

    (f) dislikeness for work at one time and likeness for work at another time.

    (g) his incompetence to excercise self-direction and self-control at one time and his competence to excercise self-direction and self-control at another time.

(h) his limited range of needs at one time and his wide range of needs at anothertime.

(i) his indifferent behaviour to organisational needs at one time and his concerned behaviour to organisational needs at another time.

(j) his incompetence to make decision at one time and his competence to make decision at another time.

(k) that he is not achievement oriented at one time and that he is achievement oriented at another time.

4. **There is no one best style of management** — In the same organisation, in some situations theory *X* approaches may be wholly justifiable while in others, theory *Y* approaches are preferable. It is far more preferable not to proceed with any pre-conceived stereo types but rather to try to understand people as they are and adopt an approach or combination of approaches appropriate to each situation.

5. **No Conclusive Evidence** — Empirical studies which attempted to test the relevance of these theories have not come out with any conclusive evidence. Some empirical studies showed that Theory *X* based approaches were associated with reasonable employee productivity and satisfaction and other studies showed that the evidence was negative. So has been the case with Theory *Y*.

One US enterprise, 'Non-Linear Systems' experimented with Theory *Y* approaches and after having failed, switched over to Theory *X* approaches.

6. **Ignores Situational Factors** — Theories fail to specify and recognise the situational factors and the contingency nature of organisational effectiveness. These theories fail to provide answers to the questions like —

(a) how far would they prove to be effective in terms of higher productivity, profitability, employee satisfaction and commitment?

(b) If they fail, what is to be done?

The probability of their success or otherwise depends not only on manager but also on subordinates and on several situational factors.

7. **Make High Demands** — Peter Drucker observed that Theory *Y* by itself is not adequate. It makes exceedingly high demands both on managers and on their subordinates. Managers in general are extremely busy people. They have little time and less patience to work out finely tuned human relations approaches. They work under high pressure. Some of them may like to conform to Theory *Y* approach but may not be able to conform by force of circumstances.

8. Theories have been formulated by reference to supervision of workers and employees at operating levels and not by reference to other managers who are subordinates to managers at other than supervisiory levels.

9. **Difference between Personal Philosophy and Professional Approach** — Managers may not allow their personal philosophies to interfere with their

professional approaches. For example, Manager who holds Theory *X* assumption may for tactical and practical reasons adopt Theory *Y* approaches.

10. **Theories Negatively Correlated** — The claim made by McGregor that his theories are not polar opposites but are simply different, is not correct since the empirical studies have showed that theories *X* and *Y* are negatively correlated.

11. Scope for making jobs meaningful and challenging is quite little for some types of jobs. If all people aspire to be assigned challenging tasks, who will do the repetitive, narrow and montonous jobs?

12. Theory *Y* approaches may lead to a decline in managerial motivation and satisfaction though they may result in increase in employee or subordinate satisfaction.

13. Sociologists agree that human behaviour in individual tends to approximate management's expectations under conventional aproach of Theory *X*. But what they do not agree to is that such a behaviour is the consequence of man's inherent nature rather they contend that such behaviour is the outcome of "industrial organisation and management philosophy, policy and practice." Thus, cause is mistaken for effect.

14. **Theory X fails to motivate people having social, eco and self-actualisation needs** — A fundamental opposition of Theory X is that it is inadequate to consider the subject of motivation. It is to acknowledge that satisfied need ceases to motivate any individual further. Since there exists hierarchy of needs, man moves from satisfaction of lower needs to the satisfaction of higher needs. Once physiological and safety needs are satisfied, social needs, ego needs and need for self-actualisation respectively become the most important motivators. Management by direction and control (Theory *X*), regardless of its hard or soft approach, is ineffective to motivate people whose important needs are social and egoistic. Once lower order needs are satisfied, rewards, promises, incentives, or threats and coercion the devices used by management under Theory *X*, cease to motivate people.

HERZBERG'S MOTIVATION-HYGIENE THEORY

On the basis of empirical research on job attitudes of 200 Accountants and Engineers, Herzberg identified two separate sets of factors as follows:

1. Maintenance Factors or Hygiene Factors or Dissatisfers or Job Content Factors.
2. Motivational Factors or Satisfiers or Job Context Factors.

   Let us study the purpose of such factors, effect of their presence/absence and examples of such factors.

COMPARATIVE STUDY OF MAINTENANCE FACTORS AND MOTIVATIONAL FACTORS

Basis of Comparision	Maintenance or Hygiene Factors	Motivational Factors or Satisfiers
1. **Their Purpose**	Maintenance factors are necessary to **maintain a reasonable level of satisfaction** among the employees. These factors are called hygiene factors because they play a role in creating a healthy congenial climate in the work-setting.	Motivational Factors are necessary **to promote strong job satisfaction, strong motivation and good performance.** These factors are called satisfiers because they promote strong job satisfaction among job holders.
2. **Effect of their absence or deficiency**	Any deficiency in or absence of maintenance factors can create **job dissatisfaction, demotivation** and **poor performance** among the job holders.	Any deficiency in or absence of motivational factors **rarely proves strong dissatisfiers**.
3. **Effect of their presence**	The presence of maintenance factors **prevents job dissatisfaction** but does not promote strong job satisfaction, strong motivation, and good performance.	The presence of motivational factors **promotes strong job satisfaction, strong motivation and good performance.**
4. **Intrinsic/Extrinsic**	Maintenance factors are job content factors and are **intrinisic to the job.**	Motivational factors are job context factors and are **extrinsic to the job**.
5. **Which needs are covered**	Maintenance factors cover **physiological, safety, social and some portion of esteem needs like status.**	Motivational factors cover the **remaining portion of esteem needs like** advancement, recognition **and self-actualisation needs.**
6. **Examples**	1. Company Policy and Administration 2. Technical Supervision 3. Interpersonal relations with Supervisor 4. Interpersonal relations with Peers 5. International relations with Subordinates 6. Salary 7. Job Security 8. Personal life 9. Working Conditions 10. Status	1. Achievement 2. Recognition 3. Advancement 4. Work itself 5. Possibility of growth 6. Responsibility

SOME OTHER OBSERVATIONS OF HERZBERG'S THEORY

1. Motivators could be build into job through job enlargement and job enrichment. **Job enlargement** is a motivational technique which involves horizontal expansion of the scope of a job to include greater variety of operations with a view to reduce the boredom and monotony associated with performing repetitive operations. **Job enrichment** is a motivational technique which involves enriching the content of the job or the deliberate vertical upgrading of responsibility, scope and challenge in work with a view to make the job more interesting, meaningful and challenging.

2. Today's motivational factors are tomorrow's hygiene factors because they stop influencing the behaviours of persons when they get them.

CRITICISM OF HERZBERG'S THEORY

Herzberg's two factor theory is subject to the following criticism:

1. The findings of empirical research were based on self-reports of the respondents which could be biased.

2. The findings of empirical research were based on unreprsentative sample of accountant and engineers who were relatively well paid.

3. Maintenance factors may generate positive motivation, satisfactors and higher performance in same cases while motivational factors may totally fail to do so in some cases.

4. Maintenance factors may prove to be motivational factors in some cases for example, higher wages to workers, higher salaries to manager may motivate them to perform better.

5. His theory ignores the fact that peple are heteroganous in their needs and expectations. For example, for some employees, good wages, job security and good working conditions may act as motivational factors while others may not show any interest in challenging and meaningful jobs.

6. According to his theory, just as it is possible to reduce job dissatisfaction without increasing job satisfaction it is possible to increase job satisfaction without reducing job dissatisfaction. This seem to be doubtful.

7. According to his theory, job satisfaction leads to good performance and job dissatisfaction leads to bad performance but there may not any cause-effect relationship between satisfaction and performance.

ADVANTAGES OF HERZBERG'S THEORY

Herzberg Theory forced organisations —

1. to re-examine some of their stero-typed ideas about work behaviour of people.

2. to redesign job to make job interesting, meaningly, and challenging to ensure job satisfaction and good job performance.

COMPARISON BETWEEN HERZBERG'S AND MASLOW'S THEORIES

Basic of Comparison	Herzberg's Theory	Maslow's Theory
1. **Basis of Theory**	Herzberg theory is based on **two factors—** Maintenance factors & Motivational factors	Maslow's theory is based on the **hierarchy of needs.**
2. **Proposition**	Maintenance factors **avoid job dissatisfaction** but do not provide motivation to workers.	**An unsatisfied need becomes a motivating factor** for the individual and governs his behaviour in that direction.
3. **Lower order needs like physiological safety and social & some portion of esteem needs**	These lower needs **act as maintenance factors**.	These needs also **act as motivators untill satisfied.**
4. **Highes Level needs like remaining portion of esteem needs and self actualisation needs**	Higher level needs act as **motivating factors.**	These needs act as **motivating factors untill satisfied.**
5. **Applicability**	It has **limited** applicability in the sense that it is more applicable to professional personnel.	It has **universal** applicability in the sense that it is applicable to all kinds of workers.

RELATIONSHIP BETWEEN HERZBERG'S AND MASLOW'S THEORIES

Relationship between Herzberg's and Maslow's Theories can be diagrammtically represented on the next page:

Relationship between Herzberg's and Maslow's Theories

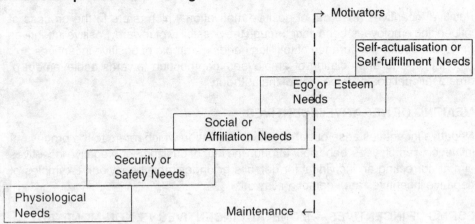

The above figure shows:

Under Maslow's Theory	Under Herzberg's Theory
1. Physiological Needs	Maintenance Factors
2. Security or Safety Needs	Maintenance Factors
3. Social or Affiliation Needs	Maintenance Factors
4. Esteem Needs	
(a) some portion (status etc.)	Maintenance Factors
(b) remaining Portion	Motivational Factors
5. Self-Actualisation Needs	Motivational Factors

INCENTIVES

After determining the needs of the people working under him, the manager should provide an environment in which appropriate incentives are available for their need satisfaction.

MEANING OF INCENTIVES

Any act or promise which induces an individual to respond in a desired manner is called an incentive. It stimulates a person towards some goal. Incentives may be either positive or negative.

NEED FOR INCENTIVES

The need for incentives arises because of the following benefits:

1. Incentives induce the employees to respond in a desired manner.
2. Incentives encourage the employees to put in their maximum efforts.
3. Incentives help in increasing employees' productivity and efficiency.
4. Incentives help in boosting employees' morale.
5. Incentives help in minimising the conflicts between management and workers.
6. Incentives help the employees to be directed towards achievement of organisational goals.

MEANING OF POSITIVE INCENTIVES

Positive Incentives arise out of positive motivation which refers to the process of influencing employees' behaviour through the possibility of reward. Positive incentives provide a positive assurance of fulfilling needs. Example of positive incentives are: recognition and appreciation of employees' contribution towards achievement of organisational goals, delegation of the authority.

MEANING OF NEGATIVE INCENTIVES

Negative incentives arise out of negative motivation which refers to the process of influencing employees' behaviour through the fear of punishment. Negative incentives aim at correcting an individual for defaults or undesirable behaviour. Examples of negative incentives are : demotion, lay off.

FORMS OF INCENTIVES — MONETARY INCENTIVES VS. NON-MONETARY INCENTIVES

To satisfy varying needs of employees, the manager should provide different forms of incentives. Since some of the needs can be satisfied by money while others cannot, the manager should provide both the monetary incentives and non-monetary incentives to the people working under him. A comparative analysis of monetary incentives and non-monetary incentives is given below:

Bases of Comparison	Monetary Incentives	Non-Monetary Incentives
1. **Meaning**	These refer to those incentives which are directly or indirectly associated with **monetary** benefits.	These refer to those incentives which are **not measurable in** terms of **money**.
2. **Purpose**	The purpose of these incentives is **to satisfy the physiological, security and social needs**.	The purpose of these incentives is **to satisfy the esteem and self-actualisation needs**.
3. **Role**	These incentives play a significant role in case of employees **at** comparatively **lower levels** of management.	These incentives play a significant role in case of employees **at** comparatively **higher levels** of management.
4. **Examples**	These incentives include wages, salaries, bonus, leave with pay, LIC premiums, medical reimbursement, free house, free car, free servant etc.	These incentives include grant of higher status, recognition, assignment of challenging jobs, workers' participation in management, suggestion system, opportunities for growth etc.

Conclusion — From the above discussion, it can be said that money is not always a motivator because people are motivated by money only up to the stage they are struggling for satisfying their physiological and security needs. After satisfaction of physiological and security needs, people are motivated by non-monetary incentives to satisfy their needs such as esteem, self-actualisation. Thus, it can be said that money is not the only motivator.

EXERCISES

SHORT ANSWER TYPE QUESTIONS

1. Briefly explain the meaning of motivation.
2. Explain in brief the nature of motivation.
3. State the process of motivation.
4. Enumerate the various categories of human needs.
5. State any three types of need which govern human motivation.
6. What is meant by incentive?
7. What is the need of incentive?
8. What is meant by 'positive incentive'?
9. What is meant by 'negative incentive'?
10. Explain in brief the various forms of incentives.
11. Distinguish between monetary and non-monetary incentives.
12. Give two examples of each of financial and non-financial incentives.
13. Distinguish between the following:
    (a) Positive Incentive and Negative Incentive
    (b) Monetary Incentive and Non-Monetary Incentive
    (c) Theory X and Theory Y
    (d) Maintenance Factors and Motivational Factors
    (e) Job Enlargement and Job Enrichment
14. Write short notes on the following:
    (a) Need Hierarchy Theory
    (b) Two Factor Theory of Motivation
    (c) Job Enlargement
    (d) Job Enrichment

LONG ANSWER TYPE QUESTIONS

1. Explain briefly the importance of motivation in management.
2. Explain the need for motivating the employees.
3. What is motivation? How does it improve efficiency and facilitate the accomplishment of organisational goals?

4. "Motivation is the core of management." Explain.

5. Define Motivation and explain its nature. Discuss fully the importance of motivation. Also discuss the financial and non-financial motivators as technique of motivation.

6. What is meant by incentive? Discuss the role of financial and non-financial incentives to increase the efficiency of workers.

7. What is the need of incentive? State the main forms of incentive.

8. Explain contentions, Merits and Criticism of Maslow's need Hierarchy Theory of motivation.

9. Explain the contentions and criticism of Theory X and Theory Y of motivation.

10. Explain the contentions, advantages and criticism of two factor theory of motivation.

11. Give a comparative study of Herzberg's and Maslow's Theories of motivation. Also show the relationship between these two theories.

23 Directing— Leadership

MEANING OF LEADERSHIP, LEADER AND FOLLOWERS

Leadership is the process of influencing the behaviour of other people to work willingly towards the achievement of specified goals in a given situation. Leadership naturally implies the existence of a leader and followers as well as their mutual interaction.

According to Robbert Tannen Baum, *"Leadership is the interpersonal influence exercised in a situation and directed through communication process towards attainment of specified goals."* The leader is a person in a group who influences the group to work willingly. The followers are the other members of the group led by a leader.

According to Louis A. Allen, *"A leader is one who guides and directs other people. A leader gives the efforts of his followers a direction and purpose by influencing their behaviour.*

ELEMENTS OF LEADERSHIP PROCESS

The leadership process has the following five elements:

1. It is a **process of influence**.

2. Its purpose is **to influence the behaviour of followers** to get willing cooperation of all members of the group.

3. It **involves interaction between two or more persons**. The interaction between the leader and his followers is based on interpersonal relationship which grows out of the leader's support and help to the followers in achieving their individual and group goals.

4. It **involves pursuit of common goals** under the advice and guidance of the leader in the interest of individuals, group and organisation.

5. It is **always related to a situation**. The style of leadership differs from situation to situation.

LEADERSHIP AND MANAGERSHIP

Leadership and managership are not the same thing. A manager is a leader as well in the sense that as a leader he influences the behaviour of his subordinates to work willingly towards the achievement of common goals in the interest of his subordinates, organisation and the group as a whole. He does not depend only on his formal authority to secure group performance but exercises influence as a leader for the purpose. A manager can be more effective if he is a good leader. A manager is more than a leader in the sense that a manager performs all the five functions of management — planning, organising, staffing, directing and controlling, whereas a leader performs leadership function which is one of the elements of directing function.

A leader need not necessarily be a manager in the sense that a manager holds managerial position in the organisation whereas a leader may not hold any managerial position. For example, in an informal group, the leader may influence the conduct of his fellow members but he may not be a manager. A leader acquires powers due to the acceptance of his role by his followers whereas a manager acquires powers due to delegation by his superiors.

Thus, all managers are leaders but all leaders are not managers.

IMPORTANCE OF LEADERSHIP

The importance of leadership arises from the following functions performed by a leader:

1. **Helps in Guiding and Inspiring Employees** — Leader guides and inspires the employees towards higher performance and helps in the attainment of organisational goals.

2. **Secures Cooperation of Members of the Organisation** — Leader persuades employees to work co-operatively and enthusiastically towards attainment of organisational goals.

3. **Creates Confidence** — Leader creates confidence among the employees by his conduct and expression.

4. **Develops and Maintains an Environment Conducive to maximum work effort** — Leader develops and maintains an environment for employees to contribute their maximum efforts towards attainment of organisational goals.

5. **Acts an a Intermediary** — Leader acts as an intermediary between his subordinates and the higher level management. He communicates the expectations of management to his subordinates and of the problems and grievances of his subordinates to the top management.

6. **Acts as a Counseller** — Leader acts as a counseller of his subordinates where they face problems in connection with their performance at work. He guides and advises the subordinates concerned.

7. **Develops Work Group as Team** — Leader develops the work group as a team.

8. **Helps in Motivation** — Leader helps in motivating the employees and boosting their morale.

9. **Helps in Establishing Cordial Relations** — Leader helps in establishing and maintaining cordial relations between the management and the employees.

ROLE OF LEADERSHIP IN MANAGEMENT

The leadership plays an important role in management. The role of leadership in management is discussed below:

Level of Management	Why Leadership is needed
1. At top level	To secure the involvement and co-operation of executives in the formulation of plans, policies and objectives
2. At middle level	To interpret plans and policies and to direct, guide and influence the lower level managers towards better performance
3. At lower level	To persuade employees to work co-operatively and enthusiastically towards attainment of organisational goals

1. Leadership is needed at all levels of management.
2. Leaders try to integrate organisational goals with personal aspirations of subordinates.
3. Leader-manager represents the work groups to his superiors and other managers. He represents the organisation outside the organisation.
4. He defends the employees of the group of which he is the leader.
5. He plays the role of a friend, philosopher and guide to the followers within and outside the organisation.
6. Leaders represent the organisation and initiate actions to keep the organisation dynamic and progressive.

QUALITIES OF A GOOD LEADER

The qualities which a good leader should possess are discussed below:

1. **Intelligence** — He should be intelligent enough to examine problems in the right perspective, and to take right decision at the right time in the interest of the organisation.
2. **Communicative Skill** — He must be able to communicate clearly, precisely and effectively. He should have knowledge about the various types, methods and channels of communication. He should use the appropriate type, method and channel of communication in the given situation.
3. **Objectivity** — He should be objective (i.e., free from bias) in his dealings with his subordinates.
4. **Knowledge of Work** — He should have full knowledge of the work being performed under his supervision.
5. **Human Relations** — He should develop and maintain personal relations with his followers.
6. **Self-Confidence and Will-Power** — He must have confidence in his own ability to lead others and have the required will-power to meet the needs of every situation by adopting a suitable leadership style.
7. **Empathy** — He should have the ability to look at things from others' point of view. He should have capacity to appreciate others.
8. **Sense of Responsibility** — He should have a sense of responsibility towards the attainment of organisational goals so that he can himself be a living example in front of his followers.
9. **Awareness about himself** — A leader must be aware of his strengths and weaknesses in relation to his subordinates. He should know how others perceive him as a leader.
10. **Sound Health and Stamina** — A leader should have sound health both mental and physical, stamina, balanced temperament and optimistic outlook.

THEORIES OF LEADERSHIP

There are a number of theories which provide explanations regarding various aspects of the leadership phenomenon. The leadership theories can be classified into the following categories:

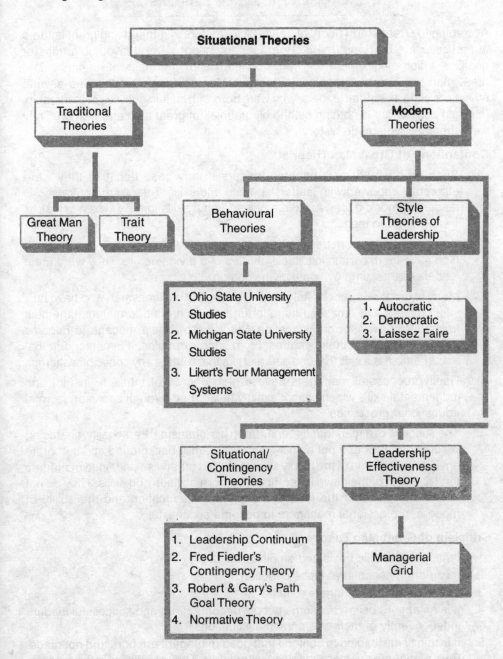

Let us discuss these theories one by one.

TRADITIONAL THEORIES OF LEADERSHIP

1. GREAT MAN THEORY OF LEADERSHIP

According to Great Man Theory of Leadership leaders in general and great leaders in particular are born, not made. Born leaders inherit several favourable traits or qualities which single them out from non-leaders or the mass of humanity. The great man like Nelson, Napoleon, Churchill, Mao-se-Tung. Gandhiji and several others are cited as natural leaders, who were born with built-in qualities of leadership. It is said that history is nothing but the biographies of great men and women. They were the ones who made history.

Contentions of Great Man Theorists

1. Such men would have become leaders in any case because they were inherently endowed with leadership traits and skills. They were not trained in leadership nor did they acquire any leadership skills in their lives; such skills were natural to them.

2. Some individuals were destined to become great leaders on their own because God gave them certain inimitable abilities of a divine nature. They were great leaders of their time by some divine design.

3. Many of great and successful entrepreneurs and businessmen who have built vast empires and amassed huge fortunes have had no formal management training, not even formal education. But still they could manage to become great successes in their ventures. From such examples, it is contended that management is a skill that one gets just like that without any conscious attempt.

4. Really successful managers have a high degree of intuition, insight and judgemental skills which cannot exactly be learned through books and formal educational processes.

5. The success of a manager depends upon his 'charisma' Personality, character, wisdom and luck and not on his education, family background and corporate environment. Some of the highly successful but otherwise untrained managers tend to boast of their own inherent and in born abilities and skills. They do not hesitate to discount the idea of management education and the ability of modern, professional managers to become successful.

Criticism of Great Man Theory

1. It has no scientific basis and empirical validity.
2. It is more a speculative piece of notion.
3. The improbability of inherent traits.
4. It is an absurd belief that some people become great and successful leaders independently of their environmental situations.
5. It is totally misleading to contend that good managers are born and not made. Born managers are mere imaginary characters. They are misfits in the modern, complex and fast changing conditions and characteristics of business.

6. If at all there are any born managers, their supply is negligible, unreliable and cannot be matched through human action with the demand for good managers. The demand for good managers can be met only by preparing individuals through formal management education and training to assume important managerial responsibilities. One need not possess any inborn attributes or qualities to become a good manager; it is both absolutely necessary and sufficient if he acquires professional managerial knowledge and experience.

7. Success in management especially under modern complex conditions, depends not only inherent and inborn qualities of management but also on formal acquisition of modern management knowledge and training. The latter serves to sharpen and brightness the former type of qualities and attributes. This implies that management education by itself is necessary but not sufficient. Aspirants for management positions should possess certain essential and basic traits. It is also conceded that such traits are necessary but not sufficient for success in management. Formal management education provides sufficient condition for success.

2. TRAIT THEORY

Trait theory is a modification of Great Man Theory. Trait theory states that—

1. There are certain identifiable qualities that are unique to leaders and that good leaders possess such qualities to a great extent.

2. Leadership qualities may be inborn or they may be acquired through training and practice. Thus, good managers need not always be inborn, they may be made.

Trait theorists identified a long list of following qualities which the good business leader possess:

(a) **Intelligence Qualities** — Good business leaders should be intelligent enough—

1. to understand the context and content of their position and function;
2. to grasp the dynamics of environmental variables, both internal and external, which affect their activities; and
3. to have a good perspective of the present and future dimensions of their organisation.

(b) **Personality Qualities — Outer personality qualities** include outward physical appearance. **Inner personality qualities** includes —

1. emotional stability;
2. maturity;
3. self-confidence;
4. decisiveness;
5. strong drive;
6. optimism;
7. extrovertness;
8. achievement orientation;
9. purposefulness;
10. discipline;
11. skill in getting alongwith others;

12. integrity in character; and
13. a tendency to be cooperative.

These qualities tend to help business leaders to organise and co-ordinate human efforts, to guide and motivate people in task situations, to make sound decisions, to achieve concrete results and goals, to resolve conflict and to manage organisational change.

(c) **Other qualities —**
1. Open mindless;
2. Scientific spirit;
3. Social sensitivity;
4. Ability to communicate;
5. Objectivity;
6. An abiding interest in people;
7. Pragmatism; and
8. A sense of realism.

Qualities of Effective Leaders according to Ralph Stogdill —
1. a strong drive for responsibility;
2. task orientation;
3. vigour and persistence in pursuit of goals;
4. venturesomeness;
5. originality problem solving skills;
6. drive to exercise initiative in social situations;
7. self confidence;
8. a sense of personal identity;
9. willingness to accept consequences of decisions and action;
10. readiness to absorb inter-personal stress;
11. ability to influence other persons; and
12. capacity to structure social interaction systems to the purpose at hand.

Leadership Qualities are necessary, though not sufficient

Although possession of the above qualities does not guarantee success for a business leader, all we can say is that they increase the probability of success and enable the leader to interact and cope with situation more effectively. However, serious deficiencies in the above qualities may be disatrous for leaders. **For example,** persons who are indecisive and indifferent do not make good business leaders. It is quite possible that presence of some vital qualities in a marked degree may offset the absence or deficiency of other qualities. **For example,** a higher achievement orientation may to some extent compensate for deficiency in tolerance and objectivity.

Criticism of Trait Theory

Trait Theory is subject to the following criticism:
1. It is not based on any research or systematic development of concepts and principles;
2. It is more a speculative theory which fails when subjected to empirical tests;
3. It is only a descriptive theory on how some people emerge as leaders;
4. It has few explanatory and predictive properties;

5. It is not possible to isolate a specific set of traits which can be consistently applied to leadership across a range of situations: cases can be cited to prove that mere possession of certain traits is not enough for one to become a leader. Nor does the absence of the so-called trait prevent individuals from emerging and proving their worth as leaders.

6. It does not try to relate particular traits to performance, behaviour and effectiveness of leaders. Some traits tend to cancel out each other. For example, pragmatism and possession of ethical sense of right and wrong do not always go together.

7. Traits which are needed for maintaining leadership are different from those which are needed for acquiring leadership.

8. An individual's traits do not make up his total personality, nor do they fully reveal about his attitudes, values, aspirations and behaviour.

9. The trait theory is inward looking towards the leader alone to the exclusion of the group of followers and the task situation, which are in fact more important for leadership effectiveness.

10. There is no way of systematically defining and measuring the incidence and intensity of traits among persons purported to be leaders. Nor is it possible to position the traits along a hierarchy of importance.

11. There is no universally agreed list of traits associated with successful leaders.

BEHAVIOURAL THEORIES OF LEADERSHIP

The behavioural theories of leadership are based on the belief that leaders can be identified by reference to their behaviour in relation to the followers. In other words, it is suggested that leadership can be described in terms of what leaders do rather than what they are. Behavioural theories have been presented mostly on the basis of research studies.

1. OHIO STATE UNIVERSITY STUDIES

These studies identified two dimensions of leadership style as follows:

Dimensions of Leadership Style	Meaning
1. Consideration	It refers to the extent to which job relationships are characterised by mutual trust, inter-personal warmth, respect, friendship and consideration for subordinates' ideas and feelings.
2. Initiating Structure	If refers to the extent to which the leader organises and defines subordinates' activities and relationships. In otherwords, it refers to the leader's behaviour in endeavouring to establish well-defined pattern of organisation.

Thus, consideration is closer to democratic style whereas 'Initiating Structure' is closer to the autocratic style of leadership.

Diagrammatic Representation of Combinations of Dimensions

The behaviour of a leader may be described as any combination of both dimensions as follows:

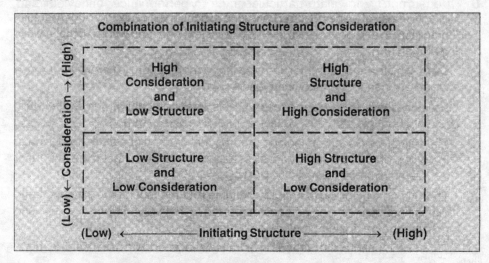

Combination of Initiating Structure and Consideration

| | High Consideration and Low Structure | High Structure and High Consideration |
| | Low Structure and Low Consideration | High Structure and Low Consideration |

(High) Consideration → (Low)

(Low) ← Initiating Structure → (High)

2. MICHIGAN STATE UNIVERSITY STUDIES, USA

These studies identified two types of leaders as follows:

Basis of Comparison	Production Centred Leader	Employee Centred Leader
1. **Belief**	Production centred leader believes that what is good for the organisation is automatically good for his group members.	Employee centred leader believes that what is good for his group members is automatically good for the organisation.
2. **Emphasis**	He emphasises job performance in conformity with prescribed standards. He is concerned about production.	He emphasises the promotion of employee satisfaction as a means of enlisting employee's co-operation for achieving organisational goals. He is concerned about the well-being of his group members.
3. **Delegation of Authority to Subordinates**	He does not prefer to delegate authority to his subordinates.	He prefers to delegate authority to his subordinates.

4.	Decision-making	He prefers centralised decision-making with himself.	He prefers participative decision-making along with his subordinates.
5.	Degree of Supervision	He excercises close control over the employees as if they were tools of production.	He excercises moderate supervision to instruct, guide and inspire the employees.
6.	Development of Future Manager	He does not permit the development of future managers.	He permits the development of future managers.
7.	Effectiveness	He may be effective in short-run.	He is usually effective in short-run & long-run.
8.	Positive/Negative Approach	He has negative approaches as he makes use of penalities to get work done.	He has positive approach as he makes use of rewards to get work done.
9.	Production	He seems to get lower production.	He seems to get higher production.
10.	Employee Satisfaction & Morale	He seems to have employees with lower job satisfaction with poorer morale.	He seems to have employees with higher job satisfaction with high morale.
11.	Job Instructions	He gives details job instructions so that employees can conform to it without introducing their own judgement or discretion.	He believes in loose definition of jobs, a general sort of planning and supervision of work.
12.	Rigidity/Flexibility of Organisational arrangements	He relies on rigid organisational arrangement such as official chain of command, official communication channels, penalities for inefficient performance or improper behaviour.	He relies on flexible organisational arrangements such as informal relations, informal communication channels, rewards to motivate.
13.	Strict/Liberal	He is strict and task oriented in his outlook and does not toleterate any slackness or indiscipline among his subordinates.	He is liberal and humanistic in his outlook.

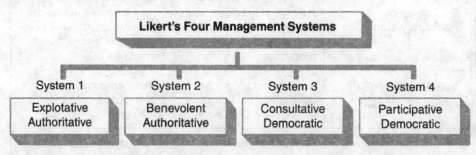

3. LIKERT'S FOUR MANAGEMENT SYSTEMS

Rensis Likert identified four management systems as follows:

Let us have the comparative study of these systems as follows:

Basis of Comparison	System 1	System 2	System 3	System 3
1. **Orientation**	Task-oriented	Task oriented	Human Relationship oriented	Human Relation-ship oriented
2. **Goal-setting**	Centralized at the top	Centralized at the top	In consulattion with subordi-nates	Jointly by leader and subordinates
3. **Decision-making**	Centralized at the top	Centralized at the top	In consulattion with subordinates	Jointly by leader and subordinates
4. **Motivation Approach**	Based on fear threats & punishments	Carrots & Sticks Approach	More emphasis on rewards than on punishment	Participations & involvement are principal motivation forces
5. **Leadership**	Highly Autocratic	Sometimes Patronising attitudes, and other times, harsh attitudes toward subordinates	Democratic	Highly Democratic
6. **Communi-cation**	Highly formal & down-ward in direction	Mostly one way traffic	Two-way communication	Open & effective communication
7. **Control**	Strict Control	Strict control	Substantial self-control but not complete	Complete self-control

8. Relation-ship	Characterized by distrust & ill-will	Master-servant relationship, low degree of mutual confidence & trust	Substantial degree of mutual trust & confidence but not complete	Group approach cordial & friendly since complete mutual trust & confidence
9. **Producti-vity**	Lower	Higher than that under exploitative but lower than that under consultative	Higher than that under benevolent but lower than that under participative	Higher
10. **Employee's Turnover & Absenteeism**	Higher	Lower than that under exploitative but higher than that under consultative	Lower than that under benevolent but higher than that under participative	Lower
11. **Quality Control**	Lower	Higher than that under exploitative but lower than that under consultative	Higher than that under benevolent but lower than that under participative	Higher
12. **Resource Wastage & Scrap losses**	Higher	Lower than that under exploitative but higher than that under consultative	Lower than that under benevolent but higher than that under participative	Lower

Research Findings

1. Participative - democratic leadership is the only valid and viable approach to optimise organisational performance and employee satisfaction because of the following reasons:

   (i) It is the positive and progressive approach to management of people at work.

   (ii) It is totally consistent with human dignity and development.

   (iii) It results in desirable re-distribution of power and influence as between the leader and his group members.

   (iv) It promotes organisational harmony and health by helping the process of removal of artificial walls between leaders and their group members.

     (v) Participative leadership fulfills a range of needs of group members — needs for information involvement, interaction, influence, responsibility, achievement and advancement.

     (vi) It also facilitates greater understanding of and control over work environment so far as the group members are concerned.

2.   For leaders operating in system 2 and 3, he suggested extensive and intensive training at all levels of management so as to move them into system 4 management zone.

Criticism

Likert's advocacy of System 4 participative democratical leadership is open to criticism. It ignores situational factors and their influence on leadership effectiveness. Participative leadership may succeed in some situations and fail in others. Its success depends upon the skills of the leader himself, the nature of subordinates, the task situation and the organisational climate.

STYLE THEORIES OF LEADERSHIP

Meaning of Leadership Style

Leadership style denotes the way in which the leaders themselves behave by way of exercising their influence and power to affect responses of other through which they have to get things done. *In other words,* the dominant behaviour pattern of a leader-manager in relation to his subordinates is known as leadership style.

Leadership Style Theories

Over the years, researchers have identified different styles of leadership. Let us discuss the various contributions to style theories.

Lawin, Lippitt and White Studies — They conducted leadership studies in 1939 on three different styles of leadership as follows:

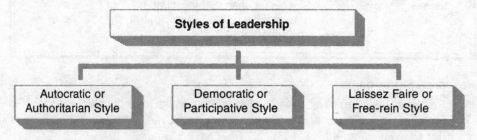

Let us discuss these styles one by one.

1. AUTOCRATIC OR AUTHORITARIAN STYLE OF LEADERSHIP

Meaning of Autocratic Style of Leadership

In autocratic style, the leader centralizes power and decision-making in himself and expects his subordinates to do what they are asked to with very limited participation.

Features of Autocratic Style of Leadership

The features of autocratic style are as follows:

1. **Centralization of Authority** — The leader retains almost full authority with himself. He delegates little authority.

2. **Centralization of Decision-making** — The leader takes almost all decisions himself.

3. **Production Oriented** — The leader is production oriented. He emphasizes production.

4. **Does not allow participation** — The leader permits little or no participation of subordinates.

5. **Close Supervision** — The leader exercises close supervision.

6. **Use of coercion** — The leader uses coercion as a means for getting the job done.

7. **Little concern for well-being of employee** — The leader has little concern for the well-being of employees, who suffer from frustration and low morale.

8. **Compels Subordinates under threat of penalties** — The leader compels subordinates to follow his orders under threat of penalties.

Diagrammatic Representation of Autocratic Style of Leadership

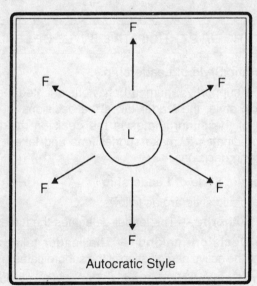

Autocratic Style

Limitations of Autocratic Style of Leadership

The limitations of autocratic style of leadership are as follows:

1. **Less Effective in the long run — According to Mc Greger,** since autocratic approach is negative in character, this approach may be quite effective in securing short run results from the group but will fail to induce the subordinates for better performance in the long run. Autocratic leaders are less effective in sustaining productivity and satisfaction of their group members in the long run.

2. **Higher Labour Turnover etc.** — It results in higher resentment, higher absenteeism and higher labour turnover rate.

3. **Low Morale** — It results in low morale due to the inner dis-satisfaction of employees.

4. **Not Permit Development** — It does not permit development of future managers from among capable subordinates.

Suitability of Autocratic Style of Leadership

Autocratic style is suitable in the following situations:

(i) When subordinates are incompetent and inexperienced.

(ii) The leader prefers centralised decisions-making.

(iii) Fear and punishment are used as disciplinary techniques.

(iv) There is little room for errors in final accomplishment.

(v) Under conditions of stress when great speed and efficiency are required.

(vi) When uniformity and consistency in decision-making are required.

(vii) When confidential matters may not permit normal consultation.

(viii) When there is very little time for participation particular in crisis.

(ix) When the leader may have more knowledge and as such may compensate for participation.

2. DEMOCRATIC OR PARTICIPATIVE STYLE OF LEADERSHIP

Meaning of Democratic Style of Leadership

Democratic style is a supportive, human behaviour oriented leadership style. In democratic leadership style, the leader takes the decisions in consultation with active participation of the subordinates in the decision making process and encourages the subordinates to make suggestions and take initiative in setting goals and implementing decisions.

Features of Democratic Style of Leadership

The features of democratic style are as follows:

1. **Delegation of Authority** — The leader delegates the necessary authority.

2. **Participative Decision-making** — The leader takes the decision in consultation with the active participation of the subordinates in decision-making.

3. **Production and Employee Oriented** — The leader is production as well as employee oriented. He emphasizes both production and employees satisfaction.

4. **Allows participation** — The leader permits participation of the subordinates.

5. **Not subject to close supervision** — The subordinates are not subject to close supervision.

6. **Allows two way Communication** — The leader encourages two way communication between himself and his followers. Subordinates are allowed sufficient freedom to communicate with their fellow members.

7. **Concern for Employees**

   The leader —

   (i)   Reposes a high degree of confidence and trust in them;

   (ii) Respects their values and viewpoints;

   (iii) Initiates group processes and discussions;

   (iv) Gives more freedom of thinking and action;

   (v)   Tries to minimize the distance between himself and his group.

8. **Creation of Favourable Climate** — The leader tries to provide a proper climate in which the group members derive the pleasure of working for themselves by working for the group and enterprise.

   He tries to bring about voluntary compliance and commitment of the group under his leadership to the common goals so that group morale positively contributes to employee productivity.

Diagrammatic Representation of Democratic Style of Leadership

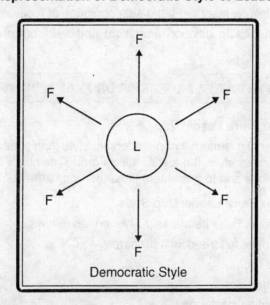

Democratic Style

Advantages of Democratic Style of Leadership

The main advantages of democratic style of leadership are as follows:

1. **Effective in Short-run & Long-run** — Since democratic approach is positive in character, this approaches is quite effective in sustaining productivity and satisfaction of group members not only in the short-run but also in the long-run.

2. **High Morale** — It results in high morale due to inner job satisfaction of employees.

3. **Permits Development** — It permits development of future managers from among capable subordinates.

Limitations of Democratic Style of Leadership

The main limitations of democratic style of leadership are as follows:

1. **Delay in Decision-making** — Decisions taken through participative decision making process may cause delay.

2. **Compromises** — Participative decision making requires compromises to meet different view points.

3. **Dominance of vocal persons** — Participative decision making process may be dominated by few vocal persons.

4. **No Individual Responsibility** — No one individual may take the responsibility for implementing the decision taken by the group as a whole.

Suitability of Democratic Style of Leadership

The democratic style of leadership is suitable in the following situations:

1. When subordinates are competent and experienced.

2. The leader prefers participative decision-making process.

3. Rewards and involvement are used as techniques of motivation and control.

4. The leader wishes to develop analytical and self-control abilities in his subordinates.

3. LAISSEZ FAIRE LEADERSHIP OR FREE-REIN STYLE

Meaning of Laissez Faire Leadership

Laissez Faire Leadership is more a non-leadership style than a leadership style. In Laissez Faire leadership style, the leader allows group members to set their own goals, to take decisions and to implement those decisions themselves.

Features of Laissez Faire Leadership Style

The features of Laissez Faire Leadership Style are as follows:

1. Subordinates have full freedom as regards —
   (i) Goal-setting;
   (ii) Taking decisions;
   (iii) Implementing decisions;

2. No Guidelines and rules of behaviour are established for the conduct of members.

3. It is directionless. The leader does not direct his group members.

4. It is inspirationless. The dealer does not inspire group members.

Diagrammatic Representation of Laissez Faire Style of Leadership

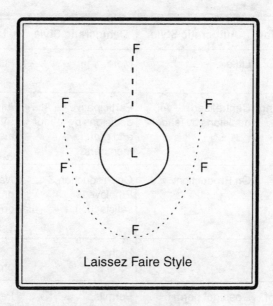

Laissez Faire Style

Limitations of Laissez Faire Leadership Style

The limitations of Laissez Faire Leadership Style are as follows:

1. It may lead to chaos and mismanagement of group goals since group markers are allowed to set their own goals.
2. It is does not promote group morale, satisfaction, and development of group cohesiveness.
3. It is directionless since the leader does direct his group members.
4. It is inspirationess since the leader does not inspire his group members.
5. It emphasises *neither* production *nor* employee satisfaction.
6. Employees are left to drifting.

Suitability of Laissez Faire Leadership Style

The Laissez faire leadership style is suitable in the following situations:

1. When the subordinates are competent and experienced.
2. When the leader prefers full delegation of decision-making authority.
3. When organisation goals have been communicated well to the group members.
4. When group members have understood the organisation goals to be achieved.

DISTINCTION BETWEEN DIFFERENT STYLES OF LEADERSHIP

Basis of Distinction	Autocratic Style	Democratic Style	Laissez Faire
1. **Delegation of Authority**	Little.	More.	Full.
2. **Decision-making**	Centralised — All decisions by leader.	Participative — All decisions by leader and group members.	All decisions — By group members.
3. **Emphasis**	On Production.	On Production & Employees satisfaction.	*Neither* on production *nor* on employees satisfaction.
4. **Employees' Morale**	Low.	High.	Does not promote.
5. **Development of Future Managers**	Does not permit.	Permits.	Permits.
6. **Degree of Supervision**	Close.	Moderate.	No supervision.
7. **Effectiveness**	May be effective in short-run.	Usually effective in short-run & long-run.	May or May not be effective.
8. **Positive/Negative Approach**	Negative as the leader makes use of penalities to get work done.	Positive as the leader makes use of rewards to get workdone.	*Neither* positive *nor* negative as the leader *neither* makes use of rewards *nor* penalities.
9. **Suitability**	When subordinates are incompetent & inexperienced.	When subordinates are competent & experienced to participate in decision-making process under guidance of their leader.	When subordinates are enough competent & experienced so as to take all decisions themselves without any direction by leader.

4. BUREAUCRATIC STYLE

It is one of the common styles prevalent in government organisations and departments. It is an impersonal, rule-ridden style. The bureaucratic leader functions in terms of established routine procedures, due processes and rules. He emphasises on activity than on achievement. He looks for formality, uniformity and conformity in the behaviour of his group members. He is rather leisurely in his approach to solving problems. He does not encourage initiative, innovation and dynamism among subordinates.

5. NEUROCRATIC STYLE

In this style of leadership, leader adopts hard driving, high pressure tactics of direction for himself and for his group members. He is restless and wants to achieve tomorrow's results today, regardless of consequences. He has a strong urge to become bigger and better by any means. Like an autocrat, the neurocrat leader leaves nothing to chance and closely supervises his group members.

SITUATIONAL OR CONTINGENCY THEORIES OF LEADERSHIP

According to Situational Theories —

1. Leadership is situational
2. Leader's qualities and behaviour can not be separated from the environment.
3. Besides the leader's qualities and behaviour, other variables in particular
   (a) the task; (b) the work group; and (c) the position of the leader within that group, are involved in any leadership situation.
4. Individuals will be leaders in some situations but not in others.
5. Different leadership styles are related to the conditions associated with different organisations.
6. **Situational Factors in Leadership** — A more moderate situational view is that leadership should be viewed in terms of a dynamic interaction between the leader, the group of followers/subordinates, the task situation and the environment. Leadership is thus multi-dimensional. The range of situational factors in leadership may be stated in terms of the following classification.

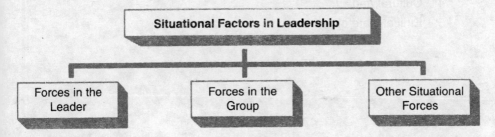

I. **Forces in the leader** — These include:
   1. Leader's specific personality characteristics;
   2. Orientations;
   3. Qualities and skills which are relevant for the function of leadership;
   4. The leader's value system;
   5. Inter personal and other skills;
   6. Self confidence;
   7. His confidence in subordinates;
   8. Feelings of security;
   9. Readiness for flexibility.

II. **Forces in the group** — These include:
   1. perceptions and attitude of group members towards (a) the leader, (b) their tasks and (c) organisational goals;
   2. needs and expectations of group members;
   3. Their skills and knowledge;
   4. Extent of group size;
   5. Nature of group structure and unity;
   6. The personality characteristics and qualities of group members.

III. **Other situational forces** — These include internal as well as external forces
   Internal Forces:
   1. The nature of the task, its complexity and technology, its importance in relation to other tasks.
   2. The structure of the organisation authority responsibility relations, organisational values and goals, policies and procedures, reward and control systems,
   3. The nature of problems which are faced by the leader and his group,
   4. The extent of pressures under which they work.

   External Forces:
   1. Trade unionism and its militance;
   2. Political conditions;
   3. Economic;
   4. Cultural and;
   5. Ethical state of society.

Three significant contributions to these theories are given below:

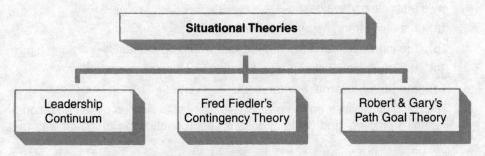

Let us discuss these theories one by one.

1. LEADERSHIP CONTINUUM

Robert Tannenbaum and Warren Schmidt depicted a broad range of leadership styles on a continuum which moves from authoritarian or boss-centred leader behaviour at one end to democratic or subordinate-centred behaviour at the other end.

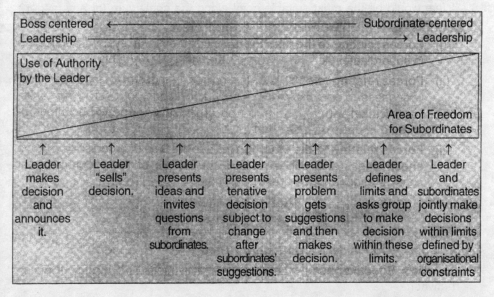

On the extreme left, under boss-centered leadership, the leader makes most decisions. Little freedom is permitted for subordinates. As we move along the continuum to the right, subordinates are more involved in decision-making and they have greater freedom of action.

Tannenbaum and Schmidt emphasised that—

1. Different leadership styles will be differentially effective under different situations. There is no one best style of leadership for all situations. A style which is effective in one situation may be ineffective in a different situation.

2. An effective leader is one who is sensitive enough to choose and adjust his style after clearly evaluating—

   (a) his own strengths and weaknesses;

   (b) the individuals and the groups with whom he interacts;

   (c) the organisational and task situation in which he operates;

   (d) the broad external environment.

3. This calls for abilities on the part of a leader (a) to size up all the situational variables properly and (b) to choose an appropriate style to match with the situation.

4. There is a high degree of interdependency among the situational forces.

5. In the long run, the leader may be able to influence some of the situational variables so as to gain more control over them.

6. Leadership operates is an open system.

7. There can be leaderless groups, in the sense that group members exercise authority and assume responsibility for task accomplishment on a collective basis.

8. What would be the most suitable point along the continuum for any leader? That depends on three sets of forces as follows:

   (i) **Forces relating to the managers** include their value system, confidence in subordinates, leadership urges, and need for certainty.

   (ii) **Forces relating to subordinates** include their desire for independence, willingness to assume responsibility, knowledge, interest in the tasks, identification with the goals of the organisation, and expectations of sharing in decision-making.

   (iii) **Forces relating to the situation** include the type of organisaiton, group effectiveness and cohesiveness, the nature of the problem under consideration, and the pressure of time.

2. FRED FIELDER'S CONTINGENCY THEORY

According to to Fred Fielder's Contingency Theory —

1. **Leader's Effectiveness** — Leadership effectiveness is a matter of match between—

   (i) a leader's personality; and

   (ii) the situation in which he functions.

2. **Two-extreme Leadership Personalities** — There are two extreme leadership personalities — Task-oriented leaders and Human Relations Oriented leaders. A leader's orientation is a measure of his characteristics, motivations, skills, values and goals.

3. **Situational Variables** — There are three variables which govern the situation in which the leader functions, as follows:

	Situational Variable	What it is?
1.	**Leader-Member Relations**	These may be **good or poor** depending upon the extent to which the leader is accepted, respected and trusted by members of his work group
2.	**Task Structure**	It may be **high or low** depending upon the extent to which the jobs of members of the work group are defined, routine and known.
3.	**Position Power**	It may be **strong or weak** depending upon the extent to which power is possessed by the leader.

4. **Situational Combinations** — Situational Variables may exist in different combinations. Eight such combinations may be listed as follows:

Situational Combination	Leader member Relations	Task Structure	Position Power	Situational Favourable ness
1.	Good	High	Strong	High
2.	Good	High	Weak	
3.	Good	Low	Strong	
4.	Good	Low	Weak	
5.	Poor	High	Strong	
6.	Poor	High	Weak	
7.	Poor	Low	Strong	
8.	Poor	Low	Weak	Low

5. **Research Findings —**

(i) Task-oriented leaders are most effective (i.e., are able to ensure good group performance) when the situation is *either* highly favourable *or* highly unfavourable. Reason is that in highly favourable situation, a task oriented leader can afford to give attention to task accomplishment. He need not worry about inter-personal relations, task structure and position power.

In highly unfavourable situation, he is able to get things done since he is supposed to be a strong leader.

(ii) Human Relations oriented leaders are most effective in intermediate situations (i.e., those lying in between the two extremes of highly favourable or highly unfavourable situations)

Appropriateness of Leadership behaviour for various group situations

Task Oriented Leaders	Relationship Oriented Leaders	Task Oriented Leaders
Very favourable Leadership situation	Intermediate favourable leadership situation	Very unfavourable leadership situation

The above figure shows that task oriented leaders tend to perform best in group situations that are *either* very favourable *or* very unfavourable to the leader. On the other hand, relationship-oriented leaders tend to perform best in situations that are intermediate (medium) in favourableness.

(iii) Situational factors need not be viewed as 'given' or 'inflexible'. They can be modified through proper means. A highly unfavourable situation can be made more favourable situation (a) by restructuring and redefining the tasks; (b) by strengthening the leader's position power; and (c) by influencing the perceptions of group members towards the leaders.

(iv) To improve group performance, the situation may be modified or improved so as to make it conducive for the leader to operate in and get effective results from the group.

(v) Leaders can not switch from one style to another in tune with the nature of the situation because switching over involves the ego of the leaders.

3. ROBERT & GARY'S PATH GOAL THEORY

According to Path Goal Theory —

1. There is a clear relationship between the behaviours of the leader and the motivation-performance-satisfaction of the group whom he leads.

2. Members of the group have certain expectations in regard to the behaviour of their leaders. Of course different groups have different expectations.

3. On the basis of members' expectations, four types of leader behaviours may be conceptualised:

Type of Leader Behaviour	What is expected from leader?
(a) **Directive Leadership**	The leader is expected to define the tasks and responsibility of his group members, set performance and reward norms, clarify rules and regulations as applicable, provide guidance, advice and instructions as necessary and monitor their performance.
(b) **Supportive Leadership**	The leader is expected to establish interpersonal relationships with the group,

		understand and share their aspirations and feelings, show concern for their welfare and promote group cohesiveness.
(c)	**Participative Leadership**	The leader is expected to keep the group informed on relevant tasks, goals and situations, involve them in decision-making, solicit their ideas and consult them often.
(d)	**Achievement Oriented Leadership**	The leader is expected to develop and utilize the skills and talents of group members, set challenging goals to them, make tasks interesting and meaningful and give some freedom to people in their jobs.

4. **Factors on which the patterns of preference of group members with regard to leader behaviour depends are as follows:**

   (a) the personal characteristics of group members (self-confidence, intelligence, skills, attitudes towards self-reliance, initiative, sense of responsibility and so on and

   (b) environmental conditions like the complexity of tasks, structure of the work group and the extent of formalisation of policies, rules, norms etc. For example, members who are deficient in self confidence look for a directive leadership. If the task is dull and uninteresting, people resent directive leadership.

5. **Who is an effective leader?**

   An effective leader is one who understands the characteristics of subordinate and the environmental situation and who matches his behaviour accordingly. On so matching his behavioural pattern the leader is likely to gain acceptance of his people by arousing their motivation to perform well, to earn expected rewards and to achieve satisfaction of their needs and aspirations in the process. In fact, such a leader helps people to achieve their goals (both organisational and personal) by clarifying the path (ways and means) to achieve them.

6. **Research Findings**

   (i) A leader can change his behaviour patterns as demanded by the needs of the situation. In a sense, leader behaviour is not an independent variable. It is dependent on the nature of the situation and the characteristics of people. Such an adaptive leader behaviour tends to be effective in generating the needed acceptance, motivation, performance and satisfaction on the part of the people concerned.

   (ii) The leader's effectiveness is contingent on his ability to capture the dynamics of the situation and the attitudes of people in a correct perspective.

(iii) Leaders are effective due to their influence on followers' motivation, ability to perform, and their satisfaction.

(iv) Subordinates are motivated by the leader to the extent he is able to influence their expectancies relating to the performance and attractiveness of the goal.

(v) Individuals are satisfied with their job if they believe that (a) performance of the job will lead to desirable outcomes and (b) with hard work they will be able to achieve the desirable outcomes.

4. NORMATIVE THEORY

Victor Vroom and Phillip Yetton's normative theory offers prescriptive guidelines on what leader should do and how he should behave in particular decision making situation effecting his group's task performance.

According to Normative Theory —

1. A leader is effective to the extent that decisions made in his unit facilitate group performance, are acceptable to the members and are made on a timely basis.

2. There are basically three decisions making methods or styles which the leader may adopt for purpose of solving group problems — Autocratic, consultative and group participative.

3. The leader should adopt different methods or styles depending upon particular decision situations. The choice of a particular method should be based on the nature of relevant decision situations.

4. There are decision rules on the feasibility or otherwise of particular decision making methods under different sets of decision situations. These decision rules are: Information rule, commitment rule, unstructured problem rule, acceptance rule, acceptance priority rule, fairness rule and conflict rule. Most of the rules appear to be self evident but simplistic. For example, they state that the autocratic method of decision making is not feasible if the quality of the decision is important, if the leader is deficient in possession of information or expertise, if the problem is unstructured and if the acceptance of the decision by the group members is critical.

Criticisms of Normative Theory

1. The theory is overly prescriptive and leaves little flexibility to leaders in their decision making.

2. It leaves out several other decision situations and decision making methods. For example, the urgency of the decision, nature of organisational policies as guides to decision making, the structure of the organisation, the extent of relationship of the problem to other problems and decisions and so on, are important aspects of decision situations which are not covered in this prescriptive theory.

3. Some decision situations may not be known to the leader untill after the decision is made. This fact rules out the feasibility of matching particular decision styles to decision making situations.

4. It also seems rule out the possibility of changing the decision situations themselves by the leader.

LEADERSHIP EFFECTIVENESS

The manager leader may be effective or ineffective depending upto the leadership style adopted by him. Effectiveness depends on the situational demands of a specific environment.

Diagrammatic Representation of Effectiveness Dimension

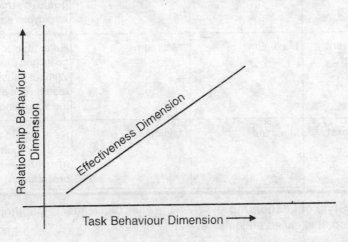

The various styles of leadership on the basis of effectiveness are as follows:

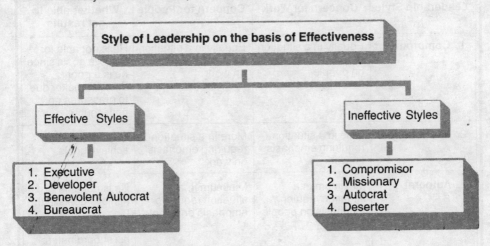

Let us discuss these styles one by one.

Effective Style of Leadership — When the style of a leader is appropriate to a given situation, it is called an effective style of leadership.

The following are regarded as more effective styles:

Leadership Style	Concern for Work	Concern for People	Whether able to get results
1. **Executive**	Maximum	Maximum	He is able to achieve goals by effective team work.
2. **Developer**	Minimum	Maximum	He is able to achieve goals by means of employees' satisfaction.
3. **Benevolent Autocrat**	Maximum	Minimum	He is able to achieve goals and procedures. Without causing any resentment among the subordinates.
4. **Bureaucrat**	Minimum	Minimum	He is able to achieve goals by means of rules and procedures.

Ineffective Style of Leadership — When the style of a leader is inappropriate to a given situation, it is called an ineffective style of leadership.

The following are regarded as less effective styles:

Leadership Style	Concern for Work	Concern for People	Whether able to get results
1. **Compromisor**	Equally in a situation requiring emphasis on people	Equally in a situation requiring emphasis on work	He is not able to achieve goals since he is a poor decison-maker due to pressures on both counts.
2. **Missionary**	Little in a situation requiring emphasis on work	More in a situation requiring emphasis on work.	He is not able to achieve goals.
3. **Autocrat**	Maximum in a situation requiring emphasis on people	Minimum in a situation requiring emphasis on people.	He is not able to achieve goals in the long run since he lacks confidence in his subordinates.
4. **Deserter**	Not at all	Not at all	He is not able to achieve goals. He has passive attitude towards his job. He is an escapist.

Determinants of Effectiveness according to Three Major Approaches

I. **According Trait Approach** — Leadership effectiveness is a function of the personal traits or qualities of the leader. Certain basic qualities of the leaders are necessary but not sufficient for the effective leadership since the possession of these qualities does not guarantee effectiveness.

II. **According to Behavioural Approach** — Leadership effectiveness is not a matters of what leaders are but rather a matter of what they do and how they behave. Leaders who have high concern for both the people and the work are said to be effective leaders. Effective leaders do regard high productivity and employee satisfaction as consistent and complementary to each other.

III. **According to Situational or Contingency Approach** — Leadership effectiveness is a function of interaction among at least three variables: the leader, the group of followers and the tasks situation.

Here effectiveness is defined in terms of the task performance and satisfaction of the group of followers. It is determined by **situational factors** like:

1. Personal qualities of the leader which enable him to secure willing co-operation of the followers through his personal influence on their behaviour;

2. His authority or power position (how much authority or power he possesses, the extent of his knowledge, skill and competence and the degree to which he can utilise them);

3. The expectations and behaviour of his subordinates.

4. The expectations and behaviour of his superiors.

5. The expectations and behaviour of his fellow managers (peers).

6. The aspirations, attitudes and skills of the group members;

7. The complexity of relations between the leader and group members and the task situation, technology, organisational or task structure;

8. The requirements of tasks to be performed by subordinates.

9. Relationship among tasks, division of labour, freedom available for doing the tasks;

10. The degree of imposed control; and

11. The rewards associated with performance.

12. Organisational policies.

Leadership effectiveness in this context depends upon the ability of the leader to adopt different behavioural styles to match different situations. There is no one best leadership style for all situations. Leadership effectiveness can be secured or enhanced by tailoring the style to the demands of each situations.

LEADERSHIP EFFECTIVENESS THEORY

MANAGERIAL GRID

On the basis of an idea that a leader may combine his concern for people and concern for production with different degrees of emphasis on each, Robert Black and Jane Mouton developed the concept of 'Managerial Grid' in 1964.

What is Managerial Grid?

The managerial grid refers to a diagrammatic representation of the possible combinations of concern for people and concern for production on a two dimensional space.

What are the steps involved in the preparation of Managerial Grid?

The following steps are involved in the preparation of managerial grid:

Step 1 → Divide each axis into 9 units — 1 representing the lowest degree and 9 representing the highest degree of concern on each scale.

Step 2 → Represent a leader's concern for production on horizontal axis. Production becomes important to the leader as his rating goes up the horizontal axis.

Step 3 → Represent a leader's concern the people on vertical axis. People becomes important to the leader as his rating goes up the vertical axis.

Blake and Mouton argued that a leader's managerial style is a point on the grid. They have identified 5 combinations of styles, for illustrative purposes, out of 81 (i.e., 9 × 9) possible combinations. These 5 combinations are outlined as follows:

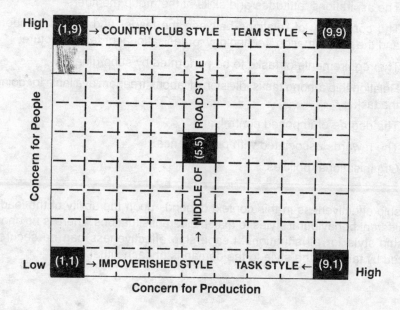

Combination	Style	Interpretation
(1,1)	**Impoverished Style**	The leader has **minimum concern for both people and production**. He has casual attitude towards getting things done from people and maintaining relationships with people. He regards people as lazy and underdeveloped.
(1.9)	**Country Club Style**	The leader has **minimum concern for production and maximum concern for people**. He tries to keep people happy expecting that an amiable climate will motivate people to work with enthusiasm.
(9.1)	**Task Style**	The leader has **maximum concern for production and minimum concern for people**. He adopts a directive style to get things done from people and arranges conditions of work in such a way that human elements interfere to a minimum degree.
(5,5)	**Middle of Road Style**	The leader has **moderate concern for production and people**. He does not push too much in *either* direction but tries to achieving a satisfactory balance between the requirements of production and of people. His approach is that of **"live and let live"**.
(9,9)	**Team Style**	Adequate organisation performance is possible through balancing the necessity to get work while maintaining morale of people at a satisfactory level. His behaviour may fluctuate between being tough on people to increase productivity and being nice to people to increase their sagging morale. The leader has **maximum concern for both people and production**. He tries to bring about an integration and harmony between the needs of people and of production. He creates a highly encouraging organisational climate of commitment, co-operation trust and hope. Work accomplishment is from committed people. Interdependence through a common stake in organisation purpose leads to relationship of trust and respect.

Conclusions given by Blake and Mouton

1. The two concerns (i.e., concern for production and concern for people) are independent and can be present together.

2. (9.9) style is the most desirable style in the long-run.

3. Grid concept can be used to enable managers to identify their current leadership behavioural position.

4. Managers who have lower concerns for production and people can be exposed to some training programme to enable them to move to (9,9) style.

5. A manager will often use one managerial grid style when initially confronting a given problem or situation. However, if this approach does not resolve things satisfactory for him, he will shift to second grid style which is called manager's back up style.

MORALE

MEANING OF MORALE

Morale is the state of mind or attitude of an individual or group towards the work and environment. A favourable attitude is an indication of high morale while an unfavourable attitude indicates low morale. High morale leads people to attach greater importance to group goals as compared to their personal goals and reduces absenteeism and labour turnover. On the other hand, low morale leads to inefficiency, waste, low productivity, high degree of absenteeism and labour turnover. Morale is an important factor which contributes to the willingness of people to work, leads to their happiness and determines their productivity. High or low morale may affect the achievement of organisational goals.

FACTORS DETERMINING THE MORALE

The factors determining the morale are as follows:

Factor Influencing Morale	Morale tends to be high...	Morale tends to be low...
1. **Organisational Objectives**	If employees **consider** the organisational goals to be **useful and important**.	If employees **does not consider** the organisational goals to be **useful and important**.
2. **Organisation Structure**	If organisational structure **defines clearly** the lines of superior-subordinates **relations**.	If organisational structure **does not** define **clearly** the lines of superior subordinates relations.
3. **Communication**	If there is **free and frank communication** between the superior and the subordinates.	If there is **no free and frank communication** between the superior and the subordinates.

4. Compensation	If there is **satisfactory** levels of wages and salaries as well as system of rewards and incentives for higher efficiency.	If there is **no satisfactory** levels of wages and salaries as well as system of rewards and incentives for higher efficiency.
5. Opportunities of Advancement	If **there is an opportunity** of advancement in the career through promotion.	If **there is no opportunity** of advancement in the career through promotion.
6. Working environment	If there is an **adequate provision** for safety, healthcare and welfare of employees.	If there is **not an adequate provision** for safety, healthcare and welfare of employees.
7. Job Satisfaction	If employees **derive** personal satisfaction from the work they do.	If employees **does not derive** personal satisfaction from the work they do.
8. Leadership	If leadership **enables** the subordinates **to achieve their goals** and aspirations.	If leadership **does not enable** the subordinates **to achieve their goals** and aspirations.
9. Network Behaviour of Co-workers	If members of the work group are **co-operative** and there is **mutual faith** and understanding among them.	If members of the work group are **not co-operative** and there is **no mutual faith** and understanding among them.

Leadership, Motivation and Morale

Effective leadership makes a positive impact on the motivation and morale of the subordinates due to the following reasons:

1. Leadership provides satisfactory work environment and thus ensures job satisfaction.
2. Leadership recognises the needs and aspirations of subordinates.
3. Leadership provides for a proper system of monetary and non-monetary rewards and incentives.
4. Leader's concern about the well-being and advancement of careers of subordinates.
5. Use of democratic leadership style to allow subordinates to involve and participate in decision-making.

EXERCISES

SHORT ANSWER TYPE QUESTIONS

1. Explain the term 'leadership'.
2. State briefly any four qualities of a good leader.
3. State the elements of leadership process.
4. Explain in brief the nature of leadership.
5. Distinguish between leadership and managership.
6. "All managers are leaders but all leaders are not managers." Comment.
7. State the factors influencing the effectiveness of a leader.
8. Distinguish between Leadership and Managership.
9. Write short notes on the following:
   (a) Leadership Traits
   (b) Leadership Styles
   (c) Leadership Continuum
   (d) Leadership Effectiveness
   (e) Managerial Grid

LONG ANSWER TYPE QUESTIONS

1. "Leadership, is an influence-interaction process." Comment.
2. What is leadership? Discuss the importance of leadership in the management of a business organisation.
3. Discuss the role of leadership in management.
4. Discuss the qualities of a good leader.
5. "A good leader helps his subordinates to solve problems by themselves." Comment.
6. "A good leader is one who understands his subordinates, their needs and their source of satisfaction." Comment.
7. Explain the relationship among leadership, motivation and morale.
8. "Leadership abilities of manager are not totally inborn or genetic, they can be acquired or learnt also" comment.
9. What is leadership? Discuss the various styles of leadership.

24

Directing— Communication

MEANING OF COMMUNICATION

The term **'Communication'** has been derived from Latin Word **'Communis'** which mean commons.

There are a number of definitions of the term 'communication'. A few of them are being reproduced on next page:

1. *"Communication is the sum of all things, one person does when he wants to create understanding in the minds of another. It involves a systematic and continuous process of telling, listening and understanding."*

   — Allen Louis

2. *Communication has been defined as "the transfer of information from one person to another whether or not it elicits confidence."*

— ***Koontz and O Donell***

3. *"Communication is an exchange of facts, ideas, opinions or emotions by two or more persons."*

— ***George Terry***

4. *Communication is defined as "the process of passing information and understanding from one person to another, it is essentially a bridge of meaning between people. By using the bridge of meaning a person can safely cross the river of misunderstanding."*

— ***Keith Davis***

Thus, Communication is the process of transmitting the message and receiving the response to that message. The person who sends the message is known as '*sender*' and the person who receives the message is known as '*receiver*' and the response to that message is known as '*feedback*'. Since the feedback requires another message to be communicated by the sender and so on, the communication process becomes a circular process.

NATURE AND CHARACTERISTICS OF COMMUNICATION

The characteristics of communication highlight the nature of communication. These characteristics have been shown below:

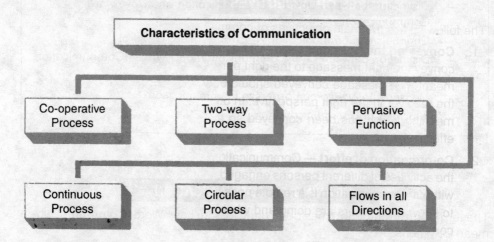

Let us discuss the characteristics of communication one by one.

1. **Co-operative Process** — Communication is a co-operative process in the sense that it involves the participation of at least two persons - one who transmits the message and the other who receives the message and responds to it.

2. **Two-Way Process** — Communication is a two-way process in the sense that it involves both sending the message and receiving the response to that message. It is not complete unless the receiver of the message has understood the message and his reaction or response is known to the sender of the message.

3. **Pervasive Function** — Communication is regarded as a pervasive function because it is required at all levels of management (top, middle or lower) and in all departments (planning, manufacturing, marketing, finance or personnel).

4. **Continuous Process** — Communication is a continuous process in the sense that it is required by superior, subordinate and fellow members on continuous basis to understand what management expects from subordinates and what subordinates expect from management and to keep the wheels of operations running smoothly.

5. **Circular Process** — Communication becomes a circular process when the response to the message (**also known as feedback**) requires another message to be communicated by the sender, and so on.

6. **Flows in all Directions** — Communication may flow vertically upward or downward between superiors and subordinates, horizontally between persons occupying similar ranks in different departments as well as diagonally between persons at different levels in different parts of the organisation.

PURPOSES OR OBJECTIVES OF COMMUNICATION

The following are the main objectives of communication:

1. **Conveying the right message** — The main objective of communication is to convey the right message to the right person, i.e., to the person for whom it is meant. The message conveyed should be well understood and accepted by the receiver in the right perspective. In other words, it should carry the same meaning which has been conveyed so that it may be translated into action effectively.

2. **Co-ordination of effort** — Communication is an effective tool for co-ordinating the activities of different persons engaged in running a business. Co-ordination without communication is a remote possibility. The individuals or groups come to know what others are doing and what is expected from them only through communication.

3. **Good industrial relations** — Communication develops good industrial relations as it conveys the feelings, ideas, opinions and viewpoints of one party to the other party. The two parties—the management and the subordinates come closer through communication. They understand each other and dispel any misunderstanding. Thus, it promotes cooperation and good industrial relations.

4. **Development of managerial skills** — Communication helps managers to understand human behaviour at work. Communication of facts, ideas, opinions, information, feelings etc., and value to the knowledge of managers about various happenings, in the organisation and behaviour of people. Thus, communication is a process of learning.

5. **Effectiveness of policies** — The organisation formulates policies and programmes to guide the workforce. These should be conveyed properly to those who are really responsible for the execution of work to achieve the organisational objectives. Only effective communication can translate the policies into action. Effectiveness of the policies can be judged from the success which surely depends upon an effective communication system.

The above objectives of communication, lead to a boosting the morale of the people and thus ensure the success of organisation.

STEPS IN THE PROCESS OF COMMUNICATION

The process of communication includes the following steps:

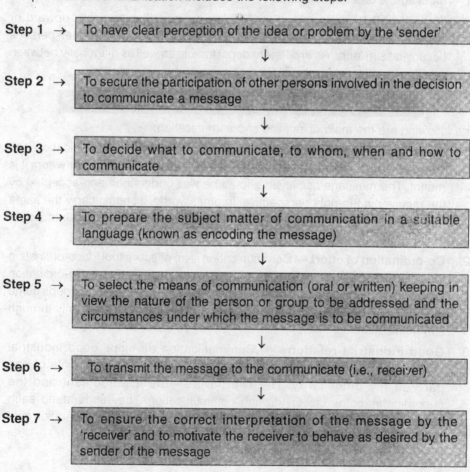

Step 1 → To have clear perception of the idea or problem by the 'sender'

↓

Step 2 → To secure the participation of other persons involved in the decision to communicate a message

↓

Step 3 → To decide what to communicate, to whom, when and how to communicate

↓

Step 4 → To prepare the subject matter of communication in a suitable language (known as encoding the message)

↓

Step 5 → To select the means of communication (oral or written) keeping in view the nature of the person or group to be addressed and the circumstances under which the message is to be communicated

↓

Step 6 → To transmit the message to the communicate (i.e., receiver)

↓

Step 7 → To ensure the correct interpretation of the message by the 'receiver' and to motivate the receiver to behave as desired by the sender of the message

↓

Step 8 → To evaluate the effectiveness of communication to determine whether and to what extent the receiver has positively responded to the message

ELEMENTS IN THE PROCESS OF COMMUNICATION

The basic elements in the process of communication are shown below:

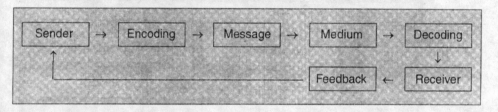

Let us discuss them one by one.

1. **Sender** — The sender is a person who initiates the process of communication. The sender may be a superior, a subordinate, a fellow member, a customer, a creditor or any other outside person.

2. **Encoding** — It refers to preparing the subject matter of communication in a suitable language. Its purpose is to translate the thought of the sender into a language or code that can be easily understandable to the receiver of the message.

3. **Message** — It refers to the encoded subject matter of the communication which is to be transmitted.

4. **Medium** — It refers to means of communication which carries the message from sender to receiver. It serves as a link between the sender and the receiver.

5. **Decoding** — It refers to the conversion of the message by receiver into meaningful terms so as to make it understandable.

6. **Receiver** — The receiver is a person who receives the message of the sender. The receiver may be a superior, a subordinate, a fellow member, a customer, a creditor or any other outside person.

7. **Feedback** — It refers to the actual response of the receiver to the message sent to him. It enables the sender to check whether the message sent has been properly understood by the receiver.

IMPORTANCE OF COMMUNICATION

The communication derives its importance from the following benefits which flow from it:

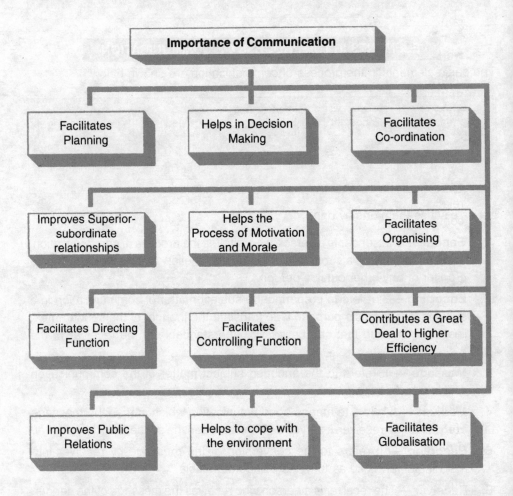

1. **Facilities Planning** — Communication facilitates planning by providing such information as is needed by planners.

2. **Helps in Decision-Making** — Communication facilitates decision-making by providing the required information needed. The quality of decision made in an organisation depends largely on the amount and quality of information available to the decision-maker.

3. **Facilitates Co-ordination** — Communication facilitates co-ordinating by providing proper upward, downward and horizontal interaction between members of different departments or sections at all levels of authority.

4. **Improves Superior-subordinate Relationships** — Communication helps in

improving relationships between superiors and subordinates by removing misunderstanding and providing clear and accurate information in time.

5. **Helps the Process of Motivation and Morale** — Communication helps the process of motivation and morale building through sharing of information, consultation and discussion. It helps in moulding attitudes also. Prompt redressal of subordinates' grievances by superiors motivates employees to work efficiently.

6. **Facilitates Organising** — Communication facilitates organising function of management by providing information about the duties, responsibilities, authority, relationships, positions and jobs. Delegation and decentralisation of authority is accomplished in an organisation.

7. **Facilitates Directing Function** — Communication facilitates directing function by providing proper interaction between managers and their subordinates and between members of work groups. It improves superior-subordinate relationships by promoting exchange of ideas and information between them continuously.

8. **Facilitates Controlling Function** — Communication facilitates controlling function by providing feedback of actual performance against planned targets.

9. **Contributes a Great Deal to Higher Efficiency** — Effective communication contributes a great deal to higher efficiency in job performance. It ensures willing co-operation of others due to close understanding of ideas and instructions established through communication.

10. **Improves Public Relations** — Communication helps in maintaining and improving good relations with the customers, suppliers, shareholders the Government and the society at large by providing and receiving the required information. It helps in developing a good public image of the organisation.

11. **Helps to cope with the environment** — Communication helps the organisation to cope with a rapidly changing business environment by supplying the information relating to changes taking place in business environment.

12. **Facilitates Globalisation** — Communication facilitates globalisation of business operations by providing facilities to establish links with different countries.

TYPES OF COMMUNICATION

The communication may be classified on the basis of relationship and direction of the flow as shown below:

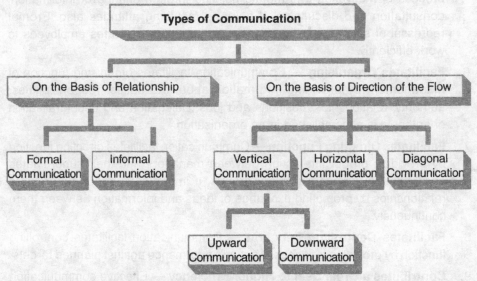

Let us discuss the types of communication one by one.

(a) **Formal Communication** — It refers to the communication which takes place on the basis of organisational relationships formally established by the management. It is used for the transmission of official messages within or outside the organisation. It follows the officially established chain of command. It is mostly expressed in written form.

Advantages — The major advantages of formal communication are as under:

1. **Orderly and Systematic** — Formal communication is orderly and systematic.

2. **Possible to fix responsibility** — It is possible to fix responsibility for the action taken on the basis of formal communication.

3. **Serves Organisational Needs** — Formal communication serves organisational needs.

4. **Easy Tracing of Source** — The source and direction of flow of formal communication can be easily traced.

5. **No distortion of Message** — Message flowing through formal channels may not be distorted.

6. **Facilitates Functions** — Formal communication facilitates planning, organising, directing, decision-making and controlling functions.

7. **Does not lead to rumours** — The network of formal communication often does not lead to to rumours.

8. **Follows chain of command** — Formal communication follows the official chain of command and hence provides support to the authority of superiors over the subordinates.

Disadvantages — The major disadvantages of official communication are as under:

1. **Slow Moving Process** — It is a slow-moving process particularly when it is routed through more than one authority level.

2. **Lack of Personal Involvement** — Personal involvement is lacking because formal communication is mostly conveyed in an impersonal manner.

3. **Chances of Not Providing Accurate Information** — There are chances of not providing accurate information particularly when such information is likely to have unfavourable effects.

(b) **Informal Communication** — It refers to the communication which takes place on the basis of informal or social relations among people in an organisation. It is usually used for the transmission of personal messages within or outside the organisation. It does not follow officially established chain of command. It is mostly expressed in verbal form. It is the result of social interaction among the members of organisation. It may take place among the persons placed at different levels and in different departments. The network of informal communication is known as '**grapevine**' because the origin and direction of the flow of informally conveyed messages cannot be easily traced as in the case of a vineyard. The grapevine often leads to rumours (i.e., the portion of the message which is not true).

Advantages — The major advantages of informal communication are as under:

From the point of view of Members

1. **Serves Social Needs** — Informal communication serves social needs of the members of the organisation by enabling them to develop friendly relations through informal exchange of ideas and information.

2. **Helps to discuss other matters** — Informal communication helps the members to discuss the matters which cannot be done through the official channel.

3. **Helps Members not linked through official chain** — Informal communication helps the members who are not linked through the official chain of command, to communicate.

From the point of view of Management

1. **Serves to fill in Gaps** — Informal communication serves to fill in the gaps, if any, in formal communication.

2. **Fast Speed** — Informal communication travels faster than the formal communication because it is not required to follow scalar chain of command.

3. **Helps to know employees' attitudes** — Informal communication enables the management to ascertain the employees' attitudes and reactions to plans and policies.

4. **Provides Emotional Relief** — Informal Communication provides emotional relief to the subordinates and reduces tension in labour-management relations.

Disadvantages — The major disadvantages of informal communication are as under:

1. **Chances of Distortion** — Messages flowing through informal channel tend to be distorted as different persons pass on the same with different outlook and interpretations.

2. **Rumours** — Its network (known as grapevine) often leads to rumours and develops misunderstanding.

3. **Unsystematic Erratic** — It is unsystematic and erratic and hence cannot be relied upon.

4. **Chances of Leakage** — Confidential information often leakes out through informal communication.

5. **Difficult Tracing of Source** — It is difficult to trace the source and direction of flow of informally conveyed message.

6. **Not possible to fix Responsibility** — It is not possible to fix the responsibility with respect to informal communication.

DISTINCTION BETWEEN FORMAL AND INFORMAL COMMUNICATION

Formal and informal communication can be distinguished as follows:

Basis of Distinction	Formal Communication	Informal Communication
1. **Meaning**	It refers to the communication which takes place following the officially established chain of command.	It refers to communication which takes place independently off the official lines of communication.
2. **Speed**	It is **slow**-moving process particularly when it is routed through more than one authority level.	It travels **faster** than the formal communication since it is not required to follow scalar chain of command.
3. **Fixing of responsibility**	It is **possible to fix the** responsibility with respect to formal communication.	It is **not possible** to fix responsibility with respect to informal communication .
4. **Nature of message**	It involves **work-related matter**.	It may involve **work-related matters or social matters**.
5. **Direction of flow or nature**	It is **orderly and systematic**.	It is **unsystematic and erratic**.

6. **Needs served**	It serves **organisational needs**	It serves not only the organisational needs but also **social needs** of the employees of the organisation.
7. **Channel of communication**	It is mostly expressed in **written form**.	It is mostly expressed in **verbal form**.
8. **The source and direction**	It's source and direction of flow can be easily **traced**.	It is **difficult to trace** its source and direction of flow.
9. **Distortion of Message**	Message flowing through formal channels **may not be distorted**.	Message flowing through informal channel **tends to be distorted** as different persons pass on the same with different outlook and interpretations.
10. **Rumours**	Its network often does **not lead to rumours**.	Its network (known as grapevine) **often leads to rumours**.
11. **Manner of conveying**	It is mostly conveyed in an **impersonal** manner.	It is mostly conveyed in **personal** manners.

II. On the Basis of Direction of Flow

(a) **Vertical Communication** — It refers to communication that takes place between persons occupying superior and subordinate positions in the organisational hierarchy. It may be sub-divided into: (i) downward communication, and (ii) upward communication.

 (i) *Downward communication* — It refers to communication that takes place from higher level positions to lower level positions. Plans and policies communicated by top management to middle level management, rules and procedures communicated by middle level management to lower level management and orders and instructions communicated by lower level management to operatives (workers) are the examples of downward communication. These communications may be oral or written. The written communications are conveyed through (a) notices, (b) circulars, (c) handbooks, (d) orders, (e) memoranda, (f) Instructions etc.

Purpose — The purpose of downward communication is —

1. to communicate Plans & Policies;
2. to communicate Rules & Procedures;
3. to communicate Orders & Instructions.

Example — The downward communication has been illustrated below:

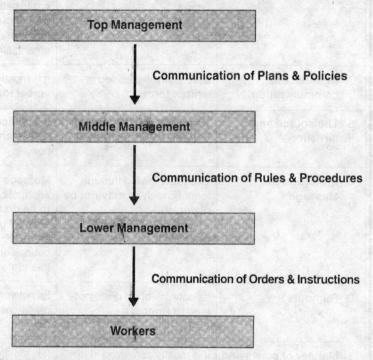

Advantages of Downward Communication — The advantages of Downward Communication are as follows:

1. It helps in explaining the organisation's policies, plans, and programmes, work methodology and other necessary information, to the members of the organisation,

2. It is used as a means to control the activities of the subordinates by intimating them the quality of their performance on the jobs,

3. It helps the subordinates to know what is expected of them, and puts a check on the unreasonable demands of the superiors, and

4. It brings satisfaction to people and helps motivate them.

Limitation of Downward Communication — The major limitation of downward communication is that the information has to pass through various hierarchical levels, and is interpreted and reinterpreted at each intervening level. The message may possibly reach the bottom in a distorted and changed shape. This loses the very objective of the communication.

(ii) *Upward communication* — It refers to communication that takes place from a lower level position to a higher level position. These communications may be oral or written. Information by subordinate workers to foreman, by foreman to assistant-manager, by assistant-manager to manager, by manager to general manager or by chief executive to board of directors are examples of upward communication.

Types — Such communication is of two types:

1. **Feedback of Information** in which subordinates convey a message to the top executive in response to the latter's original communication. Sometimes, managers at higher levels solicit information about the performance of subordinates on the job in response to orders and instructions issued to them, their feelings about the job and work environment.

2. **Voluntary communication** from the subordinates to convey their complaints, grievances, suggestions and opinions. It may also include innovative ideas, reaction to a particular policy, rules, or behaviour of any person on the job; (i.e., subordinates work performance,) clarification of orders, instructions, policies etc., and personal or family problems.

Purpose — The purpose of upward communication is —

1. to communicate the progress of work;
2. to communicate the work performance of subordinates;
3. to communicate the problems relating to work;
4. to communicate the opinions and suggestions;
5. to communicate the complaints and grievances;
6. to communicate to get clarification with regard to orders, instructions, method of work etc.

Example — The upward communication has been illustrated below:

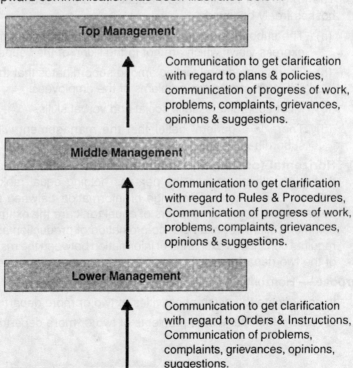

Advantages of Upward Communication — The advantages of Upward Communication are as follows:

1. It helps the top to know the attitudes, behaviour, opinions, actions and feelings of the workers on the job. On the basis of such information, the management may improve its behaviour, introduce motivational and other plans in the organisation, and improve its controlling function.

2. It creates confidence and trust in the superiors,

3. It develops confidence among subordinates that they can convey their feelings, grievances, complaints, suggestions, opinions, etc. to the top and can contribute more to the achievement of organisational objectives.

Limitations of Upward Communication — The limitations of Upward Communication are as follows:

1. Generally, upward communication is ignored or distorted or coloured at the intermediate levels because:

    (a) The top management is quite unwilling to listen to the juniors in the hierarchy.

    (b) It may contain negative points which adversely affect the person at the intermediate level.

2. Another problem of upward communication is caused by status differences. The lower level functionaries hesitate in communicating messages to their bosses freely because:

    (a) The subordinates are afraid of action being taken against them if they express views which are not to the liking of their superiors.

    (b) There is a general feeling among subordinates that the management is not interested in the problems of the employees.

    (c) Most subordinates lack social and verbal skills.

    (d) There is a general belief that the management will not respond to subordinates' suggestions.

(b) **Horizontal (or Lateral) Communication** — It refers to communication that takes place between the persons holding equal ranks in the same or different departments. Exchange of information between two departmental heads or two or more managers of equal rank are the examples of horizontal communication. For example, co-ordination of production and sales activities requires continuous exchange of information between the respective managers of the two departments.

Purpose — Horizontal type of communication is necessary —

1. to co-ordinate the different activities of two or more departments, and

2. to resolve the interrelated problems of two or more departments.

Example — The horizontal communication has been illustrated below:

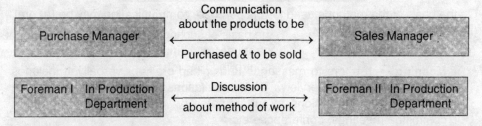

Advantages of Horizontal Communication — Horizontal communication has the following advantages:

1. It helps in co-ordinating the activities of different departments at the same level.

2. Different departmental heads may sit together and thrash out problems of wastage of time, money, labour, and materials.

   Limitation of Horizontal Communication — The main problem in lateral communication, which very often arises, is the difference in approach and vision of different functionaries, who advocate things from their own angles; this affects the productivity and efficiency of the organisation adversely. The problem may be advertised through the pattern of horizontal communication.

(c) **Diagonal Communication** — It refers to communication that takes place between persons holding different ranks in different departments. This type of communication takes place only under special circumstances. For example, a cost accountant asked sales representatives about some reports for some analysis and the sales representative's sent their reports directly to the cost accountant.

DISTINCTION BETWEEN UPWARD COMMUNICATION AND DOWNWARD COMMUNICATION

Upward communication and downward communication can be distinguished as under:

Basis of Distinction	Upward Communication	Downward Communication
1. **Meaning**	It refers to the flow of communication from a subordinate to his superior in the hierarchy.	It refers to the flow of communication from a superior to his subordinates in the hierarchy.
2. **Purpose**	Its purposes include to inform management about (i) the progress of work, (ii) the performance of subordinates, (iii) problem in relation to work, (iv) opinions or suggestions, (v) complaints and grievances, and to get clarifications with regard to instructions, procedures and methods of work.	Its purposes include to inform about organisational plans and policies, orders and instructions, roles and procedures etc.

CHANNELS OF COMMUNICATION

On the basis of the methods used for the purpose, communication may be (a) oral, (b) written, and (c) gestural.

(a) **Oral Communication**

Meaning — It refers to messages transmitted orally or verbally. It includes face to face contact, interviews, joint consultations. It usually takes place when superiors give instructions to subordinates or when discussion is held in committee meetings, conferences etc.

Advantages — The major advantages of oral communication include the following:

1. **Permits clarification of doubts** — It permits detailed explanation and clarification of doubts.

2. **Takes less time** — Oral transmission takes *less time* if the message is brief.

3. **Useful at operational level** — Oral transmission is particularly *useful at the operational level*.

4. **Gives Personal touch** — Oral transmission gives communication a *personal touch*.

5. **Permits to know immediate reaction** — Oral transmission is especially useful when the sender wants to know the reaction of the receiver quickly.

Disadvantages — The major disadvantages of oral communication include the following:

1. **No verification** — Oral transmission cannot be verified afterwards.

2. **Time consuming** — It may be time consuming as it happens in meetings, seminars and conference.

3. **Not taken seriously** — Oral transmission may not be taken seriously by the parties involved.

4. **Difficult to act** — It may be difficult to act on oral communication if details are missing or forgotten.

5. **Costly for Distant Places** — Oral transmission is more costly for distant places.

(b) **Written Communication**

Meaning — It refers to message transmitted in written form. It includes the messages in the form of letters, notices, circulars, memoranda, notes, manuals etc.

Advantages — The major advantages of written communication include the following:

1. **Facilitates Verification** — Written communication can be verified from the written records.

2. **Precise Terms** — Written communication can be expressed in precise terms after due thought.

3. **Suitable** — Its contents can be suited to specific requirements.

4. **Taken Seriously** — Written communication is taken more seriously by the parties involved.

5. **More Economical** — Written communication is *more economical* especially when the subject matter to be conveyed is lengthy or where it is intended to be conveyed to a large number of persons.

6. **Easier to Act** — It becomes easier to act upon written communication.

7. **Only means for distantly placed persons** — Written communications serve as the only means of exchange of ideas and information where the communicator and the communicatee are separated by long distances.

8. **Lengthy communication** — Written communications are ideal in case the subject-matter to be conveyed is too lengthy or where it is intended to be conveyed to a large number of persons simultaneously.

9. **Record** — Written communications can be safely preserved for long periods of time and they can be referred to in future also.

10. **Repeat value** — A written communication can be used again and again which is not possible in case of verbal communication.

Disadvantages — The major disadvantages of written communication include the following:

1. **Takes More Time** — Transmission of written communication *takes more time* especially when the sender and receiver are at places far away from one another.

2. **Expensive** — Written communication is *very expensive* especially when the lengthy messages are to be sent by telegram or fax.

3. **No Personal Touch** — Written communication does not give a personal touch.

4. **Secrecy Difficult** — It is difficult to maintain complete secrecy about a written communication.

5. **Not permits to know immediate reaction** — Written communication is *not useful* especially *when* the sender *wants to* know the *reaction of the receiver quickly.*

DISTINCTION BETWEEN ORAL COMMUNICATION AND WRITTEN COMMUNICATION

Oral and written communications can be distinguished as under:

Basis of Distinction	Oral Communication	Written Communication
1. **Meaning**	It refers to a message sent or received verbally.	It refers to a message conveyed in written form.
2. **Verifiability**	It **cannot** be verified afterwards since there is no evidence to verify.	It **can** be verified from the written record.
3. **Economy**	It is **not economical** for distant places.	It is **more economical**.
4. **Precision**	It may **not** be very precise.	It **can** be expressed in precise terms.
5. **Speed**	Its transmission takes **less time**.	Its transmission takes **more time**.
6. **Action**	It may be **difficult to act** on oral communication if details are missing or forgotten.	It is **easier to act** upon a written communication.
7. **Seriousness**	It may **not be taken** seriously by the parties involved.	It is **usually taken** more seriously by the parties involved.
8. **Personal or impersonal**	It tends to be **personal**.	It may tend to be **impersonal**.
9. **Usefulness**	It is particularly useful **at the operational level** of management.	It is particularly useful **at top and middle levels** of manage-ment.

(c) **Gestural Communication —** It refers to communication by actions. Communication through gestures is often used to make verbal or written communication more effective. **For example,** a trade union leader, while addressing a meeting, uses different gestures by hands, movement of eyes to make his point. Similarly, when a foreman pats his worker on his back and says 'keep it up', it is gestural communication used to appreciate the work of a worker. It is important to develop and maintain inter-personal communication. It may take place in the form of —

1. Facial Expressions;
2. Movements of Hands;
3. Movements of Head;
4. Movements of Lips;
5. Wink of an eye etc.

Circumstances under which written communication is preferred over oral communication?

Under the following circumstances written communication is preferable over oral communication.

1. Where records are to be kept;
2. Where formal message is to be delivered;
3. Where the message is addressed to large number of persons;
4. Where accuracy of message is to be emphasised;
5. Where future reference and verification is required.

BARRIERS TO EFFECTIVE COMMUNICATION

Barriers to effective communication are the obstacles which create confusion, misunderstanding and may even lead to breakdown of the communication process. The major barriers to effective communication are given below:

1. **Multiplicity of Organisational Levels in the Hierarchy** — The organisational structure having multiplicity of organisational levels in the hierarchy often becomes an obstacle to effective communication. Information may be withheld at a particular level or passed on with changes. This happens particularly when communication of correct information is likely to have an adverse impact.

2. **Language Barrier** — The language used for communicating a message may also be an obstacle to effective communication. This happens particularly when the pronouncement of words is not clear in verbal communication, words are not clear in written communication or words having different or more than one meaning have been used.

3. **Status Barrier** — The difference in the status of sender and receiver may also be an obstacle to effective communication. For example, subordinates often withhold or pass on distorted information to please their superiors because they do not like to reveal their mistakes to them.

4. **Physical Distance as a Barrier** — The physical distance between the sender and the receiver of any message may also be an obstacle to effective communication. This happens particularly when the sender of a message is interested in knowing the reaction of the receiver of the message quickly but verbal communication is not possible.

5. **Emotional and Psychological Barriers** — These barriers arise from motives, attitudes, judgement, sentiments, emotions and social values of participants. These barriers often arise due to lack of mutual trust and confidence. People having strong attitudes and feelings either reject or refuse to accept the

messages affecting them emotionally. These barriers create psychological distance that hinders communication.

6. **Semantic Barriers** — These barriers arise from the limitations of the symbolic system. The same symbol may carry different meanings to different people. The purpose of communication will be defeated if the receiver draws wrong inference about the symbol used by the sender.

7. **Lack of Organisational Facilities** — People generally fail to communicate effectively due to lack of organisational facilities such as meetings, conferences, complaint or suggestion boxes, open door system etc.

8. **Organisational Rules and Regulations** — The rigid organisational rules and regulations also act an obstacle to effective communication when these rules restrict the flow of certain messages, prescribe the subject matter to be communicated and the channel through which it is to be communicated.

9. **Specialisation Barriers** — The differences between departments due to specialisation create an obstacle to effective communication because each department is more concerned about its own work and does not pay attention to other departments.

10. **Inattentiveness** — Inattentiveness of the receiver also act an obstacle to effective communication. The purpose of communication is defeated when the receiver shows inattentiveness to the message conveyed.

MEASURES TO OVERCOME BARRIERS TO COMMUNICATION

To overcome barriers to communication the following measures should be adopted:

1. **Priority** — The inflow and outflow of communication should be regulated by determining the priority of messages to be communicated so as to concentrate more on important messages and to reduce the chances of getting important messages ignored.

2. **Feedback** — Feedback means the response or reaction to the initial message and includes the receiver's acceptance, action, behavioural response.

3. **Appropriate Language** — Appropriate language should be used to express the message in clear terms. Vague expressions should be avoided. The words which may have different meanings should be avoided. Researches have shown that oral communications together with their written versions are more effective in bringing about the desired response. The sender must use the language with which the receiver is familiar.

4. **Listening Ability** — A receiver of the message should listen to the verbal messages carefully so as to avoid misunderstanding and confusion. A sender should also be prepared to listen to what the receiver has to say and respond to his questions, if any. Keith Davis has developed 10 guides to effective listening.

    (a) **Stop talking** — You cannot listen if you are talking.

    (b) **Put the talker at ease** — Help a person feel free to talk.

    (c) **Show the talker that you want to listen** — Look and act interested.

(d) **Remove distractions** — Don't doodle, tap, or shuffle papers.

(e) **Empathize with talkers** — Try to put yourself in the other person's shoes and understand the problem from his point of view.

(f) **Be patient** — Allow plenty of time. Do not interrupt a talker.

(g) **Hold your temper** — If you are angry, you fail to understand and appreciate the meaning of words.

(h) **Go easy on argument and criticism** — Do not argue. Remember you cannot win arguments, even if you win, you lose.

(i) **Ask questions** — This encourages a talker and shows, that you are listening. It helps to develop points further.

(j) **Stop talking** — A person who is constantly talking is not listening or learning. Listening requires two ears, one for meaning and one for feeling.

5. **Control Over Emotion** — Both sender and receiver of the message should have control over their emotions. They should ensure that the content of the message is not affected by any negative impact of emotions.

6. **Non-Verbal Signature of Compliance** — In case of oral communication, the sender should observe the actions of the receiver to ascertain whether they are in conformity with the intent, purpose and understanding of the message.

7. **Mutual Trust and Faith** — The parties involved in communication should have mutual trust and faith between themselves. They should feel free to make suggestions and correct each other's views without there being any misunderstanding .

8. **Providing Organisational Facilities** — Communication may be mode more effective by providing organisational facilities such as meetings, conferences, complaints or suggestion boxes, open door system etc.

9. **Two-way Communication** — The organisation's communication policy should provide for a two-way traffic in communication—upwards and downwards. It brings two minds closer and improves understanding between the two parties, the sender and the receiver. A sound feedback system should be introduced in the organisation so that distortion in, and filtering of, messages should be avoided. There should be no communication gap.

10. **Strengthening Communication Network** — The communication network should be strengthened to make communication effective. For this purpose, the procedure of communication should be simplified, layers in downward communication should be reduced to the minimum possible. Decentralisation and delegation of authority should be encouraged to make information communication more efficient, through frequent meetings, conferences, and timely dissemination of information to the subordinates.

11. **Promoting Participative Approach** — The management should promote the participative approach in management. The subordinates should be invited to participate in the decision-making process. It should seek cooperation from

the subordinates and reduce communication barriers.

12. **Credibility in Communication** — One criterion of effective communication is credibility. The subordinates obey the orders of their superior because they have demonstrated through their actions that they are trustworthy. They must practice whatever they say. The superior must also maintain his trustworthiness. If the superior is trusted by the subordinates, communication will be effective.

13. **Selecting an Effective Communication Channel** — To be effective, the communication should be sent to the receiver through an effective channel. By effective channel we mean that the message reaches its destination in time, to the right person, and without any distortion, filtering, or omission.

PRINCIPLES OF COMMUNICATION

The principles which can be followed to make the communication system more effective are given on below:

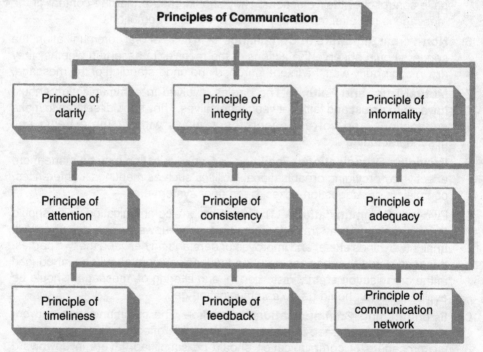

1. **Principle of clarity** — The idea or the message to be transmitted should be clearly worded so that it may be interpreted by the receiver in the same sense in which it is communicated. There should be no ambiguity in the message. For this purpose, the idea to be communicated should be very clear in the mind of the sender. It should be kept in mind that the words do not speak themselves, but the speaker gives them meaning. If the message is clear, it would evoke an appropriate response from the other party. It is also necessary that the receiver must be conversant with the language, the inherent assumptions, and the mechanics of communication.

2. **Principle of integrity** — Communication should be aimed at motivating people to take action as agreed upon. In this process, the superiors rely upon the subordinates and under assumption that their integrity is unimpeachable. It is because the integrity of the organisation is related to the level of integrity possessed by the subordinates. No communication may evoke a response from the subordinates if their integrity is doubted. The superiors should trust the subordinates, accept their view points and never doubt their intention, in executing the task entrusted to them.

3. **Principle of informality** — Formal communication system is cornerstone of a formal organisation, and it leads to transmittal of messages. But, sometimes, formal communications prove ineffective in evoking the needed response from the subordinates. In such cases, the superiors should adopt the strategy of making use of informal channels of communication: they may contact, if necessary, the subordinates personally or through someone else to persuade them to translate their orders into action. Informal communication at times proves for more effective than formal communication.

4. **Principle of attention** — In order to make the message effective, the recipient's attention should be drawn to the message communicated. Each one is different in behaviour, sentiments and emotions, which determine the degree of attention. For this purpose, the superior must note that he himself should not expect from his subordinates what he himself does not practice. So, a manager cannot enforce punctuality if he himself is not punctual: **"Actions speaks louder than words."**

5. **Principle of consistency** — This principle implies that communication should always be consistent with the policies, plans, programmes and objectives of the organisation, and not in conflict with them. Messages which are inconsistent with the policies and plans of the organisation create confusion in the minds of the subordinates about their implementation; and, such a situation may prove detrimental to the organisation's health.

6. **Principle of adequacy** — The information should be adequate and complete in all respects. Inadequate and incomplete information may delay action and destroy understanding, and create confusion. Inadequate information also affects the efficiency of the sender and the receiver of the communication.

7. **Principle of timeliness** — All message should be transmitted at the proper time. Any delay in communicating message serves no purpose except to make them merely historical document as it loses its importance after some time.

8. **Principle of feedback** — One of the most important principles of communications is the principle of feedback. The communication must have feedback information from the recipient to know whether the recipient has understood the message in the same sense in which the sender has meant it, or whether the subordinates agree or disagree with the contents of the message. It also helps in understanding attitude of the people.

9. **Principle of communication network** — Communication network means the routes through which the communication travels to its destination, i.e., the

person for whom it is meant. A number of such networks may exist in an organisation at a given point of time; but the management should consider the effectiveness of the communications network in the given situation, and its effects on the behaviour of the recipient before it finally chooses the network.

The above principles, if followed, will make the communication effective. An effective system of communication should be installed in the organisation so as to promote better industrial relations.

EXERCISES

SHORT ANSWER TYPE QUESTIONS

1. State the meaning of communication.
2. Explain in brief the characteristics of communication.
3. State the objectives of communication.
4. Enumerate the steps involved in the process of communication.
5. Enumerate the elements in the process of communication.
6. What is 'formal communication'?
7. What is 'informal communication'?
8. Enumerate the types of communication according to the direction of flow.
9. What is meant by 'downward communication'?
10. What is meant by 'upward communication'?
11. What is meant by 'horizontal communication'?
12. What is meant by 'diagonal communication'?
13. Distinguish between upward communication and downward communication.
14. Enumerate the various methods or channels of communication.
15. What is meant by 'oral communication'?
16. What is meant by 'written communication'?
17. What is meant by 'gestural communication'?
18. Under what circumstances will you as a manager prefer written communication over oral communication?
19. Enumerate any three circumstances where oral communication is preferred over written communication by a manager in an organisation.
20. Distinguish between the following:
    (e) Formal communication and informal communication
    (f) Upward communication and downward communication
    (g) Oral communication and written communication
21. Write short notes on the following:
    (a) Grapevine
    (b) Diagonal channels of communication

(c) Horizontal channels of communication

(d) Barriers to Effective Communication

(e) Guidelines for Effective Communication

(f) Role of Communication in the process of control

LONG ANSWER TYPE QUESTIONS

1. "Communication is sharing of understanding." Comment.

2. Explain briefly the importance of communication in management.

3. Explain the process and importance of communication.

4. What is formal communication? Briefly describe its advantages and disadvantages.

5. What is informal communication? Briefly describe its advantages and disadvantages.

6. What is informal communication? How is it different from formal communication on the basis of mutual relationship among the members and speed of communication?

7. Differentiate between formal and informal communication.

8. What is meant by 'communication'? Differentiate between oral and written communication.

9. "A good system of communication makes use of both oral as well as written messages." Explain.

10. Discuss the merits and demerits of written communication

11. Discuss the advantages and disadvantages of oral communication.

12. "Informal channels of Communication are more "Humane" and "Homely". Discuss"

13. What are the barriers to effective communication? Suggest the measures to overcome such barriers.

14. Discuss the guidelines for effective communication.

15. Discuss the principles of communication.

25 Controlling

MEANING OF CONTROL

Control is the process of verifying whether actual performance is in conformity with planned performance and taking corrective action where necessary.

More specifically, **control involves:**

1. knowing what work is to be done as to quantity, quality and time available;
2. verifying whether work has been or is being carried out in accordance with the plan;
3. analysing deviations (i.e., difference between planned performance and actual performance) to ascertain the causes thereof;
4. adopting remedial measures to correct the deviation; and
5. suggesting revision of plans, if necessary.

OBJECTIVES OF CONTROL

Controlling serves mainly the following two purposes:

1. to check and ensure that performance of work is in accordance with the organisational plans, policies and programmes;

2. to detect deviations (or deficiencies) in performance, if any, to rectify them (if possible and necessary) and to prevent their repetition in future.

NATURE AND CHARACTERISTICS OF CONTROL

The characteristics of controlling function highlight its nature. These characteristics have been shown below:

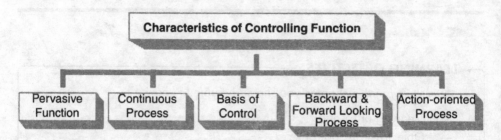

Let us discuss them one by one.

1. **Pervasive Function** — Control is a pervasive function in the sense that it is required at all levels of management in every type of organisation. Every manager performs the controlling function irrespective of his status and the nature of his job.

2. **Continuous Process** — Controlling is a continuous process in the sense that it involves review of performance and revision of standard operations on a continuous basis. As long as an organisation exists, control continues to exist.

3. **Basis of Control** — Planning is the basis of control because planning lays down the standards attainable against which the actual performance is compared under controlling function. The concept of control presupposes the existence of planning. Without planning, no control is possible.

4. **Backward and Forward Looking Process** — Control is a backward looking process in the sense that it compares actual performance which has been or is being carried out with the planned performance. Control is a forward looking process in the sense that it improves future planning by suggesting revision of existing plans and targets and adoption of new plans on the basis of information derived from past experience. It looks at future through the eyes of past. Therefore, control is both a backward and forward looking process.

5. **Action-Oriented Process** — Control is an action-oriented process in the sense that the manager starts comparing actual performance with the planned performance immediately after the actual activities have been undertaken and, in order to prevent recurrence of deviations, a manager modifies and improves the existing plans. Control has no meaning if no corrective action is taken and then it will be simply backward looking. A good control system always facilitates timely action in the form of corrective measures to prevent the recurrence of deviations in future.

IMPORTANT OF CONTROL

Controlling function derives its importance from the benefits which flow from it. These benefits are shown below:

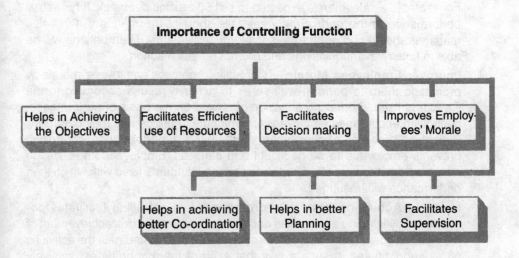

Let us discuss them one by one.

1. **Helps in Achieving in the Objectives** — Controlling facilitates achievement of organisational objectives by providing means of determining —
   (i) whether plans are being implemented;
   (ii) whether there is any progress towards achievement of objectives;
   (iii) whether there is any deviation between actual and desired results;
   (iv) whether there is any need to revise the existing plan targets or to adopt a new plan.

2. **Facilitates Efficient Use of Resources** — Controlling facilitates efficient use of human and non-human resources by ensuring —
   (i) the quantity of work as per plan;
   (ii) the quality of work as per plan;
   (iii) the work performance within the time allowed as per plan;
   (iv) the required work performance of requisite quality with the given resources as per plan (i.e., ensuring performance at a cost not more than that specified in the plan).

3. **Facilitates Decision-Making** — Controlling facilitates decision-making through enabling the managers to find out the deficiencies in work performance and to take appropriate decision to rectify those deficiencies.

   Control and decision-making are considered to be Siamese twins. The process of control is complete only when corrective measures are taken. This requires taking a right decision as to what types of follow up action is to be taken.

Controlling involves in detecting the deviations and their causes. Controlling helps in quick decision-making by bringing together all the units of action.

Controlling enables the management to take decisions for future course of action also.

For example a salesman is expected to sell 50 articles per week. If his actual performance at the end of the week falls short of the standard, the sales manager should find out the reasons for it immediately. Then only he will be able to take relevant decisions and prompt remedial action.

4. **Improves Employees' Morale** — Controlling improves employees' morale by prompting them to perform well so as to achieve results according to the standards fixed. By making provision of reward on the basis of performance, controlling encourages employees to contribute to the best of their capability. By making provision of punishment on the basis of performance, controlling prevents employees to be negligent and careless. Employees know well in advance what they are expected to do and the standards fixed with which their performance will be judged.

5. **Helps in Achieving better Co-ordination** — Controlling facilitates co-ordination by keeping all activities and efforts directed towards achievement of the planned goals. Controlling forces each manager to co-ordinate the activities of his subordinates in such a way that each of them contributes positively towards the objectives. Since this follows throughout the organisation, co-ordination is achieved in the organisation as a whole.

6. **Helps in Better Planning** — Controlling facilitates planning by providing important information on the basis of which existing plans may be revised and new plans may be adopted.

7. **Facilitates Supervision** — An effective control system facilitates supervision in an organisation by comparing actual performance with the standards fixed and finding out the deviations, if any, to know the root cause of it.

RELATIONSHIP BETWEEN PLANNING AND CONTROLLING

Planning and controlling are interdependent and Interrelated activities. They are interdependent in the sense that —

1. Planning provides basis (i.e., standards) for the controlling activities. In the absence of planning, the controlling activities cannot be performed because no fixed standards are available with which actual performance may be compared. It cannot be determined whether the performance is good, bad or reasonable.

2. Controlling ensures realising planned goals efficiently and provides basis for improvement in future plans. In the absence of effective controlling, planned activities cannot be properly implemented in accordance with the plans and programmes of the organisation and there cannot be improvement in future plans.

Controlling is the process of (a) measuring deviation of actual performance with the standards, (b) detecting the causes of deviations, and (c) suggesting the corrective measures to avoid deviations in future. These quantum of deviations, their causes and suggestive measures are the basis for future planning and for revising the targets, for improving staffing, and for making changes in the techniques of supervision, motivation and leadership.

Planning and controlling are interrelated and, in fact, they reinforce each other in the sense that —

1. planning based on facts makes controlling easier and effective; and
2. controlling improves future planning by providing information derived from past experience.

Planning without controlling is meaningless and controlling without planning is blind. Their mutual relationship can be judged from the figure.

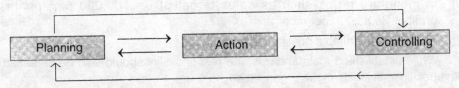

Planning is Looking Ahead and Controlling is Looking Back

Planning is looking ahead in the sense that it lays down the standards to be achieved in future. Controlling is looking back in the sense that it measures the actual performance relating to the past and compares it with the standards laid down. Controlling is not only looking back but also looking forward in the sense that it helps in the adoption of new plans and revision of the existing plans on the basis of comparison of actual performance with the prescribed standards.

STEPS IN THE PROCESS OF CONTROL

The process of control includes certain steps to be followed. These steps are shown below:

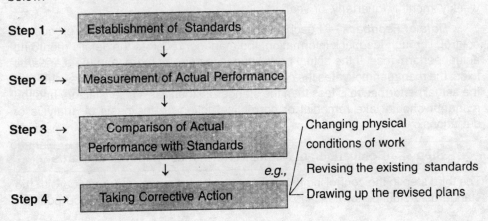

Let us discuss the steps involved in the process of control one by one.

Step 1 → Establishment of Standards

The first step in the controlling process is to establish standards. Standards represent the planned performance to be achieved during a specified period. Standards are the yardsticks with which actual performance is to be compared. These standards should be fixed in the light of objectives set by top management. These standards should be specific so that one may know in clear terms what is to be achieved and the checking of performance may became possible. These standards should be expressed —

(i) in physical terms such as production target of 10,000 units per month, maximum rejections of 10 units per batch of production of Rs 10,000 units per month;

(ii) in monetary terms such as sales target of Rs 100,000 per month, profit of Rs 30,000 per month;

(iii) in any other verifiable qualitative terms.

While establishing the standards, the responsibility should also be identified with specific individuals in the organisation.

Step 2 → Measurement of Actual Performance

The second step in the control process is to measure the actual performance. To facilitate the comparison of actual performance with the standards fixed, the actual performance should be measured and expressed in the same units as the planned performance. The performance should preferably be measured in quantitative terms as far as possible. Where quantitative measurement is not possible, the performance should be expressed in terms of qualitative factors. For example, the performance of industrial relations manager may be measured in terms of attitudes and morale of workers, and frequency of strikes. The measurement of actual performance may be *either* through personal observation *or* regular oral and/or written reports. Such measurement and reporting of performance may be done at periodic intervals, say, weekly, monthly, quarterly, or yearly.

Role of Feedback — Feedback plays a very important role in the process of control. Through feedback information, the manager receives the details regarding actual performance. If the actual performance is up to or more than the standards fixed, the manager motivates the concerned person. But if the feedback reveals that the actual performance is less than the standards, then it is not satisfactory and the manager should take remedial or corrective action on the basis of analysis of deviations.

Step 3 → Comparison of Actual Performance with the Standards

The third step in the controlling process is to compare actual performance with the standards. Actual performance is compared with the standards for two purposes:

1. to find out the extent of deviations (i.e., the difference between the actual performance and planned performance);
2. to identify the causes of deviations if the deviations between the planned performance and actual performance are significant.

Such a comparison should be done as close to the point of performance as possible. It assists in quick location of defects and results in correction with minimum losses.

The causes of factors responsible for deviation may be defective material, defective machinery, defective process, defective handling etc.

Meaning of the Term 'Deviation' in Controlling

Controlling as a function is the process by which actual performance is compared with the standards fixed to get the feedback. The results of comparison can be nil difference, positive difference or negative difference. Nil difference means that the performance is up to the standard, positive difference means that the actual performance is more than the standard fixed and negative difference means that the performance is not up to the mark and, therefore, remedial action is required. *This difference, positive or negative, in controlling, is known as 'deviation'.*

Step 4 → Taking Corrective Action

The last step in the controlling process is to take corrective actions on the basis of factors causing deviation between standard fixed and actual performance. Such corrective action is taken to prevent the recurrence of deviation in future. A corrective action may involve a change in methods, machinery, rules or procedures, improving physical conditions of work or changing the nature of supervision. It may be noted that where the deviation cannot be corrected through managerial actions, the standards may have to be revised.

Some of the examples of corrective action are suggested below:

Causes of Deviation	Corrective Action to be Taken
(a) Defective material	Change the quality specification for the material required.
(b) Detective process	Modify the existing process.
(c) Defective machinery	Repair the existing machine (if it can be repaired) or replace the same (if it cannot be repaired).
(d) Incapable labour force	Change the workforce, the method of selection, training of workmen (depending upon the knowledge why workmen are incapable).
(e) Defective supervision	Change the nature of supervision.
(f) Defective physical conditions of work	Improve the physical conditions of work.

Control by Exception — The concept of control by exception states that while measuring the actual performance with the standards laid down, it is necessary to establish the range of deviations beyond which the attention of top management is needed. Only the deviations of exceptional nature should be reported to the top management. If all deviations are considered, no deviation will be treated properly. For example, if postal expenses increased by 10%, the deviation is not important to require managerial attention. On the other hand, if materials cost increases by 2%, it should receive immediate managerial attention. Therefore, it is rightly said, "If managers try to control everything, they may end up by controlling nothing."

The application of this concept helps in conserving the managerial time, talent and efforts so that it can be applied to more important areas.

Illustration 1 In section *A* of a particular department 50 workers are employed. They are assigned the daily work in the form of 60 units per worker per day. Only 3 workers were in a position to achieve the standards fixed. Suggest the remedial action to be taken by the departmental head.

Ans.: Out of 50 only 3 workers-were in a position to achieve the standards of 60 units per worker per day which may be due to the following reasons:

(i)   Unrealistic standards; or

(ii) Untrained staff.

In the first case, standards fixed should be reviewed properly on scientific basis, and standards should be fixed again.

In the second case, proper training should be provided to the workers.

FEATURES OF A GOOD CONTROL SYSTEM

Since the process of control consists of certain steps which are interrelated, it may be called as 'system of control'. To be effective and to serve its purpose, the system of control must satisfy certain requirements. These may be regarded as the prerequisites (i.e., features) of effective control system. These features are shown below:

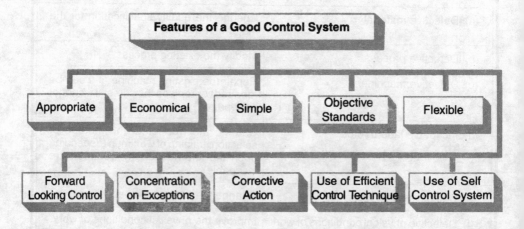

Let us discuss the features of a good control system one by one.

1. **Appropriate** — The control system must be appropriate to suit the requirements of an organisation. The control system should be designed after considering the nature of organisation (manufacturing, trading or service), size of organisation (large, medium or small), functions of departments (production, marketing or service) within an organisation.

2. **Economical** — The control system must be economical. In other words, the cost of setting up, implementing and maintaining a control system should not exceed the benefits derived from it. The control system must justify the expenses involved. A control system is justifiable if the savings anticipated from it exceed the expected costs in its working. Small-sized organisation cannot afford elaborate and expensive control system.

3. **Simple** — The control system must be simple and easily understandable to the controller and the controlled. The control system should provide reports regarding performance in a simple and easy way. There should not be any difficulty of interpretation of reports on performance.

4. **Objective Standards** — Effective control system requires objective, accurate and attainable standards. There should not be any scope for subjective interpretation. Standards should be factually determinable and verifiable. If the standards have been set accurately, the controller can evaluate performance and provide reports in an objective manner.

5. **Flexible** — The control system should have the flexibility to adjust itself to the changing requirements of the organisation. It should be adaptable to new developments including the failure of the control system.

6. **Forward Looking Control** — An effective control system should be forward looking in the sense that it should be directed towards future. It should report the deviations from the plans quickly in order to safeguard the future. It must ensure timely detection and prevention of their repetition in future.

7. **Concentration on Exceptions** — An effective control system should be control by exception. It is called control by exception because according to this principle only significant deviations from the standards require management's attention as they constitute exceptions. The control system must focus attention only on those factors which are critical to performance.

    If managers try to control everything, they may end up controlling nothing because an attempt to go through all deviations tends to—

    (a) to be tedious;

    (b) to be time consuming;

    (c) increase unnecessary efforts; and

    (d) to decrease attention on important problems.

    For example, if postal expenses increased by 10%, the deviation is not important to require management attention. On the other hand, if materials cost increases by 2%, it should receive immediate managerial attention. Therefore, it is rightly said, "If managers try to control everything, they may end up by controlling nothing".

8. **Corrective Action** — An effective control system should not only point out deviations but also must lead to timely corrective action to prevent their repetition in future.

9. **Use of Efficient Control Techniques** — An effective control system should use efficient control techniques. Control techniques are said to be efficient when they detect deviations from plans and make possible corrective action at an early stage with the minimum of unforeseen consequences.

10. **Use of Self-Control System** — The different units or departments should be so planned that they control themselves. These sub-systems of self-control should be lead together by the overall control system.

Symptoms Which Indicate a Faulty Control System

The symptoms that would indicate a faulty control system are given as follows:

  (i)   Unrealistic (too high) standards;
 (ii)   Poor communication system or network;
(iii)   No clear-cut fixation or delegation of authority;
(iv)   Continuous poor performance of workers; and
 (v)   Decline in quality of goods produced.

TECHNIQUES OF CONTROL

There are various techniques of control. Some of them are shown below:

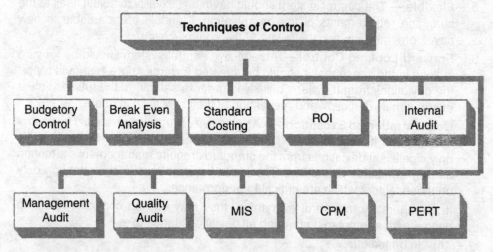

Let us discuss these techniques one by one.

1. BUDGETARY CONTROL

The three key elements of the management process are planning, execution and control. Business management must plan its activities in advance, carry out the plan and institute appropriate techniques of observation and reporting to ensure that deviations from the plan are properly analysed and handled.

Meaning of the term 'Budget'

According to C.I.M.A., London. *"A budget is a financial and/or quantitative statement, prepared and approved prior to a defined period of time, of the policy to be pursued during that period for the purpose of attaining a given objective. It may include income, expenditure and the employment of capital."* A budget is a plan covering phases and operations for a definite period in the future. It is the form of quantitative expression of policies, plans, objectives and goals laid down in advance by top management for the concern as a whole and for each sub-division thereof.

The main **characteristics of a budget** are:

1. **Prepared in Advance** — It is prepared in advance and is derived from the long-term strategy of the organisation.

2. **Relates to Future** — It is related to future period for which objectives or goals have already been laid down

3. **Expressed in Quantitative/Financial Terms** — It is expressed in quantitative form, physical or monetary units, or both.

Meaning of Budgeting

Budgeting is the art of building budgets.

Meaning of Budgetary control

According to C.I.M.A., London "Budgetary control is the establishment of budgets relating to the responsibilities of executives to the requirements of a policy and the continuous comparison of actual with budgeted results *either* to secure by individual action the objective of that policy *or* to provide a basis for revision." The fundamental principles of budgetary control may be stated as under:

1. Establishing a plan and target performance, for each of the activities of the business for the budget period.

2. Recording of actual performance during the budget period.

3. Continuous Comparison of the actual performance with that planned.

4. Ascertainment of the variances and analysis of reasons therefor, and

5. Taking corrective action such as revision of budget in the light of changed circumstances.

Budgetary control forms an integral part of any management control system. In a budgetary control system, each of the large number of budgets monitors actual performance relating to target (budgeted) level of performance for a sub-goal of the firm's activities. **For example,** comparison of budgeted and actual sales shows whether the performance in relation to the sale sub-goal is satisfactory or not. The attainment of the sub-goal in turn contributes to the achievement of overall goal of satisfactory level of profit. Thus, budgeting is viewed as a process constructing a set of sub-goals for a given goal of profit attainment.

Objectives of Budgetary Control System

The objectives of Budgetary Control System are given below:

1. To determine targets of performance for each section or department of the business for the budget period.

2. To lay down the responsibilities of each of the executives and other personnel so that every one knows what is expected of him and how he will be judged.

3. To provide a basis for the comparison of actual performance with the predetermined targets.

4. To ascertain the variance (i.e., differences between actual performance and budgeted performance) and analyse the reasons therefor.

5. To take the necessary corrective action.

6. To provide a basis for revision of current & future policies.

7. To draw up long-range plans with a fair measure of accuracy.

8. To ensure the best use of all available resources to maximise profit or production subject to the budget (or limiting) factors.

9. To co-ordinate the various activities of the business.

10. To centralise control.

11. To decentralise responsibility to each manager.

12. To show the management where action is needed to remedy a situation.

13. To act as a guide for management decisions when unforeseeable conditions affect the budget.

14. To engender a spirit of careful forethought, assessment of what is possible and an attempt at it. It leads to dynamism without recklessness.

15. To plan and control income and expenditure of manufacturing or training operations so that the most practicable profits are obtained.

16. To plan and control capital expenditure in the most profitable direction.

17. To plan and control the financing of the business so that adequate working capital, including liquid resources are available for carrying out the policy of the business.

18. To plan and control expenditure on research and development.

19. To combine the ideas of all levels of management in the preparation of the firm's plans.

Step involved in the preparation of Budgets

The following steps are involved in the preparation of budgets:

Step 1 → Appointment of Budget Controller

Although the Chief Executive is finally responsible for the budget programme, it is better if a large part of the supervisory responsibility is delegated to a special official designated as Budget Controller or Budget Director. Such a person should have knowledge of the technical details of the business and should report directly to the President or the Chief Executive of the organisation.

Step 2 → **Formulation of Budget Committee**

The Budget Controller is assisted in his work by the Budget Committee. The Committee consists of all the Heads of various departments, viz., Production, Sales, Finance, Personnel, Purchase, etc. with the Managing Director as its Chairman. It is generally the responsibility of the Budget Committee to submit, discuss and finally approve the budget figures. Each head of the department should have his own Sub-committee with executives working under him as its members.

Each member will prepare his own budget which will be discussed at the committee meeting before a final shape is given for co-ordinated action. The important function of a budget committee are as follows:

(a)   To define general policies of the management;

(b)   To receive and review budget estimates;

(c)   To approve budget estimates;

(d)   To analyse variances and recommend corrective action where necessary; and

(e)   To co-ordinate budget programme.

Step 3 → **Fixation of Budget period**

The period covered by a budget is known as budget period. There is no general rule governing the selection of the budget period. The length of the budget period depends upon the nature of the plan and circumstances of the business. **For example,** industries which are subject to fashion change use short budget period whereas industries involving long-term expenditure with relatively little change in product design use long budget periods. **For example,** (i) a shoe industry uses short-term budgets and (ii) a telephone manufacturing company uses long-term budgets. Normally, one year is a normal period for budget because it coincides with the accounting year. A common practice however, is to have a series of budget periods. Thus, sales budget may cover the next five years while production and cost budgets may cover only one year. The capital expenditure budget may cover even 5 to 10 years; the yearly budgets may also be broken down into monthly periods. Long-term budgets may be supplemented by short term budgets. Thus, **For example,** a long-term budget for three to five years may be supplemented by short-term budgets for one year or less.

For control purposes, the budget period may be divided into shorter periods. The period of time covered by a budget and the resulting comparative statement of actual and budgeted expenditure should be largely determined by the requirements and outlook of the persons whose activities are planned in the budget. **For example,** a foreman may need a weekly budget and report on certain costs because he exercises day-to-day control over such expenditure. The departmental manager with a broader outlook, may not be interested in short-term fluctuations. Normally, the control period covers a month.

Step 4 → **Identification of Budget factor (or Key factor or limiting Factor)**

The factor which sets a limit to the total activity is known as budget factor, key factor or limiting factor. **For example,** if production can not be increased inspite of heavy demand, due to non-availability of raw-material/power, raw-material/power is called here key factor. The key factors should be correctly identified and their extent of influence must first be carefully assessed.

Examples of Principal Budget Factors (or Key Factors)

Item	Budget Factor (or Key Factor)
(a) Materials:	(i) Availability of supplies. (ii) Restrictions imposed by the Government like, quotas.
(b) Labour:	(i) Shortage in certain key processes.
(c) Plant and machinery:	(i) Insufficient capacity for lack of space. (ii) Bottlenecks in certain key processes.
(d) Sales:	(i) Low market demand. (ii) Insufficient advertising due to lack of funds.
(e) Finance:	(i) Long-term finance. (ii) Short-term funds.
(f) Management:	(i) Lack of managerial time for additional work.

It would be desirable to prepare first the budget relating to this particular factor, and then prepare the other budgets. An illustrative list of key factors in certain industries is given below:

Examples of Key Factor in Specific Industries

Industry	Key Factor
Motor Car	Sales demand
Aluminium	Power
Petroleum Refinery	Supply of crude oil
Electro-optics	Skilled technicians
Hydro power generation	Monsoon

A key factor is not necessarily a permanent factor. It is often a temporary one. In the long run, it may be possible for the management to overcome the limitations imposed by a factor by raising funds necessary to finance capital expenditure, finding alternative sources of raw material or substitutes for raw materials; in the short run by working overtime, hiring equipment, etc. Thus, the aim of locating limitations is to seek harmony among the various factors of production from the beginning and to maintain it throughout the budget period.

Step 5 →   Identification of Budget Centers

It is a well known saying that "costs are the best controlled at the point of incurrence." Thus, for example, in the case of production cost the point of control will be at the supervisor or operator level. In this way, suitable areas of control have to be selected. These areas should not be too large because the span of control should be limited. Normally, the areas chosen should conform to the natural responsibilities of executives. Such areas are known as budget centres. A budget which refers to a budget centre is a department budget. A budget centre may again consist of a number of cost centres representing different groups of machines.

Step 6 →   Preparation of Budget Manual

The budget manual is a schedule, document or booklet which shows, in written forms budgeting organisation and procedures. The manual should be well written and indexed, a copy thereof may be given to each departmental head for guidance.

Contents of Budgets Manual — Budget Manual should include the following matters:

1. Introduction: A brief explanation of the principle of budgetary control system, its objectives and benefits.

2. Procedure to be adopted in operating the system. For example, 'distribution instruction', will specify as to whom various budget schedules are to be sent.

3. Definition of duties and responsibilities of (a) operational executives, (b) budget committee and (c) budget controller.

4. Nature, type and specimen forms of various reports. It also specifies the persons responsible for the preparation of the reports and the programme of distribution of the reports to the various officers.

5. The account code and classification used by the company.

6. The budget calendar showing the dates for completion of each part of the budget and submission of reports.

7. The budget periods and control periods.

8. The follow-up procedures.

Advantages of Budget Manual — The following are the advantages of Budget Manual:

1. An overall well co-ordinated plan, provided by budgetary control system, shows what role each manager is expected to play in maximising the profits.
2. Any problem arising from the operation of a budgetary control system can be settled through the manual.
3. New employees get acquainted with the procedure involved in the operation of the system by referring to manual.
4. Methods and procedures become standardised.
5. Since co-ordination is maintained, there is no overlapping of instructions. There is in other words synchronisation of all efforts which leads to the attainment of the objectives with minimum of friction.

Advantages of Budgetary Control System

1. **Facilitates the carrying on of Business Activities in efficient manner** — The use of budgetary control system enables the management of a business concern to conduct its business activities in the efficient manner.
2. **Facilitates Control of Expenditure** — It is a powerful instrument used by business houses for the control of their expenditure. It infact provides a yardstick for measuring and evaluating the performance of individuals and their departments.
3. **Reveals Deviations** — It reveals the deviations to management, from the budgeted figures after making a comparison with actual figures.
4. **Facilitates Effective Utilisation of resources** — Effective utilisation of various resources like men, material, machinery and money is made possible, as the production is planned after taking them into account.
5. **Facilitates Revision of Plans** — It helps in the review of current trends and framing of future policies.
6. **Facilitates Implementation of Standard Costing System** — It creates suitable conditions for the implementation of standard costing system in a business organisation.
7. **Inculcates feeling of Cost Consciousness** — It inculcates the feeling of cost consciousness among workers.

Limitations of Budgetary Control System

The limitations of budgetary control system are as follows:

1. **Estimates** — Budgets may or may not be true, as they are based on estimates.
2. **Rigidity** — Budgets are considered as rigid document.
3. **No Automatic Execution** — Budgets cannot be executed automatically.
4. **Lack of Staff co-operation** — Staff co-operation is usually not available during budgetary control exercise.
5. **Expensive** — Its implementation is quite expensive.

2. BREAK EVEN ANALYSIS

Meaning of Break-even Analysis

The term **'Break Even Analysis'** is used both in the narrow sense and in the broader sense.

In the narrow sense, 'Break Even Analysis' refers to a technique of analysis which is used to determine the 'Break-even Point'. **Break-even Point (BEP)** refers to that volume of operations at which total costs are just equal to total sales. It is a point where there is *neither* profit *nor* less. At BEP contribution (i.e., Sales – Variable Cost) is just equal to fixed costs. A firm will incurr loss if the sales volume decreases beyond this point and can earn profit if the sales volume increases beyond this point.

In the broader sense, 'Break-even Analysis' refers to a technique of analysis to study the relationship between Cost, Volume and Profit at different levels of operations. It is used to determine —

(i)   the amount of profit/loss at various volume of operations;

(ii) the volume of operations required to earn a target profit;

(iii) the impact of change in cost on profit;

(iv) the impact of change in selling price on volume and profit.

In its broader sense, it is also called as Cost-Volume-Profit Analysis (or CVP Analysis)

How to perform Break-even Analysis

Break-even analysis may be performed both graphically and algebrically.

Graphical Analysis — The graphic presentation of the break-even analysis is called the break even chart. Break-even chart shows—

(i)   the relationship between Cost, Volume and Profit;

(ii) Break-even point i.e., the point at which there is *neither* profit *nor* loss.

(iii) Margin of safety i.e., the difference between Actual Sales and Break Even Sales;

(iv) Profit/loss at various levels of activity.

Example — An example of a Break Even Chart is given below:

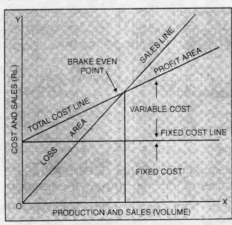

Algebric Analysis — Algebrically Break-even point can be computed in any of the following manner:

(i) Break Even Point (*in units*) = $\dfrac{\text{Total Fixed Cost}}{\text{Selling Price Per Unit} - \text{Variable Cost Per Unit}}$

(ii) Break Even Point (*in value*) = BEP (in units) × Selling Price per unit, or

= Total Fixed Cost × $\dfrac{\text{Selling Price}}{\text{Selling Price Per Unit} - \text{Variable Cost Per Unit}}$

Assumptions of Break Even Analysis

Break-even Analysis is based on the following assumptions:

1. All costs can be separated into fixed and variable components.
2. Fixed costs will remain constant.
3. Variable cost will change in direct proportion to the volume of output. In other words, variable cost per unit will remain constant.
4. Selling price of the product will remain constant.
5. There is only one product or in the case of multiple products, the sales mix will remain constant. (i.e., sales of various products will always be in some pre-determined proportions).
6. Entire production will be sold.
7. Productivity and Operating efficiency will remain constant.
8. Product specifications and methods of manufacturing and selling will remain constant.
9. General price level will remain constant.

Limitations of Break-even Analysis

Break even alayisis is fundamentally a static analysis it assumes almost everything constant (e.g., constant total fixed costs, variable cost per unit, selling price, productivity, sales mix in case of multi products etc.). The limitations which make the assumptions to be unrealistic are given below:

1. All costs can not be separated into fixed and variable components with accuracy.
2. Fixed Costs may change because of change in management policy or after a range of activity.
3. Variable cost per unit may change because of operation of law of increasing returns or decreasing returns.
4. Selling price may change because of increase or decrease in output, market demand & supply, competition etc.
5. In case of multiple products, the sales mix need not necessarily be constant.
6. In case of multiple products, separate break even points are to be calculated. This poses a problem of apportionment of fixed costs to each product.
7. Entire production need not necessarily be sold in practice.

8. Productivity and operating efficiency may change because of change in method of production, incentive plans, training & development.

9. Product specifications and methods of manufacturers and selling may change because of change in policy of management.

10. General price level may change.

11. Break-even analysis ignores the capital employed which is one of the important factors in the determination of profitability.

In spite of its limitations, the break even analysis is a useful management device if it is constructed and used by those who fully understand its limitations.

3. STANDARD COSTING

Standard Costing is one of the cost control techniques. It may be noted that it is not a method of costing like job costing, process costing.

Meaning of Standard

Standard means a criterion or a yardstick against which actual activity can be compared.

Meaning of Standard Cost

Standard Cost is the cost **what should have been** under a given set of operating conditions.

Standard Cost is "a predetermined cost which is computed from management's standards of efficient operations and the relevant necessary expenditure, on the basis of engineering specifications of all the factors affecting cost, in advance of production during the period to which the standard cost is intended to relate."

Distinction between Standard Cost and Estimated Cost

Standard Cost differs from Estimated Cost in the following respects:

Basis of Distinction	Standard Cost	Estimated Cost
1. What indicates?	Standard Cost indicates what cost should be?	Estimated Cost indicate what cost will be?
2. How determined?	Standard costs are determined on a scientific basis.	Estimated costs are obtained by adjusting past figures to possible future changes.
3. How useful?	Standard costs are useful for cost control.	Estimated costs do not serve any such purpose.
4. Which firm uses?	Standard costs are used by a firm having Standard costing system in operation.	Estimated costs are used by a firm having historical cost system.
5. Whether Recorded?	Standard costs are recorded in the regular system of accounts.	Estimated costs are not recorded in the regular system of accounting.

Meaning of Standard Costing

Standard Costing is one of the cost control techniques.

According to terminology of Cost Accountancy, CIMA, London, *"Standard costing is the preparation and use of standard costs, their comparison with actual costs and the analysis of variances to their causes and points of incidence."*

On the basis of above definition, the steps involved in the techniques of standard costing are as follows:

Step 1 → Fixation of realistic (i.e., attainable) standards for each element of cost.

Step 2 → Comparison of the actual costs with the standard cost and findout the difference between the two known as variance. A variance which increases profit is called favourable and which decreases profit is called unfavourable or adverse.

Step 3 → Analysis of variances to ascertain the reasons for the variances.

Step 4 → Presentation of information to the appropriate level of management to decide upon the corrective action to be taken.

Objective of Standard Costing

The main objective of standard costing is to control cost through variance analysis.

Advantages of Standard Costing

The main advantages of standard costing are as follows:

1. **Facilitates Planning** — Standard costing facilitates planning since setting up standard involves careful analysis and scrutiny of different activities of a business.

2. **Facilitates Effective Delegation of Authority** — Delegation of authority becomes effective since the people concerned know what they have to achieve and by what standard they will be judged.

3. **Facilitates Cost Control** — Standard Costs facilitates cost control by —

   (i) revealing exact degree of efficiency in various operations through comparison of actual figures with standard figures.

   (ii) revealing exact causes of deviation of actual figures from standard figures through variance analysis.

4. **Facilitates Motivation** — Standard costing facilitates motivation through standards which provide incentive and motivation to attain standard output of standard quality. Workers who attain standard output may be rewarded. This increases efficiency and productivity.

5. Right person can be rewarded & promoted since performance can be judged objectively.

6. **Facilitates Coordination** — Standard costing facilitates co-ordination between different functions by bringing different functions such as purchasing, production, selling, accounting together while fixing standards.

7. **Facilitates the use of MBE Principle** — Standard costing facilitates the use of management by Exception principle since the management need to concentrate only on the areas and problems which require its attention through study of variance analysis.

8. **Facilitates the formulation of Pricing Policies** — Standard costing facilitates the formulation of pricing policies for prospective orders.

9. **Facilitates the formulation of Production Policies** — Standard costing facilitates the formulation of production policies for various products by providing predetermined cost are each element of cost on the basis of engineering specifications.

10. **Facilitates Cost Reporting** — Standard costing through variance analysis provides a ready means of interpretation of information for the management for the purpose of control and decision-making. Ready reporting enhances the value of reports.

11. **Reveals the areas of avoidable wastages & losses, idle capacity** — Standard Costing through variance analysis reveals the areas of avoidable wastages & losses and idle capacity.

12. **Facilitates Cost Audit** — Standard Costing facilitates cost audit since if variances are satisfactorily explained, the accuracy of costing can be safely assumed.

13. **Provides economical means of costing** — Standard costing provides economical means of costing in the sense that once the standards have been fixed some records can be kept in quantities only. This eliminates much clerical effort in pricing and balancing items on stock ledger card. The standard cost of goods produced can be calculated immediately just by multiplying the quantity by the unit standard cost.

14. **Provides uniform valuation of Inventory** — Standard costing provides uniform valuation of inventory by valuing inventory of raw-materials, work-in-progress and finished goods at standard costs and by transferring the difference between actual and standard cost to a variance account.

15. **Provides forward looking approach** — By adoption of standard costing system, the whole concern is imbued with a dynamic forward looking mentality.

16. **Provides Objective measurement of Operational Efficiency** — Standard costing through setting of standards, enables to measure the operational efficiency of workers and other members of the staff objectively against those standards.

17. **Creates Cost Consciousness** — Standard costing creates cost consciousness among executives which increases efficiency and productivity.

Limitations of Standard Costing System

The limitations of standard costing system which make it difficult to work a standard costing system successfully are given below:

1. **Setting of Accurate Standards** — It is difficult to fix accurate standard costs. Standards may be *either* too strict *or* too liberal. Inaccurate and unreliable standards do more harm than benefits.

2. **Revision of Standards** — Standards require revision because business conditions constantly keep on charging. Revision of standards is costly and some firms may ignore it.

3. **Adverse Effect on Morale & Motivation** — Non-achievement of unrealistic standards may have an adverse effect on the morale and motivation of the employees.

4. **Unsuitability** — Standard costing system is costly and unsuitable in job-order industries where the production is of a non-repetitive nature.

5. **Expensive** — In case of small concerns it is expensive to operate standard costing system.

6. **Duplication** — Where the system has not yet been fully accepted, there is duplication in recording in as much as inventory pricing etc. have to be done both at standard and actual price.

7. **Difficulty in Setting Standards** — Sometimes it becomes difficult to set up standard costs in view of the uncertain economic conditions, great fluctuations in prices.

8. **Not Facilitate Cost Reduction** — Standard costing facilitates only cost control and not cost reduction.

It may be seen that the aforesaid limitations are not so serious as to make the system unworkable. These limitations can be overcome by taking special care in the setting up of the standards and in educating the staff at different levels.

Distinction between Standard Costing and Budgetary Control

Although basic principles of Standard Costing and Budgetary Control are same, yet they differ in the following respects:

Basis of Distinction	Standard Cost	Budgetory Control
1. Basis of Comarison	Control is effected by comparing actual figures with **standard figures** of actual output.	Control is effected by comparing actual figures with **budgeted figures** of sales, production, capital assets etc.
2. Scope	The scope of standard costing is comparatively **narrow** since it covers mainly production costs.	The scope of budgetary control is comparatively **wide** since it relates to all business operations, sales, capital and financial expenses.
3. Main Concerned	It is mainly concerned with the **ascertainment and control of each element of cost.**	It is mainly concerned with the **overall profitability and financial position** of a business.
4. Projection	It includes projection **of cost accounts** only.	It includes projections of **financial accounts as well as cost accounts.**

5. Recording of Variances in accounts	Variances (i.e., differences between actual figures and standard figures) are normally **revealed** in different cost accounts.	Variances (i.e., differences between actual figures and budgeted figures) are normally **not revealed** in different accounts.
6. Can it be operated in part?	It **can not be** operated in part. All items of expenditure included in cost units are to be accounted for.	It **can be** operated in parts. It is possible to carryout even for a particular type of expenses say Advertising Expenses, Reserach & Development Expenses.
7. Summary or Detailed Analysis	It involves the carrying out of detailed variance analysis in respect of each cost element in minute **detail** and thus facilitate in taking correcting action. Thus, it is comparatively technically improved system.	It involves budgeting and control of total expenses and revenues based on estimates. Thus, it is comparatively **broad** in nature.

4. RETURN ON CAPITAL EMPLOYED/RETURN ON INVESTMENT (ROI)

Return on Investment (ROI) is a technique of controlling overall performance.

1. **Meaning** — This ratio measures a relationship between net profit before interest and tax and capital employed.

2. **Objective** — The objective of computing this ratio is to find out how efficiently the long-term funds supplied by the creditors and shareholders have been used.

3. **Components** — There are two components of this ratio which are as under:

    (i) **Net profit before Interest and Tax;**

    (ii) **Capital Employed** which refers to long-term funds supplied by the long-term creditors and shareholders. It comprises the long-term debt and shareholders' funds.

    Notes:

    (i) *Non-Trading Assets do not form part of capital employed (e.g. Advance for purchase of Fixed Assets, Capital Work-in-Progress, Non-Trade Investments)*

    (ii) *Income from Non-Trading Assets should be excluded while calculating the Net Profit before Interest & Tax.*

Tutorial Note: Some accountants feel that the figure of 'Capital Employed' should be fairly representative of the capital investment throughout the accounting period and therefore, they prefer to make use of the concept of 'Average Capital Employed' which can be obtained by dividing the aggregate of capital employed at the beginning and at the end of the accounting period, by 2.

4. **Computation** — This ratio is computed by dividing the net profit before interest and tax by capital employed. It is expressed as a percentage. In the form of formula, this ratio may be expressed as under:

$$\text{Return on Capital Employed} = \frac{\text{Net Profit before Interest and Tax}}{\text{Capital Employed}} \times 100 = \ldots \%$$

Alternatively, ROI can be computed by taking the product of Net Profit Ratio and Capital Turnover Ratio.

$$\text{ROI} = \text{Net Profit Ratio} \times \text{Capital Turnover Ratio}$$

$$= \frac{\text{Net Profit before Interest and Tax}}{\text{Net Sales}} \times 100 \times \frac{\text{Net Sales}}{\text{Capital Employed}}$$

5. **Interpretation** — This ratio indicates the firm's ability of generating profit per rupee of capital employed. Higher the ratio, the more efficient the management and utilisation of Capital Employed.

6. **Uses of Return on Investment** — The Return on Investment is a very important concept in the field of operational management and the financial management. Its managerial uses include the following:

(i) It is a **measure of overall profitability** of an enterprise.

(ii) It can be used to measure and compare the **performance of various divisions** within an enterprise.

(iii) It can be used to compare the **performance of various enterprises** within an industry.

(iv) It can be used **for evaluating Investment Decisions** (or Capital Budgeting Decisions or Capital Expenditure Decisions) Investment Decision is a decision to invest in long-term assets. Other things remaining the same, the projects yielding higher Rate of Return on Investment may be selected.

(v) It can be used **for planning the Capital Structure**. Capital Structure Decision is a decision to decide upon the proportion of various sources of long-term funds viz., long-term debts, preference shares, equity funds (including retained earnings). A financial manager should not take the financial risk by employing the funds carrying fixed financial charges if he is not in position to generate a Rate of Return on Investment greater than the Rate of Fixed Financial Charges.

(vi) It can be used for **determining the price of a product/contract**. The price of a product/contract should be fixed in such a way that a reasonable rate of return on investment is obtained after recovering the operating cost of that product/contract.

7. **How to Increase ROI** — ROI can be increased in any one of the following five ways:

1. By increasing sales volume proportionately more than the increase in total investment.

2. By reducing the total investment proportionately more than the decrease in sales volume.

3. By increasing the sales volume proportionately more than the increase in cost of sales.

4. By reducing the cost of sales proportionately more than the decrease in sales volume.

5. By any other combination of aforesaid ways.

5. INTERNAL AUDIT

Meaning of Internal Auditing

According to the Institute of Internal Auditors, USA, *"Internal auditing is an independent appraisal function established within an organisation to examine and evaluate its activities as a service to the organisation".*

Objective of Internal Auditing

According to the Institute of Internal Auditors, USA, *"The objective of internal auditing is to assist members of the organisation in the effective discharge of their responsibilities. To this end, internal auditing furnishes them with analysis, appraisals, recommendations, counsel and information concerning the activities reviewed".*

Thus, internal auditor has to conduct an appraisal of the various operational functions and provide advice and recommendations on the activities and operations reviewed by him.

Scope of Modern Internal Auditing

The Institute of Internal Auditors defines the scope of internal auditing as *"the examination and evaluation of the adequacy and effectiveness of the organisation's system of internal control and the quality of performance in carrying out assigned responsibilities."*

Steps involved in Internal Audit

The following steps are involved in Internal Audit:

Step 1 → Review of Reliability and Integrity of Information and the means used to generate such information.

Step 2 → Review of the systems established to ensure compliance with those policies, plans, procedures, laws and regulations which could have a significant impact on operations and reports and determining whether the organisation has complied with them or not.

Step 3 → Review of the systems of safeguarding assets to assess the risk of losses from theft, fire etc. and verification of assets.

Step 4 → Appraisal of the economy and efficient use of resources with which resources are employed. **According to the Institute of Internal Auditors,** an internal auditor should determine whether—

    (a) operating standards have been established by the management for measuring economy and efficiency;

    (b) established operating standards are understood and being met;

    (c) deviations from operating standards are identified, analysed and communicated to those responsible for corrective action;

    (d) corrective action has been taken;

Step 5 → Review the operations to ascertain whether results are consistent with established objectives and goals and whether the operations are being carried out as planned.

Thus, the modern concept of internal auditing not only covers the traditional functions but also the modern functions. The coverage by modern concept of internal auditing can be seen in the following chart:

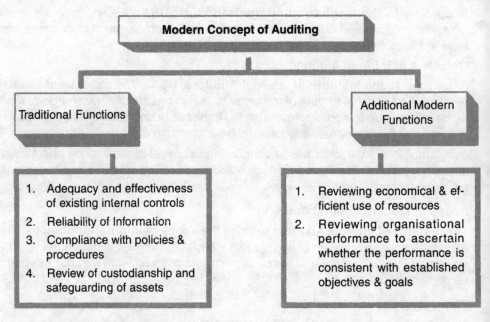

Modern Concept of Auditing

Traditional Functions

1. Adequacy and effectiveness of existing internal controls
2. Reliability of Information
3. Compliance with policies & procedures
4. Review of custodianship and safeguarding of assets

Additional Modern Functions

1. Reviewing economical & efficient use of resources
2. Reviewing organisational performance to ascertain whether the performance is consistent with established objectives & goals

Need for Internal Auditing

The need or internal auditing arises mainly due to the fact that the organisations have grown in size and operations and it has become necessary for the management of such organisations to have a team of specialists to review the procedures and operations of various units and report cases of non-compliance, inefficiency and lack of control so that necessary action can be taken without further delay.

6. MANAGEMENT AUDIT

Meaning of Management Audit

Management Audit is a systematic examination, analysis, appraisal and evaluation of the functioning, performance and effectiveness of various management processes and functions of an organisation.

It is an audit to examine, review and appraise the various policies and actions of the management on the basis of certain standards. It is a comprehensive and critical review of all aspects of management performance.

Features of Management Audit

1. It evaluates the actual performance and compares them with the predetermined targets.
2. It concentrates on the results and not on the files.
3. It concerns itself primarily with the results and with the ratios of inputs and outputs.

4. It measures in quantitative terms various inputs that a manager uses in terms of wages, materials, overheads or capital resources.

5. It measures output in terms of quality, return or performance targets.

6. It evaluates the performances by relating inputs with output.

7. Thus management audit is highly result-oriented.

Usefulness of Management Audit

Management Audit can be useful in the following situations:

1. A progressive management may like to get a management audit conducted to assess the performance of various managers.

2. An outside agency (say government) may be interested in getting management audit conducted with a view to examine the efficiency of the management of a particular enterprise.

3. A bank or financial institution may like to get a management audit conducted before advancing loans or before agreeing to participate in the equity capital of the enterprise.

4. Foreign Collaborators may also like to get management audit conducted periodically to assess the managerial abilities of their associates.

Objective of Management Audit

The overall objective of management audit is to assist all levels of management in the effective discharge of their responsibilities by furnishing them with objective analysis, appraisal, recommendations and pertinent comments concerning the activities reviewed.

Steps involved in Management Audit

The following steps are involved in management audit:

Step 1 → Identification of the objectives of the organisation

Step 2 → Breaking down of overall objectives into detailed plans for various segments

Step 3 → Review the organisation structure to assess whether or not it can effectively achieve the overall objectives and detailed plans. If possible, identify the specific responsibility centres.

Step 4 → Evaluate the performance of each responsibility centre and compare it with the objectives and targets

Step 5 → Forming opinions and conclusions on the basis of analysis of evidence and information so collected and generated.

Step 6 → Suggest a realistic course of action for future guidance of management and for reform of processes and practices of management of the organisation in question.

Techniques of Management Audit

A management auditor can adopt and case a number of techniques such as—

1. Inquiry by raising questions
2. Examination of documents and records
3. Confirmation from various persons to confirm the already obtained information.
4. Own observation of pertinent activities and conditions in the organisation
5. Correlation of information collected through various techniques so as to reach meaningful conclusions.

Appraisal Areas of Management Audit

Depending on the preferences and perspectives of the top management, management audit may cover all or some major facts of functioning of the organisation and its management. Usually the following appraisal areas are covered under any comprehensive management audit programme.

1. The management audit team should review the process of management by framing questionnaires with respect to:
   (a) objectives;
   (b) planning;
   (c) organisation;
   (d) control;
   (e) systems and procedures.

2. The management audit team should review various functional areas to assess their role in achieving the overall objectives of organisation. Questionnaires should be framed with respect to the following functional areas:
   (a) Purchase Management;
   (b) Inventory Management;
   (c) Production Management;
   (d) Marketing Management;
   (e) Personnel Management;
   (f) Accounting;
   (g) Finance.

Who Conducts Management Audit?

Management audit can be conducted by in-house team of experts or outside team of management consultants. Since management audit requires an inter-disciplinary approach, the team should consists of various experts from different disciplines like accountancy, operations research, industrial engineering, social science. Each member of this team should have the following qualities:

1. He/she should have an analytical mind;
2. He/she should have an ability to look at a management functions from the point of view of the organisation as a whole;

3.   He/she should have proper training;

4.   He/she should have an expert knowledge of the science of management;

5.   He/she should be acquainted with salient features of various functional areas.

This team should have a clearly defined authority from the management. Management audit can not be effective unless it is fully supported by the top management.

7. QUALITY AUDIT

Meaning of Quality Audit

Quality Audit is a systematic examination, analysis, appraisal and evaluation of the quality systems and processes with a view to ascertain whether or not such systems are effective and efficient.

What Quality Audit includes —

Quality Audit includes:

1.   Review of management responsibility for quality;
2.   Quality Systems;
3.   Contracts;
4.   Design Control;
5.   Document Control;
6.   Purchasing;
7.   Supplied Production;
8.   Product Identification;
9.   Process Control;
10.   Inspection & Testing;
11.   Measuring and Testing Equipments;
12.   Quality Records;
13.   Internal Quality Audits;
14.   Statistical Quality Techniques.

Steps involved in Quality Audit

The following steps are involved in quality audit:

Step 1 → Reviewing the auditee's quality documentation such as quality manual

Step 2 → Determination of level of adherence to the standards specified by ISO 9001/9002/9003

Step 3 → Evaluation of complex technical processes and quality systems

Who conducts Quality Audit?

The quality audit is conducted by a Lead Auditor or a Lead Assessor who has satisfied certain training requirements prescribed in this behalf.

Is Quality Audit essential?

Quality Audit is an important condition to obtain ISO 9000 certificate. ISO 9000 is a series of international standards on quality management and assurance. The basic purpose of this series of quality standards is to enable an organisation to establish quality systems, maintain product integrity and satisfy the customers.

8. MANAGEMENT INFORMATION SYSTEM

The term 'Management Information System' consists of The three words viz. Management, Information and System which have been explained below:

Management — The term 'Management' refers to a set of functions and process designed to initiate and coordinate group efforts in an organised setting, directed towards promoting certain interests, preserving certain values and pursuing certain goals. It involves mobilisation, combination, allocation and utilisation of physical, human and other needed resources in a judicious manner by employing appropriate skills, approaches and techniques. It is a process of conceiving and converting certain worthwhile ideas into results by getting things done through people by offering them monetary and other inducements in return for their contributions.

The functions and processes of management are wide-ranging and closely inter-related. As creator and activator of productive organisations, the functions of management range all the way from design of the organisation, formulation of organisational goals, strategies, policies and plans of action, determination of tasks and their distribution among the activity units, employment of personnel, installation of reward systems, communication and control system to ensure that what is planned is achieved, facilitation of organisational change and adaptation resolution of organisational conflict, and so on.

In short, 'Management' may be thought of as the sum total of those activities which relate to the laying down of certain plans, policies and purposes; securing men, money, materials, and machinery needed for their goal achievement; putting all of them into operation, checking their performance: and providing material rewards and mental satisfaction to the men engaged in the operation.

Information — "Information" as defined by Webster, is the communication of knowledge or intelligence; .... knowledge derived from reading, observation or instructions; especially unorganised or unrelated facts or data.

Although the terms information and data are commonly used as synonymous, but it is important to distinguish between the two. Data are raw facts, unassembled and usually unrelated to one another. Business organisations produce enough data e.g., A machine breaks down five times in a day. There are ten employees on a particular job etc. Data are not only produced by business organisations but externally as well.

Only by processing the data in some way we obtain information. Information can be thus defined as a collection of related pieces of data.

System — According to Murdick and Ross, "System is a set of two or more elements, such as people, things, and concepts, which are joined together to attain a common objective". But *C Davis defines a physical system as* "a set of elements which operate together to accomplish an objective. We can also think a system, as a group of interrelated components or parts which function together to achieve a goal. Thus, system can be described by specifying its parts, the way in which they are related, and the goal which they are suppose to achieve. For example, human body has a particular set of parts — right arm, a left leg, a stomach, a head etc.— these various body parts are related by means of connecting networks of blood vessels and nerves.

Management Information System — Management information system can be viewed as an information network within the business system which supports the decision-making responsibilities of management. Thus we can define management information system as an integrated man/machine system for providing information to support the operations, managerial and decision making functioning in an organisation. The system utilises computer hardware and software, manual procedures, management and decision models, and a data base. Accordingly managerial information structure must be of a pyramindical shape and it should be in conformity with the pyramidical patters of the structure of the particular organisation i.e., at higher levels, the information needed is more filtered, brief but meaningful whereas lower the level the broader should be the information base.

Diagrammatic Representation of MIS

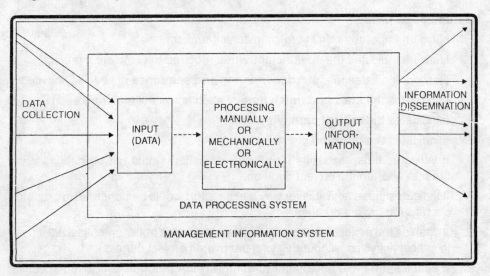

Chart → Showing MIS & DPS Therein

9. CRITICAL PATH METHOD (CPM)

Meaning of CPM

A network is a graphical representation of a project, depicting the flow as well as the sequence of well-defined activities and events. A network path consists of a set of activities that connects the networking beginning event to the network terminal event. The longest path through the network is called the critical path and its length determines the minimum duration in which the said project can be completed.

NetWork (or Arrow Diagram)

A network is a graphical representation of inter-relationship of the various activities of a project. While drawing network, the following rules must be kept in mind.

1. An activity cannot occur untill all activities leading to it are complete.
2. No activity can start untill its tail event is reached.

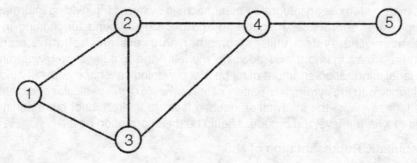

Usefulness of CPM

CPM plays an important role in project planning and control.

1. Network indicates the **specific activities** required to complete a project.
2. Network indicates the **interdependence and sequence** of specific activities.
3. It indicates the **start and finish time** of each activity of the project.
4. It indicates the **critical path**.
5. It indicates the **duration** of critical path.
6. It indicates those activities for which extra effort would not be beneficial in order to shorten the project duration.
7. It indicates those activities for which extra effort would be beneficial in order to shorten the project duration.
8. It enables the project manager to **deploy resources** from non-critical activities to critical activities without delaying the overall project duration.
9. It enables the project manager to **assign responsibilities** for each specific activity.
10. It enables the project manager to **allocate resources** for each specific activity
11. It can be used as a **controlling device** to monitor activities of the project by comparing the actual progress against planned progress.

12. It can be used to determine **possible alternative solutions**.

13. It can be used to determine various **cost variances** for initiating corrective action by comparing the actual costs against budgeted costs of the project.

14. It enables the project manager to determine a **revised plan and schedule** of the project by recomputing the project's critical path and the slack of non-critical activities using the actual duration of activities already finished and the revised estimated duration of activities not yet finished.

Assumptions of CPM/PERT

1. A project can be sub-divided into a set of predicable, independent activities.

2. The precedence relationships of project activities can be completely represented by a non-cyclical network graph in which each activity connects directly into its immediate successors.

3. Activity times may be estimated *either* as single point estimates or as three point estimates (i.e. optimistic, pessimistic or most likely) and are independent of each other.

4. Activity duration is assured to follow the beta distribution, the standard deviation of the distribution is assumed to be 1/6th of its range.

   Mean (t_e) is assumed to be $= \dfrac{t_0 + 4t_m + t_p}{6}$

   Variances in the length of a project is assumed to be = sum of variances of activities on the critical path.

5. The duration of an activity is linearly related to the cost of resources applied to the activity.

   The aforesaid graphical representation showing the inter-relationships of the various activities of a project is called 'Network'.

Steps Involved in Critical Path Analysis

The working methodology of Critical Path Analysis (CPA) which includes both CPM and PERT, consists of following five steps:

Step 1 → Analyse and breakdown the project in terms of specific activities and/or events.

Step 2 → Determine the interdependence and sequence of specific activities and prepare a network.

Step 3 → Assign estimate of time, cost or both to all the activities of the network.

Step 4 → Identify the longest or critical path through the network.

Step 5 → Monitor, evaluate and control the progress of the project by replanning, rescheduling and reassignment of resources.

10. PERT

Meaning of PERT

PERT stands for Programme Evaluation and Review Technique. PERT is event oriented. PERT is a probabilistic model i.e. it takes into account uncertainties involved in the estimation of time of a job or an activity. It uses three estimates of the activity time - Optimistic, Pessimistic and Most Likely. Thus, the expected duration of each activity is probabilistic and expected duration indicates that there is 50% probability of getting the job done within that time.

PERT is primarily concerned with project time. It enables the project manager to schedule and co-ordinate the various activities so that the project can be completed on scheduled time. PERT is generally used for those projects which are not of repetitive in nature (e.g. Research and Development Projects) and where time required to complete various activities are not known in advance.

The process of PERT analysis includes the following steps:

Step 1 →	Identification of the activities of the project.
Step 2 →	Estimation of activity time.
Step 3 →	Defining inter-dependence relationships between the activities.
Step 4 →	Drawing the net work.
Step 5 →	Using the network to obtain the scheduling data.

Distinction between CPM and PERT

CPM and PERT differ in the various respects:

Basis of Distinction	CPM	PERT
1. **Orientation**	CPM is **activity** oriented i.e. CPM network is built on the basis of activities.	PERT is **event** oriented.
2. **Nature of Model**	CPM is a **deterministic** model i.e. it does not take into account the uncertainties involved in the estimation of time for execution of a job or an activity.	PERT is a **probabilistic** model i.e. It takes into account uncertainties involved in the estimation of time of a job or an activity. It uses three estimates of the activity time –optimistic, pessimistic and most likely. Thus, the expected duration of each activity is probabilitistic and expected duration indicates that there is 50% probability of getting the job done within that time.

3.	**Emphasis**	CPM places dual emphasis **on time and cost** and evaluates the trade off between project cost and project time. It enables the project manager to manipulate project duration within certain limits by deploying additional resources so that project duration can be shortened at an optimum cost.	PERT is primarily concerned with project **time**. It enables the project manager to schedule and co-ordinate various activities so that the project can be completed on scheduled time.
4.	**Use**	CPM is generally used for those projects which are **repetitive** in nature (e.g. construction projects) and where one has **prior experience** of handling similar projects.	PERT is generally used for those projects which are **not repetitive** in nature (e.g. Research and Development Projects) and where **time** required to complete various activities are **not known** in advance.

Usefulness of PERT

1. **Facilitates Planing** – PERT facilitates planning. Planning involves the formulation of objectives and goals that are subsequently translated into specific plans and projects. The planning phase of the project is initiated by PERT because it requires the establishment of project objectives and specifications, and then, it provides a realistic and disciplined basis for determinining how to attain these objectives, considering pertinent time and resource constraints. Planners are required to specify not only all the activities necessary to complete a project but also their technological dependencies. PERT calculations then lay out clearly the implications of these inter-dependencies and aid the planners in finding problems that might be over looked in large complex problems. PERT provides a realistic way of carrying out more long range and detailed planning of projects including their co-ordination at all the levels of management. In developing a detailed and comprehensive project network, users often make significant improvements over their original ideas, they do a better job of early co-ordination with supplier, engineers, managers contractors and all other groups associated with the project.

2. **Facilitates Controlling** – PERT facilitates controlling. The function of control is to institute a mechanism that trigger a warning signal if actual performance is deviating (in terms of time, cost or some other measures of effectiveness) from the plan. PERT is unique in its emphasis on the control phase of project management because it uses statistical analysis along with probability

calculations concerning the project completion by a certain period. As a result, it is easier under PERT to revise the plan each time changes are introduced in the network. With the information from PERT, the manager is in a better position to know where troubles may occur, supervision may be needed and where resources may be shifted to keep the project on schedule. It also helps in controlling the project by checking off progress against the schedule and by assigning the schedule manpower and equipments. It enables the managers to analyse the effects of delays and to revise the network in case any changes are required.

3. **Facilitates the Application of MBE Principle** – PERT **facilitates the application of the principle of management by exception** by identifying the most critical elements in the plan, focusing management attention on the 10 to 20 per cent of the project activities that are most constraining on the schedule. It continually defines new schedules and illustrates the effects of technical and procedural changes on the overall schedule. Thus, the manager can control the project in a better way.

4. **Acts as Project Management Technique** – Programme Evaluation is a **project management technique**. The project to be planned is broken into inter-dependent activities and a network of arrows is constructed to depict these dependency relationships, each activity being represented by one arrow. PERT, however is particularly suited to innovational projects (viz. oil exploration or introducing a new product) for the activities of which it is not possible to estimate the timings precisely.

5. **Provides Feedback Information** – PERT provides valuable feedback information about the status of the project. The management is provided with a convenient yardstick against which progress of various activities especially those which are critical may be measured. This information is extremely important for control. For example, any delay beyond the schedule completion time of an activity will be brought to management's attention. The cause of the delay can be investigated and remedial action taken. This increases the likelihood of completing the project.

However, the success of the technique depends on the management's response to the feedback information provided. If this information is merely field and no remedial action is taken, the purpose of the technique is defeated. It is important to recognise that there is no self-correcting mechanism built into the model that will cause automatic remedial action. Such action has to be initiated by the persons using the technique. Another problem that may destroy the success of PERT model is the tendency of many activity managers to delay in the reporting of the current status of progress. This causes delays in the updating of time schedule and the management begins to operate with outdated information which could be disastrous. To resolve this problem, it is crucial for the project manager to inform all activity managers about the relative importance of their activity's impact on the total project and where they 'fit in' in the overall project's success.

In short, there is nothing wrong with the PERT network technique. If the feedback information provided by it is properly utilised by the management, it will act only as wall decorates in a business enterprise. However, if proper remedial action is initiated for various information provided by it, PERT can prove to be a dynamic tool for planning, controlling and scheduling a project.

How to incorporate uncertainty in pert model

Uncertainty can be incorporated in PERT network by assuming that the activity time has a beta distribution. This enables us to calculate the expected activity time and its standard deviation. For this purpose we have the following three diferent estimates for he completion time of an activity.

Optimistic Time (T_0) Optimstic time for an activity is the minimum time required to complete an activity if everything goes all right. i.e. under ideal conditions.

Normal Time (or Most Likely Time) (T_m) Normal time, is the most probable time which an activity will take. This is the time which lies between the optimistic time and the pessimistic time.

Pessimistic Time Pessimistic time, is the best guess-estimate of the maximum time that would be required to complete an activity if bad luck were encountered at every turn. The estimate does not take into account such natural catastrophes as flood etc.

Expected Time Expected time is the average time that an activity will take if it was to be repeated on large number of times and is based on the assumption that the activity time follows beta distribution. It is given by the relation –

$$t_e = \frac{t_0 + 4t_m + t_p}{6}$$

where t_0, t_m, t_p are the optimistic, most likely (or Normal) and pessimistic times.

Activity Variance Activity variance is the square of 1/6th of the difference between the pessimistic and optimistic guess-estimates, i.e.

$$\sigma^2 = \left(\frac{t_p - t_0}{6}\right)^2$$

Project Variance Project variance is the variance of the critical path duration which, in turn, is the sum of variances of the activities on it. From central limit therein it follows that critical path duration is normally distributed. As such variance can be put to use for finding the probability of completing the project by a given date. The physical interpretation of this term is that if the project were to be repeated on myriads of occasions its duration follows a normal distribution with the variance explained above. The formula presumes beta disribution of activity time.

Thus, Project Variance = Sum of Variances of Critical Activities.

_____ **EXERCISES** _____

SHORT ANSWER TYPE QUESTIONS

1. State the meaning of control.
2. State the objectives of control.
3. State the nature of control.
4. "Control is a pervasive function." Explain.
5. "Control is a continuous activity in an organisation." Explain.
6. "Control is forward looking." Discuss.
7. "Controlling is looking back." Comment.
8. "Control implies taking action." Explain.
9. "Control is action-oriented." Explain.
10. Enumerate the main steps of the control process.
11. State the relationship between planning and controlling.
12. How is control related with planning? Explain briefly.
13. Outline the main features of a good control system.
14. Explain any two features of a good control' system.
15. How does control simplify the task of a supervisor?
16. What is compared with what in controlling?
17. What is feedback in controlling?
18. What is meant by the term 'deviation' in controlling?
19. What is meant by control by exception?
20. "Instead of controlling every deviation, the management should concentrate on important deviations." Explain.
21. With what is the performance compared under control?
22. State any three reasons for the faulty control system.
23. Point out any three symptoms that would indicate a faulty control system.
24. In section A of a particular department 100 workers are employed. They are assigned the daily work in the form of 50 units per worker per day. Only 4 workers were in a position to achieve the standards. Suggest the remedial action to be taken by the departmental head.
25. Enumerate the various techniques of conrol.
26. Write short notes on the following:
    (a) Control by Exception
    (b) Critical Point Control
    (c) Current Control
    (d) Pre Control and Post Control
    (e) Limitations of Budgetary Control
    (f) Break Even Analysis

(g) Management Audit

(h) Management Information System

LONG ANSWER TYPE QUESTIONS

1. Explain briefly the importance of control in the process of management.
2. How does controlling help in achieving objectives and improving employees' morale?
3. Explain briefly the various steps in the process of control.
4. "Planning and control are mutually inter-related and interdependent." Explain the statement.
5. "Planning is looking ahead and controlling is looking back." Explain.
6. Explain briefly the features of a good control system.
7. Define control. Discuss the requirements of an effective control system.
8. "An ideal control technique is the one that checks every bit of performance." Comment.
9. Explain the various techniques of control.
10. What is Budgetary Control? Explain the essential elements of budgetary control. Also explain its benefits.
11. Explain the concept of Management Audit. State few major areas which could be the searchlight of management audit.

APPENDIX

REVISIONAL QUESTIONS

PART A - BUSINESS ORGANISATION

1. Define Business System and explain its features. State briefly the various sub-systems of business system.

2. Define Business and its main characteristics. Discuss briefly the scope of business.

3. Discuss the social responsibilities of business.

4. Discuss fully the various entrepreneurial decisions which must be taken while promoting a new business enterprise.

5. Discuss the factors to be considered while selecting the location of plant.

6. Discuss the factors to be considered while selecting a suitable form of organisation.

7. Discuss the factors to be considered while selecting a suitable channel of distribution.

8. Discuss the factors to be considered while selecting a suitable medium of advertising.

9. Discuss the factors which influence the requirements of Working Capital in a large scale business.

10. Discuss the factors which influence the requirements of Fixed Capital in a large scale business.

11. Discuss the factors which influence the capital structure of a public limited company.

12. What is small business? What is the importance of small business in Indian Economy? What is government policy towards small business in India?

13. Define the term 'Public Enterprise'. What is the rationate of public enterprise? What are the main problems of public enterprises in India?

14. Distinguish between the following:
    (a) Private Company and Public Company;
    (b) Life Insurance, Fire Insurance and Marine Insurance;
    (c) Advertising and Salesmanship;
    (d) Share and Debenture;
    (e) Equity Share and Preference Share;
    (f) Over-capitalisation and Under-capitalisation;
    (g) Wholesalers and Retailers;
    (h) Multiple Shops and Chain Stores;
    (i) Public Enterprise, Public Corporation and Public Company.

15. Write short notes on the following:
    (a) Nature and causes of Business Risks;
    (b) Social Responsibilities of Business;
    (c) Qualities of a good salesman;
    (d) Statutory Corporation and Government Company;
    (e) Advantages and Disadvantages of Advertisement;
    (f) Rationale of Public Enterprises;
    (g) Importance of Small Business;
    (h) Government Policies towards Small Business in India.
    (i) Steps in Import Procedure
    (j) Steps in Export Procedure
    (k) Services of Wholesalers and Retailers

PART B - MANAGEMENT

1. Define Management and discuss its nature and functions.
2. Is the management science, art or profession? Discuss.
3. Define Planning and discuss its significance and limitations.
4. What is managerial planning? Explain its characteristics. Discuss briefly the various stages involved in the planning process.
5. What is meant by delegation of authority? Explain briefly the principles of delegation.
6. What is meant by the term 'decentralisation of authority'? How is it different from delegation of authority? What are the factors that influence decentralisation of authority in an organisation?
7. Describe the procedure involved a business enterprise for the selection of employees.
8. Discuss the need and importance of training personnel and explain the various methods of imparting training to employees.
9. Define Motivation and explain its nature. Discuss fully the importance of motivation. Also discuss the financial and non-financial motivators as technique of motivation.
10. What is leadership? Discuss the various styles of leadership.
11. Define communication. What are the common barriers to communication in an organisation? How can they be overcome?
12. Describe the important techniques of controlling.
13. Distinguish between the following:
    (a) Administration and Management;
    (b) Unity of command and unity of direction;
    (c) Unity of command and functional foremanship;
    (d) Time Study and Motion Study;

(e) Taylor's scientific management and Henry Fayol's Principles of Management;

(f) Organising and organisational structure;

(g) Formal organisation and informal organisation;

(h) Line and line staff organisation;

(i) Line and staff and functional organisation;

(j) Line and functional organisation;

(k) Authority, responsibility and accountability;

(l) Centralisation of authority and decentralisation of authority;

(m) Delegation of authority and decentralisation of authority;

(n) Recruitment and Selection;

(o) On the Job Training Methods and off the Job Training Methods;

(p) Internal Sources and Exeternal Sources;

(q) Direction and Supervision;

(r) Positive incentive and Negative Incentive;

(s) Leadership and Managership;

(t) Formal communication and Informal communication;

(u) Upward communication and Downward communication;

(v) Oral communication and Written communication.

(w) Policies and Objectives

(x) Policies and Strategies

(y) Policies and Procedures

(z) Procedures and Rules

14. Write short notes on the following:

(a) Limitations of Planning;

(b) Types of Plans;

(c) Principles of Delegation;

(d) Functional Organisation;

(e) Procedure of Selection of Employees

(f) Advantages of Training;

(g) Methods of Training;

(h) Span of Control;

(i) Importance of Direction

(j) Importance of Motivation;

(k) Styles of Leadership;

(l) Barriers to effective communication;

(m) Principles of Effecting Communication;

(n) Motivation, Morale and Leadership;

(o) Importance of controlling;

(p) Techniques of controlling;

(q) Feedback in controlling;
(r) Deviation in controlling;
(s) Control by exception;
(t) Good Control System;
(u) Meaning and Objectives of Budgetary Control.